AS150735

Dumfries and Galloway Libraries, Information and Archives

This item is to be returned on or before the last date shown below.

SCD

1 1 MAY 2010 CD
2 2 JUN 2010 CD
2 8 JUL 2010 CD

-1 OCT 2010 CD

3 0 JUN 2012 CD

1 4 JAN 2014 EW

355 359

Central Support Unit
Catherine Street Dumfries DG1 1JB
tel: 01387 253820 fax: 01387 260294
e-mail: libs&i@dumgal.gov.uk

CUSTOMER
SERVICE
EXCELLENCE

N RENEWAL ON OUR WEBSITE - WWW.DUMGAL.GOV.UK/LIA

D1346053

Praise for Martin Windrow's *The Last Valley*:

'Hard to praise too highly ... meticulous and magnificent ... Windrow is master of every detail ... gripping reading'
Max Hastings, *Sunday Telegraph*

'Martin Windrow's book is nothing less than a landmark in miliary history'
Richard Holmes

'I know I'm never going to read a better book this year'
James Dellingpole, *The Times*

'Martin Windrow has pulled off a remarkable feat'
John Crossland, *Sunday Times*

'Enthralling ... Windrow gives one the very essence of battle ...
His character sketches are deft and acute'
Allan Massie, *Literary Review*

'Great lucidity and humanity ... moving ... judicious ... vivid'
Martin Woollacott, *Guardian*

'An extraordinarily good description and analysis of the events, so that non-experts can get a real understanding ... It is Keegan, with footnotes.'
Colonel John Wilson, *British Army Review*

OUR FRIENDS BENEATH THE SANDS

The Foreign Legion
in France's Colonial Conquests
1870–1935

MARTIN WINDROW

AS | Dumfries and Galloway LIBRARIES

| 1 | 5 | 0 | 7 | 3 | 5 | Class 355·359 |

Weidenfeld & Nicolson
LONDON

For Graham – with thanks for a thousand miles of the
djebel and the *bled*; for the hilltop of Astar, and for
racing the thunderstorm from Skoura to El Mers.

First published in Great Britain in 2010
by Weidenfeld & Nicolson

An Hachette UK company

10 9 8 7 6 5 4 3 2 1

© Martin Windrow, 2010

All rights reserved. No part of this publication may be
reproduced, stored in a retrieval system, or transmitted,
in any form or by any means, electronic, mechanical,
photocopying, recording or otherwise, without the prior
permission of both the copyright owner and the above publisher.

The right of Martin Windrow to be identified as the author
of this work has been asserted in accordance with the
Copyright, Designs and Patents Act 1988.

Maps drawn by John Richards; © Martin Windrow

A CIP catalogue record for this book
is available from the British Library.

ISBN 978 0 297 85213 1

Typeset by Input Data Services Ltd, Bridgwater, Somerset

Printed and bound in the UK by CPI Mackays, Chatham ME5 8TD

The Orion Publishing Group's policy is to use papers
that are natural, renewable and recyclable products and
made from wood grown in sustainable forests. The logging
and manufacturing processes are expected to conform to
the environmental regulations of the country of origin.

Weidenfeld & Nicolson

The Orion Publishing Group Ltd
Orion House
5 Upper Saint Martin's Lane
London WC2H 9EA

www.orionbooks.co.uk

Contents

MAP 1 Neuilly, north-west Paris,
April 1871

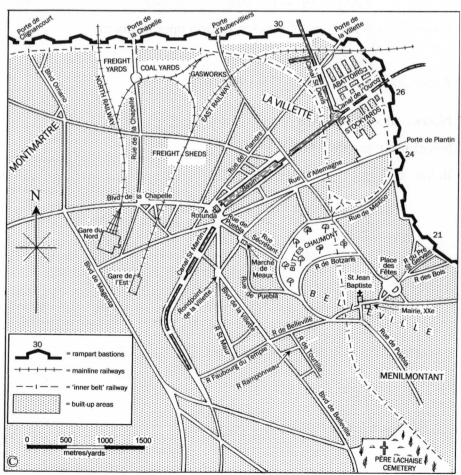

MAP 2 North-east Paris, May 1871

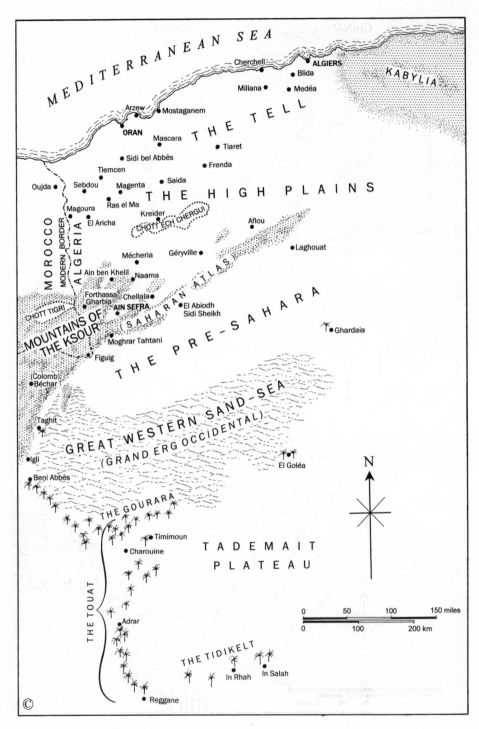

MAP 3 Western Algeria, c. 1871–1900

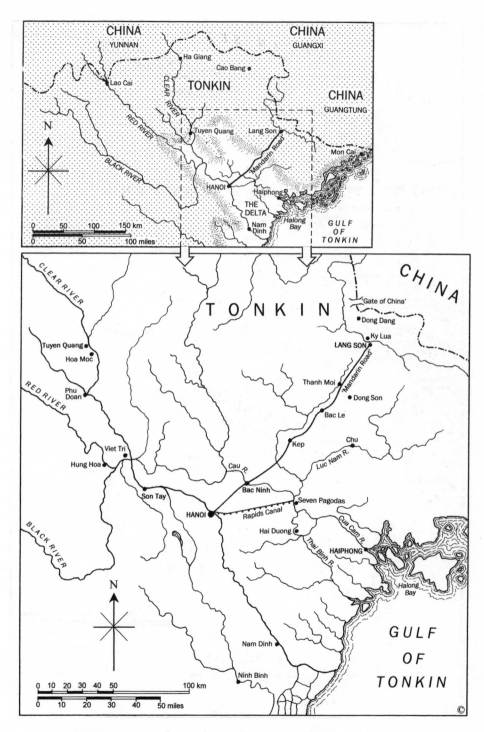

MAPS 4a & 4b Tonkin, and area of operations 1883–85

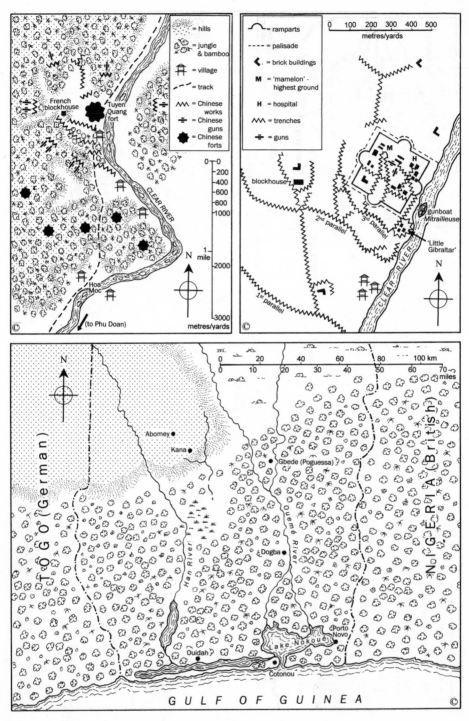

MAPS 5a & 5b Vicinity and siege of Tuyen Quang, 1885

MAPS 6 Dahomey, 1892

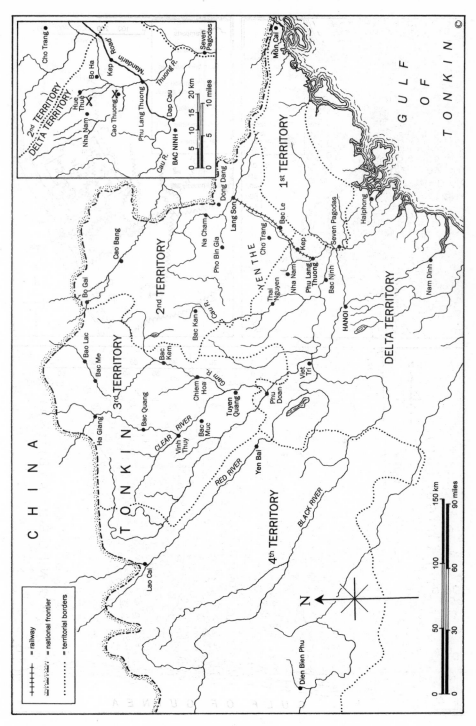

MAP 7 Tonkin, c.1895, with detail of the Yen The region, c.1892

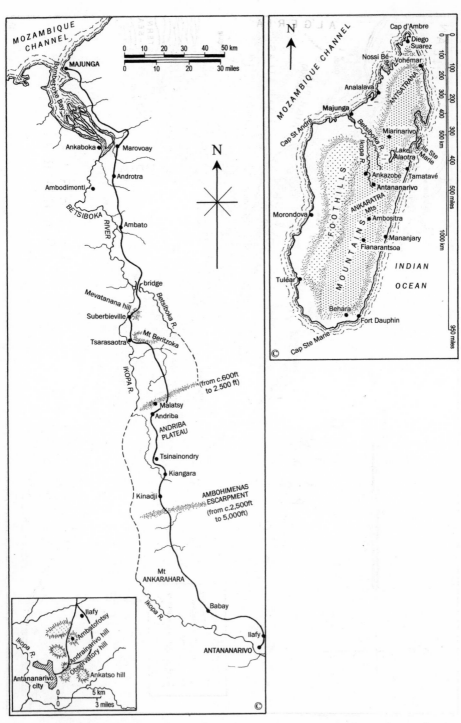

MAP 8 & 9 The advance from Majunga to Antananarivo, 1895; and general map of Madagascar, 1895-c.1905

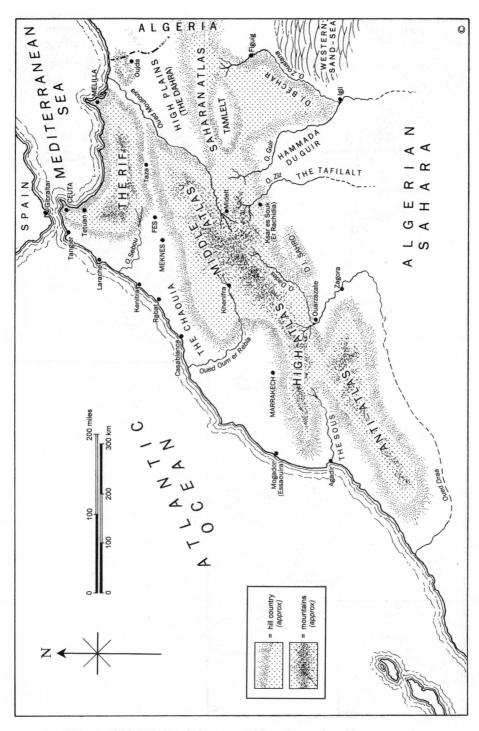

MAP 10 Morocco, c.1900

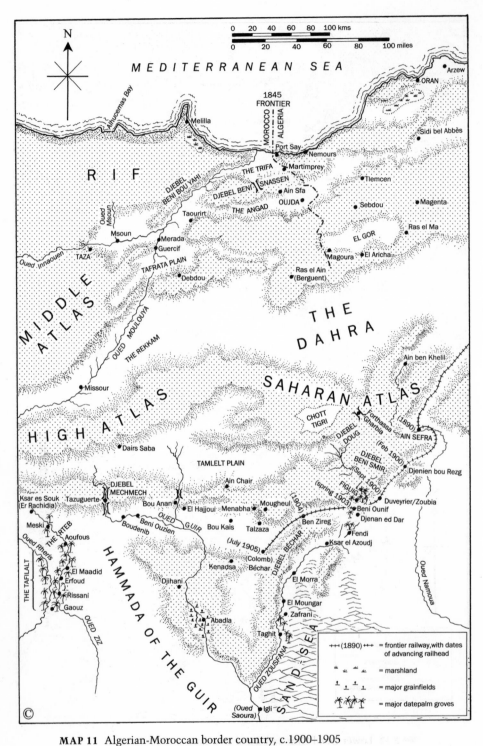

MAP 11 Algerian-Moroccan border country, c.1900–1905

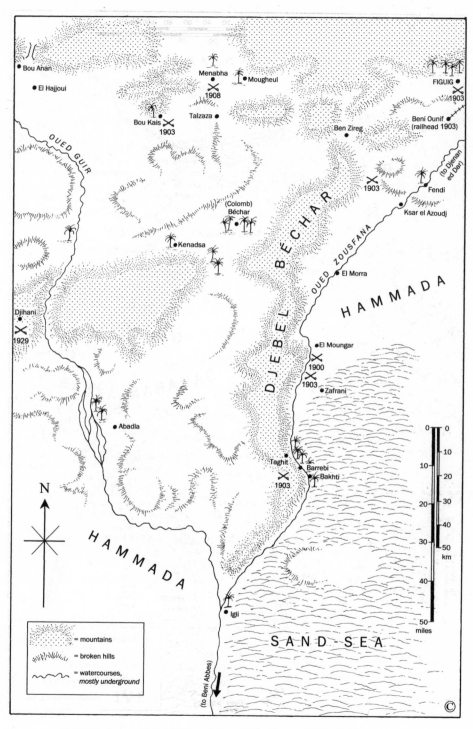

MAP 12 Lower Oued Guir and Oued Zousfana, c.1900–1905

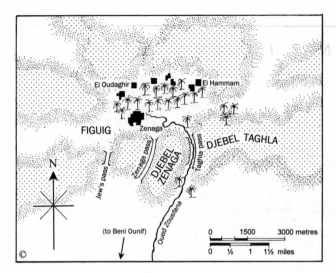

MAP 13 Figuig, May–June 1903

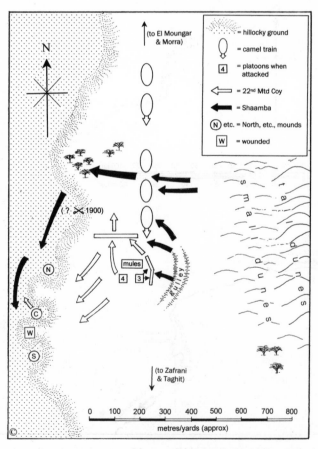

MAP 14 El Moungar, 2 September 1903 (after Holtz)

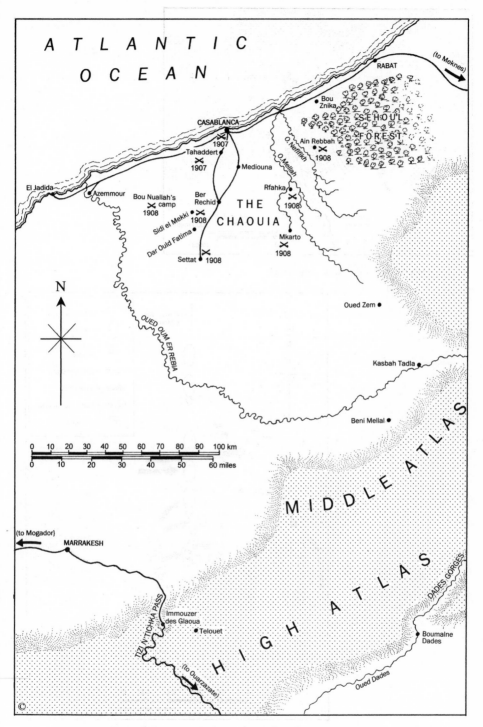

MAP 15 Central Western Morocco, from the Chaouia to the High Atlas

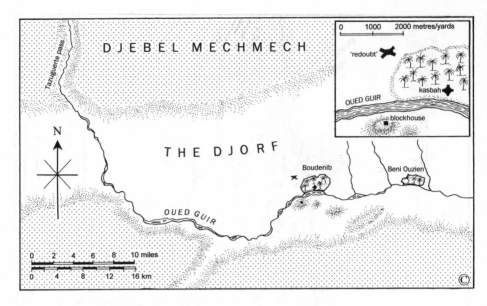

MAP 16 Boudenib, September 1908

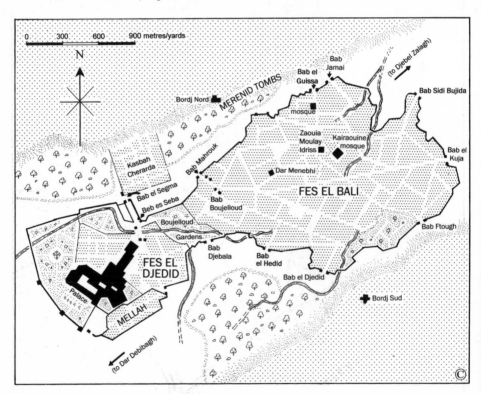

MAP 17 Fes, May 1912

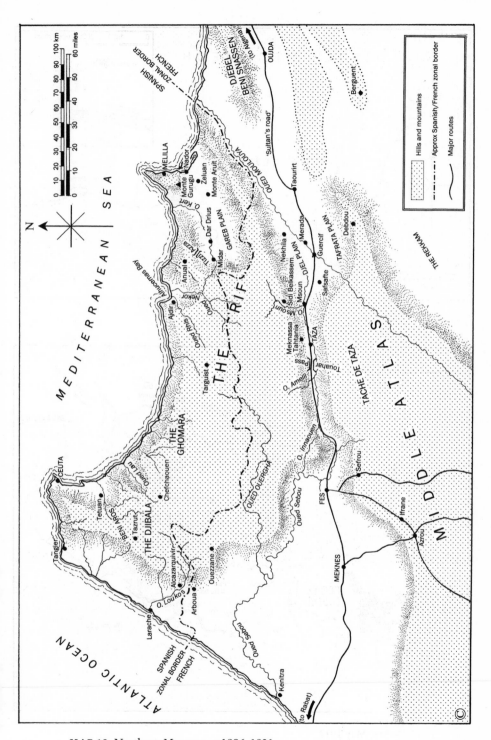

MAP 18 Northern Morocco, c.1906–1921

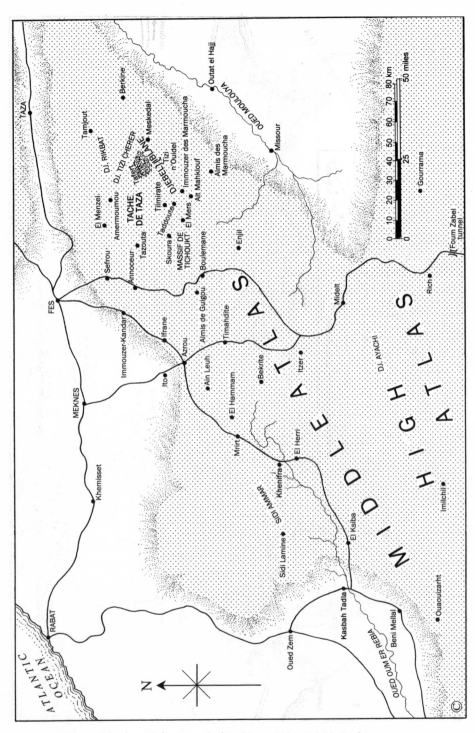

MAP 19 The Middle Atlas: the Zaian front, and the Tache de Taza

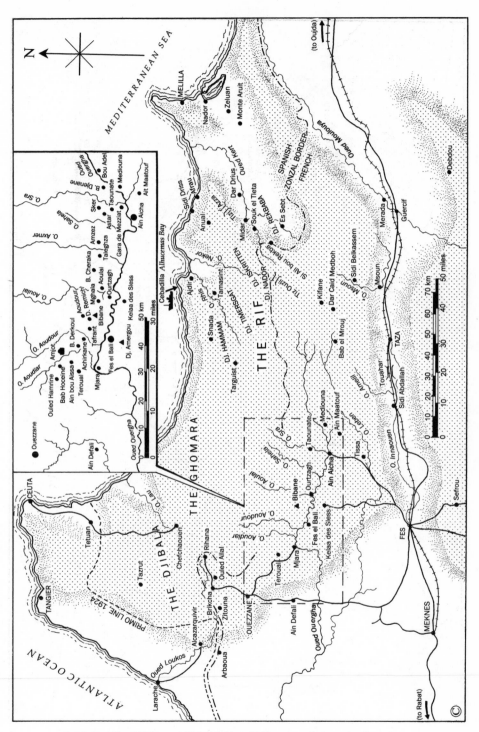

MAP 20 The Rif Wasr, 1925–26; (detail) the central Ouergha front

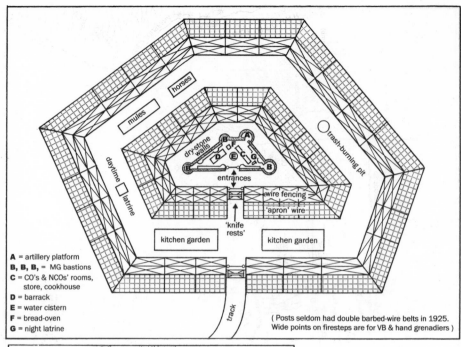

mules

horses

drystone walls

B · A
D F
E C G
B · · B

entrances

trash-burning pit

daytime ☐ latrine

wire fencing

'apron' wire

'knife rests'

kitchen garden

kitchen garden

A = artillery platform
B, B, B, = MG bastions
C = CO's & NCOs' rooms, store, cookhouse
D = barrack
E = water cistern
F = bread-oven
G = night latrine

track

(Posts seldom had double barbed-wire belts in 1925. Wide points on firesteps are for VB & hand grenadiers)

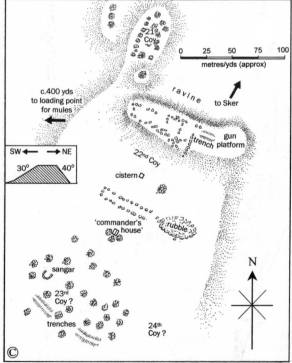

21st Coy

0   25   50   75   100
metres/yds (approx)

c.400 yds to loading point for mules

ravine

to Sker

gun platform

trench

SW ◄—— ——► NE
30°   40°

22nd Coy

cistern ☐

'commander's house'

rubble

N

sangar

23rd Coy ?

trenches

24th Coy ?

Ⓒ

MAP 21 Recommended post layout, Morocco, 1920s–30s (after Vanègue)

MAP 22 Remains of post at Astar, 2007

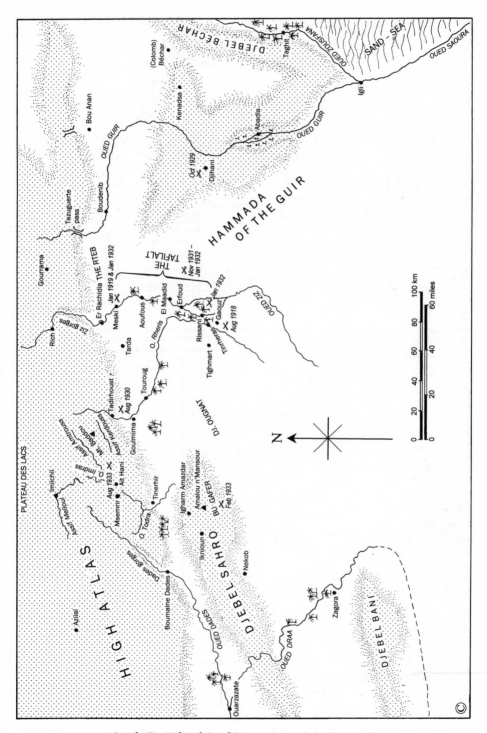

MAP 23 South Central and South-East Morocco, c.1930–34

SAND - SEA

DJEBEL BÉCHAR

OUED SAOURA

OUED ZOUSFANA

Taghit

(Colomb)
Béchar

Kenadsa

Igli

OUED GUIR

Abadla

Oct 1929

Djihani

OUED GUIR

HAMMADA
OF THE GUIR

Bou Anan

Boudenib

Tazuguerte
pass

THE RTEB

Jan 1919 & Jan 1932

THE TAFILALT

Nov 1931 –
Jan 1932

Gourrama

Er Rachidia

Meski

Aoufous

El Maadid

Erfoud

Jan 1932

ZIZ Gorges

Rich

Tarda

O. Rheris

Rissani

Gaouz

Aug 1918

OUED ZIZ

Touroug

Tighmart

Tinmeflest

Goulmima

Tadirhoust

Aug 1930

PLATEAU DES LACS

Imilchil

Assif Melloul

O. Imdias

Mt. Baddou

Assif Kerouss

Assif Amrouss

Aug 1933   Aït Hani

Msemrir

Tinerhir

O. Todra

DJ. OUGNAT

Ighram Amazdar

Amalou n Mansour

BU GAFER

Feb 1933

Azilal

HIGH ATLAS

Dades Gorges

Boumaine Dades

OUED DADES

Iknioun

Nekob

DJEBEL SAHRO

OUED DRAA

Zagora

DJEBEL BANI

Ouarzazate

N

100 km

60 miles

80

60

40

20

40

20

0   0

©

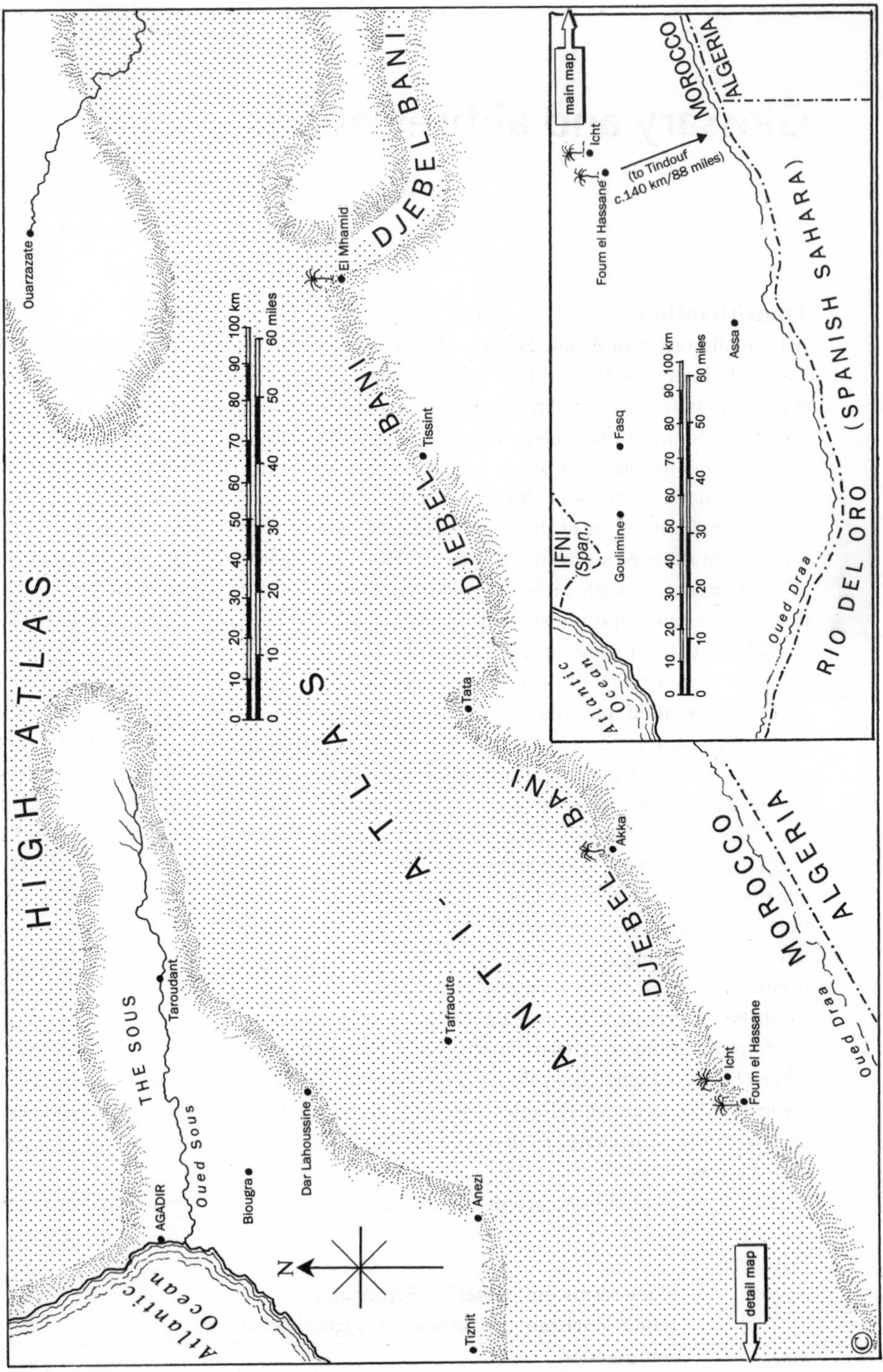
HIGH ATLAS
ANTI-ATLAS
DJEBEL BANI
THE SOUS
Atlantic Ocean
Oued Sous
Oued Draa
MOROCCO
ALGERIA
Ouarzazate
AGADIR
Taroudant
Biougra
Dar Lahoussine
Tafraoute
Tiznit
Anezi
Tata
Tissint
El Mhamid
Akka
Icht
Foum el Hassane
N
0 10 20 30 40 50 60 70 80 90 100 km
0 10 20 30 40 50 60 miles
detail map
main map
IFNI (Span.)
Goulimine
Fasq
Assa
(to Tindouf c.140 km/88 miles)
RIO DEL ORO
(SPANISH SAHARA)

MAP 24 South-West Morocco: the Sous and the Anti-Atlas, c.1929–34

Glossary and abbreviations

Transliteration

All transliteration of Arabic is basically phonetic; it always involves the insertion of chosen Roman vowels, and there are often several alternative Roman consonants, so sources transliterated into French, English, Spanish and German over the past century inevitably confront the reader with inconsistencies. The choice of rendering the term for a watercourse as *oued* or *wad*, for example, for a walled village as *ksar* or *qsar*, and tribal name prefixes as *ouled* or *awlad, beni* or *bani*, is clear enough, but others are less so. I lost count of the number of spellings for the Middle Atlas Berber tribe rendered in these pages as the Ait Segrushin, and of the apparently random spellings of place names on both early and modern maps printed in different countries – for instance, the mountain heartland of the Ait Atta Berbers is variously given as the Djebel Sahro, Jebel Sarho or Jbel Saghru.

After a brief moment of insanity when I contemplated trying to standardize all spellings, I recalled that this book is not intended for linguistic specialists, and I took an entirely arbitrary decision: linguistic purity and consistency have been ruthlessly sacrificed to clarity of recognition. Most Arabic names are given in the French forms found in general sources (using, e.g., *djebel, oued, Chaouia, Tahami el Glaoui* rather then *jbel, wad, Shawiya, T'hami al-Glawi*), but even so I have not been rigidly consistent (e.g., preferring *Dawi Mani* over *Doui Menia*). For Berber names I have usually copied the forms used by Professor Ross E. Dunn and/or David M. Hart. I have omitted diacritical marks; and I have sometimes deliberately chosen among alternative spellings to reinforce the differences between similar names for different persons and tribes (in a very few cases a common alternative spelling is given in parentheses after the first use of a name).

A similar problem faced me in the chapters on African and Indochinese campaigns, where I have adopted a similarly cavalier solution. Vietnamese names are usually given in their separated syllables without hyphenation, e.g. Tuyen Quang, but these days it would be pedantic to insist on Ha Noi or Hai Phong instead of the familiar elided forms.

In this, as in all other matters, any errors and infelicities are entirely my own.

Glossary

aman	peace terms (lit. 'water' in Berber dialect)
amil	senior Maghzan (q.v.) official (at Figuig and Oujda)
amir	commander
'bigors'	French Naval/Colonial artillery – see RAM/RAC

bled	open country
cadi	Islamic judge
caid	tribal chief
chott	depression, dried lake
dar	house, mansion
djebel	range of mountains or hills
djich	small raid, raiding party
douar	tent village
faqih	teacher
goumier	North African native auxiliary soldier of short-term enlistment
harka	large war party, expedition
imam	religious teacher, officiating preacher at mosque
kasbah	fortress-village
khalifa	viceroy
ksar	walled village
maghzan	Moroccan central government
moghazni	North African native local gendarme
medina	Arab city
mellah	Jewish quarter, ghetto
marabout	holy man
'marsouins'	French Naval/Colonial infantry – see RIM/RIC
mehalla	army
'moblots'	*gardes mobiles* militiamen
oued	river, watercourse
partisan	North African tribal irregular in French service
pasha	governor
sharif	descendant of the Prophet
sheikh	leader, elder
souk	market
suppletif	see *partisan*
'turcos'	French Algerian native light infantrymen – see RTA
ulama	council of Islamic scholars
zaouia	centre of religious brotherhood, 'abbey'

Abbreviations of French unit titles, etc

I, II, etc.	Battalion of a regiment; e.g. I/2nd RE 1st Bn/2nd Foreign Regiment
Bat d'Af	Bataillon d'Infanterie Légère d'Afrique (Africa Light Infantry – penal)
BCP	Bataillon de Chasseurs à Pied (Light Infantry)
BILA	see Bat d'Af
GOC	general officer commanding
LE	Légion Étrangère (Foreign Legion)
RAC	Régiment d'Artillerie Colonial (Colonial Artillery)
RAM	Régiment d'Artillerie de Marine (Naval Artillery)
RCA	Régiment de Chasseurs d'Afrique (Africa Light Horse)
RE	Régiment Étranger (Foreign Regiment)

REC	Régiment Étranger de Cavalerie (Foreign Cavalry)
REI	Régiment Étranger d'Infanterie (Foreign Infantry)
RIC	Régiment d'Infanterie Colonial (Colonial Infantry)
RICM	Régiment d'Infanterie Colonial du Maroc (Morocco Colonial Infantry Regiment)
RIM	Régiment d'Infanterie de Marine (Naval Infantry)
RS	Régiment de Spahis (Native Light Horse)
RTA	Régiment de Tirailleurs Algériens (It is conventional today to translate *tirailleurs* as 'Rifles' in a nod to their British Indian Army equivalents, but in the context of this book the literal translation 'Algerian Skirmishers' seems more apt.)
RTC	Régiment de Tirailleurs Coloniaux (Colonial Skirmishers – West African)
RTM	Régiment de Tirailleurs Marocains (Moroccan Skirmishers)
RTS	Régiment de Tirailleurs Sénégalais (Senegalese Skirmishers)
RTSM	Régiment de Tirailleurs Sénégalais du Maroc (Morocco Senegalese Skirmishers Regiment)
RTT	Régiment de Tirailleurs Tonkinois (North Vietnamese Skirmishers)
RZ	Régiment de Zouaves (North African Europeans)

Picture captions

Photograph Section One:
1 The Legion's unexpected battlefield in the streets of Paris, spring 1871. This is the Rue Peyronnet in the western suburb of Neuilly (today, Rue Peronnet, three streets north of the Avenue Charles De Gaulle). During 16–19 April 1871 it marked the left-hand edge of the Foreign Regiment's perimeter in the street-fighting against Dombrowski's National Guards; this and the parallel Boulevard d'Argenson one block south were the most heavily shelled part of the regiment's sector, where four days in the line cost the Legion 129 casualties.

2 The ruins around the canal harbour of the Basin de La Villette, crossed by the Foreign Regiment on the morning of 27 May 1871. Most of the visible devastation was caused not by shellfire but by the previous day's massive fires and explosions in the large grain warehouses. (Both images Eugene Schulkind Paris Commune Collection, courtesy University of Sussex Library)

3 A gateway of the citadel at Bac Ninh in Tonkin; the town was stormed by General de Négrier's légionnaires on 12 March 1884, but the Chinese regular garrison fled without defending the citadel itself. The outer defences of the town – and of Son Tay, which the Legion did have to storm – were almost identical. Note the fringe of bamboo spikes projecting downwards from the wall parapets, and the huge pile of bricks raised to block access to the gate tunnel for troops assaulting across the moat bridge. (Engraving Lancelot, from Hocquard's photo)

4 Small single-screw Navy gunboat on the Clear river, probably at Phu Doan, December 1884. French troops relied upon the rivers for many tactical movements, and on the gunboats themselves for fire support and some transport – here several dozen troops are shown crowded onto the deck. This is presumably the same class of vessel as *Mitrailleuse*, the gunboat anchored off Tuyen Quang fort during the siege; note the single gun at the bow, and the armoured crowsnest mounting what looks like a light 'Gatling'-type revolving cannon. With a crew of 12 ratings, these boats were an ensign's command – a dream posting for any adventurous young officer. (From Hocquard)

5 The fort at Hue Thué in the Yen The highlands was skilfully held by troops of the Tonkinese rebel mandarin De Nam, and a major French operation was required before it was captured at the third attempt in January 1891; the Englishman

Frederic Martyn of II/1st RE had taken part in a failed attempt the previous month. The drawings made later by a 2nd Brigade intelligence officer show elaborate Chinese-style brick walls protected outside by *panji*-sticks, both in the open and concealed in 'wolf-traps' (left); beyond these were a palisade and a thick abatis. (From Manington)

6 This squad, probably from II/1st RE, are halted in the jungled Yen The hills near Cho Trang in 1892. They wear white sun helmets and grubby khaki-drill jackets from Naval Infantry stores, and only the lightest patrol kit, with a single cartridge pouch to save weight. The Tonkinese Skirmishers wear their dark blue cotton uniform with a flat-topped bamboo 'salacco' hat. Cho Trang was a notoriously dreary and unhealthy post, where the English légionnaire George Manington narrowly survived blackwater fever. (Jean Vigne)

7 To keep the forts in the Sud-Oranais supplied, single convoys of up to 4,000 camels, spread out over miles, were not unusual – and neither were losses of up to 30 per cent during the round trip. A working camel with a load of c.300lb needs water every third day and at least 60lb of forage daily, and these were often impossible to find on the Zousfana tracks. A camel can go for up to five days grazing on camel-thorn alone, but it then needs grain feed and a couple of days' rest in good pasture, and if it gets thirsty it stops eating. Many drivers skimped on grain to increase their profits; losses were also aggravated by careless loading and overwork by the drivers, who for the sake of the French compensation (and the saleable hide) sometimes deliberately ill-treated beasts that could have survived with proper treatment. (SIHLE, courtesy Jacques Gandini)

8 On prolonged marches in the Sud-Oranais the men could load their packs on the baggage camels and carried only light equipment, but their fatigue clothing and their boots suffered badly from the thorn-scrub and sharp stones. Even this blurred photo shows the raggedness of their uniforms after a few weeks in the wilderness. (Courtesy Jacques Gandini)

9 Water camels resting at Boudenib, c.1910. Two of these 50-litre (c.11-gallon) iron-bound wooden kegs was the maximum safe load; up to four times as much could have been carried in native water-skins, but these were not available in sufficient numbers, and white troops did not understand how to care for them. The kegs leaked even if well prepared, and more than 5 per cent wastage per day had to be expected. A battalion of 1,000 men needed at least 300 camels to carry five days' water, the normal reserve in the Sud-Oranais. (Photo Garaud)

10 The Taghla pass, looking northwards towards Figuig oasis; the Oued Zousfana flows through it on the west side below the Djebel Zenaga, with the steeper wall of the Djebel Taghla beyond the sandy corridor on the east bank. This was the route followed on 31 May 1903 by Captain Bonnelet's 18th (Mounted) Company 1st RE. (Photo Bourgault)

11 Classic image of a sergeant (left) and three légionnaires of 2nd RE at Figuig during the brief occupation following the bombardment in June 1903. This postcard bore the postmark 'Beni Ounif de Figuig', from the garrisoned railhead that had been established 5 miles south of the oasis. At that date full decorations were worn on the campaign uniform; the tall légionnaire, second left – whose two re-enlistment chevrons show that he has served since at least 1893 – displays medals for Tonkin, Madagascar and Colonial service, but unlike his comrades he is still a private 2nd class. The covered képi with sun-curtain, and the broad blue body belt, were not actually exclusive to the Legion; they were also worn by the Bats d'Af. (Photo Leroux)

12 Looking roughly south from the walls of Taghit fort; the minaret at left shows how close the fort was built to the *ksar* below. At right is the signal station on the summit of the western ridge above. This photo cannot date from earlier than 1905, when General Lyautey ordered the signallers' station to be improved into the substantial blockhouse visible here, named Fort de l'Éperon; during the attacks of August 1903 it was a much more rudimentary position. (Courtesy Jacques Gandini)

13 Algeria's Great Western *Erg* begins immediately on the eastern edge of the oasis of Taghit on the Oued Zousfana. The French fort there was built in 1901, on a ledge of the cliff rising above the west side of the palm groves – i.e., behind the photographer's left shoulder. During the attacks of August 1903 the mixed garrison, including légionnaires from 22nd (Mounted) Company/2nd RE, came under fire from the high dunes only 300 yards away.

14 Père Charles de Foucauld of the White Fathers at his hermitage at Beni Abbès, with Captain Roger de Susbielle, the Native Affairs officer for the lower Zousfana region. Susbielle, commanding at Taghit, kept in intermittent touch with the missionary, who had been a cavalry officer and a resourceful intelligence agent before he found his vocation; in September 1903 Father de Foucauld rode to Taghit to help care for the wounded of El Moungar. After nine years at Beni Abbès, in June 1910 Foucauld would move eastwards into the central Sahara and build a second hermitage c.35 miles from Tamanrasset, 8,500ft up in the Ahaggar mountains, where he wrote the first dictionary and grammar of the Tuareg language. He was killed by hostile tribesmen in December 1916 during the Senussi risings. (Photo J.C. Humbert, courtesy Jacques Gandini)

15 The 'proprietor' from a two-man Legion mule team, with their loaded mount (see Fig 22 below for a note on the gear usually carried). Apart from the curtained képi replacing a sun helmet, this man is typical of the légionnaires of Captain Vauchez's 2nd Half-Company, 22nd (Mounted)/2nd RE who were ambushed at El Moungar on 2 September 1903. He wears the white fatigue blouse and trousers, with his blue waist sash under his rifle belt and Y-straps; the only other items carried on his body are his haversack, waterbottle and slung Lebel. (Musée de l'Empéri, courtesy M. Raoul Brunon)

16 Lieutenant Selchauhansen, mortally wounded at El Moungar, was an artillery officer in the Danish Army who had obtained a Legion commission in 1894, serving thereafter both in North Africa and in Madagascar. The story that the Danish Prince Aage was inspired to join the Legion by a boyhood meeting with Selchauhansen seems to be groundless. (SIHLE, courtesy Jacques Gandini)

17 El Moungar, looking west towards the *djebel;* in the foreground, stones cover the mass grave of the légionnaires killed on 2 September 1903. The obelisk, raised later, stands about 13ft high on the central of the three low mounds defended by Captain Vauchez's half-company – this feature's undramatic contours gave very little natural protection. Both the monument and the grave received large memorial plaques; these were desecrated by passing tribesmen over the decades, but when the Saharan traveller Ivan Baumgarten visited the site in 1987 the obelisk still stood. (Courtesy Jacques Gandini)

18 In the first years of the 20th century fortified stations marked the advance of the railway down the Zousfana; Ben Zireg, built in 1904, was between Beni Ounif and Colomb Béchar. Although this was essentially a military route, little frontier villages sprang up along the railway to service the garrisons. The tracks also brought increased prosperity to the Arab merchants in the south-eastern oases, by opening up a quicker and cheaper export route than the long and dangerous caravan tracks westwards to the Tafilalt and then north across the High Atlas. (Courtesy Jacques Gandini)

19 The colour party with the flag of 1st RE gives a detachment from the regiment a send-off from the railway station at Sidi bel Abbès on their way to Taourirt in eastern Morocco, via the frontier town of Oujda; from there they will march on foot. The 3rd, 5th and 6th Battalions of 1st RE operated in 1907–11 on the high plains around the Moulouya river, where Taourirt post was established in June 1910. In May 1911 a company from VI/1st RE came to grief at Alouana during General Girardot's operations to draw tribal attention away from the uprising around Fes provoked by Sultan Moulay Hafid. (Courtesy Jacques Gandini)

20 Before the First World War – and for many years afterwards – the only means of evacuating casualties from wilderness battlefields were (left to right) the mule *cacolet*, with two chairs; the mule litter, with two stretchers for prone men; and the camel litter with the same load, here with canopies rigged. Although morphine might be available, all gave a ride somewhere between the uncomfortable and the agonizing, usually lasting several days, and the wounded suffered terribly from the sun and the flies. This photo is captioned 1903. (Courtesy Jacques Gandini)

21 Légionnaires of 1st (Mounted) Company, 1st RE in camp at Safsafte while escorting a convoy westwards from Guercif to Msoun, which was occupied in May 1913. The soldier at left is dressed for sentry duty, in the mule companies' typical field uniform of sun helmet, white fatigues, broad blue sash, and black leather equipment with cartridge pouches for his M1886/93 Lebel magazine rifle; in camp, he wears canvas shoes instead of hobnailed boots. Several men wear the red-and-blue képi, with or without a khaki cover – it was always a more popular headgear than the 'melon' helmet. The man in the right background with his hands on his hips, wearing a brass-buttoned white jacket with gold forearm stripes, is their sergeant. (Photo N. Boumendil)

22 Well-known photo of a Mounted Company soldier giving his '*brêle*' a trickle from his 2-litre waterbottle. The mule's official load was, ahead of the saddle, a bolster-shaped 44lb sack of oats; the men's greatcoats rolled in their tent-sections; two wallets with picket line and pin, cooking gear and camp tools; and usually, on top of it all, a chance-gathered bundle of firewood. Below and behind the saddle were a pair of big saddlebags; two spare waterbottles; spare horseshoes and nails; rolled blankets; reserve ammunition, and anything from two to fifteen days' rations for the men. (Musée de l'Empéri, courtesy M.Raoul Brunon)

23 Mounted Company légionnaires working on the gateway of their new post, while to the right others in patrol kit lead in saddle- and pack-mules. Left, in front of the gate pillars, are a lieutenant or warrant officer with a white sun helmet, and another just in from patrol, wearing tinted goggles on a khaki helmet over a wrapped white *cheich*. The post is unidentified, but it is certainly in the frontier country of the Sud-Oranais and eastern Morocco, and the photo dates from before the First World War. (SIHLE, courtesy John Robert Young)

24 Looking southwards across the broad bed of the Oued Guir from the *palmerie* and *kasbah* of Boudenib, at the red rock *gara* where Lieutenant Vary of VI/1st RE and his 75 men defended the blockhouse on the night of 1/2 September 1908. Ruins – apparently of a later construction on the same spot – are just visible on the skyline of the tabletop, about one-third of the way in from the left escarpment. The distance from the camera is about 1,000 yards. (Author's photo)

25 The Boudenib blockhouse, seen from the south on the day following Vary's defence, after at least one 80mm mountain gun had been brought up. On the previous night the tribesmen had massed in the foreground of this photo before attacking the blockhouse from three sides. Beyond the *goumiers* at the left is the dark *palmerie*, far below and beyond the river to the north. (Photo Garaud)

26 Guercif, on the Oued Moulouya in the middle of the high plains, was almost half way from the Algerian border to Fes; Lyautey's patrols westwards from Taourirt reached here in 1910. Guercif is a typically Spartan enclosure, basically a *caravanserai* with a watchtower (from which this photo was taken). There is a firing step along the inside of the crenellated walls, and around the basic buildings plenty of room has been left for the tents, animals and baggage of convoys stopping overnight. (Photo G. Tecourt)

27 Légionnaires building barracks at Taourirt post, c.1911; the Legion always did its own construction work. The defensive walls of a new post were raised first, and barracks and other internal buildings were only added when the first permanent garrison was installed, usually the following winter. (Courtesy Jacques Gandini)

28 On the great open plain of the Chaouia behind Casablanca, General d'Amade's Landing Corps manoeuvred in open rectangular formations that might be a mile across, with the infantry forming the faces and the artillery, baggage, and herds of rations-on-the-hoof in the centre. At other times two of these 'squares' were formed, one for offensive action and one protecting the impedimenta. (From Rankin, photo Reginald Kann)

29 Men of one of the Legion battalions in action at Settat, 15 January 1908, during General d'Amade's first march to that town. The forward face of a 'square' deployed for action in a single rank, so a battalion occupied about 1,000 yards of frontage, with its ammunition mules close behind. A second battalion waited in support, drawn up 450–850 yards behind in line of platoon columns, ready to deploy where and when they were needed. The artillery were *'en batterie'* close to these supports; cavalry always guarded open flanks, and General d'Amade kept a modest reserve under his own hand. (From Rankin, photo Reginald Kann)

30 These Arab tribal horsemen of the western Moroccan plains are in fact French-allied *'partisans'* – or at least they were, on the day the photo was taken – but their appearance is indistinguishable from the cavalry who attacked General d'Amade's battalions on the Chaouia in spring 1908. (Photo Gillot & Ratel)

31 'Honour to the Brave': after d'Amade's success on the Casablanca plains the 6th Battalion, 1st Foreign were recalled to Sidi bel Abbès in August 1908. Like any unit returning from active service VI/1st RE were given a lavish welcome, both by the regiment and also by at least some of the town's civilians. The fact that postcards commemorating such events were put on sale by a commercial studio – even if only in Algeria – showed that by this date the Legion's renown was well established. (Photo N.Boumendil)

32 The sale of a postcard celebrating the courage of an individual légionnaire is remarkable testimony to the public mood in Algeria, though not unprecedented: the blinded Légionnaire Haberthur had been publicized in this way in summer 1910. During General Alix's operations in north-eastern Morocco in 1913 after the establishment of the Protectorate, Sergeant Panther of I/1st RE was wounded while saving the life of Lieutenant Grosjean after their company commander had been killed, in an attack by Beni Bou Yahi tribesmen on the camp at Nekhila on 10 April. Panther himself would be killed in June 1917, as a warrant officer leading a platoon of his regiment's 1st (Mounted) Company in the hills north of the Taza corridor. (Photo N. Boumendil)

33 This and the other photos on this page were published in July 1913 in a major article in the magazine L'Illustration which was clearly part of an official attempt to improve the Legion's image at a time of intensely hostile German propaganda. This légionnaire of the 2nd RE photographed at Saida, wearing full field marching order and sun helmet and sporting the Colonial Medal with a campaign clasp, was said to be an Englishman named 'De Bulmerinq' – one suspects a phonetic approximation.

34, 35 Portraits of many nationalities of légionnaires were published in *L'Illustration*. A Cuban, 'Domingues', gives the lie to the claim that the Legion accepted only white recruits. The original caption for the Austrian, 'Bezdicek', claims that this veteran of 15 years' service and many campaigns was a former captain in the Austro-Hungarian Army; it is perhaps not too fanciful to see in his face the melancholy of the disgraced gentleman-ranker? His name, if genuine, may indicate a Czech, at a time when that people were agitating for national autonomy.

36 This barrack room shown in the *L'Illustration* feature conforms almost exactly to Frederic Martyn's description of the Quartier Viénot in 1889. The men have been carefully posed as if at their ease – in fact the mattress and blankets had to be folded away during the day. Such rooms were about 75ft long and 20ft wide, with windows at each end and doors in each side wall. The rifle rack is at the far end, and the cabinets hoisted up below the ceiling contain the squad's tableware for meals. Each man's clothing is meticulously stacked on the shelf above his bedspace, with his equipment hanging below behind a towel forming a curtain.

37 This platoon, apparently photographed on the plains of north-eastern Morocco, have stacked their rifles during a halt, but thirty-odd dropped knapsacks are not evident here, so they were probably posed during a short-range local operation close to the column. Note the sentries spaced out individually about 100 yards beyond, between the platoon and the higher ground.

38 A fine natural study of two officers representing mainstays of the old Armée d'Afrique before the Great War; when on column, Legion units were almost always covered by cavalrymen of the Spahis. These two unidentified veterans are a lieutenant colonel of the Legion, wearing a caped greatcoat over his service uniform, and an Algerian captain squadron commander of Spahis. In 1874 it had been ordered that captain was the highest rank an Arab officer could attain, and after 1897 this ceiling was actually lowered to lieutenant. (AdeQ Historical Archives)

39 A cheerful group of officers, with a civilian guest, picnic in the field in north-eastern Morocco during operations against Ouled Salem tribesmen in 1913. The officers wearing the native *cheich* scarf/turban and *djellabah* robe over their uniforms (near left) are named as Captain d'Alencon and Lieutenant Pollet, leading Arab auxiliaries. General Maurice Baumgarten (standing right) was Lyautey's reliable deputy at Oujda; in May 1914 he would lead the eastern force, including two battalions of 1st RE, in the final elimination of the 'Taza gap'.

40 The Bastille Day ceremonies at Taza in July 1914 were effectively a repeat of the occasion on 18 May when the flag of 1st RE was paraded in front of General Lyautey and 6,000 troops to celebrate the link-up there of Gouraud's and Baumgarten's forces from west and east, opening up the 'Taza corridor' between Fes and Oujda for the first time. From 1910 the field dress of légionnaires in Morocco had increasingly been the M1901 khaki drill Colonial Troops issue; the képi-cover was removed for parades. (Courtesy Jacques Gandini)

41 At Taza, soldiers lift the badly wounded Major Met, commanding officer of I/1st RE, out of a horse ambulance after an agonizing journey in the summer heat. At Sidi Belkassem on 5 June 1914 he had led his battalion into the attack up a slope, with the bugles playing his favourite march 'Karoline'; a bullet shattered both his legs, and one would have to be amputated. His battalion successfully petitioned the high command for 'Daddy' Met's promotion. (Photo Réty, courtesy Jacques Gandini)

Photograph section two:

42 Hilltop post in the Rif, 1925–26; Clérisse captions this as Kifane, a post in the eastern sector which managed to hold out. Its appearance is probably fairly typical: the walls are a patchwork of dry stone, timbers, and what may be either mud bricks or earth-filled ammo boxes, with rough loopholing. (Photo Gillot & Ratel)

43 An outlying blockhouse of the post above, seen from the open connecting trench that linked it to the main garrison. Such flanking positions, held by only a handful of men to cover a water point or a masked approach to the post, were extremely vulnerable. (Photo Gillot & Ratel)

44 The summit of Astar, looking roughly east to west, with (at left) the dark neighbouring hill that was occupied by the Rifians throughout the action of 4–5 June 1925. At centre is the narrow summit shelf, today surrounded by the remains of drystone walling showing the position of the upper range of buildings; the exposed gun platform at the post's north-eastern corner is just outside the photo to the right. The figure just visible sitting on the ruined wall at centre right gives an idea of scale. This photo shows the sharply sloping ground of the defended area south of the summit shelf; in 1925 this was the interior of the post, defended on 4–5 June by Captain Pechkoff's 22nd Company of the Cazaban Battalion. (Photo Graham Scott)

45 Looking north-west and downwards from the north-western corner of the summit of Astar, at the shoulder from which 21st Company covered the main western approach to the post; today cactus growth follows the straight traces of the original defensive positions. The English légionnaire Adolphe Cooper served in 21st Company, but his memoir gives no details of holding the hilltop after the original assault. Note the steepness of the northern ravine immediately below the summit shelf. (Author's photo)

46 There are few known photos of Legion rankers during the Rif War that show enough specific detail to be worth publishing. These men are clearly inside one of the Colonial Troops' posts built on the hilltops before Abd el Krim's offensive; note the loopholed drystone walls. Incidentally, under magnification it is clear that these légionnaires have two types of light machine gun, and thus need two types of ammunition resupply – 8mm rimmed for the old 'Chauchat', and 7.5mm rimless for the new FM24. (SIHLE, courtesy John Robert Young)

47 The English memoirist Adolphe Cooper posed for this studio shot shortly after enlisting for his first hitch in 1914, aged 15 years. His service was interrupted by his wounding at Gallipoli in 1915 and subsequent discharge, but he re-enlisted twice after the Great War. He served under Major Cazaban in VI/1st RE in the Rif, and among the officers he knew and admired were Captain Pechkoff of that battalion and Lieutenant Djindjeradze of 4th REI and 1st REC. Cooper took his final discharge as a sergeant in 1930.

48 Major Marcel Deslandes, the former Line sergeant who distinguished himself in the Rif in command of II/1st RE. After leading a famous charge at Bibane on 25 May 1925, he fell at the head of his men near Bab Hoceine on 18 July. (SIHLE)

49a Breguet 14A2 reconnaissance/bomber aircraft on the airfield at Taza, autumn 1925 or spring 1926; about 300 Breguet 14s represented some 80 per cent of the equipment of the *Aéronautique Militaire* in the Rif and Tache de Taza campaigns. A rack for 16x 10kg (22lb) anti-personnel bombs – attached tail-first – can be seen under the fuselage, and the observer mans a pair of Lewis machine guns on a mounting ring that allows depression for firing at ground targets. The 'Pierrot' insignia of Escadrille BR 7 is a reminder of the hasty reinforcement of Colonel Armangaud's 37th Air Observation Regiment in Morocco. The 32nd RAO in France transferred its Sqns BR 201 and 219 to the 37th in early September 1925, and must have grabbed this machine from another of the regiment's squadrons to make up the detachment's strength, without taking the time to repaint it. (Photo Henry Clérisse)

49b Renault FT-17 two-man light tanks, armed with a machine gun or a 37mm cannon, were committed in Morocco for the first time in August 1925 north of Ouezzane, where they supported – among other units – II/1st REI. Here they roll forward across the almost dry Oued Ouergha on their way to the front. (Photo Coutanson)

50 The terrain of the upper Oued Nekor valley in the eastern Rif, where I/ and III/2nd REI distinguished themselves during the final offensive of May 1926 as units of General Ibos' Moroccan Division. This is one of some 14,000 aerial photos taken during the campaign, covering nearly 6,000 square miles; this to some extent compensated for the lack of adequate maps of this unexplored region of the nominally Spanish zone. (From Clérisse)

51 The brothers Abd el Krim el Khattabi. While Mohammed – seated – provided the vision, the inspiration and the public face of the Rif rising, Mhamed, younger by about ten years, was the quiet military organizer; indeed, some Europeans who met them thought the younger brother the more impressive personality. Note the modesty of their appearance; despite his ambitions and his power, Mohammed Abd el Krim was never seen in any costume more showy than this plain *rezzah* turban and *djellabah*. (UPI)

52 Hubert Lyautey, apparently photographed as a four-star *général de corps d'armée* during the First World War, when he was in his early sixties. This portrait by Henri Manuel closely resembles the slimmer-faced Lyautey of his active fifties, with a penetrating pale blue gaze, and a dark moustache despite his silver hair.

53 Marshal Lyautey, in an official portrait taken at some date between 1921 and 1925, so at least 66 years old. He now shows a greyer moustache and thickened features, perhaps due to his serious ill-health from 1923 onwards.

54 Group of légionnaires of 3rd REI off-duty in Fes in the early 1930s; the tall soldier in the background is an Englishman, No.3254 Albert Neal, who before his discharge in 1936 had been promoted sergeant and awarded the Croix de Guerre TOE. These men all wear the bleached képi-cover with winter walking-out uniform; they proudly display at the left shoulder the double *fourragère* lanyard of the Légion d'Honneur and Croix de Guerre awarded in October 1918 to this regiment's predecessor, the RMLE, for nine citations while fighting on the Western Front – a distinction shared by only one other French regiment, the RICM. (Courtesy John Neal)

55 Légionnaires Cyril Conway (left) and Albert Neal photographed in handsome 'whites' at Er Rachidia, March 1935; they had enlisted together in Marseille in February 1931. From the early 1920s white walking-out dress was encouraged, to give battalions some extra 'swank', but it was not an issue uniform. The 4th Foreign seem to have been the first to blossom, followed by the 2nd and 3rd; when the repentant sinner Corporal Adolphe Cooper served with III/4th REI in 1929 he was determined to be the most dazzling soldier in his company, and bleached his whites with Eau de Javel disinfectant and cinders. (Courtesy John Neal)

56 After the Rif and Tache de Taza campaigns of 1925–26 Legion infantry spent much of their time – and after 1933, almost all of it – labouring on Morocco's roads and other building projects. (AdeQ Historical Archives)

57 Tattoos – more or less crudely executed, usually by the soldiers themselves – were a long-standing tradition in the old Legion, as one of the rare outlets for individuality. There are many accounts of men tattooing defiant obscenities on their hands, feet or even foreheads, and some extraordinarily ambitious 'illustrated soldiers' are recorded. In 1912 d'Esparbes published a photo of a légionnaire whose entire torso was the canvas for an intricate and lubricious scene of 'Venus Awakening' on a draped bed, attended by three winged lovers, and the same author claimed to have seen with his own eyes the legendary 'Fox Hunt' tattoo. This légionnaire of the 4th REI in the

1930s has been fairly restrained: on his right arm can be made out a crescent and palm trees, and a snake coiled round a sword with the motto *Pas de chance* – 'No luck'. The illegible declaration on his collarbones, above a strange Picasso-like profile and the sultry beauty, seems to end with the words ' ... *j'en rien*' – which has a suitably nihilist ring to it. (Courtesy R.G. Harris)

58 No.2388 Légionnaire Robert Lincoln, photographed at Meknes in the early 1930s in clean white fatigues with the Legion sash. This Londoner – who looks like a man who could look after himself – enlisted in 1930 at the age of 23 and served for five years with the 2nd REI. At the time of his discharge in 1935 he was serving with the regiment's Mounted Company, then still equipped with mules, so it is not impossible that he saw action under Captain Fouré at Bu Gafer in 1933. Bobby Lincoln died in London in 1986. (Courtesy Jim Worden)

59 A Legion senior NCOs' canteen, probably at a regimental depot, in the early 1930s. Legion sergeants and above did not have to frequent squalid local grog-shops, and had the pay to stand each other drinks more varied than the rough red *pinard*. As in the old British Army, to get – and keep – a sergeant's stripes made an enormous difference to a soldier's status and prospects. Assuming that they avoided bullets, microbes and cirrhosis, most men who achieved this rank re-enlisted for the maximum term, earning a pension and valuable civic privileges on their eventual discharge. Foreign-born légionnaires earned French citizenship by a single five-year hitch, and naturalization was expected of men with ambitions for promotion. (Photo Sretchkovitch, courtesy Jacques Gandini)

60 & 61 Légionnaires in action in the cedar-clad alpine terrain of the Atlas, where after 1914 the Legion did far more of its soldiering than in the open desert. These may be men of the Mounted Company/2nd RE, photographed in summer 1932 during operations against the Ait Haddidou tribe, around the Assif Melloul valley south of the Plateau des Lacs in the High Atlas. The soldier in the foreground of the left-hand picture may be Bobby Lincoln; in the right-hand photo, note also one of the Berber *partisan* scouts, who were always indispensable. (Courtesy Jim Worden)

62 Southern Morocco, July 1932: the Georgian Lieutenant Prince Djindjeradze, a troop commander in 4th Squadron/1st Foreign Cavalry. He wears a covered képi and the 1st REC's *gandourah* field smock over his uniform. The English légionnaire Adolphe Cooper, who had been his orderly in 1929 when Djindjeradze was a platoon commander with III/4th REI, claimed that he and the other two company officers turned a blind eye to the unfortunate death in action, from a bullet in the back of the head, of a sadistic NCO. (Family collection)

63 Djindjeradze's troop trumpeter in IV/1st REC, Légionnaire Slavko. The Foreign Cavalry created a definite style for themselves when in the field. They wore képis with long *couvre-nuque* sun-curtains, abandoned by Legion infantry since the First

xl OUR FRIENDS BENEATH THE SANDS

World War; the *gandourah*, then worn by no other Legion enlisted men, was bleached a creamy white; a pale khaki *cheich* scarf was crossed on the chest; and sometimes these baggy khaki *seroual* desert trousers replaced the regulation breeches and leather leggings. (Family collection)

64 Studio portrait of an unidentified légionnaire posing in summer *grande tenue*, 1930s. The regimental number on his collar patch cannot be made out, but the long sun-curtain on his képi-cover almost certainly marks him as a cavalry trooper, since only the REC are known to have worn this *folklorique* item by this date. (AdeQ Historical Archives)

65 Prince Aage of Denmark was a big, high-spirited man who became popular with both his brother-officers and his men once he had proved himself free of any royal conceits. He was a 'group-oriented' rather than a 'goal-oriented' commander, who might be seen in louche city nightspots treating his subalterns to champagne and caviar, and sitting in on drums with the jazzband with his képi tipped at a rakish angle. The close friend with whom he is photographed here, in Marrakesh on New Year's Eve 1936, is an American expatriate named Dorothy Gould. She and Aage were also friends of the Georgian Prince Djindjeradze, whose family believed that he later owed her his freedom from internment by the Germans after the 1940 Armistice. When a Nazi commission obliged the Vichy regime to let it comb out 'undesirables' from the Legion, she apparently offered 'Djinn' a marriage of convenience that enabled him to sail for the neutral USA. (Family collection)

66 The terrain of the Djebel Sahro, photographed in hot October weather in 1997. This is the Tadout n'Tabla plateau, north and east of the village of Nekob; when Captain Spillmann's *goumiers* and *partisans* advanced across it against the Ait Atta in February 1933 it was bitterly cold and lashed by icy winds and rain. (Photo Andy Grainger)

67 A Legion infantry encampment in the Moroccan mountains in the early 1930s. The tents are pitched and rifles stacked inside the low dry-stone *murettes d'Afrique* that were built around every night camp, and pack-mules of the *train de combat* are picketed just outside, under the eyes of the armed sentry. At right foreground, the officers are gathered for a meal – the *popotte* or officers' dining mess was a sacred tradition, even in the field.

68 The French monument to the dead of 1933, raised at the foot of the final heights of Bu Gafer. The ruins are those of a police post installed after the submission of Assu u-Ba Slam. (Photo Andy Grainger)

69 View from one of the triple summits of Bu Gafer; in 1997 the ground was still scattered with the fragments of shells and bombs. The Ait Atta guide pictured here, aged about 67, negotiated the climb without any apparent fatigue; he had recently added a new 28-year-old wife to his household. (Photo Andy Grainger)

70 u-Skunti, the Ait Murghad chief who led the final defence of Mount Baddou in August 1933. His features are characteristic of the Berbers of the High Atlas. (Photo Ward Price)

71 Berber *partisans* during the Mount Baddou campaign, indistinguishable from the rebels led by u-Skunti. The Legion officer in the right background, in *cheich* and *gandourah*, is a model of 1930s battlefield *chic*. (Photo Ward Price)

72 Légionnaire Ronald House of II/2nd REI, photographed by Ward Price during the Mount Baddou operations. A Londoner, House was a man of his hands in more ways than one: a drummer in the regimental *clique* when in garrison at Meknes, he had reached the finals of the 1932 French Army boxing championships in Morocco, and his skill with a pencil was also employed by his unit. About ten days before this photo was taken he was recommended by his company commander for the Croix de Guerre TOE, for going out alone in front of a very recently secured ridge position and sketching the terrain. Note that he is holding a map – not a usual accessory for a private soldier. (Photo Ward Price)

73 Another Engish légionnaire of II/2nd REI – his trail-worn, unshaven appearance typical of the Legion on campaign in Morocco – photographed while building the inevitable *murettes* to consolidate a newly occupied ridgetop during the Mount Baddou operations. He was a Leeds-born former Royal Navy petty officer named Hunter, who had enlisted when unable to find work at home. He was quite satisfied with Legion life, and told Ward Price that the hard labour was easier than he had known when working as a lumberjack in Canada. (Photo Ward Price)

74 General Antoine Huré reviewing légionnaires in the field after the submission of u-Skunti's rebels on 26 August 1933. (Photo Ward Price)

75 The 6th Squadron/1st Foreign Cavalry were the first Legion unit to be mechanized, receiving their first vehicles as early as February 1929, but it was 1933–34 before they were fully equipped and operational with armoured cars and carriers. During Colonel Trinquet's advance into the far south-west in February–March 1934, VI/1st REC operated a troop of three armoured cars and three troops each with five of these Berliet VUDB armoured recce carriers. These fragile vehicles had a three-man crew, four-wheel drive and independent suspension. (SIHLE, courtesy John Robert Young)

76 Photographed during Colonel Trinquet's 1934 thrust to the frontier with the Spanish Sahara, these are armoured cars of the 4th Foreign Infantry's Composite Automobile Company (CMA), which Charles Milassin would join the following year. The AMD Panhard 165/175 TOE had a four-man crew including two separate drivers, one for driving forwards and one for going in reverse – a not unusual arrangement at that date. Note the carbines and bayonets clamped inside the open door. The company's working dress was then a suit of *bleu mécanicien* denim, like any French factory worker. (Photo Henry Clérisse, courtesy Francois Vauvillier)

77 One of the four squads of the *peloton portée* of CMA/4th REI at Foum el Hassane had two M1914 Hotchkiss MGs; on their twice-yearly 2,000-mile tours through the Western Sahara each gun and crew travelled in a truck, 'loaded for bear' with 5,500 rounds of ammunition. Since the tilt over the truck's rear body was made of thin sheet iron they suffered badly under the desert sun. Here they pose with, at right, two notably smarter senior NCOs. (Courtesy Charles Milassin)

78 Despite the remoteness of their post, CMA/4th REI lived as comfortably as they could under the paternal command of Captain Gaultier. Jazzbands seem to have been popular in 4th Foreign – Major de Corta's 3rd Battalion also maintained one. Here, at Christmas 1936, Légionnaire Charles Milassin is on drums; note the company badge. The dark-skinned soldier on banjo may perhaps be the Légionnaire Abd el Halim whom Chief Warrant Officer Milassin remembered. (Courtesy Charles Milassin)

79 The Panhard 179 *camion blindé* carried – in considerable discomfort – an NCO commander, driver, machine-gunner and seven riflemen, with two light machine guns. Ergonomics was then an unknown science, and the men's physical wellbeing was not given a high priority in this early experiment with mechanized infantry in a desert environment. (Courtesy Charles Milassin)

80 In December 1939, on the eve of world-changing events, the newly naturalized and promoted young Sergeant Milassin poses in the smart walking-out dress of a Legion career NCO at Tindouf. Half of the 4th Foreign's motorized company were often based at this major Saharan post just over the Algerian border from Foum el Hassane. (Courtesy Charles Milassin)

81 A veteran légionnaire of the strong detachment sent by 1st REI to Paris to take part in the 14 July 1939 Bastille Day parade – the first time the public saw the white képi-cover officially worn for ceremonial.

At the end of the First World War the Legion's uniforms had been a motley mixture of French and US surplus khaki tunics, trousers and sidecaps, and even some regimental colour parties were unable to lay hands on half-a-dozen képis for parades. Légionnaires were set apart from Metropolitan troops only by the seven-flamed grenade badge, and the green of their collar numbers, piping and rank stripes. Thereafter the accretion of special distinctions would be a semi-official process, nudged along by unit COs and only documented and authorized retrospectively. Some wartime khaki képis began to be issued from 1923, and in June 1926 the Legion – uniquely – was authorized the pre-war red-and-blue design, with a khaki cover for field use. By 1931 the 2nd and 3rd REI were wearing a white cover on parade; an order of August 1933 authorized general issue of a white cover for parade and walking-out and a khaki one for the field, though the latter was often bleached in defiance of regulations. Green re-enlistment chevrons were authorized in September 1929; the three on this soldier's left sleeve show that he is serving his fourth five-year contract (but is still a private 2nd class, despite his Médaille Militaire). The green-and-red *epaulettes de tradition*, discontinued in 1914, were restored from November 1930, by the centenary celebrations of March 1931 the légionnaire stood out from lesser breeds as colourfully as Colonel Rollet could wish.

82 Ain ben Tili is in the tri-border region of the Western Sahara, near the meeting-place of the frontiers of Morocco, Mauritania and Algeria. In the 1930s the fort there was a regular way-point on the twice-yearly, two-month-long desert patrols made by Charles Milassin's motorized company of the 4th Foreign Infantry from Foum el Hassane, and in 1993 its abandoned walls were still serving the same purpose for patrols by UN soldiers from the MINURSO mission. (Photo David Craig)

83 The partly legible gravestone at Ain ben Tili is that of a *brigadier* – corporal – of the mechanized Legion cavalry squadron V/1st REC, who died here on 12 December 1934 during joint operations by all the motorized and camel companies in the northern Sahara, including CMA/4th REI. (Photo David Craig)

Preface

THERE ARE SOME VISUAL CLICHÉS so woven into our common culture that a cartoonist can evoke a whole back-story with a few economical lines; they pass down the generations with archaic details unchanged, because they offer a useful narrative shortcut – like the long- bearded castaway under his single palm tree, or the burglar with a striped sweater, domino mask and swag-bag. One of them features the boxy outline of a fort amid sand dunes, and a soldier in a big dark coat and a cap with a white sun-flap. His advance beyond a French system of visual shorthand into that of the wider world can be dated with some accuracy to October 1924, when John Murray first published P. C. Wren's novel *Beau Geste*. Almost immediately, the légionnaire joined the cowboy, the explorer/big-game hunter and the brilliantly intuitive detective in the pantheon of popular heroes. The cartoon came to encapsulate a certain military concept: a simple, old-fashioned, rather brutal form of soldiering completely separated from the values and concerns of civilian life. It implied the voluntary endurance of harsh discipline, physical hardship and occasional deadly danger, far from home and for little reward. Although that description has, of course, also applied to much other military experience the world over, for some reason the cartoon légionnaire has maintained his grip on the stereotype.

IN SIMPLE TERMS, THE AIM OF THIS BOOK is to try to explain just what the légionnaire was actually doing – in both a historical and a military context – in that landscape, and in others equally inhospitable: to describe where these places were, for what purpose he was sent there, how France used him when he got there, and what happened to him.

It is certainly not a general history of the Legion, of which there are arguably too many already. Since the publication in 1991 of Professor Douglas Porch's magisterial *The French Foreign Legion, A Comprehensive History* – to which, like all subsequent writings on the subject, this book owes a great deal – it will be at least a couple of generations before the world needs another. Some histories (though not, emphatically, Professor Porch's) adopt a tight focus on a chronological listing of the Legion's battles; rather than simply duplicating that record, I have tried to set the légionnaire in the physical, military and political context of the campaigns in which France employed him (although the political material is necessarily restricted to not much more than a series of 'bluffer's notes'). I have also tried – by means of occasional snapshots from individual careers – to suggest the continuity that is central to the character of any seasoned military organization. This book does not pretend to be a work of primary research, for which neither my training nor my circumstances qualify me. It is a synthesis of secondary sources, including some of the obscurer French-language material, which I hope may cast light for English-speaking readers on the Legion's classic period of colonial conquests.

Since I am not an academic, the period described here is not bounded by strictly defined academic limits, but it suits my purpose. I have taken as my point of departure the Franco-Prussian War of 1870–71; since this shaped French military affairs (and to a large extent, the consciousness of the French nation) until 1914, it seems impossible to omit an introduction both to the army that fought it, and to the Legion's modest part in it. After the next decade of total preoccupation with preparing for revenge on Germany, from 1881 France began to make a parallel investment in its previously haphazard drive to acquire a second overseas empire, to compensate for the loss of its first to Britain in the 1760s. For various reasons, I believe it can be argued that its earlier conquest of Algeria between 1830 and roughly 1860 stands rather apart, although this is summarized in Chapter 2. I have ended the story in 1935, the year following the submission of the last undefeated tribesmen in Morocco, since that Hadrianic moment marked the end of the period when France was acquiring rather than seeking to hold its empire.

While the raising of the Legion predated these campaigns by 50 years – and while it had already won a strictly local reputation in Algeria, the Crimea, Italy and Mexico – its huge enlargement, and its widest employment, were a direct consequence of the dynamic expansion of the French colonies that started in the early 1880s. In 1875 the Legion was a single regiment of 4 battalions totalling 3,000 men; by the early 1930s it was a corps of 6 regiments with 18 battalions and 6 cavalry squadrons, plus 5 independent companies of mounted infantry, 4 of sappers and 2 artillery batteries, with a peak strength in 1933 of more than 33,000 men. It was those colonial campaigns that created the image of the Legion that we still recognize: the Legion of sun-flapped képis and agonizing desert marches, of fever-haunted jungle forts and desperate last stands. It was for those campaigns that the Legion provided the ultimate insurance – the 'heavy infantry' backbone, often rather ponderous but completely reliable – within the mixed columns and expeditionary forces that France assembled.

When I first considered the old Legion's campaigns as a subject for a book they presented, of course, a particular problem. Some years ago I wrote an account of the battle of Dien Bien Phu, the culmination of the French Indochina War of 1946–54. That subject had an obvious progression – the classic 'three-act story arc'; by comparison, the story I was now addressing seemed less shapely. I only began to relax into the task when I recognized that after France's episodic lunges for the components of an empire before 1900, the second part of the story moved towards a natural climax, as the task, the instruments and the man (in the person of General Hubert Lyautey) all came together. France's overseas adventures led it, and eventually the greater part of the old Legion, to Morocco – the last and greatest theatre of the drama, where for thirty years the Legion undertook some of its most intense and characteristic soldiering.

THE NATURE OF THE OLD LEGION'S CAMPAIGNS was naturally dictated not only by terrain and climate but by the adversaries it was sent to fight. Westerners think in terms of *a* war – a finite historical episode; it has causes, both sides have aims and objectives, and it follows a roughly linear progress. But to many of the peoples whom the colonial armies confronted a century ago, the idea of a specific war had little meaning; they regarded warfare as a normal, often a more or less constant aspect of their way of life. The novelist Charles Frazier has put into the mouth of a nineteen-century Native American character the complaint that, 'These new white people took all the fun out of war and just won and kept winning, as if that was all that mattered'.[1] One of the most characteristic figures of turn-of-the-century Morocco, the great robber baron Ahmad er Raisuli, was quoted to the effect that the colonialists brought security, but at the cost of narrowing a man's horizons: 'In the old days everything was possible. There was no limit to what a man might become. The slave might be a minister or a general, the scribe a sultan. Now a man's life is safe, but he is forever chained to his labour and his poverty.'[2]

Given that during Raisuli's lifetime the limited Spanish penetration of his territory put purely notional constraints on his continued accumulation of gold and spilling of blood, this lament must be understood as poetic rather than literal, but it does illuminate a particular view on life. It is a view that is still encountered in some parts of the world even today. After returning from some months spent 'embedded' in an infantry battalion in Helmand province, Afghanistan, in 2007, Dr Duncan Anderson recounted conversations with local fighters. One of them refused to believe that the British Army's deployment there was anything more than an (entirely honourable) revenge for the costly defeat of the Berkshire Regiment at Maiwand in July 1880; and another asked, in honest puzzlement, who – while all these British warriors were in Afghanistan – was doing the fighting back home in Britain?[3]

Another intriguing parallel between the French colonial experience and the current situation in Afghanistan concerns civil development. In his important study of British operations there in 2006–7, *A Million Bullets* (London; Bantam, 2008), James Fergusson quotes a British officer as urging that development personnel cannot achieve anything if they are forced to wait until peace is firmly established over large areas. They, too, should be embedded with the troops, with the remit and the resources to begin work immediately any local success is achieved, because it is precisely that work that will give the local people a stake in the establishment of stability. (A Cabinet Office appreciation released in April 2009 seems to recognize the force of this argument; it is, of course, the pure Galliéni/ Lyautey doctrine of the 'oil patch', described in Chapter 6 of the present book.)

Raisuli's complaint ignored another feature of the Moroccan campaigns that might seem counter-intuitive: the fact that as soon as they had been defeated, clans who had resisted the French fiercely, and had paid bloodily, were quick to enlist in French service under their own chieftains in order to continue fighting their neighbours in the eternal cycle of mutual raiding. Throughout their history, weaker tribes had always sought alliances with stronger, and the prestige of a chief rested not only on his physical courage and leadership qualities but on his persuasive ability to achieve such alliances.[4] It is a paradox that a century ago, at a time when most Europeans never even examined what today we might call their racial arrogance, not all relationships across ethnic divides were dictated by today's sulphurous preoccupation with racial identity. To grasp the character of some of the colonial campaigns visited in this book we have to make a leap of imagination further back than the ideologies of the twentieth century, which have collectively demonized the enemy of the day. The behaviour of some Moroccan groups suggests that yesterday's enemy might have been seen as no more intrinsically 'bad' than the rival runners in a race.

Given all this, it seemed sensible to introduce the accounts of the Legion's campaigns with brief descriptions of those non-European enemies, in an attempt to give them a little more dignity than the anonymous brown mass in the rifle-sights with which some commentators have been content.

A DEFINING CHARACTERISTIC of colonial soldiering was the limited numbers of men involved, and thus the limited scope of combat operations. Attuned to Western military history, we automatically expect the account of a war to build steadily towards a climactic conclusion – a decisive victory and defeat. This seldom, if ever, applied to colonial campaigns. On the European side, the sheer physical difficulty of moving and supplying armies in roadless wilderness, and keeping the troops healthy enough to march and fight in difficult and disease-ridden country, imposed its own limitations. In most cases their opponents were disunited, unable to assemble large forces in the field or to support them for long (a fact that makes the great exception – the Abd el Krim brothers' campaigns in the Rif hills in 1921–6 – all the more remarkable). After the initial advances, the natural rhythm of such campaigns became that of counter-insurgency warfare: an endless cycle of small patrols and convoy escorts punctuated by ambushes, and by occasional exhausting – and often vain – attempts by larger columns to bring elusive enemies to battle. This does have one compensation for the reader: just as in the American frontier campaigns (a story with some similarities to that of the old Legion), when combat did occur it tended to be dramatic and on a human scale. The names that spring from the dusty pages are usually those of desperate company actions, when no more than a couple of hundred men suddenly found themselves fighting for their lives, against great odds. These incidents tend, with repetition, to get 'name-checked' in a fairly perfunctory way; rather than attempt to include them all, I have tried here to bring the specific character of some of them to life in a little more detail.

Consequently, I have made a number of detours from chronological history to examine a few specifics of how the French Army actually carried out this sort of soldiering, since I have always believed that too many accounts of military operations fail to address the physical and tactical realities as experienced at the level of small units and individuals. I have tried to keep the text digestible by banishing to the end-notes the more relentless detail of weapons, equipment, organization and various other subjects – including some references to a few battlefields that I was able to visit. Hard-core readers who share my taste for this sort of thing can always use two separate bookmarks while reading.

FINALLY, IN ANY REVIEW of the history of a European colonial military corps, the 800lb gorilla in the corner of the room is, of course, colonialism itself. Since it cannot be ignored, we should be honest enough to take at least one steady look at it, and this seems to me a better place to do so (with an appeal for the reader's patience) than scattering relevant comments throughout the body of the book.

The author cannot summon up any interest in attempts to judge long-dead generations by the liberal consensus of our own day, or in adopting shifty pieties of phrasing. Out of its own cultural neuroses, each society and generation chooses or invents its own demons – whether it calls them heretics, witches, degenerate Jewish cosmopolitans, imperialists, godless Commies, infidel crusaders or eco-polluting smokers. Those who insist upon studying our ancestors only through the narrow prism of twenty-first-century racial sensitivity are surely as blinkered in their way as the white supremacist bigots they denounce. By definition, such mental tunnels blind us to context, and context is everything. It is a bleak fact that human life has always depended fundamentally upon competition for territory and resources, and a broad view of history suggests that aggressive 'imperialism' has been the default setting of human affairs on most of the world's land masses for some 7,000 years. Seen against those countless strata of ashes and skulls, any claim that some special wickedness was committed by a few brief generations of white men in pith-helmets must surely fail. Historically, the process of territorial conquest has been as unremarkable as water running downhill; while it is one of the grimmer strands in the human story, it is such a constant that it hardly seems to admit of analysis simply in terms of 'right' and 'wrong'. If we wish to understand ourselves we had better face the fact that we are not herbivores.

In nineteenth-century Africa and Asia the results of such confrontations were obviously decided by the superior weapons and more advanced military organization available to the European invaders. It is equally obvious that we cannot simply stop thinking once we have accepted those brute facts; if we dismiss any moral dimension at all, then we may be tempted towards the sort of perverted Darwinism that rationalizes genocide. We all acknowledge today that the mainspring of European colonialism was ruthless greed. When we confront the long-term consequences in, say, the former Belgian Congo, it is almost inconceivable that any alternative history could have had a worse outcome. But the whole world is not the Congo, and in order to avoid sounding like Nazis it is surely not necessary for us to overcompensate to the point of going into sentimental denial about the nature of pre-colonial cultures. To characterize these in terms of Arcadian innocence is adolescent fantasy. All of the societies conquered by France in the nineteenth and early twentieth centuries were ancient, and some were richly complex, attracting the sympathetic fascination of many cultured colonizers; but it does not necessarily follow that they were the more admirable in any absolute sense.

IN MOROCCO, FOR EXAMPLE – the arena of many of the events described in this book – indigenous rulers were chronically unable to provide their people with stability or protection. At the end of the nineteenth century, the sultanate was still respected as the focus of religious authority, and (theoretically) as a just arbiter between the feudal and mercantile interests through which society functioned. In practice, however, the sultan's authority depended on his having the energy, guile and military strength to gather taxes and enforce decrees, and if he lacked these, then local power was quickly usurped by others. Where a national or regional ruler could indeed wield that power, there was no effective check on his behaviour. To say that the machinery of such pre-modern states at every level was, by today's anglophone standards, brazenly corrupt and self-seeking is simply a category error: government was a structure designed for individual aggrandizement, in the absence of any real concept of a public commonwealth that we would recognize. The whole point of acquiring power in such societies was (as it still is, over large parts of the world) to share advantage and riches with one's own extended bloodline and followers at the expense of others; this is not recognized as misgovernment, but as a leader's moral duty towards his own dependants.

In Morocco the ruling elites were unashamed predators, who competed for dominance in cycles of rapacity that recall those of early medieval Europe. At every level they extended their wealth and power at best by armed protection rackets, and at the frequent worst by massacre and pillage. The far-sighted ruler might keep the exploitation of the ruled within sustainable limits, but he had to balance this against a need to demonstrate and reinforce his authority and the dominance of his group by exemplary violence. This was achieved by putting other men to death, decorating his gates with their severed heads, throwing their women to his soldiery and seizing their goods.

In the great majority of Morocco that was outside the practical control of the sultanate, robbery with violence and murder bedevilled populations struggling for subsistence. In the harsh northern hills the Rifian Berber farmers glowered at their neighbours – even their relatives – from loopholed blockhouses. In the southern wilderness of the pre-Sahara, where the oasis villages were built as walled castles, the clans of semi-nomadic pastoralists thrived or dwindled by aggressive competition for grazing-land and water, the exploitation of the productive oases and the profitable control of caravan routes. Waging blood-feuds against neighbours, raiding strangers and ambushing unlucky travellers were not occasional aberrations committed by criminals, but simply what many men did when they went out to work in the morning. In an unpredictable and marginal natural environment, life depended upon the calculation and pursuit of short-term advantage. The French may have brought new forms of exploitation to Morocco, but to claim that these were, by definition, 'worse' than the old ways seems a perverse stance for humanitarians to adopt.

On reading the history of the colonial years, we may be repelled by European rhetoric about the white man's 'civilizing mission' when we compare the most idealistic of the words with the most callous of the deeds; but despite many extreme cases to the contrary, the words were not invariably cynical, nor the deeds always shameful. It would, of course, be absurd to claim that any of the nineteen-century colonial armies were motivated by a protective care for their African or Asian fellow humans; but that did come to be true of individual officers, and it is undeniable that in practical terms colonial garrisons did bring at least some protection. We may surely say that to the colonized subsistence farmer, any reduction in the risk of tribal enemies or bandits stealing his flock and crops, looting and burning his home, cutting his throat and carrying off his daughters was presumably welcome. Preventing that happening was a job that could only be done by hard men, shaped by a harsh world; but the colonial soldiers were still just men like any others, as mixed in their qualities and failings as those of any other time or place.

With that thought I gratefully turn away, leaving the gorilla in peace in his corner; he has, after all, been dead for some time now.

AMONG THE SOURCES LISTED in the select bibliography, I must pay particular tribute to the basic orientation guide for anyone interested in French colonial military history: Dr Anthony Clayton's *France, Soldiers and*

Africa (Brassey's Defence Publishers, 1988), which was recommended to me by a French publisher as simply the most thorough and accessible single text in either language. Another important source is Professor Ross E. Dunn's *Resistance in the Desert: Moroccan Responses to French Imperialism 1881–1912* (Croom Helm, 1977), which first opened my eyes to the academic research carried out by ethnographers into peoples who – by happy coincidence for me, if not for them – became the old Legion's opponents. I particularly wish to record my debt to the researches of Jacques Gandini of Calvisson, France, author of books published during the 1990s under his own name and that of Extrêm'Sud Editions. Monsieur Gandini was most generous with copies of rare photographs from his collection, and his book *El Moungar* (1999), which draws upon extensive work in the Legion archives and those of the (then) Service Historique de l'Armée de Terre and the Archives d'Outre-Mer, was an indispensable source for Chapters 9 and 10. (All my more recent attempts to contact M. Gandini and his publishers have failed; if by chance any reader can advise me of a current address, I would be grateful.)

Among primary accounts, I was lucky enough to find the vivid and absorbing memoir of Dr Charles Édouard Hocquard – *Une Campagne au Tonkin* (Hachette, 1892, reprinted by Arléa in 1999 with meticulous annotation by Philippe Papin). Those who are enthusiasts for the novels of Patrick O'Brian would discover in Dr Hocquard a sort of real-life Stephen Maturin, whose boundless curiosity is matched by the wonderful clarity of his written French.

Just as I recognize the obvious limitations of sanitized official accounts of events, and the often self-serving nature of senior officers' memoirs, I am all too conscious that junior ranks frequently tell lies about their own lives – on the page, as well as in the pub. When reading veterans' memoirs I have allowed a discount not only for lapses of memory but also for the tendency of story-tellers or their ghost-writers to reshape, embroider or simply invent in order to give the public of their day the type of material that they expected. Some cross-checking has occasionally been possible, but in the end the sifting process can only be a matter of reasoned guesswork. When in doubt, I have tended to omit particular anecdotes; I am thankful that much of the real historical value of such memoirs in fact lies in their more mundane passages.

I owe my publisher particular thanks for allowing me an unusual amount of space both for the photographs that I have collected over the years, and for proper captions; I hope that both will help bring alive for readers the men and the events described. I am equally indebted to John Richards for his patient and careful work on the sketch maps. The names of many obscure spots mentioned in early accounts are absent from modern maps; in fact, of course, some may only have figured in the handwritten notes of junior officers, who were obliged to include in their after-action reports some roughly phonetic version of a name told them by a camel-driver or a *goumier*. However, the sites of several historical engagements can be located, at least to within a mile or so.

MY OPPORTUNITY TO VISIT even a handful of the Legion's Moroccan battlefields in the autumn of 2007, through the generous and patient help of my nephew Graham Scott, has been among the greatest pleasures of this project, and in Graham's unique case I am happy to make an exception to my usual rule of listing my acknowledgements in strictly alphabetical order. Our travels in the south of the country taught me valuable lessons about the unique conditions of desert visibility, immediately answering questions that had long puzzled me in the bald accounts of several actions. That I was able to find the hilltop of Astar in the Rif, and to walk the ground described in Captain Pechkoff's account of the fighting of 5–6 June 1925 – ground still scattered with artillery fragments – was due to Graham's determination; to the efforts of our interpreter Hassane el Khader; and to the pure good luck of an encounter in the hillside scrub with a remarkable paratrooper-turned-farmer named Abd el Malek. In the Middle Atlas, on one of the more memorable afternoons of my life, it was Graham's experience of driving 4x4s in extreme terrain on six continents that got us across the Tichoukt Massif to El Mers before the pursuing thunderstorm could wash out the rudimentary track zigzagging along 16 miles of sometimes unstable ledges.

My other grateful acknowledgements for help during the preparation of this book are as follows: to John Ashby, for generously sharing his files on P. C. Wren; the late M. Raoul Brunon, of the Musée de l'Empéri, for photos; Dr Simon Chapman; René Chartrand; Dr Anthony Clayton; Roger Cleeve; Major Gordon Corrigan; Captain David Craig; Mick Crumplin; Adjudant-Chef Philippe Dalfeur, 1er RE (Chef du Secrétariat de *Képi Blanc*); Kerry Denman; Jim Dowdall; my agent Ian Drury, of Sheil Land Associates; Martin Earl, of HP Bookfinders; Peter Edwards; Gerry Embleton, for locating – yet again – an elusive and indispensable source; Will Fowler, as so often; John Franklin; Penny Gardiner, warrior-queen of editors; Andrew Grainger, editor of the British Commission for Military History journal *Mars & Clio*, for sharing his photos of the Djebel Sahro; John Hadidian; Ian Heath; Vincent Lieber, Château de Nyon, Switzerland; Keith Lowe, of Orion Publishing; the late Adjudant-Chef Charles Milassin (4e REI, RMLE, 2e REI); Kate Moore; Dr David Murphy; in particular, Thamaz Naskidaschvili, Paris, for his tireless researches on my behalf; John Neal; Brian Nicholls; Dr David Nicolle; Ronald Pawly, Antwerp; Alex de Quesada, Tampa, Florida; Frank Reeves; Sylvan Rossel, Swiss National Library, Berne; Philip Smith; John Thompson; Francois Vauvillier, Paris; Jean Vigne; Rosemary Weekley; my brother Dick Windrow, for his patient and generous assistance in the virtual world; the late Jim Worden, and John Robert Young, for photographs. In Morocco: Abd el Malek, Hassane el Khader, Takki el Bakkali, Frédéric Sola and Jurgen Moller. Finally, to the staff of the London Library, the British Library, the School of Oriental and African Studies, and the University of Sussex Library.

MCW

RINGMER, EAST SUSSEX, MAY 2009

Prologue: 'Bloody Week'

The public deludes itself with the most erroneous ideas about the true nature of military valour. There are no heroes . . . I have never seen any. What I have seen is men doing their duty worthily and conscientiously, that is to say aiming and firing, taking cover just enough to have some shelter but not enough to hinder them from shooting, standing up when ordered and advancing without allowing themselves to stop because of the enemy's fire, even at its most intense.

Captain Léonce Patry, 1897[1]

IN THE END, it had hardly taken an hour to capture the hilltop gun battery that had threatened the advancing French troops for days past. Below, staff officers murmured in pleased relief as their sweeping binoculars picked out blue figures with tell-tale red képis and trousers spreading out over the summit – searching the undergrowth, herding groups of prisoners, or simply resting around the captured cannon, swigging from their waterbottles in the muggy heat. From the brow of the hill, the soldiers could gaze curiously down between the unfamiliar oriental trees over the ancient city that spread out for miles along the loops of the river. To the west, great columns of dirty smoke rose to meet the low late-afternoon clouds from the fires that had destroyed the central district, still glowing sullenly here and there despite the torrential spring rains of the past two days.

The hill had been planned as tomorrow's objective, but the leading infantry had made faster progress southwards than expected, reaching the bottom of its slopes by mid-afternoon that day. With enemy cannon thundering from the summit, General Montaudon had decided that whatever Corps had at first intended, he could not keep his division simply sitting there under fire. His Metropolitan regiments of young conscripts had done surprisingly well, but they always needed careful handling, and the past few days of street-fighting had put a continual strain on their nerves. Men forced to remain inactive under fire for too long have time to listen to their fears; a contagion of uncertainty can pass from man to man, and it becomes difficult for their officers to persuade them to leave cover and move forward when the order is finally given.

Montaudon had formed his brigades in a semi-circle around the north and west sides of the hill; his flanks were secured by other divisions; on his left, his colleague Grenier had led his men nearly a mile further southwards, bringing the hilltop under artillery and machine-gun fire from behind. At 4pm Montaudon had given the signal, and his infantry had surged forwards willingly enough. In the centre of the north slope one of his three battalions of the Foreign Legion had shown the way, ignoring caution and simply charging with fixed bayonets. In the event, casualties had been remarkably light.

WE MAY PERHAPS ALLOW OURSELVES to imagine a handful of those légionnaires on the hilltop in the aftermath of their assault. Lieutenant Dupont of the 5th Battalion is about to order them to make sure that no armed adversaries are still hiding under cover – there is supposed to be a big cave somewhere nearby. These were the first soldiers to reach the battery, and their officer is in high spirits; with any luck this exploit will earn him a citation for the coveted red-ribboned Cross, which will help him towards promotion. His eye falls on a squad sitting around a cannon tipped sideways on a patch of torn-up turf, one spoked wheel splintered and its bronze barrel splashed silver by the hail of shot from one of General Grenier's *mitrailleuses*. There are a couple of ripped corpses in odds and ends of blue uniform tangled up in the trash of broken ammunition boxes, dropped shells and gun-tools. The thought occurs to Dupont that these *salauds* had been as lazy as they were ignorant – they had been here for weeks, yet they had built no breastworks around the guns to protect the crews.

One of the mutilated bodies seems to be rather small and slight, and a pale young soldier, himself only a few months in uniform, is staring down at it in horror, crossing himself and muttering in some foreign gutteral: 'É hanù en Tad, hag er Mab, hag er Spered-Santel – Elsé revou groeit . . .'. Some of the other youngsters also seem too preoccupied to be of any use as scouts; best let the sergeant pick his own men from the *vieux moustaches*. The

NCO is a man in his late thirties, with a leathery, pockmarked face under his whiskers; he is set apart not only by the gold sleeve-stripe on his threadbare blue greatcoat, but also by a silver medal on his chest, which hangs from a white ribbon with an exotic eagle-and-snake symbol.

At his officer's order the sergeant nods, twitches the peak of his képi down, unslings his rifle, grunts at two or three of the other older men, and leads them southwards off the summit. They move in a loose, watchful scatter, down towards the gap between two small lakes; on their left, a dramatic fissured pinnacle thrusts up nearly a hundred feet, crowned by a small, shining-white temple. On his way down the slope the sergeant pauses to stare at a weird, leafless tree that seems to consist entirely of sharp-pointed dark brown scales – they remind him of a lizard he saw once in Mexico. He comes back to himself with a start at the slamming of a volley from behind the trees a hundred yards away; then he relaxes, as he hears a rattle of rifle-bolts and a voice chanting measured orders – it's just an officer having prisoners shot.

Even a veteran of the Mexican expedition might have been startled to learn that within a couple of weeks the French generals would have massacred nearly 20,000 men, women and boys. This was, after all, their own capital city – for this imagined scene on 27 May 1871 takes place, of course, in the arboretum on the Buttes-Chaumont in Paris.

BY 1 APRIL 1867, when this park had been ceremonially opened by Napoleon III, Emperor of the French, his luck and audacity had already been failing him. While Chancellor von Bismarck pressed ahead with the unification of Germany under Prussian dominance, Napoleon's incorrigible meddling abroad had cost him any chance of foreign alliances. At home, the hectic outward glamour of the Second Empire could no longer conceal the syphilitic decay beneath. With the grip of his dictatorship slipping, Napoleon tried to liberalize his regime, but each easing of controls simply encouraged his enemies to snatch for more. The extremist 'Red clubs' that had previously played hide-and-seek with his police in the twilight now openly preached a Jacobin uprising, while constitutional Republicans extended their electoral hold on Paris and most other cities. Meanwhile, the emperor's long-argued and sensible plans for correcting the Army's chronic lack of trained reserves were obstructed by a combination of politicians suspicious of any move to 'bring the population under military control' and sclerotic generals instinctively defending the status quo.

Tired, discouraged and painfully ill, Napoleon increasingly let himself be swept along by events, and in July 1870 they dragged his empire over a cliff. A diplomatic quarrel with Prussia was handled with peevish stupidity, of which Bismarck took such expert advantage that within two weeks the Paris crowds were baying for a march on Berlin. To the incredulity of many commentators, on 19 July 1870 France rushed into a war against 'the greatest military power that Europe had yet seen, in a bad cause, with its army unready and without allies'.[2] Nevertheless, even pessimists had never imagined that the gleaming military machine crafted by Generals von Roon and von Moltke would destroy or encircle France's two field armies within just six weeks. The Army proved itself outclassed in every aspect of pre-paredness, organization and staffwork, and in much of its operational lead-ership. Many regiments fought bravely when given a chance to do so; the Germans made costly tactical blunders and paid a high price in lives; but most French generals allowed themselves to be herded blindly around the countryside until their badly supplied armies could be destroyed in detail. By mid-August Marshal Bazaine's army of 180,000 was already encircled at Metz, and at Sedan on 2 September Napoleon himself passed into captivity with 100,000 of Marshal MacMahon's troops. Three days later his empire fell, unlamented, and a Third Republic was proclaimed under a provisional 'government of national defence'.

Bismarck declined to oblige its ministers with an immediate peace settle-ment, and Moltke continued to drive a broad corridor across northern France to the Channel and the Atlantic. On 20 September, the cavalry of two German armies linked up to encircle Paris, and Moltke soon established an 'Iron Ring' around the capital. The new French government (based first at Tours, and later at Bordeaux) was little more than a title, still trying to invent itself day by day; nevertheless, the response to what was now a 'people's war' was immediate. While Parisians flocked to join the National Guard, the Republic – in the person of the 32-year-old war minister, Léon Gambetta, who escaped Paris by balloon on 7 October – began conscripting men for replacement armies in the south and north-east, to be built around those fragments of the Imperial regiments that remained at liberty.

THE CRIPPLING INCOMPETENCE of the French Army's mobilization that summer had not prevented white and Arab regiments from the Algerian garrisons from reaching the front, but the four battalions of the Foreign Legion (the Régiment Étrangère, RE) had not at first been summoned. They were legally prohibited from serving on French soil, and many of these 3,000-odd mercenaries were Germans. Since returning to Algeria from Mexico in 1867 they had been used largely as a labour corps, distracted from their road-building only by cholera, typhoid and a few indecisive bandit-hunts. At first they were simply moved around to replace the garrisons shipped off to Marseille; but after the disaster of Sedan orders arrived on 6 October that the RE was to send two battalions to France without delay.

There was nothing incompetent about the Legion's mobilization. In just four days, most German légionnaires were transferred into the 3rd and 4th Battalions, and the 1st and 2nd (I/ and II/RE) were landing at Toulon. By 14 October they were 400 miles to the north-east at Pierrefitte, and that day Colonel Deplanque's 60 officers and 1,457 men were reinforced with a battle-shocked group of about 450 other foreigners. These were the surviving one-third of a 5th Battalion (V/RE) of duration-only volunteers hastily raised at Tours during September, who had been driven out of Orleans after hard fighting on 11/12 October against General von der Tann's Bavarians. Filled out with various drafts from French units, the Foreign Regiment was allocated to XV Corps in General d'Aurelle de Paladines' new Army of the Loire.[3]

Gambetta, eager to break the siege of Paris from the south, sent d'Aurelle north to retake Orleans; but after winning France's only outright victory, over the (heavily outnumbered) Bavarian corps at Coulmiers on 9 November, the Army of the Loire was forced backwards from Loigny on 2–3 December. Lieutenant-Colonel Canat led what was left of the Foreign Regiment on an agonizing retreat through the snows of the cruellest winter in memory, and by the time the troops reached Saint Florent on the Cher on 10 December they had dwindled to a single 1,000-strong battalion.[4]

On 18 December, at Chappelle Saint Ursin, the Legion survivors provided the backbone for a new three-battalion 'marching regiment' patched together with 2,000 Breton conscripts – boys who did not speak French, had never fired a rifle, and wanted only to go home. Some of the experienced Legion NCOs and soldiers were dispersed amongst them, but the new regiment's combat value was limited. On 7 January 1871 the troops were loaded into freezing trains to go and join General Bourbaki's Army of the East, near Montbéliard in the Franche-Comté.[5] On 15–17 January, Bourbaki's attempt to relieve the besieged fortress of Belfort failed in the hills around Héricourt, despite odds of two-to-one in his favour; his freezing, hungry army was pushed back in a near rout, and 85,000 men sought internment in

Switzerland. The remains of the Foreign Regiment were not among them; they were at Besancon on the Doubs river when, at the end of January, news arrived of a general ceasefire.[6]

DESPITE THE REPUBLIC'S almost unbroken series of defeats, including the surrender of Metz on 27 October, Paris had held out under siege for four months. The capital's defences enclosed an area measuring about 7 miles by 6, with a population of nearly 2 million; it was never in danger of actual assault, since its ramparts were too formidable and its garrison too large. It was guarded by a ring of artillery forts up to 3 miles outside the walls themselves, which were massive earthworks faced with brick and masonry, surrounded by a cavernous ditch dominated by 93 artillery bastions. Within this ring the military governor, General Trochu, had (on paper) several hundred thousand men, including the equivalent of nearly 30 regiments of regular troops and 6 more of sketchily trained Gardes Mobiles. In theory, he also had under command 59 regiments of the 'active' Garde Nationale de Paris, but in practice these were barely capable even of manning the static defences, and were a threat to public order.[7] Parisians had rushed to enlist in their district (arrondisement) units, but many from the desperate workers' slums joined simply for the pay and the food rations, and most received no meaningful training at all. Many were outspokenly hostile to the 'quitters' of the regular army, and furiously resisted any attempt to bring them under military discipline.

While the German besiegers, too, would suffer from hunger and sickness during the bitter winter to come, inside the city Trochu faced problems unknown to Moltke, and these would have direct consequences in the events of March–May 1871. From the beginning, Parisian political factions used the leverage of their National Guard alliances to insist upon sorties that usually had no discernible military goal. These lunges outside the ramparts by the regular troops of Generals Vinoy and Ducrot were uniformly unsuccessful once they got beyond the 3-mile range of the city's heavy guns, but their failure inflamed the Parisian radicals, who openly insulted the soldiers as cowards. Throughout the siege, hopes were periodically raised and then dashed by reports of various advances and retreats by the armies of the Loire and the North, but no breakout to link hands with a relief force was ever feasible. In December, food and fuel ran desperately short, and the civilian death rate from hunger, cold and sickness rose inexorably. On 5 January 1871, while Parisians haggled over the price of horses' hooves and dogs' heads, the Germans extended their shelling from the forts to the city itself.

On 18 January, Bismarck delivered an exquisite insult when, in the Hall of Mirrors at Versailles, he proclaimed King Wilhelm I of Prussia the Kaiser of the new German Reich. In a spasm of fury another sortie was hurled out, which cost 3,000 French casualties (probably 400 of them shot in the back by confused National Guardsmen). On 19 January, General Faidherbe's Army of the North was beaten at St Quentin; on the 20th came news of the final defeat of Chanzy's Army of the Loire at Le Mans, and soon afterwards reports of Bourbaki's fiasco outside Belfort. On the 22nd, 'Red' National Guards exchanged volleys with Mobiles defending the Hôtel de Ville (the city hall). The following day, Foreign Minister Jules Favre requested a meeting with Bismarck, and an armistice was signed on 26 January.

ELECTIONS WERE HELD for a new government to conclude a final peace, and the National Assembly returned at Bordeaux on 8 February was dominated by provincial conservatives. They appointed as prime minister the 73-year-old Adolphe Thiers, who, on 26 February, signed preliminary terms of capitulation: France would give up the border provinces of Alsace and northern Lorraine and pay a huge war indemnity. The Assembly ratified these terms, by an 80 per cent majority, on 1 March – the day that 30,000 German troops paraded down the Champs-Élysées. On 3 March they left the city, but continued to surround the eastern half of the ramparts north of the Seine (from Saint Denis, at roughly '12 o'clock', to Charenton at '5 o'clock'). By then, however, Paris was already on the verge of insurrection against the Assembly.

Relief at the raising of the siege was quickly forgotten in the Parisians' rage over what they saw as a treacherous surrender; Army officers were attacked in the streets and policemen were lynched. The National Guard formed a representative Federation, and these Fédérés swore to resist any attempt to disarm them. The Federals accused the provincial deputies of wishing to restore a monarchy, and they persuaded many soldiers of the garrison to their viewpoint. Guard units from well-to-do districts dissolved as the nervous middle classes fled the city, and a Red element – represented by a self-created Central Committee – grew stronger. Parades on 26 February had brought some 300,000 men on to the streets, at a time when General Vinoy's garrison had been reduced by the armistice terms to at most 15,000 distinctly shaky regulars. That day, Guardsmen seized some 200 cannon

from artillery parks and dragged many of them off to working-class strongholds on the hills of Montmartre and Buttes-Chaumont.

Prime Minister Thiers entered the capital on 15 March; he and his
Republican ministers were well to the Left of the Assembly, but as negotiations with Bismarck continued under the threat of German cannon, they
knew it was essential to establish the new government's authority. Thiers
ordered Vinoy to carry out a coordinated occupation of strategic points on
18 March, to recover the artillery and arrest dissident ringleaders, but this
attempted *coup de main* failed. Huge, hostile crowds gathered, and Army
officers, lacking any realistic rules of engagement for dispersing them, were
helpless to prevent their confused and nervous men from standing aside, or
even fraternizing openly. In Montmartre the 88th Marching Regiment fell
to pieces; two generals were seized in the street, and that afternoon – despite
the protests of the young district mayor, Dr Georges Clemenceau – both
were murdered and mutilated by a drunken rabble of men and women. The
prime minister's reaction was immediate, but surprising: by nightfall on
18 March, Thiers' government and Vinoy's troops were leaving Paris for
Versailles, 7 miles to the south-west. The psychological distance this placed
between the Army and the Parisians was as significant as their physical
separation.[8]

BARRICADES WERE THROWN UP in the streets and the red flag was
hoisted. In the absence of any coherent organization, the Central Committee
of the National Guard seized the reins, and on 22 March Guardsmen fired
on an unarmed rally by conservatives in the Rue de la Paix. The demands of
ideology had already forced the Central Committee publicly to defend the
lynchings of Generals Lecomte and Thomas, which caused widespread
disgust; now these dozen more killings strengthened Thiers' position. A
parallel mental entrenchment appeared in Paris; after hasty elections, on 28
March a new Red-dominated municipal council installed itself in the Hôtel
de Ville under the name of the Commune of Paris.

The word Commune, which has a long history in France, had nothing to
do with 'Communism'; it simply meant a municipality enjoying a degree of
self-government. However, once the Commune had been proclaimed, the
many competing groups that gathered beneath its flag each clamoured to
define it in their own preferred terms. Heated disputes raged between the
leaders of various factions; during April and May rival commissions and sub-
committees sprang up almost daily, and mutual denunciations led to arrests

at gunpoint. From the first, the baying of bloodthirsty Jacobins could be heard amidst the babble, growing louder as the weeks passed. The Reds were contemptuous of the dithering uncertainties of the moderates, and some genuine sociopaths were to elbow their way to prominence as events careered out of control. In the protective shadow of Charles Delescluze, the ineffectual old Jacobin figurehead, younger men – notably, the security commissars Raoul Rigault and Théophile Ferré – would seize their opportunity to enjoy life-and-death power. Nothing approaching a coherent plan of action was ever achieved; but the Paris poor believed (wrongly) that they had nothing to lose, and collective memories of both cathartic mob violence and brutal repression in 1830 and 1848 opened their ears to extremist rhetoric. And all the time, out at Versailles, Thiers was recovering his nerve.

The Thiers government spoke for the provincial constituencies of the National Assembly. Over the past 80 years 'deep France' had grown sick of having ready-made regimes imposed on them by conspirators in Paris, and they now wanted peace on almost any terms. The provinces had elected men whose instincts they trusted, and for once parliament had a genuine mandate from the country at large. Frightened by violent disorder and threats to property rights, the rural, Catholic population heard in the title 'Commune' an echo of the Terror of 1793–4, which had unleashed widespread horrors on the western provinces. The middle-class tendency to interpret the worst excesses of any Communards as revealing the essential character of the Commune itself was entirely predictable – as was the government's exploitation of those fears, to justify the military confrontation for which it was now trying to equip itself. Whether that attempt could succeed remained questionable, however; the immediate fear was of a National Guard assault on Versailles in overwhelming numbers, and there was real doubt that Thiers' 55,000-odd soldiers, militia and gendarmes could – or would – even defend the new government.[9]

On 27 March 1871 the Foreign Regiment were ordered from Besancon to Versailles by rail, and when they arrived on 1 April they had 66 officers but only 1,003 rankers on strength.[10] How many of them could strictly be described by now as 'légionnaires' is unclear; we might guess at a total of perhaps 350 men from the original I/ and II/RE from Algeria still in the ranks among the Bretons and French odds and ends. It was normal to equalize battalion and company strengths as far as practical, and – with a critical shortage of seasoned sergeants – to spread experienced corporals and privates-first-class among the youngsters as stiffeners. If that was the case here, then the RE's 1st, 2nd and 5th Battalions would have had only about 330 men each, divided into 6 field companies of some 55 men, of whom perhaps 1 in every 3 was a veteran. The high ratio of officers noted on 1 April did not last; by 26 May the colonel was concerned about being able to provide each company with even 2 officers, so many of the original 66 must have been transferred to fill critical vacancies in other regiments. Close personal supervision of the troops was vital at a time when the loyalty of many units was dubious.

IT IS NOT A FIGURE OF SPEECH to say that the Imperial army, made up of long-term conscripts and volunteers, had been almost destroyed during the summer of 1870, since only ten of 100 Line regiments had survived. Otherwise the infantry of the National Defence armies of September 1870 to January 1871 were so-called *régiments de marche*, bearing the number of a regular Line unit but actually assembled from its depot companies and those of two other regiments, bulked out with new conscripts and 'reservists'.[11] The depot personnel were the essential staff of pen-pushers, storemen and other old sweats necessary to process new recruits; although many were unfit, most at least knew their job by rote, and a few other ex-regulars had also volunteered to return to the colours. However, the great majority of the rank and file were baffled young peasant conscripts, and the 'reservists' bore no resemblance to the genuinely trained *Landwehr* of Bismarck's armies. At this date French reservists were not veterans who had been discharged after years of service, but the products of that pre-war system that Napoleon III had tried in vain to reform. Even conscripts who drew 'bad numbers' in the lottery had been divided into 'first and second portions'; for lack of funds to equip, train and embody them the latter had been sent home again, to report for a brief spell of instruction each year. The training these 'second portion' men had behind them when they were mobilized was (at the very best) three months, at least a year previously.[12]

These 'marching regiments' were led by an equally diverse officer corps. Some had been dug out from behind desks, others had volunteered or been recalled from retirement. About two-thirds of pre-war captains and lieutenants had been commissioned ex-NCOs, and many in the National Defence armies were very newly promoted from the ranks, serving beside military school cadets with perhaps a year's theoretical instruction, and young volunteers from the educated classes with even less.[13] While some of the ex-sergeants were battle-wise, the need for literacy meant that such men were disproportionately drawn from the administrative NCOs. Whatever their backgrounds, all were products of a tradition that demanded unquestioning obedience to superior rank and to the textbook, and actively discouraged initiative. The haste with which their improvised regiments had been assembled meant that few officers had known their superiors or their subordinates for more than a few weeks, and the introduction of a new manual of infantry tactics in 1869 added to the confusion. In a period when the company officer's tasks on the day of battle were to turn his colonel's broadly expressed orders into reality on the ground, and to control and encourage his men by persuasion and example, these were serious handicaps.

In 1870 an infantry battalion still moved and fought *en masse*, wielded by its commander as a single weapon. The first steps in infantry training were therefore reasonably straightforward: men had to learn how to move together on command; to handle and care for their weapons and bivouac kit; and to shoot reasonably straight when ordered to deliver volleys. This last was not an easy skill to acquire even if (as was seldom the case) there was plenty of time and ammunition for range practice. The large-calibre, single-shot rifles of those days had a robust kick and spewed out a blinding cloud of powder-smoke, and to many returned veterans and reservists the new Chassepot introduced in 1867 – the French soldiers' only edge over the Prussians – was as much of a mystery as it was to new conscripts. (Since old soldiers always delight in making recruits' blood run cold, they probably exaggerated the grisly stories about the tendency of the long firing-pin to break and jam in the forward position, so that chambering the next round too smartly could cause a premature discharge that would blow the bolt straight back into the firer's face, taking his thumb with it.)[14]

In any case, no training could prepare raw recruits for the shocking and confusing reality of battle. To obey orders under fire (especially artillery fire, which was a new experience even for most veterans) demanded habits of mind that could only be learned through patient example and encouragement by familiar and trusted NCOs and lieutenants, and these were in short supply. Some of their officers were intelligent and humane, some of the NCOs fatherly and resourceful, some of the veterans comradely and encouraging, but taken as a whole the 'marching regiments' of the National Defence armies were of uncertain quality when they went into action in autumn 1870. The inevitable breakdowns of the system under campaign conditions had left many of them cold, famished, ragged and rudderless, and by March and April 1871, when they began arriving around Versailles to reinforce the compromised Paris garrison troops, many had been tested to the brink of collapse.

THE RANK AND FILE were disheartened by their winter defeats and privations; bewildered by the political turmoil and wretchedly supplied, sheltered and fed, most of them longed only for their discharge. Except for a few regulars who had broken parole to escape from Metz, their junior officers were equally brittle; appalled by the thought of civil war, significant numbers now took 'sick-leave' or applied for transfers. Left without vigorous leadership, with their morale in their boots (if they had any), the troops were sullen at best, and there was a good deal of open talk about refusing to fire on fellow Frenchmen. The central factor in the remedies applied during April was the return from German captivity of many more regular officers, who were both instinctively loyal and ignorant or impatient of the complex politics of the moment.[15]

On 6 April, command of the new Army of Versailles was given to Marshal MacMahon, whose previous record and wounding at Sedan insulated him from the contempt in which the troops held most Imperial generals. Under his stern but commonsense leadership, the returning professional officers filled all staff posts and unit commands, and many more junior vacancies. These regulars were much better equipped, by experience and conviction, both to discipline and to cajole their men into obedience and reasonable efficiency. They spent a great deal more time with the rankers than had been usual, awarding swift but just punishments and also real encouragement. Parisian soldiers and other suspected malcontents were identified and posted away, although the unfamiliarity of officers with their composites of detachments made this a rather hit-or-miss process. Coming at a time when reservists, volunteers and men from Alsace-Lorraine were also being demobilized, this purge cost some regiments hundreds of men. While MacMahon had about 120,000 troops by late May, some divisions and brigades went into action at less than half their establishment strength.[16]

Pay, wine rations, food, shelter and medical care were all improved. There was an attempt to keep Parisian newspapers, whores and booze-pedlars out of the camps, and pro-government papers were distributed. The men were exhorted to remember their soldierly duty, regaled with reports of Communard outrages, and told that it was this godless criminal rabble who were prolonging the war (and their own military service) needlessly.[17] In a nation with a long history of centralized despotism, the countryside's instinctive suspicions capital played some part in opening their ears, but a genuine hunger for national unity at a time of disaster was more significant. The rank and file would never be remotely enthusiastic about attacking Paris, but as the weeks passed, routine and obedience became the line of least resistance, and some of the troops' resentments were gradually steered away from authority-figures and towards the Communards.

While there was little mutual respect between regular and wartime-commissioned officers, all believed that they could not put 1870 behind them and build a new France until the ugly boil of the Commune had been lanced. Prime Minister Thiers visited the camps every day; as an old journalist he understood the power of words, and even some of the most ardent republicans became true believers. Paul Déroulède, a progressive young Parisian man of letters, was so scaldingly determined on revenge against Prussia that he 'took the képi as one takes the veil'; for such agonized patriots the path to the Prussians lay on the other side of the 'secessionist' Commune. Déroulède's képi would be in the midnight-blue of the 30e Chasseurs à Pied, then brigaded with the 39e de Marche and the Régiment Étrangère.[18]

NEITHER SIDE COULD GUESS the other's intentions, and on 2 April a government probe to the western suburb of Courbevoie sparked confused skirmishing; both sides ran away, but the *Versaillais* Colonel Boulanger of the 114th Line had five prisoners shot. Reports of this were exaggerated, and the enraged Communard leaders ordered a major sortie for the next day: three columns totalling 30,000 men would march on the Buzenval heights, Meudon and Châtillon.[19] The Central Committee had already carelessly allowed government troops to occupy the vital artillery fort of Mont Valérien, due west of Paris, and the events of 3 April would confirm their incompetence. National Guard officers were elected by their men, and many owed their epaulettes more to rhetoric, indulgent slackness and generosity with wine than to any military qualifications. Moreover, Jacobins like Delescluze were not just ignorant of, but actively hostile towards military training. In thrall to the revolutionary myth of the irresistible rush by impassioned patriots, they wrongly believed that the national *levée en masse* of 1793 had saved the fledgling First Republic by sheer ardour, proving that free men –

sufficiently politicized – did not need the rigid 'Prussian' training of the brutalized 'slave-soldiers' of the old monarchies.

This had always been sheer fantasy: enthusiasm, rifles and red flags do not transform an eager crowd into soldiers capable of coordinated action and endurance under fire. The National Guards, hardly engaged during the Prussian siege, were quite ignorant of real war, yet were unaware of their ignorance.[20] To take only the most mundane practical example: the majority of the National Guard had been armed not with the bolt-action Chassepot, which was in short supply, but with previously muzzle-loading percussion-lock rifles converted to breech-loaders by the so-called *tabatière* ('snuffbox') modification. The *tabatière* 'threw high'; to hit a man in the body at 150 yards you had to aim at his knees, and at his feet when the range closed to 100 yards. This went against all natural instinct, and in 1871 many of the virtually untrained National Guardsmen must have wasted their bullets in the air above their adversaries' heads.[21]

On 3 April 1871, the confidence of the amateur generals that the 'royalist' soldiers of Versailles would not stand and fight proved to be mistaken. Advancing without reconnaissance against troops holding old Prussian positions, the Federals – some of them unprovided with ammunition, and some drunk – were badly shaken by shells from Mont Valérien. A minority fled at once, most others were later dispersed by the hard-charging General Gallifet's cavalry, and the last surrendered at Châtillon the next morning. The captured leaders, and any suspected of being Army deserters, were shot at once (some of them, again, by the bloodthirsty Colonel Boulanger), thus establishing a trade in mutual reprisals that would escalate over the next eight weeks.[22] The city gates were shut and rail traffic was halted, but tens of thousands of citizens continued to flee Paris – especially after the Commune passed their ominous Law of Hostages on 5 April.

AFTER THE FAILURE of the 3 April sorties, the Central Committee of the Federation appointed as operational commander one Gustave Cluseret, who at least had wide (if dubious) military experience. A former officer cashiered for theft, Cluseret had fought in the Crimea before embarking on murky overseas adventures, and he was at least enough of a soldier to recognize that its internal anarchy was crippling the National Guard. There was simply no functioning chain of command; untrained unit commanders were sent conflicting instructions by various organs of the Commune, and district mayors often refused orders for the deployment of their battalions elsewhere in the city. Indiscipline and absenteeism were endemic, and members of some fancifully titled local gangs spent most of their time getting drunk, unchecked by their imitation officers. Too many of the latter saw command not as a serious function but as a political reward, entitling bully-boys to strut around festooned with sashes and pistols like *banditti*. Cluseret made an attempt to separate men with some potential from those best ignored, but he would claim that he never had more than 30,000 of the former. He appointed as his chief-of-staff the only serving regular Army officer who had joined the Commune, a young lieutenant-colonel of sappers named Louis Rossel. Cluseret's operations officer was also reliable: Jaroslaw Dombrowski, a Russian-trained veteran of the 1863 Polish insurrection, who was sent to command at Neuilly in the west.

Thiers, a politician for forty years, could judge the mood of crowds; he recognized that even though the Army of Versailles was improving by inches it was still a tool that would break in his hand if he swung it hard. The troops must be committed gradually, with manageable objectives; they must be rested often, cared for and rewarded, and above all they must never be exposed to the risk of heavy casualties. Nobody understood the strength of the Paris defences better than Thiers – it had been he who supervised their construction in the 1840s, when he was King Louis-Philippe's prime minister. He knew that there was one weak point: at the Point du Jour, where the Seine emerged through the far south-west corner of the ramparts. He never imagined that his infantry could actually storm fortifications; his method would be to besiege the western half of the city, strip it of its outer forts (particularly Fort Issy, commanding the Point du Jour), ratchet up the pressure, and wait for some opportunity to arise. The Prussian-held eastern perimeter was porous; plain-clothes agents slipped in and out at will, and there was always a chance that some Communard faction might be persuaded to enter secret talks.

In the meantime, the first troops were sent forward: to the south, to begin the reduction of Fort Issy, General Cissey's II Corps; and to the west, to bite their way into the Neuilly defences lying outside the ramparts, Ladmirault's I Corps, which included Montaudon's division – one of whose units was the Régiment Étrangère.[23]

ON 7 APRIL THE FOREIGN REGIMENT marched through Courbevoie towards the Neuilly bridge, to the thunder of nearby government artillery duelling with Federal batteries at Porte Maillot (see Map 1). Rested, well-fed, and with pay in their pockets to spend in any convenient *café-cabarets*, they were brigaded under General Dumont alongside the Breton 39th Marching Regiment and the 30th Light Infantry Battalion.[24] The bridge was blocked off by a Federal barricade; the RE were held in reserve, sheltering behind houses and listening to the crashes of preparatory shellfire and the unmistakable 'coffee-grinder' stuttering of hand-cranked mitrailleuses softening up the objective. In the middle of the afternoon the 39th charged, and by nightfall the barricade had been turned into a forward battery for Versailles artillery. Next morning, Dumont's brigade was relieved and marched back to its camp; this modest baptism of fire had cost the Legion three killed and five wounded.[25]

After a week's rest, the Foreign Regiment were back in Courbevoie; late on 15 April, the senior officers crossed the Seine by boat to reconnoitre positions on the north side of the Avenue Neuilly.[26] Anchored on a central gun battery, their sector comprised island-blocks of houses and gardens, linked by a trench across the avenue and by side-street barricades. That night, the companies slipped across the bridge in succession under intermittent blind shelling; dawn, and increasing artillery and rifle fire, revealed their positions as less than solid. The pleasant, leafy streets of bourgeois Neuilly were killing-grounds swept by crossfire. The most exposed positions were those held by V/RE on the left flank, between Rue Peyronnet and Boulevard d'Argenson; here the defenders had to abandon one corner of their 'frame' when a shelled house collapsed, and they improvised barricades inside the gutted villas from rubble, furniture, pianos and mattresses. However, although the National Guardsmen were fighting very much better than they had in the open fields, they still hesitated to assault. After one half-hearted attempt on the afternoon of 16 April was driven back, Communard officers and their men could be heard shouting curses at one another. This was not a question of 'cowardice'; the psychology of an infantry combat is more rational than that.

Effectiveness in battle depends upon both training, which gives a man a familiar rhythm to follow when he is scared and confused, and – very largely – upon encouraging leadership, by soldiers who at least give the appearance of being calm, knowledgeable and confident. Most National Guardsmen sorely lacked both of these supports, and without them it was hard to be 'brave' if confronted by what a flat-nosed ounce of soft lead could do when it struck human flesh and bone at about 900 miles per hour. In defence of houses and trenches, groups of friends had the comfort of each other's close presence and could choose when to show themselves briefly to take a shot. But making an assault meant coming out of cover, and even moderate marksmen with Army Chassepots could lay down a dangerous curtain of fire over the first 200 or 300 yards of the closing distance before a man armed with a 'snuffbox' rifle had any hope of replying effectively. Captain Léonce Patry, who had commanded both regular *lignards* and National Defence conscripts, wrote that the latter had mostly fought just as well as regulars with two to six years' service behind them; but also that

> Nothing is so hard as to lead forward under enemy fire men whose nerves are on edge after being stationary for a long time and who have thereby unlearned the exercise of their will ... the men, once in skirmish order and well ensconced behind some shelter, in the end do not go forward unless they really want to ... Hence it is very difficult for company officers to carry along all their troops, and extraordinary and incessant efforts are required to push them forward and lead them right up to their objective. Those who have not fought in a war as infantry subalterns can have no idea of the forcefulness required ... to get the men in hand ... and to make them advance against the enemy.[27]

THE FOREIGN REGIMENT'S 2ND BATTALION came up to take their turn in the exposed sector, at one point (oddly) choosing to reinforce a barricade by dragging heavy glass carboys in panniers across from an abandoned factory; these proved to contain perfumed toilet-water, and the sweaty, dust-caked légionnaires splashed themselves liberally. On the left flank a Federal shell plunged into an occupied house, killing Captain Giraud and a corporal, mortally wounding Sub-lieutenant Maumias and injuring three privates. Although firing artillery on more or less fixed lines from the Porte Maillot a mile away hardly demanded much expertise, the Federal artillery in fact had some skilled gunners and plenty of ammunition.[28] On the night of 19 April the légionnaires were relieved and withdrew across the Seine. Their four days and nights in the front line had cost them a casualty rate of about 12 per cent – 3 officers and 15 rankers killed and 111 wounded. Decorations were awarded, and on 20 April, while camped in the Parc de Villeneuve-l'Étaing, the légionnaires received reinforcements of 6 officers and 370 bewildered young conscripts from the 20th and 52nd Marching, bringing each battalion up to about 430 all ranks. In the light of recent experience the regiment was ordered to form a specialist sapper platoon.

On 27 April, the légionnaires of I/RE and V/RE crossed the river again;

this time the 1st Battalion took the left sector, and – unusually – came under heavy infantry attack at once. By now Neuilly looked like a miniature Stalingrad *avant la lettre*. The British eyewitness Colonel Stanley described every tree cut to pieces and the ground covered with spent canister-shot, broken-up dud shells and flattened bullets; guns were emplaced behind improvised breastworks in once lovely gardens, whose railed walls were broken down to provide access. Disembowelled houses revealed upper floors wobbling from one remaining wall, the smashed wreckage of everything from billiard-tables to mirrors, and the enemy dead left lying for days in the spring heat.[29] However, the légionnaires' morale was reportedly good; by now most of them knew every trench corner and blind window, food came up regularly, and 'trench days' earned extra wine and rum rations.

After a few days they were pulled out again, and it was not until the end of the first week in May that they were back in the line at Neuilly. This time they were on the southern perimeter, between Avenue de Neuilly and the Bois de Boulogne. Life was safer here than in the shattered streets north-east of the bridge; there were a few casualties during patrol clashes, but the most memorable event was an encounter between a small Legion outpost and a terrifying figure that turned out to be an orang-utang escaped from the zoo, pursued by its agitated keeper shouting 'Don't shoot! Don't shoot!'.[30] On 11 May, a rebel attack hit the légionnaires' right flank from the Bois, but was driven back; reserves came up to block any repetition, and thereafter shellfire was the only threat. The soldiers soon figured out the pattern of firing, timing their chores in the open to coincide with the Federals' habitual mealtimes before getting back behind shell-proof cover. On 14 May they were withdrawn again, and sent out to police quiet sectors in the villages of Gennevilliers, Asnières and Bécon and the suburb of Clichy. The spring heat was building, and inside the city the defence was crumbling.

IN LESS THAN FIVE WEEKS the Commune's leaders ('leadership' implies too much solidarity) had fatally undermined the efforts of two nominal military commanders. After a scare at Fort Issy, Cluseret was arrested on 30 April as a 'royalist traitor' – the usual hysterical currency of the Commune; he was replaced by Louis Rossel, who would be hamstrung by the same conspiratorial disunity as his predecessor. He was frustrated in his attempts to organize new inner barricades and redoubts, and to concentrate the hundreds of neglected cannon to some serious purpose. He ordered the formation of infantry 'battle groups', each with its own guns, from among those

Guardsmen who seemed willing to fight – now perhaps 20,000, from a theoretical strength of five times that many. The response was disappointing; as always, most men refused to serve outside their own home districts.[31] A long struggle over the control of operations led, on 3 May, to the creation of an all-powerful Committee of Public Safety dominated by extremists, but the factional wrangling continued. Most of Rossel's orders were either ignored or countermanded; when his plan for a counter-attack to ease the pressure on Fort Issy on 7 May was rejected he resigned, was threatened with arrest, and went into hiding.

On 8 May, after a final crushing bombardment, the surviving defenders finally abandoned the shell-ploughed mound of Fort Issy, thus freeing the approaches to the Point du Jour. The visibly dying old Charles Delescluze was now co-opted to head the Committee of Public Safety, but his military instructions extended no further than an appeal to the gods of 1793. Mac-Mahon's shelling was relentless, and his counter-batteries had smashed many Federal guns; the National Guard were conscripting civilians at gun-point; untreated wounded lay in rows along the kerbs, while companies without orders wandered aimlessly. The Prussians had blockaded the eastern gates to prevent food coming in, and some 300,000 Parisians had fled the city. Meanwhile, Communard leaders argued passionately over future social legislation, and State Prosecutor Rigault began to drag batches of his 3,000 hostages in front of summary tribunals.[32]

Seen from outside the ramparts, however, the recapture of Paris still threatened to be difficult and costly. Attacking through city streets is a meat-grinder of infantry: every move from cover to cover invites fire from concealed defenders, and units can quickly become dispersed and lost in the maze, overlooked by cliffs of deadly windows. The broad, straight central boulevards of Hausmann's redeveloped city centre were shooting-galleries for artillery. If the side streets had been intelligently blocked, then working around the flanks of Communard positions would be a slow and bloody business, and the Paris mob had a proud Revolutionary history of building formidable barricades. In 1871 the traditional type – basically walls of carts, cabs and horse-buses in-filled with prised-up paving blocks, sandbags and furniture – could hold back infantry, though not artillery for long. However, others were real fortifications straight out of a field engineering manual: massive squared-off stacks of paving blocks and sandbags, at least twice a man's height, tens of yards thick, and incorporating textbook emplacements for cannon and mitrailleuses.

WHAT LATER BECAME INFAMOUS AS 'BLOODY WEEK' began almost as farce. On the afternoon of Sunday 21 May, sheer carelessness in the Federal manning of the Point du Jour ramparts allowed the returned ex-prisoners of war of Douay's IV Corps to simply scramble inside without a shot being fired. A mishandled counter-attack was beaten back, and the Versaillais got beyond the only viable inner barrier along the Ceinture railway line. Rampart bastions were cleared and other gates opened for troops and cannon; early the next day, Clinchant's V Corps regulars worked their way clockwise up the inside of the ramparts on Douay's left, reaching the Étoile at the top of the shell-battered Champs-Élysées; meanwhile, in the south, Cissey's motley II Corps got in through the Porte de Versailles and headed north. Some 50,000 men were now inside the walls; the piece-meal Federal defence of western Paris collapsed, and by nightfall on Monday 22nd, MacMahon, from his headquarters with the artillery on the dominating hill of the Trocadéro, could plan an articulated advance eastwards on both banks of the Seine.

Although firing went on throughout the long May days from first light to full darkness, no needless risks were being taken with the soldiers' lives; determined to avoid chilling his army's lukewarm morale with heavy casualties, the marshal had strictly forbidden frontal attacks on barricades, and advances were made in unhurried bounds with generous covering fire.[33] MacMahon's *pantalons rouges* observed the tactical rules that still govern urban fighting to this day, and kept out of the fire-swept streets whenever possible. Artillery was plentiful enough to provide each brigade with at least a section of two guns to support the advance of its assault battalions. The cannon were set up at corners, to sweep both main streets and cross-streets; meanwhile, the infantry tried to outflank each obstacle by finding a way down a parallel street, crossways through alleys and yards, or into and along the continuous rows of houses from the inside. The slow pace of the Versaillais advance gave the Federals time to build about 500 new barricades during the week 21–28 May, but although many would be defended bravely, they were thrown up without coordination, and usually lacked interlocking fields of fire at the vague junctions of district battalion sectors.

The famous Federal artillery on the hill of Montmartre – the catalyst for the whole confrontation – remained neglected and more or less silent through lack of preparedness and of orders, and the hilltop village was attacked on the morning of Tuesday 23 May from three sides. Resistance (by both male and female units) was bitter in places, but it was piecemeal, and by 1pm the hill was in government hands.[34] However, that Tuesday saw a much stiffer Federal defence of the central city, on both banks of the river. Fighting was particularly intense against IV Corps on the Right Bank, on a front of Place de la Concorde – Madeleine – Opéra, and behind this on the Rue de Rivoli.

Artillery duels were fought at close range, the concussion carpeting the streets with sucked-out window-glass, and where the shells struck they holed and gutted multi-storey blocks, bringing down roaring avalanches of rubble. Sharpshooters in upper storeys and on rooftops made the open streets murderous, and the echoing noise even of rifle-fire was deafening. The crossfires clipped off showers of leaves and scored the trunks of trees, and wounded men left blood-trails as they dragged themselves towards doors that remained stubbornly closed. The cost was not only in human lives: under the howl and crash of gunfire, mounted couriers were constantly clattering back and forth, and the main streets were crowded with horse-drawn gun-teams, ambulances, and infantry being moved around in horse-buses. The troops sometimes had to inch past maimed horses screaming and kicking in pools of blood and excrement on the cobbles.

Forced back from the Place Vendôme, the Communards set fire to any building that they could not hold. When they finally retreated down Rue de Rivoli towards the Hôtel de Ville during the long spring dusk, the blazing Rue Royale and Tuileries palace were lighting up the sky like a rival sunset; most of the Palais Royale and many other historic buildings also caught fire from wind-blown sparks or were deliberately torched, and the Louvre and Nôtre Dame were only barely saved.[35] Meanwhile, Rigault's henchmen started killing hostages, with slow and horrible inefficiency, at the St Pelagie prison. As Paris burned, the myth of the *petroleuses* put any woman seen carrying something in the street in peril of summary execution; both sides indulged in a spiral of vengeful killings, goaded on by civilian mobs.

On Wednesday 24 May, the Hôtel de Ville was abandoned and burned by the Communards; in the afternoon, Rigault became trapped in the Latin Quarter and was killed. That morning General Lefèbvre's 2nd Brigade of Montaudon's division had come in through the Porte de Clignancourt in the northern ramparts; by noon they had captured the Gare du Nord, and by 7.30pm, the Gare de l'Est (see Map 2). Some of his soldiers slept that night in the Gare du Nord, though fitfully: Federal shells from the Buttes-Chaumont smashed through the high glass vaults and exploded inside, driving them from the concourse and platforms where today's British travellers alight from Eurostar trains.[36] During the evening Rigault's creature, Théophile Ferré, had the Archbishop of Paris and five other prominent hostages murdered at La Roquette prison. That night the Foreign Regiment were warned, as they gazed from the village of Asnières outside the ramparts at the huge red glow in the eastern sky, that their brigade would enter the inferno before dawn.[37]

IN THE EARLY HOURS of Thursday 25 May, Montaudon brought Dumont's 1st Brigade marching in through the Porte Maillot in the west and clockwise around the inside of the ramparts. After a long trudge under a blazing sun they reached the North railway freight and coal yards; the 30th Light had to outflank and capture a barricade blocking the upper Rue de la Chapelle, but that evening Dumont linked up with Lefèbvre's 2nd Brigade. The division spent the night of 25/26 May more or less along the line of the East railway, with the Legion in rear reserve between the North railway and Boulevard Ornano.[38] The great fires were not much more than a mile away now, and sometimes a dull rumble could be heard as some seven-storey block collapsed into itself, sending huge gouts of flame licking into the sky. That evening, old Delescluze found the bullet he sought when he tottered up an abandoned barricade across the Boulevard Voltaire. Under cover of night, perhaps 5,000 remaining Communard fighters were falling back to sell their lives dearly in their eastern heartland – the industrial squalor of La Villette, and the narrow slums of Belleville and Ménilmontant.

They had a strong perimeter to defend, especially in this northern sector. Passing in through the northern ramparts, the Canal St Denis ran south to join the Canal de l'Ourcq coming in from the north-east. The latter made a straight, broad moat through the warehouses and quays of La Villette, all the way south-west to the Rotunda customs house at the junction of Boulevard de la Chapelle and Boulevard de La Villette.[39] South of that crossing, the dog-leg of the Canal St Martin ran all the way down to Rue du Faubourg du Temple. Well behind these water obstacles, the Federal artillery on the hill of the Buttes-Chaumont covered the northern and western approaches to Belleville. The Versailles corps were now converging: Ladmirault's I Corps, including Montaudon's division, from north to south; Clinchant's V and Douay's IV from west to east; Vinoy's Reserve closing the bottom of the bag and pushing northwards, while behind them Cissey's II Corps mopped up in the south-east.

*

THE STIFLING HEAT BROKE in a torrential downpour on Friday 26 May, stopping the spread of the great fires even if it did not put them out. Part of Dumont's 1st Brigade, stretched between the Gare d'Orléans freight sheds and Bastion 30 on the ramparts, was launched eastwards at the Canal St Denis, but they only captured a bridge at about 3pm. The battalions of the Foreign Regiment seem to have been separated, with one element fighting alongside the 39th Marching up on the East railway; there Dumont's left wing went on to clear several bastions down to the Canal de l'Ourcq, and stopped for the night in the noisome shelter of the huge city abattoirs.

At the same time, down to the south-west, another Legion element was on the right flank of 2nd Brigade, struggling to overcome barricades at the eastern end of Boulevard de la Chapelle and to clear an approach to the major Federal stronghold in the Rotunda.[40] They captured ten cannon and a *mitrailleuse*, and Private Gagneux was cited for the Military Medal for killing a Federal officer and seizing the flag of the 124th Battalion. (His captain had four of the prisoners shot. This was not a case of mercenaries bringing African habits to the streets of Paris; Metropolitan units routinely shot prisoners during Bloody Week and, given that the Communards were trying to kill as many fellow Frenchmen as possible with artillery and machine guns, this cannot be surprising. Versaillais atrocities such as the massacre of wounded and doctors in dressing stations are more so.)[41] On the left of these légionnaires, a rush by a battalion of 2nd Brigade's 119th Line finally forced the Federals back from barricades on three sides of the Rotunda, allowing troops to get across the square into the mouths of several streets south of it, though still under fire from the customs house itself.[42] During this fighting a sugar refinery and canal warehouses full of grain, alcohol, tar and timber caught fire, blazing with explosive ferocity despite the rain and forcing the evacuation of several streets. At some point during the night of 26/27 May the last Federals abandoned the Rotunda and fell back to the east, though many of the streets round about were still blocked and defended. (By that night the last 50 hostages from La Roquette prison had been murdered in the Rue Haxo.)[43]

According to General Montaudon's memoir, Dumont's 1st Brigade spent what must have been a comfortless night on the division's left flank, in the stinking abattoirs and stockyards beside the Canal de l'Ourcq. During the night Montaudon received new orders from I Corps: Grenier's division would come down from behind his left shoulder to clear the eastern ramparts towards the south, down to the Porte de Pantin. Montaudon was to shift his weight to the right, maintaining contact with Grenier but 'acting depending upon circumstances', to clear the way for an attack on the hill of Buttes-Chaumont on Sunday the 28th. Operations would commence at 11am on the 27th, and commanders were reminded to make the maximum preparatory use of their attached artillery and engineers.[44]

Montaudon's 2nd Brigade (Lefèbvre) were already facing eastwards across the Canal St Martin, and at first light on the 27th the divisional commander ordered Dumont's 1st Brigade down from the abattoirs to link up with Lefèbvre's left flank. The Foreign Regiment must have marched south-west down the Canal de l'Ourcq, since they got into action close to the Rotunda in today's Place de Stalingrad. They took a barricade at the bottom of Rue de Flandre, rounded the end of the barge-harbour at Basin de La Villette, crossed the square past the Rotunda, then captured more barricades at the ends of Rue d'Allemagne and Rue de Puebla. On the afternoon of the 27th they worked their way south down the latter street.[45]

The drill was automatic by now. Scouts went first, dodging from doorway to doorway and shooting at any suspicious windows to draw fire. Orders had been shouted to householders to keep their shutters open but their windows closed; anyone showing himself at an open window paid the fatal price of stupidity, and any sniper instantly revealed himself by the thick puff of powder-smoke. The sapper squads came next, to demolish any abandoned barricades or to circumvent any defended ones by breaking into flanking houses and yards with the leading infantrymen. A gun team then rumbled up, unlimbering at the corner of a block to shell the barricade if it was in the line of sight, prevent movement across the street if it was not, and command the sidestreets; firefights in this heavy weather filled the streets with clouds of choking powder-smoke, unsighting the riflemen of both sides. Inside the houses, meanwhile, the sappers with their heavy axes and crowbars, and infantrymen with their boots and rifle-butts, smashed 'mouse-holes' through the flimsy plank or lath-and-plaster partition walls, working their way along the row from house to house until they could fire down on the barricade from an upper storey. After a last blast from the cannon, their comrades below could rush what remained.

As each assault unit made progress, the battalions that followed it, accompanied by gendarmes and loyalist 'National Guards of Order', searched houses for hidden snipers and arms and interrogated the residents. By 27 May, many National Guardsmen had dumped their weapons and uniforms, and most were careful to have not even a belt or tunic-button in the house where they were found. God help any man caught with powder-stained hands or a bruised right shoulder; he probably would not even live to join the long, bedraggled columns of prisoners being escorted by cavalrymen out to the Bois de Boulogne, where the merciless General Gallifet's firing-squads were busy. When prisoners were taken under arms, many were summarily executed, but most reprisals were not the work of the assault troops. Neither did they loot – beyond individual petty thefts – or rape, nor was there even much drinking; the Communards were more conspicuous for that. Always on the look-out for wavering discipline, the Versailles officers kept a tight grip on their men. The same could not be claimed for the irregular Seine Volunteers who accompanied I Corps; anti-Communards who had been forced out of the city in March, they relished the chance to settle political and personal scores.[46]

By 3pm on the 27th, the Foreign Regiment had got far enough down Rue de Puebla to secure the Marché de Meaux, though under shellfire from the Buttes-Chaumont that now loomed over the rooftops straight ahead of them, just 500 yards away up at the end of Rue Sécretant.[47] Off to their right, 2nd Brigade had got across the Canal St Martin to attack Federal barricades in the Rond-Point de La Villette. In earlier centuries this had been the site of the huge Montfaucon gallows, a great square frame of gibbets standing nearly 50 feet high, in what was then a wasteland between the medieval city and the hilltop fields around the quiet rural hamlet of Belleville.

THE BUTTES-CHAUMONT had a colourful history over recent decades. Away from the Seine in the centre, old Paris had enclosed a surprising amount of open space, but during the prosperous reign of Louis-Philippe development had accelerated. The population of Belleville mutiplied, as odd clumps of shacks and cottages grew together; the dirt lanes were eventually paved and lit, linking boomtown developments of solid houses with rickety tenements served by a notorious area of bars and brothels.

The catalyst had been the Buttes themselves, a 150-foot hill feature where gypsum – the raw material for 'plaster of Paris' – was mined and processed. The quarries on and to the east of the hill were called 'America', either because of the destination of much of their product or (more pleasingly) because they were at the edge of the inhabited world. During the boom years, when the hill was riddled with tunnels dug by primitive capitalists, this was an uncontrolled frontier where men could make their fortunes or get killed with equal ease. Powder-blasting and the thudding of steam crushing-mills deafened Belleville from dawn to dusk, and coal-fired furnaces smoked day and night. Men frequently died in collapsing tunnels, and roadways far from the hill began to subside into the random burrows it sent out. As the unrestricted diggings were gradually abandoned, the destitute and the predatory moved in, and this wilderness of craters and spoil-heaps acquired a sinister reputation. The population of Belleville was further swollen, and radicalized, during the 1850s–60s, when industrialization and Hausmann's redevelopment of the central city drove the poorest classes outwards into jerry-built slums to live as best they could on starvation wages.

In 1862, Napoleon III decreed that the eyesore should be turned into a public park, and by an extraordinary effort his civil engineers, public works officials and gardeners got it ready for its grand opening in time for the Universal Exhibition of April 1867. The honeycombed hilltop was filled and carved into a landscaped horticultural garden-cum-arboretum around several artificial lakes, overlooked by a dramatic 90-foot pinnacle crowned with a shining copy of the Temple of Sybil at Tivoli. Rich and poor alike could stroll along winding paths beside waterways flanked by exotic trees and plantings gathered from all over the world, marvelling at a 60-foot grotto complete with brand-new stalactites, while waterfalls splashed down rock-faces cloaked with climbing plants.

By the afternoon of 27 May 1871, this hilltop and that of Père Lachaise cemetery a mile and a half to the south were the last two important positions that the Communards held.

BY LATE AFTERNOON on 27 May the hill was surrounded on three sides, with Montaudon's 1st and 2nd Brigades in a rough semi-circle from the centre of the north slope down to the west, and although the Buttes were supposed to be tomorrow's objective the divisional commander decided not to wait. His flanks were secure; on his left, Grenier had taken a brigade right down to Bastion 21 behind the hill and was delivering supporting fire from 12-pounders and *mitrailleuses*. At 4pm Montaudon gave the signal for the assault; the details of the attack are unclear, but we do know that it did not take long. The Foreign Regiment had had enough of cautious step-by-step advances; two companies headed the central assault column, simply charging up the steep Rue Sécretant 'under a hail of bullets' and throwing themselves up the slopes in front of them. After a fairly brief fight they reached one of the summits and planted the tricolour, while the 36th Marching from 2nd Brigade stuck theirs at the top of the western slope, and Abatucci's brigade from Grenier's division then came panting up from the 'American quarries' to the east.

The defenders were attacked from two, later three, sides simultaneously, after being bombarded from about 1,300 yards by 120mm guns and raked by *mitrailleuses*; this was well within the latter's effective range for an area target such as a gun-battery, which is exactly what they had originally been designed to shoot at. We might speculate that the two Federal batteries were neither well sited nor properly protected from fire by breastworks (these were certainly neglected at Montmartre). Whatever the reason, light Versaillais casualties confirm that the *pantalons rouges* cannot have had to charge gun-muzzles hurling out canister-shot. The Legion casualties are not recorded, but seem to have been less than twenty; three lieutenants were cited specifically for their behaviour here, and Lieutenant Dupont's men were reportedly the first to reach the Federal guns.[48]

To the south, the two Federal batteries in Père Lachaise cemetery had also fallen, to General Vinoy's naval troops. There was still plenty of light, and while Montaudon established his staff on the Buttes he wanted to get men down into the streets to the south – presumably to prevent the Federals consolidating a front facing the south side of the park to resist the final crushing of Belleville the following day. The légionnaires of I/ and II/RE were at first ordered to remain on the hill for the night, no doubt beginning the task of dragging corpses together for the pyres that would send stinking smoke over the city for days afterwards. The V/RE moved down out of the park and south towards Place des Fêtes, accompanied by the Seine Volunteers.

At about 6pm they reached the entrance to this large, open marketplace and fairground, where the Seine Volunteers charged a barricade – presumably across the Rue de Crimee or des Solitaires – and lost their Major Delbos in the taking of it. He was their second commanding officer to be killed in four days (Major Duriue had fallen in Montmartre), and we may guess that they added to their reputation for shooting prisoners out of hand. The V/RE passed through into the square and towards a barricade on the far side. A group of Federal stragglers were sitting drinking in a bar close to it; when they opened fire a Wild West gunfight ensued, with shots being traded under tables and up the stairs. The légionnaires cleared the house, then burst out of it on to the barricade, taking it for the loss of two men killed. Other companies bumped into significant resistance just beyond the square, and the 5th

Battalion CO called his men back; he wanted no confused firing in the dark streets, and established his unit in a 'hedgehog' at Place des Fêtes for the night, reinforced on its wide perimeter by three companies of II/RE sent down from the Buttes.[49]

THE LAST COMMUNARD FIGHTERS were mopped up on Whit Sunday, 28 May, as the cordon around the remaining blocks of the 19th and 20th Districts was pulled tight by I Corps and the Reserve. The Federals were now surrendering in large numbers, but soldiers found that it was still perfectly possible to get themselves killed that morning. From 5am there was a brisk exchange of fire between opposing positions in the streets of Belleville, until cannon on the Buttes intervened to start the légionnaires on their way. On the left, V/RE moved eastwards to the ramparts, clearing barricades along Rues du Pré St Gervais and des Bois. In the centre, II/RE ran down streets at the double; by 10am the tricolour was flying from the church of St Jean Baptiste, and the Commune's last headquarters in the 20th District town hall soon fell. A British witness trapped at the *mairie* described a soldier of the Legion calling for everyone to lay down their weapons and surrender; the Englishman went forward, and made sure his name was recorded as having been taken unarmed.[50]

On the regiment's right, I/RE took their last barricade at the corner of Rues de Belleville and Puebla; General Grisot wrote that this last day cost the RE two killed and 14 wounded. It was west of Rue de Puebla that the diehards of the Federal 191st Battalion went down fighting, around Faubourg du Temple and Rue Saint Maur. Most of the shooting was over by 2pm on Sunday afternoon, but what seems to have been the very last barricade was taken at about 6pm by men from the Legion's brigade-mates, the 30th Light Infantry. It was there, at the corner of Rue de Tourtille and Rue Ramponneau, that the Versaillais apparently suffered their last casualty: the passionate young Lieutenant Paul Déroulède, badly wounded in the arm, would get his Cross for seizing a red flag.[51] That night, all three battalions of the Foreign Regiment were back in bivouac on the Buttes-Chaumont, where their drums and bugles beat 'Retreat' to remind Parisians that the Army now owned the hill.

Total Versaillais casualties since the beginning of April had amounted to 877 killed (including three generals) and 6,454 wounded; during Bloody Week perhaps 3,500 Federals were killed in action or died of wounds.[52] The Foreign Regiment spent 29 May gathering up weapons and disposing of Communards in Belleville. Although the regimental diary admits with some regret that 'large numbers' of prisoners were shot locally on 28–29 May, there is no apparent evidence that the RE played any part in the mass executions carried out in cold blood during the next fortnight.[53] On 30 May the RE were sent to the barracks of La Pépinière; these former quarters of the Imperial Guard had been left in such a state of wrecked squalor by the Communards that it took the légionnaires four days to clean up.

IN THE ANGUISHED HANGOVER from that 'Terrible Year', the French state and its army faced a painful period of introspection, and during this demoralizing exercise the presence in France of l'Armée d'Afrique would be neither necessary nor welcome. Since the participation of foreign mercenaries would have been positively embarrassing in MacMahon's victory parade at Longchamp on 29 June, on the 10th a ministerial decision was taken to return the Foreign Regiment to Algeria. The next day the légionnaires left Paris by rail for Toulon, where on 15 June they embarked on the *Drôme* for Mers el Kebir.[54] They belonged, after all, to a colonial regiment. However indistinguishable their behaviour in the streets of Paris from that of the improvised units of the Metropolitan Army, they had been raised and trained for a different sort of soldiering.

1. The Tools of Empire

*With a whole Metropolitan regiment I could not venture
two hours' outside the town – with a single company of
the Legion I could make a tour of Tonkin.*
General Francois Oscar de Négrier[1]

THE FRANCO-PRUSSIAN WAR that culminated in the destruction of
the Paris Commune was the first in which regiments raised specifically for
service outside France had been employed in the defence of 'the Hexagon'
itself. In comparison with the use there of three regiments of Algerian
'turcos', the illegal shipping of half the Legion to France had attracted
little comment, but the distinction between Metropolitan troops and those
transferred from North Africa was not solely racial. French colonial troops –
in the generic, rather than the specific administrative use of that term –
were tacitly understood to have a different character from the Metropolitan
Army, and to have entered a different implicit covenant with the state.
These were not French farmboys, conscripted into uniform to spend seven
years in some other part of France before re-entering the life of their family
and village. Colonial troops enlisted voluntarily, breaking not only their
personal bonds but also many of their ties with the national family, to soldier
far away in the service of a more robust military doctrine. In crude terms,
they were a tool designed for dirtier work in harsher fields, and a glance at
that work should perhaps precede a summary of their history and organization.

THE DEFINING TASK of such troops was to kill those members of native
populations who resisted the advance of the Europeans. If native fighting
men could not be brought to battle and defeated immediately, then subjection was achieved by running off their flocks and destroying their villages,

orchards, crops and stored food, thereby inflicting starvation on their families until their leaders submitted. The human reality behind the phrase 'destroying their villages' varied widely in practice. In North Africa a 'village' might be anything from a *douar* – a scatter of tents, overrun with a minimum of drama and bloodshed after a couple of volleys, to a *ksar* – something resembling a medieval castle, that had to be shelled and stormed, house by house, at the point of the bayonet.

The French Army in the late nineteenth century (though not its native auxiliaries) was a disciplined force; its officers allowed petty looting for the cooking-pot, but well understood the dangers of unleashing their men to sack without control. But if some soldiers raised in today's liberal democracies can occasionally behave barbarously during wars fought among populations that they perceive as wholly alien, then we can hardly be shocked that their great-grandfathers did the same. There were, of course, cultural differences between various national armies, and compassionate exceptions among Christian believers, but in those days any sense of global shared humanity was shallowly rooted. The colonial soldiers of those times and places lived in a past that is doubly a foreign country to us, and they did things differently there.

It is easy to condemn such brutalities automatically, but we should beware of self-righteous cant; these soldiers were the organic products of a world that most of us would find terrifying. Statistically, it is safe to assume that only a tiny minority of the readers of this book have ever known lives of real Third World hardship, hunger, superstition, and arbitrary violence without appeal. For the nineteenth-century European underclasses such experiences might be the norm, and illiteracy denied most of them any understanding of a better world. When men born into such conditions were offered regular meals, a comprehensible system of reward and punishment, clearly defined tasks and a sense of collective self-esteem, they could be shaped into a weapon, but it would remain a rather indiscriminate one. It is dauntingly difficult for us to imagine ourselves into the minds of unreflective men – both the illiterate and the educated – who lived on the far side of the absolute historical watershed of the First World War. Before that uniquely traumatic experience most people simply did not question the need for wars nor the moral status of those who fought them, and the things that might sometimes happen on campaign were no business of civilians; after all, the adversaries that they were fighting never took prisoners themselves, except with the very worst of intentions.

French colonial forces shared with all other such armies not only the values of their times, but also the lack of the external check that would be introduced – however haphazardly, and often unjustly – by the late twentieth-century mass media. In the absence of the babbling international conversation that deafens our own age, events had witnesses and some had chroniclers, but they did not have a world-wide reactive audience. After a distasteful episode the occasional letter from an indignant officer might reach his friends, but seldom any wider echo-chamber; in a deferential age there was a strong ethic, sincerely held by decent men, of discretion owed to the respected institutions of army and state. There were exceptions – in France, notably, when such a letter revealed the deranged butchery of two Naval Troops officers named Voulet and Chanoine in West Africa in 1899; but usually, the sound of brutalities committed far off in the wilderness died away into silence after the passage of a few miles and a few days – if they were even considered to be brutalities, in that environment.[2] In justice, it must be said that by the turn of the century crimes such as those of Voulet and Chanoine were exceptional, particularly north of the Sahara. The more intelligent commanders insisted that gratuitous brutality was both contemptible and counter-productive, and generally the troops' attitude to civilians was one of callous indifference rather than active cruelty, leavened with episodes of sentimental kindness to children and their mothers. Ill-treatment is not an absolute: there are degrees, and we can assume that these differences were significant to the native populations.

Once peace had been established in new colonies the French forces planted small dispersed garrisons to maintain local security. As the initial violence receded in the memory (for the native peoples it had been, after all, only one incident in a history of violence stretching back to time out of mind), so workaday contacts brought at least a degree of mutual toleration. There was little French intrusion into daily life, and most inland communities never even saw a white man. After a while, some benefits of the new stability might become apparent: a check upon tribal warfare, safer travel and increased internal trade, and – if they were lucky – some material improvements to their way of life.

However, when a native people submitted to white administration there was always a vaguely defined frontier with the territory of those still unsubdued – the tribes of either a masterless hinterland or a neighbouring native state. Rebels could find safe refuge over these borders, and the free tribes also tended to raid the peaceful and thus more productive subdued tribes, who looked for protection to the colonial garrisons. Field columns would be assembled from among these troops, to march out once again; and so the process would be repeated, as European flags crawled steadily across the maps towards one another. The regiments that carried them showed a diversity of character that sometimes went beyond simple national differences.

UNLIKE GREAT BRITAIN – whose all-volunteer battalions might be posted anywhere from Aldershot to Canada or to Burma – France had raised particular units specifically for service overseas. Initially, however, in the 1880s–90s, the expeditionary forces for colonial conquests were a mixture of troops from three distinct organizations.

The first was the Metropolitan Army, 'le biff' – the young conscripts fulfilling their years of obligatory military service. The second were the Naval Troops; these were volunteers before the mid-1870s, a mixture of volunteers and conscripts from then until 1893, and thereafter solely volunteers once again. The third was l'Armée d'Afrique (from 1873 designated the 19th Army Corps), raised mostly in Algeria from both Europeans and Arabs. The Africa Army's infantry was composed of white Zouave and (penal) Africa Light Infantry conscripts; Foreign Legion volunteers; and native volunteer Algerian Skirmishers ('turcos'). The cavalry were the Chasseurs d'Afrique (Africa Light Horse), who were white conscripts leavened with some volunteers both white and native, and the Arab volunteer Spahis.

The Naval Troops (Troupes de la Marine) traced their history back to a company raised for overseas service in 1621. Their development had been complex, but by the late nineteenth century their mission was defined as protecting naval bases both in France and the colonies, while also providing temporary task-organized units (régiments de marche) for global operations, specifically in sub-Saharan Africa, Asia and the distant oceans. After the Franco-Prussian War four large regiments were based at Cherbourg, Brest, Rochefort and Toulon, with an unusual, baggy structure. A Régiment d'Infanterie de Marine might administer as many as 45 companies (instead of the conventional 12 of a Metropolitan Régiment de Ligne), of which 18 were usually serving overseas at any one time. In the early 1870s the Naval Infantry ('marsouins') totalled about 20,000 men and the Naval Artillery ('bigors') another 3,300. The first experiments in forming ad hoc West African auxiliary companies into regular battalions had also added some thousands of Senegalese Skirmishers, led and administered by Naval Infantry cadres.[3]

This corps was administratively a historical leftover; the defence of home naval bases was now simply an aspect of overall national defence, and since 1856 the traditional tasks of embarked soldiers had been taken over by specially trained sailors (fusiliers-marins). Since the admirals wanted to spend their budgets on the Fleet, they neglected their land units badly, while reflexively snarling at the many recommendations that these simply be turned over to the War Ministry. Trapped by this inertia, officers of the Naval Infantry endured inferior career prospects and prestige to those in both the Fleet and the Army, until the Tonkin (North Vietnam) campaigns of 1883–5 raised the service's profile and began to attract high-flyers.

The death rate from disease was high among the Naval Troops, but higher still in the Metropolitan regiments sometimes deployed to colonial theatres. Shipping the conscripted sons of French voters to far-off, fever-ridden hellholes was eventually admitted to be politically unsustainable, militarily ineffective, and a distraction from their proper task – that of training for revenge against Germany for the disasters of 1870–71. The folly of sending Metropolitan units on such expeditions became a matter of scandal when the Madagascar campaign of 1895 cost the mixed Army/Navy/African expeditionary force some 5,000 deaths from tropical disease (nearly one-third of its strength), the highest price being paid by the Metropolitan troops.

In 1900 the Army finally prised the Naval Troops – equivalent in peacetime to a whole army corps – from the grip of the admirals. An Act of 7 July 1900 transferred them to a separate 8th Directorate of the War Ministry under the title of Colonial Troops, with their own general staff and their own career structure; they also kept their anchor badge and all-blue uniforms for reasons of morale.[4] Significantly, however, the conscription law of 30 July 1893 – which had seen their numbers drop by some 10,000 between 1897 and 1900 – remained in force. The Colonial Troops received no annual quota of conscripts, and had to fill their ranks entirely by voluntary enlistment; substantial bounties were offered, with pensions and reserved civilian employment after discharge. Despite its title, however, la Coloniale was not given back any monopoly of overseas operations.

Since the early 1880s the predominance of the Naval Troops in every overseas theatre beyond North Africa had fanned inter-service rivalries, with consequent jockeying for political influence and funding. The Army, too, needed a solid core of stoic white infantry who could be sent anywhere in the world as an armature for the Arab regiments that provided most of the Army bayonets for colonial campaigns. Over the period 1883–1914, this tough spine was increasingly provided by the mercenaries of the Foreign Legion, whose numbers were steadily multiplied during those years from four to twelve battalions. One consequence would be an increasing sense of rivalry – robustly expressed during chance encounters in alleyways and brothels – between the French soldiers who wore the blue trousers and anchor badge of *In Coloniale*, and the mercenaries sporting the red trousers and seven-flamed grenade of *la Légion*.

EVEN DURING THE THIRTY YEARS of vigorous colonial expansion before 1914 there was a general public vagueness about the Légion Étrangère, which had almost never been seen on French soil: many people had heard of it, but few felt any real curiosity. From the upper slopes of the Metropolitan military establishment the Legion was regarded as a functional but mildly embarrassing afterthought, little better than a labour corps. It was confused by civilians and even by some soldiers with the '*joyeux*' of the Africa Light Infantry – Bataillons d'Infanterie Légère d'Afrique (BILA or 'Bats d'Af') – the distinctly grim units in which convicted civil criminals had to fulfil their military service obligation, and to which military offenders were sometimes transferred.[5] The French Army's leadership under the early Third Republic was an uneasy amalgam of Bourbon monarchists (both Legitimists and Orléanists), Bonapartists and Republicans, but in an officer corps sharply conscious of the wide divisions within its own ranks, at least the more educated and monied could unite in regarding the Legion as an impossibly unfashionable bunch of dim roughnecks. Intellectuals from the École Poly-technique and exquisites of the cavalry assumed that it was led by black sheep or the socially untouchable, who were condemned to serve in lethally unhealthy postings far from the career-enhancing gossip and networking of officers' club and city salon. Neither in France nor abroad, however, was the Legion's image as a military underclass specifically due to the fact that it enlisted foreign soldiers.

The word 'mercenary' has been used and understood in different ways since the early 1960s, when the collapse of the former Belgian Congo first brought it into the headlines. In fact, there has always been a clear distinction between the hired freelance seeking high short-term rewards, and the foreign-born professional soldier accepting unremarkable wages for long-term service. It takes a rather wilful ignorance to refuse to recognize the essential difference between, say, the *affreux* of mid-twentieth-century Africa and the Royal Gurkha Rifles, though both could loosely be described as mercenaries. Given the possibility of confusion, however, the historical resonance of the term demands some examination.

WRITERS FORAGING for a ringing epigraph have sometimes chanced upon A. E. Housman's poem *Epitaph on an Army of Mercenaries*, but those splendidly stoic lines have nothing whatever to do with the Foreign Legion. Housman wrote it in September 1917, on the third anniversary of the First Battle of Ypres, in order to honour the regular soldiers of the old 1914 British Expeditionary Force who had fallen in their tens of thousands while resisting the German invasion of Flanders. To define long-service professional soldiers of our own national army as 'mercenaries' is not a usage many of us would recognize today – when it would embrace, among others, the whole armed forces of the English-speaking world – but in Housman's day the term did not carry today's baggage of disdain. It simply described soldiers who enlisted voluntarily for pay rather than being conscripted by compulsion; in the nineteenth century, and still when Housman wrote his praise-song over the graves of the BEF, the word was simply a technical description, which could apply equally to home-born and foreign volunteers. In the past, European powers had routinely hired foreign troops in formed regiments; equally, many officers were permitted, even encouraged, by their governments to rent out their skills to other friendly rulers.

The unthinking presumption that a nation's army should, in honour, consist only of men born in that country is of recent origin. The very concept of a national standing army dates only from the seventeenth century, and its birth certainly did not make the medieval practice of employing foreign soldiers obsolete. For instance, a quarter in modern Gdansk is still known as 'Old Scotland', and it is estimated that in 1600 no fewer than 37,000 Scots were living in Poland to provide a pool for mercenary recruitment. The Thirty Years War (1618–48) saw the beginnings of permanent national forces, and during the 1620s King Gustavus Adolphus was conscripting about 2 per cent of Sweden's male population for regional regiments each year; but at the same time he was also employing very large numbers of Germans and more than 30,000 Scottish, English and Irish soldiers.[6] Long-term employment of whole foreign brigades (notably, Swiss and Irish) was a permanent feature of several eighteenth-century European standing armies. While

Britain's naval strength allowed it to avoid military conscription, its small volunteer army was supplemented by many foreign mercenary units led by a mixture of skilled professionals and political emigrés.

During the Revolutionary and Napoleonic wars between 1793 and 1815, Britain's field armies included many battalions of Germans other than King George's Hanoverian countrymen, and also of Frenchmen, Dutchmen, Belgians, Swiss, Italians, Sicilians, Corsicans, Maltese, Greeks, Albanians and Croats – to say nothing of its non-European garrisons in the West Indies, South Africa, Asia and the East Indies.[7] Neither was this trade all in one direction, for the flow reversed in parallel with political developments. The aftermath of Waterloo threw many British ex-soldiers into penury, and some 5,500 of them sailed off to fight for Simon Bolivar in the South American wars of independence, led by officers many of whom had also served under Wellington.[8] French and Italian officers, in their turn, travelled as far afield as the Punjab to rent out the skills they had learned under Bonaparte.

WHEN LOUIS-PHILIPPE, THE LAST KING OF FRANCE, raised the Légion Étrangère on 9 March 1831 specifically for service in Algeria (see Chapter 2), there was no disgrace in regular mercenary soldiering. A foreign regiment on the payroll was simply another state asset – indeed, in 1835 Louis-Philippe passed the original formation over as a gift to the Queen Regent of Spain during the Carlist civil war (though he had to re-raise it almost at once). By 1870 the Foreign Legion may not have been fashionable, but militarily it was perfectly respectable. This respect had not been earned by its hard labour and savage little battles in Algeria – in which the French public showed little interest – but during 'proper' wars: the foreign expeditions mounted by Napoleon III in the 1850s–60s.

The last surviving son of the great Corsican adventurer's brother Louis had grown up in exile, but after the Orléanist monarchy fell to the 1848 Revolution this tireless conspirator had managed to get himself elected president of the Second Republic, France's first experiment in democracy. The 'prince-president' proved an untrustworthy guardian for this political infant: in December 1851 a slick military coup raised him to absolute power, massively endorsed by a popular plebiscite and consolidated by means of purges and police spies. A year later he was proclaimed Emperor of the French, taking the regnal name Napoleon III in deference to his dead cousin, 'l'Aiglon'. The emperor inherited the conditions for a decade of impressive industrial and economic growth that expanded a newly wealthy, and thus broadly contented bourgeoisie. Since his Bonaparte blood was his only real claim to power, and resurrecting French prestige his only real policy, he launched a number of military expeditions during his first decade on the throne, and his generals from Algeria won him some of the laurels with which he hoped to distract Frenchmen from his domestic police state.

When a French army fought alongside the British in the Crimea in 1854–5, four battalions of the Legion spent freezing months in the trenches before Sebastopol. In May 1855 their Colonel Viénot was killed in a night attack on the city's Malakoff bastion, and in September a hand-picked company of légionnaires carried scaling ladders for the final successful assault; however, despite its thousand dead in the Crimea, the Legion was still virtually unknown outside l'Armée d'Afrique itself. In 1859 Napoleon decided to meddle in northern Italy's war of independence from Austria, and the Legion distinguished itself at Magenta in June. Another colonel, de Chabrière, fell at the head of his men, and as the légionnaires fought their way into the town their corps commander, General Patrice MacMahon (himself descended from an emigré mercenary) was said to have remarked 'The Legion's there – this job's in the bag!'. Before the Crimea the Legion's ability to face modern armies in battle had been questioned, but now the mercenaries were given a place of honour in the victory parade through Milan. The prohibition on their ever serving on French soil that had been decreed at their raising in 1831 was briefly relaxed, and Parisians were mildly intrigued by their participation in the triumphal march through the capital on 14 August 1859. Within a few years, however, the Imperial gambler's luck ran out, and the légionnaires found themselves among the chips thrown down for his losing bet.

'*L'AVENTURE MEXICAINE*' began as an international attempt to recover debts owed by the government of President Benito Juárez of Mexico. With the United States safely embroiled in its own Civil War, in December 1861 Spanish, French and British troops landed at Veracruz on the east coast to seize the customs house. The Spanish and British sensibly withdrew in April 1862; but Napoleon (and his forceful Spanish empress, Eugénie) allowed himself to be convinced that a Catholic client state could be created for France in the Americas. Mexican conservatives, incensed by the threat to their privileges posed by the Zapotec Indian reformer Juárez, assured French envoys that the people would rise up in support of an intervention. Apparently believing them, Napoleon used French bayonets to install the unemployed Austrian Archduke Maximilian as a vassal Emperor of Mexico, at the head of the reactionary party in this civil war.

The anticipated easy victory did not materialize, and by April 1863 the French army was tied down by the difficult siege of Puebla, 150 miles inland and the key to any advance on Mexico City. Colonel Jeanningros' Foreign Regiment were not in the trenches but on the lines of communication, dispersed through the pestilential 'hot lands' below the escarpment to guard 75 miles of the road up from Veracruz against frequent attacks. Although they had only been in sub-tropical Mexico for a month they had already paid a heavy toll to the 'black vomit' and malaria. On 29 April, when the 3rd Company of the 1st Battalion were ordered to march back down the track to meet and escort an important convoy carrying up stores and pay for the siege army they numbered only 62 NCOs and men and one officer, Sub-lieutenant Vilain. Two officers of the regimental staff volunteered for the mission: the standard-bearer, Sub-lieutenant Maudet (like Vilain, an ex-NCO), and the adjutant-major Captain Jean Danjou. A veteran of Sebastopol, Magenta and Solferino, Danjou was recognizable to all by his articulated wooden left hand, carved for him in Algeria in May 1853 after a signal gun had blown up in his fingers. In the pre-dawn darkness of 30 April 1863, he led the company out of Chiquihuite and down the track; the cliché is that they 'marched into legend', but it was a legend that took many years to spread very far.

This is not the place for yet another detailed account of what became – long afterwards – the Legion's holy day. The defence of the stableyard of La Trinidad farm at Camaron (immortalized by a misspelt report as 'Camerone') has been pored over by historians with the same reverent pedantry accorded to the defence of Rorke's Drift.[9] In brief, about 45 légionnaires who survived a first attack in the open held the walls against nearly 2,000 Mexicans throughout a furnace-hot day, with virtually no water. Before he was killed, Danjou made them swear not to surrender; they fell fighting, one by one, rejecting two more calls to lay down their arms and save their lives. Late afternoon found only five left on their feet: Sub-lieutenant Clément Maudet, Corporal Philippe Maine, and légionnaires Victor Catteau, Gottfried Wenzel and Laurent Constantin. They decided to die fighting; firing their last shots at point-blank range, the five charged the enemy with the bayonet. Catteau tried to protect his officer and died with 19 bullet wounds, despite which Maudet fell mortally wounded; but the Mexican Colonel Cambas prevented his men from killing the other three. In accordance with Cambas' promise to Corporal Maine, the provincial governor Colonel Don Francisco de Paula Milán had the French wounded taken from the field and treated as well as circumstances allowed; of the légionnaires taken alive, 20, or possibly 22, would survive captivity. The convoy, warned of the ambush, had halted, and reached Chiquihuite in safety on 4 May; and on 19 May, Puebla finally fell to General Forey's siege army.

When Colonel Jeanningros' column approached Camerone on 1 May they rescued from his hiding-place in the cactus Drummer Casimir Laï, wounded nine times. In a ditch behind the farmhouse they found the stripped corpses of 23 dead, but were forced to leave them where they lay until they were able to return two days later. When they finally buried what the vultures and coyotes had left of Jean Danjou, his wooden hand was nowhere to be seen. In 1865 Colonel Thun of the allied Austrian Legion in Mexico wrote to Jeanningros that one of his officers had found it some 75 miles away, in the possession of a French-born rancher named L'Anglais (but that this patriot wanted 50 piastres for it). The recovery of this 'precious souvenir' attracted the attention of the French commander-in-chief in Mexico, Marshal Bazaine, but only because he himself was a former Legion sergeant who had fought in Algeria.

When the Legion were shipped home to Algeria in February 1867 the wooden hand went with them in the baggage of Colonel Guilhem. In time it would become the Legion's most sacred relic; but the great annual ceremony of which it forms the centrepiece today was choreographed only in 1931, and the anniversary does not seem to have been specifically celebrated even at unit level before 30 April 1906 (when a historically minded lieutenant in a tiny post in North Vietnam paraded his platoon and told them the story). The 3rd Company's stubborn defiance, unto death, was admired in the expeditionary army, and the emperor himself instructed that 'Camerone' should be embroidered as a battle honour on the regimental flag. He also ordered that the names of the company's three officers be inscribed in gold on the walls of the Hôtel des Invalides, the shrine to French Army tradition in Paris, but the fact that this instruction was not obeyed until eighty-six years later suggests that the Legion still did not carry much weight with the military establishment.

After Camerone the Mexican civil war dragged on for four more years, and French troops increasingly became involved in self-defeating counter-insurgency. In 1865, Union victory in the American Civil War brought General Phil Sheridan down to the Rio Grande with a corps of 50,000 men to make threatening noises. The 'Mexican adventure' ended in death by firing squad for Maximilien and in humiliation for Napoleon, and thereafter most Frenchmen were inclined to forget about it as quickly as possible. Their focus of attention now lay to the east, where Prussia's astonishing defeat of Austria–Hungary at Sadowa in July 1866 had forced the other European nations to adjust themselves to a drastically revised balance of power.

In October 1866, while the French expeditionary force was retreating towards Veracruz for withdrawal, it was announced that the Legion would be left behind in Mexico to continue serving Maximilien, just as it had been gifted to Queen Isabella of Spain thirty years before; if the order had not been countermanded on 16 December almost nobody today would ever have heard of the French Foreign Legion. The regiment sailed for Algeria in February 1867, leaving behind nearly 2,000 dead, probably 80 per cent of whom had died of disease.[10]

EIGHT YEARS AFTER CAMERONE, as we have seen, a few hundred men of the old Foreign Legion would visit the French capital for a second time, in a less celebratory mood than in 1859. At the earliest opportunity they were shipped back to Algeria, where – as in Metropolitan France – the fall of the Second Empire had unleashed both political turmoil and violent rebellion.

2. 'France Overseas'

What could be more legitimate than to oblige the convenience of 2.5 million Arabs to give way to the higher interests of 40 million Frenchmen?
Napoleon Lannes de Montebello, 1871

Should any misfortune have attended the march of the column, and a retreat become necessary, these Arabs, hitherto so timid, will not hesitate to engage in a hand-to-hand fight. The wounded, if left behind, are mutilated, and the pursuit assumes, by day and night, every feature that will try the nerves of the best troops.
Major J. North Crealock, 1876[1]

THE BARBARY COAST OF ALGERIA was the frontier between the worlds of Mediterranean Europe and Africa, but some stretches of the shore-line were deceptive. The hills that rose immediately inland, cradling the white coastal towns, were often blue-green with aromatic *maquis* and tall maritime pines, like the coastal hills of Provence. Elsewhere they were treeless, their tan flanks sprayed with a dark speckling of scrub, and any illusion of familiarity was fleeting; when the breeze blew off the land, the soldiers waiting on deck picked up a scent that was not France.

Behind the coast lay the *Tell*, a band of country stretching right across the 600-mile width of Algeria and reaching inland for about 70 to 100 miles. Between the hills, the valleys and plains were watered green by clouds from the sea, making it the only continuously fertile zone in the whole of Algeria. The northern slopes of the mountains were shaded by forests of cork-oak, holly-oak, conifers and cedar on the upper shoulders. The highest peaks, rising to 7,000 feet, were snow-capped for five months of the year; the winter rains and spring snow-melt fed countless watercourses that irrigated fruit orchards in the valleys and wheatfields on the plains, and near the coast there were still stretches of the stagnant malarial marshland that had killed so many of the early immigrants and soldiers. Between May and October the climate was Mediterranean, but this was still Africa; in late September the sirocco wind from the Sahara might last for three days at a time, raising the temperature to a dry, brain-baking 110°F (43°C) in the shade, kicking up dust-devils, sifting fine orange powder into every cranny, and sometimes blowing strongly enough to break windows.[2]

By the 1870s this area of roughly 70,000 square miles had been brought under extensive cultivation by a single generation of white settlers, and these *colons* had achieved a great deal in thirty years. The plains and valleys between the chains of mountains were a granary and vegetable garden; many of the hillsides were dark with olive groves, and since the 1860s some had been planted with vines, though others were useful only to the goats that foraged through the crackling scrub. Most of the immigrants who were transforming this land had come from Spain and Italy, desperate for a better life than tiny patches of poor soil and rigid, introverted societies had allowed them, and here they had found the masterless horizons of which their ancestors could not even dream. Of a total European population of about 280,000 in 1870, some 120,000 were pioneer farmers, whose lonely homesteads were scattered across the Tell around isolated villages linked at long distances by a sparse network of bad dirt roads. When men travelled, they rode armed; since many of them had carried from Europe a visceral hostility to the 'Moors', their daily lives were almost completely divorced from the more than 2 million Muslim Arabs among whose tribal territories they worked their jealously guarded land grants.

South of the Tell lay the 'high plateaux' – more than 30,000 square miles of treeless steppes. Stony and uncultivatable, they were nevertheless covered by an ocean of the salty esparto grass on which the flocks and herds of *colon* ranchers and Arab seasonal nomads thrived. In summer the temperature under the immense blue vault of the sky might be 100°F (39°C), but it could rise and fall dramatically with little warning. Snow fell up here in winter; it did not usually lie for long, but occasional freak years could see men trapped by blizzards and frozen to death as late as April. Rainfall on these prairies was unpredictable, and there was hardly any running water; what the storms did drop disappeared quickly far below ground, and despite the occasional shallow ponds lying in broad depressions, good wells were few and far between.

Along the southern edges of the high plains, ranges of mountains came slanting up from the south-west in extensions of the great Atlas; in the western province of Oran (see Map 3) they lay on the furthest southern frontiers of even military penetration into the 'Sud-Oranais', but in the centre and east – the 'Algérois' and 'Constantinois' – they slashed right up to the coast. They were separated into parallel blades by corridors of plain; here, too, water tended to lie in shallow, brackish lakes, which evaporated in summer but still fed stripes of thick vegetation. From the alpine landscape of Greater Kabylia behind the central coast east of Algiers, other spurs and massifs stuttered roughly south-eastwards again down towards the Tunisian border – Lesser Kabylia, the Hodna plateau, the Aurès and the Nemenchas, their parched and jumbled strata cut by the hidden green gorges of streams. Here, from natural fortresses of peaks and canyons, the fiercely independent Berber highland clans had defied Arab *amirs* and Turkish *beys* for twelve centuries, and in 1870 their nominal submission to the French was recent and sullen.

South of the mountains, in a vague margin slanting roughly south-west to north-east from Ain Sefra through Laghouat to Biskra, the inhabited world petered out. Below this there was nothing but the silent, mysterious immensity of the Sahara desert, the haunt of scorpions and evil ghosts. There were men who had always crossed it, down fragile chains of wells whose secret whereabouts were passed from father to son, men who risked their lives for the sake of riches to be found in the far oases; there were others there who lived by preying on them; but for the great majority of Europeans and Arabs alike, the Far South was another planet.

FRANCE'S RESUMPTION of the business of colonial empire, after a 70-year hiatus since the 1760s, had been almost accidental. Its first extra-European conquest was Algiers, one of the lairs of the Barbary pirates and slave-raiders who still preyed on Mediterranean shipping as they had done for centuries. General Bourmont landed his troops close to the city on 14 June 1830 for what was intended to be a temporary and local punitive expedition against the Dey of Algiers. At first the French tried to pacify a few small coastal enclaves on what was then a distant fringe of purely nominal Turkish suzerainty. They installed garrisons resembling human islands along the edges of this bewilderingly exotic, enticing and dangerous world, but they discovered that while Arab chiefs were always ready to accept bribes, they seldom stayed bribed for long. France had no plan beyond extracting some diplomatic profit from Istanbul in return for an early with-drawal. The boundaries of French control were uncertain and temporary, as was the policy of Paris governments, and there was no identifiable Arab leadership with whom to treat on more than a local basis – this was an entirely tribal society, in a constant state of flux.

The French governorship alternated between hopeful conciliators and adventurers; periodic military defeats provoked harsh revenge and 'mission creep', and Paris soon grew indignant about the death rate from disease among the Metropolitan troops.[3] This encouraged the raising of local Arab units to take over the burden: spahi cavalry and *turco* infantry, formed from groups of auxiliaries already serving under their own subsidized chiefs. The same imperative saw the re-raising in 1836 of a certain obscure unit of foreign mercenaries, a year after its original formation had been casually signed over to Queen Isabella II and shipped off to Spain as a political gift.

In February 1841, the mercilessly clear-sighted General Thomas Bugeaud de la Piconnerie was appointed governor-general of what since October 1839 had been called 'Algeria'; unenthusiastic about the original expedition, he had previously been sent to buy off (also to his own enrichment, it must be said) the ambitious Amir of Mascara, Abd el Kader. When the policy of subsidy and coexistence failed, Bugeaud was sent back to Algeria with strong reinforcements and a remit to pursue outright conquest. He was a veteran not only of Austerlitz – where he had fought as an infantry corporal – but also of Marshal Suchet's army in the Peninsula, and his experience of counter-guerrilla warfare in eastern Spain had brutalized him. Bugeaud argued that simply reacting to attacks by the far more mobile Arab horsemen would always fail; instead he sent columns out to destroy their villages and prevent them from planting and grazing. His tactics of mounting these ruthlessly destructive *razzias* against the tribes were effective but cruel. He himself described them unflinchingly as a '*chouannerie*', using the term for the French Revolution's pitiless harrowing of the royalist Vendée in 1793.

Bugeaud's long tenure of command, until September 1847, enabled a systematic series of operations and the crushing of subsequent risings in many parts of northern Algeria, and by the time of his departure he had largely broken the northern tribes' primary resistance. Others continued his ruthless work, and by 1854 French rule (or at least, freedom of movement) extended south as far as the Saharan Atlas range that barred the way to the desert. The Foreign Legion – as just one among other corps, both white and Arab – had fought in many of these campaigns.

BUGEAUD'S GOVERNORSHIP had a legacy more significant than mere pacification. Like some old Roman, he was convinced of the benefits of ruling the Arab population through their own aristocracy, but he had also encouraged white immigration, dreaming of planting *colonia* of ex-soldiers. However, among the subsequent waves of settlers, poor peasants from Spain, Italy and Malta nearly equalled the numbers of the French. Despite the generous land grants that were periodically offered to lure small farmers, few Frenchmen other than short-term speculators felt any inclination to seek their fortunes in North Africa.

The settlers who did come sweated out their lives, like frontier pioneers everywhere: they grubbed up rocks and stumps yard by painful yard, drained malarial marshes, ploughed and fertilized, and dug lonely graves for their children as drought and pests killed their crops. Some gave up the struggle, drifting into the coastal towns to seek wages, or selling their holdings to the expanding estates of richer men and being reduced to mere sharecroppers; but others toiled on stubbornly to build a future. As their numbers grew (from about 25,000 in 1840 to 280,000 in 1872, of whom some 160,000 were French-born or naturalized), they proved insatiable in stripping the local tribes of their communal farming and grazing land. The *colons* missed no opportunity to deprive Arabs of their rights to property, representation and justice – by purchase, trickery, and manipulation of both local and Paris politicians. Inducements offered to the Arabs themselves sometimes took the form of pretended access to French civil rights, but these carried the impossible price of giving up observance of Islamic law and were accepted only by a tiny handful of *assimilés*.

Algeria's history presents a remarkable contrast to that of Britain's overseas dominions; while the latter increasingly sought separation from the 'Old Country' and were eager to accept responsibility for their own future, the Algerian *colons* pressed for ever more thorough assimilation into the polity of France. The Second Republic of 1848 granted universal male suffrage in France, of which white Algeria was blandly declared to be an integral part. The French in the colony acquired the right to send deputies (members) to the Paris parliament from the three *départements* of Oran, Algiers and Constantine, and non-French whites gained representation in local government. However, the application of much of the French legal code was initially limited to those areas that qualified – by demographic criteria – for heavily settled 'civil' as opposed to sparsely settled 'military' status. In the former the *colons* had a large measure of freedom of action, but in the latter the French Army, under the military governor-general, stood in their path.[4]

The consequence was relentless pressure, through their deputies and lobbyists in Paris, to free as much territory as possible from the Army control that frustrated their rapacity. The settlers' spokesmen pursued a long campaign to get the decision-making process called back to Paris, where remote and ignorant ministers would be more amenable to pressure from special interests. Anything that weakened the authority of the tribal chiefs *(caids)* furthered their cause, and in 1858 they succeeded so well that the incumbent of a newly created (though short-lived) Ministry of Algeria and the Colonies defined his policy as 'the breakdown and dissolution of the Arab nation', removing most of the chiefs' powers and 'taking the tribe to pieces'.[5] One of the emperor's leading intellectual opponents, Lucien Prévost-Paradol, would write that 'It is necessary to bring in laws designed exclusively to favour the expansion of the French colony, leaving the Arabs thereafter to compete as best they can, on equal terms in the battle of life' – a striking interpretation of the concept of *égalité*.[6]

It may be counter-intuitive today, but it is undeniable that the paternalistic rule of the Army district officers of the Bureau Arabe – set up by Bugeaud in 1841 to have sole control, under the governor-general, over relations with the natives – was the latters' best protection from the settlers; it was certainly recognized as such by the *colons*. A number of these officers genuinely worked to improve the lot of local populations, not only in terms of security of property and respect for religion and culture, but also by advances in agriculture, infrastructure, health care and education.[7] Their reward was the furious hostility of those who saw the Army's proper role simply as enforcing European privileges.

This hostility between the colonists and the military reached a climax in 1863–9, during a period of reforms instituted by Napoleon III following a personal tour of inspection in 1860. His programme was a typically well-intentioned but muddled attempt to use the Army's authority to reconcile settler and Arab interests, but he was promptly demonized by the *colons* as 'the Arab Emperor', and his project as a tyrannical *'régime du sabre'*. The settlers more than recovered their lost ground during the weakness of his 'Liberal Empire' in 1869–70, and news of the collapse of the regime and the humiliation of the Army in the summer of 1870 was greeted in Algiers with furious glee. However, in the aftermath of the German victory the vainglorious local Committees of Public Safety discovered that the Army still had its uses.

THE DEPARTURE OF HALF THE LEGION for France in October 1870 – on the heels of the great majority of the Zouaves, Algerian Skirmishers and Africa Light Infantry, as well as the Line units that had been stationed there – left Algeria with a total garrison of only 32,000, many of them Garde Mobile militiamen. However, no trouble was anticipated from the desperately weakened Arabs; in 1866–8 a series of natural disasters – swarms of locusts, animal epidemics and droughts, followed inevitably by famine, cholera, typhus and the plague – had killed some 300,000 among the Muslim population (perhaps more than 12 per cent). The unconcerned *colons* believed that the only Arabs who needed watching were those still unsubmitted tribes in the vague military borderlands between western Algeria and Morocco; here no frontier line had been agreed further south than about 90 miles from the Mediterranean coast, and this wild west of Oran province was therefore in a permanent state of uncertainty.[8] Some tribes traditionally acknowledged the sovereignty of the Sultan of Morocco, others did not, and in the empty spaces between them herdsmen and raiders circulated at will.

The French had treaty rights of 'hot pursuit', and in 1859 General Martimprey had led 15,000 men against the bellicose Beni Snassen tribe of the hills behind the coast north of Oujda (see Map 11).[9] In 1864 the south-west had erupted when the powerful Ouled Sidi Sheikh, a loose confederation of linked clans with high religious prestige, encouraged a large but strictly temporary alliance of tribesmen from eastern Morocco to cooperate in a great raid into Algeria, and their pillaging extended as far north as the Tell. Although the Sultan of Morocco had been willing to leave border security to the French, the diplomats at the Quai d'Orsay had been nervous of invoking French military prerogatives, and it was not until April 1870 that General Wimpffen, commanding Oran Division, had been allowed to march 3,000 troops deep into south-east Morocco as far as the lower Oued Guir valley, a vital grain- and date-basket for all the tribes. Following this reprisal, the tribes astride the southern border were content to lick their wounds during the Franco-Prussian War.[10]

In autumn 1870 the Algerian authorities were therefore not unduly concerned that the almost entirely German 3rd and 4th Battalions of the Legion – bulked out with about 500 new German recruits from France, and some Belgians – were now the only white troops in Oran province apart from unimpressive *colon* Mobile Guards based in the northern towns.[11] On 10 October, III/RE were sent to replace a Bat d'Af at the bleak post of Géryville on the high plains (today, El Bayadh), with detachments to smaller posts nearby. Most of IV/RE went to Saida, with one company at the Legion HQ at Mascara.[12] That winter the légionnaires were both chilly and somewhat unkempt, since the stores had been ransacked to outfit the I/ and II/RE for France, and the battalions left behind were short of greatcoats, woollen trousers, knapsacks and belt equipment; they carried their kit in blanketrolls and ammunition in their pockets until well into 1871. Luckily the tribes of the Oranais remained quiet, if watchful.

IN OCTOBER 1870 it was the settlers who erupted first. Led by an Algiers lawyer, Vuillermoz, they defied the military authorities and launched a secessionist movement. A newly arriving governor-general did not even dare to come ashore, and commissioners sent out by the National Defence government in January–February 1871 were ignored, despite sweeping concessions that put local military commanders and Arab Bureau officers under the control of the *colon* authorities. The advances made by the settlers since 1868 had greatly concerned the Arab *caids*, whose personal authority was directly threatened. The withdrawal of garrisons, the news of the defeat and fall of the Empire, and the open contempt with which officers were now treated by the settlers had all cost the Army, in their eyes, its all-important *baraka* (that prestige and luck which is earned by strength and the favour of Allah). Now they interpreted the Paris government's 'Crémieux decree', granting collective naturalization to Algerian Jews, as a threat to their religion.[13]

The spark was struck in the Constantinois in the east. In January 1871 preparations to ship the 5th Squadron, 3rd Spahis to France led to a mutiny at El Guettar; Arab troopers murdered their officers and, with local rebels, briefly besieged the town of Souk Ahras.[14] In mid-February the Ouled Aidoun tribe attacked El Milia, 95 miles north-west of Souk Ahras. On 14 March a chieftain named Mohammed el Mokrani brought his tribal league out in rebellion, and on 16 March some 6,000 Ouled Mokran and allied tribesmen wiped out a village fully 170 miles south-west of Souk Ahras. The rising was reinforced by a Berber religious brotherhood led by the *marabout* Sheikh el Haddad, who declared *jihad* on 8 April, and within a few days the rebellion was spreading throughout Kabylia and beyond.[15] Tribes of Arabs and Berbers alike came out one by one, from the Hodna right up to the Collo peninsula, and as far west as the hills around Algiers.

This rebuke to Vuillermoz's initial boast that 'four men and a corporal' would be enough to restore order gave Prime Minister Thiers his opportunity to bring the shocked *colons* back under some kind of control. From the perspective of Versailles in March/April 1871, the Algiers separatist movement must have seemed to echo events in Paris and other French cities as yet another threat of national dissolution. Thiers named Admiral de Gueydon as governor-general, sending him with reinforcements to put down both white and Arab risings – the one by a stern show of force, the other by using it. Gueydon landed on 9 April; the garrison would soon be raised to some 85,000 men, of whom 22,000 would be actively engaged. By the end of April it was reckoned that they were facing about 100,000 rebels actually under arms; in the Constantinois and Algérois many *colon* farms were attacked or abandoned, civilians were massacred, and half-a-dozen villages and posts were cut off. Army columns now began a pitiless campaign of repression, which had essentially crushed the rebellion by mid-September; the rebels lacked all coordination, and each band was outgunned by the troops sent against it. However, at least 1,000 soldiers (and perhaps twice that number) were killed in the course of 340 engagements recorded between March and December 1871.[16]

WHILE NEWS OF THE UPRISINGS naturally electrified the whole colony, the tribes of the Tell and the high plains south of Oran remained quiet; the Kabylies were no kin of theirs, and the local chiefs' main concern was to deny the Ouled Sidi Sheikh in the south any opening to ravage their territory again as they had done in 1864. However, it was an attempt to counter the magnetic attraction of that formidable tribe that led the Legion into its only battle in the Oranais during the 'great rebellion'. In mid-April 1871, two small mobile columns were assembled on the northern plains to march west and show the flag among the clans in the wooded border hills. The larger and more northerly, with IV/RE and two companies from III/RE, marched from Saida to Sebdou and back; on the way, 6th Company, IV/RE – almost entirely composed of new recruits, so at this date largely German – were detached southwards to the village of Magenta, where they joined a smaller mixed column led by Lieutenant-Colonel Demesloizes.

The colonel was presumably glad to see Captain Kaufman's 218 white-covered caps slogging down the valley towards him: he had two light guns, two squadrons of mainly white Africa Light Horse, and a couple of hundred irregular Arab mounted auxiliaries *(goumiers)*, but his only infantry were three companies of hardly trained local Mobile Guards. The colonel had reports that an Ouled Sidi Sheikh chief, Si Kaddour ben Hamza, was planning a link-up with men of the Mehaia tribe somewhere south of Sebdou. Demesloizes marched about 50 miles south-west to the southern edge of the arid moorland of El Gor, camping on the night of 16/17 April east of Magoura (see Map 11) . Next morning his scouts brought word of a strong war party not far to the north, heading westwards for Morocco. Leaving the *'moblots'* in camp to guard the baggage, the colonel took the Legion company, his cavalry and his guns after the tribesmen.

Demesloizes caught up with them about 3 miles from Magoura. His two small cannon opened fire, and hundreds of Arab horsemen charged – a flutter of robes and head-cloths above the boiling dust, contorted faces, a thunder of hooves and crashing muskets, looming nearer and larger at frightening speed. A cavalry charge was much less dangerous to well-armed and ordered infantry than it seemed, but it took seasoned soldiers to understand that, and it says much for Kaufman's youngsters that they kept their nerve, listened to the shouted orders, and broke up this first rush with rifle volleys. Even if the Arabs had waited until they were 200 yards away before kicking their mounts into a gallop across the scrubby grassland, the soldiers would still have had nearly half a minute before contact, and with bolt-action Chassepots even green soldiers should have been able to get off three rounds each. Once the charge closed to 100 yards a horse was a sizeable target; many of the 200 légionnaires ought to have made a hit of some kind, while the Arabs' flintlocks, fired from the saddle, would have been much more noisy than dangerous.

The tribesmen regrouped, and then charged the hovering *goumiers*, who turned tail (as they were expected to). The trumpets of the two pale-blue-and-crimson cavalry squadrons yelped them forwards into a counter-charge with the sabre, but the crowd of Arab riders parted and sucked them in, and when the troopers rallied and cut their way back out of the mêlée the saddles of both the captains were empty. Demesloizes' bugler cracked his cheeks to call in one of the disordered squadrons as they fell back past the blue-and-white line of légionnaires, and the colonel formed what was described as a 'small, irregular square', with about 70 légionnaires in each of three faces, the troopers in the fourth, and the two guns in the centre. Covered by the other squadron, this little formation then retreated slowly across the grassland, pausing to fire when the enemy got too close, until they reached a rise where they could take up a proper defensive position. They held off further mounted and foot attacks for about an hour, until the tribesmen gave up; the steady conduct of the young Germans in their first action was particularly praised.[17]

Reunited with the baggage and the nervous Mobiles, Demesloizes continued his mission, not reaching a rendezvouz with another Legion company at Tlemcen until June. Both finally returned in late August to the HQ at Mascara, where they found the three Legion battalions that had returned from fighting the Prussians and Communards. Oran province was not troubled further during the uprising.

THE TROOPS FIGHTING IN THE ALGÉROIS had needed support against the Kabylies, however, and in May the governor-general ordered the Foreign Regiment to provide a 500-strong detachment. With only two battalions in total this was easier ordered than accomplished; however, three companies of III/RE were scraped up from Mascara and Saida, and these 12 officers and 585 men formed a marching battalion under Major Gache. Reaching the village of Alma on 27 May, they were incorporated into a mixed column under Colonel Desandre, along with six depot companies of Zouaves and Algerian Skirmishers. The column marched on 30 May, to link up with other troops under General Cérez and relieve the besieged village of Dra el Mizan; this was accomplished on 5 June, when the Legion battalion pursued the Berbers back up the heights above. Until mid-July they carried out aggressive sweeps – in General Grisot's euphemism, 'visiting' villages – along the Oued Sahel and on the southern slopes of the Djebel Djurdjura, the southern wall of Greater Kabylia.

The troops suffered a modest but continual drain of casualties in this hill fighting. Skilled snipers from concealed positions, the Berbers never willingly defended ground, preferring to fall back into thick cover after doing as much damage as they immediately could to the leading company. Then they would disperse, only to close in again on the flanks and rearguard, by day or night; indeed, a favourite tactic was to tempt troops forward to occupy exposed ground that they would later have to abandon at dusk, giving the Kabylies a chance to pounce as they fell back. Only converging columns had a hope of forcing them to stand and fight; cavalry were no use except for couriers and escorts, and to get results columns ideally needed up to half-a-dozen battalions of infantry, with mule-packed mountain artillery, engineers and medical troops to make them self-sufficient, and several thousand pack-mules – lines of communication were too vulnerable in the wooded hills to count on any resupply catching up with the column later.

Ideally, the force was led by an infantry vanguard marching without packs, followed by a detachment of sappers to clear natural obstacles, and then the main force. Behind these came what the French called the 'convoy' – the baggage train, escorted by cavalry and infantry on its flanks: first the artillery, then the ambulance unit, then the service troops, baggage and led animals. Last of all came a strong rearguard, again marching without packs; both vanguard and rearguard were accompanied by *cacolets* – mule-litters for casualties.[18] As the column reached each dominating height to right or left, infantry had to leave the line of march and struggle up through rocks, scrub and trees to 'picket' the hilltops, climbing down again to form the rearguard as the column passed them, in a constant rotation on both flanks. When the column had to thread through a pass it halted until strong pickets had been pushed through and beyond the defile and up on to the heights on both sides. Units took turns for these exhausting duties, but by late in the day every battalion was tired out.

Crossing any ridge rising across the line of march was particularly dangerous, since the patient hill tribesmen were past masters at rushing a crest as soon as it had been abandoned and firing down into the retreating rearguard. The rearguard had to follow the column down the far slope 'by echelons' – in leapfrogging companies, taking turns to pause and cover each other's next bound, while scooping up any earlier flankguards as they went. They had to keep in close order (not easy in broken terrain) so as to concentrate their firepower on the crest behind them, always falling back along a flank so as not to mask the fire of the men covering them. Care had to be taken never to muddle companies together during these manoeuvres, so that men were always led by their familiar officers; the senior officer commanding the baggage train had to remain with the rearguard at all times, controlling its progress with an eye on the tail of the column ahead.

Crossing a river through a valley bottom required a coordinated square-dance by a strong advance guard, flank guards both up- and downstream, and the rearguard. Anyone who has ever walked in any kind of strung-out column knows that it 'concertinas' repeatedly, as the terrain slows or speeds up different groups independently. It took skill and unremitting concentration for officers to avoid potentially fatal dislocations to a column of several thousand men and mules; a four-battalion force with support and service units might be strung out over nearly 2 miles, as it moved like an inchworm through broken country full of hidden enemies. Fifteen miles between first light and late afternoon was an excellent rate of progress in the hills, and any temptation to cut corners could be disastrous (in 1856 one careless column in Kabylia suffered the loss of an entire battalion and a half).[19]

WHILE MAJOR GACHE'S MARCHING BATTALION of III/RE had been struggling up and down the hills of Kabylia, I/, II/ and V/RE had arrived back from Paris; they were stationed at Mascara, Sidi bel Abbès and Tiaret respectively, thus giving the northern Oranais a garrison strong enough to ensure its tranquillity. On 17 July, Gache's unit in the Algérois were ordered back to Mascara, but when they marched into Maison Carrée to board the trains on the 25th they found new instructions. They were to march on westwards to Miliana and join a column under Colonel Nicot of the 11th Provisional Infantry – mostly returned prisoners-of-war from Germany – operating against the Beni Menacer tribe between Miliana and Cherchell on the coast (see Map 3). Nicot had ten other companies of odds-and-ends; it took a week to organize the column at Miliana, and only 600 mules were available to carry their ammunition and rations for ten days – about half the usual requirement of pack-animals.[20]

The troops marched on 2 August, getting an enthusiastic send-off from the frightened townspeople; they were to climb towards a second column coming up from Cherchell through the steep wooded hills and gorges between the Oued Chélif and the coast. On the 5th, two companies took a dozen casualties as they clambered up slopes thick with holly-oaks to the pass of El Anacer, and reckoned that they only reached the crest thanks to the quick reloading of their Chassepots compared with the muzzle-loaders of the enemy – in thick cover the Berbers' long-barrelled flintlock *bushfars* were as deadly in practised hands as rifles.[21] On 20 August the Kabylies began submitting, and on 5 September Major Gache marched his légionnaires back into Miliana. No longer in danger, the *colons* this time gave them the contemptuously cold reception to which soldiers in Algeria were now accustomed.[22]

MADE VENGEFUL BY THEIR FRIGHT, the settlers used the crushing of the rebellion as their opportunity finally to destroy the foundations of what remained of Arab tribal independence. Once the Army returned to barracks the Arab Bureau and the *caids* were stripped of their prerogatives, and many hundreds of thousands of acres of tribal land were simply confiscated. Over the years that followed, impossibly severe collective fines forced the sale of as much again; many communities were utterly beggared, and others were still paying off the debts twenty years later. General Hanoteau of the Arab Bureau had accused the settlers of dreaming of 'a bourgeois feudalism, in which they will be the lords and the natives the serfs', and after 1871 this dream became reality.[23] The settlers' final victory in their long struggle with the Army limited military control to the remote fringes of the Sahara, and their political triumph under the Third Republic bred in them a well-founded confidence in their immunity from effective opposition in Paris, where Algerian affairs were handled by the Interior Ministry. From the early 1870s many people even in Metropolitan France sincerely believed the jaw-dropping myth that Algeria was simply 'France Overseas'.

IN FRANCE ITSELF, MEANWHILE, the young republic was wrestling with the task of redesigning the French state. The National Assembly remained firmly monarchist; the moderate Adolphe Thiers presided over the provisional *de facto* republic – at that date, literally with a small 'r' in official documents – from September 1871 to May 1873, though hampered by his minority in the Chamber of Deputies (the lower house of the Assembly). In November 1873 the Assembly replaced him with Marshal MacMahon, whom they expected to be friendlier to the monarchist cause; they voted the old soldier a seven-year presidential term, but in the event his loyalty to the rule of law would prove stronger than his reactionary sympathies. The Third Republic, as formally constituted, was belatedly born out of the inability of the wrangling parties to agree any alternative. In February 1875 a constitution was finally approved – by a single vote – and elections in 1876 at last returned a Republican majority to the Chamber (though not yet to the Senate or upper house).

However, until MacMahon's honourable resignation from the presidency in January 1879, following a trial of strength with the Chamber over constitutional prerogatives and the spiteful purge of several generals, monarchists of various stripes retained a strong grip over the executive for most of the decade.[24] Officers who had been given emergency promotions and commissions in the National Defence armies struggled – usually in vain – to hang on to their ranks and careers as their dossiers were examined by General Changarnier's 'revising' commission of old-school regulars. When the commission had finished its work the officer corps had largely the same complexion as it had in the summer of 1870; throughout the 1870s any officer of 'exaggerated' Republican opinions was wise to keep them to himself, and military bands were even forbidden to play the *Marseillaise*.[25]

Inevitably, the post-mortems into the events of 1870 drove some senior scapegoats into the wilderness and reforms were tentatively sketched out, but overall the serious failures of organization and command at the highest levels were not subjected to any very painful parliamentary scrutiny. (There were, after all, nineteen generals sitting in the Assembly, and more than 10 per cent of its members were either active or retired officers.)[26] In most respects the Army would make its own mind up, in its own time and in decent privacy. However, there could be no ignoring the huge advantage in numbers enjoyed by the Prussians in 1870 – some 400,000, plus 200,000 trained reservists, against 250,000 with no reserves. The need to remedy that disparity was urgent, since during the 1870s many believed that a war of revenge against Germany to liberate Alsace-Lorraine – *'la Revanche'* – would not be long in coming.

Since 1832, the ranks of the French Army had officially been filled by voluntary enlistment for a seven-year term, but (massively) topped up by a conscription lottery of that year's 20-year-olds. This effectively excused the roughly 20 per cent from the middle classes who drew a 'bad number', since for a sum equivalent to about two years' pay for a labourer they could hire a proxy to serve in their place.[27] Bounties encouraged re-enlistment after the first seven years, and the NCOs were found from among these *rengagés*. The new conscription law of 27 July 1872 stated that all 20-year-old Frenchmen must personally report for military service; proxies were forbidden, though students in higher education might be exempted. On their discharge after five years with the colours, the 'first portion', then about 25 years old, would pass successively through the Active Reserve (four years), the Territorial Army (five years), and the Territorial Reserve (six years), until the Republic released them from their obligations at the age of 40.[28]

An essential factor in French politico-military affairs during the early decades of the Third Republic was the political Left's instinctive distrust of all generals, and they resisted reforms to streamline the Army's system of high command for fear that it might be turned not against Germany but against them. Such fears were understandable – given that anyone aged over about 35 could clearly remember the military coup whereby Napoleon III had taken power – but they were groundless. However instinctively conservative, the officer corps as a whole was far more passionate for national stability and order than for political power (by 1878 even General Gallifet, the 'butcher of the Bois de Boulogne', had become a loyal republican and a willing colleague of the socialist Léon Gambetta).[29] Though they were never convinced democrats, the chafing of the generals under intrusive political scrutiny was largely a learned response to the political favouritism that had bedevilled them under the Second Empire, and they recoiled from any hint of confrontation with the legitimate government.

On the Left, although some Radicals still yearned for the *levée en masse* in place of what they persisted in regarding as a sinister state-within-a-state, most Republicans recognized the absolute need for strong defence forces, and also that in the country as a whole the Army was now respected and popular. The Left hoped that virtually universal conscription would not only remove the notorious immunities that the wealthy had previously enjoyed, but would also dissolve the mental wall between the rank-and-file and the political nation, thus insuring against any threat of a reactionary clique using the Army against the people. For their part, the Right dreamed not of a 'nation in arms' but of a 'school of the nation'; they hoped that mass subjection to military discipline (and a quiet return of the Church through the barrack gates) would inoculate the youth of France against radical ideas, and return it to civilian life as a new generation of sturdy, obedient and right-thinking patriots.[30]

A law of March 1875 fixed the strength of the Line infantry at 144 regiments each (eventually) to be increased from 3 to 4 battalions, each of 4 rifle companies, giving the regiment a peacetime strength of about 2,000, plus officers and depot personnel. The Foreign Regiment, now officially reverting to its old title of Foreign Legion (which had always been used anyway), would conform to this organization, but would have about 50 per cent more manpower.[31] The whole Legion was to be stationed in Oran province in western Algeria, with regimental headquarters at Sidi bel Abbès, a small town about 40 miles south of Oran city. Significantly, from now on the Legion would be not only the largest European regiment in the French Army, but the only one made up entirely of volunteers.

IN 1871, FRANCE HAD BEEN ANXIOUS to embrace any Alsatians and Lorrainers who chose to leave the lost provinces. Between June 1871 and 1880, new enlistments in the Legion were officially (though not in fact) completely reserved for Alsace-Lorrainers, who were now technically foreigners but who could qualify for French naturalization by a single five-year term in the Legion.[33] The 5th Battalion disbanded in December 1871; its Frenchmen were transferred to Line units, any remaining war-duration volunteers were discharged, and other foreigners were posted to I/RE.[34]

The influx of patriotic young Alsatians and Lorrainers made the Legion of the later 1870s a notably willing and well-disciplined force by contemporary standards. Its mettle was not tested in battle, but in February–March 1877 some 500 Alsatians of the 3rd Battalion stood up well to a punishing Legion march in the old style. General Flogny formed the usual type of mixed column to show the flag on the high plains and down into the Sud-Oranais – one battalion each of Zouaves, Algerian Skirmishers and Legion, a squadron each of Africa Light Horse and Spahis, and an artillery battery. The III/LE left Sidi bel Abbès on 6 February; a three-week march via El Aricha and Ain ben Khelil took the column down to Ain Sefra and Thiout between the northern fingers of the Saharan Atlas, where they bivouacked for a week. They finally returned to the comparative comfort of Sidi bel Abbès on 26 March after a round trip of more than 350 miles, without encountering any resistance.[35]

Such marches covered about 28 miles in each ten-hour day, starting at first light and ending in the late afternoon; the men were rested for ten minutes every hour, and made an hour-long halt at mid-morning to brew coffee. Trained légionnaires took pride in their endurance on these marches along stony tracks or across the grassland, and a number of memoirs from about a decade later describe them. The first few days were hard, but once men got into a rhythm they marched at ease, rifles slung, smoking their pipes, sometimes singing or humming some popular song. The officers, who rode, occasionally ordered the drums and bugles to play if tired spirits needed lifting up the next long slope. Private Silbermann recalled a five-day march over the plains from Saida to Géryville, starting at 5am after a 3am reveille; below Ain el Hadjar, 8 miles south of the barracks, all signs of cultivation petered out into sand and gravel, broken only by clumps of grey thyme scrub, and later the endless sea of halfa grass. (In the whole five days Silbermann's unit encountered only one other human being: a Spanish settler riding up from Géryville, revolver and dagger at his hips, who passed them unsmiling, without a word.)

On the treeless steppe there was no firewood at all, and campfires were made with thorn-scrub and the dried camel-dung that was to be found all along the tracks. At the long halt for mid-morning coffee, each man had to tip a quarter-litre of water from his canteen into the squad cauldron – no contribution, no coffee.[36] The men were allowed 2 litres per day each, plus 15 litres for each squad to cook the evening meal, from the reserve carried on each company's three baggage-camels; wells were too far apart to be reached every night, and their yellowish, bad-tasting water needed hard boiling. The food was bulky enough but dull – a typical evening meal might be rice studded with a few *lardons* of fat pork. The men slept on the hard ground in sixes, wrapped in their greatcoats and a single blanket, in ridged bivouac-tents buttoned together from their individual canvas sections. In bad weather on the high plains the wind blew the tents apart, rain might fall for days on end, and sometimes the cold and discomfort made sleep impossible.

A well-fitting pair of boots was vital – broad in the foot, about half-an-inch longer than the toes, snug at the heel to prevent slipping and blisters, with the uppers heavily greased with tallow. No socks were worn; the men were issued with Russian-style foot-cloths to wrap round their feet, but hardened marchers often preferred to go barefoot inside their greased boots. Despite the regular route-marches during their basic training the newer men found marching for weeks on end hard going. The campaign packs weighed about 80lb, with big dixies and other camp gear teetering on top; the men wore coarse linen blouses under their coats, and when these became sodden with sweat the pressure of the pack straps chafed the skin raw. The folklore about stragglers being left to their fate was just that; one of the company subalterns always rode at the rear to keep men moving, and Silbermann describes NCOs pulling young men along by their waist-sashes while their packs and rifles were divided among their stronger comrades.[37]

Within a few years French tactics on the southern plains, for which this tiring but uneventful excursion by III/LE had been textbook training, would be tested once again.

THE ESSENTIAL NATURE of any French column on campaign was that it was composed of mixed arms, and always had a scatter of native auxiliary horsemen to act as forward scouts. The ideal mix of regulars was a colourful box of soldiers: a pale-blue-and-crimson squadron of Africa Light Horse and one of red-and-white Spahis, for solidity and superior acclimatization respectively; at least three battalions of infantry – pale-blue Algerian Skirmishers for agility and dash in the attack, and blue-and-red légionnaires for a rock-like base of firepower in the defence; and a two-gun section or four-gun battery of black-and-red artillerymen, for 'shock and awe'.[38]

The potential enemy on the plains comprised both concealed crowds of warriors on foot and highly mobile Arab horsemen – sometimes more than 1,000 of them. Expert at judging a marching column, they were easily able to fall back from a contact and hook around the flanks and rear, and dangerous when they did so. Marching across the plains, the column had its auxiliaries swirling well ahead as a mobile 'door-bell'; the *goumiers* would always flinch from a sudden contact, but their task was simply to race back with the warning. Half the regular cavalry rode within sight but some way off on a flank, while the other half hovered in a protective line behind the infantry. In dangerous country the infantry marched in a single large open square – up to 1,000 yards on a side – enclosing the baggage-train and the guns. The foot soldiers still had to *mamelon* (literally, 'to tit'), sending out platoons or companies to the flanks to picket any high ground as the square advanced; enemy warriors on foot were skilled at lying in wait under apparently minimal cover, and the *goumiers* were sometimes careless.

If enemy horsemen were encountered, the French cavalry engaged first, but it was important that they remained well within range of the infantry's massed rifles. To the frustration of these *sabreurs* they were seldom able to charge home against adversaries who simply drifted apart like smoke, seeking to lure them on and then close in from flanks and rear to trap them. Five hundred yards from the infantry, a single squadron of 160 (if kept on a tight rein) could safely attack 1,000 native riders; at twice that distance, it was risky to tackle half that number – the troop horses were much more heavily laden than the Arab steeds, and when they got blown and slow their riders were always vulnerable to surprises.

It was unusual for the tribesmen to press home an attack on the main column. War for them was motivated by a mixture of *machismo* and hard-eyed economics, so their chosen prey were small detachments and isolated convoy escorts. When they did strike a column their aim was normally to divert it from a line of march that threatened the tribes' villages or nomadic camps and herds. If they did try to break up the column the infantry battalions each formed their own smaller squares, ideally in a mutually supporting diamond or triangle pattern, with the baggage, guns and cavalry between them in the centre. Protected from all sides by the volley-fire of the infantry, the gunners could fire shrapnel to break up enemy con-centrations, while the cavalry awaited a chance to charge out and pursue a retreat. Once it became clear that the cost of securing any loot was going to be prohibitive, the attackers usually sheered off.

However, like all successful irregulars, the Arabs were accomplished counter-punchers; they understood how to retreat before a strong advance, staying in watchful contact until the chance came to turn and claw at its eventual withdrawal. If a column was retreating – deep in unfamiliar country, tired, far from water, slowed down by its baggage-animals and ration-bullocks, perhaps with significant numbers of sick in its mule- and camel-litters – then the tribesmen would close in eagerly on its rearguard and flanks. They watched like wolves for the slightest opportunity to cut off water-parties or isolated flank guards, and soldiers who straggled or got separated suffered cruel deaths.[39] The Arabs might hook ahead to poison the next well with a rotting carcass; night camps would be relentlessly fired on by snipers to rob the nervy soldiers of their sleep, and infiltrated to cut throats, grab rifles and run off beasts. If the troops betrayed real signs of weakness or lack of alertness, allowing gaps to open up, then limited all-out assaults might be attempted. The Arabs did not expect to achieve grandiose massacres, and were happy for the chance to devour even a single platoon; in their culture, prestige was nourished by taking back to their families and elders any kind of material loot – particularly animals, modern rifles and precious ammunition (though sometimes more gruesome souvenirs). The further a column marched into the deceitful monotony of the wilderness, the greater the danger of its vigilance dissolving in the hypnotic rhythm of the march, and the higher the price it might have to pay.[40]

IN APRIL 1881, THE QUIET LIFE ENDED for many French garrisons when the government led by Jules Ferry and Léon Gambetta ordered a French occupation of Tunisia. This ramshackle and only nominally Turkish coastal *beylik*, neighbouring Algeria to the north-east, was hopelessly in debt to European bankers. The infant Italian state, desperate for some foreign adventure to give credibility to its claimed nationhood, was taking a predatory interest, but Britain did not want any single power to occupy both shores of the Mediterranean narrows. Bismarck was happy to encourage France into any military distraction from its eastern frontier, especially one that would cost it a potential European ally in Italy. About 5,000 troops from the Africa Army in Algeria (but none from the Legion) were among the 30,000 committed to an overland and seaborne invasion of northern Tunisia in the last week of April, and initial resistance was feeble. From the first, senior

Africains were looking back over their shoulders, and in late May and June the War Ministry agreed to send home the troops from Algeria and many from France.[41]

At the same time, however, something alarming was happening in the Oranais, and the *colon* newspapers were shrieking again. Since 1878 a preacher from Figuig calling himself Bou Amama had been attracting followers to his *zaouia* or religious centre at Moghrar Tahtani, a small oasis on the southern slopes of the Mountains of the Ksour in the south-western Oranais.[42] By 1880 he was preaching holy war against the French, in the name of the seventeenth-century founding saint of the Ouled Sidi Sheikh. With many of the traditional chiefs of that confederation either in exile in Morocco, or making their own deals with the French to restrain their warriors' raiding, his message was appealing to those whose memory of Wimpffen's reprisals was fading after ten years. The religious prestige of such a charismatic *marabout* could occasionally weld together pan-tribal alliances; with the whole of Algeria groaning under the triumphalist *colons*, and tribes being displaced southwards by their land-grabbing, Bou Amama found many listeners. On 22 April 1881 the assassination of Lieutenant Weinbrenner, the Arab Bureau chief at Géryville, sparked a general uprising all over the western high plains. This was vigorously exploited by the Ouled Sidi Sheikh and their allies, for whom it was simply an excuse for a traditional pillaging *razzia*.

The Army hastily gathered troops from scattered garrisons, to cover the Tell and to grope for contact with the main body of rebels. The Legion's four battalions were then stationed in a wide belt across the south-west of the Tell, with only half of II/LE down on the high plains at Géryville. The III/LE were ordered south from Sidi bel Abbès and IV/LE from Tiaret, thus theoretically guarding the corridors up into the Tell on both west and east sides of the 100-mile-wide Chott Ech Chergui depression. On 24 April, Major Laffont took the other two companies of the 2nd Battalion by train from Mascara to Saida; there he gathered up another two companies from I/LE, and marched this *ad hoc* battalion south to Krafalla the next day. His plans to march further were frustrated on the 26th by the arrival of a senior officer.

Colonel Innocenti of the 4th Africa Light Horse took command at Krafalla, where a battalion of Zouaves and another of Algerians arrived on the 27th. They were quickly followed by General Colignon, who took control of operations. The general considered Krafalla inadequate as an assembly point, and marched the troops to Tafaroua to organize his column there. On 3 May it was ordered to Géryville, arriving on the 8th and remaining in that windswept and inhospitable spot for a further five days. The légionnaires called it Geléville – 'Frozentown'; icy in winter and baking in summer, it stuck up in the middle of the dusty prairie like a desolate set for a Western film. Apart from two forbidding stone barracks for a Legion company and a Spahi squadron the village boasted only a single street of low, gloomy houses and shacks, and even ten years later only four Frenchmen lived there.[43] The arrival of a couple of thousand men pitching their tents on the flats around the barracks must have put a considerable strain on Géryville's notoriously sparse supply of firewood, and possibly the chilly nights of early spring were responsible for the fact that General Colignon retired at this point to sick quarters. Command reverted to Colonel Innocenti; it was 14 May before the already footsore column finally began to march to any purpose, heading south-west to follow up reports that Bou Amama was gathering men at El Abiodh Sidi Sheikh, the shrine revered as the burial-place of the tribe's ancestral saint (see Map 3).

On 19 May the column, with its 1,800 baggage-camels, made contact with elements of about 4,000 warriors at a place called Moualok, about a day's march short of the wells at Chellala. Accounts of the action that followed have that lack of unanimity and precision so often found in reports of embarrassing failures. The enemy clearly made a frontal attack on the big moving square, in a corridor between hill features. Major Laffont's Legion marching battalion, deployed in line as the leading face of the square, repulsed the charge with volley fire; the infantry were then ordered by Colonel Innocenti to drop their packs and advance. Apparently this order was resented as unnecessary – the légionnaires did not like being parted from their essential camping gear, and prided themselves on being able to fight in full marching order. The cavalry colonel's order to follow the apparently withdrawing enemy also flew in the face of all experience, and it left the prize of the enormous baggage-train in the rear guarded only by a half-squadron of Innocenti's 4th Africa Light Horse. The exact sequence of events then becomes cloudy, especially the role played by the rest of the cavalry; but the essential fact is that while the infantry were fighting forwards, a large force of Arab riders hooked around their right flank, driving fleeing *goumiers* confusingly ahead of them, and overran the baggage-train. The French lost 72 men killed (mostly from the cavalry escort), 15 wounded and 12 missing – a killed-to-wounded ratio that speaks eloquently of the warriors' having time to carve up the casualties at their leisure. The baggage was looted and many of the beasts were run off.

To the fury of the légionnaires, their dumped packs were also pillaged; when the shaken column camped that night at Tazina they had a comfortless time of it, and their sleep was disturbed by taunting attacks on the outlying *grands-gardes*.[44] On 20 May the force resumed its march to Chellala under nagging sniper fire (most of its screen of *goumiers* having been dismissed). Arriving within sight of a large Arab encampment there at about 5pm, Colonel Innocenti declined to attack until morning. By dawn on the 21st, unsurprisingly, Bou Amama was gone. He and his warriors rode north, passing within a mile and a half of Géryville, and thence into the Tell – some 200 miles from their starting-point in the south-west.

During June these raiders made a number of attacks around the settler towns of Saida and Tiaret; they looted, burned crops, killed farmers, and persuaded French-paid irregulars to change sides and join them. This caused fury among the *colon* leaders and real fear among their isolated constituents. Three French columns lumbered about the prairies trying to trap Bou Amama, but found themselves lunging into empty air behind him as he flickered away again into the broken terrain of the Chott Ech Chergui. (A probably unjust impression of tactical fumbling is not helped when we read of one Sub-lieutenant Scohier of Colonel Innocenti's command – not a Legion officer – who got himself killed while making his night rounds of camp sentries at Naama by foolishly allowing his sword-scabbard to trail noisily along the ground.) The Legion's commander Colonel de Mallaret led III/LE down from Sidi bel Abbès to Kreider to link up with Innocenti and General Detrie; for two months Bou Amama more or less played with Detrie and the other two columns, before their converging pressure finally pushed him over the Moroccan border in July to take refuge in the Oued Zousfana valley.[45]

COLONEL FRANCOIS OSCAR DE NÉGRIER succeeded Colonel de Malleret in command of the Legion in July 1881. Négrier, wounded at St Privat in August 1870, had shown his impatience of convention when he broke parole to escape from Metz. He would soon confirm it, when he forced Ouled Sidi Sheikh chiefs to exhume the sarcophagus of their hereditary saint from the shrine at El Abiodh that had been the focus of rebellion, and carried it off under an honour-guard for a reverent reburial in a suitable tomb at

Géryville. He told the chiefs that in future they could come and pray to it there, where he could keep an eye on them.

His first tactical innovation was to revise the order of march of the columns he led, breaking up the single large square into two distinct elements. The baggage-train, field ambulance and artillery reserve would move under a strong flank escort of infantry; meanwhile a separate manoeuvre element would be formed with the *goumiers*, cavalry, the bulk of the infantry and a 'ready' section of guns, free to strike out without being tied to the slower-moving baggage.[46] Négrier's interest in every detail of his profession even extended to having his légionnaires make up for themselves, out of scrap cloth or leather, an extra chest rig to carry reserve ammonition for their Gras rifles high across the torso, instead of stowed away inside the knapsack.[47] However, the main tactical problem, in what was essentially counter-guerrilla warfare, was the French imbalance between mobility and firepower.

Arab war parties could carry their few 'logistic' needs on horseback, and so could cover the ground much faster than French mixed-arms columns. If French cavalry pressed ahead alone to catch raiders, the troopers often lacked the firepower to defend themselves adequately, let alone to inflict a significant defeat; their squadrons were usually outnumbered, and the Arabs were too wise to stand and meet a sabre-charge. The daily routine of horsed units, more demanding than for infantrymen, left comparatively little time for practising marksmanship on the range; in the cavalry firearms training traditionally had a rather low priority, and the troopers' carbines were anyway shorter-ranged than infantry rifles (and kicked even harder). When they did dismount to form a skirmish line, one man in four had to serve as a horse-holder for his comrades, and the consequent thin line of kneeling men was always vulnerable to being outflanked and overrun by adversaries who stayed in the saddle. What was needed in action was the massed firepower of steady infantry; but infantry could not catch the nimble raiders.

One solution was mounted infantry – foot soldiers mounted for travel but fighting dismounted; they, too, needed horse-holders, but their massed rifles and infantry training made them more dangerous than troopers. During the spring of 1881 the 2nd Algerian Skirmishers had tried mounting one company on native ponies; that December, Négrier was in the field with a column including III/ and IV/LE and a battalion each of Zouaves and Algerians, and this time all of them made a limited trial of the mounted infantry concept. At the wells of Ain ben Khelil on 8 December, Négrier formed a platoon of 50 selected men and gave them 50 locally requisitioned mules.[48] Mules were cheaper than horses, and plentiful in North Africa, having been used for riding since ancient times all over the Mediterranean world. Intelligent, robust and sure-footed, mules are much less nervous than horses, less fussy about their food, and have hard hoofs that stand up well to stony ground. In every respect except sheer speed a mule is at least the equal of a horse, and speed was not the point – endurance was. Ridden mules could keep going at a man's marching pace all day long, for six continuous days, carrying their own and the troops' rations, and delivering their riders still fit enough to go into action instead of wilting under the huge infantry packs.[49]

Colonel de Négrier would write: 'The purpose is not to go fast, but to keep going for a long way and a long time ... The battle is not decided by the number of riflemen but by the number of kilometres – it is a question of *marching*.'[50] What he called his 'light group' soon proved its worth by covering something like 100 miles in a 48-hour forced march; it surprised Bou Amama's ally Si Sliman in the Chott Rhabi in late December 1881, forcing him to flee into Morocco leaving his complete camp and 4,000 sheep. The livestock were auctioned, and each légionnaire was given 15 francs' prize money – roughly nine months' Legion basic pay, and a huge incentive that must have become the talk of every barracks canteen.

At the same time Major Marmet at Ain Sefra tried a significant variation; he formed a 100-strong half-company of his 2nd Algerian Skirmishers with just 50 mules – one for each pair of men. The mule carried its own and both men's rations and kit; one man rode, the other marched, changing places every hour. Carrying only rifle, ammunition, light haversack and water-bottle, the marching man had no difficulty in keeping up with the mule-rider at a speed of about 4mph. Period marching diaries show up to 50 miles a day over easy going, and an average of 37 miles even in rocky terrain – twice what a horsed cavalry unit could manage in such punishing country. (Horses had to be walked or led for much of the time, and 35 miles per day was about their limit even on good European roads.) The soldiers and their mules ('*brêles*') could keep up this rhythm for several days at a time, if necessary making a forced march over the final stage to close with the enemy. The two-men-per-mule principle had a subtler advantage than mere economy and the halving of the number of mule-holders: by making the men march on their own feet half the time, it reminded them that they were still infantrymen. The need for this reminder would be underlined in red the following spring.[51]

THE 'SUD-ORANAIS' was still largely unexplored in early 1882. The nearest substantial French post was at Géryville; that at Ain Sefra, about 120 miles to the south-west, was in the process of being built, but other named spots on the map were simply waterholes. In April 1882, General Colonieu, with a mixed column that included Colonel de Négrier and two Legion battalions, was camped at Ain ben Khelil while his reconnaissance patrols spread out across the wilderness. One party was led by a 32-year-old infantry officer on General Colonieu's staff, Captain Henri de Castries; he was a scion of a noble family with generations of prominent military service to France, and had recently married into another family of Army aris-tocracy.[52] The captain led his little column out on 20 April, heading south and west to make a topographical survey. They went westwards through the Djebel Doug pass at Forthassa Gharbia, and by the 26th they were in the large Chott Tigri depression about 60 miles from Ain ben Khelil. (The term *chott* is usually translated as the bed of a dried-up salt lake, but any mental image of miles of cracked mud-scales is quite mistaken. These low-lying areas may be very large, embracing various kinds of surface, and the only common factor is the largely invisible groundwater that supports vegetation and grazing.)

The escort, commanded by Captain Barbier of III/LE, comprised his infantry company from that battalion; Lieutenant Massone's 23-man squad from the Legion's new mounted platoon, each of them riding his own mule; a *peloton* of Africa Light Horse, and a few *goumiers* – perhaps 250 men in all.[53] Arab drivers led pack-camels, and drove a few sheep on the hoof for the pot. They were moving at a leisurely rate of about 10 miles a day, to allow Captain de Castries to make his observations and draw his maps, and this also gave the escort the chance for some opportunist sheep-rustling. On 25 April a trooper carried back to Colonel de Négrier the report that there had been a slight encounter near the wells of El Merir: some Beni Gil tribesmen had fired a few shots before 'abandoning' about 1,800 sheep, a flock so large that it obliged the captain to disperse numbers of his infantrymen as shepherds. (It is hard to believe that this was not provoked by the bonanza enjoyed by the mounted infantry four months earlier).

At first light on 26 April the party broke camp at a spot called Temid ben Salem and marched on across the Chott Tigri. In the early years of the twentieth century Professor Augustin Bernard described its terrain as 'seamed with gulleys – the waterholes are numerous and the pasture generally abundant'; the account from the Legion archives mentions sand dunes, deep gulleys and clumps of dwarf palm – 'a curious region, full of hidden dangers'.[54] By 6am the sun was already hammering down, and in this broken, low-lying ground the men struggled to drag the superheated air into their lungs. In the vanguard even the mules of Massone's mounted squad were panting, struggling almost knee-deep up soft dunes and slipping on the down-slopes. Suddenly, from ahead and then on both flanks, a fusillade rang out: the Beni Gil sheep-guards had not been alone. The estimates of Arab numbers at Chott Tigri vary widely, but the lowest guess is some 900 riders and 1,500 on foot, neither figure being intrinsically impossible.[55]

CAPTAIN BARBIER HAD TO GET HIS MEN OUT from among the dunes and gulleys, where the enemy could fire down on them from every side and riders could suddenly appear out of cover at short range. He turned the column about and headed for a table-topped *gara* feature that they had recently passed, leaving Massone's all-mounted squad as the rearguard. The Italian officer made the fatal error of not dismounting his men and, when fighting from the saddle, they were no match for the Arabs. They disappeared among a yelling whirlwind of tribesmen, and within a moment Massone, his NCOs and half his légionnaires were down and most of the mules had been shot or hamstrung. When the Arabs briefly wheeled away to reload their muzzle-loaders, an old soldier led the knot of survivors up a dune, where they shot the remaining mules and used their bodies as a parapet. A second rush ignored their thin volley and simply swarmed over them. At such close range the heavy lead balls from smoothbore muskets could smash through bone with ease; although they did not transmit as much splintering energy as rifle bullets they could, for instance, pass through the skull and carry part of the brain out the other side, or blow a shoulder or hip joint right out of the body. The concentrated force of a sword-cut delivered by a horseman could sever an up-flung arm, cleave the skull down to the eyebrows, or take off the top like that of a boiled egg.[56]

Barbier's leading platoon under Lieutenant Delcroix were fighting their way back towards the abrupt *gara* or mesa thrusting about 120 feet above the floor of the depression, but some of the Beni Gil were racing them to it. With a few of the Africa Light Horse, the platoon ran a gauntlet of fire from Arabs converging on foot from their flanks and rear, but broke through, and managed to drive the few tribesmen who had arrived first off the top of the *gara*. Delcroix's men then threw themselves down on the lip and opened fire on their pursuers, covering the retreat of the rest of the company, who were fighting on the move in a little square. When they finally came panting up the slopes the wounded Lieutenant Weber was among them, but not Captain Barbier, who had been killed when Arab riders overran the baggage-train.

Captain de Castries took command on the tabletop, which was a strong position with good fields of fire. The Arabs were distracted by looting the baggage-train and the bodies, and now they had lost the advantage of the ground their attacks became increasingly half-hearted as the légionnaires' steady fire punished each attempt. After a while Sub-lieutenant Mesnil was able to take his platoon back down to try to bring in any survivors; remarkably, they found a couple from the mounted squad, and Private Androesco also carried in Barbier's corpse on his back. At about noon Castries was able to send off a Light Horse trooper to try to summon help from Ain el Khelil; and at some point in the early afternoon, no longer surrounded, he led his men down the *gara* and set off to the north-east, with their wounded but not their dead. There was some pursuit, but not in strength, and volley-fire persuaded these riders to shy away; why get shot, when their brothers were busy dividing the loot without them?

The soldiers pushed on at a killing pace, and Castries did not allow them to halt until they reached the waterhole of Galloul in the foothills of the Djebel Doug during the night. There they were given two hours' rest before wearily getting on the march once more. Colonel de Négrier, who had been alerted by the message-rider on the evening of 26 April, led 500 men 30 miles south that night, and the two parties met early on the morning of the 27th. After a long halt the whole force marched back to Chott Tigri along the survivors' tracks; they reached the battlefield that night, later gathering up the dead for burial, and on 2 May the battalion reached the camp at Ain ben Khelil once again.

The casualties comprised about one-third of Castries' command: 2 officers and 49 rankers killed, 2 officers and 26 rankers wounded. Again, the higher ratio of dead to wounded was typical for a unit that had been broken up and overrun, and the dead were very badly cut up; Barbier's decapitated body bore 9 bullet wounds and 7 sabre cuts. The Legion account claims that hidden on the body of the old légionnaire who had led the last stand of the mounted squad they found an Officer's Cross of the Legion of Honour.[57] At least one lesson was learned: Colonel de Négrier reduced the mule-string of his mounted company to one for every two men, and he hammered home the message that the Compagnie Montée were infantry, and must always fight as such.

CAPTAIN HENRI DE CASTRIES (1850–1927) was an uncle of Brigadier-General Christian de Castries, who on 7 May 1954 surrendered the fortress of Dien Bien Phu in North Vietnam to Vo Nguyen Giap's People's Army. By coincidence, North Vietnam would be Négrier's, and the Legion's, next theatre of war.

3. *La Mission Civilisatrice* and the Straw Hat Trade

God offers Africa to Europe. Take it – not with the cannon, but with the plough ... Pour your surplus of strength into this Africa, and in one blow solve your social problems – transform your proletariat into proprietors. Go on – build! Build roads, harbours, towns; grow, cultivate, colonize, multiply!

Victor Hugo, 1879, addressing a banquet to commemorate French abolition of the slave trade

Let me have 600 men of the Foreign Legion, so that if it comes to that, I can at least die with decency.

Colonel Joseph Galliéni to M. Lebon, Colonial Minister, March 1896, on being offered command in Madagascar[1]

MUCH EUROPEAN COLONIZATION in Africa and Asia proceeded by a haphazard series of largely unplanned steps, with trade as the catalyst. Library shelves groan under detailed analyses of particular cases, but – in order to highlight by comparison some aspects of the French case – a sort of generic narrative of a 'British model' might run as follows.

First contact typically led to the establishment of small coastal forts where handfuls of white traders lived on the edge of the great unknown. In sub-Saharan Africa, the pioneer traders of the seventeenth and eighteenth centuries were as often as not the slavers, to whom African rulers willingly sold their captives in return for European goods – above all, for woven cloth and firearms. The slow suppression of the Atlantic slave traffic from 1807, led by Britain, gradually transformed trade with Africa into the pattern that had long been the norm in Asia, with exports of cultivated and raw materials taking the place of the appalling commerce in human beings. (The slave trade remains an indelible stain on European and American history, but it is barely relevant to late nineteenth-century colonialism – except in the sense that the colonizers had some success in stamping out the much more ancient operations of the Arab slavers supplying North African and Middle Eastern markets.) At first the white men relied for protection upon the local rulers whom they enriched, but increasing investment demanded greater insurance, and traders began recruiting and arming local warriors directly. In the interests of profit, white men manipulated local rivalries; white-governed territories were extended, and local peoples were displaced or conquered – though as often by the newly powerful client rulers as by the white men themselves.

When the investment reached a high enough perceived value to the home government, then events, rather than any long-nurtured imperial conspiracy, would finally prompt the despatch of white government troops – a decision often taken reluctantly, and against vigorous domestic opposition on grounds of expense or diplomatic complications. Once these garrisons had been installed, reasons to expand their areas of control would soon present themselves; this process was urged, or simply undertaken, by the traders, officials or soldiers on the spot, who could usually come up with plausible arguments by the time a slow boat presented the distant home government with a *fait accompli*. Eventually, however, the home government would accept the need to tidy up the map, usually with an eye on the competitive advances of other colonial nations, and the complete annexation of new territory or a native state would follow. (During the eighteenth and nineteenth centuries essentially the same process took place, of course, on the expanding continental frontiers of the United States.)

THE HISTORY OF FRANCE'S COLONIAL CONQUESTS differs somewhat, even at this comic-strip level, from the outline above; and the difference most relevant to the subject of this book is that while in most territories annexed by Britain in the nineteenth century the soldiers arrived last, in France's conquests they usually arrived if not first, then certainly a great deal earlier in the process. One of the reasons that this was necessary was the comparative success, achieved in the mid-eighteenth century, of British *laissez-faire* opportunism over a French obsession with central control.[2]

By the early seventeenth century, English and Dutch trading companies had been founded to exploit the opportunities of newly discovered sea routes. English merchant-adventurers, chartered by the Crown but operating without significant home support or control, were happy to give patriotic names to their settlements and to hold them as nominal national property so long as they enjoyed freedom to exploit them. Emigration for settlement, where it occurred, was normally unhampered by state or Church interference. Such a relaxed approach was unthinkable in France, whose overseas traders and settlers were hedged about with restraints unknown to their competitors. There the monarchy (closely partnered by the Catholic Church) attempted, despite the huge distances and glacially slow communications, to retain all meaningful control in Paris. French colonization was, from the start, a state-sponsored geopolitical project, rather than simply an opportunity for businessmen to make money and for emigrants to build a new life.

By the end of the seventeenth century, England's violent religious and political schisms had at last given birth to constitutional reforms that broadly satisfied the national instincts for a balance between effective authority and individual liberty. The division of powers enshrined in the 1689 Declaration of Rights set clear limits on those of the monarchy, and would allow forms of representative government to evolve gradually under the protection of the rule of law. Since Britain's affairs would increasingly be dominated by a productive mercantile middle class secure in its property rights, this system would also benefit the growth of the country's overseas colonies. France, too, was ripped apart by savage wars in the sixteenth and seventeenth centuries, but in her case they culminated not in a constitutional settlement, but in the establishment, by Louis XIV (r.1643–1715), of an absolute royal and religious despotism supported by a parasitic aristocracy. Two linked consequences of Louis' triumph were the tightening of arbitrary controls over colonial activity, and the distortion and corruption of national finances.

The outstanding example of the outcome is provided by North America, where New France (Canada) strikingly failed to attract the number of settlers, or to generate the wealth, needed to counterbalance the growing strength and confidence of the British colonies on the Atlantic seaboard to the south. Conventional explanations always over-simplify causes, but it is broadly true that what became Britain's Thirteen Colonies were peopled by restless individualists of all classes who abandoned the Old World and risked everything to build new and unfenced lives; consequently they multiplied, pushed the frontiers outwards, and prospered. This did not happen in French Canada, which remained to a great extent a simulacrum of rigid, almost feudal France. Old France always had to subsidize her 75,000 colonists, while by 1750 the population of Britain's colonies exceeded one million and was playing a vigorous part in the British trading economy.

The ultimate test of strength and will came in the 1750s, as one front in the sprawling Seven Years' War. Both Britain and France drew a significant proportion of their riches from the sugar islands of the Caribbean, by means of the infamous 'triangular' Atlantic trade – of manufactured goods from Europe to Africa, to buy slaves for sale to Caribbean planters, who provided highly profitable sugar imports to Europe. Old France gave priority to the protection of its Caribbean islands, which in terms of wealth creation were the oilfields of their day, and since it had a weaker and more thinly stretched navy than Britain, this put New France at risk. The colony received too few troops, diverted from those European land fronts that naturally preoccupied Paris more than London, and their transatlantic lines of supply were vulnerable. Britain had the breadth of naval strength to fight everywhere; and above all, while it was much less rich than France in absolute terms, it was willing to spend a great deal more of its wealth on overseas campaigns.[3] By 1763 the combination of French colonial mismanagement overseas and fiscal mismanagement at home had doomed both Canada and the small French foothold in India to capture by Britain.

Ten years of comparative neglect of the Royal Navy then allowed France to take revenge in 1778–81, sending crucial help to Britain's now-rebellious American colonies; but the expense of Grasse's fleet and Rochambeau's expeditionary force helped to cripple Louis XVI's financially chaotic regime in the last years before it collapsed into the flames of the Revolution. In the eighteenth century French anti-clerical intellectuals such as Montesquieu, Voltaire and Rousseau had argued that acquiring colonies was a vicious and debilitating habit, and during the Revolutionary and Napoleonic wars France remained preoccupied by continental European fronts. By the time of its final defeat in 1815 its navy, and thus its transoceanic trade, had long been virtually destroyed; as the Industrial Revolution hit its stride, the world's wide horizons lay open to British merchants protected by British warships.

THE CASE FOR A REVIVED COLONIAL EFFORT had been argued during the Second Empire, though the emperor's unpopularity limited the audience.[4] The active expression of the argument was left to the initiative of admirals, acting almost independently under a colonial directorate within the Navy Ministry. In 1853 New Caledonia in the Pacific was added to France's small cabinet of foreign curiosities, and the following year an energetic Naval Troops governor, Faidherbe, began to explore beyond the enclave of St Louis on the Senegalese coast of West Africa. During 1859–67 the Navy acquired Cochinchina (South Vietnam), and under the early Third Republic continued to pursue a piecemeal series of local initiatives, notably in West Africa.

In the last quarter of the nineteenth century, the footholds that France had acquired spasmodically on African and Asian coastlines would increasingly be seen as jumping-off points for a more purposeful colonialism, and voices arguing for such a project began to be heard from a number of quarters. In 1874 a young academic, Paul Leroy-Beaulieu, published his widely read and influential *On Colonization by Modern Peoples*, arguing that an advanced society had an economic, intellectual, social and moral duty to colonize, for the sake of its own survival and prosperity and for the benefit of humanity as a whole.[5] France was caught up in the international enthusiasm for exploration and scientific discovery that was characteristic of this period – as was an energetic Catholic missionary movement, which urged a national duty to shed 'the light of French Christian civilization' on lands sunk in dark ignorance and barbarism. More pragmatic supporters of a blue-water policy were the commercial interests, particularly those clustered around the ports of Bordeaux and Marseille. Imaginative military men in the Naval Troops and Africa Army needed new outlets for their energies, and although it would have put their careers at risk to take a public stance on such matters, some senior officers had political and journalistic connections that channelled their opinions into the public debate.

The thirty-odd years of France's greatest colonial dynamism were to begin in 1881. Spurred on by the realization that it was being left behind by the other powers in the global search for raw materials and new markets, and hungry to re-establish national prestige after the humiliations of 1870–71, France was in a hurry. Its psychological inability to relax central government control had cost it the opportunity to ride into an empire gradually on the backs of merchant-adventurers, and it had thus missed out on the mature stage of mercantile imperialism represented by, for example, the East India Company's slow expansion of British authority in the subcontinent between the early eighteenth and mid-nineteenth centuries. After this long intermission, the only way for France to realize its revived enthusiasm for colonies was to send military expeditions to brazenly kick-start a French government presence in new territories, immediately following the first swashbuckling phase of commercial penetration. Thus, during this second major chapter in its colonial story, France more or less reversed the sequence generally followed by British colonialists.

It is noticeable that many French enthusiasts for colonialism were on the political Left. As early as 1839 the socialist Louis Blanc had written, in his influential essay *The Organization of Work*, that 'the genius of France is essentially cosmopolitan: to go beyond herself, to spread herself across the world ... that is the role which History has long assigned to France'. He appealed to 'the invincible ardour of our will', and claimed that Algeria had been placed conveniently just across the Mediterranean by the laws of Providence. The attraction of colonies for theorists of the utopian Left was that they would provide a laboratory in which confused ideas for a new social order could be worked out in practice, among peoples powerless to resist such engineering. While supporters of overseas adventures were to be found at many points on the arc of French politics, in the 1880s the most coherent imperialist doctrine would be argued by governments of the moderate Left led by Jules Ferry and Léon Gambetta.[6]

UNDER THE THIRD REPUBLIC French prime ministers seldom saw a second Christmas in office. Embedded in mutual distrust, politicians were as intent on denying their rivals effective power as on harnessing it constructively themselves. Parliament was divided not between disciplined parties of clear ideological definition, but between many factions spread right across the spectrum from Catholic reactionaries to extreme Radicals. Administrations were formed by temporary and fragile coalitions of interest; these were usually clumped somewhere in the Republican centre, but occasionally included inhabitants of more marginal political territory who could, for a while, deliver the votes of a few more deputies. (For a rough modern model of the practical dynamics of the late nineteenth-century National Assembly we might take, perhaps, today's Israeli Knesset.) Governments were vulnerable to partisans of particular issues or regional interests; chronic instability made it difficult for any cabinet to sustain coherent policies, which were also subject to ambush by the entrenched bureaucrats who were the only uninterrupted tenants of the ministries. One consequence was that a limited number of individual politicians rotated into and out of office on several occasions. One of these was Léon Gambetta; the past decade had slightly sobered the wild-bearded young balloon-rider of 1870, but in a Chamber with many cynical careerists he was still a charismatic conviction politician.

In 1881 Gambetta headed a Republican faction that was important to another led by the more stolid figure of Jules Ferry, who had become prime minister in September 1880. Gambetta had for years been a supporter of outward-looking policies; Ferry had never previously shown any interest in colonialism, but early in 1881 Gambetta (himself convinced by a loose cannon in the Foreign Ministry) converted him to a sincere belief in the need to act boldly in Tunisia. The withdrawal of most French troops from Tunisia in May–June 1881 was influenced not by Bou Amama's coincidental rising in western Algeria but by the prospect of elections in October; this reduction quickly proved premature, and the need for a subsequent 'surge' – naval bombardments and a second major landing – saw Ferry voted out of office on 10 November. He was succeeded by Gambetta, who himself lasted only until 30 January 1882, but during those three months he showed an energy recalling his glory days in 1870–71; perhaps his most relevant reform was to take colonial affairs away from the Navy Ministry and give them to a new under-secretariat in the Trade Ministry. After a brief interregnum, on 16 February 1883 the revolving doors deposited Jules Ferry in the prime minister's office once again, and he immediately demonstrated that his stumble over Tunisia had not diminished his newly found passion for the colonialist cause.[7]

THE ARGUMENTS FOR THAT CAUSE, as articulated by Ferry, were threefold. The first was commercial: only colonial expansion would secure for France the raw materials and the new markets for its manufactures without which its economy would be crushed by foreign competition. The second was humanitarian: how could France, the birthplace of the Enlightenment, shirk the task of leading towards reason and civilization those unfortunate lesser peoples still mired in ignorance and cruelty? The third was the straightforward appeal to national interest and pride: France could not resign herself to the role of a second-class power – its people 'would not easily be content to count for no more in the world than a large Belgium'.[8] Having lost the balance of power in Europe to Germany, France would wither into irrelevance if it did not reassert itself on a wider field, and it would become powerless to defend those overseas interests if it did not plant garrisons and naval bases in those regions not already swallowed up by other nations. The civilized countries were 'extending their ancient rivalries into faraway fields of competition; the politics of the hearthside, of immobility, of withdrawing into ourselves, are nothing but an abdication'. France would remain great only by 'carrying everywhere it was able its language, its customs, its flag, its weapons, its genius'.[9]

The main obstacle to this ambition was simply the stubborn indifference of the French public as a whole to the world beyond their shores. To an introverted and still largely rural society, far horizons were more frightening than attractive, and twelve years after Sedan military adventures did not command much enthusiasm even among xenophobes. There were also many who were happy to provide reasoned counter-arguments. Liberal economists condemned colonies as uselessly expensive distractions from the urgent task of industrialization at home: rather than finding undemanding new markets for goods with which the developed world was already saturated, France should throw itself into the competitive search for more modern products. Military conservatives argued against distractions from 'the blue line of the Vosges'. The ultra-nationalist Paul Déroulède (last encountered at the barricade in the Rue Tourtille on 28 May 1871, and now the moving spirit of a League of Patriots) spoke for many who mourned for Alsace and Lorraine and disdained the prospect of colonial sideshows: 'I have lost two daughters – and you offer me twenty servant-girls?'. Speaking for the Radicals in the Assembly, Georges Clemenceau (who as mayor of Montmartre had briefly enjoyed some influence in the Commune) declared his unabashed enthusiasm for what Ferry dismissed as the politics of the hearthside: 'Personally, my patriotism lies in France ... Do you not find the tasks of increasing the sum of knowledge and enlightenment in our own country, of developing its wellbeing, of increasing liberty and extending rights ... do you not find these tasks sufficient ... ?'

Any cause that could arouse the visceral opposition of both Paul Déroulède and Georges Clemenceau was unusual: significantly, neither the Right nor the Left had a monopoly of either pro-colonialism or anti-colonialism. The dispute would bicker on for thirty years, quite separately from the major ideological confrontations that would dominate French politics, and it would be March 1894 before even a separate Colonial Ministry was finally created.[10] During the 1890s the colonial lobby led by the deputy for Oran, Eugène Étienne, would belatedly bring together supporters from right across the spectrum of party and faction to work for this one cause – businessmen of the French Colonial Union, devout Catholics of the Movement for the

Propagation of the Faith, members of the burgeoning Geographical Societies, soldiers, sailors and social visionaries.[11] On the one hand, since this single-issue pressure group was not particularly aligned with either of the deep tendencies in French society, it could never form a truly decisive parliamentary block. On the other, since the colonial lobby was increasingly well organized, funded and publicized, the serial instability of French governments throughout the period would, at particular moments, give the deputies who did support it opportunities to punch well above their weight in the Chamber.[12]

Those moments would include any occasion when some British slight to France's tender self-esteem inflamed public resentment. It must be remembered that during the thirty years following 1871 nearly every Frenchman instinctively loathed Britain with almost as much intensity as he did Germany; and since it was Britain, not Germany, that would sometimes frustrate France in the arena of colonial competition, chauvinists were always happy to blame any misfortune on the ancient enemy. French progressives might praise Britain's stable political institutions, flexible education and easier relations between the classes, but patriots were constantly aggrieved by the international success of 'Anglo-Saxon' industry and commerce and the perceived arrogance that it bred. Some French commentators revealed an extraordinary indignation that simply making and selling things should be rewarded with such undeserved wealth, power and respect; in their world view, to elevate pragmatism above abstract principle was ignoble, and commercial enterprise was simply greed.[13] While Britain's self-esteem was anything but tender, and its long-established imperial position was far beyond the reach of French rivalry, it was no less inclined to automatic hostility. As early as May 1884 a Mr Cust, Honorary Secretary of the Royal Asiatic Society, delivered a paper on France's colonial ambitions to the Royal United Services Institution in London after returning from a tour of Algeria:

> It is openly asserted by French publicists that the only chance for France maintaining her position as a Great Power in Europe is to found colonies in Asia and Africa, and the cherished desire of the French nation is to have a great African Empire. To give birth to such colonies as Australia and Canada they are confessedly unequal, as owing to well-known domestic habits their population is stagnant, and has no annual surplus of thousands to throw off. To govern great subject empires such as India they are not qualified, for they

have not as a nation sufficient self-restraint to be content with the affairs of empire and to leave the property in land of the subject races absolutely unviolated.

What they mean by a colony is a country like Algeria, in which French citizens are encouraged to settle on lands from which the ancient proprietors have been ousted, not, however, cultivating them entirely by themselves, but by the agency of the indigenous races reduced to serfage. Their object ... is to make such colonies the strictly guarded commercial preserve of the mother country, the raw products ... being collected mainly for the advantage of the conquering race. The manufactured products of the mother country are to be poured into the subject country, all competition [from] other European countries being barred by protective duties: the *raison d'être* of a colony is to constitute an exclusive mart for the home manufacturer.

Even in the mode of acquisition ... the French nation has a method of its own. Neither the Russian nor the English nation can plead innocence in the matter of annexation, but, when each case is examined, it will be found that there has been no deliberate design conceived beforehand of seeking an entirely new country for conquest ... The French nation, however, usually selects the spot which seems suitable to their operations; an explorer is sent forward, and makes a Treaty which founds rights; the Treaty is of course broken by the Native Power – and it is naively admitted that it is meant to be broken; and invasion and annexation follow ... [14]

WHILE WE CAN ALMOST HEAR THE GROWLS of agreement from behind a dozen heroic moustaches, Mr Cust's audience need not have been too concerned about France's 'exclusive mart for the home manufacturer'. By the late 1890s the British Empire covered 11 million square miles, with a population of around 400 million people. Between 1880 and 1914 the French empire would expand from about 270,000 square miles to just over 4 million, but its population from about 5 million to only 48 million. The initial expense of military invasion was negligible: that whole column of the ledger, worldwide, from 1830 to 1913, totalled only 1 milliard francs (a thousand million, or a billion) – equivalent, in 1900, to just two years' French government revenue from taxes on alcohol. But over the same period the cost of continuing military occupation and pacification was 8 milliards, and that of investments in civil infrastructure another 4 milliards – the latter, money that economists argued would have been better spent on France's own mines, railways and ports, to allow its industry to serve more efficiently customers with a lot more to spend than Arabs, Africans and Indochinese.

Set against these capital outlays, in overall terms of profit and loss the return on the empire was questionable. An analysis of its value in 1913 shows that while its colonial trade represented 13 per cent of France's global exports and 9 per cent of its imports, the total trailed in third place behind its trade with Britain and Germany. While the absolute volume of French trade with French colonies was perhaps twice that achieved with them by foreign countries, foreigners did not have to provide inwards investment, so their profit margins were much wider. Moreover, both British and German industry proved more alert in discovering and satisfying the actual preferences of the French colonial marketplace (for example, Lancashire textile mills were quick to tailor their production to match the strict sumptuary laws that governed Indochinese clothing, while French agents persisted in trying to sell bolts of cloth in standard French measurements.)[15] Individual French industries and the shareholders of private companies did, of course, make considerable profits out of the new empire; but while the colonies did contribute materially to the growth of some sectors of the French economy, overall they mainly saved existing lame ducks rather than spurring vigorous new activity that would earn future dividends on the world market. Among the ailing industries saved by the new colonial trade was one based around Marseille: the manufacture of straw hats.[16]

If this seems a rather modest return on the gold and blood invested, nevertheless, in spring 1883, Jules Ferry was convinced that such an investment was absolutely necessary in North Vietnam.

PHYSICALLY AND HISTORICALLY, the thousand-mile north to south length of Vietnam – in the nineteenth century still collectively called by its old Chinese name of Annam, 'the pacified south' – is divided into three distinct parts, traditionally described as two rice-baskets joined by a carrying-pole. The north, Tonkin, is the heavily populated Red river delta (hereafter, simply the Delta), walled in by forested hills and mountains astride its borders with China – with Yunnan province to the north-west, and Guangxi to the north-east. Its capital Hanoi and all other important towns were sited on the navigable Black, Red and Clear river complex slanting down from Yunnan to empty into the Gulf of Tonkin (see Map 4). South of the Delta is the heart of the old kingdom, the narrow carrying-pole specifically known today as Annam; here the seat of national authority was established in the imperial city of Hué on the Perfume river. Further south still, beyond the wild Central Highlands, is the second populous rice-basket: Cochinchina, where the southern capital Saigon sat on the lower Mekong river.

Tonkin was colonized by China in ancient times, and in the nineteenth century it still looked northwards; what we call Annam and Cochinchina had evolved separately during centuries of conflict with Cham and Khmer peoples from the west. The whole country was unified by King Gia Long only in 1802, while still acknowledging a formal allegiance to the Dragon Throne in Beijing. So long as face was preserved by obsequious courtesy and regular tribute, the Chinese court was unconcerned about internal affairs in a country whose people they regarded as uncouth (at home, the Annamese monarch styled himself an emperor; to the Chinese, he was emphatically a mere king). Many Cantonese had emigrated to form discrete communities that dominated commercial life in towns all over Vietnam, and Annamese culture and forms of administration had been modelled on those of China since ancient times. Authority devolved from the monarch's court through a classically educated mandarin class who, with their hordes of scribes, formed a distinct elite of 'the lettered' ranged in many gradations of prestige and wealth. The introverted mandarin class did not provide the population with much practical executive leadership, and its surface of formal state authority concealed conspiratorial patterns of local rivalries, alliances and client obligations. In an outwardly rigid society, power and status were in fact fluid and negotiable over the longer term.

Vietnam's lowland population was overwhelmingly rural, spread out amid paddy fields along the waterways in innumerable small, virtually self-sufficient villages living on their twice-yearly rice harvests. Gia Long's reforms in the early nineteenth century had virtually destroyed the former feudal landowning class in the countryside, so there were no large land holdings. Wealthy merchants were found only in the cities; over most of the country there was little internal trade above local artisan level, so there was only a rudimentary cash economy. The only real roads were the main north–south 'Mandarin Road' to China and a few tributaries linking it to the larger towns, and most travel and movement of goods was by the many rivers and canals. Life was Confucian, centred on family and village, and comforted by the rituals of a relaxed Buddhism merged with Taoism and ancestor-worship; every community had both its little Buddhist pagoda and its shrine to the ancestral spirits. After 2,000 years of dynastic civil wars and intermittent struggles for liberation from China, the Vietnamese people had learned innate habits of secrecy and concealment. In times of upheaval the peasantry were preyed upon by pitiless bandits, but in the deltas the main threat to their lives and livelihood came from periodic floods that wiped out the harvest and caused widespread famine. Their most resented burden was not the rice-taxes but the system of forced labour obligations (corvées, in the French term) administered through local mandarins, by which all public works were carried out.

The jungle hills around the edges of the Tonkin delta were inhabited by minority tribes of many ethnic origins; these were typically tough, self-reliant highlanders, and formal Annamese or Chinese authority was almost irrelevant to their lives. Throughout Vietnam lowlanders regarded all mountainous regions with dread, as the haunts of bandits, tigers, disease and evil spirits, and in at least three respects their fears were well-founded.

THE FIRST EUROPEAN TRADERS who landed in the sixteenth and seventeenth centuries proved to have less staying-power than the Catholic missionaries, who made significant numbers of converts.[17] In 1787 the passionate engagement of Father Pierre Pigneau de Béhaine in Cochinchina led him to befriend a young refugee southern prince, Nguyen Anh. Béhaine negotiated limited French help for his protegé – a few ships, cannon, and engineers to supervise the building of forts – in return for trade concessions, mainly at Da Nang (Tourane). Béhaine's judgement of character was sound; Nguyen Anh later fought his way to power over the whole country, and his sovereignty as King Gia Long was recognized by China in 1804. However, this energetic and centralizing reformer had the intelligence to keep the French at polite arm's length. After his death in 1820 his successors turned violently against their Christian converts, and French missionaries were periodically martyred.

Eventually, since Napoleon III counted upon the support of the Church at home, in late 1858 Admiral Rigault de Genouilly was ordered to occupy Da Nang as a reprisal against King Tu Duc for the recent execution of several missionaries. This proved impractical, but in February 1859 Rigault fought his way into Saigon and installed a garrison that managed to hold out under a fitful siege until Admiral Charner landed a stronger force in February 1861. The French then expanded their grip to include several other cities in the Mekong delta. In 1862 Tu Duc's most pressing concern was a rebellion led by a pretender in Tonkin, and that June he signed the Treaty of Saigon, ceding to France the southern capital and the three provinces that lay east of the Mekong. In 1867 the French simply annexed the other three provinces of Cochinchina; guerrilla war grumbled on, but thereafter the Navy governors in Saigon maintained an uneasy peace with Tu Duc's court at Hué.[18]

By this time Tonkin was being ravaged by the overspill from the catastrophic series of uprisings in China against the Manchu Ching dynasty collectively known as the Taiping Rebellion (1851–66). As Manchu armies harried their southern provinces, a plague of assorted freebooters crossed the mountains, and reduced to chaos most of the country between Lang Son in the north-eastern hills and Son Tay on the middle Red river. Tu Duc's appeals belatedly brought Chinese troops to garrison some towns, but the medicine proved almost as painful as the disease. This state of anarchy both frustrated and attracted the French, because Tonkin was potentially more than just another rice-basket like the cul-de-sac of Cochinchina. In 1867 it was established that the upper Red river in Tonkin was actually one and the same as the Hoti river of Yunnan. The Opium Wars of the 1840s–50s, and the mortgaging of the Ching dynasty to Western powers during the Taiping Rebellion, had opened China's eastern ports and great rivers to almost unrestricted commercial exploitation. However, direct access from the south into Yunnan – currently in the hands of Muslim rebels, and known to be rich in mineral resources – held out to either the British from Burma or the French from Cochinchina the prospect of a client trading partner independent of Beijing.

While the prize was alluring, the obstacles were many. To bring French boats all the way upriver from Haiphong on the Gulf of Tonkin to Manghao in Yunnan would depend on securing the simultaneous agreement of King Tu Duc's court in Hué, his mandarins in the northern capital at Hanoi, his *de jure* overlords in Beijing, Chinese governors in Yunnan, and whoever might currently be in *de facto* control of the chaotic upper Red river badlands – a daunting house of cards for any European to build. Even on those rare occasions when clarity rather than an elegant vagueness was the desired object, negotiation with Chinese or Annamese officials (who always had varying agendas of their own) had a rich potential for misunderstanding that went far beyond the real difficulties of translation. By May 1883, the attempts of various impatient Frenchmen to gain access to Yunnan had detonated a number of unintended consequences.

THERE WAS A SHARP DISTINCTION between the legal authority of both the Chinese and Annamese governments and their discontinuous physical ability to control events in their wild borderlands. Regional governors exercised stewardship in their monarch's name with wavering degrees of honesty and efficiency, but provided that the necessary outward forms of respect were observed then both court and regional mandarins were usually pragmatic enough to accommodate themselves to the realities on the ground. Those realities involved, as often as not, reaching mutually satisfactory agreements with local strongmen whom neither monarch nor governor had the military resources to suppress.

Although the Taiping Rebellion had devastated huge areas of central China, the original outbreak had occurred among the misty mountains of Guangxi in the far south, across the Tonkin border from Cao Bang and Lang Son. As Manchu authority was restored in Guangxi in the mid-1860s, a brigand named Liu Yung-fu – a junior boss in a gang known as the Yellow Flags – led a few hundred men south to seek his fortune, under a black flag that he had seen in a dream.[19] He eventually built a stockade on the Red river opposite Son Tay; instead of simply marauding, however, he hired out his services to the local governor, turned against his original Yellow Flag chief, and received from Hué an honorary commission as an Annamese government officer. He later moved up the Red river, controlling and 'taxing' the stretch between Hung Hoa and the Yunnan border at Lao Cai, where further co-operation with a Manchu general earned him a parallel commission in the Chinese Army. By 1873 his cunning, ruthlessness and instinctive grasp of the unspoken rules had earned this bandit chief the letters patent that transformed him into a general and a man of status with two governments. From China he received payment and rifles for his Black Flag followers, whom he organized into battalions and companies and ruled with a merciless discipline.[20]

At Hanoi, in December 1873, the arrogance of a merchant-adventurer named Jean Dupuis and the violent impetuosity of a naval officer, Francis Garnier, had created a confrontation over navigation rights on the Red river between the Annamese court and Admiral Dupré, the French governor in Cochinchina. By the time the shooting stopped many Tonkinese had died, fighting both against and (in the case of Christian converts) alongside a company of French *marsouins*; but the Black Flags – employed for lack of other reliable troops by the Annamese governor Prince Hoang – were parading the heads of Lieutenants Garnier and Balny d'Avricourt around the Delta villages.

A line was ostensibly drawn under the affair in March 1874, when a treaty was signed between the French and King Tu Duc's government; Garnier was written off as a hothead who had exceeded orders, and the French withdrew from Tonkin except for a lightly guarded consulate in the Hanoi 'concession'. The treaty formally recognized French rule over the whole of Cochinchina; but it also promised French help to Hué against any attack, and declared Annamese independence from all foreign powers. These clauses had fateful consequences: in French, but certainly not in Annamese or Chinese eyes, they both gave a pretext for French armed intervention in Tonkin at some future time, and withdrew recognition of Chinese suzerainty over Tonkin and Annam. The treaty also opened the Red river to trade, but – to France's growing frustration – that clause remained in practical abeyance, since Liu's Black Flags (enjoying increased prestige and recruitment, thanks to the head of Francis Garnier) physically controlled the upper reaches.[21]

DIPLOMATIC FENCING CONTINUED for years between Saigon and Hué, and between Paris and Beijing (now ruled by the iron-willed Dowager Empress Tzu Hsi). King Tu Duc was in an impossible position: with Tonkin overrun by marauders, he was trying to maintain his authority without military resources, while simultaneously satisfying two external powers. France continually escalated its demands, and China, while expecting obedience without being able to provide protection, was sponsoring the Black Flags who stood in the way of French access to Yunnan.

The election of the Ferry and Gambetta governments in 1881–3 unchained the frustration of the Yunnan enthusiasts, and the civilian governor of Cochinchina, Le Myre de Vilers, secured the endorsement of Paris for an attempt to resolve the impasse over the Red river. He would pressure Hué to accept a limited French expedition specifically against the Black Flags; this would ostensibly be acting on Tu Duc's behalf, in a broad interpretation of the 1874 treaty clause promising French help against the king's enemies. Accordingly, Le Myre despatched to Hanoi two gunboats and 230 Naval Infantry under Captain Henri Rivière, whose orders were to reinforce the 100-man consulate guard, and to carry out a police action against the Black Flags and any other 'pirates' blocking river traffic.

The French always used this term, partly for reasons of public relations, partly because the Chinese and other freebooters lived mainly by preying on trade up and down the rivers and coastal sea lanes. No single English word seems to describe their actual character precisely, since Liu Yung-fu's relationship with the Hué government was always ambiguous. His Black Flags were essentially mercenary soldiers who received pay and ammunition from China, nominally to act on behalf of Hué but actually beyond the control of the Annamese court. Liu exploited the areas he occupied like a robber baron (as did the otherwise lethargic Chinese regular garrisons that the governor of Guangxi had planted in north-eastern towns). Villages were looted and taxed, men were forced to build forts and work the fields for their occupiers, and women were carried off for Chinese slave-markets. The smaller groups that infested the Delta were simple bandits, who emerged briefly from their hideouts to pillage and kill. It is estimated that by 1882 as many as 80,000 freebooters and outlaws of all kinds were at large in Tonkin, since many men from the communities destroyed during these years of anarchy had little choice but to turn bandit themselves. During the 1870s, some up-country regions had become virtually depopulated.

HENRI RIVIÈRE WAS A PUBLISHED POET and novelist with ambitions for election to the Académie Française. However, five years previously this burly middle-aged Norman had also played a leading part in crushing a jungle rebellion in New Caledonia, and it was that less nuanced side of his character that responded to the icy reception he received from the mandarins at the Hanoi Citadel on 2 April 1882.[22] When another 250 *marsouins* arrived upriver on 24 April he presented the Annamese with an impossible ulti-matum and only a few hours in which to consider it, and the next day he repeated Garnier's impetuosity. He, too, shelled and assaulted the Citadel, capturing it within a couple of hours and inflicting hugely disproportionate casualties. There were furious protests, shocked disclaimers, and a great deal of undercover diplomacy, but Rivière stayed in the Citadel under the tricolour flag. There were no immediate Annamese reprisals; the Black Flags were the only other credible force in Tonkin, and Liu Yung-fu played hard to get (first with the Annamese Prince Hoang, and later with a hawkish Chinese mandarin, Tang Ching-sung) in order to extract better terms.

When President Grévy called upon Jules Ferry to form a second gov-ernment in February 1883, the prime minister halted the Foreign Ministry's conciliatory talks with Beijing (which was anyway preoccupied by Japanese aggression in Korea). Reinforced to about 1,250 Naval Troops plus local Christian auxiliaries, Captain Rivière was emboldened, on 27 March, to take the city of Nam Dinh by storm. In his absence the small garrison left in Hanoi held off a surprise attack by both Black Flags and Chinese Guangxi regulars from a garrison at Bac Ninh. At Son Tay, the Chinese mandarin Tang urged the Black Flag chief Liu to gather all his men and any willing locals to attack the French invaders, with the blessings of both governments. Liu sent insulting messages to Rivière, daring him to come out and fight, and on 19 May 1883 the French commander obliged him, personally leading 450 troops north out of Hanoi on the road for Son Tay, along a causeway through the paddy fields.

They had only marched a few hundred yards when they fell into an ambush near the Paper Bridge – almost exactly where Garnier had lost his head ten years previously. By the time the French made good their escape 50 had been killed – including Henri Rivière – and 76 wounded, and French heads pickled in brine were exhibited to enthusiastic crowds for months thereafter. A French offer to ransom Rivière's corpse was unfortunately misinterpreted by the Black Flags, who hacked it to bits, under the impression that each of them could claim a separate bounty for his own gobbet of flesh.[23]

IN DEATH, CAPTAIN RIVIÈRE had served his prime minister's purpose admirably, and '*Ferry le Tonkinois*' rode the tide of public indignation. Without dissent, the Chamber voted his government the funds for an expedition 'to avenge France's glorious children', and the first 3,000 reinforcements were soon heading east of Suez. While they were still at sea, in July 1883, King Tu Duc died, leaving a child as his designated successor. The dominant figures on the regency council, Nguyen Van Tuong and Ton That Thuyet, were determined to thwart France; while sending urgent orders to mandarins throughout the country to resist any French advance, they substituted an elder prince, to rule as King Hiep Hoa.[24]

On 16 August 1883 the French envoy Harmand delivered an ultimatum to Hué calling for national surrender within 48 hours; in the absence of a response, Admiral Courbet's warships destroyed the forts at the mouth of the Perfume river, *marsouins* were landed, and on 25 August representatives of King Hiep Hoa signed a draft treaty accepting a French protectorate over Annam. France was to take over all dealings with China; all Chinese troops must withdraw from Tonkin; French troops would be solely responsible for expelling the Black Flags, and for ensuring the safety of French navigation on the Red river; and French officials installed in the major cities would supervise government finances. The king was allowed to retain some measure of autonomy in lesser Annam – the central provinces of the country – but he would be hemmed in by French rule over Tonkin and Cochinchina. Further pressure to sign had simultaneously been applied by 1,500 Navy troops shipped up from Saigon under General Bouet, although attempts on 15 August and 1 September to bundle the Black Flags out of Son Tay failed before the unexpectedly solid defensive works.

For both Paris and Beijing the situation had to be considered with an eye to wider international sensitivities; France was the stronger by far, but the other Western powers had all invested heavily in China. Unilateral French operations on the Chinese mainland were out of the question, and a naval war along the Chinese coast would infuriate Britain, Germany and the United States. While different factions in both the Quai d'Orsay and the Chinese court argued about how strong a line it was wise to take – with some murmuring about a possible demarcation agreement to share Tonkin – the late summer of 1883 saw a military stalemate in the paddy fields. The Black Flags, Chinese garrisons, bandit gangs, and locals stirred up by the regents continued to destabilize the Delta, waging guerrilla warfare wherever opportunity offered.[25]

IN JULY 1883, THE FOREIGN LEGION establishment had been increased from four to six battalions, and by the end of the following year only two of these would still be in Algeria.[26] The 5,000-odd Navy troops in Vietnam and locally recruited Annamese Skirmishers were inadequate for what might turn into an all-out war with China; Admiral Courbet requested reinforcements, and some of these were drawn from North Africa. On 27 September 1883 a marching regiment embarked at Algiers, comprising a battalion each from 1st and 3rd Algerian Skirmishers and Major Donnier's 600-strong 1st Battalion of the Foreign Legion.[27]

4. The Year of the Five Kings

*As soon as we had passed this crest the appearance of
the landscape changed abruptly, as if by a magic wand.
Just now it had been a laughing country, of shady woods
full of flowers and birdsong; on this side it was a chaos
of high, arid mountains, sad and desolate ... The
Annamese called this desert 'the country of hunger and
death'.*

    Dr Charles Hocquard, 10 February 1885[1]

THE FRENCH TRANSPORTS made landfall in Halong Bay, where white-painted warships lay at anchor amidst a fairytale stone forest of natural pillars thrusting up from the blue-green water. Native sampans and naval pinnaces darted around the ships, while the heavily laden troops clambered nervously down into strings of lifeboats to be towed in through the labyrinth by steam launches. In November a fog hung over the sea, and the constantly shifting mudbanks in the mouth of the Cua Cam river played hide-and-seek with even the Vietnamese pilots. When the mist lifted it revealed a low ceiling of leaden grey cloud, muddy red riverbanks, and beyond them a flat chequerboard of green fields stretching away towards a line of blue mountains in the northern distance. Progress was slow, depending upon the water level, the skill of the pilot sounding at the bow with a pole, and the alertness of the French sailor at the helm.

At the inland port of Haiphong, tiny and squalid on its mudflats, the Legion battalion transferred to larger boats for the journey up the Cua Cam to Seven Pagodas, then west along the Rapids Canal to its junction with the Red river at Hanoi (see Map 4). The soldiers were happy enough; the officers had drawn a cash allowance for food in addition to standard Naval Troops rations, and Haiphong had provided rice, eggs, chickens and pork. Well fed, and snug under their greatcoats against the occasional drizzle, the légionnaires lounged like sightseers for two or three days as the boats made their sinuous way between fields squared off with raised dykes and sown with rice, maize and thickets of sugar cane. Every few hundred yards they passed a bamboo-and-thatch village, each shaded by a clump of fruit trees, plumed with a few tall, straight areca palms, and defended by a hedge of thick bamboo. Wading fishermen netted the shallows for prawns and crabs, children ran along the banks waving, dogs barked, and at every bend the boats disturbed ducks and white egrets. The waterways were crowded with traffic, and further amusement was provided by the sight of big junks loaded with troops and stores stuck fast on mudbanks waiting for the flooding tide.[2]

The Legion battalion arrived in Hanoi on 18 November 1883. There, on the west bank of the Red river, perhaps 100,000 people were crowded into a triangular city stretching roughly 3 miles in each direction to its fringe of suburban villages. The sluggish water was about 1,000 yards wide here, but there were no proper landing stages, so after the boats threaded their way to shore through the jam of launches, barges and junks the soldiers had to wade through treacly black silt. They clambered up treacherous mud steps into a scene of purposeful pandemonium, as hundreds of coolies with bamboo carrying-poles and ropes scurried to unload the boats constantly arriving from Haiphong. Beyond a riverside road bordered with almond trees, roofs showed above the loopholed palisade that surrounded the French Concession. Once the newcomers had been formed up by their bellowing NCOs they were marched inland along packed streets of thatched wooden cabins and rows of narrow-fronted brick houses with oddly stepped rooflines, broken here and there by the sculpted towers of whitewashed pagodas. Their destination was the other focus of the occupation – the Citadel, on the north-west edge of the city.

This was the largest in the country, but its architecture was typical of all the strongholds of the Annamese royal government that the légionnaires would occupy. It was essentially a separate quarter within the city; inside a stagnant, reedy moat loud with bullfrogs, high, thick brick walls enclosed a rectangle measuring nearly 2 miles on the long sides, with five monumental gatehouses set in protruding half-moon bastions. Protected by an inner rectangle of walls in the centre of the great compound was a magnificent Chinese-style palace built to accommodate the king on his occasional visits, splendid with carved gables, upswept eaves and varnished red-tile roofs with decorated ridge-lines. An octagonal brick 'flag tower' rising close to the palace was now used by the French for their optical signalling system.[3] Around the inside of the Citadel's outer walls handsome mansions once occupied by the governor and his mandarins were set in pleasant tree-shaded gardens, and one corner of the enclosure was filled with big brick granaries where the gathered rice-taxes were stored. Otherwise the wide expanse between the walls and the central palace had been empty, but the French now fulfilled its original purpose by crowding it with temporary buildings of clay cob, timber, bamboo and matting to accommodate the swelling garrison.[4]

MAJOR DONNIER'S LÉGIONNAIRES did not have long to explore the wonders of the Orient. The rainy season of May to November, when insupportable heat and constant downpours made military movement nearly impossible, was over. In the second week of December, Admiral Courbet, now reinforced to about 8,000 troops, took advantage of his limited window for operations: the end of the monsoon made cross-country marches possible, but before long water levels for the essential river traffic would start to sink again. His first objective had to be the Black Flag stronghold of Son Tay about 25 miles upriver, where Liu Yung-fu was again taunting the French to come on if they dared.

Courbet sent Lieutenant-Colonel Maussion's Naval Infantry upriver on junks and gunboats, but the Legion, Algerian *turcos* and local troops marched up the west bank through a heavily cultivated landscape of paddy fields and orchards. The légionnaires were still in their blue greatcoats and red trousers, and had not yet been issued with Naval Troops' pith helmets; they trudged along under 50lb packs, envying the coolness of the *'desmoiselles'* who marched ahead of them. These Annamese Skirmishers, in their little bamboo hats, loose black cotton uniforms and red sashes, were burdened with nothing but their weapons; their women – who always accompanied them on campaign – carried the rest. (Their nickname was unsubtle: since Vietnamese men seldom grew more than 5 feet tall and were slightly built and beardless, and since both sexes wore trousers and folded their long hair up in a chignon, off-duty légionnaires were prone to embarrassing mistakes.)[5] The causeway road through the fields was straight and quite broad, with hump-backed bridges across the many creeks and irrigation ditches. The column passed isolated, tree-shaded pagodas, and every few hundred yards a hamlet; at their approach dogs barked madly, gongs sounded, and everyone got out of sight – or, if surprised far out in the fields, took off their broad hats and bowed deeply.

The town of Son Tay, lying with its north side against a bend of the Red river, was a considerable obstacle. Turreted gatehouses rose at the cardinal points of an enclosure of thick mud-brick walls about 14 feet high, loopholed for rifles and light cannon along upper galleries; these were topped with bamboo hoardings from which rows of wicked spikes pointed out and downwards. A wide, deep moat ran around outside the walls, and the narrow strip of earth between them was planted along much of its length with a hedge of growing bamboo, up to 12 feet tall and thick enough to explode impact-fuzed shells before they struck the brickwork. The flats outside the moat were obstructed by a bristling double line of interlaced bamboo barricades; X-shapes of sharpened stakes were lashed tightly side by side along crosspoles to form dense *chevaux-de-frise* as high as a man's head – what the Legion's German NCOs called 'Spanish riders', and as basic to all Vietnamese defences as barbed wire is to Europe.

Although division and indecision had hampered the build-up of Chinese garrisons during the rains, about 1,000 Yunnan regulars had joined the 3,000 mercenaries at Son Tay but, to Liu's frustration, the mandarin Tang had only been able to contribute a few hundred Guangxi soldiers. The 5,000-odd Annamese troops who were also in the area were of very uncertain morale, and Liu had contemptuously driven them out of town into the outlying villages. In Son Tay itself, Courbet's 5,500-strong expedition still faced about equal numbers of fighting men, many of them installed behind solid walls with perhaps 100 muzzle-loading light cannon and 'rampart guns'.[6] As the French approached Son Tay on 14 December they came up against the first palisaded villages, which had to be taken by troops deploying laboriously across the flooded fields. When the two causeways they were following converged towards the defended village of Phu Sa south of the town the resistance became stiffer; both dykes had been cut and the far sides of the gaps blocked with earth and bamboo defences. These were taken without too much trouble, but at the Y-junction of the dykes more serious fortifications had been built, and were held and flanked by Black Flag riflemen.

LIU YUNG-FU'S MEN were no mere guerrillas who would run from a couple of volleys or shells; they were aggressive, quick to seize any chance in combat, moved under command in disciplined companies, were good shots with rifles mostly as modern as the légionnaires' Gras, and were not afraid to fight face-to-face. Taller and stronger than the Annamese, Liu's soldiers proudly kept the Manchu hairstyle – the front of the head shaved and a long pigtail at the back, rolled up under a small turban when in battle. They wore long loose blouses, broad trousers and puttees of dark blue or black, identifiable by lacking the big coloured disc on the chest and back that distinguished Chinese regulars; swords, long knives or bayonets were thrust into their coloured sashes, and they carried plentiful ammunition in belts or vests looped for cartridges. Observers unanimously describe the Black Flags as more skilful and motivated than the Chinese regulars who fought beside them in 1883. Like the légionnaires, the Black Flags were mercenaries, but in Chinese eyes they too were a patriotic expeditionary force, and – like the Legion – they had earned that reputation in battle.[7]

On the confined 20-foot frontage of the causeway it was difficult for the French to get their artillery up and into action, and the infantry fought throughout 14 December without managing to break through the Chinese works. At nightfall they had to fall back along the two dykes to the outworks they had already taken; they had little rest, and repeated harassing attacks were only driven off thanks to the unusually bright moonlight. The next morning they found that the Chinese had abandoned their ramparts and fallen back into the town, taking with them the heads of the French dead who had unavoidably been left on the field the night before. A Chinese poster found at Son Tay, dated 11 December, listed bounties for enemy heads: 40 *taëls* for that of an Annamese Skirmisher, 50 for a *turco* or légionnaire, and a sliding scale of 100 and upwards for French officers, depending on their number of rank stripes. (This eager head-hunting put considerable pressure on French medical personnel to stay close behind the fighting line, going forward to rescue the wounded immediately.)

On 15 December the French guns were dragged up along the dyke and brought into action, joining the gunboats on the river in shelling the walls and gates of Son Tay, though apparently without achieving any serious breaches. Maussion's Naval Infantry landed and assaulted the north river gate, but without success. The morning of the 16th found Major Donnier's I/LE forming up under cover of the paddy-dykes of Phu Nhi village, facing the town's west gate across 300 yards of open fields. At 1pm the bugles sounded and the légionnaires moved forward, coming under fire from the walls as soon as they left cover. French shells did not make much impression on either the walls or the bamboo *chevaux-de-frise* (which yielded and sprang back under anything but a direct hit), but they did smash up the

wooden hoardings and clear riflemen off the broad wall-walks, and soon 3rd
Company were within 50 yards of the west gatehouse. A platoon rushed
forwards across the moat bridge, but this led them to a blank-faced half-moon
bulge of brickwork surmounted by a crenellated tower. The légionnaires had
to turn to one side and follow the wall round until they reached side
entrances in the bastion, which led into the arched tunnel of the inner
gateway. When they got there, they found it blocked with bamboo entanglements and the gate itself bricked up.

The rest of the battalion gradually made their way across and pressed up
against the base of the walls; when the French artillery necessarily ceased
fire the Black Flags swarmed back to the parapets, to shoot and drop ceramic
powder-grenades down on them (one of those killed here was the quartermaster, Captain Mehl, a veteran who had left his proper post in the rear
to join the assault party). The artillery opened fire again on another sector
of the wall, and by about 5pm had created a practical breach. The 3rd
Company clambered up the ramp of smashed bricks, led by a big Belgian
private named Minnaert, who tore down a black banner and stuck an improvised tricolour at the head of the breach. Once the outer wall had fallen, the
légionnaires drove the Chinese back through the streets into the formidable
citadel in the centre of the town – a scale model of that at Hanoi, with its
own moat and bastioned walls about 500 yards on each side.

With the prospect of another costly assault ahead, the French troops
rested around the town that night; but when they probed forward next
morning they found – remarkably – that the entire remaining garrison had
somehow slipped away in the darkness, and local civilians were already
inside the citadel, looting the mandarins' houses. The Chinese left enormous
stores, and more than 1,000 corpses; the final number killed may have been
at least twice that many, since after finding their comrades' heads stuck on
bamboo stakes the French did not take prisoners. The French losses at Son
Tay were 83 killed and 320 wounded.[8]

The Legion battalion loaded their wounded on to riverboats and marched
back to Hanoi, where they spent the rest of December. To his disappointment, Admiral Courbet soon reverted from his overall command to
that of the naval squadron only, since Paris recognized that steering this
campaign would demand professionals in the art of land warfare. During the
winter months the number of troops in Vietnam almost doubled, and by
February 1884 they would form a 15,000-man expeditionary corps commanded by Navy General Charles Millot. Its two constituent brigades were

to be led by Navy General Brière de l'Isle (1st Brigade, Hanoi), and Army General Francois de Négrier, whose command of 2nd Brigade at Hai Duong would bring a reunion with his familiar légionnaires. The Legion contingent was reinforced on 28 February by the arrival from Algeria of Major Hutin's 2nd Battalion, 800 strong, bringing with them nearly 200 replacements for the already fever-worn 1st Battalion.[9] One of the French ships that left Toulon that winter was *L'Annamite*, a steamer of the Messageries Maritime company, which sailed on 11 January 1884 carrying a battalion of the 23rd Line, two artillery batteries, 30 horses and 60 officers, including Médecin-major de 2e Classe Charles Hocquard – a uniquely valuable witness to the coming campaigns.[10]

WHILE THE FRENCH REINFORCEMENTS settled in, their adversaries were not idle. In January 1884, at the new Black Flag base at Hung Hoa further up the Red river, Liu Yung-fu – recovering from a wound received at Son Tay – was visited by the Chinese governor of Yunnan province, Tsen Yu-ying. Liu had been disgusted by the feeble support received from Guangxi, but Tsen promised that he was bringing 12,000 Yunnan troops across the border and down the river corridor. On the strength of this, and his promise of future support in Liu's own territory, Tsen succeeded in persuading Liu to lead his Black Flags – now reconstituted to about 3,000 men – eastwards to join the Guangxi garrison at Bac Ninh, reportedly the next French object-ive, in the first week of March.

The Cau river and its southern continuation, the Thai Binh, flow roughly parallel to the Red river and to its north-east; Bac Ninh lay on the west bank of the Cau about 20 miles across country from Hanoi, and perhaps 30 miles north-west of the French base at Hai Duong further down the Thai Binh (see Map 4). Bac Ninh was an important hub of road and river transport where a Chinese garrison guarded the Mandarin Road; this led north-east to the strategic town of Lang Son about 70 miles away in the Middle Region, just inside the Tonkin–China frontier. When Liu arrived, he discovered that although the garrison had constructed about two dozen rather flimsy forts immediately surrounding Bac Ninh, the outlying hills were mostly unguarded, and the Guangxi troops themselves were unimpressive. They numbered several thousand; they had plenty of equipment, stores and modern weapons (single-shot Snider, Remington and bolt-action Mauser rifles, even some Krupp field guns); they blew their trumpets a great deal; but their training and morale left much to be desired. Their pillaging had

also earned them the hatred of the locals – not something to which Liu
Yung-fu usually gave a thought, but here the Guangxi troops had allowed
weapons to fall into the peasants' hands. Confirmed in his prejudices,
Liu took his Black Flags up into the neglected western hills to await
developments.[11]

General Millot's spring campaign was a conventional two-pronged
advance on Bac Ninh, by Brière de l'Ile's 1st Brigade moving east from Hanoi,
and Négrier's 2nd moving north from Hai Duong. (It seems to have been on
this occasion that somebody attributed to Négrier a spectacularly stupid
exhortation to the Legion battalions: 'Légionnaires, you are soldiers in order
to die; I am sending you where men die.' This has the unmistakable whiff
of journalistic invention; there is no identifiable authority for the alleged
quotation, and it contradicts everything in Négrier's known record.) The
preparations took several days of apparent but deceptive chaos, while per-
spiring staff officers endured contradictory orders, querulous demands, misplaced documents, colliding working parties and strayed couriers. At each
brigade base more than 5,000 troops had to be brought in from the outlying
pagodas where they had been lodged, to be assembled, kitted out and given
their movement orders.[12]

Each brigade needed about half as many coolies to carry its rations and
baggage as it had soldiers; these were conscripted by the mandarins, who
routinely pocketed the generous pay the French offered, telling their people
that this was a compulsory corvée. Tons of stores had to be broken down by
the harassed commissariat into two-man pole-loads of about 70lb, while
boxes and carrying-frames were knocked up on the spot by every carpenter
who could be found. Army tinned meat and biscuit had to be supplemented
with rice and fresh meat or fish, and in the procurement of these and other
necessities the ever-efficient Chinese merchants proved of far more use than
the few expatriate French businessmen.[13]

At last all was ready, and 2nd Brigade – with its coolies, about 7,000
men – set off at first light on 6 March. The troops were to be shipped up the
Thai Binh to its confluence with the Cau at Seven Pagodas in locally hired
craft, and in the shallow-draft French Navy river gunboats that were such a
valuable asset in all the colonial campaigns.[14] On the 7th they passed through
Seven Pagodas, then marched westwards across country north of the Rapids
Canal; the plan was to rendezvous with 1st Brigade at the village of Chi, due
south of Bac Ninh, and then to strike north together. Like many military
plans, it did not long survive, but on this occasion because Négrier made

better progress than expected; a sketch map by Captain Carteron shows 2nd Brigade not heading straight westwards for Chi but veering off increasingly to the north, in the direction of Bac Ninh.

The 1st Brigade – 9,000 men all told – started its march eastward on 8 March. Avoiding the more direct route of the well-defended Mandarin Road, General Brière marched along south of the Rapids Canal, aiming to cross it and link up with Négrier at Chi. The 3-mile column had to keep to the dykes criss-crossing an enormous plain of paddy fields; some of the solid causeways between villages were several yards wide, but most dykes were mere field-boundaries so narrow that the men had to march in twos. Their thousands of boots soon tore up the soft surface, and since the dykes were only inches wider than the wheels of the artillery's 80mm mountain guns the column was repeatedly delayed by guns slipping down the muddy slopes, to be retrieved only with backbreaking effort by gangs of coolies hauling on ropes while infantrymen slithered down to get their shoulders under the weight. Progress slowed to little more than half a mile an hour, and the mud-slathered troops were soon heavy-footed and staring, panting in the humidity and using their rifles as walking-sticks.

While sympathetic, Dr Hocquard – forced to dawdle at the rear with his ambulance unit – was fascinated by the chance to survey the scene from 300 feet above. Just ahead of him in the column, towed along by gangs of blaspheming artillerymen, were two bobbing observation balloons, and since the brigade was often at a standstill the enthusiastic Lieutenant Julien of the *division d'aérostiers* was happy to take the doctor up for a bird's-eye view.[15] Spread out below him was the monotonous rectangular mosaic of reddish dykes dividing up the pale green of the winter-sown rice. At long intervals across the plain tall areca palms flagged the presence of little villages shaded by banana groves, and here and there a white pagoda glinted against the vast dark umbrella of an ancient, buttressed banyan tree, thrusting up from roots like anacondas and offering enough tempting shade for a whole company.

At last the column got out of the paddies and began to make better speed across a plain planted with sugar cane and vegetables. The couriers and officers were able to remount their led horses and rush busily up and down the column; the big French horses that many officers had shipped out had quickly sickened as a result of the local climate and unfamiliar forage, so they were obliged to swallow their pride and employ Tonkinese ponies that made them look ridiculous. These were thickset, enduring, and as sure-footed as goats on the narrow dykes, but they stood only about 12 hands at the withers (chest-height on a man), attracting old jokes about mounting by standing with one's legs apart and letting the pony walk between them. They could carry a European at least 25 miles in a day, were unfussy about their feed, and had only one unnerving habit: they could not trot – they had nothing in the gearbox between a walk and an all-out, bone-jarring gallop, and at the slightest encouragement they took off like a rocket. (When the elegant cavalryman Major Lyautey was introduced to them ten years later, he would write home: 'It is neither a horse, nor a bicycle, it is a kind of machine on which you sit astride in defiance of all the rules, and which goes ahead under you like something mechanical, at a devil of a pace ...')[16]

ON 11 MARCH, THE NAVAL INFANTRY and *turcos* of 1st Brigade turned north to cross the Rapids Canal. General Brière knew that 2nd Brigade on the north bank had been veering right, away from the planned rendezvous at Chi but closer to Bac Ninh. For three days now the Legion had been bundling half-hearted Guangxi soldiers out of forts and off hills, and by that night Négrier was impatiently awaiting the arrival of 1st Brigade on his left. They faced a belt of forts defending the eastern approaches to Bac Ninh in an arc, from Trong Son hill on their left to the Cau river on their right. On the morning of the 12th, Brière's binoculars clearly showed Chinese forts on hills about 3 miles to his north, bedecked with forests of multicoloured flags. At around 11 am, 1st Brigade heard Négrier's cannon off to their right front, fighting through villages 4 miles away on the Dap Cau road. He had hooked right and was pushing towards Bac Ninh from the north-east – and the troops in the forts facing 1st Brigade to the south could also hear the gunfire, from the direction that was their way home to China.

French infantry tactics of the 1880s stressed the importance of the aggressive attack even against a well dug-in enemy, but these tactics were not simply a question of 'heads up, keep going and damn the casualties'. Négrier was a commander who was known for disdaining the mindless attack-at-all-costs, preferring tactics calculated to save his men's lives whenever he could, but on this occasion the Chinese refusal to fight in the open left him no option.[17] Attacks were made in line – that is, by companies or battalions strung out side by side across an extended front – to the sound of drums and bugle-calls. During the advance the men were halted to fire volleys before moving forward again, and did not charge with the bayonet until the last moment. The importance of artillery to silence the enemy's guns and to thin and demoralize his riflemen before the attack was well understood, as was the distinction between using some infantry units to deliver 'preparatory fires' of massed volleys to clear the enemy parapets, and others to make the shock assault. If the terrain forced a unit to close up and advance in a narrower, deeper formation, then large numbers of sharpshooters were sent skirmishing ahead to soften up the enemy by heavy sniping. (The desirability of putting in simultaneous flank attacks to divide the enemy's fire was, of course, second nature.)

Brière's brigade advanced northwards on Bac Ninh across a plain of paddy fields studded with indifferently fortified hills; when they got within range the artillery pounded the forts, and the infantry shook out into lines and waded across the flooded paddies. The forts wreathed themselves in gunsmoke, but not for long; as soon as the muddy French infantry began to climb the slopes the garrisons pulled out, and by 4.30pm Brière had infantry on top of Trong Son hill. His 1st Brigade halted to camp for the night, but General de Négrier did not; at 9.30am the next morning a courier brought Brière word that 2nd Brigade had occupied the town the night before.

When the Chinese in Bac Ninh had seen tricolours appearing one by one on hilltops along the whole arc from the south to the north-east, they had panicked. By 6pm the Legion's 1st Battalion were facing the north-east gatehouse across the usual moat bridge; it did not seem to be held in any strength, and Négrier ordered an immediate attack. Artillery blasted the huge leaves of the gate; by 6.30pm légionnaires were tearing the splintered timber aside, and once again the now-Corporal Minnaert pushed through first (though he was jostled for the honour by Sergeant Christophel, who wanted a Military Medal of his own).[18] There seems to have been hardly any infantry fighting; the Legion lost only 2 killed and 12 wounded, and when they got inside they found the town mostly abandoned and scattered with the debris of hasty flight. The Chinese had run for the north with as much loot as they could carry. All the corpses wore the uniforms of Guangxi regulars; the Black Flags, watching from the hills west of the town, had quietly slipped away, and were already cruelly ravaging the countryside on their way back to their base at Hung Hoa.

The enthusiastic looting of Bac Ninh by the porter-coolies, carrying burning torches after dark, became worrying when it was realized that the alleyways and shacks were strewn with abandoned munitions; next day Dr Hocquard found a house where loose gunpowder lay ankle-deep. The strongly fortified brick citadel could have forced the Legion to pay a bloody price if it had been defended stoutly. In its courtyard the soldiers proudly arranged their main trophies: an unused battery of Krupp guns, a Nordenfeldt machine gun and a large number of flags, including two splendid generals' banners of richly coloured silks (which in time would find their way back to Sidi bel Abbès).[19]

The consensus was that the Black Flags had been much tougher adversaries than these Chinese regulars, who had failed to exploit their numbers or their firepower against French troops who were at the disadvantage of advancing deep into enemy-held territory. French officers argued that the Chinese could not 'manoeuvre' – their commanders seemed to lack the initiative and skill to bring them out of fixed defences and move them around. The essence of battle command was, after all, to attack after creating an advantage by movement and timing, in the manner of a wrestler picking his moment and his grip, but the Chinese had simply waited for the French to come to them. That might still have been a winning tactic – they could have inflicted heavy, perhaps decisive casualties if they had held their positions stubbornly and used their firepower to the full – but they did not. They had artillery, but seldom used it properly; when French shells started to hit the outlying forts the garrisons had abandoned them without attempting to hold the walls against the coming infantry assaults, in which the defenders should have had all the advantages. It was only the lack of French numbers to encircle them first that allowed the Chinese to escape in their thousands. As for the légionnaires, they simply concluded that these 'Celestials' did not dare to stand and fight them. They would learn in time that there was more than one kind of Chinese regular.[20]

ONLY A FEW WEEKS AFTER the French had driven the Guangxi troops back into the hills south of Lang Son, General Millot led both his brigades from Son Tay towards Hung Hoa; the Yunnan troops also fell back before them, up the Red river corridor towards the border at Lao Cai. Accepting, furiously, that the Delta was lost to him for the time being, Liu Yung-fu blew up his magazine, burned down Hung Hoa and marched most of his Black Flags north-west after the regulars, driving thousands of wretched local slaves with him. On 12 April, it was the two Legion battalions that occupied the ashes of Hung Hoa, marching up from the lowlands into ever-steepening ranges of wooded hills. The Black Flags had completely depopulated the countryside, but as they passed the orchards of deserted villages the troops discovered for the first time the juicy delights of guavas and lychees.

Their commanders were more interested in the abandoned fortifications: for miles around Hung Hoa the Yunnan regulars had prepared the terrain for defence with professional skill. Spider-webs of zigzag trenches converged on squat dugouts with rifle slits at ground level, their tree-trunk roofs concealed with turf; they were built in interlocking series, with communication trenches leading back to forts. These main positions were surrounded by cleared fields of fire sown thickly with sharpened *panji*-stakes and barred with *chevaux-de-frise*; concentric systems of inner trenches and palisades covered the approaches to low, thick redoubts of rammed earth, complete with embrasures and inner gun platforms. Some French officers were thoughtful, as they gazed up into the waves of forest canopy stretching away to the purple mountains in the north.[21]

The légionnaires of Lieutenant-Colonel Duchesne's II/LE were left at Hung Hoa in garrison. Donnier's I/LE then made a voyage from Viet Tri – the node for river transport on the Clear, Red and Black rivers – as far north as the shallow upper reaches of the Clear, and an exhausting four-day march through forested hills took them to the old abandoned fort of Tuyen Quang, where 3rd and 4th Companies took up residence while the other half of the unit returned to Hanoi.

THE LÉGIONNAIRES WERE TIRED OUT and anaemic; the sky was permanently sealed by oppressive grey clouds, and up in the highlands the eve of the May monsoon brought chill morning fog and occasional downpours. Back down in the Delta, however, the heat was building towards its summer peak; the humidity was staggering for Europeans who had only disembarked about three months previously and who had been sent on operations without a chance to become acclimatized. The hospitals were full, and Dr Hocquard put much of the blame on the unrealistic loads the men were obliged to carry; a few weeks on campaign left them so worn down that they were easy prey for fever. June temperatures of 96°F (35°C) and high humidity prevented skin evaporation; the sweat ran off a man's fingertips as if from a dripping tap, and even raising an arm felt like lifting a weight. Food spoiled in hours – the market price of a freshly killed chicken fell from 80 centimes to 20 between 7am and 1pm. While the French troops were as yet surprisingly free from cholera, the deadly local water – in the words of a later chemist, 'a broth of cultures' – still made dysentery a constant fact of life despite precautionary orders. A parched man had no way to boil water when he snatched a chance to refill his bottle on the march, from a ditch filled with run-off from fields fertilized with human excrement.[22]

By far the most widespread scourge, in both the Delta and the hills, was the endemic malaria, which ensured that an alarming proportion of any Legion company were always sick – sometimes dangerously so – for days on end. The literature was unhelpful, recommending that 'men must not fall asleep without covering their stomachs with their sashes' and that they cover their eyes when sleeping in the open air. Koch's theoretical work on bacteria and the identification of the anopheline mosquito as the vector were still 10 to 15 years in the future, and even the modern-minded Dr Hocquard noted that it was unhealthy to sleep near reedbeds because of their 'miasma'. Although quinine had been known for about 50 years, before the First World War its correct use and dosage were still matters of controversial guesswork. In the 1880s–90s it was wrongly believed to be simply a curative rather than a preventative, so often was not given until symptoms appeared, by which time it was too late. Moreover, some doctors gave daily doses of only 200mg when five or six times that amount would have been more appropriate.

Between 1884 and 1888 the death rate from malaria in Tonkin was 68 per 1,000 cases – a not apparently dramatic 7 per cent – but men who recovered continued to carry the parasites and suffered recurrent attacks thereafter, potentially multiplying that percentage each time. In heavily infested areas repeated reinfection left them particularly vulnerable to the much more dangerous blackwater fever. The first symptom of this, before the tell-tale dark urine and jaundiced skin became apparent, was a shivering chill and collapse; consequently there was a great deal of misdiagnosis as simple malaria, especially among troops who were days from the nearest doctor. Quinine was ineffective against blackwater fever, and continued dosing was actually harmful; the only possible treatments were complete rest, nursing care and a diet of fruit juices, broth or milk – none of which was readily available in a bamboo hut up-country. Fatalities from blackwater fever routinely ran at 20 per cent of cases, and often rose to 50 per cent.[23] Just as lethal, and as basically untreatable, was scrub typhus, spread by rat mite larvae on the undergrowth and elephant grass; unlike other diseases this was more dangerous for older rather than younger soldiers, since it attacked the heart, lungs and circulation.

*

IN BEIJING, THE DEFEATS of the spring of 1884 enraged the Dowager Empress, but a court faction led by a military realist, the Viceroy Li Hung-chang, had increased their influence. On 11 May, at Tientsin, Li agreed draft peace terms with a Captain Fournier; these allowed for a Chinese withdrawal from Tonkin (including both regulars and Black Flags) without an explicit surrender of suzerainty. Fatally, however, the timetable for the withdrawal – into Guangxi by 6 June, and into the more distant Yunnan by 26 June – was the subject of a later private conversation that was not written into the formal treaty, and Fournier was too eager to cable news of his success. He informed General Millot of those dates, and Prime Minister Ferry announced them to the National Assembly on 20 May.

On 6 June, announcing that Chinese suzerainty had been signed away by Beijing, the French envoy Patenôtre imposed a further treaty on the Anna-mese king at Hué, insisting on the destruction of the ancient silver seal of fealty to the Dragon Throne. This was not King Hiep Hoa who had signed the Harmand treaty the previous August; the regents had done away with him in November, replacing him with yet another puppet, Kien Phuoc. This disposable figurehead would also die suddenly, on 31 July, and the regents enthroned the 14-year-old Ham Nghi – the fifth King of Annam since the previous July.

Any hope of immediate peace was short-lived. Unaware that Li Hung-chang had not dared to discuss the withdrawal dates with Beijing – whose orders to their troops were therefore simply to hold their present positions and await instructions – General Millot sent a battalion under Lieutenant-Colonel Dugenne north-east from Bac Ninh to occupy Lang Son, the strategic town just short of the Chinese border. On 23 June, after a march delayed by washed-out roads and monsoon weather, the column came upon a Chinese post north of Bac Le. When its commander asked for time to seek further instructions, Dugenne gave the Chinese officer an hour to pull out. His attempt to enforce this bad-tempered ultimatum cost him 22 men killed and 60 wounded, and a painful retreat from what the French ridiculously called 'a treacherous ambush'.[24]

The international situation then spiralled out of control, as Jules Ferry, Admiral Courbet, and the war party at the Dowager Empress' court embroiled France and China in a costly and ultimately pointless naval war on the mainland coast and Formosa that lasted nine months, from August 1884 to April 1885. It was against that background that some of the Foreign Legion's most notable actions were fought in Tonkin – where, on 27 August 1884, Liu Yung-fu of the Black Flags was formally named as a Chinese general with responsibility for local operations.[25]

WHILE PARIS AND BEIJING MANOEUVRED, and Admiral Courbet shelled Chinese ports, the Expeditionary Corps faced three distinct enemies: Chinese regulars from Yunnan and Guangxi; the Chinese-sponsored Black Flag irregulars; and local outlaws, whose banditry was sometimes lent a colour of patriotism by the encouragement of the hostile regents in Hué. Villagers both on the upper rivers and deep inside the Delta continued to suffer from persistent raiding by large numbers of these 'pirates'. In the Delta, French counter-insurgency was hampered by the involvement of local mandarins incited by Hué. While enjoying a degree of immunity from French arrest, the mandarins passed information to gang leaders; with their connivance the pirates acted in many areas as a pseudo-government, levying protection-money for their own and the mandarins' profit. Both sides depended on spies and informers, but since only a tiny handful of officers learned Vietnamese, the French were always at a great disadvantage. The rest were reliant on interpreters of questionable loyalty from among the 'lettered' minority, whose employment made them obvious targets for bribery. Minor operations up and down the waterways brought little but heatstroke and frustration; a company or two of local Skirmishers and French infantry, either marching across country or landed from boats, would usually arrive too late to catch the raiders, and most of the few successes were the result of chance encounters. Just a day's journey from Hanoi, isolated posts and gunboat crews would see the glow of burning villages almost every night.

While the Black Flags mainly haunted the upper river valleys, in the lowlands the bandits were usually local criminals dispersed in small groups in hamlets whose elders were bribed or terrorized into providing refuge. They kept in touch with one another – there were two loose networks, in the western and eastern Delta – and pooled their strength to attack promising targets.[26] A few men had flintlocks or very occasionally a more modern firearm, but most carried swords and lances. They approached a village after dark by several separate paths, surrounding it quietly while a few scouts crept forward to reconnoitre the defences. The typical village was protected and masked by a high earth bank planted with a thick bamboo hedge rising to perhaps 12 feet; the ironwood gates could defy a battering-ram, and a look-out kept watch from a stilted bamboo platform. Cutting a stealthy gap through the hedge was difficult – the village dogs slept lightly, and an alert watchman often had time to rouse his neighbours. At the sound of the alarm the villagers would rush to barricade their houses and arm themselves with machetes, fishing-tridents, hunting bows and fire-hardened bamboo spears; if the attackers were few and spotted early they might be driven off empty-handed. But if the raiders numbered scores – or even hundreds, which was not unknown in these years of anarchy – then the houses would be burned down over the villagers' heads while the bandits pillaged, killed and raped at leisure, often taking women with them when they left.

During a gunboat trip up the Clear river in December 1884, Dr Hocquard's eyes were drawn by the behaviour of feeding birds to three corpses that came bobbing past, two men and a woman; they had been impaled lengthways on thick bamboo stakes, and various hacked-off body parts were festooned around their necks on cords or stuffed into their mouths. All types of 'pirates' made examples of villagers who resisted them unsuccessfully, and with only word-of-mouth to spread their message they expressed it in the most unmistakable and eye-catching ways.[27] When the appalled doctor exclaimed at this sight, the young Navy lieutenant told him that he routinely saw such evidence of Black Flag activity upriver; a few days previously he had passed four bodies impaled along a single stake. Considering (if we can bear to) the mechanics of creating such a human *brochette*, it becomes easier to understand French complacency over the Annamese law sentencing captured pirates to death by instant beheading. French witnesses to these executions who published protests in the liberal press perhaps failed to take sufficient account of the local context.[28]

ON 8 SEPTEMBER 1884, GENERAL BRIÈRE DE L'ILE passed his 1st Brigade to Colonel Dujardin and took command of the Tonkin Expeditionary Corps. By that date the CET counted about 18,000 all ranks; the six infantry regiments numbered some 16,900 men, of whom nearly half (7,300) were Vietnamese, and the rest marching regiments each comprising three battalions of Naval Infantry, Algerian Skirmishers, Legion, *joyeux*, or Metropolitan Line infantry.[29]

As the 1884 rainy season came to an end, Brière reacted to Chinese activity far south of Lang Son. There were reported to be two groups of about 5,000 and 3,000 regulars; to create some fresh air between them and the north-east approaches to the Delta, Brière despatched General de Négrier

with three parallel columns totalling perhaps 3,500 men. In the east, Lieutenant-Colonel Donnier was to lead four Legion and two Line companies up
the Thai Binh and Luc Nam rivers towards Chu; to Donnier's west, Négrier
himself would take nine Line companies and strong artillery up the Mandarin Road to Kep, while Major de Mibielle's Algerian battalion would float
between them according to need.[30] On 6 October, Donnier advanced upriver
with three gunboats, landing infantry to picket ahead up the banks. Two
Legion companies ran into resistance at once, but Donnier drove the Chinese
back steadily, capturing the defended village of Chu on the 10th. By nightfall
his force had suffered 32 killed and 119 wounded, including Captain Beynet
of the Legion and 2 other company commanders. Some Chinese units
retreated quickly after contact, but others did not.

On 8 October, Négrier's 1,500-odd Line soldiers reached the village of
Cham a few miles short of Kep, to surprise Chinese troops holding a series
of defence works and forts across their path and on heights to their right.
These were not the sort of Chinese who had fled before them at Bac Ninh.
One unit manoeuvred aggressively under artillery and infantry fire, using
the terrain well to get a determined counter-attack within 150 yards of the
gun line, and stood their ground returning fire for a good ten minutes before
withdrawing (one of their bullets broke Négrier's leg). The Chinese in the
fortified village itself showed themselves to be courageous and seasoned
soldiers, holding out for three hours under shellfire and throwing back two
assaults. During the five-hour battle Dr Hocquard (whose horse was killed
under him) could not persuade his ambulance coolies to follow him forward
and recover the wounded, whom he had to tend as well as he could in the
front line under the inadequate cover of a bamboo thicket. The heat was
pitiless, and Hocquard describes a man with smashed legs dragging himself
towards a patch of shade with his clawed hands. The village finally fell to
the third attack, in savage close-quarter fighting among the blazing houses;
then, at last, the sky clouded over and a blessed drizzle began to fall on the
delirious wounded. In the last redoubt the Chinese forced Négrier's *lignards*
to kill them all where they stood.

In a pagoda that night Hocquard was extracting bullets in a pool of
candlelight, with a line of wounded laid out on the shadowed stone floor
under the remote gaze of the Buddha. The French had suffered 32 dead and
61 wounded; it would have been many more had the Chinese been better
shots with their Remingtons and Mausers, but they habitually fired with
the butt tucked into their armpit rather than shouldering it properly, so

most shots went high. Some of their officers had shown real leadership and the troops great individual bravery, giving the lie to the French slander that they would never stand a charge; they had left perhaps 600 dead on the field.[31]

Nevertheless, General de Négrier was still confident that he could take Lang Son (his nickname was *'Mau-len'*, from the Vietnamese for 'Hurry up'; for German légionnaires this was also a pleasing pun on 'grumble'). For the time being Paris forbade this for political reasons, and while his leg mended during November and December 1884 he was limited to sending out aggressive columns through the hills. When Négrier was finally let off the leash, the Chinese would enjoy by chance the advantage of a coordination that they seemed unable to achieve by design, and the eventual outcome would be memorable both for the Legion and for the French prime minister. First, however, the eyes of General Brière's staff at Viet Tri were drawn in another direction.

TUYEN QUANG, HELD SINCE JUNE 1884 by Major Fraudet's two companies from I/LE, stood in the path of Liu Yung-fu's ambition to take Black Flags and Yunnan regulars back down the Red and Clear river corridor, and during September, Fraudet's patrols found many signs that they were arriving. The old fort sat on the west bank of an elbow of the Clear river (about 150 yards wide here), in a swampy bowl overlooked by steep, wooded hills to the north, west and south and opposite on the east bank. There was hardly any cultivated land on the riverbank, but fishermen occupied hamlets spread a few hundred yards apart down the west bank below the fort.

On the night of 12 October 1884, shots were fired at the walls and the nearest village was burned, and this harassment was repeated with increasing frequency and boldness over the following weeks. In this unhealthy post Fraudet's 3rd and 4th Companies had been badly weakened by dysentery and fever, and he had too few fit légionnaires to risk sorties out of sight of the walls. Escorted supply boats came up from Phu Doan in the first week of November, but when the empty junks returned downriver on the 12th and 16th they were ambushed, and the gunboats *Trombe* and *Revolver* had to fight their way through. By now the fort was under fire almost every night, and General Brière decided that the garrison should be replaced. On 16 November a convoy sailed from Viet Tri under command of the Legion's Colonel Duchesne: 1st and 2nd Companies I/LE, two companies of Naval Infantry, one from 1st Tonkinese Skirmishers, and an artillery section.

The upper Clear river was shallow, and the junks and gunboats had to pick their way between rocks and gravel banks in cold, misty weather. By 18 November they were into rapids and gorges north of Phu Doan; the shallow-draft gunboats could keep going but not the junks, so the troops had to disembark on the west bank and march in Indian file through the thick forest from Hoa Moc, to cut across a big eastwards loop of the river (see Map 5a). On the morning of the 19th they ran into about 200 entrenched Chinese; during a brisk three-hour fight a Legion platoon became lost while moving through the forest, but by pure chance came out on the Chinese flank and drove them off. About 60 Chinese bodies were found; 8 *marsouins* and a légionnaire were hastily buried, and the column pressed on, carrying their 22 wounded. Late that afternoon they arrived at Tuyen Quang, where the gunboats joined them on the 20th.[32]

For three days, while the garrisons changed over, Duchesne sent out strong fighting patrols, but on 23 November he headed downriver to install the Naval Infantry companies at Phu Doan. Tuyen Quang was provisioned for four months, and entrusted to just over 600 soldiers – two-thirds of them légionnaires – led by the 36-year-old Major Marc Edmond Dominé, and supported by the small gunboat *Mitrailleuse* anchored opposite the fort. The infantry had 500 rounds per man; the gunners had two little 40mm and two 80mm mountain guns, all rather weary, and the sailors two light Hotchkiss pieces (with only 2,500 rounds – not a generous supply for quick-firers). Dominé was an intelligent but rather dour man, a St Cyrien from a modest background, who had been heard to boast that his grandfather and seven great-uncles had all been sergeants at Waterloo. He had been wounded with the 2nd Zouaves in the Sud-Oranais, and a second bad wound during the Franco-Prussian War had left him with a permanently disabled right arm, but he had transferred to the unlovely 2nd Bat d'Af in order to get out to Tonkin. The légionnaires at first regarded him with blank-faced reserve, but that would change.[33]

The fort itself was a square enclosure of dry-laid masonry walls about 9 feet high and 3 feet thick; it measured 300 yards on each side, with half-moon bastions in the centre of each – that on the south-east was within a few yards of the riverbank (see Map 5b). Roughly 30 yards inside the curtain wall the yellow earth rose in a steep bank, then sloped up to a hilltop about 120 feet above river level in the northern part of the enclosure. The four guns were emplaced on this '*mamelon*', which was crowned with a number of brick pagodas used as the headquarters, stores, hospital and officers' quarters. Over the next few weeks the garrison worked hard to improve the neglected defences, under the keen eyes of the sapper Sergeant Jules Bobillot (a 25-year-old former Parisian journalist), though hampered by the fact that there were only 27 picks and 40 shovels in the fort. Many shelters and internal trenches were dug, to allow free movement under cover and to seal off, if necessary, parts of the enclosure. Outside, a ditch and palisade fronted the walls all around, and the fringe of the jungle was cleared back where possible. There were a number of pagodas here and there on the riverside flats, and the nearest, between the southern corner of the fort and rocky outcrops on the riverbank, was fortified and tied into the perimeter; this salient commanding the southern approaches was christened 'Little Gibraltar', and would be held by Captain Dia's Tonkinese company. A blockhouse was also built on a wooded spur that overlooked the walls from only 200 yards to the west. But however Dominé improved his fields of fire, the enemy's would be better, and he had just 550 infantry to cover a perimeter of 1,200 yards.

Native scouts and French patrols reported sightings and contacts, and intelligence suggested that there were at least 5,000 Yunnan regulars and Black Flags within 10 miles to the west and south. The fort had no signal lamp, and all communication with Phu Doan and Viet Tri was by native couriers on foot or in light, fast 'basket-boats'. On 7 December campfires were seen to the north-west, and a company sortie ran into a reported 500 Chinese. On the 17th the last supply convoy reached the fort; when the sampans left they took back about 30 sick men from the garrison (Dominé had worked to improve the sanitation, but the damp hollow of Tuyen Quang was still something of a cesspit). On 21 December, Captain Cattelin's légionnaires fought a successful patrol action, and there was firing at the walls on the night of the 22nd. (The next day the wives of the Tonkinese Skirmishers appeared; forbidden to accompany their men, they had slipped away from Phu Doan into the forest, braving tigers and Black Flags to join them at the fort.)

On 31 December the blockhouse reported that about 500 men, screened by skirmishers, had approached within 1,500 yards and then withdrawn. This sounded ominously like regular troops practising. The night of 10 January 1885 was the first of several in succession when Black Flags tested the alertness of the garrison, shooting blind at the parapets to draw fire. Growing numbers of campfires were seen in the hills every night; and as the cold fog lifted at mid-morning on 16 January, lookouts spotted men digging, perhaps 600 yards to the south. The work continued steadily, and the shape of a classic 'first parallel' emerged – a continuous line of trenches facing the south of the fort.[34] Assembled by morning drum signals, gangs of men could be seen carrying timber and fascines (brushwood bundles) to shore up the earth being shifted in baskets; this was not the work of Black Flags but real engineering, by Yunnan troops who had learned their art from the Muslim ore-miners of their province. A few shells from the fort dispersed them briefly, but Lieutenant Derappe did not have the ammunition for a continuous bombardment. Soon another trench was snaking forwards from the parallel, around the southern face of the blockhouse spur west of the fort.

THE FIRST MAJOR ATTACK struck the post at 5.30am on 26 January. Rifle fire was heard from the south, and villagers came fleeing from the glow of flames through the fog to huddle in the ditches outside the walls. Under cover of the morning murk three columns each of about 700 attackers approached Little Gibraltar, the northern wall, and Sergeant Weber's 18 légionnaires in the blockhouse. Flanking fire from the fort and the gunboat repulsed all these attempts, which left about 50 dead on the field for the reward of only two French wounded; but in the south the Chinese fell back only a few hundred yards to a dyke well ahead of their first trench line, and they continued to fire from its cover.[35]

After the failure of these direct assaults, for several days both sides concentrated on digging. The Chinese extended their sideways trenches and pushed saps (zigzagging approach trenches) forwards, under constant covering fire from four rampart guns that swept the parapets from high ground. The garrison deepened their internal trenches and shelters, and completed a short covered trench from the east gate to the riverbank for water parties. A Legion platoon of picked snipers harassed the siege work; on 27 January a bugler would blow a call each time they made a hit, but that stopped when Private Taube was killed by a Chinese sniper.

It was clear that the blockhouse garrison would soon be cut off and doomed to fall to a night rush, when the fort guns would not be able to support them; but by day Derappe could still ensure a clear path for Sergeant Weber, who brought his men in without loss on 30 January. The Chinese immediately occupied the spur and began work on a gun battery; there was already scattered shelling from hills to the south-west, and the next day guns also opened fire from a height on the east bank. By 1 February, Sergeant Bobillot had reported that a second parallel was being developed from a sap-head 160 yards from the south-west wall, and by the night of 5/6 February saps had reached the fort ditch on both west and north corners; the palisade was gapped, and trenches sprouted sideways to clutch the base of the walls. When the inevitable infantry assaults did come, it was clear that their main objectives would be the north-west wall and the west corner, thus limiting the amount of useful flanking fire that Little Gibraltar in the south could deliver. The textbook response would have been infantry sorties with powder charges to kill engineers and wreck the works, but any such attempt by daylight would have been suicidal under the continuous short-range firing at the parapets. Some 6,000 incoming rounds of all calibres were counted during a single day, and the garrison were suffering a steady drain of dead and wounded.

On 7 February, Chinese guns on the blockhouse spur opened fire, and at such short range they quickly perfected their aim; bombardment now became the norm, forcing the garrison into their trenches for all movement around the perimeter. On the 8th, Sergeant Bobillot spotted earth piling up behind a trench facing the north-west wall: the Yunnan engineers were starting to tunnel a mine, to set off explosives under the walls. Bobillot responded by starting a counter-mine, with his few sappers instructing rotating gangs of legionnaires.[36] From now on Chinese mines from round the whole western quadrant seemed to breed almost nightly, and Bobillot was hard-pressed to keep track of them. On 10 February, Major Dominé noted that the shelling included air-burst shrapnel and some kind of incendiary.

On the night of 12/13 February infantry massed in trenches about 40 yards outside the north-west wall, and in the pre-dawn darkness the first mine was blown; it cracked the wall and blew a hole through under the parapet, but it did not make a breach. The Chinese attacked anyway, trying to drive the légionnaires from the parapets and scramble over; but when they gave up after about 45 minutes they left the ditch piled with their dead. As soon as the morning fog cleared the relentless bombardment and sniping resumed. The following night another mine went off, this time blowing down 15 yards of wall at the west corner. The Chinese rushed up the rubble ramp into the breach only to find that it was funnel-shaped, so that Captain Moulinay's légionnaires were able to hold the narrow inner break – though at a cost of five killed and six wounded – and the breach was later sealed off with a hasty trench and palisading. Corporal Beulin was promoted sergeant on the spot for leading four volunteers to bring in a comrade blown outside the wall (although he proved to be dead already). The next night there were no assaults; Lieutenant Goulet, Sergeant-Major de Berghes and 30 of their Tonkinese Skirmishers celebrated the Tet new year with a successful sortie from Little Gibraltar, giving the besiegers good reason themselves to be nervous of the dark.[37]

DURING THE FOURTH WEEK the siege ground on without assaults, although each night the duty officers had to keep their platoons alert for any alarm (and each night young Ensign Sènés slipped ashore from the gunboat and up the water trench to the south-east gate, to get the latest news and orders from Dominé). The stench of the unburied dead outside the walls was nauseating; to break the defenders' rest and work on their nerves the Yunnan soldiers constantly blew trumpets and the Black Flags their moaning conch-shells, and every night men crept close to Little Gibraltar and shouted enticements and threats to the Tonkinese Skirmishers. By day the légion-naires took their turns to work on the defences and in counter-mines, or sniped their tormenters when a clear shot made it worth the cost of a cartridge. The Chinese never stopped digging; the French officers obsessively swept the surroundings with their binoculars, trying to predict the next threats, but the saps were now protected and masked by palisades.

Bullets whined off the stone parapets whenever a man showed himself, and all movement outside the communication trenches was made at a crouching run; their own digging had turned the greasy yellow earth of the enclosure into a squalid building-site, and the brick pagodas were battered and holed by shells. By 1885 the légionnaires' curtained képi had been replaced with a conspicuous white cork helmet, but these were darkened with drab cloth covers; many men had acquired loose, dark-coloured Viet-namese *cao ao* in preference to their issue white linen blouses, and after weeks in trenches their red or white trousers were too filthy with earth to draw fire. While the days were sometimes warm, the nights here in the hills could be bitter, and the men were glad of the heavy blue wool tunics that the Legion had drawn from Naval Infantry stores – perhaps especially on those dreary mornings when they hastily buried another comrade before the fog lifted. Dr Vincens did what he could for the growing numbers of wounded lying on the hard, straw-covered floor of the hospital pagoda, but the heavy soft-lead bullets of those days made huge, bone-smashing wounds fouled with shreds of dirty clothing, and shock and sepsis were frequent killers. When a nominally Catholic légionnaire was wrapped in a native mat and dropped into his last cold bed he was usually sent on his way with a verse read by the compassionate Captain Borelli; there were few Protestants here, even among the many Alsatians, and Pastor Boisset could do little but help tend the wounded.[38]

Being passive targets and unable to strike back tempts frustrated soldiers to take risks (Lieutenant Naert's men amused themselves by popping up to empty latrine-buckets down into the nearest trench). Major Dominé was a tirelessly encouraging commander; the légionnaires now trusted him completely, but his orders that they build a new central redoubt had discouraging implications, and he understood that for the sake of morale he had to balance caution with occasional outlets for their frustration. In the early hours of 18 February, Sergeant Beulin was allowed to lead 24 volunteers out before dawn to hit a new sap that had been spotted; it was not a success – they did plenty of damage and killed five engineers, but lost four of their own number. On the 18th the Chinese unveiled more guns on the blockhouse hill and the bombardment intensified; Lieutenant Derappe reckoned that the batteries now had two field guns, three howitzers and two mortars. Morale among the Tonkinese Skirmishers slumped that day when their Captain Dia was killed in Little Gibraltar, and among the whole garrison when the popular Sergeant Bobillot took a mortal neck wound.

Major Dominé had been kept in intermittent touch with Viet Tri by a series of extremely courageous Vietnamese couriers making the 80-mile round trip down river and back by small boat and on foot. Now, on 21 February, he sent a message asking – for the first time – when the fort could hope for relief. He was a realist, and he knew that for the past six weeks the bulk of the Expeditionary Corps had been committed to a major operation far away on the Lang Son front, but concern for the strength and health of his garrison now obliged him to ask for help. That day the sapper Corporal Cacheux warned him that he believed the Chinese were ready to explode another mine.

THE MOST INTENSE FIGHTING of the siege began soon after 6am on the morning of 22 February. Shouts and movement were heard in the mist outside the north-west wall, and Captain Cattelin called his guards back from the parapet just before a deafening explosion wrecked 15 yards of it. As the stones pattered down, Chinese infantry came clambering up into the breach through the smoke, but rather hesitantly. Captain Moulinay (a promoted sergeant-major from the Franco-Prussian War, and a veteran of Son Tay and Bac Ninh) confidently led his duty platoon in a charge that drove them back easily – at which point a second mine exploded right under the légionnaires' feet, killing Moulinay and the men around him, and the Chinese surged forward. As a few blackened and stupefied survivors crawled back, Major Dominé passed them at the head of Sergeant Cremp's reserve platoon – and a third mine blew, only about 10 yards to one flank. The fighting lasted until 7am, and in the end the assault was repulsed, but only at the price of 14 killed and about 40 wounded. (Pastor Boisset recorded that the explosion had driven both Moulinay's thighbones up into his groin). Private Hinderschmitt went down the breach four times to bring in wounded men, but two were shot dead on his back as he carried them up; he himself was hit on the fifth attempt, but 20 cursing légionnaires charged out without permission and dragged him and the other casualties inside – they were determined not to see their mates' heads raised mockingly on bamboo stakes above the nearest trench.[39]

At this rate the three weakened companies would soon be unable to cover their perimeter. After two more days of shelling, sniping and crippling lack of sleep, at about 4.45 on the morning of 24 February the Chinese tried different tactics. This time there was no preliminary mine; they gathered quietly in the fog at the very foot of the roughly barricaded breaches in the west corner and the north-west wall, then rushed up in force. At both points they reached the head of the breach and fired inside the fort, and both Sergeant-Major Hurbaud and Sergeant Thévent fell during the guards' struggle to hold the stormers back. Then Captain Cattelin arrived at one breach with a meagre half-platoon, bugle braying, and Warrant Officer Reber at the other, and both succeeded in clearing the parapets with the bayonet; the corpses they later rolled back into the ditch wore the uniforms of three different Chinese regular units. Corporal Cacheux reported signs of no fewer than five more mines.

Before dawn on 25 February guards at the west corner heard movement in time to take cover; when a mine blew they were able to occupy the breach immediately and meet the assault head-on. Another rush hit the old north-west breach, but again Cattelin led about 25 men in a counter-charge and threw them back; the night cost the Legion another 4 dead and 12 wounded. However, under cover of darkness that evening a messenger slipped into the fort with a reply to Dominé's appeal of the 21st: word had reached Phu Doan that far off in the eastern hills the Expeditionary Corps had finally taken Lang Son a week earlier, and that a relief column was well on its way. Lang Son was less than 100 miles away on the map, but twice that on the march;

the defenders began obsessive but pointless speculations about feasible routes, rates of march, terrain and the effects of the weather. They needed every encouragement Dominé could give them during the next three sleepless nights, during which the Chinese attacked relentlessly.

On the night of 27/28 February a mine blew under the south-west wall, and successive assaults hit this and the other breaches over the following four hours. The fighting came to hand-to-hand at the hasty barricades built across the tops of the rubble ramps; the Chinese threw powder-charges and fire-pots into the faces of the defenders, who lost another dozen men before the storming parties grudgingly fell back over their heaped dead. The garrison now had to guard six breaches, totalling 120 yards of holed wall. While more could still handle their rifles in static positions, Dominé had only about 180 légionnaires still fit to take part in counter-attacks. Some 300 shells hit the fort each day, as well as perhaps 2,000 rounds from rampart guns and small arms.

On the night of the 28th another messenger slipped in: Colonel Giovanninelli was only a few miles away with 3,000 men. In the early hours of 1 March, lookouts saw flares in the southern sky. There were no assaults that night, and the next day the shelling was slacker, though the rifle fire on the parapets was undiminished. Every man strained his eyes and his imagination towards the south (it was on 2 March that one sergeant's mind finally broke, and he blew his own brains out). In mid-afternoon they heard the dull thunder of cannon fire, but the echoes among the hills gave no real idea of direction or distance. On the night of 2/3 March more flares were seen, and Dominé fired his own in reply, but these silent reachings-out in the darkness conveyed nothing beyond the bare reassurance of survival. Before dawn the garrison heard a faint rattle of rifle fire far away, but then nothing more.

The morning of 3 March was eerily quiet; outside the walls nothing could be heard through the fog but the occasional squabbling of buzzards and big white-collared crows as they picked at the rotting dead. When the mist began to lift the silence was unbroken – not a shot was fired, and there was no sign of life in the trenches. After an hour or two Dominé sent out a patrol, which soon confirmed the extraordinary truth: the Yunnan troops and Black Flags had simply gone, leaving nothing but their trash and their abandoned corpses. More men were sent out, to pick through the nearly 5 miles of trenches and dugouts that surrounded the fort; in just one redoubt – inexplicably – they stumbled on a handful of Chinese, and Private Streibler became the last man to die when he threw himself in front of Captain Borelli, saving his Officer's life at the expense of his own.[40]

At about 2pm on 3 March 1885 – the thirty-seventh day of the siege – the first Algerian scouts of Giovanninelli's relief force came cautiously through the fringe of the forest from the south. In the dank hollow of Tuyen Quang, 'All the approaches – churned, blasted, lamentable – were covered with corpses, and the carrion rotted in the air . . . The pestilential emanations of all these putrid corpses turned your stomach.' At last able to leave the fort, Pastor Boisset, too, was wandering about the battlefield: 'What a spectacle! What desolation! What ruin! . . . Our liberators cannot believe their eyes.'[41] Twenty-four hours later the commander-in-chief himself, General Brière de l'Ile, addressed extravagant praise to Major Dominé and the dirty, sallow-faced soldiers drawn up before him on the flats by the river. Of 400-odd légionnaires, about one in three had been killed or wounded.[42]

Among the relief force, Captain Cattelin's légionnaires saw men of the 3rd Company of their battalion, who had a story of their own to tell.

FACED WITH A WAR against China, the ministry had made a number of decisions that directly affected the Legion. On 15 November 1884, the 3rd and 4th Battalions were ordered from Algeria to join the first two in the Far East, and after a six-week voyage, Major Schoeffer's III/LE disembarked at Haiphong on 12 January 1885. (Major Vitalis' IV/LE was diverted to join the force that Admiral Lespès had landed on the north coast of Formosa in October 1884. They would arrive in the stagnant and over-extended Qui Lung beachhead on 21 January 1885, to join a brigade that in three months had been reduced by cholera and scrub typhus from 1,800 men to 600 capable of bearing arms, and whose dead were being dug up nightly by Chinese infiltrators for the sake of the bounty on French heads.)[43]

While these battalions were at sea, the name of their regiment had been changed; a decision to expand the Legion led on 14 December 1884 to a decree dividing it once again into 1er and 2e Régiments Étrangers, each to be raised to four battalions as soon as possible (the 1st Foreign was com-manded by Lieutenant-Colonel Grisot, who fourteen years previously had fought with V/RE in the streets of Paris). The two battalions already in Tonkin became the 1st and 2nd of 1st Foreign Regiment (I/ and II/1st RE), and the newcomers the III/ and IV/2nd RE.[44] Collectively, of course, the corps continued to be known as the Foreign Legion.

On 7 January 1885, General Brière de l'Ile was freed from the divided control of the ministries of the Navy and of War; from now on the Tonkin command would answer to the latter alone, whose latest minister, General Lewal, authorized Brière to react vigorously to Chinese movements north-east of the Delta. The troopers *Comorin* and *Chandernagor* had brought him two fresh battalions (Schoeffer's légionnaires and Major Comoy's *turcos*); these would be useful for a drive in strength towards Lang Son and the Chinese frontier, provided that he could solve the considerable problems of gathering enough supplies, and the coolies to carry them, at his forward base at Chu. The shortage of porters was serious; despite exceptional inducements offered there were never enough, and French agents sought contract labour as far afield as Hong Kong. Without enough porters, the troops had to carry more ammunition and five days' rations, raising the weight of their packs to about 80lbs – much too heavy in this terrain and climate, particularly for the young Line conscripts.[45]

Chivvied by steam launches, scores of heavily loaded junks, sampans and gunboats ferried men and matériel up the Luc Nam river to camps of bamboo hutments, Chinese tents and house-sized stacks of boxes and barrels stretching 2 miles over the grassy plain of Chu. Dr Hocquard gives a vivid picture of the diversity and bustle of the camps in late January, as some 7,200 troops and 4,500 coolies prepared for the march on Lang Son. The porters had been tempted with lavish rates of pay given directly to them rather than to their unscrupulous mandarins, plus new hats, palm-leaf rain-capes and blankets in the red colour of happiness. One useful novelty was the arrival, after General Brière's repeated requests, of some big Algerian mules to supplement the ponies used to pull and carry his artillery.[46]

On 23 January news reached Brière of the siege of Tuyen Quang, but the momentum of his campaign could not be dissipated; Major Dominé's légionnaires would have to hold off the Yunnan incursion as best they could until the Expeditionary Corps had settled matters with the Guangxi army.

ON 3 FEBRUARY 1885 the Lang Son column left its camps at Chu and headed north for the hills. The force took two hours to pass Dr Hocquard's field ambulance unit waiting to take its place at the rear of 2nd Brigade, which included two battalions of the Legion.[47] The sun burned off the mist as the muddy track appeared slowly climbing into the hills, revealing forest and tall elephant grass closing in on each side. General Brière was again avoiding the direct Mandarin Road north, and had chosen a more punishing parallel route through the heights to its east; that night they camped in the

rain, forbidden to light tell-tale fires. Next morning found the troops inching
up a narrow path on the flank of a 45° slope, with creeper-covered rockfaces
on their left and a steep drop to the treetops of the valley on their right.
When they reached the crest, an uninterrupted succession of bare mountains
stretched ahead, with the narrow Deo Van pass twisting its way into them
between steep heights riven with gulleys. Négrier's 2nd Brigade was in the
lead – Dr Hocquard's journal:

> To prevent any surprises, infantrymen had to follow the crests along the left
> and right of this deep pass. From the bottom of the valley we could see the
> little silhouette of each soldier outlined against the sky. Heavily burdened,
> delayed from minute to minute by a rock that had to be climbed, a gulley
> that had to be jumped, the footsloggers made only slow progress ... Already
> night was falling; great black clouds covered the sky, the rain fell in torrents
> ... lightning-flashes flared every few moments, followed almost at once by
> violent rolls of thunder ...[48]

The force came up against three Chinese positions on 4 February, and the
Legion and the 2nd Bat d'Af were sent into the attack up a precipitous slope
crowned by the fort of Thai Ho Ha. Artillery were ordered to climb a hill
just under a mile away to give support; the mules stumbled their way up an
incline of rolling stones, slipping and falling in holes and gulleys masked by
long grass. The légionnaires and 'pimps' were invisible while they descended
the near slopes, but from a ridge Hocquard could soon track their progress
by the waving elephant grass in the valley below; the French guns fired over
their heads, but the fort remained silent. Eventually the doctor saw a single
légionnaire emerge from the foot of the valley, pulling himself up the slope
by grabbing at the undergrowth; other blue-and-white figures followed him,
and soon the whole Legion battalion and two companies of *joyeux* could be
seen clambering steadily up towards the fort – Hocquard particularly noted
that they were still wearing their big marching packs.

The artillery ceased fire; the Chinese fort was still silent; but suddenly,
when the légionnaires were about 400 yards below the palisades, these were
wreathed with the smoke of a crackling fusillade. The légionnaires paused
only to dump their packs, then continued to climb; at 200 yards their buglers
sounded the charge: '... we saw them bound, jumping into the ditches,
crawling up the parapets and disappearing inside the walls. Thick smoke
hid the entrenchments and the action. After ten minutes' fighting ... the
Chinese were running back down the slopes, abandoning their flags.' The

day cost the lives of 17 men including Captain Gravereau of II/1st RE, and 99 others were wounded.[49]

The advance continued on the 5th, laboriously fighting its way past one hill position after another. At the aid station in the rear, wounded officers translated the sounds for Hocquard: first the far-off, muffled crackle of the vanguard's rifles; then the continuous firing of a company sent against a fort, like tearing cloth punctuated by the occasional boom of artillery. Over 10 miles, the doctor counted at least 30 captured or abandoned forts on bare hills on either side of the track. The hostile country closed in again behind the column as they advanced; they had left the occasional outpost on a height, but no secure line of communication back to Chu. For lack of men to escort them back, Hocquard's wounded had to be carried forward with the column, four coolies struggling with each stretcher; at difficult places on the narrow, switchback track the casualties were sometimes tumbled painfully from their litters.

On 6 February the 'Celestials' continued to retreat before the column, abandoning below the heights of Dong Son a large camp of bamboo barracks, where the column rested for three days while ration convoys caught up with them. Two companies and a battery were left here, with 'the malingerers and the lame', when the column marched again on 10 February. The valley road following the Hoa river was pleasant; flocks of jewel-coloured parakeets shimmered through attractive woodland, where orchids grew on old mossy trunks above carpets of wildflowers. The path itself was squalid with the discarded gear of the Chinese retreat; there were fresh graves by every cold campfire, and the French began to find abandoned dead in the elephant grass. (They had often wondered how the Chinese managed to remove their casualties from the battlefield so quickly, and now they found dragged corpses with a noosed rope around the ankles.) The terrain became suddenly more forbidding when the path led steeply up into the bare 1,500-foot mountains separating this route from the Mandarin Road away to the left; ahead lay only 'a chaos of high, arid mountains, sad and desolate ... The Annamese called this desert "the country of hunger and death"'.

After the busily populated lowlands the terrain of this lonely Middle Region seemed mysterious and sinister. The Chinese had long since reduced the scattered villages of the Tho highlanders to charred ruins; unlike the river-jungles to the west, the patches of forest seemed empty of game, and on every side silent hills brooded down on the thin line of troops pushing deeper into the unknown. They were steep, closely packed cones, like a child's drawing of hills; they pushed in aggressively, invading the soldiers' sense of space, their lower slopes dark with trees and impenetrable scrub, the upper shoulders naked green or pale with dense elephant grass. Some broke off into sheer limestone cliffs veiled with hanging lianas, and any little glen of abandoned paddy fields was crowded round by what the French called *calcaires* – weirdly abrupt pillars and blades of karst left by eons of unequal erosion. Fissured and riddled with caves under a cloak of scrub, these natural castles provided an agile enemy with vantage points and hideouts practically unreachable by European troops. All round the horizon the hills climbed, wave after wave, into saw-toothed mountains; sunlit peaks against a blue sky can be uplifting to the spirits, but here China's southern jaws were constantly shadowed by a dismal grey ceiling. The entire landscape seemed to breathe menace from concealment.

An optical telegraph station was set up at the head of the Deo Quan pass, with lines of sight back down to Chu about 20 miles south, and westwards along a transverse valley to the Mandarin Road; there the powerful telescopes could make out dark masses of outflanked Chinese troops marching north for Lang Son.[50] The two brigades took turns in the lead as the column climbed higher up the eastern flank of the mountains, on narrow tracks or earth-cut steps; they passed still-smoking abandoned forts, and waded swollen streams where bridges had been destroyed. On 12 February the Chinese stood, to fight; the 1st Brigade were leading the way through the morning mist across a valley of paddy fields when they came under fire from forts on the left. The Naval Infantry and Algerians took two lines of fortified hills by early afternoon, at a cost of 30 killed and 188 wounded; one sweeping charge by the *marsouins* passed close by Hocquard's forward dressing station, attracting heavy fire that killed three of his patients and shot a canteen out of the hands of a fourth. The tents had not yet come up when nightfall brought heavy rain, and Hocquard was grateful when a passing company of Tonkinese Skirmishers demonstrated their usual uncanny skill by quickly raising sturdy little bamboo and tree-branch shelters over the wounded. Thunderous downpours lasted all night, and few men got any sleep.[51]

At about 10 on the morning of 13 February 1885, the leading troops of 1st Brigade let out a spontaneous cheer as they breasted a ridge and looked down on a wide cultivated plain scattered with villages, pagodas and occasional *calcaires*. An hour later they were marching into the deserted town of Lang Son, the object of French ambitions for nearly two years. Now, at last, General Brière could spare troops to rescue Major Dominé; the fact that he chose to accompany them in person suggests that the garrison at Tuyen Quang had never been far from his thoughts.

THE RELIEF FORCE MARCHED after two days' rest; Négrier's brigade were to stay at Lang Son to watch the frontier, and it was Colonel Gio-vanninelli's *marsouins* and *turcos* who took the Mandarin Road road south for Kep and Bac Ninh on 16 February.[52] It would take them 15 days to cover about 190 miles of bad roads (or no roads at all). By 27 February they had reached Phu Doan, where Giovanninelli picked up reinforcements – two small mixed battalions under Lieutenant-Colonel Maussion, including a company and a half of I/1er RE.[53] From there they marched up the west bank of the Clear river, which would allow resupply by boats. The relief force had met no resistance by the night of 1/2 March when they camped about 3 miles short of Hoa Moc, the village where they would have to swing left to cut off the river bend. From there they sent up flares in the hope that there was still somebody alive at Tuyen Quang to see them, and at first light on the 2nd they set off on what they expected to be the last day of the march, groping up a narrow wooded valley that obliged them to move in three successive groups.

The thick forest limited visibility, and at about noon the leading scouts reported Chinese fortifications only 300 yards ahead, on a line of hills that slanted from behind them to the left, and forwards across the line of march, reaching the river to their right front. There were about 25 separate works; those blocking the route straight ahead, nearest to the river, seemed to be the strongest, and any force attacking these would be under fire from others to the soldiers' left flank and rear. At about 1pm a probing company of Tonkinese Skirmishers were rushed by Black Flags from a trench hidden only 30 yards away in the bush, and the many casualties were beheaded on the spot. After a brief bombardment, at about 2pm Giovanninelli wheeled his Algerian Skirmishers left and up the hills forming the Chinese centre; it was a nightmare climb through 9-foot-high bamboo, and as they broke into the first defences a mine exploded under them.

At about 4pm, Giovanninelli committed his second group, the Naval Infantry wheeling in their turn and attacking uphill on the Algerians' left. Visibility in the thick jungle was down to 10 yards, preventing anything but a primitive frontal attack, and losses were very heavy. The Chinese had built successive lines of thick palisades, masked by the forest; artillery seemed to have little effect, so the infantry had to be led by sappers with axes and powder-charges. They were under intense fire as they tried to break gaps, and the Yunnan style of dugouts – with heavy roofs and rifle-slits at ground level – were deadly to men who often could not spot them until they opened fire at the last moment. Although some positions had been stormed by the time darkness and fog ended the fighting at about 6.15pm, the troops could make no further progress; some pessimists on General Brière's staff even suggested abandoning Dominé to his fate until higher water allowed gun-boats to come up river and shell these forts.

The shivering, worn-out soldiers tried to sleep on their arms in a worry-ingly discontinuous perimeter of captured trenches and jungled hillside, but they were jumpy; the Chinese above them kept up a sharp tapping on the bamboo, fired at the briefest flare of a striking match, and slipped down to collect heads from casualties left helpless in the undergrowth. At about 3am on 3 March they launched a heavy attack; Major Comoy's Algerians responded with a furious blind charge into the mist, while Giovanninelli brought up his last reserve – Maussion's rag-bag of légionnaires, Algerians and Tonkinese – and sent them up on the far left flank. The attack was repulsed, but the men in the front lines must have been tense as the first grey light allowed them to pick out vague shapes close to them in the mist. There was no sound except the dripping of water from the bamboo; and when a Legion captain, sick of waiting, sent a patrol forward, they (like Dominé's men a few miles north) found that the Chinese had slipped away in the night – again, except for a single drunken or forgotten outpost, which was quickly wiped out. The relief force stumbled down the defile to Yuoc village, and that afternoon Dominé's lookouts at Tuyen Quang saw the pale blue vests of the *turcos* filtering through the trees. The battle of Hoa Moc was the costliest of the campaign so far; Giovanninelli lost nearly 500 men killed and wounded, and one source suggests a great many more than that.[54]

When General Brière went back downriver to Hanoi a few days later he was no doubt intent on studying the latest report from General de Négrier, whom he had had left at Lang Son two weeks previously with a single weakened brigade.

AT LANG SON, the Mandarin Road crossed a bridge over the Ky Kung river and continued north for about a mile to the wealthy little Chinese merchant town of Ky Lua; beyond this the plain ended in a hulking cul-de-sac of cliffs, and the road turned sharply left to follow the border hills north-westwards. When the two Legion battalions had arrived on 13 February 1885 they found only the debris of hasty flight, and within days Ky Lua had become the brigade's main camp.

Négrier's immediate problem was feeding his men, since in this bare and devastated country even rice and buffalo-meat were hard to find. Everything had to be portered painfully up from Chu along the precarious tracks, and rations even of tinned meat and Army biscuit had to be cut in order to last until the next convoy.[55] After a week at Lang Son the seven-battalion brigade was still at only about half-strength due to the casualties of the advance, sickness and fatigue, and Chinese troops were reported to be digging in around Dong Dang, a village 8 miles to the north-west. There the road ran parallel and close to the frontier, both of them aligned almost north to south, and the actual crossing into China was in the hills north-east of Dong Dang. The general decided that he needed to clear the Celestials right out of Tonkin, and on 23 February he left only a single company in Ky Lua to guard the sick when he marched for Dong Dang with his three Line battalions, two from the Legion, one Bat d'Af and one of Tonkinese.

Chinese troops were driven out of Dong Dang in a brief, methodical action, their attempt to fire the village being foiled by the speed of the Tonkinese Skirmishers, and in the late afternoon Négrier marched on north-wards.[56] The frontier crossing was only a couple of hours' march through the hills, at the end of a narrow defile; the approach was marked by a tiger's head carved into a rockface, but when they arrived at Cua Ai the soldiers found the renowned Gate of China something of an anti-climax. The claustrophobic gorge was blocked by a small, deserted complex of stone buildings pierced by a vaulted passageway. The men bivouacked for the night on the greasy turf, while inside the buildings Dr Hocquard shared a pile of abandoned rice sacks with huge and active rats.

The next morning he found a 'pretty machine gun' abandoned on the terrace in perfect condition, sheltered by a little straw shed. To the north, the view into China was cut off immediately by a tall mountain, with the road curling away round its foot, guarded by forts on flanking hilltops. A search of the buildings turned up rifles, many boxes of Italian and German cartridges, dynamite and – oddly – spools of waterproofed electric cable. Négrier had his gunners pile the munitions in the gate tunnel and light a long fuse when they left; Hocquard heard the muffled roar as the column reached Dong Dang. There the general posted Major Diguet's II/1st RE, with a platoon of Tonkinese and a couple of mountain guns, before taking the rest of the brigade back to Ky Lua. On 13 March (sadly for the historian) the admirable Dr Hocquard left Lang Son and marched south with his wounded. At Chu he learned of the relief of Tuyen Quang, but less welcome news reached him in Hanoi at the end of the month.[57]

THE COMMANDER-IN-CHIEF informed Négrier on 17 March that Paris had cabled him to say that negotiations with Beijing might benefit from a robust stance on the border. Since Yunnan troops and Black Flags were still showing aggression on the upper Black, Red and Clear rivers, Négrier could not expect immediate reinforcement, but Brière reassured him that he had explained to the ministry that Négrier's supply position made any major offensive action impossible. Nevertheless, Négrier had reason for concern: the veteran General Feng Tzu-tsai had at least 8,000 Guangxi troops camped at Bang Bo only 5 miles beyond the frontier, with more arriving daily, and scouts reported two new Chinese forts now being built inside Tonkin close to Dong Dang.

On 22 March, firing was heard from the north; when Négrier arrived at Dong Dang with two battalions he learnt from Major Diguet that Chinese troops had attacked that morning but had been driven back by the légionnaires without difficulty. With so few men, Négrier decided that passive defence was an invitation to General Feng to get troops south of Lang Son to cut him off, but that a bold attack on Bang Bo might cool Chinese ardour. He marched for the frontier at 7am on 23 March, with the equivalent of three weak battalions – fewer than 2,000 men.[58]

At about 10.30am Major Farret's 143rd Line ran into the new Chinese entrenchments on slopes on the Tonkin side of Cua Ai. They and the 111th failed to take the first fort, but an attack by Diguet's légionnaires showed *le biff* how it should be done, and the second position was abandoned by its defenders under shellfire. Négrier then led his men through the wrecked Gate of China and about a mile into enemy territory; they took two lines of works, and the artillery drove off an attempted manoeuvre against their right flank before the brigade bivouacked for the night. At 9am on 24 March the general ordered the 111th Line forward against the third and last set of positions, while Lieutenant Colonel Herbinger, commander of the Line marching regiment, led the 143rd and the Tonkinese Skirmishers around to the right.

Survivors told Hocquard that in time both regiments took their objectives, but that at about 3pm a massive counter-attack hit the French, forcing the Line troops out of the captured works and into a general retreat. There was some disorder, redeemed only by the Legion battalion's stubborn rear-guard fighting from hill to hill all the way back to Dong Dang. Official losses for what was called the battle of Bang Bo were 72 killed and 190 wounded, of which II/1st RE suffered 12 killed and missing and 52 wounded. The worst aspect for the légionnaires was that some of their wounded had to be left on the field, with predictable consequences.[59]

The first report of this action to reach Paris caused uproar in the National Assembly. The Ferry government was under constant pressure for its inept handling of negotiations with Beijing, for the expense of a Chinese war that Ferry refused even to admit was a war, for the obviously pointless stalemate on Formosa, and (always) for its hollow boasts about suppressing 'piracy' throughout Tonkin. Elections were imminent, and Ferry had to face down his critics with declarations that reports of a setback on the border were inaccurate – Lang Son was still firmly in French hands.[60]

Négrier decided that the isolated position at Dong Dang was indefensible against such numbers, and fell back to Ky Lua, where he was grateful for the arrival of some 1,700 replacements to fill the gaps in his weak battalions.[61] On 27 March the Chinese probed French outposts; early on the 28th their scouts fired on Captain Romani's company of III/2nd RE, and the lifting mist then revealed Guangxi regiments flooding down the road from Dong Dang. Despite the efforts of the artillery, some of the infantry at first recoiled under the weight of numbers, but they rallied and went forwards again, driving the assault off with heavy losses. Only Chinese skirmishers remained in contact, and the flags of the massed columns disappeared over the skyline. French casualty returns listed only 7 killed and missing and 37 wounded – fewer than the cost of the original capture of Dong Dang a month before; but one of the latter was General de Négrier, who was shot in the chest at about 3.30pm. Since no full colonel was present, brigade command passed by seniority to Lieutenant-Colonel Herbinger of the 3rd (Line) Marching Regiment. Accounts of what happened next were shamefully massaged, and the exact truth is lost to us.

HERBINGER HAD GRADUATED FIRST in his St Cyr class of 1861, and after field experience in Mexico and the Franco-Prussian War he had been appointed professor of tactics at the War College (École Supérieure de Guerre).[62] He was obviously a gifted officer, but he may have flinched under the sudden weight of this unexpected responsibility. At all events, he immediately took the decision to abandon Lang Son and retreat that night. He sent a message down the chain of optical signal stations to General Brière, saying (in part):

> I will profit by the night to fall back on Dong Son [Pho Vy] and Thanh Moi
> in two columns. Impossible to maintain our positions for lack of
> ammunition and rations. I personally am going towards Cut and Thanh Moi.
> Major Schoeffer of the Legion takes command of the [Pho Vy] column.

Having already taken this decision, Herbinger consulted the wounded General de Négrier, who dictated to Lieutenant Dégot the following memorandum:

> In my view, it is a matter of holding the important crossings on the roads
> [south of Lang Son] to Pho Vy and Thanh Moi – getting rid of everything
> that could be a nuisance – and in that situation watching what the enemy
> does while only leaving a rearguard at Ky Lua, while all the troops hold
> themselves on the heights of the left bank [?] in such a way that if – as
> I believe – the enemy do not want to attack, it becomes needless to evacuate.
> Lieutenant-Colonel Herbinger, who can see the situation, is the best judge,
> and I only give him this advice as my personal view.[63]

Herbinger would quickly become the designated scapegoat for a retreat that was claimed to be unnecessary, but officers who were present had mixed opinions. Servières of the 2nd Bat d'Af protested that his battalion could have held Lang Son alone; Négrier would write that the Chinese had been soundly beaten, and the fact that they did not pursue the retreat showed that evacuation had indeed been needless; but Schoeffer of III/2nd RE believed they would have attacked again the next day, with every advantage. The available food and ammunition stocks are also disputed; certainly, légionnaires were able to fill their pockets with cartridges from broken chests before leaving, and the commander-in-chief claimed that the garrison had twenty days' rations in hand. Whatever the soundness or otherwise of Herbinger's decision, it was executed badly, and his haste in ordering a move before the fast-approaching nightfall of 28 March was certainly to blame for that.

As the light faded, confusion gripped the camps and streets, and the destruction of stores and equipment – prompted by a lack of porters and mules – was haphazard. Captain Martin's battery of naval 4-pounders were tipped into the river, and a paychest with about 600,000 francs in silver was also dumped. (It was later suggested, with wonderful innocence, that the cash could have been divided up between the troops for the journey, and collected again later.) Kegs of spirits were not smashed but merely abandoned, and inevitably some men got drunk; Herbinger singled out II/1st RE for particular blame, but Major Diguet furiously defended his légionnaires, and we should recall that there was also a Bat d'Af at Lang Son whose uniforms were identical. More than one Legion memoir states that the men were ashamed and upset by what they thought an unnecessary retreat after a successful defence.[64] (The modern reader's willingness to convict Herbinger of needless fears is perhaps illogically influenced by the fact that in October 1950 a second panic withdrawal from Lang Son – after a considerably worse defeat – marked a turning point in France's war to retain its Indochinese colonies. Indeed, for readers familiar with that war, other place names in this chapter – particularly Dong Dang – will have a sinister resonance.)[65]

At 10pm on 28 March, Herbinger took the first column of Line troops and the Bat d'Af out of Lang Son on the Mandarin Road, followed shortly afterwards by the Legion and Tonkinese Skirmishers, who retraced the route of the advance through the hills via Dong Son. The columns arrived back at Chu on 30 March and 1 April respectively, without any interference from the Chinese. By then General Brière de l'Isle had made what was arguably the worst mistake of this whole episode. On 29 March the Paris newspapers carried the leaked text of a cable from the commander-in-chief to the Ministry of War:

> Colonel Herbinger, short of munitions and worn out by earlier battles, tells me position untenable and he is forced to retreat – enemy strength growing, we appear to have the whole Chinese army against us … Whatever happens, hope to be able to hold Delta, but government must send reinforcements – men, munitions, animals – urgently.[66]

It may be over-cynical to pay too much attention to the final request when speculating about Brière's motives in choosing such apocalyptic language. Two days later – by which time Brière was clearly adjusting the noose around Herbinger's neck – he sent the ministry another cable that flatly contradicted his first:

> The evacuation of Lang Son … and above all the precipitous retreat are due to a weakness in the command after the wounding of General de Négrier. The 2nd Brigade at Lang Son still had 20 days' rations and sufficient

ammunition to await the convoy that was on its way and of which they had been informed. The Navy 4-pdr battery was thrown into the river by order, and without protest from Major de Douvres. The abandoned money (130,000 piastres) [was] also thrown away by order, and all this after the success of our counter-attacks. The same haste [is evident in] the evacuation of Dong Son, with even less justification. The Chinese seem at present content to occupy their former positions north of Deo Quan and Deo Van [passes]. In sum, our situation is not compromised and better than the alarming reports suggest.[67]

This attempt to backtrack blithely ignored the fact that his own first cable had been entirely responsible for the 'alarming reports' reaching Paris. On 8 April – after giving provisional command of 2nd Brigade to Colonel Borgnis-Desbordes of the Naval Artillery, and inspecting the troops at Chu – the commander-in-chief issued an extraordinary order of the day to all ranks:

'... by a bitter joke of destiny, at the very moment when the Chinese columns were retreating hurriedly under the impact of your counter-attack, you learned that your valiant chief General de Négrier – that brave among braves – was being carried to the dressing station. In consequence of this misfortune the command fell into hands insufficiently prepared for it ...'[68]

That Brière de l'Ile chose to criticize an individual senior officer to his troops left no doubt that Herbinger was, professionally speaking, a dead man walking. (To our eyes, it also seems a reckless incitement to disrespect and indiscipline – though we must remember that Brière was a Navy general, and Herbinger an Army officer.) But whoever the high command decided to sacrifice, the French political world had already sated its more ambitious appetite.[69]

ON 30 MARCH, JULES FERRY had addressed the Chamber to request additional funds for his war, and the Chamber had torn him apart. Observers said that the news of Waterloo can hardly have caused such a panic in parliament and press as this distant and ambiguous setback, which was denounced in the most extravagant language as a military and political disaster. Ferry was shouted down from both Left and Right, and with particular savagery by Georges Clemenceau: 'We do not wish to hear any more from you; we do not wish to discuss with you any longer the great affairs of state. We do not know you any longer; we do not wish to know you any longer!' Ferry was defeated by a majority of 155 votes, and his government fell. Considering that crowds in the Place de la Concorde were baying for his blood, 'le Tonkinois' showed remarkable strength of character in keeping the secret (as he had solemnly promised) that within a few days a peace agreement with China would be announced.[70]

On 4 April 1885, a Sino-French ceasefire was agreed through the mediation of European officials of the Chinese customs service, as a preliminary to the full Treaty of Tienstin signed on 11 June. Chinese troops would withdraw into Guangxi and Yunnan by 30 May, supervised by a joint commission, and French troops were soon back at Lang Son.[71] China formally repudiated the Black Flags, though in fact many of them – and Chinese deserters – remained in Tonkin, some almost as far down the Red river as Hung Hoa. Despite the fury over Lang Son, the new war minister, General Campenon, would be voted the funds to almost double the Expeditionary Corps to 35,000 men (among the reinforcements were the hollow-eyed IV/2nd RE from Formosa, already bought and paid for).[72] Despite Lang Son, morale remained high in the Expeditionary Corps, and when Saigon newspapers reached them in April, officers in Tonkin were astonished by the violence of the reactions in Paris. Many Army officers felt that Herbinger had not deserved to be thrown to the wolves by the Navy theatre commander, and his fate would remain a sore point for years. (When Major Lyautey met veterans on the frontier ten years later, he wrote home that 'Great responsibilities attach to this matter, and they are not always what is said and believed'.)[73]

The enlargement of the CET to three divisions brought General Roussel de Courcy out as theatre commander. General Brière de l'Ile accepted one of the divisional commands, on condition that General de Négrier should be promoted to one of the others (which he was, with his third star backdated to 29 March in compliment to his wound at Ky Lua). The Treaty of Tientsin provoked an attempted putsch in Hué on the night of 4/5 July 1885, when the regents Nguyen and Ton sent some 6,000 Annamese troops to attack the palace and the French legation, but these unsophisticated soldiers were beaten off by a single battalion of Zouaves. (A Vietnamese text quoted a soldier thus: '... stupidly, we did not grasp their strategy at all. On the contrary, we made every effort to show our power by firing continually. When they judged that our supply of powder had run out, all the French got up and fired ...'). The young King Ham Nghi then escaped into the hills with the royal treasury, and – still manipulated by the regents – proclaimed a national uprising against the French. In September he was formally replaced on the throne by a complacent older brother, Dong Khanh – the sixth King of Annam in two years.[74]

ON 24 DECEMBER 1885 THE NATIONAL ASSEMBLY considered the report of a commission of enquiry into the commitment to Tonkin; this predicted that either annexation or a protectorate would be equally disastrous for France. The Assembly rejected this report by a majority of just four votes, and it was with that slim mandate that French troops remained in Tonkin.[75] It would take them another fifteen years to pacify the jungle hills; légionnaires would play a prominent and continuous part in those campaigns – during which we shall revisit them, at a time when two colonial commanders who learned to trust them were beginning to climb towards unrivalled reputations.

5. General Vengeance and King Zinc-Nose

Punishments, to be effective, must be adapted to the
thickness of the skin that they have to get through.
Corporal Frederic Martyn[1]

ALTHOUGH THE CHURNING SURFACE of the National Assembly threw up seven different war ministers between the invasion of Tunisia in April 1881 and the Tonkin ceasefire in April 1885, in the quiet depths the movement for Army reform continued to make gradual progress. There was an unprecedented harvest of thoughtful publications, and some generals whose habits of mind had been shaped by the Imperial world applied themselves to their professional studies in middle age. Even General Gallifet – a model of the old-style Bonapartist *beau sabreur*, glossy with blood and champagne – honestly declared that 'before the war none of us knew anything'.[2]

From 1880, an École Supérieure de Guerre (Staff College) replaced the old system that had created a remote and unresponsive caste of over-specialized staff officers, and during the 1870s and 1880s there was a marked improvement in the average intellectual level of junior officers. This was true not only of the traditionally scholarly output of gunners and sappers from the École Polytechnique; St Cyr, too, began to attract an increasing proportion of intelligent young patriots who saw the Army not just as a fashionable way to spend their twenties before inheritance or a good marriage allowed them to relax, but as a lifetime career. From 1881, NCOs could no longer be commissioned directly from the ranks (except as a reward for outstanding battlefield leadership); now they had to complete a punishing course of study before sitting examinations for entry to new officer academies.[3] In the Legion, these new requirements reduced the already modest number of foreign-born officers from other than francophone countries, since passing the exam for the St Maixent infantry academy demanded much more of them than simply mastering enough French to perform a squad sergeant's duties.[4]

Despite the conscription law of 1872, wrangling continued over the exact terms of national service in the ranks of the Line. In 1884 the Chamber debated a bill that would have reduced the five years' regular service to three, but with many fewer 'bourgeois' exemptions. The usual circular arguments were silenced in January 1886 by the appointment as war minister of an officer with ambitions to absorb conscription reform within a grand root-and-branch programme of his own. Since the spring of 1871, when he had been shooting Communard prisoners as colonel of the 114th Line, General Georges Boulanger had undergone a remarkable transformation into an outspoken Republican democrat; one of his sponsors for the ministerial portfolio was Clemenceau, leader of the Radicals in the Assembly.

BY THE AGE OF 49, Boulanger could boast six wounds; he was also charismatic, energetic, an administrator of real ability, and alive to the welfare and morale of the troops. The Republican Prime Minister Charles Freycinet had confidence in Boulanger's professional gifts and assumed that as a newcomer to government he would be politically obedient, while the nationalist Right were reassured by the general's noisy anti-German patriotism. At the Longchamp review of 14 July 1886 the crowds cheered as he rode past on his gleaming black charger 'Tunis' (it is tempting to see in this choice of name – a reference to a command that had brought him no glory and a quarrel with the civil powers – evidence of his deafness to perfect pitch). Boulanger had no important enemies, but he did not need any, given the tumescence of his own ego when he became, literally, a national pin-up. Although the Freycinet government fell in December 1886, the general's popularity ensured his retention in the succeeding Gobelt cabinet. Basking in the warmth of an acclaim that he judged to be nothing but his due, Boulanger soon allowed himself to become slightly deranged.

When first in office he had presented to the Chamber a grandiose Army reform bill with no fewer than 217 articles, and was frustrated when this was nibbled to death by the usual vested interests. His haste to see a revolutionary new weapon adopted during his tenure led to the premature production of the Lebel repeating rifle, taking smokeless, non-fouling ammunition; an innovative weapon and its cartridge have to be designed in harmony as a single integrated system, but again Boulanger proved to be tone-deaf.[5] He picked hasty quarrels with older and wiser heads, and he enjoyed rather too much the sound of his own brusque, soldierly tones in parliamentary exchanges. He played to the Left by preaching the solidarity of the troops with the workers, while courting the Right by posing as 'General Vengeance'; during an irritating but manageable crisis in Franco-German relations in April 1887, he made dangerously provocative speeches that delighted the extremists of Paul Déroulède's League of Patriots. The Gobelt government fell in its turn in May 1887, and there was a public outcry when Boulanger lost his ministry and was appointed to command 13th Corps at Clermont-Ferrand.

His more thoughtful political friends distanced themselves, but Boulanger ignored all warnings that he should stop playing to the crowd and concentrate on his duties. Addicted to cheering audiences, he now posed a real threat to the equilibrium that the Army and the Assembly had achieved, with some difficulty, over the previous decade. He also had a weakness for challenging elderly politicians to duels, and his pretensions earned him Jules Ferry's contemptuous dismissal as a *'Saint-Arnaud de café-concert'*; the flavour of this is hard to convey in modern English, but 'a music-hall Franco' may come close.[6] The talkative general allowed himself to be courted by an extraordinary *galère* of political factions of both Left and Right, each of which must have painted the face they wanted to see on to the essentially vacuous dummy inhabiting his uniform.

In March 1888 an illegal electoral adventure finally earned Boulanger dismissal from the service, but this did not silence him or his noisy claque, some of whom hungered for the Army to step beyond its constitutional bounds. Representing no coherent political interest, he continued to ride his theatrical cult of personality into irrelevance, disgrace, ridicule and final exile. In January 1889 Paul Déroulède – completely misjudging the mood of the Army, and apparently forgetful of what can happen at barricades – urged Boulanger to launch a military *putsch*, but the general was not quite deranged enough for that. The Army remained scrupulously silent throughout these public spasms, but by the time of his eclipse Boulanger had already done the service real damage by seeming to justify traditional Republican suspicions.[7]

In April 1888 the generals were fortunate to get Charles Freycinet as their new war minister. Politically both Boulanger's midwife and his executioner, Freycinet was a lifelong machine politician, four times prime minister, but though sometimes criticized for indecision this so-called 'white mouse' would prove unexpectedly capable. In 1889 he presided over a reduction of the conscription period from five to three years; and, by the time of his departure in January 1893 after a unique five-year term, he had demonstrated calm intelligence, administrative talent, and parliamentary skills that had even secured a slight loosening of the political shackles on the chiefs of the Army general staff. Despite Freycinet's stewardship, however, within a few years the Army would have great cause to regret the impression that Boulanger had left on the minds of the French Left.[8]

SAFELY DISTANT FROM THE PARISIAN JUNGLE, half the Foreign Legion were living a life of routine in Algeria while providing regular drafts for the other half in Tonkin. (These amounted to about a battalion's strength of replacements each year, suggesting an annual wastage of 25 per cent in the four Tonkin units.) The first generation of British memoirists served in the early 1890s, and one book of reminiscences would be published by Frederic Martyn, a British Army veteran who enlisted in the 1st RE in 1889. His perspective on Legion life at this time thus has a standard of comparison that many others lack, and is worth quoting in some detail, alongside that of his contemporary George Manington.[9]

Martyn enlisted at a recruiting office in Paris, where he was warned of what he was letting himself in for and urged to reconsider. He mentions that Frenchmen wishing to enlist had to show their identity papers, but that those unwilling to do so simply claimed to be Belgian or Swiss and were asked for no proof.[10] Given a rail warrant for Marseille and travelling money, Martyn was shipped over to Oran on the regular mailship and from there took the slow train to Sidi bel Abbès. The most substantial buildings in this small, Spanish-looking town of perhaps 30,000 civilians were the barracks of the 2nd Spahis and the Quartier Viénot, depot of the 1st Foreign Regiment.

The recruits were marched through the main gate between guardhouses, on to a parade square lined with small trees and surrounded on three sides by a four-storey U-shaped block. In one of the side-wings Martyn was given a bed in one of the large, high-ceilinged barrack rooms, which typically had 25 or 30 beds, for a half-platoon with two corporals. The beds were simply three planks laid over two iron trestles with a straw-packed mattress and bolster, a sleeping bag of coarse sheeting and two blankets. A card with each man's name and number was pinned above his bed to the edge of a long, deep shelf; on this space he had to keep his folded clothing, immaculately stacked in regulation order in a perfectly squared tower, with his equipment hung on hooks below it behind a towel curtain. At the inner end of the room was a rifle rack, and down the middle ran a long deal table and benches; above this, iron rods from the ceiling suspended a box-cupboard for tableware, with a small petrol lamp hung below it. The men took turns as room orderly, sweeping and cleaning, fetching meals from the cookhouse for their squad, and washing their dishes.[11]

The first day was taken up with a fairly cursory medical inspection, allocation of a serial number (*matricule*) and assignment to a recruit company, a visit to the washroom, and drawing uniforms and kit from stores. The men were not allowed to keep their civilian clothes, and the sergeant-major in the company office offered to sell Martyn's for him in the town for a fair price. The uniform issue was a considerable load to carry back to the barrack room: a red-crowned kepi with the Legion's red seven-flamed grenade badge on its midnight-blue band; a midnight-blue tunic with red trim and the Legion's green-and-red fringed epaulettes for dress wear, and a midnight-blue *veste* or stable jacket for everyday; red trousers; a greatcoat of 'blued-iron grey'; two suits of coarse white linen fatigue blouse and trousers; the long sky-blue sash or body-belt; two shirts and two pairs of drawers; two pairs of carefully fitted boots; and one pair each of black leather gaiters and white linen spats.[12]

DAILY ROUTINE FOR MARTYN began at 5.30am, when the duty orderly came round the beds with a jug and the men held out their mugs for black, sweetened coffee. 'Reveille' was called a few moments later; the corporals stayed in bed until the last moment, bellowing at the others to get moving – there were only 15 minutes before 'Fall in', and only the quickest got the chance to splash their faces in the washroom before folding their blankets, rolling their mattresses, sweeping under their beds (the orderly did the rest of the floor), and clattering down to the barrack square. When most of the battalion were marched off in batches to the drill grounds outside the town, led by the fifes and drums, the recruits were left to their basic training.

Learning the rank insignia and proper compliments was followed by physical exercises and basic foot drill. The corporals repeated simple orders in both French and German as a matter of course, and had a smattering of many other languages; after six months in the ranks every man could get by in the undemanding sort of French he needed. The corporals instructed by repetition, demonstration and practice; sergeants – who had higher status than in the British Army – hardly ever intervened.[13] At 8am the recruits were dismissed to wash and to work on their kit, but lurking NCOs collared many to make up fatigue parties for which the punishment book had provided too few defaulters. Morning *soupe* was at 9.30am, and was eaten in the barrack room; the usual manifestation of this all-purpose term for main meals was in fact a meat and vegetable stew. The food was plentiful, and varied to some extent, but always provided bulk rather than diversity – beef, pork or mutton, with beans, lentils, rice or macaroni. There was plenty of fresh bread, and a daily wine ration of half a litre; the men pooled their cash to buy extras like salad and additional wine.[14]

At 10am there was a semi-formal parade for 'Report' (announcements and daily orders), then recruit training resumed from 10.30am to 4pm. This progressed from simple movements to drill with rifles. Two hours in squads under the NCOs were followed by an hour of company or battalion drill under the distant supervision of officers. These sessions alternated with gymnastics, running, bayonet-fencing, lectures and theoretical instruction from manuals. The evening *soupe* was at 4.30pm; thereafter the recruits cleaned their kit for the next day. Then it was down to the canteen, or – provided they were not on duty or the defaulters' list, and could pass inspection by the sergeant of the guard – they could go out into the town until 'Retreat' at 8.45pm. Evening rollcall was at 9pm, and 'Lights out' at 10pm.[15]

Each man was assigned to an old soldier to show him the ropes, and the wise *bleu* treated his 'Legion daddy' and his squad corporal to plenty of wine. The whole barrack room usually decamped after the evening meal to the bare, cheerless canteen, its zinc-topped bar presided over by a motherly harridan who kept a slate until the end of the evening. Booze was the *leitmotiv* of barracks life, both the great solace and the great curse of the légionnaire; pernod cost 15 centimes a shot and absinthe 40 centimes, but Algerian red wine (*pinard*) was just 5 centimes – a day's pay – for a litre bottle. The men's capacity was limited only by their pockets, and two or three bottles each was not unusual (astonishingly, it was claimed that the gold-standard for 'real soldiers' – including officers – was six bottles in a night).[16]

During his first days Martyn found it difficult to work up a polish on the grubby equipment and rifle he had been issued, but although there was a proper emphasis on personal cleanliness the NCOs were otherwise not unreasonably demanding at first, and there were ways to avoid the problem. Any man with a little money could make daily life more tolerable by paying the penniless to perform his drearier military chores – laundering his fatigues in the cold-water *lavabo*, polishing his kit and taking his turn as room orderly. By the First World War the accepted daily rate for getting another man to 'do your *truc*' was 5 centimes, thus doubling a drunkard's drinking-money; this was considered entirely fair – indeed, it was felt that a man of means had an obligation to do his bit for trickle-down capitalism.[17] All new recruits soon learned the paramount importance of having a few coins to lay down, and this raises the question of Legion pay.

In Algeria the basic daily rate for a *soldat de 2e classe* around the turn of the century was 5 centimes – a twentieth part of one franc; a *1re classe* was paid twice that, and a corporal four times as much, all wages being paid out on the 1st and 15th of the month.[18] Confusion often arises from the use of the slang term *sou*; a sou was 20 centimes, one-fifth of a franc, or four days' basic pay. Some British writers have thickened the fog by expressing the daily pay in sterling equivalents at various dates – Martyn, writing in 1911 but of his service twenty years previously, calls 5 centimes a penny, and Rankin, writing in 1908, calls it a halfpenny. Either way, it is obvious that the légionnaire could never be accused of being a 'mercenary' in the modern sense; he received only a tiny fraction of the pay of a British regular private, which was then one shilling (12 pence) a day. The basic daily rate was simply pocket-money, and hard to stretch between the necessary small purchases (soap, bootlaces, polishes) and even a modest consumption of Algerian wine and tobacco at their heavily subsidised prices. The hardest drinkers therefore funded their thirst by selling items of their own and other people's kit in the alleys of Sidi bel Abbès and Saida. Although the barrack rooms saw a constant game of larcenous musical-chairs – with the last, unsuccessful kit-thief paying the penalty at the next inspection – the crimes of a habitual drunk would inevitably be discovered, and he would inevitably end up in the cells. This was wholly unremarkable and unresented.[19]

A lucky few in the ranks actually received money from home or had banked some within reach, and others found ways to earn it locally; Martyn's memoir makes clear that it was not unusual for a man to have spending money in addition to his pay. (The rare légionnaire of really bourgeois means, like one or two of the ex-officers in the ranks, might even keep a cheap rented room in the town, perhaps with a strictly forbidden change of civilian clothes for the occasional treat of a decent night out in a hotel restaurant.)

EVERY WEDNESDAY, IN ALL SEASONS, was devoted to a route march. At first the recruits carried only rifles and belt kit and the distance was limited to $12\frac{1}{2}$ miles; the fat or unfit found this hard enough, but both the burden and the distance were steadily increased, until the men were accustomed to marching 28 miles in ten hours (with the usual halts), carrying anything between 50lbs and 80lbs – a full knapsack of clothing and bivouac kit, a full waterbottle, rations for two days, and 120 rounds. The légionnaires became proud of their endurance, and there was a competitive spirit between companies and battalions. The other essential skill of the infantryman was taken just as seriously, and during his training Manington spent every Friday afternoon on the rifle range. He described the M1874 Gras as having properties much like the British Army's Martini-Henry, so it is hardly surprising that he stressed its 'tremendous kick'. Firing such a weapon requires a very tight embrace, so that at the moment of recoil the body 'rides' the shock, moving as one with the rifle; Manington recalled that firing with a 'loose shoulder' could cost the careless légionnaire a black eye or bleeding nose. However, he praised the rifle's strong, simple mechanism, and wrote that during his tour in Tonkin, when prolonged firing caused black-powder fouling, men simply took the bolt out and washed it in a handy puddle. A high standard of marksmanship was encouraged by awarding a bugle-horn badge, and by the presentation of silver watches as shooting prizes.[20]

Basic training took between two and four months, until a man satisfied the depot company that he could drill smartly; keep himself, his clothing, his weapon and his quarters clean; shoot to a reasonable standard, and manage his bivouac gear. He was then posted to a rifle company, moving into a new barrack room among the men with whom he would serve from then on. There was some predictable hazing to put up with at first, but it soon stopped if taken in good part – Manington wrote that he never saw any example of real malice, and that the practical jokes were simply an excuse for levying 'fines' at the canteen bar. Although he might not still be with his official 'daddy', the newcomer soon learned that the Legion had a culture of parallel leadership, and a youngster was as likely to look for guidance and example to an encouraging 'old moustache' as to his corporal. In the multinational barrack rooms, experienced soldiers would often take fellow countrymen under their wing.

AN ANALYSIS OF THE NATIONALITIES claimed by enlisted men in 1896–97 gave about 26 per cent Alsace-Lorrainers, 25 per cent Germans, 18 per cent French, 17 per cent Belgians, 10 per cent Swiss, 3.5 per cent Austrians, and less than 1 per cent each Spaniards, British, Poles, Czechs, Hungarians, Greeks, Turks, Russians and assorted oddities. Martyn wrote that in five years he only ever met about a dozen other British légionnaires, all but two of them ex-soldiers. The absence of Italians from this list is explained by an officer's opinion that for some reason they habitually claimed to be Spanish, and he stresses that men often lied about their nationality, which might be a fluid concept in the age of the great empires. That of Austria–Hungary, in particular, was a factory of ethnic resentments and misfortunes, and a man might have all kinds of reasons for vagueness about his origins.

In the matter of class and working background, an averaged analysis of enlistments in six-month periods of 1885 and 1898 gives, from a total of $c.$ 1,000 recruits, 369 without any skilled manual trade. Then and for long afterwards, unskilled or simply unlucky men all over Europe could easily find themselves begging in the gutter for lack of employment, and even among those with a reasonably assured subsistence income rural life was intolerably dull and confined for a young man with spirit. Most continental countries had systems of obligatory military training, so drifters often had one skill to sell; Martyn reckoned that a very high proportion of Legion recruits had previous military experience – of his intake of 20, all but two or three. As to claimed ages, the averaged analysis of 1885 and 1898 gives 27 per cent in their late teens, 56 per cent in their twenties, 16 per cent in their thirties, and a handful admitting to 40 to 45 years. Again, the officer commenting on these figures stressed that at the younger and older ends of the spectrum hopeful recruits habitually lied, but so long as the occasional 15- or 50-year-old was equal to his duties the Legion turned a blind eye. Martyn reckoned that in fact a high proportion were in their mid-thirties, and were better soldiers on account of this relative maturity. While labourers are the largest group in the listing of previous trades, the sheer variety makes it easy to understand the Legion battalion's traditional ability to find any necessary skill within its ranks.[21]

The same analysis gives 11 per cent of the new enlistees' backgrounds in the educated and monied classes – ruined gentlemen, members of the professions and ex-officers. This relatively high figure is striking, but plausible, and there is no need to seek reasons in *Beau-Gestique* fantasies of broken hearts and stolen jewels. In the volatile late nineteenth century it was not uncommon for members of the *rentier* classes to lose everything through the failure of some enterprise or a plunge in the markets. Then, as in any generation, young men of respectable background might gamble, drink and fornicate away their legacies and their social credit, and in those days such foolishness could bring real exclusion. Personal or political difficulties might also tip a military officer into limbo, with nothing to sell but his experience.

In the case of former French Line officers, it must be remembered that since the 1789 Revolution the officer corps as a whole had born little social resemblance to that of the British Army. In both, of course, there were aristocratic minorities and inheritors of new wealth who dominated the fashionable regiments; but while the mass of British officers were the sons of the modest country squirearchy and the professions, even under the Second Empire more than 60 per cent of new French commissions had been reserved for former NCOs. These men often had only primary education and limited ambitions; if an English subaltern's dream was to command his battalion, a Frenchman's was usually to retire as a captain. If such a man stumbled, there was a much lower mental barrier to seeking a second chance in the Legion. In 1889 Corporal Pfirmann knew three ex-officers in his own company – a Bavarian, a Hungarian, and a French former captain of Cuirassiers – as well as half-a-dozen other men from what he considered privileged backgrounds.[22]

Although the respectable *pekins* – 'bloody civilians' – of Sidi bel Abbès regarded légionnaires with an utter disdain that was warmly returned, it is clear that by 1889 the Legion had long since 'achieved self-consciousness'. One of the Army innovations since the Franco-Prussian War was the establishment of regimental *salles d'honneur* – rudimentary unit museums – and that of the Legion was genuinely impressive to all but the dullest recruit. On one of his first days at the Viénot barracks Martyn and other newly inducted men were taken there as if into a chapel. Surrounded by portraits of legendary figures and paintings of heroic scenes – 'The End' at Camerone, 'The Breach' at Tuyen Quang – the adjutant delivered an inspiring address on the Legion's history and traditions. Martyn thought this an excellent way of instilling *ésprit de corps*, and felt genuine pride at having joined such a regiment. Manington, too, recalled the collective lift to morale of taking part in a spectacular general inspection parade; he described the huge, bemedalled Corporal Minnaert leading the squad of bearded pioneers, followed by the Legion's magnificent band behind their Turkish 'Jingling Johnnie'.[23]

THE FIRST RUNG OF THE PROMOTION LADDER could be attained surprisingly quickly, given the French system of identifying potential NCOs during recruit training. Frederic Martyn, with previous experience and good French and German, was picked for the *éleve caporal* course after a few weeks; he was assisting with rifle training before he 'passed off the square', and he got his two red stripes after less than three months. He noted a number of former Line NCOs and one ex-officer among the other aspirant corporals.[24]

The next step to sergeant – the important climb out of the *troupes* and into the *sous-officiers* – was harder, and took at least two years even for the brightest of the French ex-Line NCOs in the ranks. (Minnaert's exploit at Son Tay had earned him the Médaille Militaire and corporal's stripes, but it still took him another seven years to make sergeant.) Getting – and keeping – a gold stripe depended on literacy, intelligence, sustained application, a clean conduct sheet, and the sheer luck of continuing physical fitness. However, despite the official need to tick the boxes, it was also the almost unique opportunities for active service that drew keen French ex-*lignards* into the Legion, whose culture gave almost as much weight to bravery on campaign as to paper qualifications. While discipline was always fierce, Legion officers took a more paternal view of their soldiers than was the case in the rigidly formal Line, and in the matter of the 'clean' conduct sheet men who had distinguished themselves in battle would be given some leeway. While it was harder to get and easier to lose your gold stripe in the Legion, it was also easier to get it back again than in the prissier environment of Line regiments; after all, what the Legion needed was men with a taste for taking risks. Progress beyond sergeant – to sergeant-major and warrant officer *(adjudant)* – was very much a case of the higher the rank, the fewer the numbers eligible, and was almost entirely limited to native French-speakers of superior literacy and administrative talents.[25]

Seen from the ranks, Legion NCOs were as mixed a group as might be expected in any army of the day. Martyn wrote that direct bribery for a specific favour was far rarer than the maintenance of a general atmosphere of relative goodwill by the occasional drink or packet of cigarettes; this was seen as simply an extension of the universal rule that any man in funds treated his mates. Manington recalled only a few NCOs as 'objectionable' – habitually picking on the men – and soldiers who kept themselves and their kit clean and were smart and obedient seldom had much to fear. Good NCOs made it clear what they wanted, barked once and then bit hard; bad ones were unpredictable, biting without warning.[26] Unlike those of the British Army, sergeants could award formal punishments on the spot, though these had to be entered in a book reviewed daily by the company and battalion commanders. This could lead to petty tyrannies, but it also gave

NCOs higher status and thus self-reliance when on campaign, which was valuable when officers fell.

New recruits unused to discipline might respond to an order or correction with a curse; once they had been taught the folly of such defiance, few except the hopelessly awkward or the hardest cases (who could be very hard indeed) got into trouble when sober – drink was the cause of nearly all crimes and misdemeanours. Except on campaign, punishments were identical in nature to those inflicted throughout the French Army, though sometimes more severe in degree. Manington wrote: 'A regiment is not like a girls' school, and it is impossible to maintain discipline in a corps composed ... of so many hard cases unless a certain amount of severity is used.' Nevertheless, the ex-British ranker Martyn was critical of the frequency of awards of punishment drill for trivial offences.[27]

The most banal penalty was extra fatigue duties and confinement to barracks; this might involve simply peaceful drudgery, or being run ragged by frequent and unpredictable blowing of the defaulters' call, summoning them for fatigues. *Salle de police* meant performing normal daily duties but spending the nights in full kit on a plank sleeping-platform in the guard-house. 'Ordinary' arrest was a good deal more severe; it meant at least eight days in a bare cell, being brought out for six hours' punishment drill daily – typically including spells of running round the square with a knapsack full of rocks or a rifle at arms' stretch. A lower circle of purgatory was *cellule* – solitary confinement for 24 hours a day in an almost lightless cell on punishment rations; the maximum award was a month, which could drive a man without unusual inner resources half-crazy.

Beyond these punishments at unit level, the battalion commander could sentence the most serious or persistent offenders to transfer for six months to the regimental *section disciplinaire*. This sentence could be extended, in theory almost indefinitely, since the slightest misdeanour set the clock back to zero – the time already endured was '*rabio*' or extra (and the whole interlude was extra to a man's five-year engagement). The final abyss was a divisional general court-martial at Oran, where a guilty verdict meant a sentence of many years' hard labour or death by firing squad. A condemned man might be returned to his unit for execution; Private Silbermann recalled two German deserters who killed local Arabs being shot at Géryville in the presence of the local *caids*.[28]

The punishment platoons were based at remote desert camps, and provided labour gangs wherever they were needed. Silbermann did a spell of duty guarding the 2nd RE disciplinary camp at El Oussek; his memoir is somewhat sycophantic to authority throughout, but cannot hide the harshness of the regime in the punishment platoon. The guard detail lived in huts, the prisoners in eight-man bell-tents surrounded by drystone walls. Their days were mostly spent in hard labour under a burning sun – breaking rocks, road-building and other construction tasks – but alternating with drill, field exercises, lectures and inspections. Silbermann claimed that they got the same rations as the guards and normal pay, and were allowed access in rotation to a rudimentary dry canteen to make small purchases. Punishments included *cellule* in a one-man bivouac tent; but the NCOs in charge of such camps were often almost entirely unsupervised, and other Legion memoirs speak of men left all day under the desert sun in an open grave (*le tombeau*), without a waterbottle. One spell in the 'Zephyrs' was almost invariably enough to tame the most rebellious spirit.[29]

IN CORPORAL MARTYN'S OPINION, the opportunity for outstanding NCOs to seek commissions through the St Maixent academy was much superior to the British system, which denied them anything but a quartermaster's commission.[30] In 1890, ex-rankers still made up 55 per cent of subalterns in the Army as a whole, but in their promotions thereafter they naturally remained at a disadvantage compared with St Cyr graduates, who had between four and ten years' start over former NCOs, as well as informal but important social connections. In the 1880s the average Army sub-lieutenant of any background took at least ten years to reach captain, and the average captain twelve years to reach major, at an average age of 43 years (these delays increased significantly during the 1890s and 1900s). The ex-NCOs' late start up the ladder meant that they were even older for their ranks.[31]

The légionnaires took both kinds of officer – St Cyriens and ex-rankers – very much as they found them, but anyway had little contact with either sort except when in the field. A fair, considerate and (above all) brave and decisive officer was respected, sometimes idolized. One need not be too cynical about the motives of men who routinely risked and often lost their lives to bring in a wounded or dead officer; they did the same for their own comrades. One might imagine that ex-ranker officers were touchy about their new status, but again, this was not the British Army, and class background was much less of an issue. At least some St Maixent men profited by their experience of life in the ranks to show kindness and knowledgeable encouragement to their légionnaires.[32]

ONCE POSTED AWAY FROM THE DEPOTS, Algerian service in these years was hard and monotonous. (The ex-soldier Martyn denied that there was anything special about *le cafard*, the desperation that was said to drive men crazy in small posts. He judged it to be no different from the extreme boredom that made Tommies in India 'fed up', and that usually discharged its tension in a drunken brawl or some defiant spree.) In July 1890, Manington was posted to 9th Company, III/1st RE, and that September he was sent on manoeuvres in the Sud-Oranais. After alighting from trains at Méchéria, the battalion marched down to Ain Sefra, and thence into the true desert (see Map 3). After about ten days, an outbreak of typhoid fever swept through his unit – enteric or *morbus campestris*, the ancient scourge of armies and prisons everywhere.[33] A delirious Manington survived a nightmare journey back to civilization, initially being jolted about for many days in mule- and camel-litters. He wrote appreciatively of the battalion medical officer, Dr Aragon, and enthusiastically of the regime at the Legion's convalescent camp at Arzew on the Mediterranean coast, where for three months he loafed, swam and rebuilt his strength with country strolls.[34]

In November 1891, each RE was ordered to be enlarged from four to five battalions (though this would take some time to achieve in practice). Considering the unrewarding monotony of Algerian duty, it is not surprising that what légionnaires at Sidi bel Abbès and Saida prayed for was a chance of active service. By 1892 Corporal Martyn had already done a tour in Tonkin, where he had survived the ravages of blackwater fever. In late July, spending an evening in a Sidi bel Abbès café after returning from his own rest-cure at Arzew (where men just off the boat from Haiphong were almost invariably sent), he saw a report in the *Echo d'Oran* that a Legion marching battalion was to be formed for active service in somewhere called Dahomey. Orders were posted in the barracks next morning, calling for volunteers and stating that preference would be given to Tonkin veterans, who were presumed to be 'fever-proofed'.[35]

THE LEGION'S RIVALS of the Naval Troops had been pushing inland from the Atlantic coast of West Africa for the past twenty years, though such piecemeal advances were largely unplanned by Paris.[36] In France these campaigns aroused an increasing public interest that was assiduously nourished by the colonial lobby, and a six-month Exposition Universelle in 1889 entranced *le tout Paris* with its artistically recreated native buildings and troupes of carefully groomed dancers. For years some visionaries nurtured hopes of driving a railway south-west from Algeria across the Sahara and as far as Dakar, to tie a single French net over the whole bulge of West Africa from the Mediterranean to the Atlantic. (In the event this trans-Saharan route would prove impossible for any but small military expeditions, and was often lethal even for them.)

Three important leaders of West African kingdoms were successively defeated during the 1880s and early 1890s: Mahmadou Lamine, Ahmadou of Segou, and Samory Touré – a remarkable soldier who himself built by conquest an empire in southern Mali, northern Guinea and northern Ivory Coast.[37] The Naval Troops officers who led these campaigns became celebrated, but the columns they led were made up almost entirely of locally recruited Senegalese Skirmishers with only small white cadres.[38] Their eventual success depended absolutely upon the black troops' relative resistance to malaria, yellow fever and other natural scourges, and upon the use of African porters to carry all equipment and supplies. By 1892 these campaigns in West Africa had left one particular unresolved space on French maps – Dahomey, lying between the narrow finger of German Togo and the great expanse of coastal Nigeria then administered for Britain by the Royal Niger Company.

THE SHEER GEOGRAPHICAL ARTIFICIALITY of Europe's African colonies can hardly be more obvious anywhere than along the southern coast of West Africa, where a series of strips of territory ran inland from the Gulf of Guinea like the keys of a piano. In the nineteenth century the regions between Cape Palmas in the west and the Niger river delta in the east were known to Europeans by the names of their historic commodities: the Ivory Coast, the Gold Coast and the Slave Coast, the latter embracing roughly the present-day states of Togo, Benin and western Nigeria.

In Dahomey, now the southern part of Benin, a unified kingdom had been born during the seventeenth century when the Fon people of the inland plateau banded together in self defence against Yoruba slave-raiders from the east. By the late eighteenth century the Fon kingdom had expanded, conquering the southern coast and the lucrative western slave-port of Ouidah; the Fon kings became enthusiastic slave-traders themselves, and advertised the fact by adopting a flag showing a European ship. (There was, of course, slaving in West Africa long before the Atlantic trade began and long after it was abolished. Powerful leaders had a pyramid of dependants, and might choose to sell those from the lowest levels into slavery. The coastal kingdoms, fenced in by the jungles to the north, were not densely populated; working people were a scarcer commodity than land, and their ownership served as a symbol of wealth and a repository of value.)[39]

The most desirable of the white men's trade goods were firearms; the first great flow of muskets into West Africa began as early as 1660, and by 1700 the Dutch alone were shipping 20,000 tons of gunpowder to the coast each year. The original trade currency of elephant ivory and gold dust was replaced by slaves, who were easier for local monarchs to obtain and more profitable to sell. Slave-raiding became a central activity of West African kings, who exchanged their captives for more guns, which enabled them to capture yet more slaves; by 1750 hundreds of thousands of flintlock muskets had transformed the military potential and the economy of local kingdoms. Dahomey alone is reckoned to have imported more than 2,000 muskets annually even during the 1690s, and to have been exporting some 30,000 slaves a year from Ouidah by 1704. In 1682 a slave fetched only two Dutch muskets, but the Africans bargained shrewdly with the slaving captains of rival nations, and by 1717 they were charging twenty-five English or thirty Dutch muskets for each male slave. The customers for firearms had firm preferences and were far from naïve about the qualities of the weapons offered them; during the eighteenth century British arms factories eventually secured about half the total trade, producing a range of types keenly priced at profit margins as low as 7 per cent.

Although the Royal Navy began to suppress the transatlantic slave trade with some vigour after 1807, from about 1820 the Fon kings of Dahomey – whose major export was now palm oil – became even more conspicuous importers of firearms, since they pursued a singularly belligerent policy by means of a unique standing army. Their human export trade might have dried up, but the kings' hunger for captives had not; they needed slaves to work the royal plantations that produced the palm oil for export, as gifts to reward their loyal chiefs, as pressed soldiers in their army – and for human sacrifice.[40]

Although it was also practised by the neighbouring Ashanti and Yoruba, Dahomey became notorious for mass human sacrifice. When King Agaja-Dosu conquered Save and Ouidah in 1777 he is said to have sacrificed 4,000 captives, and such ritual slaughters were a feature not only of especially happy public occasions but of routine annual ceremonies at Kana, the centre of the kingdom's fetish-worship. These bloodbaths were often witnessed by Europeans, whom the kings insisted attend in order to remind the white men of their unchallenged powers. The tolerant Sir Richard Burton judged these grisly 'Grand Customs' to be a 'deplorably mistaken, but perfectly sincere' religious observance, believed by all to be essential for the continued wellbeing of the kingdom; others took a less ecumenical view, perhaps influenced by the prominence of human skulls and festoons of jawbones in the royal regalia and the decor of the palace.[41] Some of the victims were local criminals, but most were prisoners taken in annual campaigns launched specifically to feed both the slave economy and the blood-rites. Most of them were beheaded, some by the king in person and his male and female executioners; others – bound inside baskets with their heads protruding – were thrown into the hysterical crowd, who competed to bring heads to the king for prizes of cowrie-shell money. In 1892, Corporal Martyn of the Legion was told by a local headman of African porters about a Grand Custom in which hundreds of men were sacrificed, 60 of them by being buried alive.[42]

THE MILITARY MACHINE that enabled 'this West African Prussia' to prey upon its neighbours was unique in two respects, of which the first was its degree of organization. In the nineteenth century the kingdom extended only some 125 miles inland, with an area of about 10,000 square miles and a total population of perhaps 200,000 people. It is therefore remarkable that its kings were able to field armies up to 12,000 strong, with a core of perhaps 4,000–5,000 'regular' warriors all armed with state-supplied flintlocks, supported at need by a more lightly armed *levée en masse* of villagers.

Permanently based around the inland capital, Abomey, and in provincial and frontier garrisons, the standing army was divided into two 'wings' each of two divisions, commanded by four officers who doubled as the chief and deputy ministers of the kingdom. The divisions were made up of separate units that were distinguished by names and 'uniform' clothing or insignia (for example, in the 1870s the traveller J. A. Skertchly described one named the Tower Gun Company, armed with old British 'Brown Bess' muskets and distinguished by dark grey sleeveless tunics with cowrie shells sewn along the seams, and by red tassels on their belly-bandoliers).[43] The army's second unique feature was its inclusion of women warriors, inevitably called 'Amazons' by European travellers; the Dahomeyans called them *ahosi* ('the king's wives') or *kposi* ('wives of the panther'). Originally a small royal bodyguard but greatly expanded during the long reign of the warlike King Gezo

(1818–58), they numbered between 2,000 and 3,000 in the late nineteenth century. They, too, were organized in separate companies (for example, the Blunderbuss Women, and the Elephant-Huntresses); they were distinguished by special clothing and hairstyles, and also by a legendary ferocity in battle.

Although many percussion-lock muzzle-loading rifles had reached the surplus market by the 1880s, the difficulty of obtaining percussion caps apparently persuaded Dahomeyans to stick to their old British, Danish and French flintlock smoothbores, for which ammunition was in easier supply. Male and female soldiers were armed with muskets decorated with paint, cowrie shells and tassels, carrying gunpowder in rows of cartridge tubes on hide waist-bandoliers protected by flap covers, and bullets in decorated leather bags. For close work they carried broad, scimitar-like machetes, long knives or ironwood clubs. Men and women alike were trained for assaulting villages by charging barefoot and without flinching through a succession of lacerating thorn-hedges.

IN THE LATE NINETEENTH CENTURY, the French position in Dahomey was tenuous; there were trading stations on the coast at Porto Novo in the east and Cotonou further west, but any expansion was hampered by commercial and diplomatic competition from the British in Nigeria to the east and the Germans in Togo to the west. In 1864 a French protectorate over Porto Novo had been agreed; in 1878 King Glélé granted the French the right to collect customs duties there; and in April 1882 a resident officer of Naval Troops was installed at Porto Novo. In 1889, the year Glélé was succeeded by his son Behanzin, the French – citing various dubious trade treaties – also occupied Cotonou and Ouidah. They received the allegiance of the coastal chief Toffa, and demanded renegotiated terms for the export of the palm oil on which Behanzin's economy rested. The resentful king (whose name was phonetically rendered by Frenchmen as *Bec-en-zinc,* 'Zinc-nose') determined to punish Toffa and confront the Europeans, at a time when the French resident was backed only by a half-company of Naval Infantry.

In February and March 1890, Behanzin sent troops to attack the Fabre & Régis trading warehouse and the telegraph station at Cotonou. They were driven off only with some difficulty by Lieutenant Compérat and his handful of men, and on 17 April Behanzin massacred and burned villages around Porto Novo. Lieutenant-Colonel Terrillon of the Naval Infantry was shipped down the coast from Senegal, and on 20 April he advanced some miles from Porto Novo with 350 Senegalese Skirmishers, three mountain guns and about 500 of Toffa's warriors as a scouting screen. After being pushed back by a much larger force of Dahomeyans and losing 8 killed and 53 wounded, Terrillon was replaced by Lieutenant-Colonel Klipfel, who began fortifying Porto Novo, but Behanzin declined to assault the town.

In October 1890 a peace was concluded that left the French in possession of Cotonou and Porto Novo, with a usefully indefinite buffer zone between them and the Fon heartland up-country.[44] Following these encounters with French breech-loading rifles, Behanzin made efforts to re-arm his crack units (including Amazons) with modern weapons. Over the next two years he acquired at least 2,000 breech-loaders of assorted types from German traders on the Togo coast, and about 500 of these were American repeaters – Winchester and Spencer magazine carbines. To his small artillery of old ships' cannon on improvised carriages, the German entrepreneurs also added six Krupp breech-loaders, and five old French *mitrailleuses* captured in 1870.[45]

On 27 March 1892 the gunboat *Topaz*, carrying the French governor on reconnaissance up the Ouemé river, was fired upon. Paris decided to tie up this loose end, and on 30 April gave full civil and military powers to a Naval Troops officer from Senegal, Colonel Dodds. From his arrival on 18 May he began to assemble an expeditionary column of nearly 3,000 men. As an afterthought, on 17 July the War Ministry announced that – most unusually for this theatre of operations – it was to include a marching battalion of the Legion.

WHEN WORD WENT ROUND THE ALGERIAN GARRISONS that a *bataillon de marche* was to be formed, Corporal Frederic Martyn was among the first to volunteer; of more than 4,000 légionnaires in Algeria just 800 were needed, and competition was intense.[46] The Republic's hardest cases became choirboys overnight, sick men tried to fake their way out of the infirmary, NCOs argued over the precedence to which a few extra days in their rank might entitle them, and officers begged and lobbied shamelessly. That same month there had been a call for just four officers to lead a half-company to the Niger river country; although the odds of being chosen were still slim, a whole battalion's-worth of appointments (about 20, plus some staff slots) made it worth a try.[47] It was in hope of this kind of opportunity that officers had chosen a North African posting, rather than putting up with the repetitive processing of intakes of Metropolitan conscripts at home – the back-biting pettiness of garrison life and the stuffy social round of provincial towns, enlivened once a year by rigidly scripted manoeuvres. This was why they endured the dreary loneliness of Algerian outposts: the hope of a chance to escape daily supervision, see combat, test their skills, take risks, and earn medals and promotion – simply, to exercise their calling, and to be at last the soldiers they had dreamt of being when they were growing up in the aftermath of 'the Terrible Year'. At Géryville, every officer of II/2nd RE volunteered; the most senior in each rank was chosen, and they selected the subordinates and the men they wanted (this may have weakened company cohesion, but it guaranteed the quality of the expeditionary unit).[48]

Command of the battalion went to Major Marius Paul Faurax of 1st RE, chosen from among no fewer than sixty applicants. Then 43 years old, he had volunteered into the ranks of the Line in 1867 and was promoted sergeant before his twentieth birthday. The Franco-Prussian War had brought him three wounds, a battlefield commission and, by the age of only 22, admission to the Legion of Honour and a captain's stripes. He lost one of them during the post-war 'revisions', and after long years spent re-climbing the ladder of peacetime seniority he had volunteered for Tonkin, where he had led a Legion battalion in 1889–90. Faurax was under no illusions about the coming campaign, and shortly before embarking he wrote to a friend that 'Most of us setting out will never return, but we are all in good heart, full of confidence, and determined to justify the superb reputation of the Foreign Legion'.[49]

On 2 August 1892 the battalion marched out of the Quartier Viénot, led to the railway station by Minnaert's pioneers and the band, and escorted by the colonel, the colours and the rest of the garrison. Their send-off from Sidi bel Abbès was mirrored by their welcome in Oran; the whole town was *en fête*, and during the three days' wait caused by a shipping delay they enjoyed many admiring glances, slaps on the back and free drinks. They finally sailed on 7 August, aboard the *Mytho* and *Ville de Saint-Nicolas*; they were allowed ashore while the troopships were coaled at Dakar on the 14th–16th, and finally anchored off Cotonou on the 25th. There they disembarked 'in the exciting and haphazard manner peculiar to the surf-bound West African coast'.[50]

THE COASTLINE OF DAHOMEY is low and level, pounded by the Atlantic surf and guarded by treacherous sandbanks; ships had to anchor 2 miles off shore, which made all landings via lighters and small boats perilous, despite the 300-yard timber jetty built out from the beach at Cotonou. The expert Mina boatmen had to time their runs through the breakers and sandbars carefully; they were skilled swimmers, but if their boats were swamped they and their passengers might be taken by the sharks that haunted the shallows.[51] There was no town at Cotonou; behind the beaches lay a network of mangrove swamps and brackish lagoons, and it was through these that the battalion made the 20-mile boat trip east to Porto Novo, the base for the expedition. Here the légionnaires were issued with sun helmets and lightweight khaki jackets, and on 27 August they were inspected by the expedition commander, whom Corporal Martyn was surprised to discover was a mulatto.

Born of a European father and an African mother at St Louis de Sénégal, Alfred Amédée Dodds had graduated from St Cyr in 1864 and reached the rank of full colonel in the Naval Troops by the age of 45 years. 'He looked us over in a way that told us that he was a soldier to his fingers' ends, and many were the expressions of satisfaction that we had got such a leader. Our satisfaction did not diminish, either, when we got to know him better.'[52] Dodds already had nearly 2,000 troops assembled north of Porto Novo, half of them a marching battalion from the 3rd Naval Infantry Regiment with Naval Artillery support; these *marsouins* from Rochefort had the new Lebel repeating rifle, but seemed very young – they had been chosen for the campaign by lottery.[53] The third main element was a marching battalion drawn from the 1st and 2nd Regiments of Senegalese Skirmishers; other black troops were a half-battalion of Hausa Skirmishers and a squadron of mounted Senegalese Spahis.

Behind the coast the country sloped gently upwards towards an interior covered with thick tropical forest; in places this was true primary jungle with a high canopy, in others secondary jungle choked with almost impenetrable bush and tall elephant grass. About 50 miles inland the forest gave way to the *lama*, a great stagnant swamp covering some 400 square miles; this guarded the southern approaches to a more open plateau where Behanzin's capital, Abomey, rose from the scrubland. Although the 80-odd miles from the coast to the capital looked short on the map, in such terrain the only practicable route for a European force with animals, artillery and a large train of African porters was along two sides of a triangle: up the banks of the navigable Ouemé river as far as Poguessa, and then west across country to Abomey (see Map 6). The climate was exhaustingly hot and humid, and the marshy bush was a cauldron of malaria, yellow fever and more exotic diseases. After a lifetime in West Africa, Dodds knew that the main threats to his men were the exhaustion of moving across country and the disease that inevitably followed. While such casualties were unavoidable, they could be reduced by providing large numbers of porters – at first, enough to assign one to carry the rations and camping kit for every two white soldiers. Some of the stores could also be carried part of the way upriver aboard the expedition's two stern-wheel gunboats, *Opale* and *Corail.*

LEAVING A RESERVE of about 900 men at Porto Novo, the expedition struck inland at the end of August with around 2,700 troops, including non-combatants, plus apparently about 3,500 porters. Apart from a diversionary force of two Senegalese companies sent directly north-west for Abomey across country, the infantry were divided between three battalion groups of about 900 troops each. The Legion marched on 1 September, bringing up the rear on the first leg of the route up the east bank of the Oueme. They quickly left the palm groves and village maize-fields behind and plunged into mangrove swamps, elephant grass and bush, which they had to cut with machetes to enlarge trails far too narrow for large numbers of burdened men, artillery, horsemen and ration beefs. Lieutenant Jacquot reckoned they made 2 miles an hour, but Martyn wrote that it was nearer 4 miles in a day. Chopping the bush stirred up ferocious ants and jiggers, and although the soldiers carried only their haversacks, waterbottles, rifles and 150 rounds (the légionnaires still used their 'de Négrier' chest-pouches) the wet, stifling heat was insupportable. At about 5pm each afternoon they halted to clear the jungle for a square camp; at night the howling monkeys and other jungle noises made the sentries jumpy, and mosquitoes attacked in their millions – each morning the troops were made to choke down a bitter draft of quinine before they were given their coffee.

It was eight days before the Legion caught up with the rest of the force, and the battalion was then divided up. The column was now to progress in mixed groups of Senegalese, Naval Infantry and légionnaires, reminiscent of the tactics in North Africa; Groups 1 and 3 had one Legion company each, and Group 2, under Major Faurax, two companies (including Corporal Martyn's).[54] On 11 September the column resumed their march, and on the 15th they reached a patch of slightly higher ground overlooking the village of Dogba on the opposite (west) bank, where they camped, to work on improving the track. On the 16th a strong reconnaissance further upriver to Oboa found no sign of the enemy, and the next day Group 1 moved up to camp there. Groups 2 and 3 remained opposite Dogba, and on the night of

18 September Major Faurax's men were warned to be prepared for a pre-dawn start.

IMMEDIATELY AFTER 'REVEILLE' sounded at 5am on 19 September, while the men were still knuckling their eyes, shots were heard from an outlying picket of Naval Infantry. The men rushed to their piled arms, fumbling half-dressed in the dark; there were a few more shots – and then the *marsouin* picket came panting into camp, with what seemed to be thousands of dark figures dashing through the trees close behind them, roaring war cries.

Dawn was the favourite time for Behanzin's soldiers to attack – the hour when the Fon slave-raids burst upon some sleeping village. They had marched for days through the forest, wearing their drab brown or grey war tunics and carrying their food and sleeping mats on their heads in pack-frames. Well-practised in stealthy night movement and sudden changes of direction, they had evaded the French patrols to approach the camp from the east in their usual horned formation, led by a screen of scouts cam-ouflaged with cloaks and upswept collars of long grass. Some riflemen had already climbed into treetops overlooking the camp, and as the mass of warriors charged the thornbush fences, these started sniping down at the white and khaki blurs milling around between the tents. Others covered the rush from the edge of the trees – Private Lelièvre described them kneeling to fire, or sitting on little wooden stools they had carried with them. The French later reckoned their attackers to be between 3,000 and 4,000 warriors.

They were within 100 yards by the time Lieutenant Jacquot snatched up his revolver and stumbled out of his tent in his shirtsleeves to join his half-naked légionnaires, who were already blazing away into the shadows with the first rifles they could grab. On the east side the abatis held up the rush, giving Major Faurax's officers and buglers the bare moments they needed to get their légionnaires into line. Amid a pandemonium of African war cries, crashing rifle-fire, bugle-calls and bellowed orders, Corporal Martyn was firing as fast as he could reload; the dark figures cannot have made easy targets, since the maize-silk they used to wad their muzzle-loaders made dense black smoke rather than the usual white. The Navy gunners fired their first canister rounds at 100 yards' range, and the Hotchkiss quick-firers on *Opale* began to spray the trees above the infantry's heads. The attackers checked, then switched the weight of their advance to the flanks; Jacquot's men kept them outside the hedge, but in his sector Faurax had to order a charge to drive them back from the tents.

Corporal Martyn found himself fighting waves of machete-wielding warriors face to face; the 5-foot reach of his bayoneted Gras saved him, and he recalled 'throwing them off to make room for another, like a farmer forking hay'. The légionnaires were called back so as not to get trapped in the crowd, and after a moment the Fon came on again fearlessly, carrying themselves with the arrogance of conquerors and ignoring the heaps of their dead piling up around their feet. They were taller and stronger than their subject tribes, very dark-skinned, with parallel ritual scars around their deep-set eyes. After a few more volleys the Legion went forward again with the bayonet, harried all the time by the riflemen on the ground and in the trees; French losses would have been much higher had the Fon been better shots. They seemed to have mastered basic fire-and-movement tactics, with some groups making flank attacks or giving covering fire to rushes by others; but they mostly fired from the hip – in slave-raids the shock of continuous noise sufficed, and since they always greatly outgunned their tribal enemies they had never placed much importance on marksmanship. Nevertheless, even those still armed with muskets used massive charges of their weak gunpowder, and at this short range their bullets, handfuls of shot and slugs of bar iron were perfectly effective killers.

Now that the sun was up, the aim of those with modern rifles became noticeably better; officers were easy to pick out, and Major Faurax was hit – he kept going, was hit again, and fell. Corporal Martyn wrote that légionnaires presented arms spontaneously as their popular commander was carried past, and that Colonel Dodds called out that he would pay 25 francs for every sniper shot out of a tree – 'We'll fetch 'em down for nothing, Colonel!' A third Dahomeyan charge was led by a few women warriors armed with repeaters – the first time that Martyn mentioned these 'Amazons', although they traditionally spearheaded Fon attacks. A sergeant-major of Senegalese Skirmishers pressed forward, foolishly brave, and was struck down and dragged off into the bush; his body, horribly mutilated, was found later (when it doomed two captured Amazons to summary execution).

At some time after 9am the warriors finally gave up and filtered away into the forest, which was shelled blind in order to speed them on their way. Lieutenant Jacquot wrote that when the surroundings of the camp were searched after this battle of Dogba some 170 dead or dying Dahomeyans were found (Martyn reckoned about 300, and another source claims that as many as 832 corpses were finally gathered up and burned). French losses were 45 dead and 60 wounded in all, of which the Legion lost about a dozen killed; they were buried deep, and their graves hidden. The senior captain, Battreau of 1st Company, took over the Legion battalion. Marius Faurax died on one of the riverboats before dawn the following morning; the first bullet to hit him had torn open his large intestine, releasing faecal matter into the stomach cavity, and death from peritonitis was quite inevitable. That day all the troops turned to and began to build an earth and tree-trunk fort, which they named after him.[55]

BEHANZIN SENT AN ENVOY to threaten Dodds with 'the shark who will eat the French', but seemed anxious to discuss terms.[56] The French commander rejected the offer to parley, and on 27 September the column resumed its exhausting march up the east bank of the Oueme, making only about 3 miles a day as they hacked out a path; now each camp had to be entrenched for defence by men already worn out, and on most nights heavy rain fell. After a brush with a Dahomeyan rearguard at the ford of Tohoué on the 31st, the column crossed to the west bank.[57] From here, Dodds decided to march not directly towards Abomey but via the more southerly town of Kana, the kingdom's religious capital; his porters were deserting in some numbers, and he was obliged to reduce the baggage train.

Early on 4 October the force was advancing in two parallel columns, still near the river on their right, when they came up against thousands of Behanzin's troops drawn up for battle near the village of Gbede.[58] Martyn reported that although Behanzin's Krupp guns opened an inaccurate fire, their ineffectiveness did not wholly cure some Frenchmen of their habitual paranoia that British or German instructors might be working with the enemy. However, it was a traditional Dahomeyan foot-charge that actually drove the leading Senegalese horsemen back. A Hausa company were then badly shot up from the cover of elephant grass and also retreated in confusion, thus exposing the Senegalese Skirmishers to a rush by a 'battalion of Amazons', but they stood their ground until the Naval Infantry came up. The Legion were initially held back in reserve, and watched with respect as the women warriors hurled themselves on the *tirailleurs* and *marsouins*. Martyn wrote that they were armed with Spencer carbines and machetes, and handled their repeaters with more skill than their male comrades; they are also known to have carried short, adze-shaped sharpened hoes at their belts, as lethal as tomahawks for close work. They were naked to the waist, wearing only a short blue divided kilt, cartridge belts and a red fez with an eagle feather, and their officers sported a human jawbone mounted on a brass plate strung to hang over the crotch. They fought to the death, and would not surrender: 'These young women were far and away the best men in the Dahomeyan army, and woman to man were quite a match for any of us ... They fought like unchained demons ...'[59]

After about half an hour the Dahomeyans fell back to take a breather, but when the French bugles sounded 'Cease fire' they imagined the white men were out of ammunition, and charged once again. The Legion were now ordered forward, to outflank the left of the Dahomeyan line. They came under fearless attack from several hundred warriors in a surprise encounter on the edge of the tall grass, forcing the légionnaires to form individual company squares. After being ravaged with several volleys, the attackers fell back to some earth-and-timber fortifications concealed by the elephant grass, which they had been foolish to leave in order to fight in the open since Martyn recalled that even with the Dahomeyans thinned and tired out it took the légionnaires several attempts to capture these works at bayonet-point. The Senegalese cavalry then reappeared to catch the Fon in the open, and shelling from the gunboats finally drove Behanzin's warriors off to the north.

Lieutenant Jacquot estimated the number of enemy dead at about 200, and guessed that perhaps twice that many wounded had been taken from the field. Martyn gives the French dead and seriously wounded as 9 and 33 respectively; Private Lelièvre judged that they faced more accurate fire at Gbede than at Dogba, especially from tree-snipers, and this may be borne out by the fact that two of the killed and three of the badly wounded were officers. As the Legion companies searched through the scene of carnage on the battlefield, Captain Battreau picked up a discarded weapon with an exclamation of amazement. Corporal Martyn insisted – anticipating the scepticism of his readers – that Battreau found an old Chassepot that he recognized by a distinctive bullethole through the butt, and then by its serial number, as the very rifle he had carried as a sergeant at St Privat in 1870.[60]

On 6 October the Legion's capture of a bridge and earthworks defended briefly by artillery and small-arms fire cost 6 killed and 33 wounded; 95 Dahomeyan dead were found, and much ammunition abandoned when they retreated quickly to save their guns.[61] This would be the last pitched battle for more than two weeks, but the Dodds column now faced their harshest test of the campaign. They were leaving the river – and thus their line of supply, communication and casualty evacuation – to strike out westwards across perhaps 60 marching-miles of thick, unexplored bush.

THE COLUMN HAD GREAT DIFFICULTY finding clean water; the men were tortured by thirst, and because they could not resist any stagnant puddle at least one in every five suffered from the filth and indignity of marching with dysentery.[62] The blazing sun knocked men over with heat-stroke, and while several violent night-time rainstorms did periodically allow the soldiers to refill their waterbottles, they also left them soaked and chilled for hours. They were incessantly tormented by clouds of mosquitoes; one source has claimed that of every 100 white soldiers, 92 contracted fevers, and that in the Naval Infantry unit the fatality rate among these cases was a staggering 95 per cent, either on the trail or later.[63] This makes the Legion battalion's rate of casualties from disease – which Professor Porch puts at about 35 per cent – seem almost light, and explains his comment that by mid-October the *marsouin* companies had simply ceased to exist as a military force.[64]

Invisible in the thick bush, the Fon clung around them all the way – springing ambushes, cutting off watering parties, harassing the camps by night, wearing the men out and keeping their nerves at screaming pitch. Any of these daily skirmishes might cost up to 20 killed and wounded (86 in all between 13 and 15 October alone).[65] The diminishing convoy of porters, and the fast-growing numbers of stretchers to be carried, meant that the troops now had to struggle through the bush burdened by 75lb packs, which multiplied the numbers of heatstroke and exhaustion casualties as their strength gave way. Rations were reduced to hard biscuit and repellent tinned meat ('monkey'), whose contents could almost be poured from the can in this heat. The column had to pause several times, and on one occasion to retrace its steps for several days, to allow more men and supplies to come up from Porto Novo and for accumulated casualties to be carried back down the trail.

On 17 October, after six weeks on the march, fighting strength was down by nearly 60 per cent to 53 officers and 1,533 men in stinking, thorn-ripped rags, with about 2,000 utterly demoralized porters who had to be guarded and driven by the pitiless Senegalese. That day 200 casualties – some with livid yellow faces, their stretchers stained with dark vomit – started to be carried back down the trail, necessarily with an escort of two full companies of Skirmishers, which reduced bayonet strength even further. In one camp

Corporal Martyn saw the notorious *crapaudine* field punishment inflicted for the first and only time, after an Italian légionnaire struck a sergeant (who in Martyn's view must himself have been to blame). The man was left on the ground for three hours, at the mercy of black ants, with his ankles and wrists tied agonizingly together in the small of his back; after being released, he had to be invalided out.[66]

On 20 October the French had to manoeuvre in square when threatened by 3,000–4,000 warriors. The Fon artillery was more accurate than before, but hardly any of the shells went off, and the gunners' inability to set fuzes argued against the 'white renegade' myth. Behanzin also got an old *mitrailleuse* into action, its crackling sound quaintly unfamiliar to this generation of Frenchmen, and merely amusing to an old Legion warrant officer; he reassured Martyn's company – correctly – that the Dahomeyans would fire much too high. Later that day the sound of bugles blowing '*Le Boudin*' to their east announced the first of some 600 reinforcements who would come in by 24 October, together with a supply convoy.[67] On the 24th the advance resumed, now in four roughly 500-man groups each with one Legion and two African companies, commanded by Majors Riou and Audéoud of the Naval Infantry and Captains Antoine Drude and Poivre of the Legion. It is clear that by this stage the Legion was regarded as the indispensable hard core in any action, while the Skirmishers provided the advance guard, baggage- and artillery-guards and any necessary detachments and escorts.[68] Corporal Martyn recalled tough resistance on 25 October before an earthwork could be captured, but much less the next day when a fort at Kotopa was taken; the Fon seemed anxious to get their artillery out of harm's way, and Martyn reckoned French casualties over 24–26 October as only 10 killed and 75 wounded. However, despite their great losses, a smallpox outbreak, and a rebellion by their Yoruba slaves, the remnants of Behanzin's crack regiments still had fight in them. Before dawn on the 27th the camp was attacked in great strength, and Martyn wrote that 'quite a thousand [men and women] were right in the midst of us. This was a very narrow squeak indeed, and the fight lasted the whole of the day, only ceasing when we had chased the Dahomeyans to within a mile of the walls of Kana'.[69]

On 4 November – now at last clear of the dreadful bush-forest, and into more open country on the outskirts of Kana – the column ran into a modest force that Martyn reckoned put up the most stubborn opposition of the campaign, particularly by Winchester-armed 'Amazons'. The French had to form six company squares to hold off counter-attacks, and 'every one of them was as busy as the biggest glutton for fighting could desire'. The Dahomeyans held their ground even after the Spahis finally captured four of their Krupp guns, but then suddenly fell back towards Abomey, leaving about 300 dead. Martyn was surprised that the column lost only 14 killed and about 50 wounded in this action, which had lasted up to nine hours. The holy city of Kana now lay virtually undefended before them; on 5 November the artillery breached the strong mud-brick walls, and the infantry entered with almost no resistance.

The légionnaires advanced cautiously through tree-shaded open spaces between separate blocks of tall red buildings, towards a walled enclosure that occupied about one-quarter of the town. The gates to the House of Sacrifice hung open; fat flies buzzed in the dim, reeking interior, where a floor smoothly cobbled with the tops of human skulls surrounded a huge stone basin caked with dried blood.[70]

IT HAD TAKEN THEM NINE WEEKS to cover a distance that on the map measured only four days' march at North African rates; but the Fon army was broken, and the rest of the campaign was an anti-climax. Colonel (from 9 October, General) Dodds rested his men at Kana until, receiving an unsatisfactory reply to his ultimatum to Behanzin, on 16 October he put the town to the torch and marched his men the few miles to Abomey. Behanzin in his turn burned and abandoned his capital, though the légionnaires still got a chance to gawp at the great palace gateway, literally built from human skulls and bones. A Senegalese battalion and one Legion company were left in garrison when, on 27 November, the rest began their march back to the coast.

On Christmas Day 1892, Corporal Martyn embarked on the steamer *Thibet* among about 1,400 Army and Navy personnel and families of Senegalese Skirmishers. Before they docked at Oran on 11 January 1893, 5 more légionnaires had died; just 214 of the original 800 landed, of whom 69 had to be carried straight to hospital, and only about 100 were well enough to return directly to Sidi bel Abbès for the ceremonial reception and feasting. Martyn wrote that the total of about 2,300 combatants had lost 15 officers and 143 men killed outright, 3 officers and 90 men died of sickness, and 27 officers and 344 men wounded – 27 per cent casualties, and 11 per cent fatalities. The significant missing figure is, of course, those laid low but not immediately killed by disease. Had this statistic been published, in Martyn's opinion the actual total casualties would have been nearly 75 per cent.[71] Even if we assume that the single Legion company not shipped home on *Thibet* was brought up to a strength of about 200 by taking fit men from the other three companies, then total Legion dead, wounded and disabled by sickness – including those taken straight to hospital in Oran – were indeed at least 75 per cent of the original 800 all ranks. (It must be significant that in 1893 a law was passed forbidding the deployment overseas of Naval Troops conscripts unless they specifically volunteered to join such marching battalions.)[72]

Behanzin and his last couple of hundred warriors continued to evade capture in the arid northern wilderness for another year, but although the Dahomeyans had to give up the human element of the Grand Customs they remained peaceful enough – especially those tribes that had now been released from the Neronian rule of the Fon kings. Nevertheless, a strong draft of Legion reinforcements was sent out early in 1893, and one of these was a former comrade of Major Faurax in Tonkin in 1889–90: Captain Paul Brundsaux, whose six-and-a-half-foot frame and enormous forked beard would one day be immortalized in bronze on the high altar of Legion ancestor-worship. Another was Private Léon Silbermann, who left an account of exhausting marches and continuing deaths from sickness until this successor Legion marching battalion returned to Algeria and was disbanded on 3 March 1894. Silbermann claimed that his unit, too, had been reduced to about quarter-strength by disease, and that two of the stretcher cases actually died on the quayside at Oran during the welcoming ceremony.[73]

SOMEWHERE OFF THE AFRICAN WEST COAST, Silbermann's returning ship must have passed another trooper which left Oran for Senegal on 19 February 1894, carrying – among others – 10 officers and 305 men of the Legion, including the now-Sergeant Minnaert of the 1st RE. On 15 January that year, in the emptiness of what is now Mali, a Lieutenant-Colonel Bonnier of the Naval Troops had joined the list of Frenchmen for whom the deceptive lure of the name Timbuktu proved fatal. After briefly visiting that disappointing museum he and his company of Skirmishers had been wiped out by Tuareg tribesmen; their bodies were found by a more methodical Army officer, the engineer Major Joseph Joffre. It was decided that the Niger country needed some token reinforcement of white troops, and in February the Legion were ordered to embark two infantry companies.

These were formed under Captains Nicolon (1st RE) and Certeau (2nd RE), and again included a high proportion of Tonkin veterans. On 2 March – while Private Silbermann and those few of his mates who were healthy enough were gorging themselves on their welcome-home feast in Oran – Major Bouvier (2nd RE) led the draft ashore at St Louis de Sénégal.

Captain Certeau was ordered upriver to Timbuktu via Kayes, Bamako and Segou; he reached Segou only on 29 April after many delays and detours in the riverine marshes, and his company stayed there until repatriated eight months later. The only members of Bouvier's command to see action were a 20-man detachment under Lieutenant Betbeder and Sergeant Minnaert. Providing a stiffening for Captain Bonnacorti's Skirmishers, they distinguished themselves in the capture of the remote village of Bossé, lair of a slaver named Ali Kary. As usual, three-quarters of them had become casualties from wounds or sickness by the time they returned to base.[74]

The irrepressible Minnaert does not seem to have been a man much given to reflection, but we may perhaps wonder if he and his lieutenant ever reminisced – as they squelched through the reed-marshes, slapping their necks – about the taste of guavas in the cool shade of a banyan tree. During that autumn of 1894 a restless French cavalry officer at a crossroads in his career was sailing East to discover such delights, and other more substantial rewards.

6. Tiger Country

*On the night of 22/23 June 1889 Légionnaire Gatelet
was taken by a tiger while on sentry duty ... The tiger
must have jumped the wall and ditch, surprised him from
behind while he was rolling a cigarette – we found the
paper and tobacco with his dropped rifle – and carried
him out over the wall again ... Next day we found his
remains 150 yards away.*

Corporal Jean Pfirmann

*[Out here] there is not a single young lieutenant, chief of
an outpost or leader of a reconnaissance who does not
develop in six months more initiative, decision,
endurance and personality than an officer would
acquire in France in the whole of his career.*

Major Hubert Lyautey, 22 December 1894[1]

MAJOR LOUIS HUBERT GONSALVE LYAUTEY was a man whose
happiness depended upon lively and informed conversation, and in October
1894 – despite the enervating heat in the Red Sea – he may have been the
happiest man aboard the steamship *Oxus*, since his fellow passengers made
for gratifyingly mixed company. Lyautey had perfect manners, and he tasted
all his temporary companions before choosing those he would devour: some
'old China hands'; an Italian missionary bishop; the *colon* black-sheep of a
wealthy family of Lyautey's acquaintance, accompanied by a lady of dubious
marital status; a number of Dutch and English colonials including a raffish
'adventuress', and – most fascinatingly – the much-travelled niece of the
second Rajah Brooke of Sarawak.

Still just short of his fortieth birthday, Lyautey had been promoted from captain some five years younger than was usual. He was a slim man of above average height, with a fine forehead, dark brows over large pale blue eyes, and a strikingly sensual mouth hidden by the big moustache of those days. He was very much a gentleman, taking his tone as much from his mother's family of minor Norman aristocrats as from the practical soldiers and engineers on his father's side. His turnout was always immaculate, as befitted a light cavalryman; the only thing that he might have regretted as he checked himself searchingly in the looking-glass before emerging on stage was his painfully thin legs – the legacy of a serious childhood accident that had kept him in calipers until the age of 12.[2]

This confinement had made young Hubert a voracious reader, and if anything it had increased his competitive energy when he was finally released; his stork's legs had not prevented him from becoming a fine horseman, which spoke for his determination. His grandfather and great-uncle had both been artillery generals, who between them could boast memories of Wagram, Moscow and Waterloo. As a boy Hubert had loved playing with toy soldiers, and had been fascinated by his grandfather's scars from Russia. But his father, Just Lyautey, was a respected civil engineer, and at home near Nancy in Lorraine – where his adored mother presided over an elegant, cultured country-house life – the boy also loved 'playing countries', building landscapes of towns, roads and railways in his sandpit.

THERE WAS NEVER any question about young Hubert's path in life; precociously gifted, he passed the entrance exams for both the École Polytechnique and St Cyr in 1872 at the age of 16. In 1876 he passed straight into staff school, yet despite this success his diaries are full of complaints about the pettiness of the academy regimes and the uninspiring curriculum. After a year of regimental duty interrupted by bad health, in 1880 a two-year posting to Algeria opened his eyes to another perspective, and he greedily sucked everything he could from this exotically different environment. He was promoted from lieutenant to captain at the early age of 26, just before his return to France late in 1882, and after a year with the 4th Light Horse at Épinal he was picked for the staff of the Inspector General of Cavalry at Commercy. It was there that the unvarying, stifling rigidities of the Metropolitan Army began to close around his spirit like the coils of a python. He was always a man prey to volatile swings of mood, and he was shocked by what time had done to some of his elders. Long years of routine and iron regulation had snuffed out any fire or curiosity they might once have had, narrowing them into pompous martinets to whom the slightest deviation from the norm seemed offensively disturbing.

Lyautey needed some project to which he could devote his energy and which would further his driving ambition, and the life of home garrisons could not provide it. Reading, correspondence and occasional like-minded social contacts kept him in touch with the worlds of art and ideas, but he seldom found opportunities to explore them in the face-to-face discussions on which he thrived. Frustrated, he took long leaves to travel in Europe; Italy charmed him, and for a while he was intrigued by the Catholic Church – not doctrinally, but politically; at that time the divisions within the French thinking classes made papal relations with the Republic a subject of real controversy. Lyautey's family connections secured him personal audiences both with the exiled Bourbon pretender, the Comte de Chambord, and with Pope Leo XIII, and he attended a thrilling pontifical mass in the Sistine Chapel – attractively risky adventures for an officer in the Army of the anti-clerical Republic. But though briefly excited by even such light brushes with history, Lyautey soon recognized them as cul-de-sacs, and continued to cast about restlessly for an outlet for his enthusiasm.

He seemed to have found it for a while when he took up a squadron command at St Germain late in 1887. With responsibility for 160 troopers – a responsibility that he took more seriously than many brother officers, who knew their troop horses better than the men who rode them – Captain Lyautey became determined to improve the day-to-day conditions that they had to endure. The French Army was a traditionally neglectful employer, and the whitewashed and tarred stone boxes in which it stacked its conscripts were essentially prisons. Some were very old and all were cramped and badly heated, with completely inadequate washing facilities, latrines and sick quarters – mundane details, but important to the men's morale. Conscripts got little free time, especially in the cavalry, where care of the horses required many fatigue duties quite apart from the daily six or eight hours of drills and exercises. The previous year was the first in which rankers had even been granted free Sundays, and there was nothing for them to do except wander the streets of little provincial towns and visit bars and brothels.

In 1886 General Boulanger had ordered the provision of recreation rooms in barracks, but these would be slow to materialize. Lyautey installed a *foyer* for his men – a clubroom, with a billiard table, a library, reading and writing facilities and non-alcoholic refreshments. 'My aim is to give them distraction, as well as instruction and fatigues, within the barracks ... to escape from the present situation, in which after 5pm every man who is not sufficiently stupefied to go to bed is condemned to the street corner or the [wet] canteen.' These efforts, modest enough, impressed some observers sufficiently to be reported in the press, but were regarded by others as suspiciously radical. Such improvements were associated in the Army mind with Boulanger, who in that winter of 1887–8 was at the height of his dangerous notoriety, so Lyautey's timing was innocently tactless.[3]

When bored and discouraged, Lyautey occasionally found the sort of company he craved through the hospitality of a former educator and politician named Guerle, a man of wide connections in several worlds. The whole nervous system of the upper classes functioned through personal contacts and mutual acquaintances, and Lyautey was always alert to opportunities for extending his network. In Guerle's salons he mixed with liberal and literary figures (including, on at least one occasion, Marcel Proust), and he found a friend in an influential man of letters, Comte Eugène Melchior de Vogüé. The elegant and charming Lyautey was good social value; these men were not used to soldiers who could discuss the latest novels with knowledgeable enthusiasm, and their interest encouraged him to express his frustrations at the dogmatism of the military hierarchy. Vogüé suggested that Lyautey write an article on socio-military reform for his journal *Revue des Deux Mondes*. The consequent 50-page essay, 'On the Social Functions of the Officer under Universal Military Service', impressed Vogüé so much that he published it complete in the March 1891 issue. Briefly, Lyautey argued the importance of officers getting truly involved with their men, using the unique opportunity of mass conscription to combine the Army's central role with that of a school of citizenship, both educating the poor for an improved standard of life and healing the mutual suspicions between the classes.

The article was printed anonymously, but when it caused a stir Lyautey's authorship was soon revealed. To the most reactionary, he was a dangerous socialist; to the merely conventional, a muddle-headed dreamer; but to like-minded progressives (in a number of different political camps) he was a refreshing new voice. Lyautey found himself in demand as a speaker, and became a member of one of those *groupuscules* so dear to the self-regard of French intellectuals. His vanity was caressed, but his small measure of celebrity earned him the automatic distrust of some senior officers. At a time of murderous outrages by anarchists, culminating in the actual assassination of a President of the Republic, the more ossified members of the establishment were inclined to overreact to any further hint that the world was going to the dogs – such as cavalry officers publicly expressing social theories.[4]

Nevertheless, the 'socialist captain' clearly had his supporters – he sprang, after all, from a reliably conservative family. In 1893 he was promoted major, and a few months later he was posted as chief-of-staff to the 7th Cavalry Division at Meaux. His initial excitement over the favourable responses to his ideas was short-lived; as his 40th birthday approached, his spirits drooped at the prospect of long years of mind-numbing routine leading only to a colonelcy, perhaps eventually to a brigadier-general's stars before a pointless retirement. His discontents extended beyond the merely military; he wrote to his lifelong friend and confidant Major Antoine de Margerie of his unhappiness in a world

> burdened with prejudice, clichés and formulas, where during the whole of
> our adolescence and youth we were kept at arm's length from life, under the
> pretext of safeguarding and correction ... where the human and intellectual
> horizon was deliberately drawn in so tightly around us ... During these past
> ten years, what personal efforts were demanded of us, and what scandals
> roused, in order to free ourselves from these swaddling-clothes![5]

IN AUGUST 1894, MAJOR LYAUTEY was on manoeuvres at Brie when he was informed of his appointment to a staff post in Tonkin. His sympathetic biographer André Maurois suggests that friends in high places felt he would benefit from some fresh air far from the introverted quarrels of the Metropolitan Army. Others believe that he was sent into what careerists regarded as outer darkness in delayed punishment for trumpeting his ideas in 1891–2; and at least one commentator has interpreted the posting as a banishment due to official disapproval of Lyautey's undoubted homosexuality. Descriptions of Lyautey's temperament by men who served with him leave little room for doubt, and it is even plausible to interpret in this way his lament to Antoine de Margerie quoted above. To what extent he was sexually active is another question, but not an interesting one. Odd though it appears today, nineteenth-century gentlemen of devout family were indoctrinated with values of duty and self-control that enabled some of them to channel repressed energies in constructive directions, at whatever emotional cost. On the other hand, *fin de siècle* French society was more tolerant than Victorian Britain, and homosexual acts were not illegal. All that matters, surely, is that any prejudice or indiscretion there may have been did not rob France of Hubert Lyautey's talents.

He sailed in October, on the *Pei-Ho* as far as Egypt (which he gulped down like a drink during his few days ashore), and then on the *Oxus* down the Red Sea and across the Indian Ocean. Despite his innate reserve towards Britain as the great national rival, part of his pleasure during the voyage sprang from his contacts with British travellers (of which one fellow-officer strongly disapproved – did Lyautey not realize that any English wealthy enough to travel must be government agents?). He was struck by how confidently some British women set out across the world without a male protector – extraordinary to a Frenchman. He also noted that the British men returning to the East after home leave invariably spoke of their colony as their lifelong future, while 'the wasters and the needy who, with us, usually occupy similar posts' counted the years until they qualified to return to France for good.[6]

Lyautey's letters really catch fire after stopovers during the voyage revealed to him something of how Britain organized its colonial possessions and garrisons. His correspondence is full of praise for British 'strength, unity of plan, continuity of design ... promptness of execution, practical good sense, tenacity, complete adaptation to the country and the climate. In a word, everything that we do not have'. Britain seemed to 'breathe initiative':

> In front of us rises the admirable English organization – broad, supple, full of
> continuity, managed from top to bottom by gentlemen (or by those who
> know how to behave like gentlemen whatever their origins) ... there is a
> school, a doctrine, a colonial system based on experience from which they
> derive methods essentially supple and elastic in their application, leaving the
> details to be dealt with by personal initiative, with latitude to vary [broad
> guidelines] to the utmost.[7]

Bearing in mind his project at St Germain, it is not surprising to read – even from Aden, of all hellish stations – his comments on the spacious, airy quarters and the sports facilities provided for all ranks (*le sport* was almost unknown in the French forces). But it was Singapore that was his real road to Damascus; his letter to his sister of 7 November 1894 seems to have been written in a sort of daze of admiration, and it encapsulates – by contradiction – most of the things he loathed about the French Army.

He describes in detail the quarters of the Lincolnshire Regiment, set in unenclosed, unguarded parkland; the only sentry he saw was at the ammunition magazine. Separate company bungalows were built for space, coolness and ventilation, each with shaded verandahs, its own Chinese-staffed kitchen, a dining room, a spacious and well-equipped bathroom (open to all, at all hours) and separate latrines. There was a large recreation hall with billiard tables, newspapers, writing facilities, and a library whose shelves were regularly refreshed. There was an officers' mess whose ante-room was 'a sort of *salle d'honneur*, with flags, the names of battles, regimental souvenirs'; a bar, and a small theatre for entertainments; a gym, two swimming-pools, and pitches and courts for football, cricket and tennis. Lyautey and a consular interpreter were shown around by a sergeant, whom they had to unearth from his prettily overgrown bungalow in garden surroundings. When Lyautey expressed astonishment at the apparent absence of restrictions the NCO was puzzled: 'What would be the good of it? Why should we keep the place closed? The men know the hours; it is their business to be on the spot at the proper time. As for their dress, they know what would happen if they were seen incorrectly turned out.' Lyautey does not address the important fact that British soldiers were all volunteers rather than conscripts, but he writes in an ecstasy of envious pleasure:

> I revel in the sight of the application of all my ideas. These are not, after all,
> Utopian – somewhere there do exist cheerful military quarters, open,
> welcoming, where duty wears a smiling aspect, where men are men – and
> not ragged convicts, shut in, sweeping those eternal courtyards under
> querulous overseers. But what would our warrant officers in France say?
>
> What would our Engineers say, at the sight of this camp where symmetry
> has been purposely avoided, and the houses are not all aligned and of identical
> design, but dotted about as at Trianon, merely for the pleasure of the eye? ...
> I should not dare to bring even the best-disposed Engineer officer here. He
> might approve enthusiasticaly, but he would certainly want to copy the
> whole plan slavishly. It would then form a Colonial Type, the same
> everywhere, at Hanoi as at Biskra, at Tamatave as in New Caledonia ...
>
> What can one say of ... the quarters in the park, so lavishly laid out for
> amusement and study; of the liberty permitted out of duty hours; of the
> constant call on initiative, the encouragement of a sense of responsibility,
> the proof of confidence in the men one commands? ... [I despair] when
> I think that in France hardly anyone believes in or wants such things – that
> regulations, coercion, are in our blood to such an extent that even amongst

the best there is not one in ten who does not consider that all is lost if the men do not groom their horses in time with music, and peel potatoes to a measured rhythm.[8]

LYAUTEY'S DISDAIN FOR FRENCH BUREAUCRACY and inertia was aggravated after he reached Saigon; it is a recurrent theme in his correspondence, but a couple of examples are enough. The main telegraph office refused to accept French gold coins – which had been accepted in every British office across the world, and even at Kandy railway station in Ceylon. There were two telegraph lines from Saigon to Hanoi, one French, one British (extended down from China); the Army used the British one even for official despatches, since it was much faster and more reliable than the French. Again, a French officer in charge of a district up-country told Lyautey that he had employed landless Vietnamese labourers for building work in a region previously abandoned for years to the 'pirates'. The colonel wanted to give each of his workers a plot of land around the reborn village to consolidate the pacification of the area, but the civil power refused permission unless each peasant submitted an application on the same forms used to register land titles in France. Unsurprisingly, they drifted back into the forest, where many of them took up banditry simply in order to eat.[9]

It is widely conceded by French historians that colonial development was handicapped by the low quality of the civilian administration. For decades, different directorates in the ministries of the Navy, Trade, War and Foreign Affairs had fought turf wars over their responsibilities and prerogatives. When the Colonial Ministry was finally created in the year that Lyautey arrived in Indochina, it housed an assortment of jealously squabbling departments with responsibilities that either overlapped or left gaps between, and all of them starved of men with real local knowledge. The instability of governments robbed the ministry of any continuity of direction; the average tenure of a colonial governor before 1920 was just one year, and most other officials also rotated at frequent intervals. It has become a lazy cliché to accuse French colonial military officers of making policy in the saddle. Since they had often been in-country for twice as long as the often ignorant and dilatory administrators, had more contact with the villagers, and were confronted by immediate life-and-death situations without guidance from the civil power, they had little choice but to act according to their experience and instincts. (As Professor Porch has pointed out, their decisions were usually based on a rough-and-ready natural justice that was

far more acceptable to the Vietnamese than the cruel inanities of the bureaucrats – *vide* Lyautey's tale of land title application forms.)

Since the specific comparison was often made by contemporary Frenchmen, it is legitimate to note that these administrators presented a sorry
contrast to those of the British colonial service, who were selected by
demanding competitive examination from among an educational elite,
required to learn local languages, and indoctrinated with an ideal of
imperial service that passed down through generations of the same
families. This ideal hardly existed in France, where the colonies were
widely regarded as dumping-grounds for professional failures and family
embarrassments, and consequently the quality of the personnel was
sometimes shockingly low. Such posts were often sought (by political
jobbery) only as the last resort of the otherwise unemployable; of those
in Senegal, General Brière de l'Ile wrote that they were 'if not actually
compromised at home, then at least incapable of making a living there'.
Anxious above all to avoid criticism from Paris, they shied away from
taking decisions and sought refuge in the wording of regulations drafted
far away and in an almost frivolous ignorance of local conditions. As late
as 1900–14 barely 50 per cent of the recruits to the service had even
secondary education; it is hardly surprising that military graduates of St
Cyr and the Polytechnique despised them.[10]

AFTER A FEW DAYS IN SAIGON Lyautey sailed up to Hanoi, and
again he was lucky in his company: Governor-General Antoine de Lanessan
himself. Since the governor spoke freely about his frustrations and hopes,
the major clearly made himself respectfully agreeable. Paris was obsessed
with short-term profit from customs revenue and taxation, 'eating up the
corn while it is still only grass'. Lanessan was insistent that France must
try to work with the existing Vietnamese power structure, imperfect and
secretive though it might be, rather than seeking to break an armature that
had held native society together for a thousand years. The French would
always be in a tiny minority, so they must patiently persuade the local elite
that it was in their own long-term interest to cooperate. The white men
must not seek to change local habits, and must offend no traditional beliefs.
To the argument that France should not be helping to entrench the selfish
privileges of mandarins (who might just as easily be working against them),
but should 'liberate and educate the poor', Lanessan replied that hierarchy
was natural in all human societies, and cited the relative success of the

protectorate in Tunisia compared with the squalor of Algeria. Lyautey recalled from his own tour in 1880–82 what had happened to the Algerian poor when their local leadership was utterly destroyed – that method might 'satisfy the mentality of corporals, but it doesn't get you very far'. Lyautey wrote of the governor-general's approach that 'this system is distasteful to the military mind, which is a powerful argument for its good sense'.[11] The belief that a people of utterly different culture would welcome the chance to become imitation Frenchmen if the ancient framework of their own society was dismantled may ostensibly have been humane, but was actually a patronising fantasy.

Arriving in Hanoi in the pleasant winter weather, Lyautey was introduced to his duties as head of the 2nd Bureau of the military staff, and immediately found them engrossing. It was his task to collate operational and intelligence information about the grinding fight against the rebels and brigands all over the four military territories into which Lanessan had recently divided Tonkin.[12] However, Lyautey's first impressions of his colleagues were not favourable: they all seemed to hate Tonkin and despise the people, and their envious self-interest was as bad as anything he had encountered in home garrisons. They had no officers' club but lived in furtive, gossipy cliques of four or five together, mirroring the introverted society of the tiny *colon* population. On expressing his surprise at the lack of a club, Lyautey was told that such an institution would only be a trap where they would be spied upon by police informers.[13] He was pained to find that despite their lack of interest in Indochina there were no collective subscriptions to French newspapers and journals, but any need for entertaining stimulus disappeared within ten days of his arrival.

A combination of illness and absence among the staff suddenly propelled Lyautey into the post of acting chief-of-staff to General Duchemin, the commander-in-chief. He had to throw himself into a ridiculously demanding crash course of self-education on the job – about the country, the operational and logistic systems, current plans and problems, even relations with the Chinese Guangtung Army on the north-east frontier. He rose to the challenge, loving the urgent and varied work, and he found his new colleagues to be friendly, helpful and several cuts above the time-servers he had first met. These were real colonial soldiers – knowledgeable, pragmatic, widely travelled and experienced in action. Recent years had provided them with plentiful opportunities to acquire such experience.[14]

*

SINCE THE TREATY OF TIENTSIN IN 1885, contacts between the commanders of Chinese and French outposts facing one another along the Tonkin border had become warily correct. By the mid-1890s General Liu Yung-fu was far away, leading his Black Flags against the Japanese on Formosa (though still carrying Lieutenant Garnier's pocketwatch as a souvenir of his glory days); nevertheless, there was no shortage of rebels-cum-bandits, both in the high country and along the Delta rivers.[15] On the borders, Chinese officers maintained lucrative relations with the gang leaders, and their own troops often slipped over to make freelance raids that would be blandly denied at the next meeting with their French opposite numbers. The ex-soldiers and bandits sustained themselves by preying on the local tribes, with whom they had no ethnic links; they simply took what they wanted – food, women (both for their own pleasure and to sell as slaves in China), buffaloes and opium. Down in the Delta they terrorized and taxed the nearest villages and raided those further afield, and even villages within sight of Hanoi were sometimes burned. Some rebel leaders had useful contacts with mandarins, whose hand could be detected in such provocations as the kidnapping of French officials for huge ransoms (which were almost invariably paid, thus encouraging the practice).

The capture and exile of King Ham Nghi in 1888 had made the task of pacification no easier; Paris demanded quicker results than the nature of the problem allowed, while declining to provide the funds and troops that might have made a difference. Starved of men and resources, the generals tried to keep watch over the countryside by planting in the most infested areas isolated posts held by single European companies and platoons, each side-by-side with double the number of Tonkinese Skirmishers, but their radius of control was very limited. The bandits' local intelligence network was nearly always superior, and the rare French success in setting an ambush or making a surprise dawn attack on a hideout depended on the guidance of some vengeful turncoat. The little garrisons were sometimes vulnerable themselves – though usually to night sniping rather than to actual assault – and their resupply parties were doubly so. The terrain and climate were extremely punishing, and the bandits nearly always enjoyed the initiative. Even after the occasional local French success, effective pursuit was usually impossible, so the rebels simply scattered, to reassemble when the French had to turn back.

If a major rebel fort in the hills was located, territory commanders would scrape up enough men during the practical campaigning season (the European winter months) for a mixed 'shandy column' of légionnaires and Skirmishers with a few mountain guns, and the large train of porters needed to keep it supplied for a couple of weeks. Moving such a force along rudimentary jungle tracks through the highlands was slow, noisy and exhausting. Coolies could not carry more than about 35lbs in this terrain; men had to be assigned to guard and escort them – and also the wives of the Tonkinese Skirmishers, who always had to accompany any major movement carrying cooking pots and their husbands' packs.[16] This all made for long and unwieldy columns; it was predictable that they did not achieve much, and more surprising that the bandits – who often had repeating rifles and plentiful ammunition – never dared to attack such a force with determination while it was strung out in broken country. Instead they usually skirmished with its advance guard, buying time for their main group to disperse before they could be brought to battle.

Their bases had usually been abandoned long before the column arrived, but when a major fort was found, attacked, and defended, the fighting was often more difficult and costly than French commanders had expected. Until they had actually seen one with their own eyes they did not seem to appreciate that these strongholds might be cleverly sited and formidably well built. One captured by General Voyron in March 1892 (after laboriously assembling 6,300 men – about 20 per cent of the whole occupation corps) covered a square mile, with more than 100 buildings and sophisticated triple ramparts, and an Engineer officer calculated that it must have taken 1,500 coolies nine months to build it.[17] Despite operations by converging columns, the defenders of such forts could seldom be encircled before they filtered away into the wilderness, to establish a new lair somewhere not far off (they, too, used baggage porters, though in their case kidnapped rather than paid). They knew that the French could not keep large forces in the field for long – and meanwhile, the areas stripped of troops to form the columns were themselves left undefended.

French operations were thus repetitive and rarely productive, but they were not cheap. Battle casualties were modest – an average of 184 killed and wounded each year in 1893–6 – but those from fever were, as always, much higher. Although total Legion combat deaths in Indochina were only 271 in the twenty-two years between 1887 and 1909, disease killed almost exactly ten times as many, and the health of those who survived was often so wrecked that the men had to be shipped back to Algeria for discharge. As already noted, the annual replacement rate needed to keep the four Legion battalions up to strength suggests that they suffered an attrition of 25 per cent of their effectives every year.[18]

THE MEMOIRS OF THREE LÉGIONNAIRES – the Bavarian Jean Pfirmann, and the Englishmen Frederic Martyn and George Manington – provide vivid glimpses of life on column and in jungle forts north of the Delta between 1888 and 1894. There was never any shortage of volunteers for drafts, despite the occasionally shocking state of men who returned to the depot, from Indochina; for most of that time Tonkin was the only place a légionnaire could earn bragging rights and a campaign medal. This attraction was powerfully reinforced by legends of clean, compliant women, and by the certainty of colonial double pay and a campaign supplement to any eventual pension.

The 500-strong Tonkin drafts sailed from Oran on the 5,000-ton trooper *Bien Hoa*, after enthusiastic send-offs.[19] The ship could carry about two battalions; Naval Troops were embarked in Marseille before the Legion draft was picked up in Oran, and the men enjoyed light work and good food during the five-week voyage. In the Suez Canal and during coaling stops at Colombo and Singapore some légionnaires were always tempted to desert, though usually more for the challenge than with any real idea of what they would do if they succeeded. Martyn wrote that, in harbour, Naval Troops sentries were posted around the rails, and when two légionnaires made a run down the gangplank in Singapore they were shot down, to the incredulous rage of their comrades that the *marsouins* had not fired wide; for the rest of the voyage the Anchor and the Grenade had to be kept strictly segregated.[20]

Haiphong had expanded remarkably since 1883; it now had floating wharfs, and brick buildings along wide boulevards with electric lighting. After a modest evening on the town, Corporal Martyn was collared by the sergeants to help round up the rest of his draft, led astray by their first encounters with *chum-chum*. (A litre of this vile-tasting distilled rice spirit cost more than three days' pay, but men pooled their resources – a litre of *chum-chum* went a long way.)[21] The new arrivals were boated up the Thai Binh and Thuong rivers to the Legion depot at Phu Lang Thuong, set among the close-packed Bao Dai hills. A big pagoda was used as a storehouse and magazine, and when Pfirmann arrived in the winter of 1888/9 substantial new barracks of ironwood and bamboo were being built; there was the usual village for the Tonkinese Skirmishers' families, Chinese shops, and even a store run by a retired Legion NCO. This was, however, very much an operational zone, and at night the glow of burning villages was often seen. Any patrols that responded before sunrise risked ambush, but when they went looking for trouble by day they seldom found any.[22]

PHU LANG THUONG WAS A CROSSROADS for communications, being linked to the 2nd Territory headquarters at Lang Son by the old Mandarin Road. The area of operations lay to the north of the depot in the region called the Yen The (see Map 7), roughly between Thai Nguyen and the Cau river on the west and south, the Thuong river and the Mandarin Road on the east, and Van Linh in the mountains to the north. The southern Yen The was mostly a fertile plain where villagers raised tobacco, yams, and mulberry trees for silkworms. About 20 miles north of Phu Lang Thuong this rich – and therefore vulnerable – country sloped up into heavily wooded hills and the chaotic Ngan Son and Bac Son mountains. These ranges were part of the wide territory that would become infamous in the 1940s–50s as the 'Viet Bac', the almost impenetrable redoubt of the Communist Viet Minh, and its selection by General Giap for his secret bases had solid historical precedents. In the 1880s–90s the mountains had been bandit country for thirty years; they formed a corridor giving access to sources of rich booty in the south, and to suppliers and markets in the north, astride the Chinese frontier all the way between Cao Bang and Lang Son.

Pfirmann's 4th Company, I/1st RE provided rotating detachments for small posts at Kep, Bo Ha and Bac Le; he was told that their main adversaries were a band led by one Doi Van – Sergeant Van – a deserter from the Tonkinese Skirmishers. (There was a loose chain of command among the rebels; the Yen The country was the fief of one De Tam, a *lettré* who had answered the call when King Ham Nghi took to the hills, and the whole territory was essentially under the parallel rule of a former military mandarin named De Nam.) In the spring of 1889, Corporal Pfirmann was sent with Captain Bonnet's company to finish building and then to garrison the post at Bo Ha on a small, snake-infested hill above the banks of the Thuong river. The ground had already been cleared and two 50-yard-long thatched bamboo barracks built, for one platoon of légionnaires and two of Skirmishers. Now the post had to be ditched and walled; the work was urgent, but it was delayed by the need to send out frequent patrols. Prickly heat, painful boils and dysentery were a constant; the commissariat was lax about supplying mosquito nets, and quinine and bismuth – while freely given – were pre-scribed on a distinctly hit-or-miss basis. However, although there was no informed medical treatment, when Pfirmann went down with his first bad attack of malaria his mates cared for him with a tenderness that touched him.

The captain kept the men's spirits up by distributing extra wine (creatively accounted for by the quartermaster-sergeant), and encouraging evening sing-songs and theatrical turns. The 4th Company badly needed cheering up after 23 June. The first thing Pfirmann had been told on arrival at Bo Ha was that a tiger had just taken the captain's horse from its stable, and tigers were never far from his thoughts after that date, when the night-sentry Private Gatelet suffered the same fate while distracted by rolling a *cibiche* (sentries were allowed to smoke, to keep off the mosquitoes). 'We buried him on his 23rd birthday. He came from Metz, following his brother, who was a sergeant-major in the 2nd Foreign.'[23]

DURING THE RAINY SEASON IN JULY 1889 two mixed columns were assembled from six post garrisons to search the Bao Dai hills. Pfirmann's column was soon more or less lost and suffering badly from heat in the stinking jungle east of Bac Le, and two officers and several men came down with fever. The few villagers they came across were too scared of the bandits to give the troops any information, or even to sell them food unless forced to do so. In the same area a couple of years later, Manington described the terrain:

> The little track we followed passed [for nine miles] through a succession of jungle-covered valleys, and over hills hidden in primeval forests of teak, banyan, ironwood and palm trees, some of which were of enormous size, with an impenetrable undergrowth of fern, interlacing creepers, orchids and spiked rattan. In these woods the light of day was almost shut out by dense foliage; no birds seemed to live there, and the strange, weird silence was only broken now and again by troops of chattering brown monkeys, which, disturbed by our approach, would scuttle away through the branches. [24]

The Tonkinese Skirmishers normally provided the vanguard: a point man (with 'one up the spout'), followed after 40 yards by a 'cover-point' of a corporal and four men, and at the same interval again by a half-platoon under a French sergeant. The légionnaires followed after another 40-yard gap (given the Gras rifle's lack of a safety catch they do not seem to have carried it loaded), and 100 yards behind them a corporal and ten légionnaires formed the rearguard. Exact spacing was, of course, almost impossible to maintain in such thick country.[25] By now the Legion in Tonkin were issued with Naval Troops' khaki drill uniforms and helmet-covers. On column they carried 120 rounds of ammunition and reduced kit in a tent-cloth roll slung round the body horseshoe-fashion; Manington recalls filling his waterbottle with cold, weak coffee, and carrying an 18-inch *coupe-coupe* machete at his hip.

Even without knapsacks, it was still exhausting to spend long days climbing and descending steep, slippery slopes, wading streams, cutting trails – almost tunnels – through thick bamboo and elephant grass, and all in humid temperatures of up to 110°F (43°C). Although the night halt would find them completely worn out, the men slept badly; they were tormented by mosquitoes and voracious jungle leeches, and spooked by the whooping of monkeys, the sudden crashing of large animals through the bush, and the occasional cough of a tiger. They hardly ever saw the sky through the forest canopy, and marched by compass bearing – in circles, Pfirmann suspected. These short-range columns took only a few porters; they had left Kep with rations for four days, and by the sixth they were seriously hungry until the problem was solved by the marksmanship of Private Kuhn in a sudden lucky encounter with a stag.[26]

Although Pfirmann's patrol had nothing useful to show for their exertions, as small jungle expeditions went this one got off lightly. When a patrol was several days' out in the worst terrain it was impossible to carry for long men who collapsed from heatstroke or fever; their reeling comrades were themselves too near the end of their endurance and had to keep moving. Sometimes the casualty was simply disarmed and left behind, but after subsequent searches found bodies decapitated it was generally accepted that a merciful bullet through the head was the only solution. Even if the bandits did not find the poor wretch, huge jungle rats or soldier-ants certainly would.[27]

Not all probes into the Yen The highlands were as uneventful. In August 1889, General Borgnis-Desbordes ordered three small columns to converge from Kep, Phu Lang Thuong and further west in an attempt to find bandit hideouts. The first, of 230 men, comprised Pfirmann's 4th Company, I/1st RE and the 2nd of I/4th Tonkinese Skirmishers (companies in Tonkin were only about 100 strong). On 28 August, creeping along between a rockface on one side and a ravine on the other, the point party ran into a barricade and came under fire; the Legion's Lieutenant Montera and a corporal were wounded and 3 men killed, and immediately afterwards the rearguard were also attacked. Pfirmann describes making use of the smokescreen spread in the humid air by their black-powder cartridges to manoeuvre his squad into better positions; 3 of his 8 men were wounded. The ten-minute action cost 10 dead (half of them légionnaires) and 14 wounded including 2 lieutenants. Pfirmann was later thanked by Lieutenant Bonafous' Skirmishers for bringing in one of their wounded along with his own casualties – they seemed astonished that a white soldier should do this.[28]

Each Skirmisher company had a French captain, 2 subalterns and the heavy allocation of 12 sergeants, though virtually none of them spoke any Vietnamese (Manington drew an unfavourable comparison with the Indian Army, where British officers were obliged to learn the languages of their troops). Martyn thought the minority recruited from highland Thos and Muongs excellent – he even compared them to Gurkhas – but about 80 per cent of the total were enlisted down in the Delta, and were scared of the jungle. Manington described them on a couple of occasions as being skittish under fire, but he paid tribute to the lowlanders for their skills in digging and building with bamboo. The Skirmishers were friendly and most spoke a workable pidgin-French; when Manington was based at Nha Nam he became friendly with a Tho sergeant, often spending time with him and his wife in their cabin outside the fort. This NCO had distinguished himself during an assault on a bandit stockade, so much so that the rebels had called out to him to come and join them, offering 100 dollars if he brought a French officer's head with him (he told Manington that they were black liars – he would probably only have got ten).[29]

JEAN PFIRMANN'S COMBAT SERVICE came to an end less than a week after his previous action. On 3 September 1889 his company were sent to search the village of Thuong Lam, surrounded by marshland and approachable only in single file along a dyke. It had the usual high bamboo hedge and substantial earth walls (Manington said that in the Yen The these were often doubled or even tripled), completely masking the interior until the vanguard actually reached the barricaded gate. As soon as Lieutenant Chavy's leading Skirmishers began to break it down, a strong party of rebels inside suddenly jumped up and opened heavy fire from the walls on the exposed soldiers.

Chavy and his corporal were killed at once; Pfirmann's admired Lieutenant Ollivier had his horse shot under him and his orderly killed beside him, before falling himself with a bullet in the stomach. The fighting was intense and prolonged; nearby, Captain Le Nourichel of III/2nd RE heard the firing and brought his company to help, but he, too, was mortally wounded. By the time the surviving defenders fled the French had suffered 11 killed and 20 wounded; 18 of the casualties were légionnaires, 2 of their 7 dead were company commanders and one was old Private Olbrecht, who wore the Mexico Medal. The medical officer was fetched to the scene, but Lieutenant Ollivier was past all help; he had a perforated intestine and a smashed spine, and by the time his men had reached him in the swamp he was covered with leeches. Corporal Pfirmann was promoted sergeant on the spot and was cited for the Médaille, but his right arm had been smashed by bullets in two places, and his time with the company was over. He endured eleven agonizing hours in the saddle of a nervous horse before reaching Phu Lang Thuong, and then a river trip back to the hospital at Haiphong.[30]

THE BRITISH ARMY VETERAN Corporal Frederic Martyn arrived in the late spring of 1890, and at Phu Lang Thuong he was assigned to Captain Plessier's 1st Company of Major Berard's II/1st RE; Martyn admired Plessier greatly, for his calm courage and his thoughtfulness towards his men.[31] De Tam's bands reduced the Yen The lowlands to anarchy that summer, and when the rainy season ended General Godin determined to clean out one of his reported strongholds at Cao Thuong. He assembled about 1,200 men in three columns, to rendezvous on 6 November 1890 a couple of hours' march south of the bandit fort.

Marching with full packs in stifling weather – 'loaded up like pedlars' asses' – Martyn's company and one of Skirmishers reached a strongly palisaded village in a clearing in thick forest, but found it empty. They dumped packs to rest, but then came under fire from a 'deserted village' visible on a nearby hilltop surrounded by dense jungle, which turned out to be the actual fort. The pair of mountain guns opened up, but it took the infantry hours to chop approach paths through the bush. Eventually they got men around a flank and close to the loopholed stockade, only to come under heavy fire from repeating rifles; an exchange of mostly blind firing through the thick bush cost French casualties and achieved nothing. When they advanced again the following morning the rebels had already withdrawn, handling an optimistic French stop-line roughly as they went. From the overnight bivouac Martyn recalled an excellent supper of fried suckling-pig, but also the pitiful exhaustion of a company of young Naval Infantrymen from the other column. Manington had a very similar memory of a camp during the advance on a rebel fort in March 1892. Around the campfires the légionnaires smoked and sang; the Skirmishers let their long hair down over their shoulders and chatted quietly, automatically waving away the mosquitoes with their paper fans; but the young French *marsouins* talked longingly of home.[32]

DESPITE THEIR CONSTANT WEARINESS, soldiers whose nerves were not twanging in expectation of imminent action were sometimes struck by the wild magnificence of the mountain scenery. There was something undeniably magical about emerging from the bamboo on to some rocky outcrop above a cloud-filled valley, gilded by sunlight and loud with the roar of unseen waterfalls. Corporal Martyn was a tough-minded man, but he recalled the jungle in rhapsodic terms:

> Try to fancy geraniums, fuchsias, and such like flowers, thirty feet high and
> with trunks twice the thickness of a man's body. Imagine, multiplied a
> hundred thousand times, the scent of an old-fashioned flower garden thickly
> planted with stocks, wallflowers, pinks, mignonette, carnations, and any
> other sweet-smelling flowers that come into your mind. Picture giant flower-
> trees whose blossoms start the day a pure white and then change from this
> successively to the palest of pale pinks, and every other shade in the
> gradations of red until at sunset the flowers are a deep rich crimson. Palms,
> bananas, frangi-pannis, shaddocks, and every other tropical tree that you can
> call to mind ... covered with ivy and climbing plants of all descriptions until
> the whole was one glorious tangle of scent and colour. And the inhabitants
> of these virgin forests! Gorgeous peacocks, pleasing silver pheasants, flocks
> of screaming parrots and parakeets, deer, wild pig, bears, panthers, tigers –
> were all to be found there in plenty, practically unmolested.[33]

A month later the local command once again demonstrated their tendency to underestimate the enemy. On 9 December 1890 patrols were sent out to find another reported stronghold at Hue Thué. After groping their way through thick bush, Martyn's company found a hidden trail and followed it to a palisade in a clearing, where they came under fire. In the dense forest it was extremely difficult to make out what they were up against, but when they climbed higher ground and could peer down through the treetops a whole defensive complex was revealed, on two hillocks above a stream. The first palisade was simply a flanking outwork, though strong enough; from there a communication trench led down to the stream, beyond which rose a Chinese-style fort with buildings big enough for a battalion, and 10-foot brick ramparts protected by three successive outer belts of palisades, *panji*-fields, 'wolf-pits' and ditches. The only two possible approaches through the forest were narrow, and were both covered from the outwork and the fort, whose loopholed walls and protruding corner bastions allowed fire in all directions. After sketching this remarkable fortification, Captain Plessier withdrew his men (taking six casualties from snipers in treetop platforms), and reported what he had seen.[34]

Despite his warning, on 11 December a Major Fane led his Naval Infantry in an ill-planned attack and was forced to retreat with heavy casualties; on the same day, Martyn's company discovered a village transformed into a nightmare butcher's-shop on the unjust suspicion of having betrayed the site of the bandit stronghold. On 22 December yet another assault was made on Hue Thué, by about 1,000 mostly Naval Infantry and Skirmishers under Lieutenant-Colonel Winckelmeyer. Although they dragged five guns through the jungle, the infantry came under such heavy fire from Spencer repeaters that all impetus was lost before an assault could be attempted. In barely an hour they suffered were more than 100 casualties, and when Winckelmeyer fell back, many of his dead – and their weapons – had to be left behind. Only half of Captain Plessier's Legion company were involved, initially as artillery guards, but they were later scooped up to join an attack on the palisaded northern outwork. This cost them 9 killed and 24 wounded; only a couple of légionnaires got through even the outer stockade, and one of those was soon struggling to free the other from the *panji*-pit where he lay impaled through the thigh.

The renegade mandarin De Nam had apparently joined his lieutenant De Tam in person, but his men were finally forced to give up Hue Thué on 11 January 1891, after a twelve-day operation by a brigade under Colonel Frey which employed full-scale siege tactics. His shells finally set the fort buildings ablaze; after keeping up a steady fire from the ramparts until nightfall the defenders buried their dead, picked up their wounded, and slipped away through the darkness, to establish a new fortress a few miles to the north. Frey dynamited Hue Thué, and the high command immediately broke up his brigade in the apparent belief that the region was now pacified.[35]

DURING JANUARY 1891, Captain Plessier's company were ordered to build and hold a new post at Nha Nam about 3 miles south-west of Hue Thué. Martyn missed the final operation; he had come down with blackwater fever, and was lucky to survive a month in the rudimentary field hospital at Phu Lang Thuong. In February he was enjoying the care of the Sisters of Mercy in the general hospital at Quang Yen on the coast, and in March he was repatriated to Algeria. He thus missed the arrival at Nha Nam in April 1891 of his countryman George Manington, posted to the same company. Manington, too, liked Captain Plessier immediately, for his tireless energy and dry wit; he was a strict disciplinarian but very just, and the men were clearly devoted to him. Manington was assigned to a brick-making gang, which had to be guarded at all times by a corporal's squad. Inside a pre-cautionary stockade Nha Nam post was still only partly built, and the hilltop was entrenched. It did, however, incorporate two abandoned pagodas, in one of which Manington had his bed-space, and he thus had solid walls round him during his first night-time harassing attack on 5 April.

The men slept in their fatigues and kept a small shaded lamp burning, so when the alarm sounded it was the work of a moment to pull on boots and grab rifle and ammunition belt. The Englishman and two comrades manned one of the windows while the corporal blew out the lamp. Under bright starlight the forest about 400 yards north was speckled with muzzle-flashes across a front of a quarter of a mile; Manington could make out the *rat ... tat ... tat* of Winchesters being fired as fast as the lever could be worked, punctuated by the deeper, slower boom of Gras or Sniders. Bullets whirred and droned overhead, thudded into the stockade and the pagoda wall and broke tiles on the roof; one passed close by his head and *thunked* into the plastered wall behind. The rifle-flashes spread around to the left and came closer, some only 100 yards away; in Manington's room a water-pot leapt from a shelf in fragments, and a drilled tin mug clattered to the floor. He ached to return fire, but still the fort lay silent.

After half an hour Lieutenant Meyer appeared with his bugler, making the rounds of his platoon, to prepare them to give six rounds' independent fire at 100 yards' range. When the bugler at the door sounded the call, everyone happily let fly at the muzzle-flashes, though the powder-smoke quickly blinded them; when the ceasefire was blown the room was fogged with it, thickly enough to make men cough. The enemy fire had become much more scattered, and soon only one or two shots were heard receding into the distance; there was a final tinkle from a smashed roof-tile, then silence. Captain Plessier made his rounds with the surgeon, but the only casualty was the sergeant-major's dog (which recovered).[36]

*

DURING THE HOT, DRY SPRING spies reported twice-weekly convoys of food heading north into the hills, usually during the middle of the day when the sun kept the légionnaires inside. Patrols were sent out to lie up in deserted villages, and during one of these Manington had his first face-to-face fight. A nervous Skirmisher spoiled an ambush on some 60 green-clad bandits escorting a large column of coolies, but Manington brought down their point man and captured a Winchester. Short local patrols were made morning and evening, but otherwise the men had little to do. Bored post commanders tended to indulge their own enthusiasms; Plessier, typically, took the opportunity to give his légionnaires extra time on the rifle range, while up at Lang Son the captain of 3rd Company, II/1st RE set his men to dyeing their khakis green, with such mixed results that they were nicknamed 'the parakeet brigade'. The food was plentiful and varied, with village markets supplementing the commissariat rations; the 2nd Brigade commander at Bac Ninh, now General Voyron, insisted on providing the men with fresh vegetables, and woe betide the post commander who could not show him a flourishing kitchen garden when he made his tours of inspection.[37]

Plessier sent hand-picked Skirmisher volunteers disguised as pedlars or musicians out around the villages in search of intelligence, and early in the 1891 monsoon season one of them brought word of bandits holed up in a nearby village, collecting taxes. The captain led Manington's platoon and two of Skirmishers on a surprise night march; for two hours, under heavy rain that covered their noise, they filed along paddy-dykes in pitch darkness, each soldier holding the belt of the man ahead. After a chilled wait in cover just outside the village, sunrise brought a child out of the gate with three buffaloes, and as soon as the gate-bars slid open Plessier blew his whistle. Slipping, cursing légionnaires and startled buffaloes collided in the gateway; there was brief pandemonium in the narrow, twisting alleys beyond, a flurry of shots, and the headman's door was smashed down to reveal a richly dressed rebel too woozy with opium to put up a fight. At the cost of 2 slightly wounded, the result was 5 bandits killed, 6 prisoners and 9 rifles taken.[38]

The rebel chief was subseqently 'turned' when he learned that the displeased De Nam had had his aged parents executed, and he proved a valuable guide during several long reconnaissances in September. After being tried by mandarins who came up from Bac Ninh, the other prisoners were executed outside the fort; Manington's eyewitness description matches several others in every respect. Marched to the place of execution by the mandarins' guards, the condemned knelt down with remarkable calm, and their blouses were pulled down from their necks. The executioner wetted a finger in his mouth and drew a line of red-brown betel juice across the bent neck as an aiming-mark; he then struck the head off with a single blow of his heavy sword – and the others awaiting their turn smiled, and expressed relieved pleasure at his skill. Their bodies were released to their families, but their heads adorned poles as a warning to others.[39]

MANINGTON'S SHARPEST FIGHT came on 12 September 1891, when Plessier led a patrol of 30 légionnaires and 30 Skirmishers to investigate a rumour that a formerly abandoned village had been reoccupied. No trouble was anticipated, and for the sake of lightness the légionnaires were only carrying 36 rounds per man, though the Skirmishers had the full 120 cartridges in their pouches (they carried shorter cavalry rifles, but the ammunition was common to both types). Women were seen working in the fields, but they fled at the sight of the soldiers. Plessier sent most of his men forward towards the village in an extended line, leaving Lieutenant Bennet on the path with a small reserve. About 200 yards from the huts they came under heavy fire, and four men fell; when the soldiers took cover behind dykes, another group opened up on them from the left flank, and the sound of orders being shouted through brass speaking-trumpets suggested that these were semi-regulars from De Nam's main force. Bennet's reserve ran up to extend the front into an L-shape on the left, but soon the rebels could be seen advancing in a disciplined skirmish line, pausing to fire between rushes, and with so little ammunition the platoon was in real danger.

Manington recalled the confidence they drew from the example of Captain Plessier – who was wearing whites that day – walking up and down behind the kneeling firing-line with his helmet at a jaunty angle, giving calm orders, smoking a cigarette and absent-mindedly slapping his gaiters with his cane. The Skirmishers were ignoring their sergeants and firing wildly, so some of their cartridges were collected and distributed to the légionnaires. The wounded were picked up and Plessier ordered a leap-frogging retreat by squads, each pausing to give covering fire for the others' movement. They were pursued to within a mile of Nha Nam, and at one point Lieutenant Bennet thought it best to pick up a fallen man's rifle and join in the rearguard's firing – one can imagine him steadying their mood with jokes about his marksmanship.[40]

*

THE GREATEST KILLER OF LÉGIONNAIRES – blackwater fever – got its claws into George Manington's liver when his platoon were detached (without a Legion officer) to a notoriously unhealthy post at Cho Trang. Within three weeks more than half of the 30 men were down with a fever far worse than the usual malaria, the victims lapsing into delirium within a couple of hours of the first shivering fits. The garrison was so weakened that it was hard to find men to go out to meet the weekly supply party, and a soldier might have to stand guard three nights in a week. Manington, like Pfirmann, described the patient kindness shown by légionnaires to their sick comrades, but they could do little more than sponge them and pile on blankets as the hot and cold fits alternated. The post commander (a Naval Infantry lieutenant, who did not impress Manington) dished out medicine according to a symptom recognition manual, but to little effect – blackwater fever responded to no medicine. When Captain Plessier and the battalion surgeon paid a visit of inspection, Manington was evacuated on the captain's spare pony, and spent two months amid the sea breezes of Quang Yen.[41] His eventual return to Bo Ha in January 1892, on a supply sampan up the Thuong river, brought out the same lyrical streak that occasionally softens Corporal Martyn's memoir:

The evening was a beautiful one ... I lay for several hours, my loaded rifle beside me, enjoying the varied spectacle ... [The] water was very clear, and ran over a sandy bottom, studded here and there with large rocks, and between steep banks ... Along either side ran groves of tall bamboos, which seemed to salute us with a graceful nod as we glided by. Sometimes there was a break, and an old pagoda, with a quaintly curved roof of red-brown tiles, came into view. Now the river would run through a few miles of forest and jungle, offering no sign of occupation by man. Enormous trees rose superbly from the banks ... and their massive branches extended for many feet over its waters, on which their foliage threw a pleasant and picturesque shadow. From these great limbs hung numerous flexible creepers, some of them starred with orchid-like blooms of white and yellow ...

Our journey between these walls of verdure, the forms and tints of which were ever changing, was one of the most delightful of experiences ... When night came down and blotted out all colour and outline, I turned on to my back and watched the stars as they came out one by one. For an hour or so I lay open-eyed, yet dreaming, till the monotonous chant of our boatman ... finally lulled me into a profound slumber.[42]

*

ON RETURNING TO HIS COMRADES in the Yen The, Manington learned that the rebel mandarin De Nam had died – allegedly at the hands of Chinese gun-runners, furious that he had won back during a night of gambling all that he had paid them the day before – and that his lieutenant De Tam was now the power in the hills. A Legion patrol had spotted his new fort a few miles north of the ruins of Hue Thué, overlooked by a promising potential artillery position. De Tam was believed to have up to 2,000 men in and around this base, perhaps 1,200 of them armed with breech-loaders, and also had mutual assistance pacts with Chinese bandits to his west and north.[43] General Voyron planned three converging columns totalling some 6,300 troops. For weeks every available man worked to transport and stockpile stores; coolies were hired, garrisons were reduced to a lonely squad or two, and in the dry heat of spring companies of the Legion, Naval Infantry and Tonkinese Skirmishers trudged all over north-east Tonkin to concentrate at their jumping-off points. In the hills, meanwhile, smoke-signals by day and lights by night suggested that every move was being watched and reported by rebel scouts.

The first column lumbered into the forest on 9 March 1892, burdened by artillery. Remarkably, surprise was achieved and the vital hilltop for the battery was occupied three days later; Manington's Legion company then guarded the sappers and coolies who in 48 hours turned a 6-mile zigzag trail into a track capable of taking artillery. After a day of frustrating fog, the 15th dawned clear, and under cover of steady bombardment the sappers forced a path towards the fort with axe, saw and explosive. (The thunder of artillery had driven all the deer out of the forest, and that night tigers took three men and three ration bullocks.) On 17 March the fort was taken; for once the rebels left many dead behind, but De Tam and hundreds of his men scattered in all directions – including southwards, passing right between the French columns.[44]

In May 1892, Private Manington turned in his old Gras for a new Lebel repeater, with its revolutionary smokeless ammunition.[45] After 18 months in-country Manington judged his company to be an effective force – unafraid of the jungle, keen-eyed scouts, good snap shots, largely fever-proofed, and capable of initiative when deployed in dispersed squads under their corporals. Captain Plessier finished his three-year Tonkin tour (the maximum consecutive service permitted), but his replacement in command of 1st Company proved, if anything, to be even more popular. A big, friendly blond from Strasbourg, Captain Watrin could call every man by name after a couple of weeks – unheard-of in the Legion.

Manington left the company in July 1892, unexpectedly posted to a clerk's job in brigade headquarters at Bac Ninh, which in 1893 would lead to a luxurious billet in Hanoi; as a consequence he would be the only one of these three memoirists to serve out a full term in Tonkin. 'Daddy' Voyron ran a happy staff, and Manington found the work interesting; the reports he filed, of actions fought and intelligence gathered while a railway was painfully pushed north from Phu Lang Thuong towards Lang Son, gave him for the first time an idea of the wider picture. However, in August he was shocked to find himself reading of Captain Watrin's death, in an ambush among the crags north of Cho Trang – seven of Manington's old comrades had been hit while getting his body back.[46] In December 1892, Manington served briefly under a new interim brigade commander brought down from the frontier; like Voyron, Colonel Galliéni was a Naval Infantryman from West Africa.

JOSEPH SIMON GALLIÉNI was then 53 years old, but had already been a full colonel for eleven years; since most Metropolitan officers did not even reach major until they were in their early forties, this was a striking example of the rapid promotion that could be earned in the colonies. On the outbreak of war in July 1870, his St Cyr class had immediately been commissioned sub-lieutenants (the consequent demonstration of enthusiasm had to be drilled back into a seemly calm by the officer of the day, a Captain Georges Boulanger). Already reduced to half-strength by 31 August, Major Lambert's 3rd Naval Infantry Regiment made a stand against Bavarian attacks on hastily fortified farmhouses at Bazeilles. The stubborn defence of the Bougerie house the next day by about 60 men under Captain Aubert would be immortalized by Alphonse de Neuville in his painting *'Les dernières cartouches'*; and one of the 60 was Sub-lieutenant Galliéni, knocked unconscious by a bullet that creased his skull.[47]

In 1880 – already four years in West Africa – Captain Galliéni led columns deep into the country between the Senegal and Niger rivers. When one was ambushed and broken up in forest fighting, Galliéni pressed ahead with the last 30 Skirmishers, very short of ammunition and quinine, and walked into a village alone to bluff the headman into making common cause against the warriors who were pursuing him. Eventually he reached Nango, capital of the Sultan Ahmadou; intermittently delirious with yellow fever, he was held captive in a hut for ten months, but finally persuaded Ahmadou to sign a treaty – an exploit that earned Galliéni promotion and decoration on his return to France. In 1886–8 Lieutenant-Colonel Galliéni held an important regional command in operations against Samory Touré. After a spell in Paris as chief-of-staff of the Naval Army Corps, he arrived in Upper Tonkin to command the 1st, then from October 1892 the 2nd Territory, with head-quarters at Lang Son.

It was another two years before the rail tracks from Phu Lang Thuong reached the frontier; but in December 1894 Major Lyautey, acting chief-of-staff to General Duchemin, was sent north for the formal opening and meetings with Chinese notables. He had already heard about Colonel Galliéni before he met him – 'the great man here ... clear-headed, businesslike, broad-minded' – and was flattered when Galliéni immediately congratulated him on his three-year-old article in *Revue des Deux Mondes*. Lyautey wrote with vivid excitement about his journey up-country by boat and horseback, then along the frontier to Dong Dang and into China during Christmas week of 1894. Like Dr Hocquard before him, he was fascinated by scenery, costume and customs. Getting away from Hanoi gave a lift to his spirits: 'I feel so well ... after this good day, wholesome, full of experiences, a day on horseback in the open air, of satisfied curiosity ... good, healthy, strenuous life.'[48]

Hubert Lyautey's epiphany seems to have occurred during the evening he spent at Dong Dang with Galliéni and the post commander, Captain de Grandmaison. Listening to them swapping stories over drinks on the little verandah of Grandmaison's shack, watching the sinking sun paint the cliffs of China red, he suddenly recognized and responded to a picture of what life could offer a colonial officer who was capable of real dedication. His letter to his sister on Christmas Day enthused about living 'like Roman legionaries', driving roads, constructing outposts, 'opening markets, governing a little world, bringing peace, confidence, life, commerce' (one recalls the little boy 'playing countries' in his sandpit at Nancy). This revelation came the more easily for the fact that Grandmaison was a man of his own class and intellect; on shelves in the captain's hut he saw not just technical manuals and months-old publications from Paris, but a little library ranging from Tal-leyrand to John Stuart Mill – about as wide a moral spectrum as one could imagine. Lyautey must have made a good impression in his turn, and he was 'enchanted' when Galliéni hinted at the possibility of future collaboration.[49]

Lyautey had pinned some hopes on his lucky shipboard meeting with the governor-general, so he was disappointed when, in January 1895, Lanessan's political opponents engineered his abrupt recall. To be fair, Lyautey was frustrated not only at losing a powerful contact who might serve his ambitions, but also by the immediate lassitude that seized the civil administration. Until the new governor arrived, every request was stamped 'pending', and this during the brief annual season when something might be achieved before the monsoon drowned out all activity in May. However, during Colonel Galliéni's consequent visit to Hanoi for final meetings with the governor, Lyautey spent time with him, and in January his orders took him back to the frontier for several months to work with 'this inspiring man'.[50]

Galliéni's photographs suggest a longer-faced version of the portraits of Rudyard Kipling in his confident maturity, in the 1890s' cranial uniform of cropped hair and walrus moustache. It is a face full of character, and behind his thick spectacles the lantern-jawed Galliéni shares with Kipling an attractive expression of sharp-eyed curiosity and engagement with his world. He was, on the face of it, quite unlike the effusive aesthete Lyautey (who lost no time in turning his off-duty quarters in Hanoi into a stage-set of *chinoiserie*). Galliéni came from a firmly Republican background, chose to live simply, and had a dry, sparing wit. The snobbish Lyautey was slightly shocked to hear Galliéni remark of Captain de Grandmaison: 'It's odd: he's of noble birth, he was educated by the Jesuits, and yet he's intelligent.'[51] But the worldly veteran of West Africa and the frustrated theorist of the salons shared one defining quality: they both had huge practical energy and painfully low thresholds of boredom.

UP HERE AT THE CHINESE END of the highland corridor of dissident activity that connected with the Yen The and the Delta, the Chinese bandits had the priceless advantage of friendly refuge across a virtually open frontier. However, although the border was porous, during the past two years it had at least presented Galliéni with something to work with – an edge he could get hold of. His converging columns did not have to try to trap the gangs from all sides simultaneously in an amorphous wilderness, but simply to drive them in a direction which they were anyway inclined to take when under pressure – back across the border. It would take much longer to persuade them not to return, but Galliéni had no intention of merely reacting to local events; he had a plan for the long term, and the patience to apply it.

The man who had talked Ahmadou of Segou into a treaty while held as a sick, helpless captive was well able to deal with evasive mandarins trying to protect the fruits of their corruption; he negotiated politely, but was absolute in his demands that they control their side of the border. He divided his territory into battalion 'circles' or districts; each comprised a number of satellite sectors, held in roughly company strength and commanded by a captain who was required to familiarize himself completely with his patch. In those adjacent to the frontier he planted a line of little border posts on mutually visible hilltops opposite the Chinese forts, staring down their throats; the bulk of the troops were held in larger posts further back on important tracks. This allowed them to react quickly and fiercely to local incursions, and his company commanders learned that Galliéni would always shield them from any diplomatic protest over robust tactics of hot pursuit.

As the arithmetic of cross-border raiding became less profitably one-sided, the terrorized locals saw that French outposts had begun to offer some measure of protection, and began to creep back from their caves and forest hideouts to rebuild in the ashes of their villages. It was then that Galliéni demonstrated his difference from other commanders: when a local success was achieved he did not shift his attention and troops to some other point, but continued his investment. He understood that without the real support of the local people no pacification could succeed. He believed that the highland tribes had been controlled by the Chinese bandits solely through terror, and that they would multiply the effect of his own stretched forces if they were given a genuine reason to do so. That reason had to be a trust earned by delivering practical incentives, and Galliéni's incentives extended to arming the tribesmen for self-defence once they were installed in their rebuilt villages and reclaiming their abandoned fields:

> This seems very strange, but gives excellent results ... Armed villages *work* –
> more than 10,000 rifles have been distributed in the 2nd Territory – counted,
> checked and inspected once a quarter by the local French officer. So far only
> one has gone missing (the man got two years in jail and a hundred strokes).
> The locals hate the Chinese and brigands; up here we really *are* liberators –
> this is the first time in twenty years that the peasants have been able to
> harvest their crops.[52]

Lyautey's letters of February and March 1895 reveal his enthusiasm as he grasped the pattern of the 'Galliéni method'. The keys were rapid access by new roads, continuity of local efforts and civil development – not postponed until some imagined future when military pacification might have been achieved, but immediately, by the military officer on the spot, to give the villagers a real stake in achieving it:

> The brigands are all Chinese ... they ravage the country, intimidate the inhabitants ... the latter are in general anxious for our arrival, and above all that we shall remain ... [They] are hostile only when they cannot count absolutely on our support, because they know that the bandits, when they return, will make them pay dearly for any help they may have given us. But when they see us do something definite – establish posts, make roads, bring the telegraph – then they quickly make common cause with us.
>
> ... Military success is nothing unless one combines simultaneously the organization of roads, the telegraph, markets, agriculture – so that alongside pacification there spreads, like an oil stain, a broad patch of civilization.[53]

This quoted phrase of Galliéni's – the *tache d'huile* – would make a career for itself; the imagery is of oil dripped on cloth, with its margin gradually expanding outwards by automatic capillary action. The first application of the oil took tireless energy, however, and Galliéni's headquarters at Lang Son were another revelation after the torpor of Hanoi. In this buzzing workshop the colonel was everywhere – checking, counting, complimenting, hustling his small staff to serve his planned timetable for development. 'It is like America: a town is being born on naked soil ... Everything seems to spring out of the earth – such intensity of creation! The whistle of a train is heard – already two arrive here each day; between the [taped-out] boundaries of the avenues comes the sound of carpentry, and lime-kilns, mortar-mixing, brick-making ...'. Lyautey had conscientiously brought with him all the latest Army staff publications on campaign service; Galliéni made a parcel of them to send back to Hanoi – 'I don't want you to be tempted to glance at them while you are with me; [they] would only confuse you – it is on the spot, in handling men and things, that you will learn your job.' (Yet Galliéni had all the main English and German newspapers sent to him, and somehow made time to read them.) He explained his hopes for the future of the border region, and one particular piece of advice would stick in Lyautey's mind:

> Look here, I tell you all this, but I am careful not to tell them in Hanoi: [it would] terrify them, and they would stop me short. French functionaries, generals and prefects fear one thing only – broadminded ideas and long views.

Therefore I serve dishes that they can digest, I make as little as possible of all that I do, I advance in secret – tacking about, shortening the range of things, describing my most daring and revolutionary acts as matters of everyday policy and detail, as if they were mere rectifications of parish [boundaries] – and so they pass.[54]

MAJOR LYAUTEY SEEMED TO HAVE FOUND the path for which he had been searching for twenty years; it was as if a gate had opened in mental walls and he had been let out into open country for the first time in his career. His correspondence races and bubbles with enthusiasm, confidence and the sheer joy of measuring himself against demanding work, and his pleasure in practical tasks far from the Metropolitan hothouse was particularly understandable at this date. The 'Dreyfus affair' cannot be ignored: it would sour the relationship between the French Army and the Third Republic for the next decade, putting a dangerous strain on the mutual toleration that had built up between generals and politicians during the previous 25 years. In early 1895, however, the reports reaching the colonies seemed straightforward, and gave little hint of the explosive potential of *l'Affaire*.[55]

On 15 October 1894, during a period of febrile public spy-mania, Captain Alfred Dreyfus, a probationary officer of the General Staff, was arrested on a charge of passing military secrets to the German embassy. Dreyfus was a chilly, unclubbable man with few friends; he was also – at a time of growing anti-Semitism – the first Jew to be appointed to a post with the General Staff. Still protesting his innocence after weeks of interrogation and solitary confinement, he was convicted by court-martial and sentenced to life imprisonment. In February 1895, Dreyfus was discharged from the Army in a ceremony of degradation in a courtyard at Les Invalides; then he was shipped off to the tropical penal colony in French Guiana, where he was one of the few convicts actually to be confined offshore on the infamous Devil's Island. It was at this stage that Lyautey referred to the matter in a letter to his sister, on 12 February:

All the details of the condemnation and degradation of Dreyfus have reached us by this mail. Certainly, at this distance the outlook is a little different; we are more deeply saddened and humiliated than we are angered ... for the simple reason that we are somewhat suspicious ... And what adds to our scepticism is that one seems to discern a certain influence of ... the rabble, always ready to blaze up. They howl '*à la mort!*' against Dreyfus, because he is a Jew, without knowing anything . . . just as they howled a hundred years ago *'Les aristocrats à la lanterne!'*, and in 1870, *'à Berline!'*.[56]

Over the following two years there was some intermittent press speculation about the legitimacy of the conviction, but few other than Dreyfus' family were working for a review of the case. He had disgraced his calling, he had been condemned to 'the dry guillotine', and France wished to forget him.

ON THE CHINESE FRONTIER in the winter of 1894/5, Lyautey accompanied Galliéni on a tour up to Cao Bang to ginger up his outposts and confer with his northern 'circle' commander, Lieutenant-Colonel Vallière (who had soldiered with him in West Africa). The first of many mentions of the Legion in Lyautey's letters is the account of leaving 'a good new road built by the Legion' from Lang Son to Na Cham, before striking off up a frightening goat-track above the Ky Kung river on 'vicious little horses, quarrelling all the time'. They made ten-hour marches sometimes in pouring rain, leading their ponies through slippery mud along rock ledges and up and down 3,000-foot passes. They did not take their clothes off for four nights, lying down in rat-infested huts and, when sleep was impossible, smoking, talking and laughing. One tip that Lyautey remembered was that even though telegraph wires had now reached the frontier, they must keep the 'optical telegraph': the sight of the lamps flashing back and forth by night was a constant reminder to the Chinese forts that any French garrison was part of a unified system.[57]

At the frontier posts he noticed how Galliéni inspired the young subalterns, energizing and encouraging them to use their own initiative, with the result that they accomplished a great deal with minimal resources. A Lieutenant Garelly of the Legion enthused about the Tho tribesmen, backward by comparison with the Delta Annamese but prouder and more honest. A year later, when Lyautey was applying these lessons in the 3rd Territory, he would write of a Tho chief he met near Na Sa, where the people of four or five hamlets had been forced for years to take refuge on a crag honeycombed with caves, reachable only by climbing with the aid of the lianas that draped the rockfaces. In 1894–5 some 110 women and children from this district had been kidnapped by Chinese slavers, and these Tho only dared come down to the valley to bury their dead according to custom. The chief was eager to cooperate – but only if he could be sure that the French were there to stay:

[He] seems very intelligent and energetic; I spent the evening talking to him; he clearly understands what we want and is only anxious to help us; but heaven grant that no blunderers may come and reject his help, failing to appreciate the value of his assistance! It is a terror to me lest the great effort we are now making may have no result, because the right men may not be put in the right places.

In the same season Lyautey would write of another important tribal headman, a 'turned' bandit whose conversion had been a real coup for the soldiers. He walked for eight hours to present for payment a chit for requisitioned rice given him by Colonel Audéoud of the Naval Infantry, only to be brusquely turned away by a commissary: Audéoud's home base was Cao Bang, therefore the receipt must be presented there. The chief had never heard of Cao Bang, which was eleven days' march away along unknown trails. This kind of dull idiocy enraged Lyautey; what would happen the next time a hungry patrol, lost in those hills, asked for help?[58]

THE EDGE OF GALLIÉNI'S 2nd Territory snaked along the Chinese frontier for nearly 200 miles, all the way from Bo Gai north-west of Cao Bang down to a point south-east of Lang Son. Its depth west from the frontier was up to 65 miles, so it embraced the northern highlands of the Yen The (see Map 7). The mountains east of Tuyen Quang and north of Thai Nguyen were infested with bandits, but they were also cut by the meandering demarcation line between the 2nd Territory and the civilian-administered Delta, where the civilians' clumsy attempts to buy off the brigands with subsidies complicated Galliéni's freedom of manoeuvre in the troubled south-west of his territory. Galliéni convinced the new governor-general, Emmanuel Rousseau, to authorize part of his planned operations; the monsoon was threatening, but in April–May 1895 four columns converged towards the reported hideout of the rebel chief Ba Ky. Lyautey was one of the 4,000 men who marched south-west from Pho Binh Gia, acting as Galliéni's chief-of-staff. His work buried him in the minutiae of coordinating troop movements, planting logistic depots, building bridges and stringing telegraph wire; it also confronted him with the difficulty of controlling detached Naval Infantry commanders who indulged their personal ambitions 'to an unimaginable extent'. Of the four column leaders, two thought only 'of stealing victory from the other ... manoeuvring to evade the colonel, to bring about an opportunity for some sudden stroke while sheltering themselves behind an accomplished deed'. However, Lyautey's staff work was sweetened by a moment for which he had longed for nearly twenty years: for the first time, he at last heard shots fired in anger. Following the pursuit of bandits fleeing from a blazing fort he heard bullets whistle past his head; it was not much, but it was better than nothing.[59]

When the columns were dispersed again Galliéni managed to hang on to some extra troops, and led 2,000 men through unexplored jungle south-west of Bac Kan, between the Cau and Gam rivers.[60] On 11 May, Lyautey described the operation to his brother from the thankful ease of a convoy drifting down the Clear river from Tuyen Quang to Viet Tri, while a squad of almost naked légionnaires bathed their bruised and cut feet over the sides of the sampan. The column had had to wade along streams and cut trails through almost impenetrable bush, finding abandoned and overgrown villages in fertile valleys whose names the guides could not even remember. The monsoon was on its way and heavy rain fell most nights; they started before dawn, making only about 2 miles an hour before having to halt for the hottest part of the day. There were no birds to be heard in this 'accumulation of warm, damp rottenness', but myriads of insects, and the jungle floor crawled with 'every horrible creature in creation – centipedes, leeches, ants – one is simply devoured'.

During these weeks Lyautey learned valuable lessons in field command. In terrible country, with only three days' hard-tack and 'tinned monkey' left and with the so-called guides avoiding his eyes, Galliéni would give his evening patrols and ambush parties their instructions, then take a 'brain bath', settling down for an hour to read the latest book by the Italian sensation, Gabriele d'Annunzio: 'They understand their orders – it will be a couple of hours before they are in position. Never send messengers when [detached troops] are on the move – they probably wouldn't find them, and anyway it would only cause confusion.' Galliéni would later reminisce to Lyautey about this march: 'Do you recall the ascendancy we had over our men at the end of the last expedition, the links that were forged between them and ourselves, without any speeches ... merely by the impression we made on them by sharing their dangers, leading them with confidence, and sparing them the thousand-and-one small regulations that are so distasteful to the French soldier?'

On 6 May they found a pre-planted food cache at Dai Thi on the Gam river, and the next day they reached Chiem Hoa post, held by Lieutenant Pierson and his half-company of légionnaires; then they force-marched downstream for Tuyen Quang, arriving only hours before the monsoon finally turned the valley into an impassable swamp. Lyautey explored the little cemetery where Major Dominé's légionnaires had left their bones ten years before, and traced the Chinese trenches still faintly visible among the huts that now clustered around the old fort.[61]

FOR THE REST OF 1895 Lyautey was stuck in Hanoi, serving once again as acting chief-of-staff to General Duchemin, and still moaning in letters home about the civil administration. (One of Galliéni's shortcuts, to get roofs over the large food stockpile needed at That Khe during the rains, had involved licensing, and then taxing, Chinese gambling-dens. This provoked a senior civil servant to exclaim 'I would prefer to see a million francs' worth of stores lost than to think that they had been saved by irregular methods!'.)[62] Lyautey's staff work was praised by the commander-in-chief, who solicited an invitation to one of his dinner parties. The major's house in Hanoi, lovingly decorated with the fruits of antique-buying forays, had a reputation as the height of colonial *chic*, and he provided his guests not only with fine food and wines but with music and opium (he did not himself indulge, but felt that the scent of the smoke enhanced the ambience). He enjoyed his position as a liaison between Duchemin, the governor-general and Galliéni, and when the latter came back to Hanoi he stayed in Lyautey's house, where he could speak freely.[63] After three years wrestling with official inertia in Tonkin the colonel felt that he needed some time at home. After a final campaign in the southern Yen The in October–December, Galliéni booked his passage home for 10 January 1896. Lyautey wrote to his sister:

> You will not expect me, I am sure, to write much about my grief on separating from the chief to whom I owe everything since I came here. He disclosed horizons of which I had never suspected the existence, associated me with stirring work, and gave me once more an object in life. I really cannot imagine what Tonkin will be like without him ... But what is quite clear from my last interviews with my dear colonel is that I am certain to be with him again, either through his return here ... or else through his sending for me to join him elsewhere. [64]

In fact, the three months after Galliéni sailed for France would bring Lyautey more useful command experience and personal excitement than he had ever known, and would cement his growing respect for the Legion.

1 ABOVE Paris, May 1871: Rue Peyronnet, Neuilly.
(Fuller captions, and picture credits, will be found on pages xxix–xxxvi.)

2 BELOW The dock warehouses of La Villette

3 ABOVE   Tonkin: the citadel at Bac Ninh, March 1884

4 BELOW   Tonkin: French Navy gunboat on the Clear river, December 1884

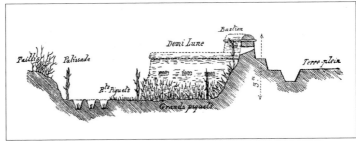

5 ABOVE   Tonkin: defences of rebel fort at Hue Thué, February 1891

6 BELOW   Tonkin: Tonkinese Skirmishers and légionnaires near Cho Trang, 1892

7 ABOVE Sud-Oranais: camel convoy on Oued Zousfana border, c.1900–03

8 LEFT Two ragged Legion scouts in the open desert

9 BELOW Camels loaded with military water kegs

10 ABOVE Figuig: the Taghla pass, looking north

11 BELOW Figuig, 1903: sergeant and légionnaires of 2nd Foreign Regiment

12 ABOVE View south and west from the walls of Taghit fort

13 BELOW The Great Western Sand-Sea – view eastwards from Taghit fort

4 ABOVE Père Charles de Foucauld with Captain de Sousbielle, commanding at Taghit, c.1902

5 ABOVE RIGHT Légionnaire of a Mounted Company with his heavily loaded '*brêle*'

6 RIGHT Lieutenant Christian Selchauhansen, mortally wounded at El Moungar

7 BELOW El Moungar: mass grave of the légionnaires killed on September 1903, with later monument on the mound beyond.

18 OPPOSITE, TOP The fortified rail station at Ben Zireg in the Sud-Oranais

19 OPPOSITE, CENTRE Colour party and departing detachment of the 1st Foreign at Sidi bel Abbès station, c.1911

20 OPPOSITE, BELOW Casualty evacuation by mule *cacolet,* mule litter and camel litter

21 ABOVE Legion Mounted Company camp at Safsafte, c.1913

22 RIGHT Légionnaire of *'la Montée'* sharing a waterbottle with his mule

23 BELOW Legion Mounted Company post under construction.

24 ABOVE North face of the *gara* at Boudenib, looking south from across the Oued Guir in 2007

25 BELOW Southern side of blockhouse on the Boudenib *gara*, 2 September 1908

26 ABOVE French post at Guercif, on the Moulouya river in eastern Morocco

27 BELOW Légionnaires at work on the fort established at Taourirt in 1910

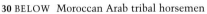

28 TOP The Chaouia, 1908: French marching 'square' crossing the plains

29 ABOVE Legion firing line at Settat on the Chaouia, 15 January 1908

30 BELOW Moroccan Arab tribal horsemen

HONNEUR AUX BRAVES

439 Groupe de Légionnaires portant les palmes offertes au 6me Bataillon du
1er Régiment Etranger, retour de Casablanca
Edit Boumendil   Phot Sidi Bel Abbè

31 ABOVE Postcard celebrating VI/1st RE's return from the Chaouia to Sidi bel Abbès, August 1908

32 RIGHT Postcard publicizing the courage of Sergeant Panther, 1913

LA FRANCE   AU MAROC
                        ORIENTAL

1276. NEKHILA — Le Sergent PANTHER, blessé au
Combat de NEKHILA, 10 avril 1913, parvint à dégager
et à mettre en sécurité le Lieutenant GROSJEAN,
blessé dès le début de l'action et menacé par un
Groupe Marocain des BENI BOU-YAHI.

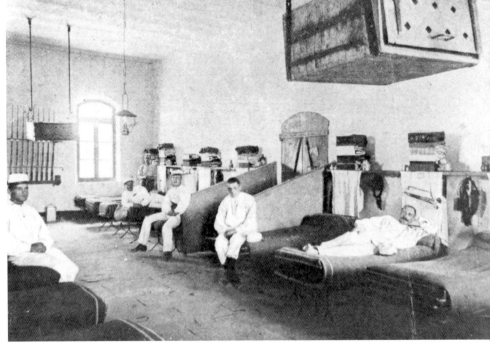

33 OPPOSITE, TOP LEFT Légionnaire in full marching order, c.1913

34, 35 OPPOSITE, TOP RIGHT A Cuban and an Austrian légionnaire, c.1913

36 OPPOSITE, BELOW Legion barrack room at Sidi bel Abbès, c.1913

37 ABOVE Legion platoon halted on the high plains, c.1913

38 LEFT Legion lieutenant colonel with Algerian captain of Spahis

39 BELOW General Baumgarten's staff take lunch in the field, c.1913

40 ABOVE Taza, 14 July 1914: the colour-party of 1st RE

41 BELOW Taza, June 1914: Major Met, I/1st RE, being lifted from an ambulance.

*

FRENCH CONTROL WAS STILL TENUOUS in the northern part of
the 3rd Territory, a V-shaped wedge of hills and mountains about 70 miles
on a side and 60 miles across, between the valleys of the upper Clear
and Gam rivers north of Tuyen Quang. Penetration had been by boat, and
outposts – many of them held by native auxiliaries – had been planted up
the valleys, on the Clear river as far north as Ha Giang about 15 miles short
of the Chinese frontier, and on the Gam up to Bao Lac (see Map 7). The
Galliéni method had not been applied here; the placing of outposts was
governed purely by river access rather than to create any systematic network
of control, and there were no armed villages, protected markets or roads.
Galliéni's work to the east had driven large numbers of bandits into this
triangle, and Galliéni's old comrade Colonel Vallière, now commanding the
3rd Territory, was eager to start applying the formula to these badlands.

In January 1896 he was given extra troops from the now quieter 2nd
Territory, and was also given Major Lyautey as his chief-of-staff for the
operation. (That month Lyautey received a delightful telegram from his
brother giving him early notice that his appointment to the Legion of Honour
was soon to be gazetted.) On 7 January he was on his way upriver to catch
up with Vallière at Bac Kem for a drive west towards Ha Giang. However,
when he reached Tuyen Quang on the 9th, he learned that a concentration
of some 1,200 bandits south-east of Ha Giang had dispersed in God knew
how many directions, and at least 400 of them, led by an old Black Flag
named Hong Cau, were raiding and burning their way south down the upper
Clear river. Vallière, with 3,000 men – the great bulk of the available troops –
was out of touch somewhere in the wilderness west of Bac Kem, and knew
nothing of this. Whichever route the brigands followed, rich and peaceful
valleys lay virtually undefended before them, and the only staff officer on
the spot to take decisions was Major Lyautey.

For the next three weeks, while struggling up and dashing down river, he
orchestrated the concentration and movements of the tiny forces of Legion
and Tonkinese Skirmishers that he was able to scrape up from scattered
posts. He ordered 100 légionnaires up from Viet Tri, mixed them with
Skirmishers in the usual one-third/two-thirds 'shandy', and began moving
60 men here, 90 men there – scrabbling to get a few dozen rifles into position
to guard vulnerable trails, while sending others into the forest to hunt for
signs of the enemy's location and direction. He had to move his makeshift
chess pieces around very approximate maps, in response to constantly

changing intelligence, and hampered by slow and unreliable communications. He sent off orders with no way of knowing if they had arrived
or been acted upon before some new rumour threatened to change the
situation entirely. General Duchemin sent him messages of confidence, but
not the troops he needed. Telegraph lines were being cut, auxiliary outposts
wiped out and river convoys massacred; sometimes signal lamps worked,
sometimes they were blinded by the weather, and he ran out of the carrier
pigeons that were his only means of contact with Colonel Vallière, somewhere out there in the mountains to the north.

The night of 13 January 1896 was a low point: Lyautey was at Bac Muc
when the bloodstained légionnaires of Captain Béranger's half-company
struggled in, led by Lieutenant Pauvrehomme with a smashed shoulder.
They were carrying their dead captain and 10 wounded, after being forced
to leave another 11 dead on the site of the ambush that had nearly done for
them all; the senior officer of Tonkinese Skirmishers (tactfully identified
only as 'Major B') had lost his pith helmet and was delirious with sunstroke.
Lyautey could do little for the wounded except give them opium pills for
the pain – 4 had probably fatal belly and back wounds. Leaving a lieutenant
with 150 men to hold Bac Muc, Lyautey had to race back to Tuyen Quang,
where only 50 guarded his headquarters; his feeding of handfuls of men up
and down river and across country often left dangerous gaps which had to
be filled by some new ingenuity.

Hanoi then ordered him back to Bac Muc to supervise personally the
withdrawal of the garrison (which he knew was madness); but when he got
there in pouring rain on 20 January he found that the Greek Lieutenant
Prokos had arrived with his 35 légionnaires and Lieutenant Talpomba's 65
Skirmishers, so now he had 250 rifles. The next day he managed to rendezvous with 150 men led east from the Red river by Major Bailly; it had
taken Lyautey eight frantic days to gather under his hand a manoeuvre force
of just 400 men, but under the circumstances they looked to him like an
army. On 22 January he was able to send detachments to guard the vital
passages of the Clear river north and south of Vinh Thuy; he thought he
would now be able to await the arrival of Colonel Vallière's main force, but
new reports of booty-laden bandits moving north towards Chiem Hoa across
on the Gam river shook the kaleidoscope once again. Lyautey had to organize
detachments under Major Bailly and his own old classmate Captain Girardot
and send them into the forest between the two rivers, while he went up to
Vinh Thuy to organize telegraph lines.

On 28 January he finally had solid word from Vallière: the colonel had smashed the strongest Chinese band north-east of Ha Giang in three days' fighting, and Lyautey need no longer fear what might come downriver from his north. Indeed, he could now join Vallière for the mopping-up phase of the campaign, as the bandits were squeezed between Bailly and Girardot from the south and Vallière from the north. With a light heart, he laid aside the responsibility of senior command and headed up river for Ha Giang with a twelve-man escort; it had all been an education, but what he yearned for was more front-line experience.[65]

LYAUTEY LOST HIS COMBAT VIRGINITY early in February 1896, when Colonel Vallière sent him into the mountains between Bac Quang and Ha Giang as second-in-command to Major Briquelot of the Naval Infantry, leading 350 men. Briquelot was weak with dysentery and Lyautey had to be ready to take over if he finally collapsed. The engagement that followed was banal, the everyday stuff of wilderness soldiering; but a man never forgets the soldiers who shared his first real experience under fire, and for Lyautey they were légionnaires.[66]

On 9 February three company groups, each only about 120 strong, advanced to try to drive Chinese bandits out of one of their lairs. Each was led by a Legion captain; Lyautey took Combettes, Pierson and a single 80mm mountain gun straight up from the valley, while Captain Certau was supposed to be working his way in along the crests from a flank. Guided by the 'friendlies' who were indispensable to any operation, at about 10am Lyautey set off; ahead lay the mouth of a narrow, dark gorge, with the smoke of bandit campfires rising pale against the forest above. Pierson took the left flank, climbing through jungle to a bare hillock that commanded the mouth of the gorge, while Combettes' légionnaires clambered up the rocks on the right. In the early afternoon Lyautey led Lieutenant Dambiermont and his reserve platoon forward out of the paddies, and as they reached the treeline they came under fire. Lyautey placed the reserve, then joined Pierson, who was pinned down by fire on the left; the gun was dragged up to the hillock and dropped shells ahead of them, while on each side of the gorge the légionnaires worked their way upwards through the bush, machetes in hand. At nightfall they bivouacked where they were, serenaded by Chinese trumpets, howls and random firing from the slopes ahead.

Before dawn on 10 February two platoons climbed on up the heights on each side of the gorge, and from the right Combettes' men reached a position to fire down into the bandit hideout. This was abandoned, and Lyautey reached it by mid-morning; at that point Major Briquelot's condition worsened, and he had to be evacuated on a stretcher. At about 2pm heavy firing was heard ahead; Lyautey could not tell if this was Certeau coming in from the north, or his own Captain Pierson's platoon. As the crackling grew more intense Lyautey became concerned – Pierson had only 30 rifles with him – so he took the 60-man reserve and followed Pierson's track up the side of the gorge:

And what a track! Hardly are we in the gorge than we find ... an inextricable chaos of rocks in ridges, in needles, torn, pitted, which one climbs for 350 feet, with bleeding hands [and] an abyss below, [only] to descend into vertical gorges and ascend again further on; but the increasing fusillade lends wings to our feet; we have an agonizing fear lest [Pierson's] cartridges give out!

... [At] every moment we expect our reconnaissance party to fall on us from above, retreating and smashed up. We are hailed from a ridge; it is Pierson. 'So it is not you in action? Who is it then?' 'I have no idea, and I'm on my way, but we can't move fast.' ... The firing redoubles ... and still there are more rocky ridges; we shall never get there. At last, at 5.30pm in the dark, here we are, the 100 of us, having dragged ourselves up to the top of a needle ... drowned in a sea of trees and less than 700 feet from the fight, but separated from it by a gulf which it is impossible to cross in the dark.

You cannot imagine what it was like: the incessant firing echoing among the rocks, the shouting of the Chinese, their war-cries and death-cries, the continuous sound of their famous trumpets – you have to have heard them to understand the shiver of fear they cause – and the anguish of uncertainty. Perched on my needle, I order the buglecall of the Legion to be sounded. It is answered; it is Combettes! We speak to each other now, though we cannot see each other. He tells us that he is on the flank of the hill, that he has been fighting alone for three hours, and that we ourselves are exactly on the right flank of the Chinese ... A salvo from the left – this time it is for us ... we can see nothing, but bullets flatten themselves against the rock, tearing the trees ... Combettes in front of us has [had] two of his men killed and four wounded ...

[It is] a night never to be forgotten. Picture 100 men clustered together on the side of a sugar-loaf with holes in it like a Gruyère cheese. No possibility of moving except at the risk of a broken neck; not a square yard of flat surface. All that one can do is to wedge oneself with ones knees into an irregularity in the rock, so as to rest a little without falling; strict orders not to light a

fire or even to smoke – [we must not] disclose our position to the rifles facing
us. On our flank facing the bandits our men [have their] rifles at the shoulder.
We are in linen, just what we wore when we dashed off . . . without any rugs
or a crust of bread . . . not even a drop of water . . . At the top, we four officers
squeeze ourselves into a cavity; it shelters us from the wind, but it is open
at the top, and now, at 11pm, comes the rain . . .

Considering his moves for the next day, Lyautey continued:

If Combettes' line of retreat with his dead and wounded is like ours, then he
cannot move: to [withdraw] in order to rally one's forces in these rocks is
death, nothing less; we should be killed like rabbits . . . The alternative is to
remain and begin the battle again from our balcony . . . [and it is] impossible
to see anything, or combine our movements.

At dawn on the 11th a 'friendly' slipped down the crag, and up again after
an hour and a half with a note from Combettes. He had spent the night 150
yards from the bandits; he now had 4 dead and 6 wounded, but his path to
the rear was not difficult. Leaving a strong guard on his 'needle', Lyautey
climbed across to join Combettes' légionnaires and advanced with them.
The Chinese – unusually – left 14 dead behind; there were blood trails,
discarded rice and gear, and drifts of empty cartridge cases (mostly
Winchester). It was on 10 February that Lyautey's Cross was officially gazetted, so technically he was admitted to the Legion of Honour while under
fire; in his letter to his brother he makes a self-deprecating joke about this,
but his pleasure is evident.[67]

BEFORE LYAUTEY LEFT the 3rd Territory he had a chance to apply
the Galliéni method himself, and he found a different but no less intense
satisfaction in the experience. On 23 February 1896 he left Ha Giang 'with
my favourite escort, consisting of Captain Pierson with sixty légionnaires
under Lieutenants Guittet and Virey . . .'. East of Bac Me he found the ruined,
overgrown site of what had been the district's main market village forty
years ago, before the Taipings came. To subsistence farmers on any continent
a local market was and is the key to survival; it is where they exchange
what little they have for what little they need, and without safe access to
such a gathering-place productive life is unsustainable.

It is always the same – visiting three or four hillocks before we find the right
one that is good from every point of view . . . interviewing the notables who

must be reassured, exhortations to the inhabitants to return, examination of
the old paddyfields, appeals to re-open the market ...

[At Lang Ca Phu] I spend my morning going over the ground and by noon
I have planned out the post. I install Lieutenant Gadoffre [of the Skirmishers]
here ... We trace out the post, find a spring whose course can be turned, a
place for brick-making, limestone to be [burned for making] mortar,
woodland for cutting timber – a rapid calculation, an estimate, a sketch, a
plan and elevation – and when I start off again at 2pm everybody is already at
work ...

When he returned on 12 March he was delighted with progress:

A real joy ... a wonderful young lieutenant, Gadoffre, the site of whose post
I only fixed 17 days ago, has already constructed it on the ridge overlooking
a deep passage ... well-placed at the intersection of tracks which for twenty
years were abandoned to brigandage. The village had been reborn [in] the
shelter of the post. These lovers of the soil, who only leave their homes when
driven out, have returned from the mountains and the jungle. A dozen
houses are already up, the headman of the canton of Yen Phu has been re-
installed. They have started to work like mad on the paddyfields on both
banks of the river. They have brought water right into the post itself. The
vegetable garden has been planted. All [is] smiles and movement; it is life
after twenty years of death ... [68]

As during his first trek along the eastern frontier, here in the north Lyautey
marvelled at the dramatic highland scenery and thrived on the physical
challenge of travelling through it on foot and horseback, sleeping beside
campfires under the stars. On the first sunny day after three months' rain
and cold:

My légionnaires are cheerful ... they march without halting, their burdens
are light and the coolies keep close together ...

... It is wonderful to think that I have become an infantryman; I never
get on my horse now except to cross the streams – though it is true that this
means pretty often. Last year I thought it more chic to wade across with
water up to my waist like the soldiers, but Galliéni convinced me that this
was idiotic: (1) because by getting wet [myself] I could not [make the others
any drier]; (2) because when the chief reaches the bivouac he writes, thinks,
orders, and has need of the rest, health and sleep on which depend the rest,

health and sleep of those he leads; and (3), because the chief is forty years old and his men twenty-five.[69]

It is interesting to see through Lyautey's eyes two different generations of Legion officer. At Viet Tri he met the old-school Captain de Traversay, a paternal 47-year-old Gascon who had graduated from St Cyr in 1869 but retired from the Army in the mid-1870s. After reducing himself to penury by riotous living he had enlisted in the ranks of the Legion, and had now worked his way back up to captain; he had decorations, the respect of his men, a passionate interest in hunting and photography, and seemed a wholly contented man. In a bivouac near the frontier Lyautey spent an evening of pleasant gossip with the younger type: Lieutenant de Meditte from Dijon, a year out of St Cyr – 'last winter he was at a dance at Marie de L's, and talks of them all and of the others whom I know there'. Clearly, the Legion's roughneck image was no longer a deterrent to gentlemen.[70] In March, Lyautey had good reason to look back on the past weeks with satisfaction:

> Could I have believed six weeks ago, after Bac Mµc, that the problem would have been solved ... and that I myself should reopen this Na Bo route which seemed to Chabrol and me, in our office at Hanoi, as something so far away, so problematic and so vague? On the innumerable white spaces on our maps ... we marked in red a mass of future outposts, without really believing in them! ... [Now] we know where we are. It has passed from the unknown to the known, from the inorganic to the organic, from the vague to the actual ... Why not congratulate oneself a little at the thought that one has taken a small part in this work? ... But all of this would have been useless, would have been mere scraps of paper, without the man of action, the *réalisateur* ... in the shape of Vallière.[71]

WHILE BANDITRY WOULD REMAIN as endemic as fever in the High Region, by 1898 the major work of pacification would be more or less complete. Until the First World War the Legion would continue to provide the hard skeleton of the up-country garrisons in the hills, and settled into a fairly peaceful routine enlivened by the occasional skirmish – particularly along the middle Red and Clear rivers in 1908–9, when various upheavals brought the name of De Tam back into the 2nd Bureau's reports. The permanent Legion presence swung between three and four battalions over these ten years, though it dwindled thereafter. One was normally based at Lao Cai on the upper Red river, with companies dispersed in forts along the

Yunnan frontier; a second at Hia Giang, to watch the upper Clear and Gam rivers; a third centred on Tuyen Quang; and the fourth at and around Cao Bang on the border with Guangxi. In 1900–1901 the garrison was temporarily increased by two Legion battalions when many Navy troops were withdrawn from the colony to take part in the international operations against the Boxers in northern China.[72]

In the Algerian depots, the appeal of a tour in Tonkin remained as strong as ever, despite the known dangers of disease; men competed to get into the replacement drafts, and the threat of being excluded was held over the troublesome. The attraction of double pay and, for 'lifers', an increased pension entitlement was less important than the simple yearning to experience an exotic faraway world. Returned veterans would speak of Indochina wistfully: a nostalgia for its beauty, its timeless calm (and its women) seemed to get into their bloodstream along with the malaria parasites, and would never let them free. The Kipling who wrote *The Road to Mandalay* would have understood them perfectly.

LYAUTEY'S LETTERS AFTER HIS RETURN TO HANOI in the spring of 1896 suggest one of his swoops into depression. Through a simple misunderstanding he had missed the chance of applying for command of the circle of Ha Giang himself; 'bereft of productive, compelling and immediate action, I am eating myself away – corroding'. He did reflect, in some wonder, on all that had happened in the bare eighteen months since that cable had reached him on manoeuvres at Brie – where he had felt himself 'chained for life to a treadmill, and . . . disheartened by successive failures to get free from it' – but he seemed unable to bank any lasting dividend of confidence from his achievements.[73]

The temptations of armchair psychiatry should be resisted, but in his personal correspondence the contrasting poles of Lyautey's character are very striking. When he is in the field, faced with practical difficulties and physical dangers that demand decision and action, then his letters are all robust energy and focused intelligence. When he is confined to the stifling world of headquarters and the obligatory social round, he is seized by gloom and apprehension. At all times his personal relationships with the men he worked beside strongly influenced his moods, and the lethargy and backbiting of Hanoi brought out his fretful side. Many of his friendly colleagues had already moved on to other postings, and he perceived other fellow staff officers as chilly and jealous, lacking the slightest interest in what was being achieved in the High Region. True, General Duchemin was as kind as ever, presenting him personally with his Cross at a private dinner party for friends and calling him 'the chief-of-staff he had dreamt of'; but Lyautey feared that public signs of favour from a commander-in-chief who would soon be going home would simply expose him to envious hostility.

In another eighteen months he would inevitably be swallowed up again by the Metropolitan Army – the great model for everything that frustrated him in Hanoi. He had been let out of prison and shown what life could be like in the open air, but he could see the gates closing on him again all too soon. Always as easily cast down as lifted up, he despaired of ever becoming a *réalisateur* himself. He considered resigning his commission, and wrote to his friend Max Weber:

> ... the plan, I imagine, would be this: to find a wife who would bring me, with her other qualities, an ample independence of means ... and henceforward to look out for an electoral seat for 1898. At 43 one can still do something in parliamentary life, and I shall try to steer towards the colonial cause and become a candidate for governor's rank.[74]

It is hard to think of a worse date than 1898 for a man of Lyautey's values and temperament to be entering the National Assembly. In the event, his 'dear colonel' would save him from a fate worse than the boredom of provincial garrison life, and would reunite him with his 'favourite escort'. Vietnam was not the only place where blackwater fever was feasting on légionnaires like a tiger.

7. 'A Calling Devoid of Allurement'

Soldiering in Madagascar for a native was a calling devoid of allurement. There was no commissariat, no pay, no outfit except for a rifle, a few rounds of ball cartridge and a bit of calico.

Bennet Burleigh, *Daily Telegraph* correspondent

'How many men do you reckon die at this hospital each day?' I asked him. 'Twenty or thirty', he replied. Taking the average as twenty-five, I made the gloomy calculation that this represented 1,500 deaths in two months, at just this hospital alone.

Private Léon Silbermann[1]

THE GREAT TROPICAL ISLAND of Madagascar lies 250 miles out into the Indian Ocean off the coast of Mozambique in East Africa. It is larger than France, almost three times the size of mainland Great Britain, and has roughly the same area as the US Atlantic seaboard states from Massachusetts down through South Carolina.

Measuring about 1,000 miles long by 360 wide at its broadest, it is shaped vaguely like a human left footprint with a long 'big toe' (see Map 9). In the nineteenth century the swampy river valleys of the northern and north-western coastal lowlands were covered with jungle. South of this region, roughly the central one-third of the island's length is divided into three distinct strips of contrasting terrain. The broad western zone is grassy savannah; from these plains slopes rise eastwards towards the island's offset rocky spine, where treeless plateaux up to 6,000 feet above sea level switchback down the island, spiked with occasional volcanic peaks rising to 9,500 feet. On their eastern edge these uplands fall away sharply in escarpments thick with mountain jungle, stepping down to a narrow, intensely fertile eastern coastal strip.

The Malagasy peoples, a diverse mixture of mainly Malayo-Polynesian and African stock, numbered about 2.5 million in 1900.[2] Depending on local conditions the tribes lived mainly by growing rice in irrigated paddy fields, maize, vegetables and fruit, and by raising longhorn oxen and fat-tailed sheep. The west, from the northern jungle inlets right down through the grasslands, was the country of the Sakalava tribes. Very dark and strongly built, Sakalavas favoured a hairstyle of matted dreadlocks; their inland communities were herdsmen and farmers, but coastal fishermen also sailed their outrigger canoes across the Mozambique Channel to Africa on slave-raids. Although intermittent fighting continued, particularly with the Sakalava, by the mid-nineteenth century the Hova people of the eastern central plateau had come to dominate a large part of central and northern Madagascar. This tribe had pale olive-brown complexions and straight Malayo-Polynesian features, and considered themselves the most culturally advanced people of the island. Their king Radama I(r. 1810–28) had aggressively extended his rule northwards and eastwards from his capital at Antananarivo (Tananarive), and southwards over the ethnically similar Betsileo people. The Hova nation was called Imerina and their state the Merina empire. Women among the Hova enjoyed equal rights and prestige, and queens were often preferred to kings, though sharing power with their consorts.

A TENUOUS FRENCH PRESENCE in 'the Red Island' dated from 1643, when Cardinal Richelieu's East Indies Company established Fort Dauphin in the far south as a trading post, but this was abandoned in 1674. During the eighteenth century French settlers on the Indian Ocean islands to the east – Macareigne, l'Ile Bourbon (Réunion) and l'Ile de France (Mauritius) – continued to trade with the eastern tribes through Tamatave, one of the few practical harbours on the east coast. The fall of the First Empire left France with ónly Réunion, and in 1817 the new British governor of Mauritius signed a treaty with Radama I, styling him King of Madagascar. (Thereafter Protestant missionaries had some success in converting the Hova nobility, and Christianity became the court religion.)[3] Undiscouraged, in 1821 the Réunion French restored an earlier foothold on the eastern offshore island of Ste Marie, and in 1840 acquired that of Nossi Bé off the north-west coast, declaring a protectorate over the northern Sakalava tribes. King Radama II

(r. 1861–63) signed a commercial treaty with Napoleon III, but his assassination by a group of aristocrats brought this to nothing. A remarkably adhesive prime minister, Rainilaiarivony, came to prominence in 1864; he was to be the husband of three successive queens, and behind their important ceremonial prestige he would manipulate effective power for thirty years, expertly juggling relations with the French and British.[4]

In 1882 the land-hungry settlers of Réunion engineered the despatch of Admiral Pierre's squadron to demand acceptance of a virtual French protectorate. Rebuffed, the admiral bombarded and occupied Tamatave, and put bluejackets ashore in the far north at Diégo Suarez. At that time Prime Minister Ferry was both preoccupied by the events unfolding in Tonkin and unwilling to provoke Britain, so he played for time. By the Convention of Tamatave signed on 19 December 1885, Imerina ceded Diégo Suarez to France and accepted a sort of phantom, unacknowledged protectorate for ten years (the French and Malagasy texts of this document varied significantly, and both sides signed it in bad faith). A resident-general was installed at the Hova capital (Le Myre de Vilers – the man who had sent Captain Rivière to Hanoi in March 1882); but while plantations were established on the east coast, and Malagasy Skirmishers were recruited at Diégo Suarez, for the most part the French officials were simply ignored. The deputies from Réunion, supported by Eugène Étienne's colonial lobby, repeatedly pressed for military occupation, and in 1890 the diplomatic roadblock was cleared by an agreement giving France a free hand in Madagascar in return for a British monopoly in Zanzibar. Paris instructed Le Myre de Vilers to demand a new and much more tightly drawn treaty, and when this was refused by the government of Queen Ranovalona III the French began planning a military operation, which they anticipated would be quick and decisive.

THE MOST OBVIOUS difficulty for a military force was the complete lack of roads in Madagascar. This was not a case of simple neglect but deliberate policy; it had distorted economic and military development, but was to the advantage of the court noblemen. In the 1820s the British had failed to persuade Radama I to build a road from the harbour at Tamatave up the eastern escarpment to Antananarivo, and periodic threats of French invasion made the continued difficulty of this obvious route to the capital an essential feature of Merina defence plans, such as they were.

Since the island had roughly the population of modern Wales spread over an area larger than France, the main limitation on Merina prosperity was a shortage of manpower. Historically the rulers had relied upon slave-raiding, both within the island and on the African coast. Growing rice, the island's staple food, was a labour-intensive activity that left few hands for work that might have increased wealth through trade; and in parallel, the lack of communications other than by rough tracks also put a premium on human porters. Except in European plantations on the east coast there was no wheeled transport, and there were taboos against using oxen as draft animals; virtually all movement of goods and passengers was by shoulder-poles, man-dragged sledges and palanquins. The Merina empire, ruled by an oligarchy of intensely competitive aristocrats clustered around the court in Ana-tananarivo, operated a system of forced state labour for all kinds of work, but alongside this a sophisticated commercial haulage business grew up to service all economic activity. Most of the porters were slaves owned by aristocratic syndicates based in the capital, who naturally profited by pre-serving the roadless status quo and keeping porterage rates high. It is cal-culated that by 1833 slaves already made up one-third of the total population of the Merina state, and two-thirds of the 50,000 inhabitants of the capital.[5]

THE FRENCH WERE NOT IGNORANT of these conditions, and spent more than a year in planning. In August 1894 a joint commission of the War and Navy ministries called for an invasion force of at least 12,000 men, to be landed not at Tamatave – some 175 miles east and north of Antananarivo – but at Majunga in the north-west, about 50 miles further from the capital along a route avoiding the defensible eastern escarpments (see Map 8). From the jungle behind Majunga the south-eastwards march towards, into and across the Merina highlands would involve three main stages: in crow's-flight terms rather than actual track miles, the first 100 miles up the Betsiboka river, through the lowlands and foothills, would end in a climb of about 2,000 feet on to the first shelf of the highlands – the Andriba plateau; some 30 miles further on, in the Ambohimenas hills, another climb up past Kinadji led to the highest pleateau, nearly 5,000 feet above sea level; after another 25 miles to Babay this central plateau dipped slightly to the high, fertile plain surrounding Antananarivo.

Since the expedition would have to be supplied from Majunga throughout the march to the capital, the planners put great reliance on the fact that for the first 80-odd miles the Betsiboka was navigable, and in October 1894 the Navy Ministry ordered the construction of a flotilla of steam tugs and lighters drawing no more than 27 inches. That same month, from the French foothold at Diego Suarez, Lieutenant Aubé of the Naval Troops reconnoitred the route south as far as the Ambohimenas and made sketches (the only available maps of the whole island were in an unhelpful 1:1 million scale). It would be impossible to obtain locally the 18,000–20,000 porters needed to carry supplies for a 12,000-man force, but it was calculated that this requirement could be reduced by 75 per cent by the generous provision of *voitures Lefèbvre* – small two-wheeled iron carts, drawn by a mule and carrying a 440lb payload. Aubé reported that only moderate work was needed to make the tracks on the inland plateau passable for these, and no fewer than 5,000 carts were ordered.[6]

In November 1894 it was suddenly announced that the whole expedition was to be organized by the Army (it is said that the war minister, General Mercier, got it by underbidding the Navy for funding by 30 million francs). While the Army had contributed troops for the basically Navy campaigns in Tonkin and Dahomey, it had not itself organized a full-scale overseas expedition since Mexico in the 1860s. This lack of experience would prove most telling in the decision that two-thirds of the infantry would be European, including four battalions of Metropolitan Line and Light volunteers.[7]

Naval Troops officers argued that the men would not be acclimatized, the Majunga route was too long, and the expedition needlessly large – while the Hova army was estimated at some 40,000 men, its morale and readiness were uncertain. These arguments for a smaller, lighter and faster-moving force were dismissed by the Metropolitan generals as typical seat-of-the-pants Naval Troops improvisation (given the rivalry between the two services, the Navy's near-monopoly of eye-catching overseas campaigns was resented). They insisted that this was a case for Army professionalism: the Merina government was known to have purchased about 25,000 breech-loading single-shot rifles, and had acquired modern artillery and British instructors.[8] On 23 November 1894 the National Assembly voted the funds for the expedition, and on 11 December the Foreign Ministry informed friendly nations that a state of war existed between France and Madagascar.

Command of the expeditionary force was given to Army General Duchesne, a veteran of both Tonkin and the débâcle on Formosa, with Army General Metzinger and Navy General Voyron to command his two brigades. The expedition totalled some 15,400 officers and men, including about 10,400 infantry in thirteen 800-man battalions: four Metropolitan, three Naval Infantry, two Algerian, and one each Legion, Malagasy Skirmishers, Hausas and white Réunion volunteers. There was an Africa Light Horse squadron for scouting, and eight artillery batteries. Engineer and Train (transport) units were almost entirely Metropolitan, but the main logistic manpower would be provided by 5,500 hired Algerian muleteers-cum-cart drivers ('Kabylies'), with 5,640 mules for the Lefèbvre carts. A Navy coastal and river flotilla of eight small warships was attached to the force, and thirty steamers were 'hired in from trade' to transport the expeditionary corps.[9]

SMALL DIVERSIONS WERE PROVIDED, between December 1894 and April 1895, by *marsouins* landed at Tamatave and others patrolling from the Diégo Suarez garrison. Another few naval companies landed unopposed at Majunga on 15 January 1895, and during February they reconnoitred inland, encountering no resistance from vassals of the Merina empire. Serious movements would not be possible before the dry season began in May, but the advance element of the expeditionary corps proper came ashore with General Metzinger on 1 March 1895 – a mixed force of Algerians, *marsouins*, Malagasies and support troops – and began unloading engineer materials and stores.

The plan called for Metzinger to establish the base camp, and then reconnoitre for 50 miles up the Betsiboka river during the tail-end of the rains in April. The second phase was to start when General Duchesne arrived with the bulk of the force in May. Metzinger's 1st Brigade would then advance south to the confluence of the Betsiboka and Ikopa rivers – the limit of navigation – by the first week in June; from there they would build a short cart road to the site for an advanced supply base at Marololo. From Marololo southwards the third-phase advance would proceed in bounds, with the leading battalions improving the tracks towards the Andriba plateau that formed the northern ramparts of Imerina, followed by the second brigade escorting the supply-cart convoys. It was expected to take another six weeks – say, until early August – to get the whole force from Marololo up on to the Andriba plateau; thereafter, the activity of the Hova army would decide events.

MAJUNGA LAY JUST INSIDE BOMBETOKE BAY, 25 miles short of the chaotic sandbars and mangrove swamps at the mouth of the Betsiboka river. An unsuspected coral reef kept large ships further from shore than had been anticipated, and heavy swells swamped some of the landing boats, making all unloading difficult and time-consuming. Building the planned wharf took months, so hastily landed crates were scattered over 300 yards of beach to lie unprotected until they were identified and collected. The ships carrying the disassembled sections of the gunboats and cargo lighters and the first 1,000 carts were late, arriving between 18 April and 7 May, and assembling and launching the boats in the choppy bay proved much harder than expected. This cancelled the riverborne element of the vanguard's planned advance in April, and although gunboats were in operation by 1 May it seems to have been at least three weeks later before the first launch towed a pair of lighters up river. Thereafter a couple of lighters every two or three days seems to have been the norm, and this shortfall in the planned river transport capacity was to have malign consequences.[10]

Seeking to replace the boats with hired porters, the Train only managed to recruit some 400 Sakalavas. About 7,700 porters would eventually be assembled by June, most of them from as far afield as Indochina, Somalia and even Algeria, which suggests a certain desperation. Crucially, the delay in getting the river supply line working meant that the heavy, narrow-wheeled Lefèbvre mule carts had to be used from the start instead of being kept for the harder ground of the uplands.[11] They immediately became bogged down on the tracks through the swampy northern jungle, and in the absence of native labour the four Engineer companies had to be diverted from skilled work to road-making.

The lords of the lowland jungle were countless billions of malarial mosquitoes. The sappers quickly became worn out by the stifling climate and by fever casualties, so survivors were relieved and saved for specialist bridging work, and many of the infantry had to take their place in road-gangs as soon as they came off the beach. Progress in building the cart road was also held up periodically by the need to bridge a succession of streams and rivers up to 100 yards wide and, in the eventual case of the Betsiboka near Marololo, 450 yards (the Merina empire relied on fords, which were often impassable at this season). In a vicious spiral, bridging materials were delayed because they had to compete with rations for the load-space on the few lighters getting up river; rations were needed for troops already weakened by the road-building that was intended to circumvent the problem of insufficient boat-space; yet the road they were building was not yet adequate to get the heavy bridging materials forward.

Despite heavy rain and floods the advance guard began to venture inland from Majunga on 25 March, without serious resistance. During April, the 13th Naval and elements of the Algeria Marching Regiment landed, and on 28 April the bulk of the Legion battalion arrived aboard the *Liban*.

THE TWO FOREIGN REGIMENTS had each been ordered, on 4 January 1895, to provide two companies for the 1st Battalion of the Algeria Marching Regiment (I/RMdA), which was officially created on 2 February under the command of Colonel Oudri of the 2nd Foreign. The 1st Battalion, formed during March under the command of Major Barre, had sailed from Oran at the beginning of April with 22 officers and 818 rankers. Private Silbermann recalled a difficult landing over the unfinished 160-yard wharf; he described Majunga as busy but filthy, with disreputable-looking European and Creole traders already erecting makeshift 'booze-shacks' in defiance of the harassed town commandant.[12]

The Legion started marching up river on 1 May, part of three columns of the RMdA, *marsouins* and Malagasy Skirmishers. (The haphazard arrival of different troopships over a month, and the need to have this latter local unit at the spearhead – where it performed consistently well – distorted the theoretical brigade organization from the start.) The columns chased Hova troops out of a 6-mile line of hill positions astride the river in front of Marovoay without difficulty but, camping in the tall grass that night, Silbermann had to stay awake to keep a smoke-fire burning – the mosquitoes were worse than anything he had known in Dahomey. On 6 May, General Duchesne arrived at Majunga; his infantry would be complete by the 11th, but his artillery, service troops, mules, drivers and stores would arrive only in individual shiploads during the rest of May and June.[13]

The expedition commander went forward to the head of the advance on 16 May to confer with Metzinger about the apparently elusive enemy. The Hovas and their famous modern artillery might be anywhere, and any general out of contact with a retreating enemy fears being lured into a trap. While the rest of the corps began to build up behind them, the advance guard had to keep pushing on through the marshy forest, trying to get a feel for the Hova dispositions and possible intentions. Between 13 and 17 May, Colonel Oudri led the légionnaires towards a strong position held by some 2,000 Hovas at Ambodimonti, to link up there with Lieutenant-Colonel Pardes' Malagasies and Algerians. The *turcos* had an undemanding encounter with a Hova column, but when Oudri and Pardes met at Ambodimonti they found the trenches empty except for 2,000 abandoned shells for Krupp and Hotchkiss field guns and 10,000 rounds of small arms ammunition, including boxes of American .45cal for Gardner machine guns. The Hovas did not seem to be the men (or women) that Behanzin's Fon had been in 1892, but so far their tactics were incomprehensible.[14]

IN TRUTH, THE HOVAS HAD NO TACTICS, because their 37,000 armed men were not an army. Among the aristocracy, motivated entirely by factional rivalries, military commands were little more than titular honours. Any of the principles of modern soldiering that European instructors had managed to instil in a few literate young noblemen were shallow-rooted, since their culture provided no seedbed. The royal court took pride in its half-dozen batteries of modern artillery, but there were few trained gunners; the guns were symbols of power rather than familiar tools, and the majority of them were kept at Antananarivo to overawe the population. The royal guards, too, were simply 'anti-coup troops', and the Hova aristocracy had never dared to equip and train a true army of their subjects. An actual majority of the common people of the Hova heartland were slaves, the rest subsistence farmers, and the rank and file belatedly conscripted in 1895 had no reason for military enthusiasm. They were also handicapped by a local warrior culture of brief raiding and pillage after ritual displays, rather than disciplined manoeuvre or sustained effort (in this they were clearly inferior to Behanzin's smaller and ostensibly more primitive Dahomeyan army). Even after the exploratory French landing at Majunga in January, the ministers of old Rainilaiarivony's government did little beyond making speeches, and the conscripts gathered in a large camp outside Antananarivo became increasingly restive and nervous. After visiting them, the London *Times* correspondent E. F. Knight wrote:

> They were a ragged lot, and discipline there appeared to be none ... When paraded before the [prime minister] or some other great man, they used to raise cheers and brandish their arms, while their officers waved their swords ... and simulated the slaughter of the foe. These were practically the sole manoeuvres, for the drill their European officers had taught them was now neglected as foreign trickery unworthy of Hova warriors.

Knight also reported that the issue of rifles gave the hungry, unpaid conscripts the opportunity to feed themselves by robbery in and around the capital. The royal guard had Remingtons, and about half the conscripts rusty Sniders, with ten or fifteen rounds per man; since there were good stocks of ammunition in the arsenals, this miserly allocation – too small to allow any useful practice – suggests distrust on the part of their government. The rest of them carried flintlock muskets or even bows and arrows.[15]

The mention of European officers raises once again a subject that obsessed some Frenchmen. The suspicion that Britain must be conspiring with the leaders of any native state that resisted them, and that any native army with some modern weapons must be led by white instructors, was exaggerated but not always wholly mistaken. The Hova regime had indeed employed a number of British officers, led from 11 November 1894 by a Colonel C. R. St Leger Shervington; however, all but one of these had left the island on 17 April 1895, in frustration at what they saw as the frivolous lethargy of the Hova ministers. In a letter to the *United Service Magazine*, Shervington claimed that for five months his team worked hard on reports and contingency plans for a government that 'would not move even an ammunition box. Promises of compliance with our advice were numerous but never fulfilled ... The most trivial circumstances were seized upon as excuses for delay.' The ministers clung to their authority over all decisions but gave little time to their military responsibilities, constantly absenting themselves for days on end on private concerns. When the advisers first threatened to resign it provoked a brief spurt of activity, but this did not last long: 'The most categorical promises were always forthcoming, but there everything ended.'[16]

BY 5 JUNE THE ADVANCE GUARD – the 1st Legion and 3rd Algerian battalions of the Algeria Marching Regiment, 40th Light Infantry and Malagasy Skirmishers – had reached and reconnoitred the north bank of the Betsiboka bend close to its confluence with the Ikopa. This would be the end of the line for riverboats, and the Betsiboka had to be crossed and secured for eventual bridging. A Hova position guarded a deep, dangerous ford, and the advance guard had only a single lighter to ferry them across in batches, a couple of hundred at a time; even so, the next day the Hovas withdrew after a brief long-range firefight, and the soldiers slogged on towards the site of the planned depot at Marololo. They themselves were being supplied – quite inadequately, and only with difficulty – by just 300 pack-mules.[17]

By late May the French were already learning the wisdom of the boast by Queen Ranovalona that she would rely upon her strongest generals, *Hazo* and *Tazo* – 'the forest and the fever'. The 50-mile cart road being shovelled with such effort from Marovoay to the Betsiboka crossing was mainly the task of the 200th Line, 13th Naval, Hausas and Réunion Volunteers, and the heat, humidity and lethal mosquitoes were already thinning the ranks of the white regiments. Marching with full packs, Private Silbermann's company took three days to cover 14 miles, and 40 of 65 men had to drop out along the way. The accompanying Chasseurs of the 40th Light were falling out in groups of 10 and 15 together, while others were visibly shuddering with fever as they stumbled on. He recorded that when the survivors reached Androtra village they found many already sick, and one légionnaire killed himself. One day's march round the flank of a mountain covered less than 3 miles, and another légionnaire hanged himself from a tree; there would be a third successful and a fourth failed attempt on 2 June. Suicide in the Legion was associated with the utter monotony of wilderness outposts, not with active campaigning, and these references suggest that there was something specially hellish about the jungle march from Majunga.[18]

Once beyond Ambato, Silbermann was among those told to take one of the big local canoes all the way back downstream to Androtra to bring food up through the rapids. The trickle of provisions coming up by boat and pack-mule had already reduced the advance guard to half rations, and what happened to arrive was a lottery. Silbermann wrote of killingly hard labour on a diet of nothing but salted rice, and of soldiers sleeping where they fell despite the mosquitoes – sodden, filthy, and too exhausted to put up tents or cook. Somebody told the Alsatian légionnaire alarming stories about the number of fever cases being buried at field hospitals further north, particularly French *lignards* of the 200th.[19]

ON 9 JUNE THE ADVANCE GUARD reached the foot of Mevatanana, a 300-foot massif overlooking Suberbieville; this had to be taken in order to safeguard the depot site at Marololo, and the Hovas were entrenched on the heights with gun batteries covering the only two possible approaches. The 40th Light and II/RMdA advanced, but as soon as a few melinite shells exploded near the batteries, all the defenders took to their heels.[20] In the abandoned batteries the troops found three brand-new Hotchkiss guns, two small brass cannon, more than 200 Snider rifles, much ammunition and some dynamite. The advance guard marched into Suberbieville the same day; this was not a village but a barracks, only partly burned by the fleeing Hovas, and the légionnaires topped up their haversacks with such small necessities as candles, matches and some tinned food. They did not find any soap, however, so they had to continue washing their clothing with river-water and sand (they were marching in khaki and white fatigues, their aching backs braced by winding their long blue sashes tightly around the midriff from breastbone to groin).[21]

This easy victory marked the end of Metzinger's first phase of forced marches, and the advance guard halted until 18 June; this astonished the Hovas, one of whom told E. F. Knight that the white men were dying 'like rotten sheep' down on the pestilential lowlands. The advance guard had achieved the original timetable in terms of the map, but the logistic backup and the progress of the rest of the corps had fallen far short. The Marololo depot now had to be built up, and every available man had to work on a 9-foot wide cart road leading up from the Betsiboka crossing, where the sappers finally finished building a bridge on 14 June. The 200th Line were still far back at Marovoay (where their Colonel Gillon had just died), and many small detachments had been skimmed off along the line of communication, so the road via Marolo to Suberbieville and forward to Tsarasaotra would be the work of the Algeria regiment and 40th Light Infantry alone – working hungry, since the only meat to be had was from a few stray Hova oxen.

For the Legion the worst nightmare began on 12 June, and it would continue for nearly three months (though the engineer shovels only reached them on 27 June, and for the first two weeks they had to make do with the light camping tools carried by every squad). Down beside the Betsiboka and Ikopa the men were often labouring waist-deep in the red swamps; on 15 June, Lieutenant-Colonel Lentonnet of the Algerian Skirmishers wrote in his diary that they could no longer count the fever victims, and that whoever had decided to send the Lefèbvre cart to Madagascar was a murderer.[22] On 17 June General Duchesne arrived at Suberbieville, together with a field ambulance unit that would soon be swamped with tottering ghosts hollowed out by dysentery, and delirious victims of blackwater fever.

Duchesne sent a reconnaissance in force to Tsarasaotra, where the 1,000-foot Beritzoka massif loomed over the route south. A large tented camp was visible on the heights of Beritzoka; its commander, General Rainianjalahy, is believed to have had 1,200 men in the front line and perhaps 3,800 more nearby. On 30 June, General Metzinger sent just four weak companies of the 40th Light and Lentonnet's *turcos* up the slopes. The Hova artillery fell silent as soon as French mountain guns opened up from 2,500 yards, and when the clambering Algerians gave them a couple of Lebel volleys at 200 yards the whole force fled. They kept going for fully 40 miles to Andriba, abandoning artillery, rifles, ammunition, food, 450 tents and all the commander's documents. French casualties for both actions on 29–30 June totalled an officer and a corporal killed, 2 officers and 14 rankers wounded. E. F. Knight was told by one Hova that they were terrified by the smokeless-powder ammunition of the Lebels – 'invisible death ... there was magic in it'.

On 15 July a camp was installed on the stony summit of Beritzoka; the jungle was behind them at last, and south from here the view was of red clay hills thinly skinned with turf, linked by steep, rocky ridges and saddles above deep river gorges. On the 18th, when Private Silbermann was sent back down to Tsarasaotra with a ration party, he arrived to find 5 funerals in progress; another 4 blanket-wrapped corpses were buried that evening, and a medical orderly told Silbermann that at least 10 more would be joining them over the next 48 hours. The Legion's Lieutenant Gustav Langlois recorded, 'All day our men make crosses [and] dig graves ...'.[23]

IN THE HOVA CAPITAL OF ANTANARIVO on 10 July the prime minister, Rainilaiarivony, had sent for the last British officer in the city. This sole exception to the departure of the European instructors was Colonel Galbraith Graves, late Royal Artillery, a former adviser who had resigned over an unsuccessful pay demand in 1890. Graves would later publish in the *United Service Magazine* an account of his service with the Hova army in July–September 1895, complete with transcripts of his correspondence with the prime minister. A subsequent acidly phrased letter to the magazine from the previous chief instructor, Colonel Shervington, does not present Graves in a good light, but it is hard not to sympathize with his frustration at the 'hopeless, thankless task' of trying to get what he calls an 'army (*sic*)' to fight.[24]

When Rainilaiarivony re-employed the Englishman and ordered him to the north-west front to advise General Rainianjalahy, Graves agreed on condition that the government undertook to release to him the men and equipment he asked for. The prime minister took all of five days to consider this, but agreed on the evening of 15 July. At another meeting on the 18th Graves also demanded freedom to appoint his own staff; the prime minister said he would consider the names submitted, but every Malagasy officer Graves requested was denied him, for political reasons. Rainilaiarivony had no clear idea of the troops or weapons already in the field, so Graves declared that he would take 5,000 men plus the artillery that was sitting uselessly in Antananarivo. The prime minister dismissed this out of hand – if the guns left the capital there would be a rising among the people. Graves finally argued him into releasing four 12-pounder Hotchkiss guns and three Gardner machine guns and, unable to wait any longer, he left Antananarivo on 23 July – without his requested staff, but with a promise that the 5,000 Hova troops would be sent after him. (Hardly any of them were; in this and other failures it is tempting to suspect the hand of the prime minister's secretary Rasanjy, who is known to have been in secret communication with the French.)[25]

On 30 July and 4 August, Graves sent back reports of his preparations at Malatsy on the northern edge of the Andriba plateau. He had dammed a stream to make the approaches more difficult, ordered entrenchments and battery positions dug, and had emplaced 'two revolver cannon with 30 rounds only, four Hotchkiss 12-pdrs with 278 rounds, one 3-pdr Hotchkiss with 700 rounds', and his three machine guns. He had at most 3,000 men to hold these positions, with just three artillery officers, and since all the so-called gunners were illiterate and innumerate none of them could use the tangent sights of the artillery pieces. He appealed to the prime minister to send reinforcements, particularly including artillery officer cadets. Given the lack of competent crews, the shortage of ammunition was almost irrelevant.[26]

On 7 August, Graves asked for gear to be sent up for moving the guns he had with him, citing plans that he had drawn up and got approved five years previously. The prime minister's replies to this and all his other letters acknowledged his reports but ignored his requests for ammunition, artillery officers and even for sandbags. Some reinforcements had now straggled in; Graves had about 4,300 men to hold twelve positions over a front of more than 5 miles. However, he still lacked rifles for a quarter of them, and complained that most of the others did not even know how to load their weapons, let alone how to fire them effectively. He now had 9 field and 2 revolver guns, but only an average of 31 rounds for each, and 8 machine guns with an ungenerous 4,500 rounds. Captured porters had told him that in one French camp 70 white men had been buried in eleven days; Graves had sent out raiding parties to shoot up the road-camps at dawn, but had heard nothing. These raids were never carried out, and on 18 August he wrote that his orders to the outposts to move forward and bring the French advance guard under fire had also been ignored.[27]

AS THE CART ROAD INCHED FORWARDS up the steep slopes to the Andriba plateau, trailing its fringes of forlorn crosses, a continuous link was established over the 155 track-miles from Majunga as far as the Beritzoka heights, giving General Duchesne direct communication with his base camp. Some of the rest of the infantry now finally caught up with the advance guard, and 'Daddy' Voyron's 2nd Brigade passed through Metzinger's 1st, reclaiming its Malagasy battalion of the Colonial Regiment on the way. On 16 August it fought its first skirmish with Hovas at the Malatsy positions guarding the gateway to the Andriba plateau. For what happened next we have the luxury of both Duchesne's report and Graves' account of 22 August.

ON 19 AUGUST THE FRENCH RECONNOITRED the steep approaches, and the next morning they advanced in three columns. Graves sent urgent orders to his gun emplacements to open fire on the little white lines and blocks flowing up and down the bare red-grey slopes, and eventually two artillery officers obeyed. French guns then sent some 50 shells into the Malatsy defences in reply; only two melinite rounds burst inside a parapet, and not a single Frenchman was within 2,000 yards of Graves' strong emplacements, but all the infantry round his No.7 Redoubt simply decamped, and the others, seeing this, began to follow them. By 8pm only one position was still manned, and Graves had no option but to fall back about 10 miles to Tafofo: 'I shall do my best, but if your soldiers will not stand, even behind 18 feet of solid earth, then I am afraid my task will be a difficult one.' From 24 August onwards Graves, near despair, began to use the word 'cowardice' openly, and while he doggedly continued to try to place obstacles in Duchesne's path his letters became little more than rants:

> If anything can be done to make this army fight, the first thing is a whole[sale] sweep of the officers ... How can you expect me to compete against one of the first powers of Europe with an army officered by men who can neither read nor understand marks?[28]

THE SITUATION FROM GENERAL DUCHESNE'S PERSPECTIVE was equally worrying. He had reached the halfway point and had his foothold in the edge of the highlands; but he could not gamble on the hope that the Hovas would never stand to fight as he penetrated into their own homeland, with an enfeebled force at the end of dysfunctional lines of supply. Getting the iron carts forward was a miserable task that took its toll of mules and men alike; many carts had run away on gradients, taking their load and their mule over the edge of drops. Others were simply dumped when the troops took the draft-mules for pack work (for which they were neither trained nor harnessed). Duchesne had urgently requested 1,000 Abyssinian pack-mules; only 430 could be found, so 800 more Algerian mules were sent out in June. There were yet more delays on the trail while the new Abyssinian pack-mules were sent forward and exchanged for the original Algerian animals, and the latter were put back between the shafts of the carts (for which the Abyssinians were not trained) – so any given *échelon* of the supply train now needed not simply enough mules, but the right sort of mules. The combat troops were harsh in their criticism of the 'Kabylie' muleteers, but these poor devils suffered just as badly as the French, and were more or less left to fend for themselves.[29]

Duchesne would report that it was on 4 August that he made up his mind to form a Light Column, of the fittest men carrying their supplies on pack-mules only, to make a dash across the plateaux for Antananarivo. However, this attempt could not be made for another month or more, while 250 tons of supplies and expected reinforcements were brought up to the Andriba plateau. By then he would be six weeks behind schedule, and the first violent mountain storms might usher in the rainy season any time from mid-October. In the meantime the road-building had to continue until 6 September, at a continuing cost in lives. Lieutenant Langlois wrote that by the end of August the four Legion companies had dwindled from 200 to 70–75 men each; the battalion then received 150 reinforcements from Majunga, so that 450 légionnaires answered the rollcall on 1 September, but that was still only just over half their starting strength. The two Algerian battalions of the RMdA had lost only some 25 per cent compared with the Legion's 60-plus per cent; but by this time disease had reduced the 40th Light from 800 to 350 men, and not one of the survivors was strong enough to be picked for the flying column. The 13th Naval had 1,500 of its original 2,400 *marsouins* left, so could contribute the best part of two battalions. Unsurprisingly, the two black battalions of the Colonial Regiment were in better shape, since the majority of the RC's 600 casualties had been among the white settlers of the Réunion battalion.[30]

The Light Column faced a forced march of 120 miles, at first through steep hills cut by rocky defiles and marshy valleys full of cactus and trees. Duchesne hoped they could average 9 miles per day, but depending upon the resistance it might take as long as twenty days to reach Antananarivo. On 9 September the men were paraded and a final selection was made of 4,240 of the fittest. Even so, Lieutenant Langlois wrote that the sight of his légionnaires almost made him weep – pale, downcast, in rags of uniforms and gaping boots, with feverish eyes glowing in the shadow of the sun helmets that seemed too large for their skulls. The I/RMdA provided 19 officers and 330 légionnaires, the two battalions of Algerians 35 officers and 1,086 *turcos;* with cavalry scouts, engineers and two batteries of mule-guns, this regiment would form General Metzinger's 1,800-strong advance guard for the Light Column. For the sake of speed they would take only 255 pack-mules carrying rations for about five or six days; this meant that the légionnaires would still have to march under the crushing weight of their full packs. (One of the fresher Legion officers, who had come up with the reinforcements, was the battalion adjutant-major, Captain Paul Brundsaux – he of the forked beard, who had already survived tours in Tonkin and Dahomey.)[31] The advance guard was to march on 14 September, followed the next day by Voyron's force mainly composed of a scraped-together Composite Regiment of about 1,300 other infantry judged fit to march. Finally, on 17 September, what Duchesne was pleased to call his 'reserve', under Colonel de Lorme of the Colonial Regiment, would bring up the rear with the bulk of the mule-train and another 830 mixed infantry.[32]

THE LIGHT COLUMN STRUCK OUT SOUTHWARDS on the 14th, and at about 7am the next morning the advance guard hit a strong hill position at Tsinainondry; thoroughly prepared by Colonel Graves to block the Riringala valley, this was held by 1,300 men with two field and two machine guns. The Legion deployed into extended line, waded a marsh and clambered up the steep central slope under intermittent artillery fire, but few of the shells exploded; meanwhile the Algerian Skirmishers turned a flank by remarkable feats of mountaineering up and down gorges and ridges. At 1,200 yards – a range that seemed impossible to the Hovas – the légionnaires lay down and began firing steady Lebel volleys. Above him, Lieutenant Langlois saw one man stand up, look around him, and bolt; two or three more did the same; then, 'as one man, like those jack-in-the-boxes pushed out on their springs, they suddenly surged out from behind their parapets and disappeared rapidly down the ... ravines that furrowed the terrain'. Graves confirmed this: 'having lost a good many, they bolted from their works like rabbits ...'. He sent General Rainianjalahy just 4 miles back, to occupy positions he had prepared at Kiangara, but when he arrived there with the rearguard at about 6pm he found nobody; he eventually caught up with Rainianjalahy some three hours later and found him asleep in bed in his pavilion, having posted not a single sentry. Total French casualties at Tsinainondry were three wounded.[33]

This spectacle was repeated on 19 September at the formidable Ambohimenas escarpment, which rose another 2,600 feet to the upper plateau. The légionnaires, Algerians and Composite Regiment clawed their way up three lung-bursting tracks towards fourteen Hova positions on the shoulders and ridges south of Kinadji. For once the Hovas attempted a counter-attack, but despite having the steep slope in their favour they were driven back; thereupon more than 6,000 defenders abandoned the whole line and retreated some 28 miles to the Ankarahara range on the southern edge of the plateau, burning their own villages as they went. Colonel Graves told the correspondent Knight that some had bribed their officers to run so that they could too. No French combat casualties are recorded, but a number of men collapsed from exhaustion. These exertions without the climax of combat were actually lowering morale; there were half a dozen suicides in the Legion battalion, and the men were silent and listless around their campfires.[34]

During the last week of September the column crossed the Ankaraharas and dropped down on to a fertile plain where villages sat among rice-paddies and fruit groves. The French were now only about 30 miles from Antananarivo; groups of Hovas continued to fall back ahead of the column but some now flowed back behind it once it had passed, so Metzinger's and Voyron's commands closed up to march in defensive formation. They took fire from a number of villages and had to deploy laboriously to attack them, but the Hovas never waited for them to arrive. The French could not be bothered to take prisoners; one Hova told E. F. Knight that when he was captured the soldiers just took his gun away and told him to go home, and the worst that prisoners had to fear was being made to carry the légionnaires' packs.[35]

FROM A HILLTOP CAMP on 26–27 September the soldiers could see, about 15 miles to the south-east, the towers, spires and domes of Antananarivo rising on its 650-foot hill above sheep-meadows and paddy fields. (The troops' relief was partly due to the prospect of those sheep; rations had been reduced steadily, from sixteen hardtack biscuits daily to just four per man.) The capital was a huddled mass of tawny-red buildings on a hill streaked with green lanes and gardens, occupying a narrow, roughly Y-shaped ridge aligned north to south. The northern slopes were invitingly shallow, but those from the west and east rose steeply to the palace complex, and an almost sheer cliff guarded the south. The city was surrounded on the whole of its southern half by the Ikopa river (see Map 8). General Duchesne decided to avoid a direct approach from the north-west; the ground was too boggy for his guns and his infantry would have had to file along paddy dykes below occupied hilltops. Instead he would keep his force well closed up as they made an unhurried clockwise sweep around the north and north-east of the city, to take some of the strong outlying hill positions and clear themselves a path in from the east. To march across the face of an enemy army was a cardinal sin, but Duchesne was not facing Soult at Austerlitz or Wellington at Salamanca (incredibly, some Hova courtiers imagined that since Duchesne did not attack frontally, his direction of march must indicate a cowardly retreat towards Tamatave).[36]

Although Duchesne did not know it, by as early as 21 September Rainianjalahy's army had been reduced to about 2,200 hungry men, and while the officers were still brandishing their swords and boasting to Colonel Graves, the government was now pressing even chained convicts into the ranks. When Graves got back to the city on 25 September he was told that Rainilaiarivony was in bed and not to be disturbed, and by the afternoon of the 27th he was still being refused an audience with the prime minister. Graves finally took the advice of the *Times* correspondent Knight and left for Tamatave. Under the circumstances, his perseverance had been remarkable, and he can hardly be blamed for securing a generous severance payment.[37]

When the slow clockwise march started in stunning heat on 28 September the Legion was assigned to protect the ration convoy, with two companies forming the rearguard; inevitably, these légionnaires were choked with dust and tormented by flies. They often had to halt while the column stretched and contracted, and some villagers even came out and offered the soldiers water and fruit; but as the baking afternoon wore on, Hova army stragglers began to hover around the slow tail of the column. The crowds grew in numbers and boldness until about 2,000 had assembled, shaking their weapons and shouting, and at last they nerved themselves to attack. Shackled to the slow-moving mule-trains ahead of them, the Legion companies could not manoeuvre beyond taking alternate turns to stop and drive the Hovas back with occasional volleys. Visibility was bad, and they were impeded by straggling pack-animals and the need to carry their casualties; the légionnaires were running low on ammunition when about 50 Senegalese drivers from the Train ran back from the convoy to resupply them. That day, from the city above, E. F. Knight had watched various bodies of Hovas making demonstrations of defiance. Shouting war-cries and brandishing their weapons, they would rush up an empty hill with apparent ferocity, but when the French got anywhere close even to artillery range they would run down again, to repeat the pantomime further off.[38] On the 29th the French continued their slow progress between scattered hills, and after a couple of skirmishes they camped early, south-west of Ilafy and about 5 miles from the city.

Early on 30 September, Duchesne attacked the outlying hill positions from two directions. Voyron's Hausas would guard the mule-train, while his 13th Naval attacked southwards via Ambatofotsy. Metzinger would hook in from the east with the Algeria regiment and the shreds of the 200th Line, with their left flank secured by the Malagasy Skirmishers. By 9.30am Metzinger had taken Ankatso hill; guns were drawn on to the summit, and before noon they opened fire on Observatory and Andrainarivo hills. Hova guns from the palace precincts replied, but fell silent after 45 minutes. The Malagasy battalion then took the Observatory and, after a slight misstep, the Algerians of III/RMdA occupied Andrainarivo, supported from the north by *marsouins* who had already taken their own objective. By 1.30pm the whole line of hills had been secured. An artillery duel then broke out between French guns on the hills and the batteries at the palace. Duchesne ordered a slow cadence, with melinite shells mixed in with the black-powder rounds. Meanwhile six small assault columns were assembled, each of two infantry companies with sappers, to force the north and east gates. The bombardment began at 2.55pm, and after 35 minutes – just as the storming parties were advancing – a white flag was raised. Within an hour royal envoys had agreed a complete surrender, and Metzinger's brigade entered Antananarivo that afternoon. In the city they found 74 guns including 30 modern pieces, enormous stocks of ammunition and some 8,000 rifles.

In actual combat, since it set out on 14 September the Light Column had lost 10 killed, 56 wounded and 12 missing. From all causes the weary, half-size Legion battalion had suffered during that period 104 casualties (nearly one man in three), of which just 14 were the result of enemy action.[39]

GENERAL METZINGER LED THE LÉGIONNAIRES out of Antananarivo for the return march north on 22 October. They marched slowly; it was 15 November before the last arrived at Suberbieville, where they saw a great dump of abandoned Lefèbvre carts. Private Silbermann recalled the trail beyond Suberbieville as noisome and depressing, lined for miles with wrecked carts and the rotting corpses of mules: 'now I could see why our rations so often failed to arrive'. They picked up the line-of-communication detachments as they marched; this would be the last column to use the road between Antananarivo and Majunga, all subsequent movements being by the eastern route from Tamatave. Like the rusting scrap-iron at Suberbieville, this was a tacit reproach to the Army planning staff.

The same might be said of the scenes that confronted Silbermann when he reached Ankaboka, where both the base camp of the 200th Line and the main evacuation hospital were situated. A chaplain was going from one hospital tent to another, giving the last rites to long rows of men in all stages of distress. A Legion medical orderly told him that for the past two months they had been burying 25 or 30 men a day at that hospital alone, and that those at Majunga were even worse. Silbermann saw these for himself some days later. When he had passed on his way up-country in May there had been only a handful of crosses in the cemetery; now he calculated that there were nearly 1,500 of them, and cartloads of coffins came from the hospitals morning and evening.[40]

Each battalion had its own two surgeons – for this campaign, twice the norm – and the central medical services (under the command, coincidentally, of the same Dr Edouard Hocquard whose memoir of Tonkin is quoted in Chapter 4) had been planned with Indochinese experience in mind. Originally 70 doctors with support staff had been provided in two field ambulance units, four 250-bed field hospitals, a 500-bed evacuation hospital and a 500-bed sanitorium, and the 350-bed hospital ship *Shamrock* was anchored at Majunga. There, three water sterilizers could process 30,000 litres a day, and lavish supplies of quinine had been shipped (eventually, about half a pound's weight for every man in the corps). It had been estimated, from Tonkin experience, that this total of 2,350 medium- to long-term beds would be filled only to 40 or 50 per cent capacity at any one time – in other words, that the expeditionary corps would never have to treat more than 8 per cent of its strength wounded or sick. This would prove to be cruelly optimistic, and the hospitals were simply overwhelmed: during the four-month campaign, one 800-strong battalion of the 200th Line would be reduced to 58 fit men, and one 200-man Engineer company to just seven.[41]

There was no lack of care by the hospital doctors and nursing sisters, at least eight of whom themselves died on the island while others had to be invalided out and replaced; but the supplies of quinine had been incompetently loaded first on to the transports, so were not retrieved from the bottom of the holds and delivered to the hospitals until too late to prevent thousands of malaria cases.[42] It was, in any case, ineffective against the blackwater fever that battened on exhausted men heavily infected with a particular sort of malaria parasite, and this killed them in their thousands – especially (but far from exclusively) those of the unacclimatized units from France, who died at twice and three times the rate of the légionnaires and marsouins. Of all those who died, the cause of death was given as malarial (that is, including blackwater fever) in 72 per cent of cases.[43]

Total figures are slightly contradictory in different sources. Those in General Duchesne's original report had to be revised subsequently, to give total deaths among French soldiers in Madagascar (including Naval Troops and the mixed Colonial Regiment) as somewhere between 4,450 and just over 4,600. To these must be added those who died aboard ship on the way home and those who succumbed after repatriation, which General Reibell later calculated at another 554 and 348, giving a total of just over 5,500; however, a standard modern French source gives a grand total of 5,756 deaths. Since the total manpower of the original expeditionary corps and its subsequent reinforcements was 18,340, this was a fatality rate of 31 per cent, and of these, less than half of 1 per cent – just 25 men – died as the result of enemy action.[44] The total dead and missing from the three battalions of the Algeria Marching Regiment was 604, or roughly 22 per cent – marginally more than the figure for the 13th Naval Infantry. Much the same percentage applied to the Legion battalion alone, which had 226 dead, only 5 of them the result of combat. What dragged the overall percentages upwards so dramatically were the deaths in the Metropolitan units: 1,039 for the three battalions of the 200th Line, and 510 for the 40th Light Infantry Battalion – fatalities of 43 per cent and a shocking 63 per cent respectively.[45] The parliamentary representatives of French voters would make very sure that Metropolitan troops would never again be exposed to such risks.

AFTER A MISERABLE VOYAGE HOME, during which the crew of the steamer Hindoustan neglected them shamefully, the légionnaires disembarked at Oran just in time for Christmas 1895. Here, the welcome was the warmest Silbermann ever experienced: the whole town was decorated, there was a garlanded Arc de Triomphe in the Place de la République, and a band led them through cheering crowds who showered oranges and cigars on them all the way to the Zouave barracks. That evening the garrison and civilians alike pressed free drinks on any légionnaire they spotted, and if he entered a *café-concert* the band struck up the *Marseillaise*. It all started again when the men from 2nd Foreign returned to their Saida depot, where they were met at the station by the colonel, the colours and the band. Many of them were soon sent to Arzew for the rest cure, but blackwater fever still came to collect a few of them even two months after disembarkation (for the sake of their morale, convalescents were forbidden by the medical officers from attending funerals). The 'Red Island' was far from finished with the Legion yet, however.[46]

WHEN GENERAL DUCHESNE ENTERED ANTANANARIVO on 1 October 1895 he declared a French protectorate over Madagascar, and in January 1896 his place was taken by a civilian resident-general, Hippolyte Laroche. This well-meaning man cast around for a group of nobles to form a plausible government under the nominal authority of Queen Ranavalona III, whose prestige was important for ensuring the peaceful acceptance of the new arrangements. Given the factional intrigues that had always characterized the ruling oligarchy, it was not difficult to find collaborators; in January 1896 the old prime minister Rainilaiarivony was sent into exile in Algeria and his treacherous secretary Rasanjy installed in his place. However, competitive conspiracies among the nobility continued unabated, as each group clawed for advantage and profit while slandering the others to any Frenchman who would listen (forging incriminating letters was a favourite activity). The two main parties were associated with courtiers close to the queen on the one hand, and with Rasanjy and a royal relative named Ramahatra on the other.

The defeat of Imerina by the French had removed any check on their former subject tribes in the north and east, and left their enemies in the south and west unpacified. The main tribal peoples were – from the northern 'big toe', southwards down the east coast (see Map 9) – the Antankarana, who showed strong Indian and Arab traits; the darker, more African Bezanozano and Betsimisaraka; and in the south-eastern forest the Tanala – expert spearmen, who carried heavy wood and ox-hide shields. The most warlike of all were the Mahalafy of the dry southern 'heel', which supported nothing but thorn-scrub and cactus; their reputation for cattle-raiding was also shared by the Bara, who lived north of them on the western savannah. North again, all the way up the grasslands to the jungle of the north-western 'toes', was Sakalava country. At first the countryside was troubled by only minor banditry, but both in Imerina and the north resentments soon gathered strength and purpose (the Malagasy word for the French was *farantsay*; in local parlance this was soon rendered as *faratay* – 'the final excrement').[47]

The rapid repatriation of half the surviving troops, under irresistible French political pressure, had left General Voyron with only about 6,000 men. Even with just Imerina and its vassal tribes to police (the west and south being still unpenetrated) he had an impossibly large area to cover. His garrisons – at Antananarivo, Majunga, Diégo Suarez, Tamatave, and Fianarantsoa in the Betsileo country of the southern plateaux – were predominantly Algerian, Senegalese and local Malagasy battalions, with a thin spine of Naval Infantry.[48] Incidents multiplied in early 1896, and in April a full-scale revolt broke out as rebels calling themselves *menalamba* attacked Frenchmen, collaborators, and the Protestant churches that they associated with the Hova regime.[49]

These outbreaks seem to have been largely spontaneous and uncoordinated, but some Frenchmen were convinced that they were orchestrated by Hova aristocrats (the more paranoid also suspected Britain's hand at work). Queen Ranavalona always denied encouraging the rebels, perhaps truthfully; but since rebellion against the throne was regarded as sacrilege, rebel leaders claimed to be acting in her name against a traitorous clique of courtiers who had sold out to the French. Violence spread not only among the Hova but also among the Betsimisaraka, the Bara, even the Sakalava, who saw the French protectorate in Ranavalona's name as perpetuating the hated rule of Imerina. Chaos spread over much of the north and centre of the island, the garrisons were forced into a purely defensive role, and soon the capital was effectively cut off from Tamatave, Diégo Suarez and Majunga. Naval Troops officers were briefing against Resident-General Laroche, and in Paris politicians and journalists took sides, with the pro-military and colonialist lobby pressing for outright annexation.

On 6 August 1896 the National Assembly voted the protectorate out of existence, declared Madagascar a French colony, and – an even greater provocation to the Hova nobility – abolished slavery. On 18 February, Colonel Joseph Galliéni had landed at Marseille on returning from his three years in Tonkin; almost immediately, Colonial Minister Lebon had offered him command of the troops on the island, and he had since accepted – on certain conditions.

*

THE FIRST AND MOST IMPORTANT promise that Galliéni extracted, unsurprisingly, was that he should have a free hand, with combined authority over both the military and the civil administration. Another – despite the fact that he was a Naval Troops officer and Madagascar was a Navy fief – was that he be given a battalion of the Legion, 'so that if it comes to that, I can die with decency'. The language might seem theatrical given the fact that the only determined enemy faced by Duchesne had been the mosquito, but it is therefore instructive.

Galliéni was a highly intelligent, seasoned and down-to-earth colonial soldier with excellent personal contacts throughout his small professional world, and he must certainly have sought information from officers on the spot while considering Lebon's offer. (The telegraph lines were open to all, and at the time those officers were garrulous with frustration.) The *menalamba* – and the thousands of half-rebels, half-bandits who were exploiting the unrest – were fighting for themselves on their own ground, and the generalized uprising involved tribesmen who were much more aggressive than the pathetic Hova conscripts herded out to face the Light Column. The rebels had gained the local initiative, against French units isolated in penny-packets over huge areas of a notoriously pestilential wilderness, with even worse lines of communication and supply than in Upper Tonkin. It would only take a modest combination of bad luck and bad judgement to produce a medium-sized disaster, and Galliéni had no intention of presiding over one. Naval troops had already been in Madagascar for more than ten years, and the fact that he specifically asked for a Legion battalion says a great deal. He had soldiered with both, and he knew which he wanted for his final insurance policy.

The ministerial decision ordering the raising of this new Legion marching battalion was dated 3 August 1896, three days before the parliamentary formalities. The unit was once again formed – with exemplary speed – from two companies each of the 1st and 2nd RE; commanded by Major Cussac, it sailed from Oran to Marseille. The first of two parties was ready to embark there for Tamatave on 10 August, and the whole unit had arrived in Madagascar by 14 September.[50]

While travelling up to the capital from Tamatave, Colonel Galliéni was ambushed and his small cavalry escort was dispersed; he emptied his revolver at his attackers and dived into the bush, evading them to catch up with his men alone. On 26 September he formally replaced both General Voyron and Resident-General Laroche (though at this date his powers were only those of a temporary appointment in a state of emergency). Long before he could think about 'oil patches' he had to identify, and stamp his authority on, a local leadership that he could work with, and he achieved this with a ruthless *coup de théâtre*. After questioning French administrators about the local power structure, he had two ministers arrested: the queen's uncle Ratsimamanga (deeply unpopular for his financial extortions), and the interior minister Rainandriamampandry (an opponent of the court party, but without powerful allies). There is no doubt that Galliéni selected them coldly as scapegoats from the two main factions. They were tried by a kangaroo court-martial on charges of complicity in the leadership of the rebellion, the serpentine Rasanjy gave perjured evidence against them, and on 15 October the two unlucky examples were executed by firing squad.[51]

In February 1897, the queen was herself exiled to Réunion; whatever her actual involvement, her presence as a figurehead for resistance could no longer be tolerated. In April that year General Galliéni was formally appointed governor-general of Madagascar with full civil and military powers. For the next nine years – at that date a unique record of continuity for the French colonial system – he would devote himself to applying the methods of military penetration and civil development that he had honed in Upper Tonkin.

THE PACIFICATION OF THIS HUGE ISLAND was carried out with only about 7,000 troops, spread between remote garrisons in the familiar system of military territories, circles and sectors. Most major movements were necessarily by ship, and apart from those in the Hova and Betsileo highlands the main bases were planted around the coasts: clockwise from Diégo Suarez, at Vohémar, Ile Ste Marie, Tamatave, Mananjary, Fort Dauphin, Tuléar, Morondova, Majunga, Analalava and Nossi Bé. The first phase of cordon-and-column operations against the *menalamba* was virtually completed by the end of 1898, although it took until 1904 to pacify all the coastal areas. The penetration of the remote west and south – mopping up small pockets of resistance, and creating 'oil patches' in areas where the Merina writ had never run – took seven years, but Paris gave Galliéni the time he needed. By the time he handed over to a civilian governor in May 1905 he had imposed law and order and made important strides in the development of infrastructure, education and health care. Limited white settlement was encouraged; this attracted experienced *colons* from Réunion but – as in Tonkin – few others except for retired Naval Troops who took their discharge locally. Galliéni not only directed his officers to learn the Malagasy language, but also set his face firmly against racial discrimination (mixed marriages were encouraged, and segregated areas in the towns were forbidden).[52]

Galliéni's only European units (apart from small detachments of Africa Light Horse as couriers and escorts) were four companies of the 13th Naval Infantry, a single battery of Naval Artillery, and the Foreign Marching Battalion. He initially had the two Algerian Skirmisher battalions of the old RMdA, but the bulk were twenty-five companies of native troops in four battalions of Senegalese and two of Malagasy Skirmishers, led as always by Naval Infantry cadres. The Legion battalion were widely dispersed in separate companies, from Imerina itself to the north-east and south-west coasts, and from high in the Ankaratra mountains to the jungles of the Majongo river valley (by common consent the unhealthiest region of the whole island, where the 3rd and 4th Companies earned Galliéni's particular praise). In 1905 the general was also quoted as saying of them that:

> The légionnaires have especially drawn attention to themselves by their endurance during our recent colonial campaigns. Their solidity under fire is equal to that of French troops and, as their physical resilience has proved superior, they have in reality played a more effective role ... during these expeditions.[53]

The légionnaires' work was Tonkin all over again: trying to follow gangs of rebels-cum-bandits to their wilderness hideouts, building outposts and the roads to resupply them, re-establishing villages, raising and arming self-defence militias, providing escorts for precarious convoys, taking a handful of casualties in encounter skirmishes and ambushes, and – always – watching the ranks dwindle under the relentless assaults of the anopheles mosquito.[54]

IN HANOI, LIEUTENANT-COLONEL LYAUTEY'S gloomy musings about resigning his commission and seeking a prosperous *marriage blanche* had been brought to an abrupt end in November 1896, when the governor-general informed him that General Galliéni was requesting his services and had agreed to hold the job open until March 1897. Lyautey's letters during his voyage across the Indian Ocean fizzed with enthusiasm, and not only about his personal prospects: he described his vision of the colonies as an essential training-ground for active administrators and officers, who might even return to revitalize a divided, cynical and lethargic France bedevilled by a general refusal to take any personal responsibility.[55] When he landed at Majunga on 3 May 1897, his old chief at once confronted him with a personal responsibility of his own – to close down *menalamba* activity in Antsatrana province in the north, where the rebellion was being led by two Hova noblemen, Rabozaka and the former royal governor, Rabezavana. A column led by Colonel Combes had achieved some success against these two in March and April respectively; now Lyautey was instructed to offer more positive incentives to Rabezavana. In confidential discussions between 29 May and 1 June terms were clearly reached; when Rabezavana came in to submit formally he was greeted with dignified ceremony, and was later confirmed in his old appointment under Lyautey's supervision.[56]

By the end of July 1897, central Imerina, from Lake Alaotra in the north to Ambositra in the south, was largely pacified, and communications had been restored between the capital and Majunga and Tamatave (in the latter case largely thanks to the 2nd Company of the Legion battalion). Lyautey and other regional commanders alternated diplomacy with force – applied by the usual converging columns of *marsouins*, Senegalese and Malagasy Skirmishers, stiffened by parsimoniously shared-out Legion companies – and with immediate civil development. At his Ankazobe headquarters Lyautey was left very much to his own devices, corresponding often with the governor-general but meeting him only infrequently; Galliéni knew that Lyautey was a sincere convert to his methods, and trusted him to make his own day-to-day decisions, both military and developmental. In January 1900, Lyautey would write in an influential article that:

> Military command and territorial command should be united in the same hands. When the senior military officer is also the territorial administrator, his thoughts when he captures a brigand's den are of the trading-post that he will set up there ... and he will plan his attack on different lines.[57]

LYAUTEY HAD COMPLAINED to his correspondents about France's apparent mood of cynicism, division and lethargy; by the end of January 1898 he would be proved right about the cynicism and divisions, and he might have wished for a little more lethargy. The name of Dreyfus was about to be thrust into the forefront of public affairs once again, and would now reveal its true destructive potential as the Army, the press and the political and chattering classes sank into an extraordinarily violent and prolonged collective nervous breakdown.[58]

In July 1897, an influential senator had been shown evidence suggesting that Dreyfus might be innocent, and that the guilty man was actually a disreputable chancer named Major Esterhazy. Rumours began to circulate, and journalists took an interest. Hitherto the authorities had met all enquiries with a serene refusal to discuss the case, but in January 1898 – while maintaining their absolute certainty of Dreyfus' guilt – they were forced to bring Esterhazy, too, before a court-martial. This acquitted him, with a perversity that shocked French and foreign commentators alike, and the result was explosive. On 13 January 1898 the controversial novelist Émile Zola – a hate-figure for the Army since the publication of his Franco-Prussian War novel, *Le débâcle* – published in the newspaper *Aurore* his famous open letter to the President of the Republic: '*J'accuse* ...'. Among those he attacked by name were the war minister, General Mercier, and the Chief of the General Staff, General de Boisdeffre. Reasoned arguments had failed, and the 'Dreyfusard' case would henceforth be pursued in extreme polemical terms.

Paris was a society as poisonously divided as the Merina nobility in Madagascar, and 'anti-Dreyfusards' were quick to hurl counter-charges. The friction ignited a political atmosphere that was even more volatile than usual, with administrations falling every few months and parliamentary factions wrestling and gouging for advantage. Throughout the whole 'affair' the partisan press of these political cliques would make sensational accusations based on the flimsiest rumours, and idle guesswork by participants in enquiries – reported through malice or simple indiscretion – would lead to an impenetrable tangle of lawsuits and counter-suits. The relatively simple case at the heart of the dispute was obscured as 'Dreyfus' became a mere slogan in the service of old suspicions and new quarrels. The simmering anti-militarism of the extreme Left boiled over, repelling some of the original Dreyfusards (including Georges Clemenceau); but during 1898 some voices of irreproachable bourgeois respectability also began to ask questions. The generals, bewildered by the variety and violence of their critics, dug in on what they believed to be their own inviolable ground; but their rampart showed the first crack when it was revealed that the original court-martial judges had been shown 'irrefutable proofs of Dreyfus' guilt that could not be revealed to the defence for reasons of state security'.

With dreary inevitability, some anti-Dreyfusards also played the Jewish card. In January 1898, anti-Semitic feeling was fanned in Algeria by opportunist *colons* who were agitating for an even freer hand than they already enjoyed. There had always been a strong anti-Semitic streak among the Spanish settlers; now Jews were suspected of voting *en bloc* against candidates seeking greater autonomy from Paris, and this distrust of the Jewish 'capitalists' was shared by local socialists. A demagogue calling himself Max Régis (Massimiliano Milano) led an autonomist/anti-Semitic front, declaring that 'the hour of Revolution has come ... We will water the tree of our liberty with Jewish blood', and for five days a violent rabble ruled the streets of Algiers.[58]

ALFRED DREYFUS WAS INDEED BLAMELESS, but the scandal did not lie in any conspiracy by the generals to railroad a known innocent. Deceived by the sheer incompetence of their intelligence office (the Statistical Section) over the identification of a handwriting sample, they had leapt to an unwarrantable but apparently sincere assumption of his guilt. General Mercier had been advised to tread softly, but he was a stubborn man, and when the arrest of Dreyfus was leaked to the press he felt impelled to go ahead with the court-martial. When the evidence proved insufficiently robust to convince a court, steps were taken by a certain Major Henry to nourish it, and the trial proceedings were manipulated to ensure a conviction. Later, goaded by their attackers, senior military figures invented increasingly unconvincing reasons for their refusal to account for their actions, while making frantic background efforts to bury the truth under yet more dubious paperwork – which had been produced for them in November 1896 by the ever-loyal Major Henry. Passive evasions and quiet pressure on individuals had degenerated into actual criminality.

More cracks soon appeared in the wall. A new head of the Statistical Section proved irritatingly persistent; Lieutenant-Colonel Picquart was no Dreyfusard himself, but he became convinced that a miscarriage of justice had taken place. When he reported this, he was first ignored, then threatened, and finally court-martialled on trumped-up charges and dismissed from the Army. In June 1898 yet another war minister, Cavaignac, seized the opportunity to show himself in a decisive light; he had no interest in the fate of Dreyfus, but believed that the career of a minister seen to drew a final line under this scandal would prosper. When his investigator told him in August 1898 that an important letter in the dossier was a forgery, he summoned Major Henry for questioning; the wretched man confessed, and the following day cut his own throat. The Dreyfusard press was exultant, and Cavaignac's insistence that a document forged retrospectively in 1896 could not invalidate a trial held in 1894 signally failed to draw the line he had hoped for.

COLONIAL RIVALRY now played its own part in inflaming public opinion, which was already infuriated by British comment on the scandal. September 1898 saw the confrontation, at Fashoda on the White Nile in Upper Sudan, between Captain Marchand's small French trans-Saharan expedition from the Congo, and some 2,000 Egyptian and British troops led in person by General Herbert Kitchener, just two weeks after his crushing victory over the Mahdist army at Omdurman. Kitchener was courteous, but declined to take seriously Marchand's claims for French rights based solely on his having pitched camp on the bank of the Nile, and the Frenchmen were obliged to move on south-eastwards towards Djibouti. In Paris, another French government fell in October, and the humiliating news from the Sudan became public on 4 November 1898.[59]

The nationalist press became incandescent over Fashoda; the Chamber voted extraordinary military funds by a margin of 471 votes to 18, and the long-festering hostility towards Britain reached such a peak that an actual shooting war may only have been prevented by the wisdom of Foreign Minister Théophile Delcassé and the British ambassador.[60] This was also a time of labour strikes, mob violence and rumours of troops being readied to take back the streets, and the press had plenty to report other than the consideration by a court of appeal of Mme Dreyfus' application for a re-opening of her husband's case. But at such a time the public were in no mood to see the Army distracted from its duty, and when the court ruled in Mme Dreyfus' favour the presiding Judge Loew (an Alsatian Jew, like Dreyfus) was accused of treacherously conspiring with British and Jewish agents.

In December 1898, during the war-fever following the Fashoda affair, it was decided to strengthen the Legion battalion in Madagascar. Additional 5th and 6th Companies were formed from the 1st and 2nd RE respectively, and these landed at Majunga on 13 January 1899. During that year the headquarters of the swollen 1,500-strong battalion was at Miarinarivo in the Imerina highlands, but the companies were dispersed all over the island, separated by up to 1,000 miles in widely differing terrain and climates.[61] In September 1899 the battalion reverted to conventional size, the extra companies being disbanded and their 'non-repatriable' personnel – that is, the men who were fittest and had the longest time still to serve – being dispersed between the other four.

IN LATE MAY 1899 – amid the clamour that might well have destroyed Lyautey had he opted for the parliamentary career path that he had considered three years previously – he and General Galliéni returned to France for several months. Galliéni had kept his promise to pacify Madagascar without asking for additional military resources, but now he needed more funds for civil development, and he had a justified faith in his protégé's powers of persuasion. While the infantryman Galliéni was locked in the trench-warfare of meetings with ministers and bureaucrats, Lyautey acted as his light cavalry, providing the more passionate advocacy at which he excelled. He networked far and wide, spreading glowing opinions of Galliéni and the work he was accomplishing at meetings both private and public.

At a time of such furiously polarized opinions for and against the military, Lyautey's colonial enthusiasms cost him a number of his old liberal friends, who followed a blindly 'pro-Dreyfusard' and therefore anti-military line. Lyautey had kept in touch with the development of the scandal through his prolific correspondence, and despite his instinctive loyalties he was deeply worried that the General Staff had betrayed the good name of the Army. Nevertheless, although saddened by the rifts that his stance caused within his personal circle, he had simply seen too many things that his literary friends never had. He defended colonial achievements as – in André Maurois' words – 'the substitution of relative peace for a state of permanent brigandage'. (In December 1899 Lyautey would address the businessmen of the Colonial Union, and his speech formed the basis for yet another influential article in *Revue des Deux Mondes*, which made him a public personality in colonialist circles.)[62]

Soon after Galliéni and Lyautey arrived in France yet another government fell, and on 22 June 1899 a 'government of Republican defence' in the Gambetta tradition was formed under Pierre Waldeck-Rousseau. That same month Dreyfus was shipped home for retrial; after more than four years in solitary confinement on Devil's Island he was ill and inarticulate – when he appeared in court at Rennes on 7 August the *Times* correspondent described him as 'an old, old man of thirty-nine'. On 9 September the court announced that Dreyfus was guilty but with extenuating circumstances, and that consequently his sentence was reduced to ten years' imprisonment. After much private negotiation between the parties, ten days later President Loubet remitted the rest of the sentence, and Dreyfus was freed. The acceptance of this pardon, which implied an admission of his original guilt, disappointed the Dreyfusards, while the remission of the sentence angered the anti-Dreyfusards. Nobody was satisfied with the outcome, but virtually the whole of France was – at last – heartily sick of the whole ugly charade, which had shamed their country in the eyes of the world. (France's sense of disgrace would soon be wiped out, however, by the delicious opportunity to lead the Europe-wide condemnation of Britain's second war against the South African Boers in 1899–1902.)[63]

In the eyes of a significant part of the French public the scandal had left the Army deeply compromised, and within three years their representatives would be inflicting painful punishment. The first generation of Republican leaders, whatever their instinctive suspicion of the generals, had managed the relationship pragmatically (indeed, their parliamentary blocs had been happy to call themselves 'Opportunists'). The Dreyfus scandal would help to create a powerful Socialist/Radical coalition – the 'Bloc of the Lefts' – that would sweep to power in the elections of 1902, and under the impulse of its strong Radical component this would introduce a relentlessly anti-military programme. For a decade to come the Naval (by then, Colonial) Troops and the Africa Army would seem to offer an even more appealing refuge to officers who craved a life of soldiering rather than political intrigues, and since these two organizations were clearly innocent of involvement in 'the Affair' they would be allowed to deliver that opportunity to many of the men who turned their faces south.

IN DECEMBER 1899, the inexorable enlargement of the Legion continued, with ministerial authorization for each of the two Foreign Regiments to form a sixth battalion; the actual rifle strength had now increased fourfold since 1875. In March 1900 it was decided to send two more Legion battalions to Madagascar, forming a marching regiment commanded by Lieutenant-Colonel Cussac, to work on the development of the Diégo Suarez naval base and roads through the tropical forest of Cap d'Ambre. The IV/1st RE and II/2nd RE landed in April and June respectively; both units would return to Algeria in 1901, leaving some men to top up the original battalion.[64]

On 7 June 1900 the long-argued transfer of the entire Naval Troops to the War Ministry as the new 'Colonial Troops' was finally voted into law; Article 8 specified that the Legion could be called upon to cooperate with them in any theatre at any time. Of the eighteen planned Colonial Infantry

Regiments (RIC), six plus additional detachments were to be based in the colonies, and the 15th RIC was shipped to Madagascar that year.[65]

THE TEAM OF GALLIÉNI AND LYAUTEY – both now promoted – were busy back in Madagascar. The governor-general appointed Colonel Lyautey his chief-of-staff and gave him command of the whole southern one-third of the island, with headquarters at Fianarantsoa in the Betsileo country. Lyautey would now enjoy the opportunity to be a *réalisateur* on a grand scale; with 80 officers and 4,000 troops, he ruled a territory one-third the size of France with a population of about one million.[66] His characteristic joy in this work would be expressed in a typical letter to his sister:

> It is splendid to lie down at night after ransacking a mail delivery that brings word, all in one day, that an advance of a day's march has been made on the Menaran; that a reconnaissance has reached the assigned objective; that two villages have been repopulated; that another 6 kilometres of road have been completed ... that an attempt to grow potatoes has been successful; that a new merchant has opened for business; that a market had been re-opened – how well one sleeps on all that!
>
> And now, to finish, you are going to give me a present. I have just found a scrap of verse in Shelley that I want to make my motto: 'The soul's joy lies in doing.' Would you have that engraved inside a signet ring, and have it sent out to me?[67]

Lyautey spent most of his time out on column and installing his outposts, coordinating security operations and civil development in the old Tonkin style. He familiarized himself with the tribal leadership in different districts and, where they seemed to justify it, he gave them a measure of autonomy, creating a radiating pattern of carefully calculated bilateral relationships under his personal control. As always he was eager to encourage commerce, but this did not deter him from taking swift and direct action where necessary. Civil development could not progress among the Bara people until his columns cleared the forests between Fianarantsoa and Tuléar (base of the Legion battalion's 1st Company) of the bandits who raided villages and ambushed French convoys. Further south, in the parched and almost impenetrable cactus forests west of Fort Dauphin (where the Legion 4th Company was based), the fierce Mahalafy had to be dissuaded from cattle-rustling from their more fortunate neighbours, and légionnaires hunted them down all the way to their bristling villages. Here, in the summer of 1901, Lyautey planted a substantial Legion fort at Behara, and not simply as a visible sign of French strength and commitment: in the shelter of such outposts he wanted peaceful marketplaces to grow, where contacts between rulers and ruled could be patiently encouraged. Pacification could only work through 'the transformation of our posts from the poles of repulsion that they are today into centres of attraction'.[68]

Lyautey always kept in mind that the Bara bandits and Mahalafy rustlers were not alien interlopers like the Chinese who had preyed on the hill tribes of Upper Tonkin; this was their homeland, and they had to be tamed rather than destroyed. He repeatedly stressed to his subordinates that they should nurture their contacts with local populations, keeping the olive-branch as visible as the sword, and never taking any hasty step that would make reconcilation impossible – above all, however frustrated they became, they must never carry out collective reprisals.[69] Nevertheless, he never entertained sentimental fantasies about the colonial relationship; shortly before he returned to France in June 1902 he wrote to Galliéni:

> Regardless of the results obtained through the economic and moral conquest
> of the native population, regardless of the degree of their submission and
> that of their leaders, we must never mislead ourselves into believing that our
> domination will ever become acceptable to them.[70]

In May 1902 his work was done; the southern military command was dissolved, and Lyautey returned to Tamatave for six weeks of debriefing and paperwork before sailing for France. There, after some home leave, in October he took up his new appointment as regimental commander of the 14th Hussars at Alencon. The Metropolitan Army had him in its grip once more.

MAJOR PAUL BRUNDSAUX had returned for his second Madagascar tour early in 1902, this time as commander of the Legion Marching Battalion based now at Majunga. Later that year he welcomed a 26-year-old junior officer who had served in his previous battalion two years before in the very different environment of the far Sud-Oranais, during a desert column to plant a garrison in a little furnace called Igli.[71]

Lieutenant Paul Frédéric Rollet was a lively, slightly built young man with bright blue eyes and a sharply trimmed dark beard, who had transferred to the Legion in December 1899 after three boring years with the 91st Line in the Ardennes. He had graduated halfway down his class at St Cyr in 1896, but he had shone at all physical activities (including an epic night march after falling asleep on a returning leave-train). In Algeria he had worked, played and hunted hard, and had been popular as a brother-officer who was willing to try anything once; he was nicknamed 'Softy', in the way that a giant is nicknamed 'Titch'. Indeed, his posting to Madagascar may have been partly due to complaints from the staid bourgeoisie of Sidi bel Abbès about the off-duty antics of a group of young 1st RE subalterns. His mother's parting advice before his embarkation was that he should not always express his opinions to his superiors quite so frankly – a trait he had inherited from his father. (General Rollet's personal report when a major and professor at the École Spéciale Militaire in 1889 had included the comment that he 'does not always show himself satisfied with what emanates from his chiefs'.) The general had personally supervised his childrens' education, and had encouraged Paul to think, question and argue.

Lieutenant Rollet was recommended for a staff post under Colonel Lyautey, but the latter was just about to return to France. Paul Rollet would serve his tour with the battalion cheerfully, rising to command 3rd Company at Anosivaro; later he would lead his légionnaires to Sakaramy to build a new post on a hill overlooking Diégo Suarez, whose development was then being directed by Colonel Joseph Joffre of the Engineers.

In 1904, the original Foreign Marching Battalion that had been shipped out in August 1896 was disbanded; its individual companies were progressively withdrawn, and on 21 July 1905 – shortly after both Lieutenant Rollet, and General Galliéni himself – the last légionnaires left the 'Red Island'. They were too valuable to use any longer on construction work in what was now a sleepy colony; for the past three years the Legion had been drawn progressively into offensive operations on a new frontier, where a recently promoted general had need of enduring and resourceful soldiers to back up his gambles.[72]

PART TWO: MAROC

8. The Instruments of Downfall 1893–9

Every one who has ever come in contact with his Majesty will feel real regret that qualities, which in another clime would have made him a liberal and enlightened ruler, have, in hide-bound Morocco, been the very instruments of his downfall.

Reginald Rankin, of Sultan Moulay Abd el Aziz, 1908[1]

MOROCCO, FORMING THE NORTH-WEST CORNER of North Africa, has an area slightly smaller than that of France, slightly larger than that of California. It is bounded on the north by the Mediterranean, on the west by the Atlantic, and on both east and south by Algeria, which is five times its size.

The whole grain of the country runs from south-west to north-east, parallel to the great mountain spine of the Atlas ranges that occupy about the central one-third of Morocco (see Map 10). A lesser range of highlands – the Rif – runs from the north-east tip of the Atlas westwards along the Mediterranean coast, like the top stroke of a figure '7'. The diagonal wall of the Atlas is about 400 miles long from end to end, and some 100 miles wide. It begins in the south-west as a fork, north and south of the triangular coastal plain behind Agadir; the southern prong is the Anti-Atlas range. The northern prong swells north-eastwards into the High Atlas, whose tallest peak, in the Djebel Toubkal, stabs up to 13,700 feet. There are only three practical passes across the High Atlas; in places these are long, easy ramps, in others they inch giddily around hairpin ledges over thousand-foot ravines. The northern part of the whole mass is termed the Middle Atlas, with peaks up to 9,000 feet. The shoulders of the mountains are thickly wooded, most characteristically with tough little holly-oaks, and above 4,500 feet they are mantled here and there with magnificent cedar forest. In the wrinkles of this alpine landscape Berber villagers have lived since time immemorial, tilling their high, hidden glens and herding goats on slopes clothed in *maquis*.

Over the country as a whole the climate, rainfall and vegetation vary enormously with latitude and altitude. As in Algeria, the wooded and watered north can resemble southern Europe; even highland valleys may be lush with fruit-orchards, and down on the Atlantic coastal plains the black soil disappears in summer under great prairies of waving grain. At the turn of the nineteenth to twentieth centuries, semi-nomadic tribes grazed their flocks and herds on the high, treeless steppes east of the mountains; again as in Algeria, the climate here resembles that of the North American high plains – searing in summer, freezing in winter. (The cliché is that Morocco is not a hot country, but a cold country with a hot sun.) These grasslands roll down southwards into gravelly plains scattered with low, wiry trees, occasionally highlighted by stripes of the dwarf palm and pale green tamarisk the that mark underground watercourses. Lesser mountains run like teeth along parallel folds in the earth, and between these blades the plains are randomly studded with abrupt buttes and giant piles of house-sized rocks. Finally, even this marginal country fades away southwards into baked stone-desert, dotted with a monotously deliberate-looking pattern of knee-high clumps of tough weeds. Here the horizons are still broken up by curtains and scattered islands of bone-dry peaks; they look young and raw, their skylines a chaotic mixture of tabletops and book-stacks, pinnacles, domes and saw-toothed crests. In this Saharan fringe, any life that requires more than camel-thorn is limited to a few intensely cultivated oases along the hidden lines of underground rivers.

THE MOST POPULATED one-third of Morocco has always been the plains that run south from the Mediterranean highlands down the western side of the country, between the Atlantic and the Atlas, and here the great imperial cities have grown up. On the coast, Rabat the Green is cooled by Atlantic breezes. About 100 miles east of it, more or less in the angle of the '7' of mountains, lie Fes the Blue – the religious, intellectual and political capital – and nearby, its rival Meknes. Some 160 miles below them is the southern capital of Marrakesh the Red, again about 100 miles inland from the Atlantic. The slanting mountain wall to the east has always divided Morocco in terms not only of climate but also of human history. While communication and trade always crossed it, the grip of governments based in the cities west of the passes was weaker in the Atlas, and tenuous in the steppe and desert to the east and south. That human history might be said to mirror the contrasts of the mesmerizing landscape – yellow-grey desert, vivid green cultivation, ox-blood castles, lion-coloured hills and silver-capped mountains, all domed by the immense African sky. Since the earliest European travellers' tales from the Middle Ages, the mysterious, almost closed world of Morocco had always been described in terms of intensely colourful extremes. Teeming activity and great riches contrasted with an emptiness where life itself was only marginally possible; clamorous noise and brutal heat, with the serene lullaby of fountains in the shade of paradise gardens and tiled courtyards; pride, generosity and ancient scholarship with piracy, slavery and hideous cruelty.

Academic careers have been built upon attempts to identify the exact origins of the Berber peoples of North Africa, who were invaded and – to a strictly qualified extent – conquered in the seventh and eight centuries AD by Muslim Arabs from the east. (The sometimes lighter colouring of hair and eyes that is still found among Berbers after 1,400 years of Arab presence has encouraged speculation, some of it entertainingly fantastic.) 'Pure' Arabs remain a minority, but over centuries of intermittent migration the two ethnic groups have mixed to a greater extent than was recognized by some Frenchmen, who sought to practise a divisive *politique de race*. In 1900 the total population of Morocco was over 4 million people, of whom at least 45 per cent spoke one of the three main Berber dialects as their first tongue, and another 20 per cent were Arabic-speakers of Berber blood.[2]

Morocco's birth as a Muslim monarchy, under sovereigns vested simultaneously with both religious and temporal authority, is officially dated to the founding of the city of Fes by Idriss II in AD 808. The sultan was simultaneously the head of the Muslim community *(imam)* and the temporal sovereign *(amir el muminin)*, and ruling dynasties sprang from both Arab and Berber stock. From the eighth century Moroccan Muslims had periodically rejected the authority of the Abbasid caliphate in faraway Baghdad, and in 1145 a Berber sultan, Abd el Mumin bin Ali, definitively broke away and proclaimed himself Commander of the Faithful of a separate caliphate of the west. This ensured that, unlike the peoples to their east, Moroccans would always be completely independent of the later Ottoman Turkish Empire. Significantly, Moroccans – unlike nineteenth-century Algerians – had a strong national consciousness, dating from the fierce resistance by the Saadid dynasty (r. 1511–1659) to attempts by Spain and Portugal to carry their Christian banners into North Africa after the fifteenth-century *Reconquista* – attempts which had left behind only the tiny Spanish *presidios* of Ceuta and Melilla clinging to the Mediterranean coast. European nations had maintained tentative contacts with Moroccan sovereigns since late medieval times, and in the 1890s Tangier, on the Straits of Gibraltar, was a bustling entrepôt from which diplomats and traders visited the imperial cities. Nevertheless, contact outside the cities was so limited by Moroccan suspicion of Christians that geographers could still count on their fingers the number of Europeans who had ever returned from the mountains that could be seen from the promenade-decks of ocean liners passing through the Straits.

THE ALAWID DYNASTY, born in the great oasis complex of the Tafilalt (the region of the lower Ziz river, south of the High Atlas), has lasted from 1659 to the present day. Moulay Ismail (r. 1672–1727), a sultan of almost demonic energy and cruelty, was the first to bring the whole country under something approaching centralized rule from his capital at Meknes. The Saadids and Alawids institutionalized the leading status in the Moroccan Muslim community of the *shurfa* (singular, *sharif*), the numerous families claiming descent from the Prophet through his daughter Fatima. This strain – indicated by the honorific name Moulay – provided the royal family (thus, the 'Sharifian Kingdom of Morocco'), but their privileges did not extend to a monopoly of power. The concept of royalty was that the sultan, in his temporal role, was the arbiter between the religious leadership, the urban merchant class who created wealth, and the feudal tribes of the hinterland whose crops and herds provided much of its raw material. In theory all were supposed to profit from this compact: the sultan raised taxes, by means of which he pursued the work of the Prophet and provided protection and justice through his ministers and judges.

A senior regional lieutenant of the sultan was termed a *khalifa;* the most important of these viceroys – particularly the *khalifas* of Marrakesh and the Tafilalt – were selected from among his relatives, but the title was also awarded to lesser, non-sharifian chieftains recognized as local governors. Appointment as a *khalifa* was a man's licence to wield the power of death in the name of the sultan while enriching himself and his family – if he had the strength to tame the locals, and the wit not to appear to his master as tactlessly over-successful. Even the greatest men were wise to approach their sovereign on their knees, pressing their foreheads to the carpet. The sultan's power was absolute, in the sense that we associate with Old Testament times, but his continued legitimacy rested on his performance in protecting the House of Islam from external aggression and in governing according to *sharia* law. The throne passed to a nominated favourite son, but legitimate succession required the endorsement of the *ulama*, the colleges of learned doctors of the Islamic faith who were based in the imperial cities of Fes, Meknes and Marrakesh.

Necessarily compressed, this summary may suggest a dignified continuity, but the true flavour of life at the Moroccan court was rather more stimulating. The number of potential alternative claimants sired in the harems ensured that the succession was under more or less constant challenge; court life was a snake-pit of intrigue, and power might rest on fragile foundations. Royal relatives lived precarious lives, and in the course of a day, even a much-caressed minister who had overplayed his hand might fall from power and riches to penury – if he was lucky. In this society, power was displayed by dazzling magnificence, serviced by abject slavery, and implemented by unremitting violence. Forgiveness was weakness, and weakness attracted hyenas. In Morocco the true symbol of public authority was not the sultan's crimson-and-gold parasol, but the row of severed heads festooning every city gate-tower.

(The Jewish ghetto was termed the *mellah* – 'salt' – in reference to one of the Jews' traditional tasks for their disdainful protectors: the salting of these ghastly trophies, which were usually hung up by means of a wire passed through an ear. The ears did not last forever, of course, and there are anecdotes of regrettable coincidences when visiting European dignitaries happened to be passing through the gates below.)

IN THE LAST YEARS of the nineteenth century the compact between the sultan's urban government – the *Maghzan* – and the tribes in the hinterland had degenerated (not for the first time) into near anarchy. The energetic Sultan Moulay Hassan I (r. 1873–94) had inherited large debts following defeat in a war with Spain in 1859–60; he needed to refill his treasury, and to strengthen himself against European pressure by demonstrating control over his territory. He spent his reign in the saddle, making repeated expeditions to enforce his authority and increase his revenues, but these efforts were often stubbornly resisted by the tribes. In this context, the term 'tax-collecting' fails to convey the true spectacle of such a progress: the sultan's resplendent tented court travelled in the midst of a colourful but barely organized army tens of thousands strong, stripping the country like a plague of locusts as they flooded across the plains and jostled through the mountain passes. The Arabic term for such a throng – *harka* – literally translates as 'a burning'.[3]

The probing by the French military into the Sud-Oranais of Algeria, just over Morocco's undefined south-eastern borders (as described at the end of Chapter 2) worried Moulay Hassan, and in 1893–4 he led an expedition from Fes down to the Tafilalt to negotiate with regional leaders in an attempt – only marginally successful – to gain some control over events. He was even less successful in achieving his main goal of restraining the shameless marauders of the Ait Atta nation (a sort of Berber equivalent of the Comanches, who will reappear often in these pages).[4] The sultan only narrowly survived the return journey; his horde had already been reduced to perhaps one-third its strength by sickness, hunger and desertion by the time the retreating rabble was caught in the High Atlas by the onset of winter. 'Under a canopy of ravens and with a rearguard of jackals', the starving remnant would have left their bones in the snowbound Tizi n'Tichka pass had they not been saved by the young *caid* (chief) of the Glaoua tribe, Madani el Glaoui, who led them to his castle at Telouet and put his whole resources at the sultan's command. Madani is described as a strikingly ugly young man, combining a horse face with the very dark colouring that he owed to his Ethiopian mother, but his large, glowing black eyes were full of intelligence. Before continuing north, Moulay Hassan rewarded his rescuer with the nominal but potentially lucrative status of *khalifa* over the tribes to the south of the mountains, and a rather more practical gift of arms and ammunition – including a Krupp field gun.[5]

Since this was the only modern artillery piece in the country outside the sultan's own arsenals, it would contribute powerfully to the spread of Glaoua influence. Madani el Glaoui (then 27 years old, and known as 'the Literate' – a significant distinction among his competitors) had previously been able to field only about half the strength of either of his two main rivals in the Atlas, the *caids* El Mtouggi and El Goundafi. He owed his wealth not to numbers but to location: he owned a valuable salt-mine, and control of the Tizi n'Tichka also allowed him to tax the rich caravans carrying produce from the southern oases over the pass to Marrakesh and thence to Fes. These resources were a temptation for his more powerful neighbours, and his

Krupp gun provided a more reliable insurance than the sultan's public endorsement.[6]

MOULAY HASSAN WAS ALREADY a sick man when he returned to Marrakesh, and he died in June 1894. He was nominally succeeded by his 13-year-old son, Moulay Abd el Aziz, who was kept in luxurious isolation while for six years a rapacious regency was exercised by the black grand vizier, Ba Ahmad ibn Musa. The vizier continued to delegate authority to the three 'lords of the Atlas', and El Glaoui expanded his territory southwards; he and his younger brother Tahami led expeditions down into the Draa and Dades valleys, defeating 'rebels', sending their heads to Marrakesh and adding their lands to the Glaoua domains.[7]

Between 1894 and Ba Ahmad's death in spring 1900, a worsening trade imbalance with the European powers caused raging inflation, and the Maghzan's treasury was in a hopeless spiral of debt and re-borrowing by the time the 19-year-old sultan emerged from seclusion in May 1900. Abd el Aziz was not a figure to command fearful obedience; he was a relatively gentle soul, whose looks were spoiled by a deeply receding chin under unsuccessful wisps of beard. His enthusiasm for Western education and technology was shared by neither the devout nor the xenophobic – descriptions that embraced Morocco's entire traditional leadership. Abd el Aziz was described as a charming, intelligent, well-meaning boy who was ill-equipped for power, and many interested parties ensured that he remained that way. His ministers exploited his interest in all things Western by distracting him with ruinously costly playthings while they proceeded to plunder the exchequer.

The deeply mortgaged treasury was also a magnet for foreign financiers and unscrupulous salesmen. Foreigners were supposed to be confined to Tangier to prevent them tainting the House of Islam, but from that nest of international intrigue advisers from competitive powers swarmed to the young sultan's court, eager to offer expensive assistance in lifting Morocco into the twentieth century. Given the Moroccans' deep distrust of Christians, the sultan's appointment of several foreigners to posts of influence caused great local resentment and suspicion. Some of these *rumis* were simply technicians who tried conscientiously to impose system on chaos, but others were avaricious rogues, and many were serving their own governments' agendas. Robbed and frustrated by his corrupt courtiers and receiving contradictory advice from the foreigners, Abd el Aziz was easily diverted from his vague plans for reform with the latest gilded toys, while his country slipped deeper into debt and disorder and his people raged that he was selling their common legacy to the Nazarenes. In the first years of the twentieth century random attacks on foreigners increased; consequent demands for reparation from the nations that were bankrolling the Maghzan had the effect of ratcheting up European privileges, and thus increasing Muslim fury.

As central control grew ever weaker, two particular regional warlords continued to defy the Maghzan with impunity. In the Djibala country of the north-west, effective power was held by the notorious sharifian brigand Moulay Ahmad er Raisuli; and in the north-east, in the mountains around Taza, a convicted forger calling himself Bou Himara (widely known simply as El Rogi, 'the Pretender') would mount from 1902 an actual challenge for the throne. Raisuli's activities complicated relations with the Spanish presidio at Ceuta, and El Rogi's with that at Melilla; his independence in an area so close to the border with French Algeria also created further complications for the Maghzan.[8]

SINCE MOROCCO APPEARED TO BE DYING as a functioning state, during the 1890s European vultures gathered around the sickbed. To complete its North African possessions France – and the leaders of its Algerian settlers – coveted this potentially rich country, and in the early 1900s it would exploit the useful provocation offered by the raids of apparently ungovernable south-eastern Moroccan tribes across the debatable borders with Oran province. Britain was well placed at court, and had manoeuvred to thwart French ambitions more or less out of habit, spurred from 1899 by France's outspoken support for the South African Boers. However, its vital interests were limited to preventing any rival power fortifying the coast facing Gibraltar, and from 1902 its diplomacy would shift towards the *entente cordiale* that was formally established in 1904.[9] Closest to Morocco was ramshackle Spain, humiliated by its defeat at American hands in Cuba and the Philippines in 1898; it was protective of its presidios on the Mediterranean coast, but lacked either a coherent plan to exploit them or the muscle to influence France or Britain. Italy's foreign policy was too unstable to predict, but anti-French sentiment was strong. A few years previously Prime Minister Francesco Crispi had been desperate for a war – any war – in the hope of creating the sense of nationhood that eluded the young state. A shocking defeat by an Ethiopian army at Adua in March 1896, and the need to deploy troops against rioters everywhere from Milan to Sicily, had cooled Italian enthusiasm for foreign expeditions, if only temporarily.[10] The young Kaiser's sullen demands for international respect had to be taken much more seriously than either Spain's or Italy's, and not only because of Germany's military strength; its interest in Morocco was solidly based on the enterprise of the German businessmen who had achieved an unrivalled commercial penetration of the country. Representatives of all these nations clustered around the court of Abd el Aziz, and their attempts to manipulate his government revealed, to a greater or lesser extent, their understanding of the actual mechanisms of local power.

MOST DESCRIPTIONS OF LATE NINETEENTH-CENTURY MOROCCO insist upon a fundamental political distinction between, on the one hand, the *bled el maghzan* or 'zone of government' – the cities and their surrounding fertile plains, under the control and taxation of the sultan's regime; and on the other, the *bled es siba* or 'zone of dissidence' – the mountains, steppes and desert where tribal anarchy defied any government constraints. Obviously, it was in the interests of French colonialists to stress the weakness of the first and the lawlessness of the second in order to justify intervention to create a new order of peace and security. While naturally biased, this argument was supported by visible facts: much of the country did indeed present a medieval spectacle of violent turmoil, and government in the European sense was indeed non-existent. We may smile at the French tendency to label all non-Europeans who opposed them as mere *'pillards'*, but a great deal of pillaging was certainly going on.

Given the attitudes of the day, France's goals seemed reasonable to its fellow Europeans, and the methods by which it would pursue them would be relatively restrained when compared with those of the Moroccans themselves. Morocco was trapped in a state of violent upheaval between the medieval and the modern worlds; its past isolation could no longer be maintained, but the external forces dragging it into the future (for reasons of self-interest) were fiercely resisted. However, the colonialists exaggerated what they claimed to be the formless chaos of Moroccan political life, which actually depended upon patterns of relationships far more complex than was admitted by those who described rigid frontiers dividing the *bled el maghzan* from the *bled es siba*. In fact the relations between particular tribal leaders and the sultanate covered as wide a range of distance or warmth as any human courtship. Few rifts were ever final, and subtly worded communication might continue through intermediaries. The degree and the tone of contacts varied with the fluctuating fortunes of groups and individuals, but the sultan's (usually) unquestioned religious authority meant that the relationship was always potentially salvageable, with even the most distant and independently minded tribe.[11] It was precisely this fluidity that would offer the French opportunities for creating temporary coalitions of interest with particular groups.

Serious studies of French colonialism in Morocco depend upon sophisticated analysis of the triangular dealings between the Maghzan, the tribes and the French; but even in a book with the present modest aims, if we are to make sense of a summary of French campaigns, then some rough-and-ready description of the tribal aspect of Moroccan life has to be attempted.

ALMOST ANY GENERAL STATEMENT about the 'tribe' as an entity invites endless qualifications from specialists, and our everyday use of the word fails to distinguish between widely varying types of group; as a description, it is no more exact than 'tree'. Tribal identity might depend on simple geography, on an actual or mythical common origin, or on various composites of client relationships and factional obligations, all of these evolving over different timescales. What we carelessly call a tribe might be the loosest association of tens of thousands of people, dispersed over large areas – perhaps a 'nation', in the Native American sense. Within these, tribes and sub-tribes thousands strong were made up of constituent clans, and the clans of lineages with some common ancestor. At the very tip of a tribal twig, a few dozen people linked by immediate ties of blood and marriage inhabited tiny hamlets scattered over a couple of hillsides, or a few neighbouring tents as they followed their flocks across the steppe.

A tribe certainly cannot be represented as a neat pyramid-shaped diagram of kinships, and – crucially – it was normally divided by internal quarrels. To pursue the tree analogy, at every level its boughs, branches, twigs and leaves grew independently of one another, at one moment in harmony, at another in competition. Some tribes had become geographically dispersed, and significant elements were to be found simultaneously in different areas of the map; migrations had spread seedlings far from the original tree trunk, some of them now growing amongst other types of tree. Within the tribal tree the sources of dynamic leadership might shift upwards, downwards or sideways with time and circumstance, depending upon bloodlines, religious prestige, intelligence and ambition, wealth, and strength in fighting men. Above all, bonds and boundaries were almost always provisional: each area of growth strove to reach the sun for itself. There is a much-quoted Arabic proverb: roughly, 'I against my brothers; I and my brothers against our cousins; I, my brothers and cousins against the world'. It was said that at any given moment, members of any group had to take account of not one but three leaders: the actual chief, his more or less impatient strongest son, and at least one resentful rival for the succession.

In Morocco, the Arab and Arabized groups tended to be associated with the lowlands, and the speakers of the Berber dialects originally with the mountains. The Berbers had no written culture; urban Arabs regarded them as uncouth and bloody-minded highlanders, and as indifferent observers of the faith. While they were, of course, Muslims, pre-Islamic beliefs were discernible in local practice, and the diligence of their daily observances varied widely. Among Berber tribes, *sharia* law had always coexisted with customary law, the latter sometimes taking precedence, and some sultans attempted to subdue outbreaks of dissidence in a spirit *of jihad* (in the early nineteenth century one of these, the zealot Moulay Sulayman, had raged at the Berbers as irreligious barbarian 'monkeys').

THE CENTRAL FACT OF TRIBAL HISTORY since the seventeenth century had been the pressure of Berber movements in search of land, broadly from the south-east to the north, north-west and west. Crudely, this was a process of competitive tribal migration by highland Berbers seeking to dispossess or dominate lowland Arabs. For example, the belligerent Ait Atta people of the south exploded from the Djebel Sahro in all directions; when they were checked in the mountains to their north they turned west, south and east, to dominate the cultivators of the grain- and date-growing oases of the Rteb plain north of the Tafilalt and the Dades valley to its west, and to compete for control of the caravan routes. Further north, in the early nineteenth century there was a great Berber revolt in the Middle Atlas; at the battle of Landa in 1818 one of Sultan Moulay Sulayman's sons was killed by the Berber 'monkeys', and the sovereign himself did not long survive the resulting crisis. To the east, French southwards expansion from the Algerian Tell to the edge of the Sahara in the 1840s to 1860s presented further dilemmas to the sultans of Morocco. Before then, at least the Maghzan had been the only major power with which the tribes could deal; now there was a second pole of influence, on the other side of ill-defined borders on the most inaccessible flank of the *bled es siba*.

After the death of Moulay Sulayman in 1822, the practical boundaries of the *bled el maghzan* had become more or less stable. Roughly, they enclosed the Atlantic coast, the plains surrounding Fes, Meknes and Marrakesh, and the strategic corridor running from Fes eastwards to Taza and Oujda, carrying 'the Sultan's Road' to the Moulouya river valley and the Algerian border. Any relative stability was due not so much to Maghzan coercion as to the success of highland tribes newly arrived on the plains in fighting off those who sought to follow them down, and the balance of tribal power at the time of French contact was still fluid. The Maghzan was obliged to grant recognition to various tribal leaders, but how heavily or lightly their recip-rocal obligation weighed on these *caids* depended, as always, on the strength, resolve and guile of the current sultan, and an inevitable consequence was that regional power accreted around individual tribal strongmen. At the turn of the century these included figures who would become central to the concerns of the Europeans – the incorrigible Raisuli in the Djibala, the brothers Glaoua in the High Atlas, and (though more briefly) the trickster El Rogi in the hills around Taza.[12] However, the early confrontations with French troops took place far from these power bases, in the southern bor-derlands between Morocco and Algeria's Oran province.

TO CONSIDER THESE BORDER MARCHES from north to south: the 90-odd miles of formally delineated frontier between western Algeria and eastern Morocco, below the Mediterranean coast, cut across the slant of forested mountains that made up the far north-eastern end of the Middle Atlas (see Map 11). The Moroccan town of Oujda lay just west of the line, but many Frenchmen always believed that the natural border should be the Moulouya river about 50 miles further west.

South of these coastal mountains lay a wedge of the high plains, about 80 miles deep and called, collectively, the Dahra. Below this, the next stripe of mountains pushing up from the south-west was the dry, naked tip of the High Atlas (called the Saharan Atlas, or Mountains of the Ksour), some 100 miles deep from north to south. Between two fingers of the Algerian end of this range lay the small town of Ain Sefra, the base for French military activity in the Sud-Oranais. Some 70 miles south-west of this, on the south-ern edge of the slanting mountain wall, was the great Moroccan oasis of Figuig, an important hub in the traditional trans-Saharan caravan routes.

South of Figuig there was only stone-desert, and after about 60 miles the gravel gave way to the first wandering dunes of the ghostly Grand Erg Occidental – the Great Western Sand-Sea.

To the semi-nomadic tribes, the notional frontier between southern Morocco and Algeria existed only as a vague idea. They did not use maps, nor see the world as divided by straight lines, but thought in terms of the ranges of particular peoples. Some communities traditionally acknowledged the religious authority of the sultans of Morocco; others did not, and inter-tribal relationships and physical movements flowed back and forth across a fluid margin whose exact edges had no meaning. The only thing that did have meaning in this desolate country was water; life was organized along and between a strictly limited number of *oueds* – watercourses, flowing as rivers in the north and in times of seasonal flood, but mostly below ground in the south, though feeding along their whole length broken chains of fertile oases. Although the tribes moved their beasts around the plains between them in a seasonal rhythm, for most practical human purposes the narrow green ribbons of these valleys and their dotted oases were the habitable peninsulas and islands in a virtually lifeless yellow-grey ocean, and the landmarks of the French penetration of south-east Morocco would all be found along three main systems.

THE EASTERNMOST, in the debatable lands between Algeria and Morocco, was the Oued Zousfana, which normally flowed on the surface as far south as Figuig (see Map 11). It then continued underground, emerging briefly at Taghit in a group of oases known as the Beni Goumi, before sinking out of sight again. Its course continued below the sands to Igli, where it joined that of the Oued Guir; from there the underground flow made its secret way south-east as the Oued Saoura, feeding oases such as Beni Abbès, until it reached those of the scattered complex called the Touat in the edge of the true Sahara (see Map 3).

About 150 miles west of Figuig, on the far side of an expanse of plateaux and hills, the Oued Guir flowed as far south as Boudenib, but for most of the year it then disappeared beneath its bed somewhere to the east. However, when it reached Abadla it frayed out into many narrow beds to create an alluvial plain covering about 15,000 acres. The water flowed on the surface here for between two and three months in winter, irrigating the tribes' main source of wheat and barley. Below the Abadla flood plain the Guir passed underground once more, to unite with the course of the Zousfana at Igli.

West of the Oued Guir, cliffs rose to the most hostile environment in the whole south-east: the Hammada of the Guir, a stark and waterless stone plateau up to 100 miles across, shaped like a north-pointing flat-iron broadening southwards towards the Sahara. In high summer it was utterly dead, but knowledgeable herdsmen could drive their beasts across it in spring and autumn. The Hammada was a rampart between the two eastern valley systems and the westernmost, richest and most politically important.

The Oued Ziz snaked south through High Atlas gorges to emerge into the desert close to Ksar es Souk (modern Er Rachidia). From there southwards it had carved a slot in the earth hundreds of feet below the lifeless expanse of stone-desert; the red canyon walls enclosed a ribbon of lush greenery, with villages every few miles along this sharply defined corridor of life. Emerging from the canyon, the Ziz crossed the Rteb plain to the great date-basket of the Tafilalt. The river usually flowed above ground here even in summer, and in spring the snow-melt from the Atlas sometimes kept it on the surface even further south. With the lesser Oued Rheris that flowed into the Tafilalt from the west, the Ziz watered an area about 13 miles long by 9 miles wide. Here, up to 120,000 residents of and tribal visitors to seven separate groups of castle-like walled villages *(ksars)*, with four subsidiary oases to the north, tended the many hundreds of thousands of date-palms that formed the basis of the trans-Atlas trade.[13]

The Tafilalt was a mostly Arab island set in a Berber sea, and it was where sultans kept their mistrusted relatives in privileged but quarrelsome exile. It was historically the main way-station for the trans-Saharan caravans; by the nineteenth century its ancient city of Sijilmasa, once the northern terminus of the trade in gold and slaves from Timbuktu, had crumbled into ruins, but the Tafilalt was still the most important religious, commercial and political centre south of the Atlas. The Maghzan *khalifa* lived in the Rissani district, though with only 50 to 100 soldiers. (More an envoy and administrator than a governor, he was largely powerless, and could not impose royal authority on any group unless he could persuade another group to support him; tribal warriors often profited by taking sides in feuds between villages, and thus came to dominate them. During a particularly devastating tribal war in 1896–1900, a Maghzan expedition led by Madani el Glaoui managed to restore order briefly, but skirmishing resumed as soon as he marched north again.)

The greater Tafilalt area supported perhaps 40 per cent of the total population of south-eastern Morocco. The whole region between the Saharan

Atlas in the east and the Ziz valley in the west, the High Atlas in the north and the Saharan dunes in the south, was home to between 200,000 and 250,000 people. These communities were both Arabic- and Berber-speaking: Arabs mainly on the high plains and along the lower Zousfana, Guir and Ziz, Berbers mainly in the eastern edge of the High Atlas, on the upper Guir and upper Ziz. The great majority of them lived by cultivating dates, vegetables, grain and fodder in the oases, and the rest by grazing sheep, goats and camels on the esparto grass and artemisia of the steppes. Between the two ways of life there was a symbiotic relationship: the semi-nomads needed access to the crops, markets, manufactured goods, scribes, holy men and news that they could find only in the oases, and often acquired date-groves there themselves. The villagers of the oases needed the meat, milk and hides of the herdsmen, sometimes their external protection, and always the lines of communication that the tribes controlled. While mutually necessary, however, these relationships were seldom peaceful for long.[14]

THE ARAB TRIBES FIRST ENCOUNTERED by the French during their infiltration from east to west were the Amur and other small groups in the Saharan Atlas north of Figuig, but these were hardly significant. The main proprietors of the Zousfana and Guir country were – from north to south – the Beni Gil, the Ouled Jarir and the Dawi Mani.

The tent-dwelling Beni Gil (the victors at Chott Tigri in 1882) were 15,000–20,000 strong, and followed their flocks across the whole width of the steppes between the High Atlas and the Zousfana and on into Algeria, some clans also owning date-groves in Figuig. South of them, astride the middle Zousfana, were the Ouled Jarir camel-herders. Though numbering only about 5,000 they were renowned raiders, and they also owned date-groves at Béchar and grainfields in the Zousfana oases. The Ouled Jarir were long-time allies of the third and most significant group, whose lands lay to the south of them.

The Dawi Mani Arabs numbered about 15,000 tent-dwellers, who insured themselves against the ever-present threats of drought, flash floods, locusts, disease and war by practising a diverse economy.[15] The centre of their range was the lower Oued Guir, where they were the biggest growers of grain around Abadla. Various segments of the tribe owned groves and fields, worked for them by sharecroppers, in the oases of both the Tafilalt in the west and the Beni Goumi area of the lower Zousfana in the east, and they migrated between these with their camels, sheep and goats in an annual cycle shaped roughly in a horizontal figure-of-eight. They assembled around Abadla in November–December to plant grain; when the spring grass appeared they dispersed both west across the Hammada towards the Tafilalt and east to the Zousfana. In May–June they converged on Abadla again for the grain-harvest, and in August they dispersed west and east once again, for the autumn date-harvests in the Tafilalt and on the Zousfana. These patterns would play an important part in the Dawi Mani responses to French pressure in the first years of the twentieth century. The Dawi Mani had a sophisticated internal structure, the *khams khmas* or 'five fifths', and despite their wide dispersal, the councils of two or more of these self-governing constituent segments might occasionally agree to take the field in joint campaigns under a temporary elected war-chief. Since they had much to protect, by the end of the nineteenth century the Dawi Mani were basically defensive, but that was always a strictly relative term, and they frequently made raids on other tribes. Their domination of oasis villages as far apart as the Tafilalt and the Touat also brought them into local conflict with the Ait Khabbash Berbers.[16]

In the first years of the new century the French would also clash with the Ait Khabbash, the outriders of the formidable Ait Atta nation, whose heartland lay far to the west of the Algero-Moroccan border but whose aggressive expansion had carried their name ever further east. From the Djebel Sahro massif, about 100 miles west of the Ziz valley (see Map 23), the constituent tribes and clans of the Ait Atta – totalling perhaps 50,000 people – had spread out in all directions since the seventeenth century, and in southern Morocco their range now extended from the Oued Draa in the west to the Touat in the east, and from Boudenib and the slopes of the High Atlas in the north down to the Saharan fringe. They were basically sheep- and goat-herders, with some camel-breeding; but at heart they were conquerors, contemptuous of sedentary Arabs and ruthless in first looting, then taking control of any oasis villages that they could. They had long ruled most of the plains north of the Tafilalt, and had extended their fingers into parts of that great honey-pot. They might capture a *ksar* by simple assault or more gradually; their protection rackets controlled much of the caravan trade as far east as the Touat, which allowed them to take over oases by a process of strangulation, extortion, and finally outright domination.

The Ait Atta could sometimes briefly assemble armies of several thousand, but usually operated in smaller numbers. They too had a 'five-fifths' structure, but even looser than that of the Dawi Mani; the 'fifth' that was active in the south-east comprised two tribes, the Ait Khabbash and the Ait Umnasf, each up to 4,000 strong.[17] Despite their rivalry for dominance of oases in both the Tafilalt and the Touat, the great expanses of grazing land on the plains allowed a degree of coexistence between Ait Atta Berbers and Dawi Mani Arabs. Sometimes Ait Khabbash and Dawi Mani tribesmen even mounted joint raids, especially southwards to steal camels from the nomadic Shaamba bedouin in the true Sahara; it was generally noted that Moroccan raiding parties might include groups of men from a number of different clans or even tribes, brought together through personal relationships. (Clans of the Ait Atta – like those of all other peoples – often fought each other, but their ancestral enemies were the Ait Yafalman, a Berber confederation in the High Atlas north of their Djebel Sahro homeland.)[18]

The central weakness of Moroccan resistance to French pressure would always be the inability to create any sort of unified, coordinated movement even at a regional level. The peoples of the south-east might appear to us as addicted to a life of gang warfare that was fatally shortsighted in the shadow of a far greater threat to them all, but that is a superficial judgement. The genuine interests of the tribes and the oasis villagers often conflicted, as did those of different elements within single tribes. The great fact of life was the desert: in this marginal environment the 'economic' arguments for or against resistance or collaboration always finally outweighed the 'political', although the two naturally overlapped. In the desert the only 'economy' depended upon retaining access to the strictly limited sources of water, food, and thus life itself. Everything came down to stark choices about group survival, choices that had always demanded flexibility.[19]

THE OASES THAT WERE THE FOCUS of both tribal and French attention enclosed the great majority of the total population, packed densely into the productive islands that were the only sources of grown food. Their economic importance was not reflected in armed strength, since most of the inhabitants were committed to intense cultivation – of date-palms, of the vegetables and animal feed grown in irrigated gardens occupying every square yard between them, and sometimes of grain in fields around the periphery. Large oases had several distinct *ksar* village communities, each inhabiting a walled warren of interconnecting two- and three-storey mud brick houses. The 'political' life of an oasis usually centred on water rights, and disputes over the opening and closing of sluices might cause vitriolic feuds.

The majority of villagers were independent Arab or Berber farmers; these boasted of being 'whiter' than the *haratin* who worked as mere share-croppers, but in fact both classes often had much African blood. This was a relic both of previous waves of conquest from the south, and of more than a thousand years of slave traffic. There were still some slaves in the *ksars*, but not many by 1900; east and south of Morocco the French had made considerable progress in stamping out that terrible commerce. When a pastoral tribe like the Ait Khabbash or Dawi Mani moved in to take over a *ksar* they seldom killed more than its active resisters, since its value lay in its continued productive activity.[20] The oases were essential to the pastoral tribes, and not just as sources of grown food and manufactured goods: here they traded the produce of their flocks and date-groves, managed their sharecroppers, met their relatives and allies, arranged marriages, submitted disputes to judges, sold their loot from raids, and planned new ones. Central to these plans was, of course, the acquisition of guns and ammunition.

MUZZLE-LOADING FLINTLOCK MUSKETS of local manufacture had been commonplace in Morocco for centuries; gunpowder was both imported and made locally and, like lead for bullets, could be bought in the markets of the larger oases. The limited accurate range of a smoothbore musket – typically, less than 100 yards – was improved somewhat by the local taste for gunbarrels up to 5 feet long, but from the early 1880s the demand for more modern weapons became intense. As in sub-Saharan Africa, there does not seem to have been much take-up of the many muzzle-loading percussion-lock rifles that were released on to the world surplus market from the 1860s. During the 1890s white armies began receiving repeaters and selling off their single-shot breech-loaders; it was these that the tribesmen demanded, and they were supplied in such numbers that by 1900 the majority of warriors even in the remote south-east had acquired them. The main suppliers were European gun-runners who shipped rifles to the Atlantic and Mediterranean ports – particularly to Spanish Melilla – from where they percolated down the trade routes into the *bled es siba*. Their great value made it perilous to entrust large numbers to vulnerable camel caravans, so they usually arrived in the oases in small batches, and some impatient warriors travelled north of the mountains to seek them out personally. Some breech-loaders were also smuggled west from Algeria despite a strict French prohibition, but a more common source of French-made weapons were the Maghzan's regular troops and auxiliaries. The sultan's neglected and unpaid soldiery were notorious for selling their weapons, often simply to buy food, and also took rifles home with them when they left the ranks.

On the frontier the French Chassepot and externally identical Gras were both apparently called the *sasbu*, and the British Martini-Henry the *bu hafra*, to distinguish them from the lowly musket generically called a *bushfar*. In the 1890s, however, the most common single type was the Remington *(mushaka)*. The supply of 1871 model Spanish Remingtons became plentiful after the Spanish Army began replacing theirs with Mauser repeaters in the 1890s; one French report of 1894 estimated that the Beni Gil alone had no fewer than 4,000 Remingtons, compared with just 200 Gras and 20 Lebel repeaters. This represented about one in five of the total numbers of the tribe, suggesting that virtually every fighting man had a breech-loader. Apart from its sheer availability and comfortable firing characteristics, the Remington 'rolling-block' was a near-perfect weapon for tribal warriors; it is extremely robust and simple, with few moving parts to get broken.[21]

Even repeating rifles were soon reaching the tribes in modest numbers – the 1873 Winchester *(sitta'shiya)* was available on the open market for those who could afford it, though supplies of Lebels depended upon theft or corruption. Although it was more often the tribesmen who had the most modern weapons rather than the inhabitants of the oases through whose hands they passed in trade, the *ksars* in the major centres were far from defenceless. A French report of 1899 on the dominant *ksar* of Zenaga in the Figuig oasis listed 800 Remingtons, 35 Martini-Henrys and 18 Chassepots, but also 47 Lebels and 75 other repeaters. (In some tribes the share a warrior received in the after-battle division of spoils was calculated on the basis of his weapon: the man who carried a Lebel could claim slightly more than the man with a Chassepot, and twice as much as the pauper with a musket – though even a boy armed only with a knife still got a half-share if he had fought.)[22]

The greatest problem for the tribes was, of course, getting ammunition for these relatively sophisticated weapons. It was no longer a question of tipping artisan-made powder and an approximately fitting ball or slug down the muzzle of a smoothbore, but of brass cartridges with integral percussion caps, and although a modest supply would be bought with each rifle these soon ran out. Used cartridge cases had to be saved carefully for reloading with local black powder and cast-lead bullets. The flimsy brass-foil cartridges of the single-shot rifles must often have become distorted during repeated extraction, and the whole process demanded work to fine tolerances. Replacing the percussion-cap set into the base of the cartridge was the trickiest part, and the materials used for this – the ground-down heads of red matches mixed with petrol – probably caused many misfires. The powder was also of variable quality, and the reliability of a cartridge that had already been reloaded a couple of times must certainly have been dubious.[23]

AMONG THE MANY OASES dotted along the borderland, Figuig on the Oued Zousfana was by far the most important, providing the centre of trade for the Amur, Beni Gil, Ouled Jarir and Dawi Mani. Here, just over the border from the Algerian Sud-Oranais, about 125,000 date-palms grew in a valley cupped by crags and hills. The 16,000-odd inhabitants lived in seven separate ksars; that of Zenaga, on the valley bottom, was as big as the others combined, and the other six watched it resentfully from higher ground (see Map 13). Figuig had no sense of political unity, and the leaders of the different ksars seldom met even to quarrel. Year-round water was provided by a complex of underground springs and tunnels feeding canals, but access to these was the cause of chronic hostility between and even within the villages.

A few hours' ride from the nearest French soldiers and their ever-tempting supply convoys, Figuig in the 1890s was a 'border town' with all that that implies. The French Foreign Ministry had long pursued a 'Maghzan policy', working patiently to manipulate the sultan's government from the top; the Quai d'Orsay was aware of his attempts to build bridges to the south-east, and did not wish to damage such little prestige as he enjoyed there. Whatever the local provocation, the Foreign Ministry had forbidden any aggressive moves by the Army on this frontier, which had remained inviolate since a clash near Figuig during a 'hot pursuit' of the rebel Bou Amama – a Figuig man – in February 1882. Ever since, and increasingly in the 1890s (as extended French activity provided them with more targets), war parties of the Amur, Beni Gil, Ouled Jarir and Dawi Mani had regularly crossed from the Djebel Beni Smir to carry out small-scale raids. To them the French were just another tribe to be robbed of beasts and a few rifles if the chance presented itself – an unusually rich tribe, yet one apparently unable to react decisively.

Figuig was for twenty years the catalyst of disputes between the Maghzan, frustrated generals in Oran Division, and Paris. The inhabitants of the seven ksars wanted the notional protection of the sultan from French pressure, but refused to pay for it with either obedience or taxes. The royal governors planted there since the early 1880s were simply a succession of powerless spokesmen hiding in the *ksar* of El Oudaghir, unrecognized by the other six villages and unable to collect tribute. The French commanders at Ain Sefra were convinced that Figuig, and particularly Zenaga, was the main source of raids into Algeria. In fact few of the sedentary population were marauders themselves, but Figuig was certainly the sanctuary where cross-border raiders planned, armed themselves, and sold their booty, and the French soldiers itched to scour out this vipers' nest.

In 1894 the project for a trans-Saharan railway was again under intense discussion, and enthusiasts for expansion south included Foreign Minister Delcassé, Governor-General Jules Cambon of Algeria, and the leader of the colonial lobby in Paris, the Oran deputy Eugène Étienne. The route favoured would have to pass through El Goléa and In Salah immediately east of the Touat oases (see Map 3), and despite the reservations of the Quai d'Orsay pressure was building to unleash the Army to pacify the borderland. If the 'Maghzan policy' could not ensure a secure right flank for the planned railway, then the soldiers must. They were already guarding the builders of their own essentially military track south from Mécheria, which had reached Ain Sefra in 1890; there it had paused, but now the steel ribbon and its fortified stations were inching south again.[24]

After 1896 the increasing proximity of the French also significantly nourished the trade of the merchants of Figuig: from that year foreign goods could be shipped into Algeria free of tariff if they were destined for the Sahara and Morocco, which undercut the duties charged in Spanish Melilla. The railway from Ain Sefra would reach Djenien bou Rezg, some 40 miles from Figuig, in February 1900, and the line of blockhouse stations was obviously destined to come even closer. The advancing railhead would bring French soldiers, but also cheap imports and – more importantly – a cheaper eastern route for exporting dates and dressed hides than the camel-caravans westwards that had to pay protection money to every tribe between the Zousfana and Marrakesh or Fes. That railway track guarded by légionnaires was the direct means by which a box of dates would soon become a regular feature of Britain's Edwardian Christmas tables.

THE PEOPLES OF THE SOUTH-EAST BORDERLAND had always lived by constantly hedging their bets, and as the rail tracks came closer the different groups were confronted with choices that they were reluctant to make. The events that finally forced them to choose unfolded not on the Zousfana, but in the winter of 1899/1900 in the Touat oasis complex further to the south-east. This was on the Algerian side of any logical frontier line, but historically subject to the Sultan of Morocco. Although Moulay Hassan had not dared to visit it during his progress of 1893–4 for fear of the Ait Khabbash, that bellicose tribe were about to have their first encounter with a new enemy.[25]

9. Sixty Thousand Dead Camels
1900–1902

*I do not believe that there has ever been a massacre
comparable to that of camels between 1900 and 1903.
The jackals and vultures responsible for cleaning the
desert were simply overwhelmed by the immensity of their
task.*

Professor E. F. Gautier[1]

SOUTH OF THE GREAT WESTERN SAND-SEA, the Touat comprised
three different groups of oases strung in a horseshoe shape open to the east
(see Map 3). From Taghit and Beni Abbès the smaller Oued Saoura oases
stuttered down south-eastwards through the desert for about 150 miles, to
link with the north-west corner of the Touat at the end of the horseshoe's
upper arm; this was known as the Gourara, with its largest centre at Timimoun. The north-south oasis line, centred on Adrar, continued for about
another 150 miles to Reggane, and from there the lower arm of the horseshoe – the Tidikelt – extended a few sparse settlements 140 miles eastwards
towards In Salah. That was where the world of the Algerian Arabs faded into
that of the Tuareg of the open Sahara. (Until the French seizure of Timbuktu
in 1894, the Touat had been the last major trans-Saharan slaving station,
and even in 1899 a trickle of poor wretches were still being driven up
here to feed the Moroccan market.)[2] The Ait Khabbash Berbers operated a
protection racket over caravan traffic into the Touat from the west, and
tyrannized several of the *ksars* in the Gourara and Adrar groups. At this
extreme eastern spearhead of their expansion they competed for dominance
with the Dawi Mani Arabs, who also profited by trading with and exploiting
several oases.

In 1892, Governor-General Cambon of Algeria had sent a group of Muslim
envoys to negotiate access to the Touat, but this had been rebuffed. An

initial military probe was carried out by Captain Théodore Pein with Algerian Spahis and irregulars in November–December 1899, and after a preliminary skirmish In Salah surrendered without a fight. In late January 1900, Major Maurice Baumgarten was checked at the *kasbahs* of In Rhar, but these were successfully stormed by Colonel Clément d'Eu of the 2nd Algerian Skirmishers on 19 March. (Usually invulnerable to other attackers, such strongholds – like the European castles of the fifteenth century – were doomed by the appearance of effective artillery.) This left the Gourara oases around Timimoun still to be occupied.[3]

The infantry available to Oran Division in the winter of 1899/1900, for all purposes, were the four-battalion 2nd Zouaves and the 1st Bat d'Af based in and around Oran itself; the 2nd Algerian Skirmishers, recently enlarged to six battalions, around Mostaganem; and the two six-battalion Legion regiments – 1st RE headquartered at Sidi bel Abbès and 2nd RE at Saida. However, the Legion had three battalions in Tonkin and one in Madagascar, and in response to international tensions two more would have to be shipped to each of those colonies in the first half of 1900, while large headquarters depots had to be maintained. Any general who was planning open-ended operations in the Sud-Oranais could not count on having all four remaining Legion battalions available to him, and while the *turcos* of 2nd RTA were acclimatized to the south they still had to be mixed with half their number of white infantry. He could send the Bat d'Af anywhere he wanted, but the Zouaves would be useless for a desert campaign, and anyway the *colons* were always sensitive to a need to keep white troops in the north to offset the presence of the native units that they never really trusted.

THE OCCUPATION OF THE TOUAT was a turning point that caused deep outrage throughout Morocco. The fundamental duty of any sultan was to defend the House of Islam against the unbelievers; these oases were the first indisputable communities of the sultan's subjects to have been occupied and garrisoned by the French, and Moroccans raged at the Maghzan to declare holy war and restore the integrity of Muslim territory. They raged loudest both in the religious colleges of the northern imperial cities, and down south in the Tafilalt, where wealthy men had widespread interests to protect; but they raged in vain. In Marrakesh, the regent Ba Ahmad would be dead in a few months, and his ministers were preoccupied with exploiting his failing grip.

In this atmosphere of frustrated fury there was a danger that regional tribal and religious leaders might assemble a *harka*, and Ain Sefra Subdivision decided that they had to cover the Touat garrison of *turcos* and *joyeux* from any threat coming out of the desert to their west. The threat was real; warriors from the Atlas, the Marrakesh plains and as far north as Fes were drifting down to the Ziz valley in search of a charismatic leader able to weld them into an active force. (To avert an attack that he knew would merely provoke a French invasion, in July 1900 the young Sultan Abd el Aziz was to name Madani el Glaoui *pasha* of the Tafilalt. Glaoua warriors partially garrisoned the oases from late 1900 until the summer of 1901, an intervention that temporarily drew the tribes' attention and thus defused the threat of a *harka* forming to march eastwards. However, at the beginning of 1900 the French could not predict this.)[5]

In February 1900, troops pushing ahead of the rail tracks down the south-eastern wall of the Djebel Beni Smir/Djebel Béchar range reached a spot on the map called Zoubia, 15 miles east of Figuig. Work began there on a station-cum-fort, to be named Duveyrier; and it was from there, on 20 March, that a column set out for another speck named Igli, some 150 miles south as the vulture flies (see Map 11).[6] Led by Colonel Bertrand, commander of the 1st Foreign Regiment, it numbered 52 officers and 2,000 men with 2,000 baggage camels. The column comprised a *turco* battalion of 2nd RTA, the V/1st RE commanded by Major Paul Brundsaux (and including the young Lieutenant Paul Rollet), the 1st (Mounted) Company/2nd RE with their mules, half-squadrons of Spahis and Africa Light Horse, a section of mountain guns and small detachments of sappers and service troops; as always, *goumiers* on horses and *méhara* camels scouted for the column.[7]

THE MARCH MET NO RESISTANCE as it slogged south from Duveyrier, with the dark bulk of the Djebel Béchar looming on its right. For the 60 miles between Ksar el Azoudj and El Moungar, the more distant line of the Djebel Mezarif showed on the eastern horizon beyond a tongue of dunes, but after that there was nothing on their left except the other-worldly skyline of the Great Sand-Sea. On 1 April they reached the important oasis of Taghit in the Beni Goumi, the people of which had never yet seen French troops. Here, where the Zousfana ran on the surface for several miles thickly fringed with palms, the passage between cliffs on the west and dunes on the east narrowed to a few hundred yards, dominated by a battered old *ksar* straggling up the rocky ledges on the right. The villagers (who owed allegiance to the Dawi Mani) manned the walls and refused Colonel Bertrand's requests to pass. In the end he simply deployed his two mountain guns *en batterie* and sent a company of *turcos* to the top of the highest dune facing the village, and after this demonstration the column were able to march through with no shots fired.[8]

It took the column another four days to reach Igli, through the worst terrain of the whole route. Brundsaux's légionnaires marched without knap-sacks, wearing only their curtained képis and white fatigues; each man's greatcoat, change of clothing and spare boots were tied in a bundle after reveille every morning and packed on the baggage camels. Each man carried only a horseshoe roll of tent-cloth, his rifle, belt order with ammunition, a haversack with one day's rations and a 2-litre waterbottle (men more often collapsed from drinking too much when they got the chance, rather than too little). The officers rode, wearing sun helmets and either whites or khaki drill to personal taste. At every night bivouac the unmistakable figure of Major Brundsaux – tall, thin and 'hard as a halberd', with his big forked beard – might appear in the tent-lines when least expected; he understood his légionnaires, and he kept as close an eye on their feet and their health as on their training and discipline.

The number of camels in the convoy was dictated by the amount of water that had to be carried. Most were loaded with two 50-litre kegs (which still leaked, despite careful presoaking), supplemented with cooler native *guerba* water-skins. The wells were sometimes more than a day's march apart, and were easily missed from only 100 yards away. Often a well was simply a hole in the sand less than a yard across and deep, and the few inches of water in the bottom was vile-tasting from mineral salts. Wells had to be dug out laboriously before a flow strong enough to water the animals was reached. The low capacity of the wells, and the large numbers of camels needed to carry a column's every necessity (even down to firewood), meant that expeditions usually marched in separated groups a day apart, so as to allow the wells time to refill after each unit had passed.

When they reached Igli on 5 April the soldiers found only a naked, tilting rockpile rising steeply from the brain-numbing emptiness of the desert. Some kind of shelter had to be contrived, and each unit constructed its own part of a desolate little shanty-village, built on the summit with piled stones and grainsacks and tent-sheet roofs. Here they would stay, eating dust and grilling in the sun, in the path of any *harka* that might ride eastwards from the Tafilalt towards the Touat – where the capture of the Gourara oases was now under way.[9]

IT WAS DECIDED TO STIFFEN the Gourara column, formed of Algerian troops from El Goléa led by Colonel Menestrel, with two companies of légionnaires, despite the fact that the nearest available were at Géryville on the high plains, a good 300 miles north of the Gourara. On 27 April 1900 Major Letulle led out the 2nd and 3rd Companies of I/2nd RE, with 9 officers and 400 rankers, to set off due south across the virtually featureless map. They were accompanied by 1,500 camels carrying 70 days' rations and 6 days' water, and by 140 mounted irregulars on whom they depended to locate the wells, which were spaced more than 100 miles apart along the planned route. This march would involve crossing part of the Great Western Sand-Sea – the first time infantry had accomplished this, in an epic that for once exactly matched the cartoon image of a lonely column of légionnaires slogging across a dazzling immensity of bare dunes. Under a sun that was already approaching the furnace heat of summer they kept up an average rate of 15 miles a day, and on 17 May they linked up with Menestrel's column at the small oasis of Tabelkoza. The twin *kasbahs* of Timimoun submitted without a fight on 26 May; and on 7 June, their wasted presence no longer required, the légionnaires began their return march to the north.

This time they were taken not across the Erg but in a huge hook around its eastern edge, via El Goléa, Ghardaia, Laghouat and Aflou (see Map 3). The summer temperature was routinely 118°F (48°C) and for the worst part of the march it was recorded at 130°F (54°C) in the shade, though for 200 miles there was no shade. The men's lightweight fatigue uniforms were reduced to rags, and boots 'crocodiled' by marching over miles of sharp rocks had to be roughly mended with bits of string or wire. Major Letulle would write that his légionnaires blasphemed constantly, but never faltered. On 26 July 1900 they reached Géryville again, having covered 1,134 miles in 72 days of marching over some of the hottest and most hostile terrain on the face of the planet; during that time only half-a-dozen of the 400 men had fallen out sick.[10]

DOWN AT IGLI, MEANWHILE, the 2,000 men of Bertrand's column were suffering badly, and a small cemetery was already filling up. There was virtually no pasturage nearby, and everything needed for human and animal life had to be brought down by periodic convoys. This complicated the equation, since the men and animals of the convoys were also mouths to be fed and watered, and while they were unloading at Igli the population of this parched oven rose to some 3,000 men and at least the same number of camels.

The convoys down the Zousfana route were themselves a wasting asset, since the losses among the camels were shockingly high. To depart slightly from strict chronology, extracts from the report of a convoy that set out in October 1900 are instructive. It was the sixth resupply convoy from Aflou to Igli, commanded by a Lieutenant Chourreu; it departed on 8 October, and was joined on the 9th by a contingent from Géryville. Chourreu's subsequent report reads, in part:

18 Oct. Crossed pass of Founassa and arrived at Djenien bou Rezg. Many dead camels from previous convoys along the track through the pass, stinking badly. The Géryville camels at the head passed through without difficulty, but those from Aflou refused to pass close by dead camels. It was necessary to shift the corpses off the track and push our camels, in twos and threes – sometimes singly – to make them pass ... On this stage the total of animals lost rose to 110; 220 [more] were requisitioned at Djenien to complete the convoy, which was accompanied [from there] by a battalion of [2nd Algerian] Skirmishers and two companies from 1st Bat d'Af, as escort and to relieve garrisons at Taghit and Igli. Apart from these troops the convoy then consisted of 16 Spahis and *moghaznis* [native gendarmes], 81 foreman-drivers, 1,375 drivers and 4,126 camels, of which 3,600 belonged to the Intendance [Commissariat]. The others were used by [the various Army units for their baggage] ...

24 Oct. Departed Djenien; arrived Igli 7 Nov. See attached table of stages, distances, report on water and pasturage, and daily losses of camels. The wells of the Igli track are little better than wells of circumstance [i.e. quite unpredictable], which had to be dug out before the convoy arrived. They gave hardly enough water for the men, horses, and the herd of bullocks that provided the convoy with fresh meat. There was no question of their providing enough to water 4,000 camels – it would have been a task of several days [at each waterhole]. Thus we had to depend on finding water in *redirs* and the rare watercourses. [*Redirs* are rock cisterns which trap seasonal rain or floodwater, shallow but sometimes up to several acres in area.]

8 Nov. Spent the day at Igli, turning over rations and equipment and organizing for the return journey. 500 of the best camels were left with their drivers at Igli, in exchange for 350 left there by the previous convoy. Similarly, 100 selected camels were left when we passed Taghit.

14 Nov. S/Lt Barthélémy, 1st RE, accompanied by [five Spahis and four native gendarmes] carried out topographical survey work on the left flank between El Moungar and El Morra. At about 1pm a raiding party of about 20 men on foot was spotted near the Djebel Béchar; they fled after an exchange of fire.

18 Nov. About 10am a recce by the cavalry escort led by Lt Solard, 2nd Spahis, ran into another raiding party of about 15 men on foot, and again put them to flight without loss.

The total of animals died or abandoned en route due to fatigue or illness, going and returning, was 1,110, of which 586 on the return journey. Those that died had usually been on previous convoys.

Chourreu's accompanying table shows an average daily march of about 13 miles, and an average daily rate of 29 camels lost. Unsurprisingly, the heaviest losses – between 48 and 62 – correlate with the days when water and pasturage are noted as scarce.[11]

This massive wastage of camels was repeated roughly every six weeks for four years; in March–November 1900 alone there were seven convoys in the Sud-Oranais, each losing between 1,000 and 1,500 animals, so perhaps 9,000 were taken out of the local economy in nine months. The camels were requisitioned from the tribes with their drivers and gang-masters, but good hire fees were paid for men and animals; the driver's daily rate of 1 franc was twenty times the pay of a légionnaire, and he got another 3fr daily for each camel. The compensation paid for camels that died was also generous, so drivers were notoriously careless of their beasts' lives, but the sheer numbers lost distorted the economy of Oran province. While the total naturally includes some 'repeat business', it is estimated that in 1900–1903 there were some 40,000 camel-hires each year, and of these, up to 15,000 died annually, so about 60,000 in total. As Professor Gautier wrote, in the face of such plenty the jackals and vultures along the Oued Zousfana and Saoura were simply unable to cope.[12]

THE REAL MILITARY BENEFIT of maintaining posts in the far south, given the escalating cost of keeping them supplied, must immediately seem questionable to us, and the fact that Oran Division was secretive in public about its operations suggests that it may have been questioned at the time. However, this was not a matter of cold military calculation; in these years the colonialist political and commercial lobby in both Paris and Algiers was riding high, and the chain of command and planning was certainly vulnerable to unofficial manipulation. In the winter of 1899/1900 the War Ministry and high command were still distracted by the furore surrounding the release of Captain Dreyfus a couple of months previously. The minister from May 1900 was General André, a Republican zealot dedicated to deep reform of the Army; his eyes were fixed on the immediate politico-military terrain, and his desk was consequently too crowded to accommodate dead camels. So long as Oran and Ain Sefra avoided any mishaps that would anger the French public, they would enjoy a fairly free hand, and in the current mood it would take some spectacular failure to anger most patriotic Frenchmen.

Fashoda was barely a year in the past, and colonial bellicosity was fanned by a hot anti-British wind – indeed, one argument for a trans-Saharan railway was that it would allow French forces strategic access to British Nigeria in case of war. In spring 1900, Colonel Bertrand's predecessor in command of the 1st Foreign, Comte de Villebois-Mareuil, was leading French volunteers fighting alongside the South African Boers (he was killed that April; the fact that his cousin was the playwright Edmond Rostand did nothing to harm the public legend of a real-life Cyrano). In this atmosphere the Quai d'Orsay's twenty-year veto over provocative moves on the Moroccan border came under serious pressure, and while Foreign Minister Delcassé still argued the importance of the 'Maghzan policy' to shield France from criticism by the other powers, he was also a believer in the Saharan adventure.[13]

SMALL-SCALE NUISANCE RAIDS repeatedly crossed the frontier zone during summer 1900, usually mounted by the Dawi Mani and their allies the Ouled Jarir. These gangs of a dozen or two riders hit mainly the herds and flocks of peaceful clans, but occasionally also vulnerable convoys of civilian and military traffic and the camps of the advancing frontier railway. On the lower Zousfana, on 26 June Major Brundsaux of V/1st RE marched a couple of companies up from Igli to Taghit with engineers to study the site for a permanent post.[14] It was an inconvenient one, and there were several false starts before the fort was finally completed on a terrace of the western cliff close to the ksar. It was designed to house a garrison of one company each of Algerian turcos and Bat d' Af joyeux; but while this would cork a bottleneck for major movements up and down the Zousfana, such static infantry posts were unable by themselves to deter the border raids.

Ain Sefra Subdivision was forbidden to follow these plunderers into

Morocco in hot pursuit, and since the heavy military convoys down the Zousfana and Saoura were soaking up many of the available mounted troops as escorts, the old imbalance between firepower and mobility still hampered the French response. Individual incidents were trivial enough, but collectively they increased the frustration of the Native Affairs officers planted among the tribes on the Algerian side. Reports travelled back up the chain of command all the way to GOC 19th Army Corps in Algiers, and officers did not relish the thought of the general reading a diary of their impotence to halt a string of irritating pinpricks:

18 May. Razzia by Dawi Mani and Ouled Jarir took all the camels of the Ouled Sidi Tadj, 9 miles south of Moghrar Tahtani.

30 June/1 July. Night firing on escort camp for rail workers at Zoubia [Duveyrier]; légionnaire wounded.

1/2 July. Shots fired, and attempted theft of rifle, at Djenan ed Dar.

20 July. Murder of a Spaniard and a native policeman at Founassa by party of Ouled Jarir and Beni Gil.

22/23 July. 40 riders and foot attacked rail camp at Djenan ed Dar; sentry wounded, rifle stolen.

27 July. Theft of donkeys and military equipment from Hadjerat M'Guil [the base of the 2nd RE's 1st (Mounted) Company].

28 July. Sentries attacked at Djenan ed Dar by half-a-dozen men.

29 July. Two sentries attacked at Duveyrier, one wounded.[15]

THE DECISION HAD NOW BEEN TAKEN to halve the size of the garrison broiling on the griddle of Igli, but it was not Major Brundsaux's Legion battalion who were relieved. The Skirmishers of Major Bichemin's IV/2nd RTA were to march back to Duveyrier with the camels from the fourth convoy; they would be screened by Captain de la Robedière's half-squadron of 2nd Spahis, the usual small gaggle of goumiers and moghaznis, and Captain Sérant's 1st (Mounted) Company/2nd RE.[16]

Since Bou Amama's rebellion nearly twenty years previously, the mounted infantry companies, of both the Legion and the 2nd Algerian Skirmishers, had become an established weapon in Ain Sefra's armoury. Each of the two Foreign Regiments always had one and often two mounted companies, and since 1894 the War Ministry had finalized their organization.[17] By the late 1890s they had acquired the prestige of an elite, and could pick and choose among the légionnaires who applied to join them. They promised exhausting desert service, but – like the drafts for Tonkin –

they also offered a man the chance of combat and the right to strut. It was a sign of the tactical distortions produced by the great southern convoys that what were supposed to be highly mobile strike units were now tethered to slow camel-trains as escort troops. This denied them the chance to take the initiative – the mission for which Colonel de Négrier had specifically created them.

A company numbered just over 200 men, with rather more than half that number of mules (the extras to carry water and ammunition reserves and provide a few remounts). Although it had only the usual three officers – the captain commanding and two subalterns – the company usually operated in two independent 100-man halves (*pelotons*), each of two platoons (*sections*), one platoon in the second half-company being commanded by a warrant officer (*adjudant*). Each platoon of some 50 men comprised two squads (*groupes*), each led by a sergeant and a corporal, who could thus lead two half-squads if necessary. The officers rode their horses, and warrant officers and sergeant-majors had a mule to themselves; all other ranks doubled up in the usual way, with each pair taking turns in the saddle of their shared mule. The men rode broad, comfortable artillery saddles with their kit, bivouac equipment and rations for men and mule strapped in two big stacks over the pommel and crupper, almost enclosing the rider (who soon acquired the knack of dozing while he rode). The marching formation varied. The half who were on foot usually marched beside their riding partners, but might advance together ahead of the riders to scout crests; if danger was imminent the unit marched in square, with the men on foot surrounding the riders.

ON 29 JULY 1900 THE NORTHBOUND COLUMN from Igli reached wells at a spot called Zafrani about 15–20 miles north of Taghit (see Map 12). The wells were low, and it would take at least a day to water all the camels. Consequently, that night Major Bichemin ordered Captain Sérant to press on ahead with the first 2,000 beasts before first light on the 30th, to reunite at Fendi at nightfall on 2 August. To the modern ear the word 'convoy' suggests a column – something linear; but a camel convoy was more like a cattle drive, spread over a wide front in separate strings of four animals loosely grouped in gaggles of 100 each under a foreman-driver. With twenty of these straggling mobs to shepherd along, Sérant's mule company would need some horsemen to ride herd on them; Bichemin gave him a couple of dozen of Lieutenant Bel Habich's Spahis, and these troopers were to be dispersed in couples of look-outs around the edges of the awkward mass.

North from Zafrani the track led across several miles of flat ground to where the next water was to be found, near the foot of the western cliffs in a couple of *redirs* at a spot called El Moungar. At 3.30am on 30 July the company got under way in the chill darkness; irregulars scouted the trail ahead, followed at a distance by Spahis, and then by the légionnaires. The camel-drivers had made their usual disorganized start, and the company were trying to catch up with some of them who had gone ahead without waiting for the escort (no doubt hoping to be first at the El Moungar cisterns). At about 4am the captain became aware of a small group of Moroccans riding back past him in the darkness on his left flank. He took these to be returning *goumiers*, but the way they speeded up when they noticed the French made him uneasy. Shortly after this a *goumier* did find him, and reported that up ahead at El Moungar he had seen a large group of Dawi Mani riders and foot. Sérant sent two Spahi patrols forward; the very first dim light showed him some low, stony hummocks on the left of the track, and after quickly reconnoitring one of these he ordered most of his men up on to it. Their NCOs organized them into a square (actually, diamond) formation for all-round defence, with the mules in the centre. Meanwhile, Sérant ordered Lieutenant Pauly to take part of his 4th Platoon and the company's own baggage-camels back to the main convoy and warn Major Bichemin.

At about 4.10am Sérant heard shots, and shortly afterwards Sergeant Léger's Spahis returned at a gallop, spurring up the hillock and into the square of kneeling and lying legionnaires. In the dim but growing light before sunrise the captain saw shadowy masses of riders following them; there seemed to be about 400–500 Arabs in three separate groups, each with a flag, and they came on fast on three sides of the company's position. When they were about 500 yards away Sérant gave the order to open fire by volleys; at that distance individual targets were invisible, but firing into the mass began to do some damage at once, and riderless horses bolted past. The Arab horsemen came on, shouting insults and firing from the saddle, and warriors on foot followed them to take up firing positions among folds in the ground.

At some point Lieutenant Pauly returned from the south after reporting to Bichemin, and rode up another hillock to try to pick out a route by which his men could safely rejoin the square. At that moment the Dawi Mani charged Sérant's position again, from about 200 yards. The légionnaires fired steadily, bringing down most of the foremost riders, but a few actually got up the hillock and inside the square before they were killed. Others flowed past towards the south, and on the valley floor they ran right into Pauly's 4th Platoon, shooting down soldiers and mules alike – the square could not give effective support for fear of hitting their comrades. Four of Pauly's men marching on foot, led by Corporal Erich, showed admirable calm; kneeling and firing as fast they could work the bolts of their Lebels, they stretched about fifteen riders in the dust around them before the Arabs left them alone in search of easier prey. Légionnaires reported seeing several riders leaning down from the saddle to snatch up wounded or unhorsed warriors behind them. The rest of that group rode on to the south towards the convoy, where Major Bichemin's alerted Skirmisher battalion repulsed them and other parties with ease.

The Dawi Mani were still hovering and sniping, but at around 5.15am the different groups returned to the hummocky ground between the company square and the cliffs and joined up again; the whole war party then withdrew into the distance towards the heights of the Djebel Béchar, carrying their wounded and leading the few baggage camels they had managed to cut out. The sun was now above the eastern dunes, and its flat rays soaked the west side of the valley with golden light; Sérant ordered his légionnaires to set their sights at between 1,600 and 2,000 yards, and fired some measured volleys. Watching the result through binoculars, he spotted kicked-up dust and adjusted the fire until he saw flurries among the riders, confirming the Lebel's effectiveness even at a mile

Captain Sérant recorded commendations for Warrant Officer Peille, Private Diebolt and Private Wilhelm, all of whom had killed Moroccans face-to-face inside the square – the latter as the rider was charging the company commander, and at the cost of a bullet which mutilated Wilhelm's hand. Sergeants Favrier and Diacre and Corporal Dommanget were commended for cool courage in exposed positions while controlling their squads' fire. Of the 4th Platoon, caught in the open, their captain commended Corporal Erich and Privates Cassier, Spierckel and Berney for their calm and disciplined self-defence. From El Morra, where the dead were buried, Major Bichemin used his lamp-and-telescope equipment to signal up the line for extra medics and mule- and camel-litters to meet the force at Fendi on 2 August. The Legion casualties were at first 7 killed – all from 4th Platoon – and 9 wounded, but one of the latter soon died; the cause of death was listed as gunshot wounds in every case.

Less than a month later the fifth convoy for Igli passed the scene of the action, and Lieutenant Guillaume left a description of the debris of battle. This was scattered over several hundred yards, but particularly around the base of the hillock defended by the Mounted Company. The overworked vultures and jackals of the Zousfana had already done their best with the sun-dried corpses; the bones of men and mules littered the ground, jumbled up with broken crates, bits of harness and assorted trash. Some finely decorated Arab weapons were proof that the Dawi Mani had not returned to the scene since the fight, and Guillaume and his comrades had their pick of souvenirs. (The most magnificent, and puzzling, was a large chased silver powder flask with an inscription from the reign of Louis XIV.)[18]

THE WAR PARTY THAT ATTACKED Sérant's company was by far the largest yet encountered by French troops on the Oued Zousfana border, and although they had been repulsed at only moderate cost, the telegraph key tapped out an urgent report from Oran Division to 19th Army Corps and the War Ministry. (The GOC 19th Army Corps was then General Grisot, first encountered in these pages fighting with the Legion's 5th Battalion in the streets of Paris.) Companies of Skirmishers were shuttled up and down the convoy route like beads on an abacus, with a Legion infantry company on immediate alert at Djenien bou Rezg.

The heavy losses suffered by the Dawi Mani did not deter the tribesmen from raiding that summer, on one occasion in large numbers: on 10 August at least 400 Dawi Mani ran off herds grazing south of Igli. The list of lesser clashes scrolls on down the page: in the week of 25 August–1 September 1900 there were five separate incidents at or near Duveyrier – actual or attempted rustling of camels, ration-bullocks and sheep, attacks on the rail camps, 2 sentries killed and their rifles stolen. During September there were five more raids, on Djenien bou Rezg, Duveyrier, Hadjerat M'guil and El Morra, by between 15 and 40 tribesmen. These were sometimes identified as from the Beni Gil or Ouled Jarir; when their origin was unknown, 'Figuig' tended to get the blame – one imagines the pen-nib scoring deep into the paper. (On 4 September there was also a more serious clash in the dunes far to the east near Timimoun with a war party of Ait Khabbash, which cost the French 13 killed and 36 wounded. There were no Legion units in the Touat, which was the responsibility of the 1st Bat d'Af and 2nd Algerian Skirmishers.)

*

THE FOLLOWING YEAR there were no major incidents along the Zous-fana valley, but throughout 1901 the regular convoys to the Far South continued to litter the sands with camel-bones, and hit-and-run raiders continued to cross the border every few nights.

The most serious engagements again took place further east in the Touat, where the Ait Khabbash assembled a *harka* of up to 1,500 men at Charouine, 30 miles south-west of Timimoun. This tribe had withdrawn north-west-wards after the French occupation, but were still not reconciled to losing their extortion income from the Touat oases and their slave imports from In Salah. After travelling by night to avoid detection, they left their camels under guard in the date-groves a mile away and hit Timimoun before first light on 18 February 1901. Creeping close to the rather ramshackle perimeter, they slit the throat of a sentry and got some 30 men inside and under cover before the alarm was given. After an initial scare, Major Reibel's garrison of just under 200 *joyeux* and *turcos* cleared out the infiltrators and drove the rest away from the walls, at a cost of an officer and 9 men killed and 21 wounded; the Ait Khabbash left 153 dead on the field. A reprisal column attacked Charouine rather hesitantly on 2/3 March; at first light on the 3rd, Captain Pein's *goumiers* and Skirmishers became trapped in a bowl of the sand dunes under heavy fire, and finally withdrew after suffering 68 casualties. (During these two weeks the tribesmen had captured about 80 Lebel repeaters.)

Fighting the Ait Khabbash was never cheap; and it is worth noting that since May 1900 they had simultaneously been heavily involved further west against fellow Berbers of the Ait Murghad tribe, over control of oases on the Oued Rheris north-west of the Tafilalt. War on several fronts was as natural to the Ait Khabbash as 'the rising of the sun', and so was polishing their warrior reputation with little concern for the details. They inhabited a world of lays and legends, not cold reportage; a fact was what people were told and wanted to believe, and Timimoun was soon famous throughout southern Morocco as a mighty victory over the French. This tendency to accept the most encouraging version of events was not the weakness it is today, but a sign of high morale, and it would remain an obstacle throughout the thirty years of the French pacification campaigns. In a world without mass com-munications, each tribe's sense of its strength or weakness was more or less introverted, so each of the many groups had to be convinced individually of French superiority. The rumoured defeat of another clan on the far side of a mountain might be ascribed to stupidity or cowardice, while any trivial success – the looting of a convoy or the killing of even half a dozen French soldiers – might be wildly exaggerated by word of mouth. The display of a few captured rifles or the heads of dead Frenchmen in villages beyond the current edge of notional French control would encourage defiance on a scale out of all proportion to the actual success.[19]

MEANWHILE, THE BOY SULTAN Abd el Aziz had emerged, blinking, into his thankless political inheritance, and lengthy negotiations over a settlement of the Algerian/Moroccan frontier question had been taking place between his Maghzan and the Quai d'Orsay – much to the fury of the *jihadi* tendency among his subjects. On 10 July 1901, a protocol was signed in Paris agreeing a form of joint authority over the frontier. Ain Sefra was to maintain regular liaison with both French and Maghzan officials appointed as border commissioners, the latter based in Figuig with a modest garrison. The limit of actual French posts was to be the western edge of the Djebel Béchar; Morocco was to build posts along the west bank of the Oued Guir (these never materialized); but the wide region between the Zousfana and the Guir – the actual arena of the raiding problem – was not decisively addressed. The Algerian governor-general defined this simply as 'territories where Moroccan tribes, whether sedentary or nomadic, traditionally reside, camp and move, in relations or in habitual contact with Algerian tribes'.[20] Here the Ouled Jarir and Dawi Mani were to be offered the choice of allegiance to either French Algeria or the Maghzan, and if they chose the latter they were to be moved away from the border to new territory with Maghzan 'assistance'.

It is legitimate to doubt that any of the negotiators believed for a moment that these terms could lead to a peaceful solution. The protocol legitimized the French presence in the Touat and the Zousfana/Saoura valleys, while the Maghzan had preserved recognition of its notional authority in the south-east, but it still lacked any means to exercise it. Whatever the protocol pretended, in fact this open acknowledgement that the tribal range of the Ouled Jarir and Dawi Mani was debatable would soon give the French Army the freedom to shape the reality on the ground.[21]

ON 19 JANUARY 1902 TWO OFFICERS of the 1st Foreign Regiment, Captains Gratien and de Cressin, went out hunting in the hills of the Djebel Beni Smir above Duveyrier. They did not return, and a search party found their stripped bodies, shot in the back. On 9 February the Paris weekly *Le*

Petit Journal expressed the prevailing mood among the colonial lobby:

> France's patience is being abused by the Moroccans. Once again, an odious crime has been committed on the frontier. Two young captains of the Foreign Legion, officers with bright futures, have been killed by the natives ... If the sovereign of Morocco is unable to assure safety within his domains, it is clearly high time to consider whether it would not be opportune to come to his aid.[22]

10. Blood and Sand
1902–1903

Disciplinary Private Maret was found some 9 miles from
the battlefield, having neither eaten nor drunk for two
days, and half naked; but although feverish, he still had
his rifle, his ammunition and his courage. I took him
back to Fendi behind my saddle, and I recommend him
for the Military Medal for his admirable conduct.

Lieutenant Deze, 2nd RE, following action near Ksar el Azoudj,
29 March 1903[1]

THERE IS AN UNMISTAKABLE FLAVOUR of America's Old West in
Isabelle Eberhardt's eyewitness description of the activity that followed the
soldiers down the Oued Zousfana. The rail tracks reached Duveyrier in
September 1900:

> Recently the railway reached Zoubia, and the new European village of
> Duveyrier sprang up with vitality. Low houses of grey earth multiplied, to
> the sound of légionnaires singing their songs of exile; canteens and drinking-
> shacks opened, made of planks and flattened petrol tins; a hardy duenna
> even led a few vague prostitutes down there from Saida and Sidi bel Abbès.
> Lines of camels came to kneel in the sandy streets before travelling on to
> resupply the posts further south. Duveyrier was the spring from which a river
> of abundance flowed towards the Sahara. An apparent prosperity reigned for
> several months; people started to enrich themselves, converging from the
> country round about on this bait of easy trade ...
>
> Then one day the little track pushed on; the two shining rails passed
> Duveyrier towards another stop further on ... From one day to the next
> another town sprang up, quick as the grass of the Sahara under the first winter
> rains – and the ephemeral life of Duveyrier disappeared, leeched out of it by
> that new station of Beni Ounif de Figuig.[2]

The American parallel most temptingly suggested by the Zousfana border country early in the century is the Rio Grande frontier with Mexico some thirty years previously. Any Army attempt to create a net of surveillance and defence had such a broad mesh between its small knots that elusive raiding parties passed through it without difficulty, to rob and often to kill. The historic reply to this was to mount counter-raids in strength, tracking the tribesmen to their villages and exacting such wholesale revenge that their own leaders would bring the provocations to an end to ensure collective survival. But since the Army was forbidden to make such expeditions across the border, and since the Moroccan government was impotent, the frontier remained open for the raiders but closed to French soldiers. The French inability to strike back effectively seemed to be encouraging larger war parties to assemble, and the Zafrani incident suggested that the tribesmen might sooner or later achieve something on a rather different scale from running off livestock and killing a couple of sentries.

Nevertheless, in 1902 the Quai d'Orsay was still focused on seeking a political solution by attempting to prop up Sultan Abd el Aziz. The end of the Boer War in May that year allowed Foreign Minister Delcassé to look further into the future, and he wanted no incidents to spark sensational reports that might disturb his planned rapprochement with Britain, which would, in addition to wider implications, give France a freer hand in Morocco as a by-product. A bungled Maghzan attempt to reform the tax system had forced Abd el Aziz to seek urgent new French loans; to ensure their servicing, French customs officials were empowered to run Morocco's ports and to skim the first 60 per cent off all duty paid.[3]

Additional accords to the Franco-Moroccan border protocol, signed in April and May 1902, were hotly condemned by the religious establishment in Fes, and raids and ambushes continued. By summer, most of the token company of 150 Maghzan levies installed in Figuig in March in accordance with the protocol had deserted after selling their rifles.[4] In June, some of the religious leaders in the Tafilalt openly declared that since Abd el Aziz had failed in his duty of protection they would no longer pray in his name – a seriously subversive act that called the sultan's legitimacy into question.

Abd el Aziz was far more concerned by the threat from the pretender to his throne in the north-east, where Bou Himara – El Rogi – was building a strong following among the tribes in the hills around the strategic town of Taza. (He was a charismatic speaker, and in a society in thrall to superstition his early success was partly due to his mastery of what Walter Harris of the

London *Times* called 'rather ordinary conjuring tricks'; one of these involved, at every performance, the death of a slave by burial alive.) Now he was sending letters throughout the south-east, trying to draw others to his flag to depose the sultan and resist the French. In the summer of 1902 Abd el Aziz sent an army to crush his rebellion, and the ambitious Madani el Glaoui and his brother Tahami led a force of Atlas tribesmen to join this expedition.[5]

WHILE A SCOURGE TO HIS PEOPLE, the sultan's army was not an impressive military instrument even after it acquired some modern weapons and instructors in their use. Since it lacked any functioning system of logistics, its operational range was dictated by its ability to live off the country, a process in which payment for requisitioned goods played no part. Command of an expedition was regarded as an opportunity not only to pillage the countryside but also to misappropriate the soldiers' pay, so it is hardly surprising that they – like all other armed men in Morocco – were motivated very largely by the prospect of loot. (Abd el Aziz had given command of the army sent against El Rogi to his teenage brother Moulay el Kebir, in order to give him 'a chance to make a little money'.)

Walter Harris accompanied another Maghzan force which Abd el Aziz personally led on a simultaneous campaign against Zimmur rebels west of Meknes in summer 1902. Their advance was blocked by a ravine, and a few shots were fired at them from scrub on the far lip. A small deserted village could be seen on a grassy shelf half-way down the opposite slope, and the Dukkala regiment were ordered to clear the canyon. Clambering down to the little river and up the far side, they halted at the village, where the inevitable search for loot turned up a store of wheat:

> In the presence of the Sultan and the whole army they ... took off their uniform breeches of bright blue cotton, tied up [the legs] with string, and filled [them] with wheat ... loaded up their booty on their backs, and started to return to the army. Nothing would make them go on: bugles were blown, signals were made, orders shouted ...

Another unit was sent forward 'to see if [the Dukkalas] couldn't be persuaded to turn once more in the direction of the enemy':

> With music and singing the Abda regiment set out. They met the Dukkalas struggling up under their heavy loads ... and the Abda charged. The Dukkalas threw down their loads and commenced firing, and in a few minutes a little

battle was raging ... A ceasing of the firing bespoke a compromise. The two bodies of troops fraternized, the Dukkalas temporarily abandoned their breeches ... and returned bare-legged to the Zimmur village with ... the Abdas. Once there it was the latters' turn to step out of their nether garments, and the Dukkalas assisted them to load up ... This done, the two regiments, except for a few killed and wounded, returned together ... On the summit the enraged Sultan and his Court and the rest of the army [were] impotent to change the course of events ... all thought of crossing the ravine that night was out of the question, so the camp was pitched ...

The Dukkala and Abda regiments quarrelled over the division of the spoil, and fought on and off all the night through. Bullets were flying in every direction ... We never crossed that ravine. The next day news reached the Sultan that the army under his brother had been defeated [by El Rogi] near Taza. In all haste we turned back ... to Fes.[6]

The expedition against El Rogi had been a complete failure; defeated at Ain Mediouna on the southern edge of the Rif hills, the royal *mehala* (army) was virtually cut off around Taza for four months. When the town finally fell on 22 December 1902, the Pretender gained great prestige throughout the north-east, and also a reputation for burning prisoners alive with petrol. Madani el Glaoui, wounded three times, led the remnant of his men across into Algeria, where a French officer arranged his passage home. His younger brother Tahami fought a rearguard action before escaping southwards; he then disappeared from the scene for three years, during which he made the pilgrimage to Mecca. In the wake of this humiliating defeat Abd el Aziz moved his court from Fes (a city vulnerable to encirclement) to Rabat on the west coast. In the winter of 1902–1903 El Rogi's victory – and his steady supply of modern rifles through Melilla – enabled him to form a coalition of both Arab and Berber tribes, and in the summer of 1903 he would even briefly occupy the border town of Oujda. His pan-tribal alliance was short-lived, however, and his pretensions could not hide his essential nature as just another regional gambler for short-term prizes.[7]

AN EXAMPLE OF THE FRONTIER CLASHES that were now taking place – too small for history books to notice, but ugly enough for the soldiers caught up in them – was an incident in March 1903 near Ksar el Azoudj (see Map 12). Held by small detachments from the 2nd Algerian Skirmishers and 2nd Spahis, this was one of the way-points on the convoy route down the

Oued Zousfana. On 29 March, Lieutenant Ruffier of the 1st RE was also camped there with a work party of légionnaires who had just finished building a caravanserai at the wells. At Fendi, about 12 miles further north, Lieutenant Deze of 23rd Company, VI/2nd RE was in charge of a larger construction gang; the légionnaires' reputation for being able to tackle virtually any physical task condemned them to such work anyway, but on this occasion both parties also included men from the regimental *sections de discipline*, undergoing hard labour as punishment.

At around noon on the 29th, Captain Normand of the Engineers was checking the track north with Sergeant Sontag and 9 légionnaires when he learned that a convoy of 40-plus camels, coming down from Fendi to enable Ruffier to pack up his detachment, had been snatched by a strong party of tribesmen and taken south-west into the hills. Leaving Sontag to slog on to Fendi, the captain rode back to Ksar el Azoudj and took the troop of Spahis there in pursuit, ordering Lieutenant Ruffier to follow with all available infantrymen. Ruffier soon got on the march, with the post commander Quartermaster-Sergeant Lovy and 10 of his *turcos*, and 20 of his own men including some of the *disciplinaires*. At Fendi, Lieutenant Deze was also alerted; he marched west up a pass into the hills, with the one Spahi trooper who was in camp, his own Sergeant Hoerter and 26 men (mostly *disciplinaires*) of 2nd RE, and Sergeant Sontag and four of the 1st RE men who had come panting up the track at the last moment. Deze put his batman, Walz, on his spare horse, so he had two other mounted men for scouting and 32 marching légionnaires.

The situation was thus as follows: two separate parties each of about 30 infantrymen, and a third with fewer than that number of cavalrymen, with no mutual communication, were now climbing into a waterless labyrinth of unexplored ridges and canyons with very limited visibility, by different routes, on the off-chance of catching up with an enemy force of unconfirmed strength – and all under nominal command of an Engineer officer, who had pushed ahead with the troopers after ordering the two infantry subalterns simply to follow him. Lieutenant Deze's report is the more detailed:

> After about an hour and a half's march to the south-west we heard brisk firing on our east, behind a chaotic massif [of rocky hills] ... I marched in the direction of the firing, and [from a crest] saw Capt Normand and his Spahis ... in action against about 60 Moroccans. I gave the following orders: [I would take] Sgt Hoerter with 20 men of 2nd RE, plus Sgt Sontag and his

four 1st RE men, directly across the massif; my mounted orderly and six other légionnaires were to follow the crest south and try to reach a pass about 1,000 yards away, in order to cut off any retreat in what seemed to me the likeliest direction – a group of Moroccans were taking that route with some of the stolen camels. Walz joined up with Capt Normand and his Spahis; they tried to check the enemy movement, but Walz was seriously wounded in the foot and could not remount, the horse bolted and was captured [and the Moroccans broke past them].

I moved ahead with the main group, which prompted the retreat of the enemy, but they stayed within effective range and used the ground with marvellous skill. We did not fire, because 17 *disciplinaires* of my detachment had received only five packets of cartridges [i.e. 40 rounds, instead of the usual 120], and it was necessary to economize in an action that looked as if it might become testing.

Deze continued to pursue the tribesmen and the stolen camels over very difficult ground – abrupt hills cut by confusing gulleys – and at about 3.45pm he came within 800 yards of a group of perhaps 20 of them. He ordered his men to fire 10 rounds each; the raiders disappeared down a canyon, and when Deze reached the spot he found blood trails. He pushed on for about another 3 miles; by now he was within intermittent sight of Ruffier's party, advancing in parallel on his flank. Despite the reticent language of the subalterns' reports it is clear that during an exhausting 4 hours of scrambling through this chaotic terrain both groups became scattered. Deze wrote that at about 5pm he had with him only 12 of his own men plus 3 of Ruffier's Algerians who had joined him; Sergeant Hoerter had fallen behind with 'the men who were not such good marchers'.

At this point Deze's group came under intense fire from tribesmen on a ridge about 600 yards off. They must have had modern rifles, because one of the first shots hit Private Ghysslinck full in the chest: 'He was carried into cover and put up on one of the Spahi horses, with a man holding him from each side'. The mention of Spahis suggests that by now Deze's and Normand's parties had joined up, but relative numbers and positions are unclear in the reports; one must suspect a good deal of confusion, with each junior officer and NCO doing his best with the men he had around him, and one does not get the impression that Captain Normand had a tight grip on events. Ruffier was on a separate crest, also under heavy fire and, on two occasions, in danger of being rushed and overrun.

The sun was getting low in the sky, ammunition and water were running short, and the soldiers were taking casualties. Two groups of tired men, within sight but not in contact with one another, were dispersed in broken and unfamiliar country, and in danger of being outflanked by well-armed enemies fighting on their own ground. Against no more than equal numbers, the sapper captain had led the légionnaires into a tactical dead end, and the worst was still to come. Normand now accepted the inevitable, and ordered Deze to retreat by two leap-frogging echelons; predictably, as soon as the soldiers gave up the high ground the tribesmen closed in on their heels – Lieutenant Deze:

> Capt Normand ordered a fighting retreat through a canyon which opened at the foot of the escarpment where we were; [Ruffier and] the Skirmishers from Ksar el Azoudj were on the south side of this ravine to guard our flank. The retreat began when the wounded had been got under cover, but at that moment new groups of Moroccans appeared on both flanks and opened a violent fire at less than 400 yards.
>
> I fell back with the last echelon. The retreat was extremely painful; we were dominated from higher ground on all sides by an enemy who knew this terrain much better than we did. When falling back we found that Légionnaire Ghysslinck had been hit again, in the head, and was dead. We tried to carry the body and put another wounded man up on the horse, but this proved impossible, and we abandoned the corpse when the Moroccans got within 100 yards of us.
>
> We reached a corridor where Capt Normand was [waiting], and rallied all the men there to cover [by fire] the retreat of Lt Ruffier in the direction of Ksar el Azoudj. [This re-emphasizes that each platoon was obliged to retreat independently, on either side of the canyon mentioned above; Normand and the Spahis were with Deze and the 2nd RE men.] *Disciplinaires* Stamm and Flipsonn of 2nd RE were killed; we could not take their bodies along as the wounded were using all the horses we had.[8] We were pursued for more than a mile, but our fire succeeded in holding them back. At nightfall Capt Normand reunited the two echelons, totalling 30 men, and we continued towards Fendi. We arrived at about 9pm, with three wounded; the wounded Walz had already been brought in . . .

Deze commended his batman Walz, who had continued to fire after his right foot was smashed by a bullet, and had killed two of his assailants; *Disciplinaire* Lambinet had also shown great bravery, fighting hand-to-hand with a tribesman who tried to take the rifle of a fallen Skirmisher. *Disciplinaire* Maret, who had behaved well throughout the day, became separated in the darkness and was missing; so at first was *Disciplinaire* Bonneuil, whose left arm was broken by a bullet, but he managed to make his way back to Ksar el Azoudj alone during the night.

Further south, Lieutenant Ruffier had also been leapfrogging his men back in the face of wolfish pursuit, and his matter-of-fact report paints a frightening picture for the imaginative:

> The Moroccans, breaking out of cover, pursued us vigorously, and soon showed that they had more ammunition than we did. We retreated, holding foot by foot; at several points it came to hand-to-hand. The fight continued until nightfall; QM-Sgt Lovy of 2nd RTA and two of his Skirmishers were killed. Légionnaire Peter of my detachment was hit in the belly, and I got a bullet in the right thigh ... My horse, held by a Skirmisher, bolted in very difficult country and could not be recaptured.
>
> I wish to commend 11859 Pte Peter, who continued to march throughout the action although wounded in the belly; and 9617 *Disciplinaire* Dubois, who behaved very well during the retreat, stopping from ridge to ridge to hold back the pursuit.

The next day General Cauchemez, commanding Ain Sefra Subdivision, ordered Captain Normand out again with Deze and 60 légionnaires to search for the abandoned bodies. Eight were found and taken back to Fendi for burial; all but one had been stripped – Stamm had fallen unseen some way from the others with a bullet through the head, and was still holding his rifle and a cartridge. Only one had been mutilated: QM-Sergeant Lovy of the Skirmishers showed no bullet wounds but the signs of violent beating, and his eyes had been gouged out with a dagger. More happily, Lieutenant Deze found 8305 Disciplinary Private Maret, 36 hours after the action and a full 9 miles from the scene. Half-naked and suffering from heatstroke, he had been eating grass seeds and drinking his own urine, but when found he still had his rifle and was full of fight.[10]

THE RESTLESS COLONIAL LOBBY in Paris and Algiers took heart in the spring of 1903 from the re-appointment as Governor-General of Algeria of Charles Célestin Jonnart. A cabinet minister in 1893, he had been forced to retire the following year when he sustained serious injuries in an early motorcar accident. He had served briefly as Algerian governor-general in the winter of 1900/1901 before ill-health then forced him to take a long sabbatical. By the spring of 1903 he seems to have recovered his full vigour, and returned to the post that had always been his ambition.[11]

In the first half of May, new cross-border raids were being reported every few days, and one was in alarming strength: on the 6th, no fewer than 1,500 Ouled Jarir and Beni Gil, 600 of them mounted, lifted several hundred camels. This suggested to some that the Tafilalt's constant demands for a holy war against the French were being heeded. Impatient to take decisive control of a drifting situation, Jonnart urged that reconnaissance columns be sent into Moroccan tribal territory, and that an actual attack be made on the walled township of Zenaga, the notorious bandits' base in the Figuig oasis.

Paris agreed to the reconnaissance columns, but forbade any occupation of Figuig; however, Jonnart was free to present demands for action to the Maghzan border commissioner there, the Amil Si Muhammad Ragragi. On 23 May 1903, General Fernand O'Connor at Oran Division was ordered to prepare the two recce columns, and also (perhaps significantly) to send artillery south by rail. A meeting between Jonnart and Ragragi was arranged, to take place on the plain outside Zenaga on the morning of the 31st.[12]

The valley of Figuig is aligned east to west, bordered on the north by steep, almost continuous cliffs and on the south by a more separated series of heights (see Map 13). The direct approach from the Beni Ounif railhead to Figuig ran almost due north by the Taghla pass. Along its left side, at the foot of the moderate slopes of the Djebel Zenaga, a thick belt of date-palms followed the west bank of the flowing Zousfana river. On the east bank a corridor of sand studded with occasional palms led along the foot of the steep, sawtoothed Djebel Taghla rising on the right. A rider emerging at the northern end was confronted, across about 750 yards of open ground, by the 2-mile long east-west edge of the great palm plantation and crop-gardens packed into a semi-circular bay in the northern cliffs. To the left, in the edge of the *palmerie* down at the western end of the valley, the walls of Zenaga dominated the oasis.

CLOSE SECURITY FOR THE MEETING was provided by Captain Bonnelet's 18th (Mounted) Company/1st RE, who marched up from Djenan ed Dar early that morning. Given the all-clear by a Spahi patrol, Bonnelet moved up the pass and halted short of the northern end; his 4th Platoon was led by Lieutenant Ruffier, who had clearly recovered from his thigh wound at Ksar el Azoudj two months' previously. The 1st Platoon were sent forward to take up position on the lower knees of the Djebel Taghla on the right of the northern exit, keeping watch over the open ground to the west and north. At 9am, Jonnart rode through with General O'Connor and their escort. At about 9.50am Bonnelet heard a shot, then two more, then a rolling fire; he left Ruffier's platoon holding the mules and took the 2nd and 3rd forward on foot at the double. They had not gone more than 50 yards before they came under a scattered fire.

The Amil Ragragi had ridden down from his residence in El Oudaghir and had met Jonnart's party on the plain. When the meeting broke up half-an-hour later, the governor-general's party had not turned back for Taghla pass, but had ridden westwards with Zenaga on their right, in order to swing left again for Beni Ounif by the broader Jew's Pass. As they rode past Zenaga shots were fired at them and riders emerged from behind the *ksar*. Seeing this, the légionnaires on the lower slope of Djebel Taghla opened fire to cover their escape. Jonnart's party spurred away to safety, while Moroccans rushed to man the walls and tower of Zenaga, returning an increasingly heavy fire on 1st Platoon. This was commanded that day by a Danish lieutenant named Christian Selchauhansen – one of the Legion's few foreign-born officers at that time.[13]

Bonnelet formed his 2nd and 3rd Platoons into a skirmish line extending left from 1st Platoon, and all advanced north to the oasis by fire and move-ment, eventually taking firing cover among the palms in the edge of some terraced gardens. After about an hour, Bonnelet received the order to fall back by echelons. A withdrawal straight backwards would have left the covering echelon still mixed up in the trees and vulnerable to outflanking; instead, the captain orderered Selchauhansen to take his platoon back to their original covering position on the Djebel Taghla slope before he with-drew the other two, at first moving eastwards along the edge of the *palmerie* before turning south across the open ground under Selchauhansen's rifle sights. This was sensible, but it took a while for Selchauhansen to complete the move. When 2nd and 3rd Platoons began to move the enemy's fire redoubled, and up to 300 Moroccans emerged from Zenaga and followed the leapfrogging platoons along the fringe of the palm-forest in an apparent attempt to get ahead and cut them off from the pass. From the slope, Selchauhansen kept this force under fire while Bonnelet led a textbook withdrawal below him, pursued by growing numbers of Moroccans.

When the three platoons had linked up at the northern mouth of the pass, Bonnelet faced a classic tactical problem. If he gave up the slope of Djebel Taghla to fall back down the open corridor, his men would have no effective cover for several hundred yards until they reached a slight ridge, and their backs would be in danger from the usual following rush that was second nature to all Moroccans; but if he left Selchauhansen's platoon up on the slope to cover the retreat of the rest, they would soon be cut off. He formed a firing line to hold the enemy back while two seriously wounded NCOs were carried to the rear, and this line soon had to bend backwards at each end to fight off Moroccans trying to flank the company on both sides. As long as his men held this ground and kept up a disciplined fire all would be well; but their cartridge pouches were not bottomless, and as soon as he thinned them out to start retreating down the pass things would become delicate.

At about 11.45am a Lieutenant Catroux rode up with orders from Lieu-tenant-Colonel Cussac, 2nd RE (now returned from Madagascar to a territory command at Djenan ed Dar). Cussac had ordered most of 19th (Mounted) Company/1st RE up the pass to help Bonnelet disengage, and 150 légionnaires were advancing along the western slope above the Zousfana, from where they could give effective cover to 18th (Mounted) falling back down the sandy corridor on their right. The two companies changed places smoothly, and the 19th (plus Lieutenant Ruffier's frustrated mule-holders) went forward for a brief exchange of fire with the Moroccans, who then fell back to Zenaga. By 2pm both units were safely back at Beni Ounif.[14]

AT THE COST OF A FEW MEN WOUNDED and a brief personal scare, Jonnart had the excuse he needed for direct surgery on the twenty-year-old cancer of Figuig. By 6 June General O'Connor had shunted his units around to assemble a strong force at Beni Ounif, including two battalions of 2nd RE from Saida and Mascara. The aim was not to assault Zenaga, however, but to persuade it to surrender by an artillery bombardment; this would be delivered by one battery each of 95mm and the new 75mm pieces, and the mission of the infantry and cavalry was simply to ensure that the guns got there and back safely.[15]

O'Connor marched on 8 June; he had anticipated that it might take a day to fight through the passes into the valley, but this proved pessimistic. The infantry occupied all the passes without difficulty, and the artillery took up position facing Zenaga. At 7.45am the eight guns opened a slow, deliberate fire, taking care not to drop any overshoots into El Oudaghir. The last guns fell silent at 11am; perhaps 150 buildings had been destroyed or badly damaged, and anything between 80 and 300 people killed. During the subsequent withdrawal there was a little skirmishing with some Ouled Jarir who emerged from the *ksar* of El Hammam, but losses were light on both sides, and by 2pm all the troops were on their way back to camp.

The councils of all seven Figuig *ksars* presented themselves to General O'Connor to negotiate the best peace terms they could get, and these were agreed on 10 June. A swingeing fine would be paid; there was to be free European access to the oasis, and tribal marauders would be expelled. In return, Figuig traders would enjoy French protection in Algeria, property rights at Beni Ounif would be respected, and no troops would be stationed in Figuig. These terms naturally bound only the sedentary population of the oasis, not the visiting tribesmen; these returned to the *djebel* and the *bled*, where they soon had increased reason for concern over France's new bellicosity.[16]

HAVING NEUTRALIZED FIGUIG, Jonnart now sent a column to follow the tribes to their second centre at Béchar (see Map 11). On 22 June, Colonel d'Eu of the 2nd RTA left Ben Zireg with 1,100 men; as well as 18th (Mounted) Company/1st RE the force included significant numbers of Algerian tribal irregulars and 'turned' Dawi Mani. The colonel's mission was to read the riot act and demand hostages for future good behaviour from Dawi Mani and Ouled Jarir camped around Ouakda and Béchar, and it is significant that a respected holy man, Si Brahim, had been invited up from the *zaouia* at Kenadsa oasis to act as mediator. On 25 June the column camped near Béchar; Colonel d'Eu brusquely repossessed any obviously rustled stock, the required hostages and guarantees were provided, and he departed on the 27th. While the involvement of Si Brahim by advance arrangement argues that the colonel had been intent on reaching an agreement, the next column to set out was clearly looking for trouble.

At Béchar, Colonel d'Eu had rendezvoused with Captain Roger de Susbielle, the energetic chief of Native Affairs for the whole Zousfana, who had ridden up from his base at Taghit with 400 of his local irregulars, including Dawi Mani. On 26 June, Susbielle escorted the *marabout* Si Brahim back to Kenadsa; then his horsemen and camel-riders were joined, from El Morra in the Zousfana valley, by Lieutenants Riverain and Famie with 2nd Half-Company, 22nd (Mounted)/2nd RE. They rode north, and during 28–30 June *ksars* in the edge of the hills barring the way to the great Tamlelt steppe were severely 'visited'. Most of the men of fighting age were absent, but Bou Kais was defended by a small gang of allegedly notorious Ouled Jarir raiders. Susbielle sent the légionnaires into the alleyways with the bayonet – his own renegades were no use for such work – and burned down the houses from which the tribesmen were firing. Susbielle would later be criticized for this raid, described even by Jonnart – an admirer – as imprudently provocative.[17]

THE FACT THAT SOME DAWI MANI Arabs were now riding with French units underlines the dilemma faced by the different segments of that people in particular, though shared by other tribes. Their widespread economic activity was anchored to date-palm oases in the Tafilalt on the Oued Ziz in the west and on the Zousfana and Saoura in the east, and for all the clans the central pivot of the annual cycle was the Abadla plain on the lower Oued Guir (see Map 11). The 'Tafilalt end' of the Dawi Mani were loud in their defiance of the French, but the 'Zousfana and Saoura end' already had garrisons planted among them. The vital Abadla grainfields were clearly at risk, since the obvious next step in any French advance would be westwards to the Guir. Since 1901, the usual calculations of relative advantage – when to fight and when to negotiate – had persuaded eastern Dawi Mani on the Saoura and Zousfana to reach accommodations with the French; their vital interests were their need for access to the date-palms of the Beni Goumi oases around Taghit, and for freedom to pasture their flocks along the Zousfana without interference. Meanwhile, those western groups whose focus was the Tafilalt and the trans-Atlas trade came under constant pressure to resist the French from the blindly warlike Ait Khabbash Berbers, whose wide-ranging bands threatened reprisals against the palm-groves and caravans of the unenthusiastic. Many tents from three of the five 'fifths' of the Dawi Mani were now concentrated north of the Hammada du Guir between the Zousfana and the Tafilalt, forming an uncomfortable buffer between the French in the east and the noisy advocates of holy war in the west.

It was not as if submitting to the French involved any intolerable subjection; the Dawi Mani were not the Lakota or Cheyenne – nobody wanted to drive them from their ancestral ranges on to some starving reservation. Those who resisted the French faced eventual defeat followed by heavy fines, but after submission they passed under only the lightest of yokes. Native Affairs officers installed in local oases expected to be kept informed about the movements of unsubmitted groups, but made few other demands. Tribal *caids* were accorded their proper dignity and their authority was unchallenged. All religious observances were scrupulously respected – indeed, the French made skilful diplomatic use of *murabtin* such as the holy men of Kenadsa, who were the traditional mediators among the tribes. The French Army offered protection – or at least, reprisals – against intertribal raiders, who did not cease to trouble the *caids* just because the French had arrived on the scene.

Among submitted tribes local feuding had to be kept within bounds, but the district officers were not naive enough to imagine they could stamp it out entirely. Their small troops of *moghaznis* exercised superficial police functions, but only slave-traders, outlaw killers and 'professional' raiders had much to fear from them. Young bucks who hungered for action could always themselves enlist as *moghaznis* or (in the Far South) in the new Saharan Companies, updating their weaponry in the process and still enjoying some focused looting.[18] The important rhythms of life – herding, farming, bartering in the oases, and the occasional absolutely irresistible killing – went on undisturbed; the French did not interfere with the seasonal movements of flocks, even all the way to the Tafilalt if needs be (since these were a conduit for useful intelligence). Finally, there was the attraction of the new trading opportunities across the Algerian border; these were already lucrative enough to present competition to the Tafilalt–Fes axis, to the fury of the caravan-masters and protection-gangs of the western Dawi Mani and Ait Khabbash respectively. There were strong pragmatic arguments for accepting the client relationship offered by this powerful new migrating tribe; but while pragmatism might have the last word, in a warrior culture it could not have the first. For those not yet in immediate contact with the French, both religion and honour demanded war.

MAKING SENSE OF THE FIGHTING on the Algerian/Moroccan border required French politicians, for their part, to grasp the distinction between the small raiding party or *djich*, whose activities were the constant background music of frontier life, and the large war party or *harka*, whose more complex orchestration demanded skills and ambitions only rarely encountered. The Algerian and French colonialist press always tended to misinterpret the ambient folk music of the *djich* as the prelude to a full-blown symphonic *harka*.

As typified by Captain Normand's action west of Ksar el Azoudj on 29

March 1903, the workaday thefts and murders by parties of anything between a dozen and several score tribesmen were difficult to counter. The marauders employed the ancient skills of the hunt: knowledge of terrain, speed of movement, observation to judge the balance of threat and opportunity; the choice of approach, the stealthy creep forward, the timing of the decisive rush, a quick withdrawal. These were the short-term tactics of hot blood but relative weakness – of small, mobile groups operating at a distance from any base that had to be protected. They travelled light, each man carrying what little he needed for a few days, and even if successful they had to retreat to their home range rapidly before pursuit and retaliation could be mounted. The booty that justified the risk of raiding should ideally be easily portable – firearms, and horses that could run with the raiders; but the most lucrative prizes were flocks or camels, and since these were a dangerously slow encumbrance, rustling demanded careful reconnaissance and planning. If employed as Colonel de Négrier had intended, the *compagnie montée* had many of the same advantages as the Arab *djich* but with greatly superior firepower.

The motivation of the *djich* was economic and recreational; the *harka* was political, and ostensibly religious, since only a charismatic *marabout* had the prestige to persuade the leaders of mutually suspicious clans to assemble a single force. A small army several thousands strong, the *harka* was encumbered by tents, families and flocks, since these could not be left unguarded against rival tribes when the fighting men went to war. These moved much more slowly than simple raiders, and gave the warriors a vulnerable 'rear base' to protect. With a collective leadership, the *harka* was also infinitely harder to control than a raiding party. Tribal peoples would not stay in the field for long, and large numbers could not be held together beyond the achievement (or frustration) of immediate and limited goals. In the face of either success or failure a large force soon dispersed into separate groups obedient only to their immediate leaders – either drifting off with the loot of victory, or cutting their losses and running from defeat. The individual tent-groups were often weak in numbers, so no contingent could afford the heavy casualties of sustained fighting. The *harka* represented a hot-blooded but shortlived spasm, releasing pressure that had built up over time.

A major French mixed-arms column had to employ the cold-blooded tactics of relative strength in pursuit of long-term goals. With a necessarily strong infantry element, it could not cover distances fast; it had to be provided with food and water collectively, and its supply train was a further drag on its mobility – in that, it resembled the Arab *harka*. Its ponderous slowness robbed it of initiative, but if it was attacked, its concentrated rifle and artillery firepower made it more or less invulnerable. (Though if badly led and foolishly deployed, with its units separated in difficult terrain, they were still vulnerable to piecemeal ambush – witness Captain Pein's defeat at Charouine on 3 March 1901 – see p.284.) If the French column's objective was a walled village, this was indefensible against bombardment followed by infantry assault, and usually surrendered after the first few shells had been fired. With local resources then added to its supply train, the column could often occupy its objectives for weeks, sending out its own raiding parties until the leaders of nearby tribes were forced to come in and submit. Even if no fixed base was assaulted, the column's screen of cavalry could snatch up the flocks and herds from around the nomad camps, and its unhurried rhythm of march allowed it to drive them home. Since they were the principal economic resource of the tribes, their loss was as damaging as the sacking of a town would have been in Europe.

NEWS OF THE FRENCH COLUMNS to Figuig and Béchar and of Captain de Susbielle's *razzia* in June 1903 caused heightened alarm in the Tafilalt. As the French had long feared, angry tribesmen finally coalesced around a temporary war-leader to mount a *harka*; the required religious bridge over tribal differences was provided by Moulay Mustafa el Hanafi, head of a sharifian family from the Tizimi district of the Tafilalt, and by his warrior son Ba Sidi.

The clearing-house for all intelligence information on the southern frontier was Captain de Susbielle's base at Taghit, and from early July his agents began reporting a major convergence of warriors – not in the Tafilalt, but around the more central oasis of Boudenib on the upper Guir (see Map 11). Then, about a week into August, the daily flow of information into Taghit suddenly stopped; for four days no riders came in from the Guir, Kenadsa or Béchar, and Susbielle wondered if the *harka* had already moved far enough south to occupy the last two. He needed up-to-date information if his reports were to prompt timely troop movements, and on 14 August he sent some of his *moghaznis* riding north to join a Legion reconnaissance from El Morra across the hills towards Béchar, by Lieutenant Pointurier, with half of 22nd (Mounted) Company/2nd RE.[19]

The mule platoons made a difficult night march over the rocky hills, and although daybreak on the 15th allowed Pointurier to study Béchar oasis with his binoculars, he could not make out much inside the great *palmerie* of 90,000 trees. The Ouled Jarir ruled this place, but centuries of tribal warfare had left all but one of the villages ruined, and the hundred or so inhabited houses were enclosed inside a *kasbah*. Pointurier led his légionnaires quietly down to the concealing edge of the palm-groves and sent out his native scouts. At 8am one slipped back from the village with the news that a *harka* had left two days previously, and was heading south for Taghit itself. Ba Sidi el Hanifi was leading Ait Khabbash, Ouled Jarir, Dawi Mani, Shaamba and smaller contingents totalling about 4,500 well-armed warriors, with at least 3,000 of their families; he had taken with him the leading villagers from Béchar to prevent them warning the French, and had left guards. The *harka* had plentiful food and ammunition, but more warriors on foot than horse- and camel-riders.[20]

Pointurier had to make some fast calculations. He sent a courier to Taghit to warn Susbielle, and allowed the *moghaznis* to follow (their families were there); then, worried for the sergeant and 20 men he had left to guard his own base camp at El Morra, he led his légionnaires back there in a forced march over the *djebel*, arriving early on 16 August. Lamps were flashing and telegraph wires humming up and down the Zousfana valley, and on the 17th Pointurier received orders to take his half-company down to reinforce Susbielle's garrison at Taghit. The *harka* would probably arrive there that same day, but Pointurier hoped to reach the fort by dawn on the 18th.[21]

THE OASIS OF TAGHIT was in effect an inhabited pass, dominated by heights on both sides: the first 300-foot dunes of the Sand-Sea towered on the east, and a broken cliff of black rock rose 350 feet on the west. The old fortified village straggled up from the sand on to the ledges and terraces of this western cliff, overlooking the flowing Zousfana in its long corridor of palm-groves and vegetable gardens.

The engineers escorted here by Major Brundsaux three years previously had had to forsake the usual rectangular plan, building the fort in an angular teardrop shape close above the village, along a sloping shelf about 150 feet up the escarpment. A steep track led from the fort up to the lip of the summit, where a rudimentary drystone redoubt sheltered the signallers' lamp and telescope. Another track, down towards a spring on the valley floor, had been walled and roofed over to make a sort of raised 150-yard tunnel for water parties. The garrison in August 1903 was the usual mix of *turcos* and *joyeux* – Captain Guibert's 7th Company from II/2nd RTA, and half of Captain Mariande's 3rd Company, 1st Bat d'Af, totalling perhaps 300 soldiers – plus about 60 of Susbielle's *moghaznis* led by Lieutenant de Ganay. The fort also mounted two 80mm mountain guns.[22]

Warned by Pointurier's rider during the night of 15/16 August, Susbielle made what preparations he could. His main achievement since his arrival the previous year had been establishing peaceful relations with Dawi Mani and other clans around this whole Beni Goumi group of oases. The route of the *harka* through the southern passes of the Djebel Béchar would bring them hooking up to approach Taghit from the south, and directly in their path lay the *ksars* of Bakhti and Barrebi. On the 16th, Susbielle sent out several mounted patrols, both to watch for the *harka* and to warn anyone they could reach to concentrate in the two most defensible villages – Taghit itself, and Barrebi, just over 2 miles to its south (see Map 12).

At dawn on 17 August the *harka* was sighted about 4 miles to the south. The straggling army reached the Zousfana, pillaged evacuated villages and burned Bakhti, then turned north for Barrebi. Stoutly defended by Dawi Mani and the villagers themselves, the *ksar* beat off two Ait Khabbash attacks during the morning of the 17th. When his scouts reported this at about noon, Susbielle sent his deputy Ganay out with a fighting patrol of *moghaznis* to lure the enemy closer, backed by the rifles of Warrant Officer Gabaig with a platoon of Algerian Skirmishers; though outnumbered by more than ten to one, Susbielle had no intention of letting the warriors dictate the pace of events. A brisk engagement took place in the palm-groves some 1,500 yards south of Taghit; this drew groups of tribesmen together, providing a target for shrapnel shells from the fort. The patrol and platoon then fell back in good order, the cost being only one dead and four wounded, although one of the latter was Gabaig (who died two days later). That evening the *harka* settled down in sprawling camps between Bakhti and Barrebi; there was another failed attack on the latter village during the night, but Taghit was undisturbed.

Early on the morning of 18 August, Lieutenant Pointurier and his 90-odd légionnaires of 22nd (Mounted) Company arrived from the north and entered the fort, bringing the garrison up to about 450 rifles. At mid-morning, Susbielle repeated his probing attack to distract the enemy from Barrebi; this time Captain Mariande led out his half-company of pimps and pick-pockets, and another fight developed among the gardens and irrigation ditches crowded in the shadow of the palms. As more tribesmen were attracted by the firing the gunners sent air-burst shells 500 yards ahead of Mariande's *joyeux*. When the odds got too doubtful, the French fell back by fire and movement, and as they approached the fort Ganay led his *moghaznis* out again to cover their arrival, accompanied this time by some villagers and Dawi Mani – an encouraging sign. When the leading tribesmen reached Taghit, villagers manning the walls of the *ksar* exchanged shots with them for about an hour before the attackers retreated under shellfire. That day's fighting cost the French three killed and two wounded.

Susbielle had been told that Ba Sidi and other chiefs were encamped just over a mile to the south-east on the edge of the sand dunes, and on the night of 18/19 August he sent out a raid to try to slip between the scattered groups of tents in that direction. At 3.30am on the 19th, Captain Guibert set out with 100 of his Skirmishers and 40 *moghaznis*, backed by a platoon of the 22nd (Mounted) to cover their eventual withdrawal. Pointurier's légionnaires had been grumbling at being held back the previous day, but Susbielle had wanted them intact as his reserve in case his sortie came to grief. The intelligence about Ba Sidi's whereabouts proved to be mistaken, but at first light the Skirmishers confronted groups of enemy on foot and horseback who were drifting towards the fort. The soldiers opened fire at 600 yards, and continued to inflict casualties until the advancing tribesmen's growing numbers prompted Guibert to begin the usual orderly withdrawal by echelons, covered by the mountain guns and, for the last few hundred yards, by the rifles of the Legion platoon.

The *harka* flowed north on their heels, and divided; most continued to advance up the river towards the village and fort on the rocky western slope, but 300–400 others swung right into the edge of the Erg and on to the great sand-dune facing and overlooking the walls (Susbielle did not have enough men to sustain an outpost in such a vulnerable position). Tribesmen also occupied several buildings below the fort, and tried to climb the walls of the *ksar*, but by about 8.30am they had been driven back to the cover of the palm trees by fire from the villagers, the fort, and the signallers' perch on the summit. In retrospect, this would prove to be the *harka's* high tidemark; however, the Ouled Jarir and Shaamba on the great dune – a significant number of them armed with Lebels – opened a steady fire into the fort which persisted until nightfall. It was easy enough for the soldiers to find cover, but many of their horses and mules were killed, and the task of fetching water became perilous for men emerging from the tunnel down in the pass.

The garrison's best marksmen were placed on the battlements to deny the snipers the leisure to observe and aim carefully – against the shining sand their dark figures stood out clearly.

The 19th cost Susbielle only one dead and three wounded, but the afternoon brought disturbing news: the Dawi Mani holding Barrebi were said to have reached peace terms with their attackers. This made him nervous about the warriors holding the *ksar* of Taghit, and he moved a platoon of Guibert's Skirmishers into the village as insurance. When the bugler blew 'Reveille' on the morning of 20 August a storm of firing greeted him from the top of the great dune. Soon afterwards a troop of riders were seen galloping in from the west; Lieutenant de Lachaux, with 40 of his *moghaznis* from Beni Abbès, reached the fort at a cost of two men hit by snipers on the dune. However, by about 8.30am the sand hill seemed to be unoccupied; a foot patrol of *moghaznis* confirmed that it had been abandoned, and a squad from the Bat d'Af were sent across to take position there. At noon a mounted patrol probing towards Barrebi found that the *harka* was striking its camps. Without any discernible climax, and at a cost of just 9 French killed and 21 wounded, the four-day battle of Taghit was over.[23]

WHILE THE NUMBERS INVOLVED on both sides had been very roughly comparable with those at the siege of Tuyen Quang, in every other respect the two actions could not have been less similar (most obviously, in that Taghit was not actually besieged). The fort's site on its high ledge was probably its least important advantage – potentially, it was still overlooked from two sides, and it was vulnerable to close approach by night.[24] At Tuyen Quang the defenders had faced a disciplined army; Ba Sidi el Hanafi was not even the unquestioned leader of a large tribal following, only the temporary 'chairman' of a disparate group of such chiefs, whose squabbling never ceased. (The Ait Khabbash were intent upon sacking the village of Barrebi; the Dawi Mani contingent preferred to negotiate with their fellow tribesmen inside.) Such *murabtin* as Ba Sidi, standing outside the tangle of everyday feuds and pacts, were essential to any pan-tribal enterprise, but – in Professor Dunn's words – they 'were good standard-bearers but bad generals ... society normally had no need for specialists of that sort'.[25] Nevertheless, Ba Sidi apparently enjoyed a warrior reputation beyond his charisma as a preacher, and it may seem surprising that there is no sign of his exercising any military control over the *harka* once he had brought it to the battlefield.

Such a European concept was simply foreign to tribal culture. It is clear that there was no coordinated plan of attack, and that even those groups not preoccupied with looting wandered in and out of combat when and where they chose – most strikingly, they did not even prevent French reinforcements from getting in. They were apparently surprised by Susbielle's aggressive tactics on 17 August, but after that first sortie they seem to have taken no steps to counter its repetition. It would not have taken tactical genius to infiltrate the palm-groves nearer the fort by night and to prepare a reception for future sorties, and in general the tribesmen's apparent failure to exploit the cover of darkness is puzzling. Above all, however, Taghit exposes the absurdity of the fictional 'Beau Geste fort' scenario. Unlike Madani el Glaoui, Ba Sidi did not have a Krupp field gun. Without artillery to breach the walls, even thousands of tribesmen could not hope to storm a properly built fort held by a couple of hundred determined riflemen with water and plentiful ammunition, and they soon gave up any such attempts once casualties began to mount. (The Taghit garrison expended no fewer than 45,000 rounds of rifle ammunition and 103 shrapnel shells.)

Prisoners taken in the week after Taghit said that some 400 warriors had been killed outright and a larger number wounded. On the morning of 21 August, a patrol saw large groups about 10 miles to the north-west, straggling through the passes of the southern Djebel Béchar on their way back to Béchar and the Tafilalt. However, they also reported the tracks of perhaps 300 camel-riders – probably Shaamba bedouin – leading off in the other direction, eastwards into the dunes of the Erg. The question of whether this force would swing north or south, and with what intentions, would be answered two weeks later.[26]

NEWS OF THE ATTACK ON TAGHIT had caused a convoy heading south for Beni Abbès to be held at Djenan ed Dar. On 24 August word came of the defeat and dispersal of the *harka*; the Legion's Lieutenant-Colonel Cussac was by then at Taghit, and that day he received orders from Colonel d'Eu (interim commander of Ain Sefra Subdivision, *vice* the sick General Prot) to send 2nd Half-Company, 22nd (Mounted)/2nd RE back up to its camp at El Morra. Meanwhile Major Bichemin, commanding the delayed convoy at Djenan ed Dar, was ordered to start it again on 25 August; the inadequacy of the wells would oblige it to travel in three successive groups. Group 1 left El Morra on 31 August, escorted by Captain Bonnelet's whole 18th (Mounted) Company/1er RE and two troops from 1st Spahis. Group 2 – the smallest – would leave before dawn on 2 September, escorted by the légionnaires of Captain Vauchez's half-company of 22nd (Mounted) and a single troop of Spahis. Bichemin himself, with two *turco* companies of 2nd RTA and another Spahi troop, would escort Group 3 out of El Morra at 6pm the same evening. From Taghit, Cussac had sent word to Bichemin of the unaccounted-for camel-riders from the *harka* who had made off into the Sand-Sea after the attack on the fort. Bonnelet's Group 1 marched out as planned, and reached Taghit without incident.[27]

Captain Vauchez's half-company turned in at El Morra at 8pm on the evening of 1 September. Their sleep was disturbed from about midnight by the bellowing of groups of privately owned camels being loaded – their owners had joined the convoy for security but accepted no march-discipline, and tended to straggle out of camp hours before the escort. Vauchez roused his men with blasts of his whistle at 2am, and they got on the march in pitch darkness at 3.45am on 2 September. They numbered 2 officers, 111 NCOs and légionnaires with 64 mules, Sergeant Damiens with 20 men from V/1st Spahis, and 2 *moghazni* 'guides' (only one of whom had ever made this journey before, several months previously). Vauchez's deputy was the Dane, Lieutenant Selchauhansen, who had transferred from Bonnelet's 18th (Mounted) to fill a vacancy since the action at Figuig at the end of May.

The mule-riders rode south in two parallel lines of pairs, Selchauhansen's 3rd Platoon on the left and 4th under Vauchez on the right, each pair of riders with their two mule-mates marching on their outside flank; the whole column thus took up only about 100 yards on the trail. Vauchez and Selchauhansen rode their horses, Sergeant-Major Tissier and Quartermaster-Sergeant Tisserand had mules to themselves, and there were two led pack-mules with water and ammunition. Pickets each of a few Spahis rode ahead and on the flanks, about 500–800 yards out depending on the ground, and brought up the rear. In the darkness, when ears were more useful than eyes, the men marched in strict silence and were forbidden to smoke. In the early light at 6am they made a half-hour halt for coffee, but even so, before long they began passing strings of the privately owned camels dawdling along over about 3 miles of the track, and eventually overtook them all to take their place at the head of the convoy.[28]

By 9.30am, with the sun well up, the men had taken off their greatcoats and were marching in their white fatigues and sun helmets. They had left the well at El Moungar a mile or two behind them when Captain Vauchez decided to call another half-hour halt so that his légionnaires could eat their haversack rations while the leading camels caught up again – since the drivers let them browse on the march, the convoy was stretching and contracting. The half-company stopped in a very slight dip in the middle of a shallow corridor of low ground, perhaps half a mile wide; the good-tempered mules were roughly field-tethered in groups, rifles were stacked in tripods, and the platoons sat down to eat, south of the mule-lines. Behind the légionnaires, spread over perhaps a thousand yards of the track from the north, groups of camels were slowly catching up, eventually followed by the five Spahis who provided the rearguard (see Map 14). Along their right flank, to the west, was a rising series of stony greyish-yellow hillocks in a band several hundred yards wide and up to 60 feet high; beyond these in the middle distance ran the line of the Djebel Béchar escarpment, in slopes of dull black scree rising steeply to cliffs. Back behind their right shoulders the escort had passed a little straggle of stunted, thorny trees in a crease in the edge of the hummocks. On their left the stony ground seemed flat and featureless, studded every few yards with tufts of coarse weeds, until it rose gently into a fringe of small white sand dunes; off beyond these lay the mezmerizing progression of giant golden dunes on the edge of the Sand-Sea.

For some reason, Captain Vauchez had chosen to rest his men almost exactly on the spot where, just over three years previously, his regiment's mounted company under Captain Sérant had been attacked while coming up from Zafrani.

THE SKETCH MAP made in September 1903 by Sub-lieutenant Holtz of 2nd Spahis shows the site of Sérant's action in July 1900 as about 300 yards north of Vauchez's halt, and QM-Sergeant Tisserand's report explicitly supports this; so, minutes before halting, Vauchez's men must have passed Sérant's little battlefield within easy sight on a hillock to their right. With a practical limit of no more than two years' continuous service in the mounted companies, there would have been no veterans of Sérant's unit in the ranks that day. Still, it seems unlikely that in such an arid climate the bulky mule-skulls could have disappeared entirely, nor have been dragged far by the little fox-sized desert jackals. It is tempting to wonder whether any of the légionnaires sitting down to open their tins of sardines commented on them.

Vauchez had been with the Legion in Algeria at the beginning of August 1900 when Sérant's action was the talk of every dinner table; that month he may have been distracted by preparing for his imminent posting to Tonkin, but he had been back in the Sud-Oranais since early in 1902, absorbing the common gossip of the frontier soldiers. Marie Louis Joseph Vauchez was far from being a dullard; he was an ambitious 37-year-old former ranker from the Line infantry, with the busy energy sometimes seen in short men (he was only 5 foot 4 inches tall). His service reports describe him as capable, studious, and a man who listened to advice, but also as one who needed reining in as much as stimulation. He is described as a stickler for regulations, sober and rather short-tempered, which seems plausible for a man in a hurry to make his way up the ranks.[29] In Tonkin he had been recommended for early promotion to major, and although this had been judged premature he was clearly regarded as an officer with a future. However, during his time in the Sud-Oranais he had not learned any respect for the tribes.

In late March 1903 he and half his 22nd (Mounted) had accompanied Captain de Susbielle on a 24-hour reconnaissance west across the Djebel Béchar. Their orders from Ain Sefra had been to avoid incidents if possible, but French officers always interpreted such instructions robustly, and Susbielle's character will already be clear. When they were seen emerging from a pass facing the *kasbah* of Béchar, three parties of Ouled Jarir and villagers totalling about 150 armed men had emerged with a green banner and advanced on them; one party had swung around the flank to cut them off from the pass and had opened an ineffective fire. Three Lebel volleys at long range had been enough to send them all back to the palm-grove, and the column had then ridden disdainfully past the walls of the *kasbah*. Vauchez's Corporal Zoli later told the journalist Isabelle Eberhardt that a few days before El Moungar, the captain had joked that 'he could lead them all the way to the Tafilalt in his shirtsleeves'. When he halted his légionnaires south of El Moungar on 2 September, Vauchez did not send out any sentries.[30]

THE VAST LITERATURE on the battle of Waterloo includes apparently baffling accounts of infantry units being surprised by cavalry before they had time to form a defensive square. At first sight the terrain between the armies seems to be an almost featureless stretch of fields, but walk a couple of hundred yards south from Wellington's line towards Napoleon's and the significance of even gentle folds in the ground suddenly becomes striking. At last you can understand how a whole regiment of Cuirassiers seemed to 'rise up out of the ground', to ride straight over a battalion of Hanoverian redcoats still deployed in line. Compared with Belgian cropland, the visual trickery of the Moroccan desert is multiplied to an extraordinary degree, and it, too, must be walked if it is to be understood.

What you see in this subtly rolling terrain of dust and stones is a series of superimposed horizontal folds, like receding ripples. Over a few miles the colours of the ground can vary in a series of gradations – from yellow-grey to charcoal, to rust-brown, then pink, and back to tawny – and the surface textures may change from fine grit, through gravel, to fist-size stones on the patches of true *hammada*. But within those stretches where the colours are constant, the monotonous swells and dips rolling gently away from you give the eye no more to catch hold of than the surface of a quiet sea. The distances and the relative heights between particular patches of ground are quite remarkably deceptive. When you look at terrain like this under the noonday sun it seems that even a desert mouse skittering across it would be seen immediately – and then the dark shape of a man seems to rise up out of the ground a couple of hundred yards ahead of you like the dead awakening, shockingly close.

If you could look down on the scene from above at dawn or in late afternoon, when the light comes low and flat, then a whole jigsaw puzzle of light and shadow would be revealed; in the French term, the terrain is surprisingly *mouvementé*. The shadows are the 'dead ground' – a soldier's hiding places and corridors for movement. The bright slopes and flats between the shadows are his obstacles, and the places where he may get himself killed. At El Moungar the sun was well up the sky; but the point is not the light – the point is that the dead ground itself does not disappear along with the morning shadows. The several hundred Shaamba waiting for Captain Vauchez's half-company that day had understood its uses since they had been little boys searching for strayed goats under the threat of a whipping.[31]

THERE WAS A SLIGHT GULLEY to the east of the spot where Vauchez had halted, between him and the small white dunes. It would have been literally invisible from ground level, and the cavalry pickets cannot have checked that flank; it may be significant that they were not from the veteran 2nd Spahis but from the 1st, newly arrived on the Oranais frontier from the long-peaceful Algiers province. It was in this curving gulley and spread among the white dunes to the north of it that the nomads who had headed into the Sand-Sea after Taghit now lay concealed. The tribesmen had hidden their camels among the dunes and crept forward to wait patiently under cover for the convoy to arrive, and they must surely have grinned like wolves when they saw the escort actually halt in the middle of their chosen ambush site. Now the white-clad soldiers were sitting bunched and stationary little more than a hundred yards in front of their rifle sights, while the unsuspecting camel-train came lumbering up from the right.[32]

It was at about 9.40am, when the leading string of camels had almost reached the soldiers and others were passing the thorn-trees a little way north-west, that shots suddenly rang out from the low dunes to the east. Immediately afterwards, as the légionnaires were stumbling to their feet and running for their stacked rifles, the tribesmen in the gulley opened a heavy fire, which struck the men of Lieutenant Selchauhansen's 3rd Platoon on the near flank of the escort. As he got them into a firing line facing east, some of the Shaamba burst out of the gulley and ran across the open ground towards his left flank, intent on cutting the escort off from the leading camels; other tribesmen rushed out of the dunes further north and made directly for the camel train (see Map 14).

Under fire from enemy both facing him and hooking fast around his left flank, Selchauhansen ordered his two squads into a shallow 'V' facing both east and north. He stood behind the angle to direct their firing, but almost at once a bullet hit him in the side of the chest and he fell; when men tried to carry him to the rear he shouted at them to leave him. Captain Vauchez took 4th Platoon north behind the 3rd to form a line on their left facing back up the track, protecting the mules; he then came under heavy fire from that direction too, from up to 100 Shaamba who had charged out of the dunes and across the track, and were now in good cover around the little group of trees to the north-west. Vauchez reacted by ordering 4th Platoon to attack them, and – whether ordered or not – the left-hand squad of 3rd Platoon also went forward on the 4th's right flank, led from each end of their line by Corporal Cachès and QM-Corporal de Montès.

The decision to react to the threat by immediate counter-attack was in the Legion tradition, but it was a serious miscalculation. As the légionnaires charged, their ranks were shockingly thinned by a hail of bullets; they were soon halted and pinned down, returning fire as best they could from the notional cover of knee-high tufts of grass. Captain Vauchez himself was among those cut down almost at once, shot in the stomach, and Sergeant-Major Tissier spun and dropped with a smashed thigh. At various moments during the fighting in the open, most of the NCOs became casualties, but in the confusion the sequence is unclear. Sergeant Dannert was described groping at a belly wound through his blue sash as if trying to pluck out the bullet with his bloody fingers; Corporals Terrasson and Gierké were killed, Sergeants Perré-Dessus and Van der Borght and QM-Corporal de Montès wounded. While some tribesmen continued the fireflight on the flats and from the hillocks to the soldiers' north-west, others grabbed the leading strings of camels and urged them sideways across the track, masking more warriors who crouched and fired between them and used their cover to get across into the hillocks to the west.

Meanwhile, from the eastern flank of the halting-place, the survivors of the right-hand half of 3rd Platoon – who had lost both their sergeants – fell back under such leadership as the corporals could provide towards the higher ground to the south-west, beyond the track; they carried Selchauhansen and at least some others of their wounded, but QM-Sergeant Tisserand describes the movement as 'pell-mell', and the mule-line was abandoned. Panting and shaking, these soldiers threw themselves down into firing positions on one of the bald hillocks and in a gulley beside it. What part the Spahis played is obscure, but most of the troopers present seem to have run for the high ground before the légionnaires.

As part of the little headquarters group, Tisserand had been with Vauchez, and he was now seconding the wounded Sergeant-Major Tissier in directing the fire of 4th Platoon and the left-hand half of the 3rd. They were isolated on indefensible ground, with their right and rear wide open, and Shaamba advancing through the hillocks on their left front to cut them off on that flank too. They were all dead men unless they could get to the higher ground, and somebody gave the order. The wooden language of Tisserand's report does not address the fear and confusion of a hasty retreat in the open, under heavy fire from half-seen enemies in three directions – a retreat that must have threatened to turn into panic flight at any second. The account of an anonymous veteran published ten years later makes it clear that the movement was more like a *sauve qui peut* than a controlled 'withdrawal by echelons'.

Most of the NCOs were already down, and now Sergeant Charlier was also hit while trying to organize his squad. With bullets kicking up the dust all around and men falling, wide-eyed soldiers must have been twisting back and forth, straining to pick out some coherent order above the racket of rifle fire, men cursing, mules braying, camels bellowing and churning up the clouds of dust through which elusive figures were flitting and firing. When they finally understood where they were supposed to run, the légionnaires must have felt wounded men plucking at their legs, begging not to be abandoned; some were roughly hoisted on to their mates' shoulders, but those who could not immediately be distinguished from the already dead were left behind. So, in the end, were the plunging, unmanageable water and ammunition mules, despite the courageous efforts of Private May. (The abandoned casualties were not mutilated by the Shaamba, who contented themselves with riddling them with bullets – remarkable proof that they had ammunition to spare. One NCO's body would be found with five bullet wounds, two more through his pith helmet, and no fewer than five strikes on his rifle alone.)

THE ACTION NOW DEVELOPED around three separate hillocks above the west side of the track, aligned north to south over a distance of perhaps 500 yards; they will be called here the north, central and south mounds. To appreciate the danger faced by Vauchez's men it is important to understand that these were not dramatic, clean-cut heights like the *gara* defended by Captain de Castries' légionnaires at Chott Tigri twenty years before. In photographs, the centre mound rises like a gently sloped whaleback to perhaps 50 or 60 feet above the track, and since it seems to have uneven shoulders the perimeter to be defended cannot have been obviously apparent. Similarly, although the French use the word *ravines* to describe the low ground between the mounds, 'gulley' is really too dramatic – these were not sharp-edged trenches in the earth, but simply clearly defined dips.[33]

By the time QM-Sergeant Tisserand reached the high ground, about a dozen Spahis were holding the south mound, and the first refugees of 3rd Platoon the central mound and a dip north of it, under the leadership of the wounded QM-Corporal de Montès. The 4th Platoon and the rest of the 3rd arrived in two groups, the first a small party led by a corporal and carrying wounded, who joined the Spahis on the south mound. The bulk of the légionnaires, with the officers, the sergeant-major and other wounded, took cover in the dip between the central and south mounds. Vauchez had been boosted back on to his horse and was brought in propped up in the saddle by the wounded Corporal Liautard and Private Paris, while Private Brona carried the crippled Sergeant-Major Tissier on his back.

Throughout the next seven hours, movement and communication between the separated knots of men was difficult and dangerous; they were exposed on smooth slopes, in white clothing, and all were under fire – from the dunes and track to the east, from hillocks to the north and north-west, and increasingly from the broken ground to the west, where the Shaamba seemed determined to surround them and get up close. Lieutenant Selchauhansen was unconscious; Captain Vauchez and Sergeant-Major Tissier were both badly wounded, but both attempted to exercise command. This was hampered by their inability to see what was happening outside the dip where they were laid, by the difficulty of communication with the other groups, and (probably) by uncertainty as to who was actually in charge from moment to moment – Vauchez, too, was increasingly slipping in and out of consciousness. Tisserand's report does not give the timing of most events, and the account by an anonymous veteran contradicts Tisserand over the location of some incidents; however, the essential phases seem to have been as follows.

AT ABOUT 10.30AM, Vauchez sent two of the Spahis spurring off with a pencilled note to summon help from Captain de Susbielle at Taghit, 25 miles to the south. The two wounded 3rd Platoon corporals tried to reassemble their men on the central mound, but this was not fully achieved before both took second wounds, Cachès being killed by a bullet in the head. QM-Sergeant Tisserand took part of 4th Platoon up from the dip south of the central mound and occupied it, driving the nearest enemy back by fire. Some of 3rd Platoon then crossed to the north mound; the rest of 4th Platoon came up on to the central mound, where Tisserand found his field of fire to the north masked by 3rd Platoon. Some of the tribesmen were busy gathering up the camel train – a couple of strings were led off southwards – but this did not distract the rest, who kept up a hot fire from the north-west, east and south-east. Their attempts to gather up the company's mules and to reach the abandoned French casualties were partly frustrated by fire from the central mound.

At some point the 3rd Platoon men abandoned the north mound and regrouped on the central one, clearing Tisserand's view. The quartermaster-sergeant was now in effective command of the men who could still move around. He was one of those former French Line conscripts who had joined the Legion in the hopes of bettering himself; his rank argues a good education, and his handwriting is a meticulous copperplate, with large, flamboyant capital letters. A drawing shows a burly man in his early forties, a little thick in the jowls, with sharply receding greying hair and an old-fashioned dark moustache and 'imperial' goatee in the style of Napoleon III. It is a good-natured face, with noticeably humorous eyes under rather devilish eyebrows, but Tisserand had already taken a bullet across the head, so that day it would have been streaming with blood – nothing bleeds like a scalp wound. (Indeed, the white fatigues of all the wounded crowded in the low ground must have looked like butchers' aprons.)

As the morning wore on, Tisserand judged the most urgent threat to be from Shaamba advancing among the hillocks to his north-west. He left Corporal Zoli with a few légionnaires and Spahis to keep up the fire to the east, and led most of the other fit men to the north-west of the central mound, from where their steady firing checked the enemy. Tisserand may have advanced further, since the summary in the *Livre d'Or* calls this a 'turning movement'. However, at about 1pm a Spahi, Trooper Peroni (presumably a busted *colon* NCO), rode across on Captain Vauchez's horse carrying a message from Sergeant-Major Tissier. Tribesmen were closing in from the west, and Tissier ordered the quartermaster to fall back from the central mound to concentrate on the defence of the dip and the south mound.

Tisserand knew that the central height was too important to be abandoned, and at this point his otherwise clear report cannot be reconciled easily with his sketch-map. He says that he obeyed the order; but he left a squad under the wounded but still determined Corporal Zoli, with some Spahis, to keep up observation and fire from the central mound. It appears that Tisserand and most of the survivors subsequently regrouped some 150 yards south of Zoli's outpost, around the wounded in the dip and holding adjacent slopes of the central and south mounds; but this may not have been achieved before 1.30pm, when the sergeant-major's warning proved well-founded.

While Zoli's men on their vantage point were preoccupied by a threat from the east, other Shaamba rushed the position from the hillocks to the west and reached the end of the shallow gulley where the wounded lay (which was aligned roughly north-west to south-east). Hand-to-hand fighting took place at this point; Private Copel bayoneted a warrior grabbing for a casualty's rifle, but several soldiers were killed before the perimeter was restored by fire from the men up on the hillocks. Among the dead were Trooper Peroni and his Sergeant Damiens, and Sergeant-Major Tissier.

At the moment of Tissier's death, command devolved on QM-Sergeant Tisserand. He placed the fittest men on slopes of the central and south mounds, and those slightly wounded who could still fire lined the edges of the dip, with the worst cases lying under cover below them; the badly wounded Privates Ueber and Vandevalle cared for Vauchez, who was now semi-conscious and in great pain. The sun was brutal; the men's waterbottles were emptying fast, and since the mule with the reserve kegs had been lost, all the wounded were soon in great distress. Tisserand moved around, controlling a disciplined fire, until about 2pm, when he, too, was wounded a second time and was obliged to hand over command to Corporal Detz. Detz – one of only 2 unwounded corporals – was now the senior able-bodied man in a unit that had begun the day with 2 officers, 7 senior NCOs and 7 corporals; nearly two-thirds of Vauchez's men had become casualties, about 30 of them killed, and Detz had the responsibility for protecting almost 50 wounded with perhaps 30 fit men spread around quite a lengthy perimeter of uneven ground.

He seems to have borne it admirably, under enemy fire that did not slacken until about 4.30pm. At that point the Shaamba must have accepted that they would never get close enough to capture the rest of the company's tethered mules, so they began shooting them instead. All the camels had now been led away, and at about 5pm the shooting stopped. Detz sent a few men down to try to find water amidst the carnage, but they only brought back a few litres, which was divided among the wounded. At perhaps 5.30pm, riders were seen to the south. The battle had lasted nearly eight hours.[34]

THE TWO SPAHIS sent to bring help from Taghit probably did not arrive there before 1.30pm at the earliest. Lieutenant-Colonel Cussac did not wait until he could get his mule-infantry under way, but sent his horsemen north in succession from about 2.30pm; these were led by the Taghit *moghaznis*, followed soon afterwards by Captain de Susbielle with Dr Mazellier and two troops of IV/2nd Spahis under Sub-lieutenant Holtz.[35]

The *moghaznis* merely ensured that the Shaamba had left the immediate scene, and it was not until Susbielle arrived that the casualties received anything but the roughest first aid. Dr Mazellier was overwhelmed by his task: 49 wounded men lay in the baking dust of the gulley between the central and southern knolls, and Susbielle had to send riders south again to Zafrani simply to bring up more water. Tisserand's casualty return signed at Taghit on 5 September shows Captain Vauchez among the dead, but in fact both officers were still alive when the rescue party arrived.[36]

Vauchez had been shot through the right side of his stomach with a bullet that had exited through his right kidney. A second bullet had struck him behind the top of his right shoulder while he was lying prone, and had made a shallow tunnel down his back to exit 10 inches lower, without doing serious harm; he also had a superficial bullet-graze on the right of his neck. He had suffered badly from thirst and heat all day, and had lost a great deal of blood both internally and externally. Dr Mazellier kept him going through the night with injections of caffeine and ether, and with opium for the abdominal pain, but he vomited and restarted the bleeding several times. At 3am his pulse became fast and thready, and the worsening pain required two morphine injections; Mazellier detected the tense 'drum belly' caused by peritonitis, as sepsis rampaged through a stomach cavity infected by the bullet-torn bowel.[37]

At about midnight, Captain Pages' half-squadron of Spahis and Lieutenant Dubois' half of 18th (Mounted) Company/1st RE arrived from Taghit; Susbielle had already sent word back for reinforcements, since campfires could be seen away to the east in the Sand-Sea. In fact the next troops to arrive, at around 10.00am on 3 September, were Major Bichemin's Algerian Skirmishers trudging down from the north. These two companies had set off from El Morra at 6pm the previous evening, escorting the third section of the convoy, and had met 5 riders on foundering horses – Sergeant Ahmed ben Boukhaten and his Spahis of Vauchez's rearguard. When the battle broke out ahead of them these men had been engulfed by a chaos of civilian camels and drivers, and after exchanging a few shots with the most northerly Shaamba they had turned back for El Morra. Bichemin brought with him Dr de Lignerolles, who joined the exhausted Mazellier in making the most of their seriously inadequate medical supplies. At mid-morning on 3 September, Lieutenant-Colonel Cussac arrived from Taghit with some 300 Legion and Algerian mule-infantry.[38] The battlefield was searched for anything salvageable while the debris was dragged together and burnt; only 5 mules were found alive, and 25 dead. It was calculated that the Shaamba had also made off with 25 rifles and no less than 5,000 rounds of Lebel ammunition, together with more than 90 laden camels – booty worth a place in tribal legend.

The two doctors did their best to prepare the wounded for the ordeal of the trek to Taghit. They had few drugs and not nearly enough mule-litters – nobody had dreamt of a butcher's bill this long. The soldiers had to improvise stretchers, and since there was nothing in this desolation from which to cut 6-foot poles they must have used rifles and greatcoats. The doctors could do little but apply dressings to all wounds, and immobilize broken bones (large-calibre, unjacketed bullets striking long bones cause shattering up and down the shaft, and often compound fractures). External bleeding would have been stopped with direct pressure, and deep wounds would not have been stitched, since it had long been understood that they should heal from the inside outwards; but bullets carried infectious shreds of clothing into the body, and doctors of that day had no antiseptic techniques. No blood transfusions were possible, and neither was it then understood that exertion by 'walking wounded' (and, equally, being jolted around on mules) could cause internal bleeding that leads to shock.

Towards noon, Vauchez was placed on one of the *cacolets* ready for evacuation. He was conscious and lucid, and had been commending his soldiers for recognition when his face became livid and he lapsed into a coma, dying at about 12.30pm; his body would be carried back to Taghit. The relief force had gathered up the corpses of 34 légionnaires and 2 Spahis, and buried them in a mass grave at the foot of the bleak knolls they had defended. Before the convoy got under way at around 1.20pm, they piled rocks all over it to deter the jackals, and erected two wooden crosses. The column walked very slowly to spare the wounded, and only arrived at Taghit at 3am on 4 September. Captain Vauchez was buried there that evening, and a few hours later Christian Selchauhansen also died. When he was buried beside Vauchez the next day, it was with the Knight's Cross of the Legion of Honour which his old company commander, Captain Bonnelet, had taken from his own tunic.[39]

FOR THE WOUNDED SURVIVORS the ordeal was far from over, since the medical facilities at Taghit were rudimentary. The fort's tiny infirmary had never been designed to hold 50 patients, and the men had to be laid out on blankets over piles of dry grass on the hard floor of various storerooms. Conditions were far from aseptic, and the fort's medical officer, Dr Boulin, at first had inadequate supplies of every necessity. He was already exhausted by the Saharan summer, and was himself suffering from a distressing eye infection (caused by a jet of pus when he had been treating one of the wounded from the attacks of 17–20 August). Nevertheless, he did everything he could to help Mazellier and Lignerolles and the 2 medical orderlies of the garrison companies, and they were soon joined by 5 more orderlies sent down from Ain Sefra with supplies. The wounded would, in fact, take as much comfort from the care of an unmilitary figure who rode into the oasis soon after their arrival: a slight, bearded, nut-brown man wearing the Sacred Heart on a monk's habit of unbleached wool, with a long rosary at his belt. As soon as the news of El Moungar reached his missionary hermitage at

Beni Abbès, Father Charles de Foucauld had borrowed a horse from the post commander there and had ridden 75 miles across the desert to offer his help.

(In France, Foucauld would become one of the fixed points of Saharan legend; it is unclear if he ever made any converts, but the tribes seem to have honoured him as a holy man for his simplicity and devoted care. Once an aristocratic and dissolute subaltern of the Africa Light Horse, he had resigned his commission in 1882 at the age of 24; he was a gifted linguist, and in 1883–4 he made a long and perilous lone journey through Morocco disguised as a Jewish rabbi, gathering intelligence and observations with a concealed compass and sextant. During later desert wanderings the *sabreur-*turned-spy rediscovered his faith; he entered the Trappist order, before being ordained to the priesthood and returning to Algeria in 1901.)[40]

Foucauld stayed at Taghit for three weeks, devotedly caring for the légionnaires; Dr Boulin gave him some credit for the fact that of the 48 wounded, 10 of them serious cases, only one died – a remarkable outcome under those conditions. As the rest became stable and gained some strength, they would be sent north to convalesce in the hospital at Ain Sefra, the last arriving during November. On 18 September, Father de Foucauld rode to El Moungar to consecrate the mass grave, being met at the site by the surviving half-company of the 22nd (Mounted) from El Morra. Captain Mariande of 1st Bat d'Af escorted him, and took a photograph; there is something biblical in the image of the spare figure in his blowing white robe preaching beside the lonely grave, attended by a rough rank of trail-worn, unshaven soldiers holding their helmets. This was a period of rabid anti-clericalism in the War Ministry, but the Rue Dominique was a long way from El Moungar.[41]

The official verdict on the disaster was that the mixing of undisciplined private groups of camel-drivers in the convoy had been disruptive, that the escort for the second section had been too weak, and that the intervals between the sections had been too long, but that nevertheless Captain Vauchez was largely to blame. He had bunched his rifles at the head of the camel train instead of spreading them along the flanks; his rearguard of five troopers had been ridiculously small; and above all, his choice of halting place, coupled with his failure to send out sentries, had condemned his men to surprise attack.

THE AMBUSH AT EL MOUNGAR was not, of course, evidence of any growing threat, but a mere epilogue to the failure of the *harka* at Taghit two weeks previously. By the end of summer 1903 tribal resistance in the south-east had, in fact, more or less collapsed, and increasing numbers of Dawi Mani were making peace with the French all along the Zousfana. Sultan Abd el Aziz, entirely preoccupied by court intrigues and the challenge from El Rogi in the north-east, had effectively abdicated responsibility for the pacification of the frontier to the French. Although the 1902 accords still placed strict limits on their operational freedom, outrage over El Moungar provoked them to interpret these aggressively.

The virtual wiping out of a hundred-strong Legion unit resonated a good deal further than Ain Sefra, and caused acerbic correspondence at a high level. At Oran Division, General O'Connor tried to turn Lieutenant-Colonel Cussac and Major Bichemin into scapegoats, but neither 19th Army Corps nor the War Ministry agreed.[42] As early as 10 September, Governor-General Jonnart – then on leave in France – was expressing his views directly to the prime minister, and the head he really thought should roll was General O'Connor's (the snap of bullets past his pith helmet at Figuig still seemed to rankle with Jonnart). The governor-general argued that the divisional commander's paramount responsibility was for the logistic and operational problems of Ain Sefra Subdivision, yet command and control over that territory had been neglected. The subdivision commander and his deputy, General Prot and Lieutenant-Colonel Lane, were both seriously ill and requesting their return to France, and O'Connor was recommending confirmation of the interim commander, Colonel d'Eu. Jonnart argued that what Ain Sefra needed was the immediate appointment of an officer of energy and imagination, who should be given a broadly drawn remit. As it happened, he knew a man whom nature and experience seemed to have fashioned for just such a task.[43]

SOME WEEKS PREVIOUSLY the governor-general had attended a lunch given by Jules Charles-Roux, a former deputy for Marseille and a supporter of the colonial lobby, and one of his fellow guests had been Colonel Hubert Lyautey of the 14th Hussars. Jonnart spoke freely of the situation on the frontier, and pressed Lyautey for his opinions. While inhibited by his lack of experience of the Sud-Oranais, the colonel allowed himself to be persuaded to enthuse about the success of the 'Galliéni method' of pacification in Tonkin and Madagascar.

In the first week of September, during the public furore ignited by the first reports of El Moungar, Jonnart visited Avord camp to witness machine-gun trials in company with the War Minister. He took the opportunity to ask General André for Colonel Lyautey's appointment to Ain Sefra Subdivision, and the minister agreed. Lyautey was with his regiment on 4th Army Corps manoeuvres in the Sarthe when he received a telegram summoning him to report to the War Ministry without delay.[44]

11. The Lyautey Drill
1904–1907

The moral is that the telegraph is a dangerous machine,
and that the first act of every commander who is
operating [far] from home should be to cut the wires . . .
Major Hubert Lyautey, 1895[1]

GENERAL LOUIS ANDRÉ, who had become war minister in May 1900, was a genuinely able reformer, but he owed his appointment to his passionately Republican convictions. Not content with retiring a number of traditionalist generals, he planned a wholesale 'purification' of what he saw as malign conservative cliques within the 25,000-strong officer corps.

Simply by virtue of their background, many officers were emotionally attached to the old focuses of loyalty, and during depressing times they were naturally inclined to nostalgia. The idealistic patriotism of their youth had curdled for lack of an outlet; many of the young men who had entered St Cyr in the 1870s on a wave of enthusiasm for 'la Revanche' were now middle-aged captains, scraping to raise families on inadequate pay in stagnant provincial garrisons.[2] During the Dreyfus affair many had overreacted to the most strident attacks on the Army, and had come to believe that the nation as a whole no longer valued them.

This mood of defensive unhappiness was aggravated by the Army-baiting of the Combes administration (1902–1905), which used it to enforce its anti-clerical policies. The closing down of religious institutions caused demonstrations by the devout, and troops were ordered to ensure civil obedience – orders given in full knowledge of how distasteful the Army found them. These confrontations, painful for Catholic officers and bewildering for the conscripts, continued under Combes' successor Clemenceau, whose formal separation of Church and State in 1906 led in some cases to soldiers being ordered to force church doors in front of angry crowds. Simultaneously, at a time of financial recession, troops were being sent on to the streets to confront increasingly angry and confident labour unions. The Army hated these episodes, which often ended in bloodshed and were bound to summon up the ghosts of 1871; some officers flatly refused their orders and paid the price, and others resigned their commissions. The extreme Radicals were not merely insensitive to the soldiers' unease but delighted to force them to do the government's dirty work, which both damaged their morale and alienated them from public sympathy.[3]

Denied by French history the priceless gift of an apolitical army – England's blessed legacy since the 1690s – it had long been commonplace for successive regimes to keep themselves informed about the sympathies of individual officers, and under the Third Republic local officials made secret reports on those suspected of royalist or Catholic tendencies. When General André decided to extend and systematize this surveillance, his choice of means was tactless in the extreme, and played into the hands of conspiracy theorists: he chose to employ the network of Freemasons.[4] The 'craft' had many adherents on the Left (including Prime Minister Combes); now the widespread lodges of the Grand Orient rite were set to gathering local intelligence about the private attitudes of individual officers. Often the notes on their index cards – *fiches* – were brief and banal, but some were rather disturbingly intrusive. Of a battalion commander in the Legion's 2nd Foreign Regiment – clearly a good soldier, reacting sensibly to an ugly atmosphere – we read:

> Very able, not very sincere. He displays anti-clerical opinions, but he encourages his wife and children in Catholic worship – he seems to want a foot in both camps. He professes republican ideals, but very weakly, and he would like to see a military man as president of the Republic. Of above average intelligence, he is a brave soldier, good to his men and devoted to his duties. In a word, he is without deep convictions, and is capable of adopting whatever outward conduct best serves his views and his ambitions.[5]

While the involvement of the Grand Orient was not publicly revealed until '*l'affaire des fiches*' caused a scandal in October 1904, the fact that the ministry was seeking windows into men's souls was all too well known.[6] It was common knowledge that informers were reporting the private conversations of brother-officers, to the benefit of their own careers. In the British Army, the revelation of such behaviour would have been a matter for instant resignation from the service, if not for taking the proverbial revolver into the library (or, indeed, for flight to enlist in the Foreign Legion). In France, different standards applied, and some informers did not even request a transfer out of their regiments when rewarded with promotion. The consequences for morale can well be imagined.[7]

IN SUCH A DIVISIVE atmosphere, it is hardly surprising that the voluble Hubert Lyautey feared the worst when he received a direct summons from manoeuvres to report to the Rue Dominique. Despite his youthful flirtation with the Vatican (encouraged by a devout aunt), his letters give no hint of deep religious feeling; but he was a snobbish *haut-bourgeois* who enjoyed any opportunity for ceremonial display, and he and some of his like-minded officers had recently attended, in uniform, a service at Alençon cathedral to mark the death of Pope Leo XIII. Now his journey to Paris was passed in gloomy expectation of being handed his professional death-sentence. However, on his arrival at the railway terminus his mind was relieved, thanks to another characteristic failing of the French Army. His appointment to the Ain Sefra Subdivision with effect from 10 September was already being reported (and, thanks to Jonnart's contacts, welcomed) in the Paris press.[8]

Happy and confident, Lyautey proceeded to Algeria without delay. At Oran he was received coldly by General O'Connor, and fellow officers seemed more inclined to offer commiseration than congratulation. Ain Sefra had the reputation of a trap, where the commander risked being held responsible for a volatile situation while being denied the means to control it. However, these Jeremiahs had not enjoyed a ten-year masterclass in the Galliéni approach to colonial command, and neither did they appreciate that Lyautey's role was not simply to be the governor-general's new broom but his co-conspirator. As long as the Quai d'Orsay maintained its policy of trying to shore up and manipulate Abd el Aziz's regime while engaging in quiet diplomacy with Britain, Spain and Italy, Jonnart recognized that he must continue to pay lip service to the vague Franco-Moroccan con-dominium over the border, even though the Maghzan's gestures of cooperation there merely weakened it in the eyes of its own people. However, Jonnart's constituencies in Paris and Algiers looked to him to take active steps to prevent another El Moungar.

On 9 October 1903, at the age of 48 – when some of his classmates were still majors – Lyautey exchanged the five stripes of a full colonel for the two stars and gold képi leaves of a brigadier-general. While warning against shameless violations of the diplomatic frontier, Jonnart encouraged his new general to use his initiative. He had chosen his man partly because of Lyautey's proven ability to achieve success by intelligent subtlety rather than short-term military crudities, and his priority was to dissuade the tribes from further adventures that would threaten the peace and profits of the Sud-Oranais. Jonnart was covered in the National Assembly by the powerful bloc led by his ally Eugène Étienne, and he judged that Lyautey had the imagination to steer a middle course between the paralysed hesitancy of the Quai d'Orsay and the more primitive instincts of the Rue Dominique, while maintaining a working relationship with both ministries.

In order to give him the elbow-room he needed, Jonnart supported Lyautey's requests for unprecedented freedom to circumvent the chain of command – specifically, General O'Connor at Oran. After an initial whirlwind tour of his territory, Lyautey reported to the governor-general that his ability to do what was asked of him depended upon having complete local control over all troops and political officers, with the freedom to shape Native Affairs policy and to launch minor operations without Oran's prior approval. He would need privileged access to Jonnart himself and, when necessary, direct telegraph communications with the War Ministry over General O'Connor's head. (This was emphatically not because Lyautey wished to give even more remote echelons of command an invitation to interfere in his decisions, but because he wanted a direct channel, unmediated by the hostility of Oran, through which he could influence the reception of such explanations as he could not avoid giving.) Within the month, Jonnart had secured the War Ministry's agreement to these extraordinary demands.[9]

LYAUTEY'S BROAD PLAN was predictably based on his experience in Tonkin and Madagascar: the War Ministry understood only the stick, the Foreign Ministry only the carrot, but Galliéni had taught him how to wield both simultaneously. As he wrote to his friend Eugène de Vogüé, he never had any intention of approaching the frontier like a military hammer, but like a gimlet – 'the drill that penetrates slowly but irresistibly'.[10] He intended to pursue military and political initiatives in parallel, oasis by oasis, tribe by tribe, bending the *caids* to his will by a combination of implied threats and delivered benefits. He believed in 'showing force in order not to have to use it', but the threat could not be empty, and he would not hesitate to spill blood when he judged it to be necessary.

Previous commanders in the Sud-Oranais had planted small, isolated posts whose radius of control was limited to their immediate vicinity. Once they were installed, the demands of ensuring the resupply of their garrisons tended to distract Oran Division from a wider view of operations, and soaked up most of the available troops in essentially defensive roles – witness the pointless waste of Legion mounted companies as convoy escorts. (The new nickname for the Zousfana corridor was 'the boulevard of the Legion' – a term whose implication of repetitive traffic was a positive betrayal of Négrier's original vision for the mule companies as an offensive and rapid-reaction force.) General Lyautey stood in no danger of militarily serious defeats, but he had to regain the initiative. Historically, French generals in North Africa had done this by resorting to expensive, unwieldy and pointlessly destructive column-warfare, and there were plenty of atavistic voices in France and Algeria calling for the same old bludgeon now. In that sense, Lyautey was lucky to be cramped up against a diplomatic frontier that obviously inhibited such conventional responses. The campaign he had to win was largely one of perceptions, both French and Arab; in public-relations terms, his operations had to serve a convincing new 'narrative'. This was a task for which he was perhaps uniquely equipped, with his combination of colonial experience, practical intelligence, negotiating skills and instinctive sense of theatre. His brain could operate simultaneously on two levels – cold calculation, and a quite genuine empathy for tribal attitudes.

While refusing to fight on the tribes' terms, he must make French strength so evident that the chiefs would come to seek peace of their own accord. He had to employ light, mobile forces to deter marauders by swift but carefully focused violence, and his strike units would need a new series of advanced outposts. These must be located not simply as way-stations along established French routes, but with a longer-term strategic purpose, so that they could become as soon as possible – as in Madagascar – 'poles of attraction rather than repulsion', protecting the facilities that would demonstrate the advantages of the *pax Gallica* over the virtual anarchy of many previous years. Establishing such posts would inevitably involve some violation of the ambiguously defined diplomatic frontier, since creating 'oil patches' of stability, as a buffer for the Zousfana and the advancing railway, would require pushing the edge of military domination west of the Djebel Béchar. To an officer of Lyautey's temperament, such insubordination, winked at by the new chief on whom he had fixed his loyalty, was an acceptable – even an enjoyable – gamble.

Lyautey would maintain blandly polite contacts with the almost powerless Maghzan border officials shut up in Oujda and Figuig, while reporting
his illegal new forts to Paris simply as ephemeral 'bases for reconnaissance',
of carefully imprecise location – even bureaucrats could understand that a
main line of defence must be protected by forward outposts. As their continuing teamwork generated mutual trust, Jonnart was to further Lyautey's
education in the patient art of managing politicians and functionaries.
Echoing Galliéni exactly, he advised his protégé to present as if they were
purely provisional and local those of his decisions that would choke the
Quai d'Orsay if argued as precedents for general policy, and to turn the
provisional into the permanent by quiet stealth. A man as articulate as
Lyautey would have no difficulty in wording reports to give an appearance
of conformity with the windy abstractions that came down from both
the Foreign and War ministries. He was also an accomplished and tireless
networker, and in time he would fine-tune his skills in playing off not just
one ministry against the other, but one faction within a ministry against its
rivals.[11]

WHEN GENERAL LYAUTEY RODE into the dusty desert township of
Ain Sefra, his staff greeted him with a mountain of administrative paperwork
that had accumulated since General Prot and Lieutenant-Colonel Lane had
fallen sick, but he quickly disabused them of the notion that he was going
to be that sort of commander. Enthralled by his rediscovery, after twenty
years, of the colour and excitement of the Muslim world and the austere
glory of the desert, he spent his days in the saddle, and set a punishing pace
as he harvested local information from the Native Affairs officers and visited
every post in his territory.

He was delighted to be reunited with the Legion, and shortly after his
arrival he wrote to Vogüé that he had met the wounded from El Moungar
convalescing in Ain Sefra's military hospital. (El Moungar survivors had
to get accustomed to curious visitors; in September some of them were
also interviewed at Ain Sefra by the traveller and writer Isabelle Eberhardt,
correspondent of La Dépêche Algérienne, who in time would take her
place in Saharan legend beside Père de Foucauld.)[12] Whenever Lyautey
visited a Legion unit, he asked if anyone there had served with him
before, and he told Vogüé that a few veterans of Tonkin or Madagascar
often stepped forward with a smile and a reminder; a friendly face always
meant much to Lyautey, and even these leathery rankers represented a

reassuring continuity in this new arena.[13] Nevertheless, while the solid spine of Legion infantry was an insurance he was glad to have, they were too ponderous for his advanced operations. When he reviewed a nominally 'light column' at Beni Ounif, the infantry's towering backpacks and the large baggage train prompted him to ask pointedly what a heavy column looked like.

The burden loaded on to the French infantryman was not mere thought-lessness, but had a logical purpose: a historical inability to rely upon the commissariat to keep pace with marching troops meant that if they were to have any chance of sleeping dry, with a hot meal inside them, infantrymen had to carry on their backs everything they needed for several days and nights. In wilderness terrain, where wheeled transport was very often impractical and enough local pack-animals sometimes hard to provide, this argument had even greater force. In 1908 the British ex-colonel Reginald Rankin, covering General d'Amade's operations for the London *Times*, saw the value of this independence from a supply train, despite the burden of at least 60lbs that it placed on every man's shoulders. He was impressed by the marching-power and cheerfulness of the Legion and Algerian Skirmishers, and wrote that each soldier carried 'a complete house, with well-furnished kitchen, larder, cellar and woodshed'. At the end of the day each squad could pitch their tents, light a fire and cook their food independently of any service troops; Rankin praised this self-sufficiency in comparison with the lot of the British Tommy, who often had a long and uncertain wait for his tents and food to arrive at the night's halt.[14]

LYAUTEY'S FIRST TUG AT HIS LEAD came in November 1903, when he established a permanent French presence at Béchar (see Map 11). On 12 November, Major Pierron and the 3rd (Mounted) Company/1st RE emerged from the hills not at the *kasbah* itself, but on the plateau of Bahira Tagda about 1,000 yards north, which dominated the vital irrigation dam. The next day they started building rudimentary defences, and on the 14th the first convoy set off from Ben Zireg to bring them supplies for consolidation. The work of building was then taken over by the 2nd (Mounted), who would be the permanent garrison during the first year. Meanwhile 3rd (Mounted) spread out in all directions on reconnaissance patrols – mapping, locating wells and overnight camp-grounds and showing the flag; in seven months the company would march nearly 2,500 miles. To avoid alarming the Quai d'Orsay this 'reconnaissance base' was referred to not as Béchar but as Tagda (a name that appeared on no map), and by 29 November the governor-general was helpfully muddying the waters further by suggesting to the War Ministry that it should be christened 'Colomb', after a long-dead French general.

Thus, without a shot being fired, a post was created in what had been the border base of the Ouled Jarir. After the bombardment of Figuig, the most belligerent half of that tribe, the renowned Asasa camel-thieves, had moved westwards towards the Tafilalt; most of the Mufalha segment, whose date-groves at Béchar were now hostage to Lyautey, came in over the next few months to make terms. At the end of October 1904 the mule company were replaced with the foot-sloggers of Captain Clerc's 6th Company, II/2nd RE, who took over the building work and the static garrison. Since this fort (like several others) was not officially sanctioned by Oran Division, no materials or funding were provided, and Legion NCOs took pride in scrounging or creatively 'diverting' what was needed. Captains turned themselves into architects, the famously heterogeneous ranks of the légionnaires provided the skilled craftsmen and foremen, and defaulters did the heavy lifting.[15] (Still under the command of Major Pierron, the fort would finally be completed in October 1905, with a handsome dressed-stone gateway carved with the name 'Colomb Béchar' and the Legion's seven-flamed grenade.)[16]

In January 1904, the first mule-company patrol from Colomb Béchar reached the Abadla floodplain on the lower Oued Guir; that month the leaders of 1,250 Dawi Mani tents came in to the new fort, following the example of 300 who had already submitted at Taghit. The rains of 1904 promised the first good harvest in four years and, the Dawi Mani had to protect their grainfields. Only about 450 tents of their Ouled abu Anan 'fifth' now remained aloof around the Tafilalt, and even their leader sent a secret envoy to discuss peace in a circular way, while ostensibly maintaining his alliance with the dangerous Ait Khabbash. On 14 February, the 21st (Mounted) Company/2nd RE planted a post in a strategic pass at Forthassa Gharbia in the Djebel Doug, some 60 miles west of Ain Sefra, to control the gateway from the Chott Tigri.[17] Lyautey's shamelessly opportunistic attitude is clear from a letter he wrote to Jonnart on 13 January:

> I believe that one must see in the Franco-Moroccan accord, and in the fiction
> of a mixed police force, something very flexible and very broad that will
> permit us to cover ourselves every time we need to; to take action in places
> that would [otherwise] be inaccessible to us; to make use of agents who,

without it, would escape us. It is in this spirit that I ask to be authorized to apply it.[18]

THE KEY TO UNLOCK the diplomatic impasse with Britain was found in April 1904, when Foreign Minister Delcassé achieved the first triumph of his *entente* policy: a confidential Anglo-French agreement that, in simple terms, gave Britain unfettered freedom of action in Egypt in return for similar French rights in Morocco. From this date Britain, recognizing that Abd el Aziz's government was a hopeless partner, cashed in its Moroccan interests in pursuit of wider geopolitical prizes. It was agreed that Théophile Delcassé would be left to negotiate a parallel agreement with Spain that took account of the latter's historic coastal claims, and this would duly be signed in October 1904.[19]

The confidence born of his getting away with his advance to Béchar encouraged Lyautey to take a riskier gamble in the summer of 1904. His next objective was Ras el Ain, a strategic oasis on the high plains, nearly 150 miles north-west of Ain Sefra. This stepping stone towards the Moulouya, situated at the southern limit of the Tell, had specifically been named as Moroccan in the 1902 accords. As a centre and granary for the Beni Gil, this was an obvious place to initiate a new 'oil stain' by planting a post and marketplace.[20] Whether or not he actually believed in a serious threat from that shadowy Sitting Bull of the frontier, Lyautey raised the spectre of allegedly hostile movements by old Bou Amama when seeking approval for free-ranging operations that summer. He did not get it; the Foreign Ministry's man in Tangier, Georges Saint-René Taillandier, was closing a financial agreement with Fes that would give France virtual control over the Maghzan treasury, and he wanted no provocative sensations on the border. In June, Lyautey went ahead anyway, sending his chief-of-staff Major Paul Henrys to occupy Ras el Ain (or 'Berguent'); this was accomplished peacefully, and soon 600 tents of the Beni Gil were attracted there.[21] It soon appeared, however, that Ras el Ain might be an oasis too far.

Lyautey had few friends at Oran Division (now commanded by General Herson), and hostile stories planted in the Paris press coincided with protests from the Maghzan. At a cabinet meeting on 28 July a furious Delcassé declared that only a withdrawal from Ras el Ain could salvage his intricate negotiations with the sultan, and Prime Minister Combes sided with the Quai d'Orsay against the Rue Dominique. General André cabled Lyautey a direct order, to which he sent a fearless reply claiming that he had cleared the move with the Maghzan governor at Oujda (blithely ignoring that official's distinctly semi-detached relationship with Fes). With passionate conviction, he argued his experience that what newly occupied native communities demanded above all else was that once the French arrived, they should stay, so that the locals could adjust with confidence to the new situation. He claimed that to abandon 'Berguent' would expose it to savage reprisals, undo months of patient political work, and destroy not only his own prestige among the *caids* but the credibility of any future French promises. When Paris repeated the order, he asked to be relieved of his command rather than be forced to break his personal word to the Arab chiefs.

There is a type of personality that cannot resist over-dramatizing the expression of beliefs that are sincerely held, whether for calculated effect or simply for the love of drama. While Lyautey's arguments were essentially truthful, the purity of his motives was overstated: in letters to his sister and to Eugène Étienne, he had written that he was managing the Ras el Ain situation with 'the prudence of a snake', and that his advance there provided 'a perfect base of operations for the day when we finally decide to do something'.[22] His request for dismissal before dishonour was pure brinkmanship; in private, he was now trying frantically to contact Jonnart, who was travelling in France. Eventually he succeeded; Jonnart told the cabinet that he had specifically authorized the move, and claimed that as governor-general he had the right to be consulted over all such decisions. Jonnart was a powerful political player, and despite Delcassé's misgivings his suggested compromise formula was accepted: a parallel Maghzan garrison would be co-located at Ras el Ain, thus preserving the fiction of condominium.

Jonnart was quite unflustered by having to ride to the rescue in this way, and his letters to Lyautey continued to be calm and encouraging: 'One must be very patient ... We are in partnership, and acting for the best in our country's interests.' Lyautey was relieved and grateful; in a letter home that September he wrote: 'This discreet penetration of Morocco, which I began surreptitiously and which is hardly under way yet, is so intensely interesting that to leave now would really be cruelly heartbreaking.'[23] Retrospective permission for the new post was given in October 1904, and alongside the 800 French troops a small and pointless Maghzan garrison from Oujda was installed – the usual boys and greybeards, whose pay never arrived. To save Moroccan face, the name Berguent became official.

*

SOON AFTER TAKING UP HIS COMMAND Lyautey had begun to sharpen the tools on his workbench and to place them where he needed them. Once Colomb Béchar was occupied, the organization on the frontier was reshaped to move its centre of gravity westwards. Taghit was downgraded to a simple post, and Colomb Béchar became the headquarters of a new 'circle' and the hub of operations. Extending Lyautey's grip on the borderland involved different types of unit, each with its own capabilities; dispersed to match their strengths to local terrain and conditions, these could be braided together as needed into mixed Mobile Groups, which swung out to criss-cross the frontier marches like the coordinated beams of searchlights. (On a literal level, the mobile groups included signalling/lamp squads for mutual communication; the southern outposts not yet linked by telegraph wires also communicated by this reliable old system, via relays of lonely little stone towers manned by a few signallers – an echo of the old Roman frontiers. Lyautey repeated what he had learned on the Tonkin frontier ten years previously: 'When they see the lights replying to one another in the night, [the tribesmen] feel tangibly our power, and the liaison between our posts by mysterious and invulnerable means.')[24]

For security patrols and for screening advances, the fingertips were the irregular *goumiers*, followed by the fingers – troops of Spahis, lightened for desert operations and accompanied by pack-horses. In the Far South the fists were Major Lapperine's new Saharan Companies of horsemen and *méharistes*, but on the high plains and in the *djebel* these fighting patrols were provided by the Legion mounted companies based at Berguent, Forthassa Gharbia and Colomb Béchar. Moving light and fast with their saddle- and pack-mules and carrying up to fifteen days' rations, the companies and half-companies made *reconnaissances de police*, pursued raiders and meted out retaliation. At any one time four of the eight Legion battalions now in Algeria were serving in the Sud-Oranais on year-long tours, and early in 1904 Lyautey formed a fourth Legion mule-company. He also raised another from Algerian Skirmishers, a horsed Saharan Company at Colomb Béchar and another at Beni Abbès on the Oued Saoura.[25]

Arabic-speaking intelligence officers in the static posts established markets and clinics, and acquired agents among the tent-groups that these attracted (the title was now changed from Bureau des Affaires Indigènes to the more candid Service de Renseignements, 'Intelligence Service'). The number of these posts – garrisoned by companies of Algerian Skirmishers, Legion infantry and Bats d'Af – was reduced, but individual posts were enlarged and stockpiled with supplies, so that the mobile units circulating between them could draw upon them for provisions and thus extend their range of action. The forts normally had a couple of guns, not simply for defence but so that temporary mobile groups could be given some muscle without calling on divisional artillery assets from the north. In Legion posts these were manned by légionnaires (there were always one or two with previous artillery experience).

Lyautey also believed that the natural light-infantry qualities of the *turcos* were being stifled by treating them increasingly like European infantry in terms of logistics and missions. He drew on Algerian Skirmisher units to form *groupes francs* ('free platoons') of more lightly equipped *tirailleurs allégés*, restoring their mobility by reducing their burden to weapons, ammunition, a burnous, water and haversack rations. Re-supply trains from the posts went out to rendezvous with both the mounted companies and light infantry, so that the latter never had to carry more than four days' rations with them.[26]

Word came from the Tafilalt that in September 1904 a second attempt by Moulay Mustafa el Hanafi to raise a *harka* had failed, and 1904 was reportedly the first year during which no Arab or European was killed by cross-border raiders.

NOW AND IN THE YEARS TO FOLLOW, Lyautey revealed his talent for establishing good relationships with the Arab *caids* with whom he negotiated the gradual expansion of his 'oil stains'. In their world, the authority conferred by mere words on paper was empty, and all prestige depended upon personal qualities. They responded naturally and as equals to Lyautey's aristocratic air, and his taste for military splendour was perfectly in harmony with their own traditions – the fluttering burnous that he wore over his uniform, the splendidly harnessed horses that he rode with dash and grace, and (perhaps above all, in a culture that revered warrior lineage) the old sabre slung at his saddle – the Napoleonic blade once carried to Moscow by his grandfather. For his part, Lyautey's return to North Africa after twenty years had rekindled a love affair that was as much aesthetic as careerist. In one letter home he wrote:

> It is ten o'clock at night. My lamp is lit on my camp table, in the great tent
> that the Bach-Agha Si Eddin of the Ouled Sidi Sheikh sent me from Géryville
> ... The flap is wide open, and outside my flag shivers in the breeze; a tall,

red-uniformed Spahi is mounting guard; my officers are finishing their pipes around a red fire. A horse whinnies and tugs at its halter; the servants carry away the remains of the meal under the eye of the *caid* of a neighbouring tribe ... The moonlight quickens the night, so cool after the heat of the day.

And again, of an evening at Ain Sefra (where he held court in Byronesque rooms adorned with Arab furnishings, and was sometimes serenaded with *Leider* by an impromptu choir of German légionnaires):

> The silver reflections off the palm trees, the violet shadows of the red-earth houses, the milky [dome of the] *kouba*, the sheep roasting over a fire surrounded by bearded faces; two white-clad Arabs at prayer, and purple-cloaked Spahis passing by; in the distance, the muffled sound of flutes and tambourines; [and beyond it all] the deep, soft shadows of the great screen of mountains – this is one vast fairyland![27]

Not all his senior officers were comfortable with Lyautey's approach to frontier soldiering, but if those who were slaves to routine and respectability were irritated by his flamboyance and restless whims, many subalterns were soon eating out of his hand. A young Legion officer, Lieutenant Jaeglé, circulated a light-hearted lampoon of the general, one of a series he wrote about senior officers identified by pseudonyms – Lyautey's was 'Lieuvin de Hautevue':

> ... dry and quick to spark as a flint, lively and bubbling as Moselle wine from his own country ... Lovable by nature, he wishes to be liked, and *is* liked – with deplorable facility ... Loved by his officers, by the soldiers, by courtiers, scribes and functionaries, he himself loves women, pretty faces, flattery, workers because they serve him ... [He is] active because it is necessary to him ... A trifle deaf in one ear, tall and of youthful appearance, he listens to one speaking without seeming to, and looks at things and men with a keen, clear eye, judging them quickly and often justly. He has no time to be modest.[28]

The general took this *jeu d'ésprit* with a smile, as a fair enough assessment. Lyautey's vanity and unconcealed need for assurance of loyal, even affectionate support were weaknesses of character of which he himself was well aware; he asked that men take him for all in all, and, given his obvious talents and devotion to his profession, spirited young officers seem to have found his flaws attractively human. The rough légionnaires he led also responded happily to the slightly theatrical style that he carried off so instinctively; this general who praised and encouraged face to face, as if he meant it, made a refreshing change from the dull, distant callousness of most men with stars on their sleeves. Vanity and ostentation were woven into French military culture, and while they may repel Anglo-Saxon puritans, they are in themselves no evidence of incompetence (even George S. Patton had a weakness for ivory-handled six-shooters). Lyautey was certainly nervy, volatile and an impatient, emotionally demanding perfectionist. But he was also highly intelligent, gifted, courageous and imaginative; to those who worked for him he was loyal, generous and charming, and instinctively empathetic to mood and character, striking perfect pitch when dealing face-to-face with men of every race and rank, from an illiterate légionnaire to a Moroccan prince.

LYAUTEY WAS ACUTELY CONSCIOUS that it was the behaviour of French troops in the immediate aftermath of their arrival that would determine whether the French presence was accepted pragmatically or resisted with hatred. Self-respect demanded that Moroccans test the strength of newcomers by combat, and they expected a winner to show implacable strength and confidence. But once the French were clearly identified as victors, Lyautey's policy depended on achieving recognition that this new, strong tribe had more to offer than previous in-comers, and the losers more to gain by accommodation than by defiance. His instructions to officers in newly occupied areas were unambiguous and forceful – for instance, to those planted among the Beni Snassen of the northern frontier:

> Sector commanders must above all work to make their post a centre of attraction for the natives. Following repression, the immediate objective is to achieve material and moral pacification, by accustoming the locals to contact with us and making them appreciate the benefits – our purchase of foodstuffs and firewood, protection, arbitration of local disputes, improvement of communications, medical assistance, etc. [Commanders] must supervise strictly the conduct of our troops – particularly European troops: no provocation, no abuse of authority, no violence, no rape. As to local customs, the people's religious observances, their *zaouias* and shrines will be scrupulously respected.[29]

At this stage in his career – before the 1912 Protectorate treaty, when he himself would become closely identified with the sultanate – the comparison that Lyautey presumably intended the tribes to draw was with the Maghzan. Historically, the sultans' claims on them had been pressed by means of destructive raids followed almost at once by the retreat of the government troops, leaving their ruined victims as easy pickings for the next marauders (who were never long in arriving). Lyautey intended to justify France's claim on the *caids'* obedience by making some positive difference to their lives, without threatening either their status or their religious sensitivities. Given the historical precedents, creating a comparatively favourable impression did not demand any unusual tenderness.

THE INTERNATIONAL SITUATION suddenly became threatening early in 1905. Sultan Abd el Aziz was flirting with German diplomats, and in March, at the request of the Wilhelmstrasse, the Kaiser interrupted a Mediterranean cruise on his yacht to visit Tangier. There he made a public speech expressing support for Moroccan sovereignty and concern for Germany's commercial interests, which nerved Abd el Aziz to assert himself against the French negotiators. More damagingly, it caused a Franco-German confrontation and a war-scare in France, and when Prime Minister Rouvier undermined his position the long-serving Théophile Delcassé resigned the Foreign Ministry in June. This stirred British support for France (a sympathy the foundation of which had been Delcassé's great achievement), and an international conference over Morocco was convened in January–April 1906 at Algeciras in Spain. Thanks to Delcassé's previous groundwork, French, British and Spanish cooperation ensured that by the time the conference ended, German ambitions had been foiled and France had achieved wide recognition of her primacy in Morocco. Disappointed in any hope of enlisting German help to free him from French tentacles, on 18 June 1906 Abd el Aziz was obliged to sign the Act of Algeciras, ceding wide powers to a French-controlled central bank and Franco-Spanish port authorities.[30]

During 1905, Lyautey had continued to press for a free hand on the frontier, ostensibly to protect the advancing railway, which reached Colomb Béchar that July.[31] Although cross-border raiders were now having to take greater care, some sizeable parties were still prepared to try their luck. In January, for instance, Lyautey wrote with satisfaction of 3rd (Mounted) Company's interception, at the Oued Nesli ten days out from Berguent, of a strong Shaamba raid: the légionnaires 'made a serious *confiture* of them' (one of that company's lieutenants was Paul Rollet, back from Madagascar).[32]

Lyautey believed – mistakenly – that the departure of Delcassé would finally sink the 'Maghzan policy', and anticipated a relaxing of restrictions; his short-sighted view of this was clearly expressed in a letter to Eugène Étienne on 2 March 1906, in which he criticized

> this idea of building a strong state adjacent to your own (unless you hold all the strings); of creating unity where there was only division; of establishing an entity conscious of itself and its strength, where before there had been only something nebulous ... [33]

(In a few years' time, when he himself was faced with the responsibility not merely for achieving local pacification but for 'nation-building' on a defeated enemy's territory, Lyautey would be reminded of what Governor-General Lanessan had told him in Tonkin about the advantages of preserving a functioning native power structure.)

By spring 1906, Lyautey's tactics were bringing undeniable results, quietly and at low cost (that April, the Army were even inviting politicians and rich tourists to visit peaceful Figuig, an exotic spectacle for the discerning traveller). The markets established at Beni Ounif and Colomb Béchar were proving to be increasingly attractive to Dawi Mani and Ouled Jarir caravan-masters who were prepared to cross the Hammada eastwards, since the arithmetic of the new trade link with Algeria was simply unanswerable. A load of dates bought in the Tafilalt could be sold at Colomb Béchar or Beni Ounif at 100 per cent profit, and French sugar bought there could be sold in the Tafilalt at an even greater margin. This provocative competition with the Tafilalt–Fes trade route coincided with the Act of Algeciras, which inflamed anti-French feeling by its revelation of the shaming impotence of Abd el Aziz's sultanate, and a consequent increase in banditry raised the costs of the trans-Atlas route even further. Firebrands in the Tafilalt tried to impose, by threats, a trade embargo on the Colomb Béchar route, but this crumbled in the winter of 1906–1907.

Paris rejected Lyautey's request for permission to take another step west-wards, to Boudenib on the Oued Guir; nevertheless, his achievements were so obvious that in December 1906 he was promoted to *général de division*. His third star was coupled with appointment to the command of Oran Division (in which post he made sure that no future commander at Ain Sefra would enjoy the long leash that he had obtained for himself). Although calls for *jihad* in 1906 had come to nothing, workaday raids – particularly by Ait Khabbash Berbers – periodically crossed the Hammada du Guir all the way to the Zousfana and Saoura oases. These ventures were not without their risks, however, as Lyautey's drill continued to bite.[34]

IN 1906 THE LEGION MOUNTED COMPANIES were circulating not only on the high plains but also up on the Hammada du Guir, and exercising their rights of 'hot pursuit' under the Act of Algeciras. In a letter, and years later in a report to the War Ministry from Oujda in 1913, Lyautey expressed his glowing opinion of these units:

> The Legion Mounted Company is an excellent tool if one knows how to use it. It is essentially a unit of mounted rifles. It has all the qualities of elite infantry – discipline, endurance, steadiness under fire – but also speed and range of action.
>
> ... Since 1881 the Mounted Companies have rendered services without number. This one company in each regiment may almost be said to have made half the contribution of that regiment during the pacification of the Sud-Oranais ... Thanks to its mobility, the Mounted Company has a moral influence of great value. It is 'the Guard': it provides a considerable moral support to the native troops; and it is desirable that the conqueror should be represented by white troops in every action and in all newly acquired territory.[35]

Capable of anything between 30 and 50 miles in 24 hours, the mule companies could pursue raiders encumbered with stolen livestock with every hope of success, and if the district officers' intelligence was good enough they could sometimes intercept them before they struck. The 100 rifles of the usual half-company were enough to ensure the annihilation of any normal-sized *djich* unwise enough to stand and fight, and, given a few days' notice, a converging combination of a couple of the companies could offer a formidable threat to even an (extremely rare) war party of several hundred warriors.

If the firepower half of the equation took care of itself, its mobility was achieved at punishing cost. The légionnaires volunteered for these elite units; Lyautey did not want very big men, who were too heavy for the mules, but recruited by the same criteria as laid down for the light cavalry and dragoons – men between 5ft 5ins and 5ft 8ins tall, 22 to 35 years old, thick-set and good marchers. General O'Connor wrote that their duty was so exhausting that none stayed in the ranks for longer than a year at a time; in 1903, Lyautey found that the mounted companies' availability for operations was often compromised by their rapid turnover of personnel, and he introduced a staggered schedule of systematic replacements to counter this.[36] As the spearhead for his operations, *'la Montée'* spent a great deal more time on the march than the foot companies holding forts, and constant exertion in a wide variety of harsh terrain and weather conditions naturally took its toll; by the end of a patrol the men were dirty, bearded and often ragged. In the high summer, a missed or fouled well could put the lives of tired men and beasts in real peril; when it rained they slept in the mud in sodden blankets, and torrential flash floods were a deadly threat to campsites near watercourses. On the high plains snow could lie until late spring in bad years – in April 1908 the 2nd (Mounted)/1st RE were surprised by a blizzard on the steppe between Ain ben Khelil and Forthassa Gharbia, and suffered such high casualties that the unit was temporarily removed from the order of battle.[37]

The usual speed was the marching pace of the men on foot, but if necessary the mules could trot and the men double-march for a while; on such forced marches the men changed places more often than the usual hourly intervals. Although they marched a little to the side to avoid the dust, the men on foot kept close to the riders so that they could change places quickly, the rider pulling his mate up from the right as he dismounted to the left at the hourly whistle and the order *'Changez montez!'*. The riding man was walled in front and back by two carefully arranged stacks of equipment and rations that supported him like the high saddle of a medieval knight. The senior man in each mule-pair was known as the *'titulaire'* or proprietor, the junior as his *'doubleur'*; the former was responsible for the mule's condition, and faced severe punishment if the evening inspection found any evidence of neglect. (The heavy load needed careful balancing, and even failing to brush the hair all in the same direction before blanketing and saddling could cause chafing sores.)

Unless a légionnaire was unlucky enough to be allocated a mule that had been ill-treated during breaking by its civilian breeder, the *'brêle'* was normally a biddable companion, and in the way of soldiers most men became fond of their beasts. Natural affection reinforced the doctrine that a man's life might depend on always caring for his mount before himself, and those occasions when human survival demanded that a mule be marched to death distressed the hardest légionnaire. When shots were fired, getting the mules under cover was the first priority, and one man in eight stayed back as a mule-holder (holding the reins in the middle of a circle of four beasts, heads inward), while the others deployed into a skirmish line. Mules naturally did best on regular feed but would eat almost anything, though they were fussier than the usually more desperate horses about the state of the water they would accept. If properly treated, they were resistant to most equine diseases and were remarkably patient, hardy and enduring; on a long march over the grassy high plains a mule unsaddled and allowed to roll and kick for about 15 minutes would then march on contentedly for many more miles.

The best eyewitness description of a mule-infantry march across the Hammada du Guir itself comes from a generation later, but Jean Martin's interwar memoir is equally relevant to Lyautey's first Moroccan campaign. It was Martin's first patrol, and he was already saddle-sore and worn out by two days on the march when his half-company reached the Hammada. This completely waterless plateau had to be crossed in 24 hours, starting at night. Late in the day they climbed steep goat-tracks up the eastern escarpment in single file, reaching the lip as the blood-red sun sank behind the horizon ahead, its light 'reflected in a crescent moon glowing in the blackening sky. But even in this failing light that briefly warmed the earth to the colour of faint pink the hammada appeared bald, brooding and inhospitable as it stretched to the horizon, limitless as a dessicated sea'.

The pace was kept down to spare the mules' hoofs 'on the large, ink-black stones', but dust was still lifted by a 'wind that rose cold out of the dark plain ... Those on muleback swayed in a fitful slumber' between their walls of kit. A *grande halt* of two hours was called at midnight; each man had to pour out a contribution from the day's 2-litre ration in his waterbottle to make coffee, over small fires of twigs that they carried with them. After an hour to prevent them getting chilled, the mules were unsaddled and rested for another hour before the march resumed:

> Soon the sun rose into a sky bleached of colour, which rapidly became so heavy with heat that it seemed to hang menacingly over the heads of the silent soldiers. Those on foot moved forward with stiff, wooden steps that betrayed increasing fatigue ... A mule faltered, and had to be unsaddled and left behind. Before the day was out, four others were abandoned in the same way. The weariness felt by the soldiers was more than physical; the hammada cast a spell of profound melancholy. It offered no concessions to the senses, nothing upon which the eye could rest – no wisp of grey vegetation, no fold of ground – nothing but a lugubrious plain over which stones lay sprinkled like peppercorns on an enamel plate ...

At about noon they spotted the cairn marking the path down the far escarpment, but the first well they reached contained only a small green puddle foul with dead rats, and even the horses would not drink. It was long after dark the next night when the patrol finally reached a post, by which time men and mules alike were badly distressed by thirst and exhaustion. The Hammada du Guir was known to be something special even among seasoned veterans.[38]

AT THE END OF A NORMAL DAY'S MARCH a camp was pitched on rising ground, if possible close to a water source. However exhausted they were, the légionnaires had to turn to and gather rocks to build *murettes d'Afrique* all round the square perimeter – little walls about 3 feet high by 18 inches thick, to provide cover from night-time sniping. Bivouac tents were raised, the rifles were stacked in threes *en faiseaux*, sentries were posted outside the four corners of the camp, and armed men were sent out for water and firewood. The mules were rested, unsaddled, then allowed to roll for a while before being watered under watchful escort, fed, and hobbled to graze; the duty corporal checked each beast's condition and gave basic veterinary care, and overnight their tethers were attached to a staked-out chain. Meanwhile the evening *soupe* was cooked. Spring water might be clear, but like the more usual standing water it was always boiled; well water could not be used for cooking rice or lentils, and the fact that it would not lather soap was a sinister sign. Even on wilderness patrols the men received their wine ration (though some chose not to drink while in the field, and used their ration as currency – two mugs of wine bought a man an extra hour in the saddle). After the evening stew few men had the energy to sit up chatting over more than one pipeful of tobacco; the fires were put out and they turned in soon after sunset, ready for a pre-dawn start.[39] New men suffered badly from fatigue and sores, but once they had settled in they built up their endurance impressively. Unit diaries show surprisingly few cases of sunstroke or typhoid, though dysentery was a frequent and demoralizing problem, and blankets and boots always had to be checked for black scorpions, tarantulas and horned vipers.

A misuse that degraded the fitness of the mounted infantry over time was their frequent employment for brute labour. This was not only a matter of building the new outposts they planted, but of driving miles of new tracks between them – breaking up rocks with hammer, crowbar and explosives, levelling the debris with pick and shovel, and sinking wells as they progressed (sometimes the men were even set to digging for signs of coal and minerals). While their ability to turn their hand to any task was a matter of pride, these labour details meant camping in the wilderness for weeks on end in all kinds of weather, after which worn and sickly men might find themselves sent off on a long patrol without time to recover their strength.[40]

Such work began with mapping by the officers – there were few Engineers on the frontier, and in 1900 combat officers of all armies were still trained to make accurate sketch-maps and topographical drawings. Some officers became specialists, and the map of the Djebel Béchar along the lower Zousfana drawn by Lieutenant Poirmeur of 3rd (Mounted)/1st RE in November 1903 is an impressive piece of observation and neat penmanship. Squared up, Poirmeur's first effort was traced and circulated by Ain Sefra Subdivision, and on each subsequent sortie patrol commanders were required to extend from this original into the white spaces. After the day's march they carefully wrote up their saddle notes about the terrain and the water points, and the glow of the officer's candle through the tent-canvas each night was usually the last light showing as the légionnaires fell asleep. The paramount need to locate water obliged these officers to study geology, for which some discovered a new enthusiasm.[41] The men were no less starved of novelty than the officers; in November 1907, while the 24th (Mounted)/1st RE were labouring in miserably wet weather on a track at Gherassa south of Colomb Béchar, Sergeant Lefèvre recorded:

> Our captain is a real geologist, who communicates his sacred fire to us ...
> Everyone has become something of a collector; magnificent stones encrusted
> with ancient seashells are plentiful in these streambeds ... This work
> interests everybody, and some of the men – quite uninstructed – are soon
> earnestly discussing primary and secondary strata, and the different traces of
> antedeluvian vegetation to be found in this terrain [42]

In January–February 1907, Lieutenant Paul Rollet of 3rd (Mounted)/1st RE reconnoitred the route for a new west-east track about 150 miles in length between Berguent and Mécheria, digging exploratory wells as he went; his subsequent memorandum recommending methods and routines for units moving across the high plains soon became the basis for standing orders. On 20 June, Rollet and Lieutenant Rolland travelled this track again on motorbikes – a revolutionary means of wilderness travel at that time, and a trip not without its mishaps.[43]

THE APPEAL OF SERVICE in the desert among these hand-picked volunteers may have been increased by the generally poor state of Legion morale in these years. All period sources agree that the overall quality of recruits had fallen noticeably since the 1890s. The element from Alsace-Lorraine, still about 22 per cent of the total in 1897, had sunk to 6 per cent, and the number of new German recruits halved to 800 a year between 1903 and 1905. In 1903, Germany began a venomous anti-French propaganda campaign to discourage enlistment; this presented the Legion as a living hell of brutal depravity, and the overall proportion of Germans in the Legion dropped from 34 per cent in 1904 to just over 16 per cent by 1914. (Nevertheless, it should always be borne in mind that those who did still enlist often claimed to find Legion life less brutal than the Frederickian treatment suffered by the Kaiser's conscripts.)

The shortage of Germans meant that a much higher proportion of Frenchmen had to be accepted – from 25–30 per cent before 1900 to about 45 per cent thereafter. The quality of some of these left much to be desired, and the minimal formalities of enlistment made it impossible to filter them at the barracks gate. The soldierly and ambitious were outnumbered by 'the sweepings of the nation', since much of the best human material was now attracted by the better pay and prospects and higher prestige of the new all-volunteer Colonial Troops. This allowed *la Coloniale* to refuse to re-engage its worst soldiers, who turned to the Legion – thugs, thieves and barrack-room lawyers old in sin. They were joined by civilian criminals who would formerly have been segregated in the Bataillons d'Afrique; General André's reforms had raised the bar for crimes which condemned men to the Bats d'Af, and this put more dubious characters into both the Line and, eventually, the Legion.

Before 1906 there was no mechanism by which the Legion could legally cancel a man's contract for disciplinary reasons, and the hardest cases were vicious, stupid, predatory and controllable only by physical violence. Since bad drives out good, the best foreigners were simultaneously availing themselves of naturalization after their first hitch and leaving the Legion to join the Colonials or the Line, instead of staying on to climb the ranks as career NCOs (one such was Léon Silbermann, the Madagascar memoirist). The disciplinary problems in Oran Division led to record numbers of courts martial in 1905; a ratio of about 20 per cent of a unit undergoing some sort of routine punishment at any one time was a reassurance to colonels that their légionnaires were not turning soft, but the situation had now become worrying.

Because the relatively lower ratio of officers and sergeants to men had been a problem in the big Legion rifle companies ten years before, reforms of 1894 and 1905 raised the numbers.[44] Even so, by 1910 the need for junior leaders in Morocco had so reduced the cadre of some Legion battalions at the Algerian depots that each company had only one officer and two sergeants – chronically inadequate for proper supervision of up tp 300 men. Discipline was naturally less of a problem on active service, though the fairly frequent dispersal of battalions in separate companies put a premium on high-quality leadership. In these conditions the occasional resort to the savage field punishments that figured so prominently in German propaganda (the *tombeau* and the *crapaudine*, described in Chapter 5) becomes more understandable. It may be significant that in 1910 the separate regimental disciplinary platoons were amalgamated into a whole company (the 8th of II/2nd RE).[45]

There was another side to the coin, however. The task of leading long-service mercenaries demanded of their officers more intelligence and flexibility than was the case in the Line – even the sullen Line of those years (see below). The mere power to punish was not enough, and officers who transferred in for only limited periods in order to get some active service into their dossiers were not accepted as 'real légionnaires' by the blank-faced ranks of old sweats. The best officers soon came to understand that 'the Legion is different', and that on the day of battle it paid dividends to have soldiers behind you who enjoyed brawling and were unafraid of punishment. While always absolutely maintaining the distance required for authority and automatic obedience, company officers in the field learned to pay close attention to the individual qualities and weaknesses of their men – they became, in other words, rather more modern than their contemporaries in France. With this familiarity came judgement: when to inflict instant punishment and when to make allowances, when to drive men hard and when to lead them like a stern but understanding father.

It was a hard but not a cynical age; in the absence of any mass popular culture, men took their bearings from the attitudes of those immediately around them, and all but the very worst soldiers were susceptible to group sentiment. They identified with their company, and might boast that their captain was the bravest, the most tireless marcher, the hardest drinker, or even (so long as he was scrupulously even-handed) the most eagle-eyed disciplinarian in the battalion. In the field all ranks had to depend upon each other; an NCO who had been stupidly brutal at Sidi bel Abbès might suffer a fatal accident on the frontier, but an officer who had earned a reputation for decent fair-mindedness could be sure that if he fell wounded, his men would risk their lives to save him, or even to drag in his corpse.

DURING THOSE YEARS, officers who transferred into the Legion, and indeed into l'Armée d'Afrique as a whole, were no strangers to poor discipline, and were at least encouraged to discover that the battle-readiness of their new units far exceeded that of the Line. During the Clemenceau administration (1906–1909), the morale and efficiency of the Metropolitan Army began to crumble under the simultaneous pressures of soldiers being employed as strike-breakers and serious political interference. Thoughtful officers knew that the politically shackled General Staff organization was quite unfit to confront that of an increasingly assertive Germany.[46] Meanwhile, the whole officer corps suffered humiliations calculated to reduce their prestige, and 'politically correct' reforms that seriously hindered their exercise of command. Originally intended to improve life for the rankers, in practice some of these initiatives damaged day-to-day discipline badly, and even encouraged corruption among NCOs.

Militant 'syndicalists' publicly encouraged the troops to defy their officers and support the workers' struggle, and very large numbers of conscripts simply failed to report for military service, even though the obligation was reduced in 1905 to just two years. There was much singing of the 'Internationale' in canteens, and small-scale strikes and riots became common. Officers and career NCOs were denied the sanctions they needed to maintain discipline; they were pressured by local politicians to favour their constituents, and – if resistant – were pilloried in scurrillous press campaigns. This rot culminated in major mutinies at Narbonne and Agde in June 1907, and by the following year these excesses would finally convince Prime Minister Clemenceau that, in a world containing Kaiser Wilhelm II, the country might pay a high price for breaking the morale and efficiency of its Army.[47]

IF THE FRENCH ARMY WAS SICK in 1907, then the Moroccan government was dying. Amid a chorus of popular hatred for the foreigners and contempt for the impotent sultan, incidents of street violence against Europeans in the cities were escalating, and in the countryside banditry was spreading unchecked. In the north-east, El Rogi had actually declared himself sultan in Taza – just 75 miles from Fes – and was selling mineral-mining leases to European companies.[48] In the south, a strong movement was gradually building to replace Abd el Aziz on the throne with his elder brother Moulay Abd el Hafid, Khalifa of Marrakesh – a groundswell largely funded by Madani el Glaoui, the most powerful and far-sighted of the lords of the Atlas. The rise of Madani 'the Literate' may have been founded on a Krupp field gun, and he might still hurl his victims into medieval *oubliettes*, but his sophistication was now unique among the Moroccan warlords: this was a man who ordered Arabic transcripts of French parliamentary debates.

In March 1907 it was Georges Clemenceau, Jules Ferry's nemesis in 1885, who was obliged – by public outrage over the murder in Marrakesh of a medical missionary, Dr Mauchamp – to order French troops across the Algerian/Moroccan border. Not far across, however: they were simply to occupy and hold Oujda, the first town inside Morocco on the northern road from Algeria to Fes. As GOC Oran Division, the man who had to carry out the order was Lyautey, with a Zouave battalion, III/1st RE and a mounted company. The occupation was easily accomplished on 29 March, but his enforced passivity thereafter caused Lyautey frustration; rather than the first step in a coherent military plan, this seemed to be no more than an ill-conceived political chess-move.[49] The French government apparently believed that simply holding Oujda hostage would force the Maghzan to meet its list of demands, but the naked occupation of a major Muslim town finally destroyed any authority Abd el Aziz still enjoyed. Moreover, by forbidding Lyautey to do anything except protect his own lines of supply, the government set his troops up as targets. When Lyautey occupied Oujda, the local *caids* came in spontaneously to negotiate with this evidently powerful new chief; but when he failed to patrol vigorously and take real control of the countryside their confidence returned – in their minds, any power-vacuum was an invitation.[50] The French government's apparent assumption that Oujda could be bargained for, like some discrete pawn in an eighteenth-century border dispute between European nation states, was a fundamental misreading of local attitudes.

To the independent and competitive tribal chiefs, the seizure of Oujda was a projection of power that could have no other reason than a French determination to acquire new territory. The French *caid* wielding this power must be tested by cautious armed probes and sounded out by negotiation. If the French were truly formidable, then a local chief should conclude an alliance with them – and preferably before his neighbours did, and exploited such an alliance against him. But if this new warlord on the scene reacted passively, failing to assert his authority by punishing insolence, then his power must have reached the limit of its reach already. In such a case the Arab or Berber chief should ratchet up his harassment, proving to his neighbours that he was himself the bolder and stronger and that they would have to seek alliances with him instead. At core, this was the same equation as expressed to Lyautey by the Tho headman on the frontier of Upper Tonkin eleven years previously: 'If you come, you must stay, and I will join you; if I cannot be sure you will stay, I dare not join you.'

IT WAS IN CASABLANCA on the Atlantic coast, where a sizeable white population had installed itself to develop a fishing village into a major port, that European exploitation was probably more visible than anywhere else in Morocco. The weakness of the Maghzan governor was a temptation to European arrogance, and the foreigners and their building sites were greatly resented by both the townspeople and the tribesmen from the surrounding country.

On 30 July 1907, a dispute over the building of a railway track led to the mob murder of nine white workmen. The French consul on the spot contained the situation, but another official in Tangier sent home inflammatory reports and despatched the warship *Galilée* to Casablanca. Arriving on 1 August, the captain was informed that the situation was tense but retrievable, and that the civilians who had taken refuge in the European consulates were in no immediate danger. Then yet another diplomat arrived, and authorized a small landing party to relieve the French consulate. On 4 August, the bluejackets fought their way through Moroccan resistance, and once inside the consulate they signalled to the ship for gunfire support. The subsequent shelling of the Arab town sparked riots and looting; tribesmen poured in, many Jews and some Europeans were butchered, and the consulates were now besieged in earnest. Clemenceau ordered General Drude to sail from Algeria with about 3,000 men, who included the légionnaires of Major Provost's VI/1st RE. On 7 August, they began landing under the guns of a large French squadron and, after occupying the town with indiscriminate violence, established defensive lines on the outskirts.[51]

On 16 August, the *ulama* of Marrakesh proclaimed Abd el Aziz deposed and Moulay Hafid as the new sultan, and the latter promptly summoned all his people to join a *jihad* against the French. France declared its continued support for Abd el Aziz as the legitimate sovereign, although French troops were forbidden to fight for him against his brother. Understandably, such fine distinctions of foreign policy were lost on Moroccans, who saw the Casablanca landing simply as an invasion. The Christian occupation of an enclave in the heavily populated west, potentially within reach of the imperial cities of Fes and Meknes, provoked spontaneous resistance to the Landing Corps, and Moulay Hafid's anti-French rhetoric gave him (for a while) the status of an Islamic champion rather than simply one party to a dynastic struggle. France's pose as the defender of the Maghzan against rebellion was irrelevant; it was the French that Moroccans wanted to fight, while neither Abd el Aziz nor Moulay Hafid had the resources to pursue their civil war with any vigour.

General Drude's remit was, nevertheless, only to protect the European population, and by the end of August some 10,000 tribesmen were roaming and looting the rich Chaouia plain inland from Casablanca without interference.[52] On 3 September, Drude sent a weak mixed column, including a couple of Legion companies, towards a large tribal camp at Tahaddert about 6 miles inland, and during swirling attacks (the tribes of the region were essentially horsemen) Major Provost was killed. The following day reinforcements landed, including two battalions of 2nd RE. On 12 September, Sultan Abd el Aziz fled from Fes, where he feared for his life, to his coastal palace at Rabat; on the same day, General Drude led a larger force to Tahaddert, but his bungled tactics allowed the *harka* to escape. Thereafter, Paris ordered him to stick close to his perimeter.[53] On 26 September, 3,000 warriors sent north by Moulay Hafid to join the resistance arrived at Settat, some 40 miles south of Casablanca, but made no further threatening moves. In the meantime Drude's Landing Corps (and a token Spanish regiment, which remained inactive) sat down in a crescent of camps about 400 yards outside the town, protected by two forts on a ridge 1,000 yards out.[54]

Having created this situation, none of the parties gave any sign of having an immediate plan of action: Abd el Aziz stayed in Rabat and pawned his crown jewels to raise a war-chest, Moulay Hafid stayed in Marrakesh and importuned Madani el Glaoui for funds and men, and General Drude stayed in Casablanca. The only antagonists who were active were the warriors from the hills surrounding the Chaouia. This plain was some 70 miles long, from the Sehoul cork-forest in the north-east to the river Oum er Rebia in the south-west, and 50 miles wide, rising about 1,500 feet into hilly pleateau country to the south-east. Well watered, its black soil was in effect a single gigantic cornfield of 3,500 square miles, thickly sown with farms and villages. With the plain now a no man's land, its cattle fat and its silos full of grain, the quarrelling tribes comprehensively pillaged this rich prize.

For nearly thirty years following the landing at Casablanca, several battalions of the Legion would be continuously on active service in Morocco, which became the corps' main theatre of operations and the context in which most of the world pictured it.

12. Two Kinds of War
1908

*There can be no doubt that the panic in Casablanca
transmitted something of its fears to France, where
today a casualty list of sixty is regarded by many people
as a quite adequate reason for a change of general.*
Reginald Rankin, London *Times* correspondent, 1908

*Your dark soul deceives you into racing to your own ruin
... The courageous and noble Muslim warriors approach
you, armed for your destruction. If you are in force, come
out from behind your walls for battle; you will judge
which is the nobler, the owl or the hawk.*
Moulay Ahmad Lahsin el Saba, 1908.[1]

FROM THE WINTER OF 1907 until the spring of 1914, the Legion units
committed to Morocco would serve on two completely separate fronts.
French forces advancing from the Atlantic coast in the west and from Algeria
in the east would remain divided by the mountain heart of the country, and
even after they joined hands in the narrow northern 'Taza corridor' in 1914
their zones of operations would for many years resemble a sort of archway
shape, surrounding a slowly diminishing central area of highland resistance.
More or less simultaneous phases of the fighting on either side of the Atlas
differed in character; while operations were naturally interconnected at the
highest staff levels, the parts played in them by Legion units are more easily
understood if described in the context of local conditions rather than in
strictly chronological order.

THE WEST WAS THE THEATRE of political developments, in the imperial cities and on the plains between them, and there General Antoine Drude

was replaced in January 1908 by General Albert d'Amade, whose Landing Corps was simultaneously reinforced to 10,000 men to enable him to clear the Chaouia plain. Among the foreign journalists who flocked to cover the campaign was Lieutenant Colonel Reginald Rankin (retired) of the London *Times*; his account of organization and logistics is everything one could wish from an informed professional who took an interest in details, but it also has more accessible qualities.

In January–March 1908, d'Amade had about 8,000 combat troops.[2] These were divided between garrisons for Casablanca and (eventually) half a dozen forward bases, and a field force of two permanent 'flying columns' designated Shore and Plains; the latter were sometimes combined, and other units were often taken from garrisons to form additional manoeuvre forces. The Shore Column (in which VI/1st RE served, in a Composite Marching Regiment) was under d'Amade's immediate control at Casablanca; the Plains (including the 2nd RE Marching Regiment) was led by Colonel Boutegourd, soon based at Ber Rechid (see Map 15). D'Amade was short of cavalry, and had needed to ship in some Algerian *goumiers* irregulars. His communications were up to date; in addition to telegraph lines connecting Casablanca with forward bases, in late January a wireless link was established between headquarters and Ber Rechid.[3] (An observation balloon was taken out by the Shore column in January, but proved a useless and too-visible encumbrance.) The supply, ration and medical arrangements for the Landing Corps seem to have been efficient, as indeed was all staff work at most levels, and d'Amade was a decisive, fast-moving commander who issued brief, clear orders. The frequent rain and heavy mud were exhausting for the infantry, and a severe limitation on the movement of artillery and transport, since the Chaouia was virtually roadless and d'Amade was starved of pack-mules and light *araba* mule-carts.

On the Chaouia, the infantry would carry out classic full-scale regimental manoeuvres with supporting horse and guns, very different from the small-unit warfare on the south-east frontier. General d'Amade's first operation was an attempt to bring Moulay Hafid's men to battle around Settat, and he set out southwards across the prairie with 2,500 men on 12 January. Two miles behind the cavalry scouts, three-and-a-half infantry battalions marched in a single great square a mile across, with the guns and baggage in the middle. They moved slowly and Rankin of the *Times* was able to indulge his interest in the local flora and fauna at leisure; he was struck by the variety of wildflowers that carpeted the plain, which was treeless except 'where a rare grove of untended fig-trees languished within their broken cactus hedge, or where the dying aloe [agave] lifted its pine-like head above the tall grey sword-leaves guarding deserted farms . . . for twelve miles inland from Casablanca man has fled.'[4]

The troops bivouacked overnight in the rain, and on the evening of 13 January were joined at Ber Rechid by Lieutenant-Colonel Brulard with a battalion-and-a-half of his 2nd RE and 'a few cavalry', swelling the force to nearly 4,000 men. On the 15th they encountered large numbers of Arab riders in the valleys and hills around Settat, who denied the artillery any targets by swirling and jinking like flocks of starlings.

> Four of the infantry companies were sent forward, in a long single rank, without intervals – the Legionaries on the left, the Tirailleurs on the right, their supports about a quarter of a mile behind . . . The line advanced as one man, then halted, knelt, fired by platoons, usually in volleys, and then again advanced. It was admirably done.[5]

There was brisk return fire: 'the air was humming with bullets, but they hit nobody, and the shells fired by the only [Moroccan] field-piece . . . buried themselves in the plough[land] without troubling to burst' – yet again, the enemy seemed incapable of setting fuzes. No Arabs ventured closer than 300 yards, and when the French entered the squalid little *kasbah* of Settat they found only terrorized Jewish families who greeted them as saviours. D'Amade had been forbidden to occupy the town permanently; denied the battle he had hoped for, he had to trudge back to Ber Rechid with very little to show for it. He had killed a few dozen tribesmen, but essentially he had been punching empty air. It was a discouraging precedent for future frustrations (and the returning Arabs killed all the Jewish men in Settat).[6] During the return march Rankin found little of military interest to report, and instead filled his notebook with what really delighted him. We are inevitably reminded of Waugh's legendary William Boot of the *Daily Beast:*

> Nowhere else have I seen so many sorts of flowers in a narrow compass. There I found the beautiful pink *Cheronia exifera*, a rare greenhouse plant at home, and a white *sparaxis* with a subtle scent . . . There I first came on a drift of lupins, just opening into blue, hard by a fold in the plain crimsoned by a colony of plantains. Our familiar little friend the Virginia Stock is at home in the rocky clefts; the glorious blue of *Veronica anagallis* is a rival to the sky; here is clump of scarlet pimpernel; there, by the reed-grown pool

where the snipe are flushed, is a belt of yellow broom; the tall *lavatera* fills the hollows; and camomile, hidden by aspiring snapdragons, wafts you a greeting as you ride by.[7]

There is a great deal more of this sort of thing; Rankin was the type of writer who called cattle 'kine' (although he also had the keenly critical eye for horseflesh that one would expect of an officer and a countryman). He had an opportunity to enjoy botanizing through open woodland on 21 January, when d'Amade marched north up the coast to Bou Znika, then swung south through the edge of the Sehoul cork-forest. The general was hoping that converging columns – from Bou Znika, Ber Rechid and Mediouna – would be more productive, but he was again disappointed. The Moroccan horsemen danced around and between these separated forces with some ease, and chose to hit Colonel Boutegourd's weaker column from Mediouna before the rendezvous. His defensive square and shrapnel shells drove them off, but before the columns could converge on them the tribesmen had simply burned their own huts and floated away. (Their grain was stored in hidden pit-silos 10 feet deep, deadly for an inattentive French horseman.)[8]

It is easy to like Rankin. One day he is rhapsodizing about 'one of the loveliest flowers I have ever seen ... a marsh-marigold in leaf, a single chrysanthemum in flower; golden, indescribable'. The next, he notes that among observers crowding forward for a view of a distant action there was 'a correspondent carrying a loaded Mauser pistol pointed fiercely towards a foe about a thousand yards away, [who] filled his confrères with a deep sense of the frailty of the bonds that hold us to the earth'. One colleague a yard from Rankin had his skull creased by a rifle bullet, and a nearby artillery officer got another through wrist and lung; these everyday mishaps are recorded briefly, but in language far less engaged than his nature notes.[9]

WHAT RANKIN CALLED the most critical action of the campaign – that is, the one that most nearly ended in a defeat – was fought on 2 February, at Sidi el Mekki. Aiming to deny the tribes resources by sweeping up some 5,000 cattle reported there, Colonel Boutegourd marched from Ber Rechid before first light with VI/1st RE and two companies of *turcos* from Passard's mixed regiment, a cavalry squadron and a battery. Soon after 7am Boutegourd had left a few troopers to ride herd on the captured cattle while he probed further south, when some 5,000 Arab riders appeared and came between the infantry and the cattle. These were potentially dangerous opponents for a badly outnumbered force; most had single-shot rifles such as Martini-Henrys, but some carried Winchester repeaters (though their insistence on firing from the saddle meant that most shots went high). They were quick to spot weak points and attack them, but their lack of coordination usually prevented any systematic follow-through.

The six infantry companies retired in a square; the cloud of horsemen got within 100 yards, though thinned by a single machine gun in front of the east face. When its crew all fell, Captain Bosquet of the Legion served it alone until he had used all the ammunition within reach, whereupon he hefted it on to his back and brought it inside the square. Rankin reported that the formation had to 'double up', making its sides shorter but two ranks deep, for more concentrated fire to prevent charging riders breaking through – this has a Napoleonic flavour. Another Legion officer told the Englishman of his pride in his men's steadiness; he had seen one légionnaire pause between two shots to pat reassuringly the head of a baby goat that was sticking out of the front of his greatcoat (many légionnaires gathered their supper on the march, but a kid was rather more ambitious than the usual chickens). The column regained Ber Rechid after 19 hours of marching and fighting, with 11 killed and 41 wounded, the latter including Colonel Passard.[10]

D'AMADE'S CONVERGING COLUMN tactics failed again on 16–18 February. Colonel Taupin repeated the hook southwards from Bou Znika, while Brulard's 2nd RE marched east from Ber Rechid and d'Amade led a much larger force north-east from Settat, for a planned rendezvous at Abd el Kerim. Picking the smallest and most isolated of the three columns, on the 17th the tribes attacked Taupin in a narrow valley in the hills at Ain Rebbah; at one point his square had to fight them off with bayonets, and fell back with 39 casualties. Marching across the prairie, Brulard's Legion column were harassed by cavalry from dawn until dusk, at a cost of 30 casualties, while d'Amade's own column never fired a shot until a skirmish on the 18th.

On 29 February, Rankin was present – and critical – when d'Amade suffered another tactical setback, at Rfakha in the hills around the confluence of the Oued Mkoun and Oued Mellah. D'Amade was advancing eastwards with the combined Shore and Plains force of 5,500 men when he came to a valley where a ford crossed the Mkoun; the river ran north–south across his front, with rolling green downland beyond. While he waited impatiently for a convoy to catch up, he did not halt his whole force on the nearer bank. He pushed his five cavalry squadrons, a Zouave and a Legion battalion eastwards across the ford, while holding the other five battalions and his three batteries of 75s on the hills on the west bank. The Moroccans, using ground with great skill, then attacked the part of his divided force that had crossed the river, and the situation unravelled in a series of mishaps.

Among the knolls and dips on the French right flank Arab horsemen flowed forwards, each with a foot soldier leaping along hanging on to his stirrup, and pressed home a number of hit-and-run attacks on Colonel Luigné's Africa Light Horse. The French cavalry charged, the mêlée wheeled away, and the Moroccan riflemen who had dropped free got up from the long grass and fired into the troopers' backs. There was some confusion when two squadrons got in each other's way, and Luigné suffered 37 casualties and 30 horses killed. (The fallen troopers were found to have been grossly mutilated where they lay, some having the bound wrists that showed they had been tortured while still alive.) When two companies of Algerian Skirmishers waded the stream and came up to provide the cavalry with a base of fire, the *turcos* paid for it with half a dozen casualties from French artillery misdirected by a confused senior officer.

The Moroccans then switched their focus, moving northwards behind a ridge to emerge on the French left flank. There they rose up out of cover to fire from 50 yards into the flank of the Zouave battalion advancing in column, dropping 13 conscripts with a single volley. Rankin watched from 200 yards away, with bullets buzzing round him, as the Legion battalion came up to support the shaken Zouaves. He describes the battlefield as a shambles, in the old sense of that term; and that night an idiotic muddle of orders sent the cursing infantry marching and countermarching up and down hills in the dark for hours before they were finally able to rest and eat.[11]

It had not been the Landing Corps' finest hour, and frustration in Tangier and Paris had already led Clemenceau and War Minister Picquart to offer the command in the Chaouia to Lyautey, who had just finished a satisfactory operation against the Beni Snassen tribe in the far north-east (see below), but Lyautey was too wise to accept it. Colonel Rankin, being a military rather than a political animal, was amused that such modest casualty bills should cause fluttering at cabinet level.[12]

D'AMADE'S CEASELESS TRAMPING around the plains by day and night, and his confiscation of herds, flocks and stored grain finally began to bear fruit in March 1908. While he seldom had the tactical initiative, he had a strategy, and the Moroccans did not. His newly established garrisons and frequent columns were steadily circumscribing the tribes' freedom of movement, which their lack of central coordination rendered increasingly aimless. There was no long-term gain from darting in to kill a dozen or two Frenchmen at a heavy cost if the squares never broke, and simply kept coming back week after week. D'Amade suffered tactically from having fewer than 1,000 cavalry, so the thousands of Moroccan horsemen could break off engagements at will, but they were paying a steady price in lives to his shells and volley-fire.

The Arabs soon had no supplies of food other than what they could gather on the spot, and d'Amade usually got to this first. (Rankin – a man of his time – believed that the French might even have erred on the side of humanity; he quoted a fellow journalist being told by Sultan Abd el Aziz himself that 'the French would never do any good in the Chaouia until they plundered, plundered, plundered'.)[13] The main tribes were being forced up off the plain into the rocky southern and eastern plateaux, where their cavalry was of less value and they would be bound to stand and defend the refuges of their people and livestock. Moulay Hafid's Rehamna warriors from around Marrakesh were still bellicose, but their looting had done as much damage to the local tribes as had the French, and they were rapidly wearing out any welcome they had ever enjoyed.

On 7 March the French marched into the eastern hills again against the stubborn Mdakra tribe and Moulay Hafid's contingents, and following this action at Mkarto – during which 'Wild Boar' Passard's légionnaires made a positively Wellingtonian charge from hiding on a reverse slope – many of the local *caids* came in to make terms. D'Amade took the opportunity of the Algerian *goumiers'* departure at the end of their four months' contract to stage an impressive parade in the field, and a week later the last major action of the campaign took place.[14]

AFTER HARD MARCHING, by noon on 15 March 1908 the combined field force of about 5,500 men was at Dar ould Fatima, south-west of Ber Rechid. This country was still populated, but men of fighting age seemed scarce among the villagers watching the column pass, and an intelligence officer soon learned that warriors were gathering at the camp of a chief named Bou Nuallah about 20 miles north-west. D'Amade ordered knapsacks to be dumped and left one man in every sixteen to guard the baggage while the rest pressed on at speed. Snipers began harassing the advance from orchards and rocks almost at once, but fell back before the French; viewed from a ridge, thousands of riders could be seen eddying about on the rolling grassland below, but these withdrew in disorder as soon as the artillery opened fire. The advance became a race, with the guns unlimbering to fire every half-mile before hitching up and hurrying to catch up with the infantry again. Then Rankin saw through his binoculars what he took to be a low line of rocks stretching right across the horizon for several thousand yards. Hard though it was to believe, what he was actually seeing was an immense encampment of about 1,200 tents.

There was no coherence to the Moroccan defence; skeins of riders caracoled back and forth, shooting and wheeling away, while others on foot fired from among the separate tribal groups of tents, where French shells soon began to start fires. As the infantry went straight into the attack, the Legion were in the centre of the long line, with Algerian Skirmishers on either flank; all were tired and frustrated by their forced marches, and in a vengeful mood. Rankin followed close behind, revolver in hand, and he leaves an unflinching picture of confused close-quarter killing among the tents, with bullets flying from every direction. He describes a Spahi toppling dead from the saddle right in front of him; a Legion platoon making an about-face on the spot to return the fire of riflemen among tents they had passed; pools of blood on the grass; bewildered women and children caught in the crossfire; tribesmen throwing down weapons and trying unsuccessfully to surrender at the very bayonet points of battle-mad Skirmishers and légionnaires; and Spahis in pursuit, leaning from the saddle to sabre fleeing Moroccans. As the sun sank into dark clouds, its last rays painted the contorted faces of the soldiers red and black; from every side screams and shouts mixed with the din of gunfire and of ammunition cooking off in the blazing camel-hide tents, which added their stink to that of gunpowder and melinite.

As darkness fell, Rankin could see for miles around the glowing rings of sparks left by tents burnt down to the ground. He reckoned that not many more than 130 Moroccan fighting men had died, but the rest scattered in a panic rout. Soon after sunset, rain began to fall in torrents; the bugles blew the 'Assembly', and under a pelting downpour the sated soldiers regrouped slowly, chilled and quiet, to begin a long, exhausted march back towards their camps around Dar ould Fatima.[15]

RANKIN'S DESCRIPTION OF TRIBAL CHIEFS coming in to seek peace terms, escorted by a dashing squadron of Africa Light Horse, paints a vivid picture:

> The dark green of the corn was flecked with patches of old rose, where the bare earth stood out ... for thousands of yards the gilded marigolds turned the mountain slope to orange; the ochre and brown walls of the derelict *kasbah* were topped by snow-white towers; the red and blue uniforms of the Chasseurs were set off by their grey horses; they hedged about a group of men in whom a sense of colour seems innate. There was a white horse whose bridle, reins and blinkers were the palest blue; his high-peaked, chair-backed saddle was covered with lemon-yellow leather. A black with flashing eye and enormous mane was decked out in vermilion, his breastplate fastened to the saddle by large silver brooches. ... Most of the men wore the dark blue burnous with its white hood thrown back behind. Some few were all in white; on their feet were either red or yellow slippers, and beneath their robes you caught glimpses of orange, blue and violet skirts.[16]

The close of major operations on the Chaouia in scenes of dignified surrender perhaps allows a digression on the nature of tribal warfare in Morocco, with its apparently puzzling shifts of fortune. Despite the obviously important part played by the French artillery, it is simply not enough to write the victory down as purely tactical and won by shrapnel shells alone. This was a confrontation between two utterly different perceptions of warfare.

TRYING TO UNDERSTAND the exercise of tribal military potential by seeking European parallels is pointless. The centrally organized Western system can be represented in terms of a fixed geometry, but the power structures of an Arab or Berber tribe were various and shifting. In the context of putting fighting men into the field, it is perhaps useful to return to the earlier analogy of the tribes as trees: the *caid* or *sheikh* had to find trees from which, at a moment of ripeness, he could pick warriors like fruit.

Tribal disunity was central to the failure to resist colonial powers effectively, and some white commentators spoke of this factor in the condescending terms used of quarrelsome children; yet such condescension is quite out of place. Disunity – the process of competition between groups – is simply the defining characteristic of tribal as opposed to national societies. (In Morocco, however, there was a counterbalance to the threat of completely self-destructive chaos, since complex patterns of alliance – the *liff* – seem usually to have achieved a rough-and-ready numerical equivalence at many levels, and French intelligence officers always had to take this *liff* factor into consideration.) Persuading local tribes to submit to the French in succession lay at the heart of what would become known as the 'Lyautey method'; it greatly reduced the need to employ shrapnel shells, and it accorded with local realities.

The most obvious difference between tribal and European societies was that, in the former, the functioning of the group still depended upon personal relationships of kinship or sworn loyalty, while Western societies had long ago cut down their tribal 'trees' and shaped the timber into a series of 'boxes' – institutions, which continued to function regardless of individual personalities. Within the pyramids of boxes making up a European field force, individual qualities and relationships still contributed to the strength or weakness of any particular box, but its very existence did not depend upon them. That was not the case among the tribes. One simple reason why Western armies always defeated, eventually, pre-modern tribes – a reason as important as better weapons and greater resources – was the sheer continuity of the white man's fighting force. When he needed troops, the white commander simply had to open a 'box of soldiers' and take out what he needed. Kill the white major and half his battalion, and (given an embarassed home government and a shrill press) they could be replaced by the next troopship. Kill the clan chief and his strongest son, and that segment of the tribe would lose its dominance and cohesion; the surviving fragments would be forced to look elsewhere for a focus of power, and would be absorbed by a neighbouring group.

When a Moroccan clan that had chosen to fight another was forced to recognize that it was outmatched, then, after fighting long enough to preserve its honour, it sought the peace settlement called *aman*. This was often mediated by some figure of religious prestige, and it did not demean the losing side in their own or others' eyes – the turn of events was simply the will of God. Defeat had already cost them lives and animals; in the moment of victory the winners naturally murdered and looted – that was the point, and how else was anyone to keep score? Now, buying peace would cost them an additional more or less heavy price in goods, and sometimes in territorial rights. But after the agreed penance had been paid, the terms were understood by all concerned to be perishable; they had something like the qualified stability of a European feudal liege/vassal relationship, which might survive through several generations or only for a few years. The fundamental sense of the settlement was 'I will keep faith with you for as long as you are the strongest in this region'.

The French, too, learned to move to this rhythm; they were as harsh as was necessary until an opponent sued for peace, but by the early twentieth century the cost of returning to the fold, even after submission and a subsequent rebellion, was not set cripplingly high – the French Army in Morocco were not the *colons* of Algeria. Throughout the Moroccan campaigns defeated clans routinely enlisted in French service to fight under their own *caids* as irregular auxiliaries – so-called *'partisans'* or *'supplétifs'* – thus preserving their all-important looting rights. Many did so within what must seem to us to be a surprisingly short time after the often bloody events of their own defeat. But in their world, straightforward defeat in war, with its inevitable passages of horror for individuals, did not always breed collective long-term resentment. To see submitted and unsubmitted tribes in comic-strip terms of 'treacherous collaborators' and 'the heroic resistance' is wildly anachronistic; each tribe simply adapted to a new reality, as it always had done. As early as November 1908, General d'Amade was able to recruit on annual contracts six mostly mounted *goums mixtes de la Chaouia* each 200 strong, led by their own chiefs under French intelligence officers. These became permanent units, and were expanded; by May 1911 they would be giving such good service under the leadership of Major Henri Simon that Colonel Pein called them 'the marvel and revelation of this campaign'.[17]

THE MAJOR EVENT IN THE WEST in the summer of 1908 was the final collapse of Abd el Aziz's sultanate. Moulay Hafid had been gathering support for months, and in January the all-important *ulama* of Fes, the country's religious capital, had given him their provisional endorsement. Their conditions were that he must repudiate the Act of Algeciras, drive European troops from Islamic soil, and end the privileges granted to foreigners. Neither the incumbent nor the claimant sultan had the means to pay troops or wage serious war on one another; they sparred in a desultory way during the first half of 1908, but 'an intense desire never to come to decisive action seems to have been the common aim of both parties'. While they continued to avoid one another, in June Moulay Hafid entered Fes.

In August, the French advised and assisted Abd el Aziz to march from the coast not on Fes, but south towards Moulay Hafid's power-base at Marrakesh. When they were almost there, a minor and fortuitous clash led to the spontaneous collapse of the royal army, which fled after pillaging its own camp. Abd el Aziz returned precipitately to Casablanca, and within days he had formally abdicated in favour of Moulay Hafid; thereafter he would retire, with genuine relief, to private life in the refuge of the international city of Tangier. Before the end of August, Moulay Abd el Hafid was formally proclaimed sultan by the *ulama* in Fes. There, having built his support on a promise to expel the French, he, too, would soon find himself forced to negotiate with them as the only possible source of funding for his Maghzan.[18]

IN AUGUST 1908, the VI/1st RE were withdrawn to Algeria, soon followed by IV/2nd RE, leaving Major Forey's I/2nd RE the only Legion unit in Western Morocco.[19] Rankin (no indulgent judge) reckoned the Legion to be the best fighting men in the Chaouia – first rate on operations, if hard to handle in peacetime. He reported that when General Drude was slow to grant them the double pay customary in colonial theatres, they had pointedly sent him a tortoise painted in tricolour with the words '*Solde Coloniale*'; General d'Amade duly granted them the colonial rate of 10 centimes daily (though this was still only one-eighteenth of what Rankin paid his Moroccan cook).[20] The English ex-colonel saw all three types of French infantry in action during the campaign, but passed over the Zouaves in a perhaps eloquent silence. He reported the Algerian Skirmishers to be excellent marchers, cheerful, willing and brave, though a little inclined to over-excitement and wild shooting. The légionnaires impressed him by their endurance, swagger, marksmanship and economy of ammunition, and he paid particular tribute to their coolness in battle:

> At the second taking of Settat I saw a legionary hit in the hand as he was in the act of firing. He asked a comrade to bind it up, and then went on shooting. Five minutes later he was hit in the other hand, rather badly, and again begged his friend to bind him up, remarking that if the Moors fancied they'd stopped his work for the day they were [...] mistaken ... Finer fighting troops it would be impossible to find in any army.[21]

Generally the légionnaires of 1908 seem to have attracted better opinions than their public reputation at this time might suggest, and among those they impressed was General Lyautey.

IN LYAUTEY'S EASTERN FIEF on the Algerian border, Legion units had been active since November 1907. After the French occupied Oujda the previous March, the Beni Snassen tribe had begun venturing out of their forested hills astride the northern frontier line to raid around coastal villages inside Algeria, but Lyautey and Governor-General Jonnart had at first argued in vain for the War Ministry to authorize a major operation. Lyautey judged that a serious outbreak would follow when the harvest was in, and had long been preparing the way with political contacts and road-building. When the Beni Snassen became bolder that winter, and a patrol clash on 7 November escalated, General Picquart let him off the leash.[22]

The Djebel Beni Snassen massif, rising some 4,500 feet, stretched east to west for about 50 miles behind the Mediterranean coast, from the Oued Kiss in Algeria to the Oued Moulouya in Morocco; it was flanked on the north by the Trifa plain and on the south by the Angad (see Map 11). Cloaked in oak forest and juniper scrub, this Tyrolean landscape had been a safe refuge for the Arabic-speaking Berber tribe of the same name since 1859, and taming it would involve mountain fighting – a fundamentally different prospect from brigade-sized sweeps across the Chaouia. However, Lyautey's intelligence officers had already more or less neutralized the clans in the western half of the range; his plan was to encircle the hostile eastern tribesmen in order to cut them off from markets and supply routes, then strike into their territory from both north and south.

On 24 November 1907, following a resisted French attack on a village, a Skirmisher company and a cavalry squadron were attacked by about 2,000 warriors on the west bank of the Oued Kiss and were forced to make a fighting retreat across the river. When this was trumpeted through the hills as a great victory it brought more tribesmen out, and on the 27th a larger *harka* crossed into Algeria and inflicted some losses on troops holding the village of Ba el Assa. By now overconfident, the Beni Snassen divided into two large war parties. On 29 November, one hit the little Mediterranean coastal village of Port Say at the mouth of the Kiss, which was held by Zouaves under the comforting guns of a destroyer anchored off shore, and the tribesmen made little progress. The other force, about 4,000 strong, attacked a post at Menasseb further upriver, held by troops including the 11th (Mounted)/1st RE. The company took casualties, but the Berbers were brought under shellfire as they advanced along a gulley, and left some 300 dead on the field after pushing on with blind courage. This was the high point of Beni Snassen aggression, and the sight of tribesmen going along their line methodically picking up empty brass confirmed the effectiveness of the cordon that was denying them ammunition from Oujda market. The next day a strong French force crossed to the west bank of the Kiss, and the warriors fell back into the hills.[23]

Now Lyautey turned to the offensive; in the first week of December he sent a column about 2,500 strong under Colonel Branlière (including III/1st RE) from Martimprey into the northern Trifa plain. The following week a second of similar strength under Colonel Felineau (including I/ and half of V/1st RE, with the regiment's mounted company) advanced along the Angad plain south of the mountains; they had their only real fight when advancing up the southern slopes to Ain Sfa on 13 December.[24] Having achieved his flanking marches, Lyautey broke his two brigades into smaller columns and sent them up into the mountains, Felineau providing the assault units and Branlière the stop-line. By the time the two met at the head of the Taforalt pass on Christmas Day, cutting the Djebel Beni Snassen in two, the *caids* had already been coming in to Oujda and Martimprey to seek the *aman* since 17 December. (Their fines were set in goats, sheep and guns; the French always tried to confiscate the more modern rifles, but the tribes habitually kept numbers of their oldest muskets for just this purpose.) Lyautey's rapid victory over a tribe of some 30,000 Berbers made a sharp public contrast with General Drude's inactivity on the Chaouia at that time, and did the former's reputation no harm. It had also brought him to his long-time objective in the northeast – the east bank of the Oued Moulouya.[25]

Lyautey expressed his triumph in a long letter to his friend Vogüé on 1 January 1908; some niggling details may have been adjusted for narrative drama, but the essentials stand up. He called the campaign 'a mathematician's joy ... this time I have been left royally in peace, and from the very beginning I have not been bothered by anyone or anything':

> Yesterday [my troops] carried out for me the finest raking manoeuvre you could imagine. Four columns coming up from the south drove simultaneously into these hitherto inviolate gorges and cliffs, while Branlière's column, from the north, blocked all the exits. This surprise movement was carried out by night, under conditions calling for incredible boldness ...
>
> At 4am I was at the mouth of a pass to greet the heads of the columns, driving all their captures [flocks] ahead of them ... A company of the Legion were passing: '*Bonjour, mes légionnaires*', I called; '*Bonjour, mon général – tout va bien!*' came back from 200 throats with a single voice ... With an instrument like that in my hand, I could go anywhere.[26]

ON THE SOUTH-EASTERN FRONTIER, the provisional proclamation of Moulay Hafid in January 1908 put heart into the resistance. Some Ziz valley tribesmen went north-west to fight on the Chaouia, and since most leaders in the Tafilalt were still hedging their bets in those days of three simultaneous 'sultans' (Abd el Aziz, Moulay Hafid and El Rogi) the focus of anti-French rhetoric also moved further north, to the edge of the High Atlas. There, a sharifian holy man had been preaching *jihad* since 1907, and was now in direct correspondence with Moulay Hafid. Moulay Ahmad Lahsin el Saba headed a *zaouia* at the remote oasis of Dairs Saba just east of the mountains (see Map 11). In February 1908, clans of Ait Izdig, Southern Ait Segrushin and Ait Aysha Berbers began gathering there to plan an attack on Colomb Béchar, and early in April between 3,000 and 4,000 warriors set out eastwards.[27]

The largest part of Lyautey's division – about 4,000 men – were still tied down around Oujda, but in the south General Vigny of Ain Sefra Subdivision sent out three modest columns to search for this rumoured *harka*. These troops included four separate foot companies of the 2nd RE (the dispersal of their battalions arguing Vigny's shortage of units), and two mounted companies of the 1st Foreign.[28] On the evening of 15 April, Lieutenant-Colonel Pierron was camped at a small oasis named Menabha with a half-squadron of 2nd Spahis, a mountain gun section, a company each from Major Velly's 2nd Algerian Skirmishers and the 2nd RE, and half of 24th (Mounted)/1st RE under Captain Maury.[29] The Spahis and the 24th (Mounted) had arrived first, and the légionnaires had built their usual knee-high walls before the rest of the column slogged in at about 5pm, delayed by the 800 baggage camels. The camp north of the palm-grove and waterhole was shaped in the usual square, perhaps 200 yards on a side, and the mule half-company were holding part of the east face. Two hills rose a couple of hundred yards outside the perimeter opposite the south-west and south-east corners; the latter, crowned with some old ruins, was the higher.

BY ABOUT 4.30AM ON 16 APRIL, Moulay Ahmad Lahsin's Berbers, apparently without being spotted, had crept up on three sides of the camp in the darkness. They opened up a heavy fire; some slipped straight over the wall before the startled soldiers could react, and got among the tents to start slitting throats. At the same time the little four-man outposts on the two southern hills were overrun, and Berber riflemen began shooting down into the camp from these heights. Sergeant Lefèvre of the 24th (Mounted), by then lying half-dressed behind the east *murette* with his légionnaires, recalls a scene of disturbing confusion in the pre-dawn murk: bullets zipping through the white tents, mules braying and falling, and shots from the hilltop striking men of his squad. He also describes the extreme tension of obeying orders to keep looking to their own front while hearing behind them the unnerving sounds of a Berber charge hitting and pushing back the units holding another face of the camp. Then shadows came rushing at the east wall, and Lefèvre was too busy to think. Behind him a Berber rush got right inside the tent lines; desperate bayonet-fighting broke out, wounded were killed as they lay in the aid tent, and the 24th (Mounted) soon had to fall back to hold a makeshift redoubt of feed-sacks.

This was not going to be Morocco's little Isandlwana, however, and there seem to have been two fundamental reasons why not: the camp was much more compact than that of the unlucky 24th Foot, and the Berbers were not Zulus – they wanted to loot as much as they wanted to kill. The camp, perhaps 200 yards across, was large enough to give the roughly 600 men pushed back from the perimeter enough depth behind them to fall back steadily and regroup, yet small enough that they could do so in close order without their attackers getting between the platoons and separating them into isolated knots. Once the defenders had retreated from part of the camp, the Berbers simply stopped attacking them and concentrated on pillaging – in quarrelsome competition – the part they had already captured; and this did not contain the two 80mm mountain guns.

Two little battles now developed simultaneously. The deadly south-eastern hill had to be retaken; Pierron ordered Captain Maury, with the 75 men of his 24th (Mounted) who were still fit, to break out from the east face – not then under heavy attack – and hook south to assault it. Halfway up they were stopped by the Berbers' fire, and Private Profilet was left lying in the open. Captain Maury called for a volunteer, and he and Private Guy ran out and grabbed Profilet's ankles, but both of them were then hit – the captain in the wrist and Guy full in the chest. Leaving the dead Profilet, Maury hauled Guy on to his back and carried him into cover (he died the next day). Then one of the mountain guns crashed into action and dropped a few shells on the summit, and Maury pushed his legionnaires upwards again; they drove the last tribesmen from the hilltop at about 5.30am in the first rays of sunrise, at the price of one-third of their number – Lieutenant Lacoste and 9 men killed, and another 17 wounded.

As the light increased, down in the camp Major Velly led a counter-attack by the Legion and *turco* companies, and at the third attempt they succeeded in driving the Berbers out beyond the perimeter again, where they could be brought under steady fire. Some were shot down while burdened by their loot, and by about 6am the rest had withdrawn. The Berbers' total losses were reckoned to be about 100; French casualties were reported as 19 killed and 101 wounded, of whom 11 and 57 respectively were from the Legion companies. The total of 120 casualties was the highest in any single frontier battle yet, and Pierron presumably had to face some stinging questions about sentries and outposts.[30]

THE BERBERS DISPERSED with their loot, doubtless spreading the word of a great victory, and no longer interested in continuing to Colomb Béchar; one source states that they got away with Spahi horses and saddles, mules, nearly 100 rifles, crates of ammunition and tinned food.[31] General Vigny assembled his columns into a 5,000-strong punitive force, and although unable to catch up with the dissolving *harka*, on 5 May this Upper Guir Column shelled and destroyed Moulay Ahmad Lahsin's headquarters at Dairs Saba. The holy man was not present: glowing with *baraka* from his success, he was gathering tribesmen about 40 miles to the south.

In the absence of the wounded Captain Maury, the 24th (Mounted) was led by Lieutenant Jaeglé, the cheerful young parodist who drew word-pictures of senior officers. Sergeant Lefèvre's diary describes the villages of the peaceful Ouled Nahcer tribe along the Oued Haiber as delightful, shaded by olive trees and lush with figs, grapes and grenadines. The twittering chaffinches around his tent gave him 'just for an instant the impression that I was gazing over a little laughing corner of France'. The légionnaires' appreciation of these surroundings was tempered by the fact that they had run out of tobacco and soap, their uniforms were in rags, and they were breaking their teeth on hard-tack.[32] General Vigny needed resupply badly, and when, on 8 May, rumours reached the column that anything between 8,000 and 20,000 tribesmen (perhaps with cannon) were gathering at Boudenib south-west across the mountains, he was in no shape to march directly towards them. It cost him two days to hook east and down the Bou Anan pass to meet a convoy at El Hajjoui, where, on 11 May, the troops were finally able to enjoy a pipe again after their *soupe*. On 12 May they marched due west along the north bank of the Oued Guir (some men of the mule company still in worn-out sandals, and trousers made from feed-sacks). At 1pm the next day the 24th (Mounted) were providing the left flank guard as the column approached on their left the palm-groves of Beni Ouzien, about 6 miles short of Boudenib.

THERE IS NOTHING OF 'LAUGHING FRANCE' about the terrain surrounding Boudenib (see Map 16). The Oued Guir cuts through the parched east–west wall of the Djebel Mechmech to emerge southwards from the Tazuguerte pass, and then swings eastwards across a flat, desolate plain – the Djorf. The *palmerie* of Boudenib, perhaps 2 miles from end to end and a mile across, enclosed a large *kasbah* built amid cultivated ground close to the north bank of the broad riverbed, facing a series of red rock *garas* jutting up perhaps 1,500 yards away south of the Guir.

Marching towards Boudenib from the east, the 24th (Mounted) would have passed over many miles of featureless flats, tawny or rust-coloured under a scabby skin of coarse gravel and dotted with the usual low clumps of grey weeds. Over any distance the ground tilts and sinks in subtle gradients, so that extensive palm-plantations only become visible when they are little more than 1,000 yards away; until they do, the lack of any vertical feature for the eye to seize upon makes it remarkably difficult to judge distances. Occasionally the légionnaires would have crossed shallow streams running down towards the river on their left, their beds of pale grey water-rounded pebbles contrasting with the angular brown-black gravel of the desert. In the far distance off to the right the receding *djebel* shows yellowish-cream, marked with swirls of darker strata like chocolate ripples in pale fudge. On the left, the otherwise indistinct edge of the shallow riverbed is marked by a straggling line of vegetation; as you approach the small village and palm-groves of Beni Ouzien the near bank is lined intermittently with feathery fresh-green tamarisk trees, plumed grasses and occasional cane-breaks. Water flows slowly in a broad band close to the south bank of the Guir, hundreds of yards away, but except during the winter floods and spring run-off most of its wide bed is a confusing succession of whale-backs of pale shingle, sandbars with occasional whiskers of grass, and stretches of unstable mud. Beyond the south bank, a succession of Devon-red cliffs grow closer as you move westwards.

Some 6,000 tribesmen had gathered around Boudenib, and through binoculars their tents could be seen crowding the flats west of the main *palmerie* about 6 miles away. At mid-afternoon on 13 May a courier from Major de Barry (the cavalry officer commanding this left wing) warned Jaeglé that tribesmen were waiting in the Beni Ouzien palm-grove, where the artillery would try to search them out. The 75mm batteries opened fire, both on the main camp at Boudenib and at much shorter range into the thick palm trees close on the Mounted Company's left front. This provoked heavy rifle fire; Sergeant Lefèvre saw white smoke-puffs against the dark green and heard bullets snapping over his head. In order to clear this flank for cavalry to pass down the plain, the company were ordered to assault the *palmerie.*

The légionnaires advanced towards the treeline over exposed ground now broken by shallow gulleys in the yellow clay, and men began to drop – seven in Lefèvre's platoon alone. The Algerian Skirmishers following the company on their right were still some way off; the 24th (Mounted) were isolated outside the palm-grove, taking fire from tribesmen concealed behind trees and in irrigation ditches, and the légionnaires' advance had obliged the artillery to switch targets. Jaeglé kept them moving and at last they reached the trees, killing several warriors face-to-face, but now that visibility was reduced to a few yards they were vulnerable to surprise attack at point-blank range. Sergeant Lefèvre knew that they had to cling on, because if they were driven out into the open again they would be easy targets. The 24th (Mounted) were on their own at the far left point of the French advance; on the plain north of them Moroccan cavalry had charged, some even reaching the gun line and forcing the crews to make use of their carbines.

At about 6pm, when Captain Clavel's *turcos* had at last come up on their right flank to form something like a battle-line, the Legion company pressed on westwards towards the far fringe of the palm trees. Lieutenant Jaeglé led a rush by the 2nd Half-Company through deepening shadows and towards the glare of sunset, against Berbers holding a wide gulley. He fell, shot in the body; Lieutenant Huot took over, but a bullet ripped across his left ribs almost at once, and in Sergeant Lefèvre's words 'he was obliged to take himself to the rear'. A machine gun came into action and swept the enemy off a low crest, and as night fell the 24th (Mounted) were ordered to fall back towards the baggage column, still under intermittent sniping. In his later post-mortem, General Bailloud, GOC 19th Army Corps, would criticize Vigny for committing this elite mobile company in the role of heavy assault infantry in closely wooded ground; the 24th (Mounted) had lost 15 out of the 25 dead suffered by the whole column that day.

Eventually the company took their place in the west face of a big defensive square on the plain facing Boudenib, and Sergeant Lefèvre went back to the field ambulance to check on his wounded, who numbered 15 out of the column's total of 68. Lieutenant Jaeglé died that night; he would be buried at Colomb Béchar beside his inseparable friend Lacoste, killed at Menabha the previous month. Lieutenant Huot turned out to be less seriously hurt than his sergeant had assumed. It was 10pm when Lefèvre returned to his squad; they had to dig shallow trenches for defence – there were no rocks large enough for a *murette* on this sandy billiard-table – and men slept with weapon in hand. Fires were forbidden, the wind was blowing hard out of the desert, and the légionnaires had nothing but hard biscuit to chew on.

THE NEXT MORNING the advance on Boudenib itself resumed; 24th (Mounted) were given the easier task of forming a stop-line at the edge of the *palmerie*, while their comrades of Captain Bertrand's 3rd (Mounted)/1st RE moved into the vanguard. From a range of a mile and a half the *kasbah* was shelled, but neither the shrapnel shells nor the melinite high explosive seemed to be very effective. A squadron of Africa Light Horse charged into the palm trees – supposedly without orders – and took several casualties before scattering out again. Captain Bertrand's men (including Lieutenant Paul Rollet) went into action against Berber riflemen from mid morning on 14 May and captured some buildings, but a general assault was avoided when, in late afternoon, the *harka* was seen streaming away to the west and north, and a white flag was raised on the minaret of the mosque.

On the 15th the village was searched, and prisoners were sorted into three groups: women and children were left free, the men of Boudenib itself were given the *aman*, but those from the Tafilalt and elsewhere were questioned. One source reported that among them were Marrakesh men in Sultan Moulay Hafid's uniform, and others from as far afield as Rabat, and the Sous plain behind Agadir.[33] General Vigny sent cavalry, mule companies and lightened Algerian infantry to follow the heavy tracks left by the *harka*, but without success (a staff officer's attempt to take a short cut resulted in the troops becoming lost in waterless terrain). It was decided to establish a base at Boudenib.

On 16 May, on the other side of the Atlas, Moulay Hafid made a triumphal entry into Meknes, and – far from being deterred by the defeat at Boudenib – in the south-east unprecedentedly large numbers of tribesmen began to gather. From the Tafilalt – only about 70 miles from Boudenib – the Ait Khabbash Berbers and Ziz valley Arabs who had previously held back now rallied to Moulay Ahmad Lahsin's banner, together with men from the High and even the Middle Atlas. By 20 August 1908, various groups totalling more than 15,000 tribesmen were reportedly assembling at the *marabout's* headquarters at Tazuguerte, less than 20 miles north-west of Boudenib.[34]

THE FRENCH HAD BUILT a 'redoubt' on rolling ground about a mile north-west of the *kasbah* in the palm-groves. This was an irregular quadrilateral of dug ditches and spoil ramparts, large enough to accommodate 1,500 men and 550 animals, with corner bastions mounting 75mm field and 80mm mountain guns. Perhaps 2,000 yards due south of this camp, on the northern lip of a 150-foot high tabletop *gara* above the south bank of the Guir, a small fort had been built for observation (it is intriguing that well before the First World War the French were using the German term *blockhaus*).[35]

Photos suggest that the blockhouse was an irregularly shaped quadrilateral of roughly dressed stone slabs, with loopholed walls rising about 25ft on the southern faces, but only about 10 feet high and unloopholed around the north, where there was only a narrow gap between the wall and the cliff edge. There seem to have been internal towers at the south-east and north-west corners, with walled sentry-balconies protruding at the top of each, resembling theatre-boxes. The building was set on a levelled rock platform, and at the west side the edge of this terrace dropped off in a chest-high step. A couple of rows of thin barbed wire had been strung along the stony slopes about 25 yards from the walls, but there was no outwork to protect the modest-sized door in the east wall. While the east, north and west sides of the *gara* were cliffs, a steep slope up the southern side gave access to the summit. In one photo signalling-lamp equipment can be seen in an exposed position on a northern parapet, facing the oasis and the French camp below.[36]

From 29 August onwards, lookouts in the blockhouse watched a mass of Moroccans pouring out of the mouth of the pass and spreading slowly across the Djorf plain towards Boudenib. The main redoubt to the north was occupied by VI/2nd RE, two companies from 2nd RTA, a Spahi squadron and gunners, all commanded by Major Fesch. (The leader of the *harka* sent in an envoy with a letter, challenging him in superbly medieval terms to come out from behind his walls and fight in the open – see the epigraph to this chapter.) The blockhouse above the south bank was held by Lieutenant Vary and Sergeant Koenig with 75 men – 40 légionnaires and 35 Skirmishers. They had no heavy weapons, but they did have some melinite charges and fuses, and a box of dynamite sticks presumably left over from the quarrying of stone for the construction.[37]

*

THE MISSION OF THE BLOCKHOUSE GARRISON was to spot and signal enemy movements for the commander of the low-lying main camp. On the late afternoon of 31 August 1908, Vary and his artillery-observer sergeant flashed the news of several tented camps being pitched north and west of the redoubt; this continued on the morning of 1 September, when groups of riders were moving around constantly and men on foot were converging towards the redoubt and the palm-groves south of it, surrounding the camp on three sides. By 3.30pm, Moroccans were also massing to the south of the blockhouse itself, masked from the direction of the redoubt, and Vary asked for artillery ranging shots.

The message traffic seems to fall into a pattern as the sun slipped towards the west on 1 September: Vary answered repeated requests from Fesch for information about the enemy around the redoubt (4pm, 'Gulley parallel to your west face full of infantry'), while becoming increasingly conscious of the threat to his own position (4.30pm, '75 fire not reaching the hill – you're firing too far west. Rake crests south of blockhouse, which are very thickly occupied. I don't *have* Map Sheets 3 and 4 . . .' – this presumably in reply to an unhelpful instruction). The 75mm field gun was a magnificent low-trajectory piece with an effective shrapnel round, but it was no howitzer, and from the viewpoint of the gunners in the redoubt the tribesmen threatening the blockhouse were just behind a reverse crest. Firing air-burst shrapnel shells close to an open-topped friendly position, especially after dark, was in any case a delicate task. The 80mm mountain gun could drop shells from a high angle, but (as Rankin had remarked on the Chaouia) this old-fashioned piece recoiled about 10 yards after every shot and had to be laboriously re-laid.[38]

Between 5pm and 5.20pm on 1 September, Major Fesch badgered Vary for information on enemy concentrations. The subaltern did his best, but complained that smoke was hiding the camps; he ended with a slightly wistful reminder that the *gara* summit south of him was now permanently occupied by the enemy in great numbers. Ten minutes later Vary's patience was clearly strained by a request for his count of how many shells of each calibre had been fired by the redoubt so far: 'The [enemy on the] summit south of the blockhouse are firing on me and beginning to advance. Request 75 fire if possible.' As darkness fell, waves of tribesmen moved forward across the rocky summit and brought the parapets and loopholes under constant fire (the edge of the foundation platform on the west gave them excellent short-range cover on that side). Though they could not breach the walls, as the night wore on Vary had no way of knowing if they might not bring up makeshift scaling ladders, and his walls were only 10 feet high at some points. The message log at various times during the night tells its own story, and it is easy to imagine the tones of voice if these signals had been by field telephone rather than by lamp. The following are extracts:

> 7.50pm [*Vary*]: Blockhouse under assault – request 75 fire behind, right and left.
>
> 8pm [*Vary*]: Too long – sweep 200–300 yards each side.
>
> 8.30pm [*Vary* – on being asked for an appreciation of the artillery fire]: We are surrounded – this is not the moment to show myself ... We are surrounded on all sides except the north ... Your fire is a bit over.
>
> 9pm [*Vary* – asked to report the last shots]: A bit too far to your right, and 20–30 yards short – one round fell close to us ... [Then] Good – fire for effect.

The blockhouse garrison had not eaten since morning, but thirst was a worse trial; two Skirmishers took their lives in their hands to take water around the parapets and loopholes. From 10.30pm there was a flurry of fire corrections; this seems to have been the crisis, and at some point the Moroccans came right up to the doorway in the east face. Before they could break in, a couple of légionnaires risked rising above the parapet to drop three pairs of fused melinite charges among them, with great effect. Then:

> 11 pm [*Fesch*]: Estimated number of enemy around you?
>
> [*Vary*]: Impossible to say, but I believe several thousand.
>
> [*Fesch*]: Have they reached your wire?
>
> [*Vary*]: They are up to the wire – many corpses spread all around the blockhouse.
>
> [*Fesch*]: Any losses?
>
> [*Vary*]: I am delighted with all my men – one Skirmisher mortally wounded. Continue to fire to the west.

Asked what was happening, Vary then reported that shouting indicated a renewed assault from the west, and passed a series of fire corrections. At about 2am on 2 September the tiredness of both officers after six hours' fighting becomes evident in a short-tempered exchange:

> [*Fesch*]: Why do you request so much fire when we no longer hear the enemy? The artillery must economize on ammo.

[*Vary*]: We have to economize on ammo too, and the enemy are in great numbers – so fire!

[*Fesch*]: Light up the surroundings with occasional flares, and request artillery support only when absolutely necessary.

[*Vary*]: Pointless to use flares – we can see well enough. I will ask for artillery whenever it is necessary.

At 2.30am the major seemed to be rather more focused on his lieutenant's plight:

[*Fesch*]: How much ammo have you used?

[*Vary*]: Eleven boxes – three left.

[*Fesch*]: In addition to the three boxes, how much do your men have on them?

[*Vary*]: Average of four packets [i.e. 32 rounds each]

[*Fesch*]: What about your charges?

[*Vary*]: We have thrown four … very good effect; we still have 16, plus the box of 'flutes' [dynamite sticks ?].

At 3am, Major Fesch was in a generous mood: 'Do you want a couple of shells?'. Vary replied that he was no longer under pressure from the east and could see nothing on that flank, but that there were large numbers of tribesmen to the west – 'I can even hear them insulting us. You might send them a shell?' Fesch promised to do so, and told the lieutenant above all to husband his remaining ammunition. At 5am, sunrise allowed Vary to report that he could see no significant movement nearby, just a few individuals; he told Fesch that he could see Moroccans returning to their camps in the valley, and asked for fifteen boxes of ammunition to be sent up. During the long night his men had held off five distinct assaults, three of them significant; 25 of the 75 defenders had been wounded, but only one Skirmisher died, and they found 173 enemy dead around the blockhouse walls. Although the tribesmen remained camped on the plain, there were no significant attacks on the main redoubt.[39]

COLONEL ALIX ARRIVED AT BOUDENIB from Colomb Béchar on 5 September with some 4,000 men, tired and thirsty after a forced march; one of them was Sergeant Lefèvre of 24th (Mounted) Company. Moulay Ahmad Lahsin was granted the pitched battle to which he had challenged Major Fesch, on 7 September on the plain north-west of Boudenib, when Alix advanced as if to cut the Moroccans off from the mouth of the pass. Rumour had been accurate for once: there really were nearer 20,000 than 15,000 warriors, making a ragged line of separate tribal groups up to 3 miles across.

On the absolutely featureless rust-coloured plain Alix drew his brigade up in a single diamond formation about 2,000 yards wide, and goaded the Moroccans with his 16 guns. When the enveloping mass of tribesmen flowed forwards at about 8.30am he ordered his infantry to hold their fire until the range had dropped to 400 yards, and then unleashed their crashing succession of volleys. By 9.30am the tribesmen were fleeing in disorder to the north and west, leaving the Djorf carpeted with several hundred bodies. Sergeant Lefèvre's mule-company had been in the right front face, so joined the Spahis in pursuing the Berbers for more than 6 miles up the Tazuguerte pass. The VI/2nd RE was also on the field that day; so the Legion had played a full part in the defeat of the last pan-tribal *harka* ever to form in the border country.[40]

13. Falling towards Fes
1909–12

*While Moulay Hafid was sultan ... the palace was the
scene of constant barbarity and torture. The Sultan
himself, neurasthenic, and addicted, it is said, to drugs,
had his good and his bad days ... He was possessed of
a certain cunning intelligence, and had some idea of
government, but disappointment met him. Things had
gone too far ... he gave way to temptations, and became
cruel and avaricious.*

Walter Harris[1]

NEWS OF THE BATTLE OF BOUDENIB, which left the way clear for a
steady penetration of the Upper Guir country and the easternmost Atlas,
increased the pressure on the new Sultan Moulay Hafid to deliver on his
anti-French rhetoric. However, since entering Fes and attempting to form a
Maghzan he had found himself completely unable to dispense with the
hated Europeans, who were already deeply embedded in the economy and
administration. The treasury was empty, and constructing a functioning
regime without French finance and instructors was an impossibility. In the
north-east, Lyautey patiently continued his 'drilling' operations in a great
triangle of country beyond the Oued Moulouya where the sultan's writ did
not run; in the west, the French retained their ostensibly protective role on
the Chaouia while keeping a wary eye on constant tribal warfare to the
south of it.

In Fes, the sultan was forced in December 1908 to accept the Act of
Algeciras entrenching French and Spanish rights, and to acknowledge
Morocco's existing foreign debts. His proclamation of an end *to jihad* cost
him dear in public credibility, and what little goodwill he retained was soon
squandered by the medieval ruthlessness of his attempts to gather taxes for

his mortgaged government. In this pillaging he was assisted enthusiastically by his king-maker Madani el Glaoui, whom the sultan had appointed grand vizier. Madani, in turn, appointed dozens of his own relatives to positions of local power, and his fiefdom, governed from a palace of royal magnificence in Marrakesh, soon extended over roughly one-third of Morocco. The sultan and El Glaoui were formally linked by a mutual exchange of daughters in marriage, and watched one another like cats.[2]

Simultaneously, the sultan gave formal governorship over the hill country of the Djibala in the north-west to another regional strongman. The notorious sharifian robber baron Moulay Ahmad er Raisuli had built on the position he had inherited from a formidable father, proving his extraordinary strength of will in disaster as well as triumph. He had survived four unimaginable years chained in one of the regent Ba Ahmad's dungeons, and after being amnestied by Abd el Aziz he had returned to the Djibala a crueller man, utterly determined to regain and surpass the influence and riches he had lost. By kidnap, extortion, pillage and murder, he succeeded; by 1908 Raisuli's audacity, guile and violence had made him the inevitable choice for *pasha* to hold down the restless north-western hills – ostensibly in the name of Moulay Hafid, though his personal appetite for gold, power and women acknowledged few limits.[3]

Raisuli treated Moulay Hafid 'the Scurvy' with more wary respect than he had shown the ineffectual Abd el Aziz, since the new sultan was an altogether more dangerous figure – a Koranic scholar, but also an unstable tyrant with a venomous temper. Moulay Hafid had, of course, been greedy for the throne, but his wish to save his country from the Europeans had also been sincere, and his frustration at finding himself powerless to do so – indeed, powerless to truly control any great matters of state – aggravated his worst traits. Resentful, avaricious and obsessively suspicious of treachery, he showed a sadistic cruelty in exercising those powers that he did have. He enjoyed supervising personally the work of his torturers and executioners, and in his lust to extort riches even high-born ladies of his kingdom were not safe from his dungeons.[4]

ONE OF THE SULTAN'S ITCHING SORES was healed in the autumn of 1909. In the north-east, the claim of Bou Himara, alias El Rogi, to be a rightful heir was generally disbelieved after the spring of 1903, when he left Taza to establish a stronghold at Zeluan, a few miles south of the Spanish presidio of Melilla. There he ruled like any other warlord, and though he posed as the head of a rudimentary pseudo-government, this was never established with any thoroughness. After he more or less ceased offensive operations against Maghzan forces around Oujda in 1905 his flow of loot dwindled, and he needed new sources of income to pay his small standing army and to rent the loyalty of tribal chiefs. One solution was his sale, in the summer of 1907, of lead- and iron-mining concessions south-west of Melilla to French and German-financed Spanish companies, complete with the right to build a railway serving them. This invitation to foreign intruders was unpopular with the tribes, as was his simultaneous resort to traditional tax-gathering methods.

In June 1908, El Rogi's black general, Jilali Mull'Udhu, led one of these pillaging parties westwards into the Rif, thus provoking an unprecedented alliance of the whole Ait Waryaghar tribe (French, Beni Ouriaghel) and some neighbouring clans. In September, these Berber highlanders surrounded the Pretender's cavalry on the Nekor river and shot them down as they floundered in the mud. In an attempt to rebuild his damaged prestige, El Rogi led about 1,000 men towards Fes in July 1909; on 10 August they were beaten in the Oued Ouergha valley by a makeshift royal *mehalla* with French artillery instructors, and between the 15th and 18th of that month Moulay Hafid presided over the public torture and mutilation of the prisoners. On 22 August El Rogi himself was betrayed and captured, and taken back to Fes in a cage to be exhibited in a courtyard of the palace by the gloating sultan. For three weeks Moulay Hafid attempted to make the Pretender reveal the whereabouts of his rumoured wealth. Finally, on 13 September, the sultan had El Rogi thrown to the palace lions, but when they proved too lethargic to do more than mangle him he was finished off by a slave. In his time Bou Himara had condemned many other men to hideous deaths, but it was said that he endured his own long ordeal with great courage. His most lasting legacy to Morocco was the seeds of an entirely new war.[5]

THE FIFTEENTH-CENTURY SPANISH harbour presidios on the Mediterranean coast – at Ceuta on the Straits of Gibraltar, and Melilla about 135 miles to the east – still retained something of the character of their medieval foundation (see Map 18). Each measuring only a few miles across, they had functioned for centuries as little more than sleepy gateways for trade, set down on the edge of almost unexplored tribal country, though their areas of settlement had been slightly enlarged after campaigns in 1859–60 and 1893–4 respectively. They were dependent on ships for intercommunication, and on Spain for almost every necessity – on occasion, even water had to be shipped over to Melilla from Malaga; they had no more capacity for independent survival than space-stations.

After defeat at American hands in 1898 left Spain with only a few abject remnants of her once world-spanning empire, an *'africanista'* faction urged the active exploitation of these footholds. At first, governments were inhibited by fear of foreign reactions, but Delcassé's busy diplomacy, culminating in the agreement of October 1904 and the Act of Algeciras two years later, cleared the way for Spain to expand her territories throughout a broad northern coastal zone of Morocco. This vision – to call it a programme would wrongly imply some coherent plan – was divisive. Spain was poor, backward, inefficient, corrupt, and largely under the autocratic social control of a stagnant Church and aristocracy; but she nevertheless had a vocal class of educated liberals, served by a courageously active press. Exposed to their arguments, popular opinion, at first indifferent to the Moroccan enthusiasts, would become increasingly hostile, though this hostility had few effective outlets for political action.

The arguments against a new colonial adventure were that an attempt to expand Spanish territory in Morocco would be a ruinously expensive graveyard for Spanish youth; that such a colony, cramped in the coastal mountains, could never become a net contributor to Spanish wealth; and that it would be a damaging distraction from the real work of reforming Spain herself for the twentieth century. Ranged against these voices were the Church, some commercial interests, conservative politicians and an element among their constituency, and the army. The Church's attitude to the 'Moors' had hardly evolved over centuries, and reports of rich mineral resources in the Rif hills were enough to explain commercial enthusiasm. Conservative politicians welcomed the prospect of patriotic theatricals to distract the poor from the national failure to provide them with any opportunities for a better life. Many less cynical Spaniards were also hungry for some cause to revive national pride, and some even hoped for new lives as pioneers.

The *africanistas* of the army, above all, saw their salvation in Morocco. Their dreary existence in home garrisons lacked the validation that the Rhineland frontier gave their French counterparts, and without Morocco they had no prospect of the active service that alone could bring prestige and worthwhile advancement. In a rigid and largely agricultural society governed by hereditary privilege and favouritism, the well-born who had any energy were denied careers in commerce or industry, and only the uniforms of God or the king were acceptable. But by now, few family estates could provide the necessary private income no matter how hard they squeezed their peasants, and there was a limit to the number of promotions to the rank of general that even the Spanish Army could justify. The collapse of the Cuban and Philippine garrisons in 1898 had revealed not only unreadiness and incompetence, but also shocking corruption (stores and armouries opened to meet the emergency were found to be empty, their contents sold off long ago for private gain). In the ranks, Spain's illiterate peasant conscripts were neglected, abused, and exploited as personal labourers by absentee officers, too many of whom lacked any taste for serious work at their profession. The kingdom was too poor to fund a modern army, and the officer class too poor to live honestly on its pay or its private means; yet both were too proud to give up the outward trappings of a military prestige that now rested on little more than distant memory.

Any healthy army needs well-founded reasons for pride. The Spanish Army in the early 1900s had none, and the *africanistas* saw a Moroccan adventure as the opportunity to build some. Many among Spain's modern-minded educated class knew that the scandals of 1898 had not been addressed, and that the ministries charged with directing such an adventure were idle, dishonest and profoundly ignorant. Unfortunately for the junior ranks (and, eventually, for many French soldiers and légionnaires), too many of the *africanistas* seem to have been in denial about the systemic degeneracy of the army that they were proposing to lead into action against some of the most vigorous and skilful guerrilla fighters on earth. Given Spain's own Napoleonic history, her generals should have known better.[6]

THEIR VICTORY OVER EL ROGI in 1908 gave the Rifian tribes confidence, and in July 1909 they attacked engineers preparing the infrastructure for the iron mines leased out by the Pretender south of Melilla. General Marina y Vega demanded reinforcements, and the call-up of 20,000 Spanish reservists caused a general strike and violent riots in several Spanish cities, notably Barcelona. In the meantime, General Pintos himself and more than 1,000 of his men had been killed and 2,000 wounded on 27 July at Monte Gurugu, a feature that dominated the plain on the west of the peninsula. Reinforced to 30,000 men, it took Marina's *comandancia* until the end of September to capture these heights, and by the time a truce was negotiated at the end of November the Spanish were admitting to 4,000 casualties.[7]

Over the next few years intermittent Spanish operations on the plains behind Melilla pushed a line of posts towards the edges of the mountains. The mines became productive, underpinning some other Spanish and German commercial activity, and a colonial administration was established. From 1911 local troops *(Regulares)* were raised to ease the burden on the Spanish Army, which in 1911–12 probed westwards as far as the Kert river.

Simultaneously, Spanish troops landed at Larache on the Atlantic coast and marched inland to plant a base at Alcazarquivir (El Ksar el Kebir) in the south-west of the Djibala, from which troops were later intended to spread northwards to link up around Tetuan with others advancing southwards from Ceuta. The commander at Alcazarquivir was a blustering royal favourite named Lieutenant-Colonel Manuel Fernandez Silvestre, who in 1911 began a frustrating relationship with the Pasha Ahmad er Raisuli. Raisuli's ambition was to become the *khalifa* of the whole Spanish zone and thus second only to the sultan, and Silvestre had to deal with him not only as a locally powerful warlord but also as the appointee of the Maghzan that was nominally recognized by both France and Spain. Naturally, Raisuli exploited both his armed strength and his official status to play off the Spanish against the Maghzan to his own advantage.[8]

FAR TO THE SOUTH-EAST OF MELILLA, 1909–10 saw General Lyautey making quiet progress with forces a fraction the size of those commanded by General Marina. Given a free hand by Paris, he pushed his mobile groups west from Oujda and Berguent across the great triangle of hills and high plains east of the Oued Moulouya (see Map 18), building a post at Taourirt in June 1910 and patrolling as far west as Guercif on that river – nearly half way between the old 1845 Algerian border and Fes. (While the Quai d'Orsay still insisted on the fiction of Maghzan authority, in practice the old frontier was now a dead letter.) Further south, patrols from Boudenib pushed into the edges of the High Atlas, where the usual combination of force, diplomacy and trade achieved tentative agreements with some Berber clans.[9]

Lyautey's spearhead unit from Berguent was the 3rd (Mounted) Company/1st RE, led from March 1909 by Captain Paul Rollet. In this independent command, Rollet – by now a four-year veteran of the mule companies, who had served with 3rd (Mounted) far longer than any of his men – was beginning to make a name for himself. He hardly ever mounted his horse between leaving one post and approaching another, so he covered twice the distance on foot of any of his légionnaires. He marched forty paces ahead of his company, as if he could not wait to find out what was over the next ridge, and he preferred sandals to boots, earning himself the nickname 'Captain Espadrilles'. He was as demanding of his men as he was of himself, quick to punish but as human as his rank allowed, and taking the trouble to get to know them personally. He had a sharp blue eye for every detail of organization, kit and procedure, and did not even leave it to his quartermaster-sergeant to haggle in remote markets when buying fresh provisions for his légionnaires. They liked his eccentricities and respected his strength, and they learned that he would defend them fearlessly against any perceived injustice. In March 1911, after his transfer to the western Moroccan front, Rollet disagreed loudly with the sentence of a court-martial on one of his men; although reprimanded for pursuing the matter as far as General Charles Moinier, then GOC Landing Corps, just two months later he wrote directly to the general to protest a similar judgement. Although himself a strict disciplinarian, he argued against the automatic and blind application of military law to his erring légionnaires. After all these years with them, he recognized their special character, and believed that only officers who knew them well were qualified to sit in judgement on them.[10]

An incident in the Sud-Oranais in July 1910 exemplified what could happen when even the best légionnaires were badly treated. By this date 3rd (Mounted)/1st RE was led by Captain Met, and that month no fewer than eighteen of his légionnaires caused a scandal when they deserted en masse into Morocco. Captain Met was one of those rare officers who earn the nickname 'Daddy' from their men, and he was not personally leading that half of his company when the incident occurred. The subsequent enquiry was chaired by the 1st RE's Colonel Girardot (Lyautey's old classmate, who had served under him in Upper Tonkin during the panic of January 1896). He concluded that the half-company was tired out by continuous marching when a stupidly brutal squad sergeant accused the sick Private Weinrock of malingering and denied him several turns on muleback; the légionnaire fell behind, and when his comrades later discovered that he had been killed by Arabs they deserted.[11]

The absentees were described as good soldiers, and the essential quality of this company was demonstrated on the 12th of the same month when its other half, led by Met in person, distinguished itself in an action on the east bank of the Moulouya near a spot named Moul el Bacha. It was operating in concert with Major Huguet d'Etaules' VI/1st RE, but they were separated when both units were attacked by Beni Bou Yahi tribesmen from the west bank. The fight went on for six hours; the half-company lost more than 50 per cent casualties – 9 killed and 42 wounded, of whom 5 died before they reached Taourirt. It was now routine to give casualties a morphine injection at halts, but they still suffered horribly from the sun and the flies, and under the heavy load of two *cacolets* a mule often stumbled. One soldier who distinguished himself, Private 1st Class Haberthur, paid a terrible price for his courage: a bullet hit him in the right side of the head and passed through, destroying both his eyes, and another broke his thigh while he was being carried to the rear. Most unusually for a ranker who did not yet hold the Military Medal, Haberthur was admitted to the Legion of Honour, an award that attracted a good deal of publicity through the sale of poignant photographic postcards.[12]

LATE IN 1910, GENERAL LYAUTEY'S COMMAND of Oran Division and his seven years on the frontier came to an end, by which time his troops dominated all the territory east of the lower Moulouya. His new appointment was to command 10th Army Corps at Rennes; he understood that war with Germany was inevitable, and he did not expect to progress any higher in the Army. He was well aware of the disdain in which the Metropolitan establishment held colonial soldiers lacking experience of handling large all-arms formations – like Wellington returning from India in 1805, Lyautey was a 'sepoy general'. Nevertheless, he conscientiously put himself through a staff colonel's course to sharpen up his theoretical skills, and he benefited from the fact that the new Chief of the General Staff in 1911 was General Joseph Joffre, whom he had known in Madagascar. The man who had collected up the hacked remains of Colonel Bonnier outside Timbuktu seventeen years earlier was hardly likely to see long colonial service as a disqualification for further employment.[13]

IN THE WEST, THE SULTAN had forfeited all loyalty, not only by his cruel rapacity but also by his ever deeper forced involvement with the French. In March 1910 he had been obliged to conclude an agreement for a massive new loan, and the French would now extend their lien on national customs revenues from 60 to 100 per cent.[14] From November 1910 a military mission under Major Emile Mangin, with a few French and Algerian officers and NCOs and a couple of British mercenaries, made limited progress in knocking the Maghzan cavalry and artillery into some sort of shape, but the unpaid and undisciplined infantry remained an intractable problem. Mangin discharged about 20 per cent of them and ensured that the remaining 4,000 actually received their meagre pay; this enraged the Moroccan officers who had previously intercepted it, but still did not go far towards persuading soldiers not to sell their rifles and desert, or keep them and turn bandit.[15]

In the second week of March 1911, warriors of the Beni Mtir and other tribes, rebelling against the sultan and his hated Grand Vizier el Glaoui, began to gather in the hills to surround Fes. Major Mangin had led much of the Maghzan *mehalla* north to quell unrest among the Cherarga, and this force was now bogged down under incessant rain. Moulay Hafid had his guard of 450 black slaves, but the city and the Dar Debibagh *kasbah* 2 miles south were held by only 200 Maghzan infantry and some 2,000 completely unreliable tribal levies; any defence would depend heavily on the artillery led by French and Algerian officers. A sortie to clear the approaches failed on 26 March, after which food prices began to rise in the city. On 2 April, about 3,000 men attacked Dar Debibagh and, although they were driven off by the artillery, by 11 April many of the levies defending that camp had defected to the Beni Mtir taking 1,200 Gras rifles with them.

Leaving the *mehalla* under the command of Major Brémond, Emile Mangin returned to Fes, where the European population were in fear for their lives, and the French consul Henri Gaillard was cabling Paris to appeal for a relief column to be sent from General Moinier's command on the Chaouia.[16] Fes might not be Morocco's heart, but it has long been its brain, and the French could no longer resist its magnetic pull. An occupation of the capital would violate the limits placed on French activity by the Act of Algeciras and would provoke Germany, Spain and the French Left; but in Paris the crisis coincided with the fall early in March of one of several administrations led by Aristide Briand, and its brief succession by that of Ernest Monis. At this moment of hesitation, the influence of Eugène Étienne's colonial parliamentary group was decisive; on 23 April, General Moinier was ordered to mount a relief column for Fes, and the War Ministry decided to reinforce the French corps in Morocco to 22,000. Brémond's muddy column of Maghzan troops arrived back in Fes on 26 April; they were of uncertain temper and short of ammunition, but they at least provided a deterrent for the city mob, whose hostility to Moulay Hafid frightened him into considering fleeing the city in disguise. (Yet another of his brothers, Moulay Zain el Abadin, was proclaimed as sultan at nearby Meknes on 19 April, and at Sefrou on 2 May). The reinforcement also allowed Emile Mangin to move his artillery up to the sixteenth-century Saadian forts of Bordj Nord and Sud on the hills immediately overlooking Fes.

It took Moinier two weeks to assemble a relief column and the necessarily large supply train from the troops dispersed around the Chaouia, hampered as he was by heavy spring rains and frequent attacks on columns and camps by Beni Hassen and Zimmur tribesmen. The first brigade under Colonel Brulard got under way from Kenitra on the coast on 11 May, but the whole 120-odd miles could not be covered in one push. Brulard had to establish a staging post at Lalla Ito, where he was joined by a second force under General Dalbiez with a camel convoy; this combined total of 5,700 men was then followed at a distance by the main supply train, escorted by Colonel Henri Gouraud's 1,800-strong brigade. The Legion, with only one battalion and a mounted company in western Morocco at this time, was represented by two companies from I/2nd RE in a mixed battalion with Zouaves, and by Captain Rollet's new command, 3rd (Mounted)/2nd RE. The mule company saw action at Lalla Ito on 13–15 May, after which large-scale tribal harassing attacks ceased.[17]

The Beni Mtir made attacks on the outer entrenchments at Fes on 11 May and again on the 18th, but were repulsed without difficulty. The 'first siege of Fes' ended on 21 May when Moinier's leading troops camped between the city and Dar Debibagh, and the tribes dispersed. Germany, Spain and the French Left were already loud in their criticism of the French government's violation of the provisions of the Act of Algeciras.[18]

IN THE EAST, MEANWHILE, on 19 April 1911 the Oran Division commander General Toutée was ordered to divert the attention of any tribes tempted to head through the unpenetrated 'Taza gap' for Fes by sending out two columns across the high plains of the Moulouya front. The columns were to link up at Debdou about 15 miles east of the Moulouya, and from there General Girardot was to swing west towards the river. Major Gerst's VI/1st RE left Sidi bel Abbès by train for Oujda, where they disembarked and made an 90-mile march south-westwards to reach Merada, where a new post was being built on the east bank of the Moulouya a few miles north-east of Guercif (see Map 11). Soon afterwards the 6th Battalion departed 'on column', together with III/ and part of V/1st RE, the usual screen of cavalry and a battery of guns. After clashes with Beni Ouarain war parties on 9 and 12 May, the advance continued into unknown country, southwards across the dry plain of Tafrata; this was open steppe, belonging to no tribe but ranged by many as their flocks and tents followed the seasons. On the 14th the column linked up at Debdou, about 25 miles south-east of Guercif, with the other that had marched west from Berguent, and they occupied the valley without resistance.[19]

The last stage of the march south from Guercif was a climb up to a cleft in a line of brown hills; once through it, the dusty column swung right around a shoulder and down into a steep valley between two ridges. After the baking plains, Debdou was a little pocket of paradise; when Charles de Foucauld passed this way in 1885 he described it as 'delicious'. It was hidden between one ridge rising 1,000 feet on the north-west, and almost sheer cliffs climbing nearly twice as high on the south-east, crowned with woods. From the mouth of the valley the légionnaires marched in through grainfields towards the large village of pink-washed houses spread among green gardens along the banks of the Oued Debdou. From the high plateau to the south, silver waterfalls bounced down to feed the stream, through olive groves and steep orchards of figs, peaches and grenadines. Shortly before this operation, another traveller described the scene in terms of some glen in the Alps or even the Auvergne, and it must have lifted the hearts of the weary légionnaires as they trudged down into its cool shade.

At its southern end, the Debdou valley was walled off from that of the Oued Beni Riis by a steep transverse ridge forming a blunt fishtail shape of yellow rock walls striped with green creepers, rising to at least 1,500 feet. The villages scattered over the plateau above Debdou were inhabited by people who called themselves the Ahl Debdou but were, in fact, of very mixed origins, including descendants of Jewish refugees from medieval Spain. Among Muslims, this remote country had a reputation for lawlessness and heresy.[20]

At dawn on 15 May three scouting parties, each in half-company strength, left the shadowed camp in the valley and clambered up into the first sunlight, each with an artillery officer to make notes of the 'going' for guns in different directions; they were to return and report by noon. Two parties returned before the appointed time, but by midday the two platoons from 22nd Company, VI/1st RE had not. The company commander, Captain Labordette – with Lieutenant Fradet, artillery Lieutenant Drouin, 72 rankers and a guide – had left the Debdou gorge by one of the corners of its southern 'fishtail'; this steep climb led to a promising-looking track across the plain showing traces of camel caravans coming up from the south, which Labordette was to explore. The patrol had been watched through binoculars from the camp until about 7.30am, when it disappeared over the lip; soon afterwards thick fog closed in, and at noon this prevented anyone seeing if Labordette was already climbing down again on his way back. This delay had begun to cause some unease when, at 12.30pm, Lieutenant Drouin of the artillery came in with a dozen of the missing legionnaires.

Captain Labordette had sent them back at about 8.30am when he reached the limit of the reconnaissance that he had been ordered to make. Drouin reported to General Girardot that Labordette had decided to reconnoitre a small village – Alouana – situated at the bottom of a bowl of hills below a pass. Details are hard to confirm, but a sketch-map has an inked addition placing Alouana (with rather unconvincing confidence) in the middle of an otherwise blank space a few miles north of the Debdou valley. Lieutenant Drouin reported that the company commander had claimed to see suspicious movements around Alouana before the fog closed in; leaving a rearguard up in the pass, he had climbed down the eastern slope into the bowl, and although the fog had blinded the rearguard the sound of firing had been heard.

A photograph taken soon after the event shows that Alouana was a far less enticing glen than Debdou; the nearer wall of the treeless bowl is steep (about 40 degrees), rocky, and patchily overgrown with scrub. The hamlet was on one of several features rising from the uneven valley floor to the west, which was some hundreds of feet below the surrounding steppe. Official accounts of the actions of dead officers invariably err on the side of tactful restraint, but Labordette has been described frankly in a Legion source as 'conscientious to the point of rashness', and soldiers have much shorter words to convey this idea. What had happened was later worked out from the reports of survivors, who included the twice-wounded Lieutenant Fradet.

THE COMPANY COMMANDER had sent back a half-squad to escort Drouin with his report; left perhaps a squad and a half on the crest of the pass; and then led his remaining 36 men down the steep eastern slope into the bowl. Accompanied by half of this platoon, he left Fradet with the other squad about 500 yards short of the village, and pushed on towards a group of riders and men on foot who were visible around the huts. As he approached them, Labordette came under fire.

He turned his men about to fall back on Fradet's squad, but they were soon being fired upon from the heights behind them and on both sides. Two men were wounded; thus burdened, they continued their retreat up the difficult, broken slopes, under covering fire from Fradet's légionnaires. The net closed around the platoon inexorably, as warriors surged up all over the slopes behind the cover of rocks and bushes. Fradet's men retreated some way ahead of Labordette's; progress was difficult up a long, steep, uneven slope not only studded with rocks and thornbushes but also veiled in fog. Soon a choice had to be faced: either to abandon their wounded to a certainly horrible fate and clamber up the slopes more quickly; or to form a circle around the casualties and defend them to the end. Lieutenant Fradet, who had almost reached the crest that would have saved his squad, chose the second option: they turned and went back down the slope into the murk.

Blinded by ever-thickening fog, they followed shouts heard at intervals in the gunfire that echoed confusingly from all directions, and managed to link up with their comrades low on the slope. They tried to climb out again carrying the wounded and dead; then Captain Labordette was hit full in the chest. As losses mounted it became clear that they had no chance of reaching the lip, since there were now more wounded than fit men to drag them. A slow calvary now began; Fradet regrouped the survivors half way up, and kept firing whenever a tribesman was spotted. If the fog hindered them it also gave some concealment from the enemy, but towards noon – when their ordeal had already lasted perhaps three hours – the fog lifted. The warriors shouted taunts as they fired, and some rolled rocks down at the dwindling platoon grouped around their lieutenant and their casualties.

MEANWHILE, AT DEBDOU CAMP, the rest of VI/1st RE were soon filing up the precarious path out of the tip of the 'fishtail' gorge. They were followed (with huge difficulty) by a section of two guns, but one piece soon had to be left behind so that the gunners could concentrate on manhandling the other up the steep track, while légionnaires carried shells on their backs. On their way across the steppe they ran into the retreating rearguard that Labordette had left that morning up on the pass. At the precise moment when the relief force had finally dragged the mountain gun to the rim of the slope above Alouana, the sound of firing below them ceased. The gunners soon got their piece into action; the warriors fell back from the slopes and gulleys towards their huts, but the effect of the hasty shellfire was certainly more psychological than physical.

Now the search for the dead and the survivors could begin, but before the légionnaires could clamber down to the scene of the fight the fog closed in again even more thickly, and persisted. When night fell the darkness added to the difficulties of finding and bringing up casualties through the chaos of boulders and thorn-scrub, and there was no alternative but to set up a new defensive perimeter themselves around the area where the dead and wounded had been gathered. They passed a wretched night, in visibility reduced to a few yards so that the least movement around the hillside was difficult. To make things worse, a fine, soaking rain began to fall, and at this altitude – about 5,000 feet – the night was chill; the tense silence was broken by the groans of the wounded, who could be given only the most rudimentary care and shelter.

When dawn finally broke, the fog still hung about the slopes. Part of V/1st RE arrived from Debdou with mule *cacolets*, but it was only at about 8am that the search could be resumed, after threatening moves by the Moroccans had been discouraged with a few cannon shots and rifle volleys. All day the dreary task continued; by late in the afternoon of 16 May, 29 corpses had been dragged up the slope, including those of Captain Labordette and Sergeant-Major Tonot. Just 7 wounded had been recovered alive, 2 of them very seriously hurt, and one man was never found at all. When the bodies of Corporal Bréval and Private Petersen were moved it was discovered that, when mortally wounded, they had taken the bolts out of their Lebels and tried to hide them, in the hope of denying usable rifles to their killers. (The rifle bolts were sent back to Sidi bel Abbès, to be preserved in the Salle d'Honneur of the 1er Régiment Étranger).[21]

AROUND FES AND MEKNES the arrival of General Moinier's troops had not yet entirely cooled the ardour of the rebels, but a botched Beni Mtir attack on the camp at Dar Debibagh on the night of 4 June did not prevent the departure of 6,000 men the next day for Meknes, where the claimant Moulay Zain surrendered after a brief and surgical firepower demonstration on 8 June. The tribal chiefs began coming in to seek the *aman*, the *muezzin* of the uniquely influential Moulay Idriss mosque announced that the French posed no threat to Islam, and the people of Fes (Fassis) were as eager as ever to do business. Major Ibos, a Colonial officer who wrote as 'Pierre Khorat', describes the scene vividly.

In the camps on the dusty plateau fringed by the blue-green woods of Dar Debibagh, Jewish pedlars from the Mellah ghetto offered bundled firewood and baskets of fruit, barley-bread and potatoes, quickly finding customers among men who had been on hard tack for three weeks – as did more eyecatching figures who sashayed around the tent-lines offering their services as washerwomen. In the mansions, courtyards and gardens around the sultan's palace in the 'new city' of Fes el Djedid harassed staff officers supervised the installation of headquarters, commissariat stores and the artillery park. Those with more leisure strolled, revolver at hip, in the cool shade of the Boujeloud gardens connecting Fes el Djedid with the ancient walled *medina* of Fes el Bali, around the foot of whose crumbling towers and ramparts 'a necklace of dead camels and horses' rotted peacefully in the sun, stinking.

Any orderly sent into the old city's maze of crowded *souks* on a chore for his officer was wise to hire one of the eager guides, but off-duty Colonials and légionnaires preferred to explore more casually with their mates. Inside the convoluted labyrinth of narrow alleys, archways and flights of steps, barred with sunlight and shade from the overhead mats, French soldiers with rifles slung and cork helmets at a jaunty angle tried to look worldly as they examined local handiwork and cheap European trash – embroidered slippers, gimcrack daggers, dubious postcards, and flasks of rosewater to combat the nauseating wafts from the sewers. Wobbling tables constricted their passage past hastily painted signs – 'Café du Commerce', 'Rendezvous des Bons Enfants' – where soldiers dallied, unwisely sampling various local liquids, while urchins gazed shyly at them or plucked boldly at their knees piping demands for *baksheesh*. Through this purposeful chaos of buying and selling, donkeys, mules, horses, even camels somehow threaded themselves along the lanes, their bulging loads forcing the crowds against the walls; as they picked their way past they left steaming trails of dung on the cobbles, to tempt the flies away from the butchers' purple offerings. Above the hubbub of voices the call to prayer echoed from the minarets of the great Kairaouine and the city's other mosques, water-pedlars announced their arrival by tinkling their strings of metal cups, jewellers tapped at chiselled silver, and smiths hammered sickles for the coming harvest.[22]

The old city was not exclusively a quarter for the poor and industrious; it had grown organically, and the pinched alleyways had closed in to embrace a number of mosques, *medersas* and lordly town-houses. The master of one of these, near the southern Bab el Hedid gate, was unexpectedly prevented from exploring a lucrative relationship with General Moinier. In May 1911, the sultan was happy to agree with a French suggestion that Grand Vizier Madani el Glaoui's dismissal would calm the tribes he had tormented. Madani and his many relatives were stripped of all Maghzan authority and much of their property north of the

Atlas, and when word of their disgrace spread, they had to fight even to defend their territory in the mountains.[23]

A SECOND AND MORE SERIOUS Franco-German crisis flared up in July 1911 when the Imperial Navy gunboat *Panther* anchored at the Atlantic port of Agadir, supposedly to reassure German merchants installed there. The Wilhelmstrasse considered that France's advance on and continuing occupation of Fes had torn up the Act of Algeciras, and in return demanded German control of the Sous – the south-western region around Agadir. Confronted with a major international incident, General Joffre gave President Armand Fallières a gloomily realistic assessment of the Army's readiness for war, and for five months, operations in western Morocco were put strictly on hold. Since safe corridors from Fes and Meknes to the Atlantic coast had not yet been secured, many troops were dispersed in small outposts along these routes, vulnerable and hard to resupply.[24]

At Fes, Major Ibos describes 6,000 bored soldiers with 3,600 animals enduring the sirocco in stupefyingly hot, dusty camps with bad water and no sanitation. By mid-June half the horses and mules were already dead or sick; their dung and corpses bred a biblical plague of flies, and in three weeks a hospital with only 30 beds and 2 doctors took in 140 dysentery, malaria and typhoid cases. No food convoys arrived for five weeks, and the Fassi merchants grew uncooperative, seeing French inactivity in the face of public German threats as a sign of weakness. The urgent need to improve General Moinier's communications with the outside world motivated the Engineers to perform prodigies of ingenuity in setting up a wireless station at Dar Debibagh: four flimsy pylons were improvised from wooden ladders lashed end to end, and strung with 'an immense Aeolian harp' of wires, while officers struggled with a transmitter, receiver and petrol generator knocked about during their transport on camel-back.[25]

Major Ibos' assessment of the different types of troops present is interesting, if biased by the anchor on his képi. He is prickly about the prejudices of the Africa Army, which affected to believe that Colonials were fit only for a soft life of booze, opium and native porters in balmy tropical climates. However, his complaint that the staff made no distinction in the demands they made on white or brown soldiers does suggest that the Colonials were not as hardened as the Legion, and he admits that after three months some of his companies with a starting strength of 180 had been reduced to half that by illness and exhaustion. He writes approvingly of the cheerful willingness of the small contingent of Senegalese Skirmishers included in the expedition, though admitting that their straggling tail of families appalled Africa Army officers. Ibos praises the Algerian Skirmishers for their marching, bravery, and endurance of harsh conditions, but criticizes their lack of 'ingenuity, shrewdness and application ... You look among them in vain for medical orderlies, clerks, storemen, skilled artisans in service units'.[26]

The token contingent of Zouaves is dismissed, but Ibos gives more space to the battalion-and-a-half of the Legion who were now present (between Fes and Meknes VI/2nd RE had joined the two companies from the 1st Battalion).[27] His confirmation of their reputation by this date is interesting, and – given the traditional rivalry – he is grudgingly generous:

> There is nothing to say about the Legion that one does not know already; these brave soldiers give us excellent service. Without sharing the snobbery of those who consider them the indisputable elite of the French Army, any impartial observer must recognize that they are, for the Moroccan episode, the most precious European element of the troops from Algeria. They have an intense esprit-de-corps, and the universal handiness of men who have seen and remembered much. In a short time any Legion detachment left to itself far from the telegraph, the theoretical plans or the instructions of superior authorities will make a rural home spring from the earth, comfortable and well run. The fetishistic respect paid to 'African' traditions often gives these the angular look of heavily fortified works, but the kitchen garden takes up considerable space; a flock of livestock is assembled with care ... because a varied diet is the best protection for European troops in exotic countries. Around the post ... the officers soon draw up a summary map of the region. The soldiers go quietly about their rural activities, waiting for the return of days of glory, when the herdsman, gardener, carpenter, mason and surveyor of roads will take up their rifles again and go looking – in a ravine, beyond a stream, at the foot of a wall – for the bullet that will end their obscure and changeable existence.[28]

A Franco-German agreement of 4 November 1911 finally purchased France a free hand in Morocco, in exchange for territories in the Congo and Cameroons and some guarantees for German business interests. France heaved a collective sigh of relief, and a new warmth began to be detectable in public attitudes towards the Army.[29] In Morocco, the limitations on military activity were lifted too late in the season for major operations in the hills, and

Moinier's manpower was still being drained by the demands of his lines of communication. Nevertheless, in January 1912 a brigade including the newly arrived I/1st RE was sent to drive back into the Middle Atlas hills tribesmen led by a chief named Sidi Raho, who had come down to attack the post at Sefrou south-east of Fes.[30]

THE IMPOSITION OF A FULL FRENCH PROTECTORATE became inevitable on 12 March 1912 when the Franco-German accord was ratified in Paris, and on 30 March the Treaty of Fes was signed in the courtyard of the Moroccan war minister's Dar Menebhi mansion. Its declared purpose was 'to establish in Morocco a fitting government based on internal order and general security', and Article 1 was brutally clear about which party would be making the decisions:

> The government of the French Republic and His Majesty the Sultan are
> agreed to institute in Morocco a new regime comprising the administrative,
> judicial, scholarly, economic, financial and military reforms that the French
> government judges it useful to introduce on Moroccan territory.

The utter capitulation of Sultan Moulay Abd el Hafid enraged his subjects, and within a matter of weeks Fes would once again be under siege. This time légionnaires would be inside the walls, protecting France's new pro-consul and sole intermediary: Commissioner Resident-General Hubert Lyautey.[31]

14. The Immaculate Raiment 1912–14

It has often been said that for colonization or intervention in a foreign country to be successful, it must be popular at home ... or else the political designs that underlie the policy must be clothed or concealed in the immaculate raiment of philanthropic intention. If both can be arranged for, so much the better.
Walter Harris[1]

WHILE THE MOROCCAN PROTECTORATE was certainly popular with France's colonial enthusiasts, no time was lost in reducing its military presence at Fes. General Moinier prepared to march three-quarters of his force back to Rabat and the Chaouia, and the existing military mission was immediately transformed into a skeleton staff for a new 'Sharifian Army' to be commanded by General Brulard (late of the 2nd Foreign). The French minister at Tangier, Eugène Regnault, arrived to take over civilian control on behalf of the Quai d'Orsay, installing himself in the former palace of the grand vizier.[2]

The ancient city of Fes was cupped between hills, its gently crumbling walls and towers partly surrounding a jaggedly irregular shape vaguely like two pears joined at the stalks (see Map 17). The greater part of some 90,000 Fassis lived in the 'pear' at the north-east, where teeming Fes el Bali filled the shallow valley of the Oued Fes, which meandered through and under the streets in a straitjacket of bridges and tunnels. The narrower south-western neck between the 'pears' was formed by the Boujeloud gardens, which linked Fes el Bali to the higher and more spacious medieval royal quarter of Fes el Djedid. There, clustered around the magnificence of the sultan's palace, the silent white or blue facades and high grilled windows of the mansions of the wealthy hid green *riad* courtyards, where coolness was trapped inside a secret world of tiled fountains, shady citrus trees, roses and birdsong. Immediately south of the palace (convenient for royal extortion, and providing a distraction for any rebellious mob pouring up from the warren below) was the large Mellah ghetto. The curtain walls of the twin city did not form a complete circuit embracing Fes el Djedid, so the European consulates and the Auvert hospital were installed in the more defensible southern quarters near the Bab el Hedid gate.

A belt of produce gardens and olive groves surrounded the city on most sides. To the north-east, the dark wave of trees petered out up the slopes of the 2,600-foot Djebel Zalagh, whose sawtooth ridge dominated the skyline. Closer to the north, facing the Bab el Guissa gate, a yellow cliff was pock-marked with the cave mouths of looted Merenid tombs. From the bald summit above them, the old fort now called Bordj Nord glared down on the medina, built not to defend it but to hold it in subjection; its partner, Bordj Sud, brooded on a less dramatic height facing the southern walls. To the north-west, in the gardens outside the conjoined 'pearstalks', the Kasbah Cherada housed Maghzan troops. To the south of Fes el Djedid the ground fell away and rose again over about 2 miles, to the partly wooded plateau of Dar Debibagh.[3]

BY 17 APRIL 1912, General Moinier and all but about 1,500 French troops had left for the coast; while others garrisoned Meknes and Sefrou, the only complete infantry unit at Fes was Major Philipot's battalion of Algerian Skirmishers in the Dar Debibagh camp with some Spahis, and only odds and ends were still occupying the quarters taken over by the French within the city. That day Moulay Hafid was due to leave his seething capital; but in the early afternoon, before the sultan could depart, a mutiny broke out at Kasbah Cherada.

Various reforms, real or rumoured, ignited the discontent that had been encouraged by some of the Moroccan officers (each battalion-size *tabor* had only one French officer and four NCOs). Some *askar* helped their own instructors to escape to Dar Debibagh, but they hunted down any Frenchmen they did not know. The city mob joined the mutineers, raging through the streets and breaking into houses; they murdered any white men they could catch, and then – with awful inevitability – ransacked the Mellah and massacred several dozen Jews. With the soldiers he had available and some armed civilians, General Brulard organized a perimeter among the occupied buildings inside the Bab el Hedid. Philipot's *turcos* were sent down to reinforce this, but they took about 100 casualties from mutineers firing from the southern wall of the Mellah as they passed by on the way to the Bab el Hedid. Major Fellert arrived from Sefrou and took guns up to Bordj Sud, and a few carefully aimed shells into the rebel-held quarters enabled the perimeter to hold out through the night. On 18 April a Legion battalion arrived after a forced march from Meknes, and later that day patrols pushed out from the perimeter to clear the nearer alleys of the medina.[4]

On 20 April, General Moinier arrived back at Fes; alerted on his way to Rabat, he had turned most of his column around and scraped up outpost garrisons as he came, finally arriving with the equivalent of five-plus infantry battalions, three squadrons and several batteries – about 3,000 men. Rumours of the rising were spreading fast in this populous region, and there were reports of tribesmen converging on the city. Moinier put troops on the hills to north and south, and began to mete out revenge to mutineers and Fassis with firing squads, curfews, fines and forced labour. He quarrelled bitterly with Eugène Regnault over the responsibility for the rising and the handling of its aftermath; Moinier cabled Paris for authority to declare a state of siege and take sole powers, but permission did not arrive until 26 April. In the meantime, he sent General Brulard and Major Girodon of the 2nd Foreign with small columns to push tribemen back from the eastern approaches. He achieved a temporary local stalemate, but outside Fes the facade of the French protectorate over Moulay Hafid's government was unsustainable, and the sultan himself thought only of escape. The 'immaculate raiment' was in urgent need of expert needlework, and such a task was far beyond Charles Moinier's blunt fingers.[5]

IN PARIS, THE FOREIGN MINISTRY was convinced that a military resident-general for Morocco, with full unified powers on the Galliéni model, was essential. Prime Minister Raymond Poincaré had kept the foreign port-folio for himself, and the Quai d'Orsay and Rue Dominique were less distant than under previous administrations. His war minister was the moderate Alexandre Millerand; the *Panther* crisis had sobered many minds, and Millerand was beginning to repair some of the damage done to the Army during the Combes–Clemenceau years (in January 1912 his first act had been to order the destruction of dossiers on officers' political and religious opinions). There was only one obvious choice for such a complex and challenging task as the creation and protection of a new Moroccan regime:

a cabinet meeting on 27 April endorsed Poincaré's submission of General Lyautey's name, and the following day President Fallières formally announced the appointment. With the promise of early reinforcements from France, Algeria and Senegal to bring the 18,000 French troops west of the Atlas up to 32,000, the new proconsul sailed for Algiers (on a warship aptly named *Jules Ferry*).[6]

There he conferred with Oran Division and Ain Sefra Subdivision over the approach to be adopted in eastern Morocco, where General Alix (a former commander of 2nd Foreign) was discouraged from any major initiatives while Lyautey established a grip on the situation in the west of the country.[7] Arriving at a tense Casablanca on 13 May, he submerged himself in briefings; some of the advice he received was defeatist, some stupidly bloodthirsty, but such contradictions were nothing new to him. He needed an intelligent deputy with local experience to escort him to Rabat, Meknes and Fes, and found him in Colonel Henri Gouraud of the Colonial Infantry, with whom he struck up an immediate rapport. At 44 years old, the tall, dark-bearded Gouraud was the youngest colonel in the French Army, and a man of some reputation. As a captain in West Africa in 1898 he had been lucky enough to capture Samory, the last serious leader of resistance to French conquest, and thereafter he had become a favourite of Étienne's colonial circle. After command of one of the Fes relief brigades in April 1911, he was now rather under-employed at Casablanca, and was happy to march up-country with Lyautey and two battalions of Algerians. The corridor of little posts up which they rode struck Lyautey as being as fragile as a taut wire.[8]

LYAUTEY'S ARRIVAL IN FES ON 24 MAY 1912 coincided with an immediate crisis; most of the Sharifian Army troops had necessarily been disarmed, and a renewed siege by dissident tribesmen closed around the capital just hours after Lyautey rode in. About 400 mutineers had escaped into the hills, the Beni Mtir were swarming up from the south, and another loose coalition had been led west from the 'Taza gap' by a pious sharif named Si Mohammed el Hajjami. Altogether, about 15,000 warriors threatened the eastern arc of the walls, from the Bab el Guissa in the north to the Bab Ftouh in the south-east, with plenty of dead ground to mask any assault. Inside the city, General Moinier and Ambassador Regnault were not on speaking terms; the former predicted disaster and urged the harshest measures, the latter was desperate to regain civilian control. The streets were unsafe, and the general's almost indiscriminate reprisals had for once given the Fassis good reason for the fickleness for which they were already notorious. The chieftains in the hills had sent in word that the French troops were their only targets, and some city fathers were certainly negotiating with them. The walls were in ruins at many points, and too encumbered by centuries of creeping house-building to offer a practical perimeter for Moinier's 4,000-strong garrison, while the broad valley between the city and his southern outwork of Dar Debibagh made immediate interventions from that direction chancy.

Lyautey was quartered at first in the Menebhi palace, the former Maghzan war minister's mansion in the Talaa Seghira, one of the two main arteries of the medina; as his horse clattered down its narrow, cobbled slope he heard doors being slammed with a curse. From the Menebhi roof he had a clear view of Legion companies being surrounded by tribesmen on the hilltop above the Merenid tombs to the north and making an orderly withdrawal in square. Bringing them back into the city would give the guns an unencumbered field of fire, but that was Moinier's business and Lyautey did not interfere with his immediate military decisions. Given his nature, it seems likely that Lyautey composed himself as serenely as possible for the evening's banquet, which promised to be a testing performance in front of a difficult audience. As the westering sun turned the teeth of the Djebel Zalagh pink, flocks of swifts wheeled above the city roofscape hunting rising insects, and occasionally a lanner falcon made a fast, low run to hunt them in their turn; there was an analogy there somewhere. The glittering formal dinner at the embassy was a surreal experience, with all parties keeping up the appearance of dignified confidence to a background of intermittent shots – some of them close by – and once the crash of a 75mm gun.[9]

On 25 May the rebels attacked, and the garrison suffered more than 120 casualties. In the space of 48 hours, several thousand tribesmen managed to enter the eastern walls; there was some ugly street fighting before the artillery and a flanking attack by Major Mazilier from Dar Debibagh drove them out on the 26th. Meanwhile, there was also heavy pressure on the Bab el Guissa gate in the north; Lieutenant Chardonnet lost 17 killed and 25 wounded while holding its roof and neighbouring houses with two platoons of *turcos*, under heavy fire not only from the Merenid tombs facing him but from riflemen inside the mosque behind him to the left. When the situation became critical, Sergeant Bernier's Legion squad were sent in; they promptly cleared the rebels out of the mosque, and installed a machine gun on its minaret to rake the cave-mouths opposite.

There was a lull outside the city for the next two days, but inside Lyautey was ceaselessly busy trying to undo the damage done by Moinier's heavy-handed reprisals. He sought out the Islamic scholars of the *ulama*, the wealthy leaders of the Fassi merchants and the sharifian aristocrats, all of whom Moinier had ignored. They deeply resented the unfocused fines and harsh requisitions of labour, and until the route to the Atlantic coast could be reopened the city's commerce was being strangled. The city fathers had become accustomed to offensively brusque French demands rather than elegant Arabic *politesse*, and Lyautey was in his element. He listened to grievances, negotiated, reassured, and usually ruled in their favour, beginning the patient work of turning men who were at best hostile neutrals into at least grudging allies.

These poker-games of verbal and body language over the fragrant tea-glasses were played out against a constant background mutter of gunfire, as grubbier hands than Lyautey's held the ring. Another incursion by tribesmen in the Tamdert district was repulsed on the night of 27/28 May. The next afternoon there was a concerted attack all around the northern and eastern defences, from Kasbah Cherarda right round to Bab Ftouh. At Bab el Guissa, the légionnaires' machine gun in the minaret piled up enemy dead in front of the gate; some Berbers penetrated deep inside Fes el Bali via the river, and reached the Moulay Idriss *zaouia* only a hundred yards from the Kairaouine mosque, but they were contained and killed. Altogether the attackers left about 1,000 bodies on the field that day, but for a while the issue was in such doubt that Lyautey moved his staff from the Dar Menebhi to the Auvert hospital in case a last stand around the sickrooms became necessary, and he had cans of petrol placed beside the gathered paperwork. Colonel Gouraud cleared the immediate vicinity of the city on 29 May, and on the 31st reinforcements from Meknes and Sefrou (including I/1st RE) raised the garrison to about 7,000 troops.

El Hajjami had pulled his tribesmen about 7 miles back to El Hadjerat el Kohila north-east of the Djebel Zalagh, and on the night of 1/2 June the garrison went on the offensive. Under cover of darkness Gouraud assembled five battalions of Skirmishers and légionnaires (I/1er and VI/2nd RE), two squadrons and twelve guns outside the Bab Sidi Bujida gate, and moved off at 5am on the 2nd. He towed his guns on to a ridge, shelled the mass of tribesmen, then sent his infantry forward. El Hajjami's host broke up and fled, abandoning their camp, and by that night Henri

Gouraud was a brigadier-general. On 3 June the notional Sharifian Army was disbanded.[10]

FROM THE SEMI-SECURE HUB of Fes and Meknes, Lyautey faced the task of pacifying the more accessible regions of a country that had fallen into a state of semi-anarchy, but the immediate problem was to secure the countryside around those two cities and the Fes–Rabat corridor. As soon as the siege of Fes was lifted he entrusted this task to General Gouraud, who had demonstrated a talent for both military and political action.[11]

Three battalions and two mounted companies of the Legion were among Gouraud's most valuable assets in 1912–13, taking part in many fighting columns and estabishing route security in all directions from the capital. During the first year of the Protectorate, the I/1st RE initially fought around Sefrou, holding the gateway between the Middle Atlas and the plains. This unit was later based at Souk el Arba de Tissa (modern Tissa – see Map 18), 28 miles north-east of Fes and half way to the Rif highlands, covering the hill country between the Oued Sebou and the Oued Innaouen as part of Lieutenant-Colonel Vandenberg's marching regiment. In early 1913 the battalion was transferred back to Algeria, serving thereafter on the Moulouya front with a marching regiment of Colonel Bavouzet's 1st Foreign.

Captain Rollet's 3rd (Mounted) Company/2nd RE remained in the west; over two years they would see action in seventeen combats, particularly along the Rabat corridor, and would twice be cited in army corps orders. In July 1913, a veteran who had served with the company two years previously volunteered to return to it, and would soon be cited by Rollet for the Military Medal. The tall, bony-faced Corporal Mader was a 33-year-old Württemberger who had deserted an Imperial German pioneer unit after striking back at a brutal NCO, and had joined the 2nd Foreign in December 1899. A mason by trade, he brought his skills to work on forts in the Sud-Oranais; he re-enlisted in 1904 and 1909, and served with the then-22nd (Mounted)/2nd RE on the Chaouia in 1910–11. (By 1918, Max Mader would become one of the most famous NCOs ever to serve in the Legion.)[12] During the summer and autumn of 1912, Major Forey's VI/2nd RE were with General Dalbiez's 3,000-strong column that fought the Beni Mtir, Northern Ait Segrushin and other Berbers in the Fes–Meknes–Sefrou triangle and on the fringes of the Middle Atlas.

Major Giralt's I/2nd RE were among Gouraud's 4,000 men based around Tissa during operations against the Hayana, Cherarga, Fichtala and other northern tribes that lasted until February 1913, by which time most had come in to submit; at the end of that month a permanent post was established at Tissa.[13] One skirmish in the Innaouen valley on 17 June 1912, trivial in itself, was felt to exemplify the best sort of aggressive Legion initiative. Sent out to collect water, Sergeant Leroy's thirty-man squad from Captain Nicolas' 2nd Company, I/2nd RE rescued a platoon of *turcos* from 4th RTA who were hard-pressed by tribal horsemen. This involved Leroy leading a dozen of his men in an attack across hundreds of yards of ground, and finally recovering the Tunisians' dead; when he brought all his men back to camp unhurt (and with the water) he was congratulated by General Gouraud himself.[14] The 'Admirable Conduct of an NCO of the 1st Battalion, 2nd Foreign' was written up in a monthly booklet, *La Légion Étrangère*, which had first appeared in April 1912, and the fact that such an everyday if creditable incident was reported more widely than the battalion may be significant. The corps was clearly making an effort to promote its reputation and to counter the hostile German propaganda of those years. (A small but telling detail is that in listing the names of Leroy's men Major Giralt prefixes their names with the style '*Légionnaire*' rather than the official term '*Soldat*' – Private – which is found in reports of the Zousfana campaign ten years previously.)[15]

There were two other significant publications in 1912–13. One was a 128-page paperback book entitled *The Mysteries of the Foreign Legion* by Georges d'Esparbes which, though undated, seems from internal evidence to have appeared in 1912. Written after a visit to Sidi bel Abbès during which the author was clearly given considerable access, it is intended to educate civilians about the history and nature of the Legion, and is written in a respectful, but by no means romantic tone. Like the monthly journal, it is illustrated both with photographs and with drawings by the well-known artist Maurice Mahut. For a wider public, the July 1913 issue of the mass-circulation French journal *L'Illustration* also contained a long photographic essay with many portraits and posed images of légionnaires, exteriors and interiors of the barracks at Sidi bel Abbès and Saida, and a few photos of troops in the field. The Legion was taking the propaganda war to the enemy nearly twenty years before General Rollet appointed himself the curator of its legend.

*

DURING 1913–14, the numerical importance of Legion units in western Morocco would become proportionately much less, as both the Africa Army and *la Coloniale* emptied themselves into this new war.[16] Lyautey's total forces in Morocco at the end of 1912 numbered about 57,000: of these, 45,000, including 26 infantry battalions, were on the western front (which also had the bulk of the cavalry, artillery and *goumiers*), and 12,000, including 11 battalions, in the east. The total would rise to about 62,000 by mid-1913 and nearly 70,000 a year later, but less than half of these troops were Europeans. Of these, two battalions in the west and three in the east were Legion units (plus two mounted companies in each zone).[17]

The other white infantry rotated through Morocco during these campaigns were all five of the Bats d'Af; nine Zouave battalions; and six battalions of the *Coloniale blanche* drawn from the 3rd, 13th and 26th RIC. However, following the 1905 reduction of French Metropolitan military service to two years, the period 1911–14 saw a major expansion of France's Arab and African forces, both to meet the demands of Morocco and in anticipation of a war with Germany. In 1912 an element of conscription for the Algerian Skirmishers was introduced for the first time, and in 1913 each of the four RTAs maintained a three-battalion marching regiment in Morocco. By early 1914 there were also sixteen independent companies of Moroccan Skirmishers totalling some 3,000 men, and sixteen company-sized *goums* of irregulars contributed nearly the same number. Most strikingly, a rapid expansion of the Tirailleurs Sénégalais – by conscription from 1912 – would see some 10,000 West Africans in thirteen battalions deployed to Morocco by mid-1914.[18]

TO RETURN FROM THE LEGION to a wider view of events from summer 1912: politically, Lyautey now had to embrace the 'Maghzan policy' that he had derided when he was a relatively free agent at Ain Sefra and Oran. Clearly, if the French Protectorate was to be convincing it had to have a sultan to protect, and since that sultan could not be the hated and discredited Moulay Abd el Hafid, his abdication and replacement had to be negotiated swiftly. In Rabat – where Lyautey soon moved his headquarters – Moulay Hafid dragged out the tortuous bargaining over the terms of his gilded exile, extracting a truly princely settlement by the time he finally embarked on 12 August 1912. Lyautey stage-managed his replacement by yet another brother, the 31-year-old Moulay Abd el Youssef, who had proved quietly helpful to the French as Khalifa of Fes that June.[19] This succession was not unchallenged, however; while Lyautey had been orchestrating affairs in Fes and Rabat, a genuine strategic threat had emerged from the passes of the High Atlas in the south, following the Islamic banners of Moulay Ahmad el Hiba, a stern blue-veiled chieftain from the desert.

Since late May 1912, El Hiba had been attracting a large following among the tribes of the Sous region, south-west of the Atlas, by a message of uncompromising Islamic renewal. Moulay Hafid's degradation of Madani el Glaoui had set the tribal billiard balls rolling and cannoning all over the south. With El Glaoui's grip weakened, the competing 'lords of the Atlas' were no longer reliable guardians of the high mountain passes, and Madani's old rival Abd el Malek el Mtouggi gambled on allowing El Hiba's host to cross northwards by his Tizi n'Test route. On 15 August El Hiba entered the southern capital of Marrakesh, and two days later he was proclaimed sultan. This claimant was not simply a harem-born puppet or a tribal warlord motivated by personal greed; El Hiba potentially commanded enough support for a country-wide Islamic revolution and a change of dynasty. The pressure on Lyautey to react was aggravated by the fact that, on 23 August, El Hiba forced Hajj Tahami el Glaoui to hand over to him half a dozen French hostages whom he had been sheltering in his house in Marrakesh.[20]

Lyautey entrusted 5,000 men (none from the Legion) to a barrel-chested, pike-jawed colonel of Colonial Infantry named Charles Mangin, a merciless veteran of Senegal and the Fashoda expedition who was already well known as the leading enthusiast for West African Skirmishers.[21] Mangin achieved results quickly; on 6 September he smashed El Hiba's 10,000-strong host at Sidi Bou Othman some 20 miles north of Marrakesh, and the *sheikh* had to flee into the southern desert. When Major Henri Simon reached the city, Tahami el Glaoui stole the credit for saving the hostages; and on 1 October, when Lyautey arrived in person (by motorcar) for discussions with the Glaoua, El Mtouggi and El Goundafi, these were smoothly orchestrated by Madani el Glaoui 'the Literate'. His brother Tahami was reappointed Pasha of Marrakesh, but for the time being Lyautey needed all three of the *grands caids* as allies to secure his southern flank, so he did not obviously favour one family over the others. As soon as he departed the Glaoua set about the congenial task of revenging themselves on those who had replaced them during their eighteen months of weakness.[22]

WHILE WESTERN MOROCCO was the natural focus of French attention in the first half of 1912, General Alix had been laying some foundations for future operations in the east. Troops based on the upper Oued Guir around Boudenib had been reconnoitring and improving tracks towards the upper Oued Moulouya, and making contact with tribes around Kasbah el Maghzan (modern Missour) on a route down the eastern edge of the Middle Atlas that had been explored by Père de Foucauld (see Map 11).

Further north, the Beni Ouarain, who had been quiet since General Toutée's operations in 1911, now contested French freedom of movement between Debdou and Merada, a ford on the middle Oued Moulouya. To contain them, General Alix sent 2,300 troops radiating out in columns; there were serious clashes in March and April; and when news of the 'second siege' of Fes reached the tribes of the Moulouya a large war party was reported to be gathering at Msoun, half way between Taza and Alix's advance post at Merada. Alix concentrated nearly 9,000 men under the former Legion officer General Girardot at Fritissa, just south of Guercif, and after several provocative Beni Ouarain probes and a series of skirmishes around Merada on 14 May, Alix was authorized to put troops across the Moulouya. Girardot led the crossing on 24 May, established a camp at Guercif and pushed westwards another 12 miles to Safsafte (see Map 18). On the 26th he beat a Moroccan force at Teniet el Hajj, and local chiefs came in to submit. Most of Alix's troops were back at Merada by 5 July, leaving a new post at Guercif and mobile elements divided between there and Taourirt. From Guercif patrols would reach as far west as Msoun, only 25 miles short of Taza itself. During this campaign a mounted company of 1st Foreign were praised for their endurance; of 225 men only 29 dropped out sick, compared to 129 from the 548 men of a 1st RE foot battalion.[23]

Apart from minor incidents, a relative peace then descended on the eastern front, which lasted for some months. In October 1912, Major Prudhomme led a force including half of 24th (Mounted)/1st RE for a couple of weeks' work on the Boudenib–Beni Ounif track; as a first distant warning to the mule-company légionnaires of things to come, their task was to make the route accessible to motor vehicles. The following month Generals Alix and Girardot made a tour by motorcar from Oujda via Ain Chair to Boudenib – a journey of some 300 miles.[24]

AN EVEN MORE ADVANCED piece of equipment demonstrated its worth on the Atlantic coast in December 1912. In October, Lyautey had left

Colonel Charles Mangin in command at Marrakesh – essentially an island of French influence in a Berber sea – but with instructions not to commit French troops nearly that far south, and to concentrate on pacifying the tribes north and west of the Oum er Rebia river. The mountains to the south were to be left to the three 'lords of the Atlas'; although vying for advantage, all were ostensibly allied to the Maghzan, and Lyautey had neither the men nor the inclination to involve French troops.[25] However, in December he did have to intervene on the Atlantic coast due west of Marrakesh. Inland from Mogador (modern Essaouria) a Major Massoutier was besieged in the fort of Dar el Kadi, where his situation was reconnoitred by a Vietnamese-born Legion officer named Lieutenant Do Huu Vi, making a daring flight in a Bleriot XI monoplane.[26]

Lyautey had been enthusiastic about the possibilities of aircraft from the first (perhaps encouraged by his old mentor Galliéni, who had embarrassed more conventional generals by using a reconnaissance plane to help him tear up the script for a summer manoeuvre in France). The 1st Aeronautical Group was sent out to Casablanca on 25 February 1912 with four Bleriots, soon increased to six; by May, Lyautey was even asking Paris for bombs, but the technology did not yet exist. During a programme of familiarization flights, relay stages were planned out and punctuated with emergency landing strips and fuel depots. The first true military mission was flown by Lieutenants Do Huu Vi and Van den Vaéro on 17 August, when they scouted for Colonel Robillot's column south of Fes. In November, a second section was installed on the eastern front at Oujda with five pilots and Deperdussin two-seaters, flying their first missions in January 1913. The pilots made liaison and reconnaissance flights for ground columns, though with some difficulty. In the heat of summer the 80-horsepower Bleriot could not get above 4,600 feet and air conditions were dangerous, with a great deal of turbulence; dust was constantly penetrating the engines and fuel feed, and engines overheated. Since the cockpit was above the wings, the downwards visibility was very poor, and it was difficult to navigate for lack of mapped landmarks. Frustrated by their lack of weapons, the airmen scribbled hasty sketch-maps and dropped them to ground troops in weighted bags to warn columns of Moroccan concentrations or ambushes ahead of them.[27]

SULTAN MOULAY YOUSSEF was a French puppet, but he at least played his part convincingly, being intelligent, honest, pious and dignified (and thus a shining improvement on Moulay Hafid). Behind the flimsy screen of the imperial parasol, Lyautey would rebuild the machinery of the Maghzan, playing sympathetically to traditional Moroccan instincts while restricting its responsibilities almost entirely to religious affairs. While ultimately powerless in occupied Morocco, the aristocratic and religious elites were never humiliated, and the reassuring rhythms of Islamic tradition were maintained.

Throughout his period of office (1912–25) Lyautey would wield complete authority as a combination of prime minister, foreign minister, war minister, and commander-in-chief of French and Maghzan troops. He created a French administration answerable directly to him, with the emphasis balanced between security, civil government, finance and public works. The activity of the civil departments was generally both honest and constructive. Morocco owes the survival of her ancient cities to Lyautey's insistence that new French building was to adjoin and not 'redevelop' them, and French industrial, commercial and agricultural exploitation of Moroccan resources was targeted and controlled. Lyautey believed in giving both Moroccans and Frenchmen freedom from stifling bureaucracy, but the relatively few *colons* in Morocco would be curbed in ways unknown in Algeria – most basically, in that they never enjoyed any degree of self-government or political authority over Moroccan communities.

In practice 'indirect' government, even through hand-picked Moroccan proxies, never really worked; the cultural gulf was simply too wide, and at every level the impatient French soon snatched at the steering-wheel. Nevertheless, as colonial regimes go, Lyautey's achievement was respectable, and it certainly stands as a reproof to the French record in Algeria. While his envious admiration of the British Empire had been a thread running through his correspondence since the 1890s, in fact Britain's Edwardian imperium offers no example of an individual military officer comparable to Lyautey in his years of power. It is tempting to reach back 1,900 years for a comparison, to the great military governors of first- and second-century Roman provinces. Like Agricola in Britain, in Morocco the decisive figure of Lyautey combined virtually unhampered military command with control of civil administration, diplomacy and political initiatives. In theory such a concentration of responsibility and power was, of course, potentially disastrous; Morocco was lucky that Hubert Lyautey was not open to bribery and was exceptionally hard-working.

The Commissioner Resident-General gathered around him a trusted staff and able regional commanders: Ernest Blondlat at Rabat, Henri Gouraud at Fes, Paul Henrys at Meknes, Jean Brulard at Marrakesh and Maurice Baumgarten at Oujda. At local level the eyes, ears and hands of the Protectorate in the military regions of the country were the officers of the Intelligence Service, soon renamed once again the Native Affairs Service. This handful of Army district officers – there were only 194 of them in 1913 – shouldered very wide-ranging responsibilities, and Lyautey sought to apply his long-time ideal of the 'perfect colonial type' in their selection (he used the English phrase 'the right man in the right place'). Inevitably, however, such qualities were not common; many officers were both young and ambitious, and their lack of local experience led to early misjudgements.

Lyautey constantly stressed the need for, and generally achieved, constructive teamwork between military and civil officials, and made slow but real progress in improving the quality of the latter. He recruited the best men from across the empire to head his civil departments, and modelled competitive examinations and specialized training on the British system – insisting, crucially, that the functionaries learn Arabic. He had no intention of saddling his new realm with the sort of lazy, ignorant third-raters who had so repelled him in Indochina. (In the end, however, the French administration in Morocco would still employ three times as many men as governed British India, which had forty times Morocco's population.)[28]

Naturally, all of the above applied only to those areas of the country that the French were able physically to control. Despite the fact that his old ally Eugène Étienne was the French war minister throughout 1913, there were always critics – both in Morocco and at home – who were impatient with Lyautey's necessarily deliberate pace of advance. Some were colonels and generals in love with French firepower, who had no sympathy with his doctrine of careful political preparation for each new military step; others were civilians who simply did not grasp that Lyautey faced

> two Moroccos: the one that we occupy, which is militarily weak and governed by a Maghzan without strength or prestige – and the other, much more important, which comprises the Berber masses who are deeply agitated, fanaticized and militarily strong, and who stand united against us under influences beyond our control.[29]

The military situation in late 1912 is perhaps best sketched by returning to the analogy of an as – yet incomplete archway being built to surround the untamed and mountainous centre of Morocco. The arch's western and eastern pillars were being constructed slowly from the top down, southwards from Fes and Oujda; the lintel would have to wait a couple of years, and it would be only in the 1920s that the pillars would reach a common southern base, and could be thickened inwards to extend control into the tangled mass of the Middle Atlas. For reasons of both resources and policy, the southern foundations of the arch in and south of the High Atlas had to be provided by the client Moroccan lords, of whom the Glaoua brothers would soon become unchallengeably the most powerful. Leaving the pacification of the south to them, ostensibly in the name of the Maghzan, meant, unavoidably, turning a blind eye to the continuation of traditional medieval brutalities that sickened those French liaison officers who witnessed them.[30] The French were quite powerless to curb these excesses, since even to attempt to occupy and govern this vast wilderness themselves would have been far beyond their resources. More importantly, this demonstration of French/Muslim partnership prevented tribal resistance being promoted convincingly as a straightforward anti-Christian *jihad*.[31]

AMONG THE MILITARILY IMPATIENT in the western pillar of operations were Charles Mangin and two subordinate officers, Colonels Reibell and Gueydon de Dives, any one of whom Lyautey might have had in mind when he wrote 'One must be wary of men who come to the colonies to refight Austerlitz; they are badly prepared for the patient, thankless and obscure tasks which make up the daily duties – the only useful ones – of the colonial officer'.[32] Lyautey was determined not to confront the highland Berbers prematurely, but Reibell's heavy-handed approach helped stir up the Beni Mtir and Beni Mguild tribes south-east of Meknes early in 1913. This provoked tribal attacks inspired by Sidi Raho, a charismatic Beni Ouarain religious and military *sheikh*, and such raids prompted further reactions by officers on the spot, thus dragging Lyautey into difficult mountain country where his intelligence officers had not yet had a chance to prepare the way.

In March 1913 he gave command south-east of Meknes to one of his old team from Ain Sefra, Colonel Paul Henrys, who by July had suppressed the attacks and planted a new post at Immouzer-Kandar to protect the Meknes–Fes road from the south (see Map 19). Meanwhile, however, Colonel Gueydon de Dives had hastened a confrontation further south with the large and warlike Zaian confederation that Lyautey particularly wanted to postpone.[33]

This wide-ranging Berber people had sent warriors to fight the Landing Corps on the Chaouia in 1907 and to harass the first Fes relief column in 1911; they totalled some 8,000 fighting men divided into two main branches, both of which spent summers in the Middle Atlas and winters on lowland pastures along the Oum er Rebia river. The Ait Zgougou tribe were led by Mohammed Aguebli, and the Ait Yacoub by a formidable old *caid* named Moha ou Hammou el Zaiani, who had enjoyed growing regional prestige over thirty-five years.[34]

In December 1912 – without permission, but probably with Mangin's encouragement – Colonel Gueydon had installed a post at Oued Zem about 25 miles north-west of Kasbah Tadla (see Map 19). No political effort had been made to prepare the Berbers for this intrusion; an influential war chief, Moha ou Said ('Irraoui, retaliated by ravaging the lands of submitted tribes in the area, and attacked the post directly in February 1913. Thereafter Oued Zem would be an isolated garrison, its resupply subject to repeated ambushes, and it threatened to become a focus for hostile tribes all the way from the Chaouia across to the Middle Atlas.[35] Lyautey sent General Louis Franchet d'Espérey to reinforce this sector, while Colonel Henri Simon – who had been the first leader of Moroccan *goumiers*, and was now head of his Native Affairs Service – kept the tribes to the west under control. In March 1913 both Simon and Mangin achieved victories over various tribal groupings, and thereafter Simon was given command of the Oued Zem sector.[36]

Mangin, now campaigning north of the Oum er Rebia between Oued Zem and Kasbah Tadla, was impatient to move east and take on the Zaians around Khenifra and on the left bank of the river. Lyautey understood that such a move into the middle of the Zaian pasture range would invite highland Berbers down on to the plain in retaliation, and – given the Moroccan way of thinking – that this would inevitably drag him into a grinding mountain campaign that he simply could not risk on the probable eve of a European war. He insisted that Mangin stay on the right (northern) bank, and only reluctantly agreed to a small advance patrol post – not a permanent base – being established at Kasbah Tadla. Meanwhile he sent Moroccan intermediaries led by Colonel Simon to try to negotiate with Moha ou Said.

The contact was rebuffed, and on Simon's advice Lyautey reluctantly agreed to Mangin's request to make a hit-and-run raid on Moha ou Said's large camp at El Ksiba, east of Kasbah Tadla. Mangin took 4,200 men across the river, but the subsequent fighting of 7–10 June 1913 was badly mishandled; his cavalry commander was foolishly eager, 77 men were killed and 170 wounded, and he was finally harried back across the Oum er Rebia leaving his dead behind. The French probably killed eight times as many Zaians, but in tribal terms this was a heartening victory that stiffened resistance. The Oum er Rebia was confirmed as the limit for military operations for the time being, and Charles Mangin returned to France (where the next few years would give him unlimited opportunities to exercise his particular talents).[37]

The limits of Lyautey's western Moroccan 'pillar' now ran roughly from Sefrou in the north to Kasbah Tadla in the south, then westwards along the Oum er Rebia to the Atlantic. The edges were naturally porous, and during the winter of 1913/14 his intelligence officers would pursue his favoured kind of political and trading contacts across the margins. Their aim was to prepare the way for a spring campaign to tidy up a salient around Khenifra. By so doing, Lyautey hoped to divide the Zaian confederacy.[38]

THE SPANISH ZONE TO THE NORTH of Lyautey's western pillar was a mild irritation in 1913. Following the declaration of the French Protectorate, a more far-reaching agreement between the two countries had been signed on 27 November 1912. Its terms required Spain to take responsibility for security north of a vaguely delineated east–west line through the Mediterranean littoral, but the French were sceptical of Spain's ability to do this.

The nature of the tripartite agreements between France, Spain and the Maghzan made no logical sense. France had a treaty obligation to the Moroccan throne to protect and develop the whole of the sultan's territory in harmony with the Maghzan. In long-agreed recognition of British concerns about the control of the coast facing Gibraltar, France subcontracted its duties and rights in the northern zone to Spain, whose high commissioner would rule that territory in harmony with a regional *khalifa* appointed by the sultan. The sultan would remain sovereign over the Spanish zone, and its external relations would be controlled by France; but Spain had no direct treaty relationship with the Moroccan Maghzan, only with France. Thus, Lyautey was in the position of having some theoretical diplomatic responsibility, but no power to control events, on the northern side of a border that Spain jealously insisted could not be crossed by French troops.[39]

The frontier between the French and Spanish zones was an entirely arbitrary line on the map, often simply following the supposed but unconfirmed contours. The tribes through whose historic range it passed were eventually informed that those north of it were now subject to Spanish rule and those south of it to France. Large areas on both sides of the notional border would long remain unoccupied and even unvisited by the armies of either nation. The Spanish had no coherent plan for the occupation or development of their zone, and their activities were spasmodic and piece-meal; Walter Harris would write that Spanish progress was hampered by inexperience, disorganization and lack of imagination, 'sacrificing practical results to an exaggerated sentiment of *amour propre*' – in other words, they insisted on their dignity as ruler, while being unwilling or unable to do a ruler's work.

It is important to remember that Spanish operations would always be on two completely separated fronts (see Map 18). The Spanish would never even attempt to open a land corridor across the 130-odd miles dividing the two presidios, and all communication between them was by sea. (Even when the Rif War ended in the spring of 1926, the two fronts would still be separated by at least 80 miles of country that was not only unpacified but unexplored.)[40] The line drawn across the map to delineate the southern border of the Spanish zone was roughly 225 miles long from the Atlantic coast in the west to the mouth of the Moulouya river in the east, enclosing about 7,700 square miles and a population estimated at some 760,000. This area – rather smaller than that of Wales, or roughly the same as the state of Massachusetts – was only about 5 per cent of the size of French Morocco.

In the west, the Franco-Spanish line ran across the bulge of the Djibala country about 65 miles south of the presidio of Ceuta at the Mediterranean tip of the Anjera peninsula, but by summer 1913 Alcazarquivir was still isolated at the end of a corridor from Larache, and Spanish troops had pushed only about 20 miles south from Ceuta to Tetuan (see below). Though this would be their regional capital, their wider 'occupation' amounted to no more than tentative penetrations from the Atlantic and Mediterranean coasts. In the Melilla Comandacia to the east the Franco-Spanish line ran across the mountains about 100 miles south of the tip of the promontory, but the average depth of this theoretical territory from the mean line of the Mediterranean coast was only some 30 miles. Here the area of active Spanish operations even by the early 1920s would extend only about 15 miles inland and some 40 miles laterally, from a little way east of the Melilla promontory westwards to Sidi Driss on the coast, and inland to Midar.

In the Melilla enclave, Rif tribal resistance to the mining and track-laying had more or less ended in May 1912, and such operations as the Spanish did pursue before the Great War took place south of Ceuta. At the end of 1912 the first high commissioner, General Felipe Afrau, had an expeditionary corps of some 40,000 men divided between his two fronts (then nearly half the entire Spanish Army).[41] In the Djibala his immediate opponent was Moulay Ahmad er Raisuli, who had been confirmed as the regional *pasha* by the new sultan; Raisuli exploited his position to the full, expanding his power ruthlessly from his base in the Beni Aros hills.[42]

General Afrau's first step was to occupy the town of Tetuan, about 20 miles south of Ceuta on the eastern side of the peninsula, both to rescue it from Raisuli's depredations and to install the new *khalifa* there. The Spanish advanced slowly, building a road as they went, and occupied Tetuan on 13 February 1913. When they got there the undisciplined troops, officers and men alike, treated the 'Moors' with stupid brutality. Walter Harris put it delicately: 'There was too great an exhibition of the spirit of conquest. Morocco must give of its best, and amongst its best were its women.' The Spanish soon made themselves hated; an educated sergeant, Arturo Barea, wrote that the Spanish Army turned occupied territory into a combination of battlefield, tavern and brothel. In April 1913, the Khalifa Moulay el Mehdi was installed at Tetuan, but the charade of Maghzan-Spanish alliance did nothing to reduce hostility towards the occupiers, and ambushes and skirmishing continued.[43]

IN LYAUTEY'S EASTERN 'PILLAR', General Alix decided in February 1913 that the time was ripe for more progress towards Taza from the east. He concentrated troops including the 1st Foreign's marching regiment at Merada as the base for a systematic exploration of the dreary Djel plain between the Moulouya and Msoun. As he advanced he anchored his columns on new posts including Nekhila in the north and Safsafte in the south, occupying the latter on 8 April (see Map 18). Beni Bou Yahi warriors responded by attacking Nekhila; photographic postcards were quickly published showing wounded légionnaires, including the splendidly named Sergeant Panther of 2nd Company, I/1st RE, whose left hand was smashed by a bullet as he rescued the wounded Lieutenant Grosjean after the death of their Captain Doreau. On 19 April General Alix led 4,500 men forward from Merada, surprising the Beni Bou Yahi camp and inflicting a punishing defeat.

On 9 May, Alix struck out again from Merada, leading 5,000 troops via Safsafte to Msoun, which was occupied on the 11th. An anonymous légionnaire of I/1st Foreign left an account of the final advance across a plain shoulder-deep in barley; each company was deployed in diamond formation, with its four platoons 50 yards apart. A few kilometres from Msoun they came under long-range fire, hearing an appreciable interval between the buzz of the almost-spent bullet and the muffled report of the shot; the légionnaires continued to advance without returning fire, and could soon see figures flitting among the trees and rocks.

> Soon we got close to the hills that surrounded our objective. We started to hear the whistles and cracks of bullets passing over our heads and hitting the ground around us. We were still in the barley field, with only our heads above the crops; we could easily hide ourselves, and we fired back unhurriedly, as if on the ranges … [Then] the terrain changed; we entered harvested fields, and the platoons lay down, able to adance only by successive bounds. My comrade was hit in the left arm; he continued to advance, firing now and then with his good hand. A bullet went through my haversack; several men fell and did not get up again.[44]

The tribesmen did not wait for the French to close with them, and the battalion occupied high ground around Msoun that evening. The camp outside the *ksar* was attacked without success that night by men from the dominant local tribes, the Beni Ouarain and Riata, who were no more successful on 24 May. When Riata, Branès and other tribesmen attempted a convergence, General Alix again marched from Merada, meeting them near Kasbah Ain el Arba on 28 May and defeating each of three groups individually; this definitively pacified the plains around Msoun.

The length of the old Sultan's Road from Fes to Oujda was 210 miles; when Major Ibos of the Colonial Infantry finished his summary of operations in December 1913 the remaining 'Taza block' between Tissa in the west and Msoun in the east was only 62 miles wide. Narrow-gauge rail tracks were being laid from both sides to ease the logistics; the obstacles to a final link-up were 'hardly considerable and will diminish further as time passes'.[45]

THE EASTERN PILLAR of French control had now been built from the mouth of the Moulouya on the Mediterranean all the way down to the Hammada du Guir south of Boudenib, and in May 1914 Lyautey decided to set the lintel on his archway. Any secure success in the north obviously depended on the French opening the corridor between Fes, Taza, Oujda and the supply bases beyond the Algerian frontier. Eventually this would allow coordinated operations against the 'Taza Pocket' to the south – the northern Middle Atlas – but reducing that heartland of Berber independence would take many years. In the meantime, tribes at both ends of the northern corridor had been softened up by the usual patient political work.

In April, General Gouraud carried out preliminary operations against the Tsouls tribe north-east of Fes, during which 3kg aerial bombs were used for the first time in Morocco. These were made locally, using glazed earthenware casings; the bursts produced a considerable moral effect, but the flimsy, underpowered aircraft could only carry a few of them and they had to be dropped almost blind. The tribesmen's reaction – massed rifle-fire – had both a moral and a physical effect: on 8 April 1914, Captain Hervé and his mechanic Corporal Rocland were brought down beyond the line of outposts and killed by tribesmen, and thereafter Lyautey limited the permitted radius of flights. He judged that the boost to Moroccan morale of bringing a plane down and having souvenirs and heads to show around the villages would outweigh any advantage gained by sending aircraft into actual combat. (His opinion was shared by the General Staff, who judged the experiment a failure. That summer all aircraft were withdrawn to France on the eve of war, and Lyautey would not get any back until 1916.)[46]

THE TAZA CORRIDOR was the fertile valley of the Oued Innaouen. Travelling from Fes towards Taza, the valley floor was flanked by white and grey hills cut by gulleys and almost bare except for a sparse scatter of dwarf palms growing on the lower slopes. Perhaps 50 miles from Fes the hills gradually closed in and the dirt road started to rise, to a crest about 1,800 feet high. Beyond this Touahar pass the hills fell back around a broad circular plain; 10 miles further on the town of Taza could be seen on the southern side, perched on a black rocky crag that jutted out into the valley surrounded by 'a veritable forest' of fruit trees. Medieval travellers had praised the splendours of Taza, set amid its rich orchards and gardens; but by 1884 Père de Foucauld was describing the town as semi-ruined, and in 1900 the Marquis de Segonzac called it a pile of rubble, stripped by the almost daily attacks of the Riata Berbers, who had strangled trade along this important route and reduced Taza to about 3,000 residents. The hills above the Oued Innaouen were also the territory of the Hayana Arabs, the Meknassa, Tsouls and Branès, these last two Arabic-speaking Berber tribes being the strongest.[47]

Two French forces would meet at Taza: from the west, General Gouraud led the larger roughly 45 miles from Tissa, while from Msoun in the east General Baumgarten had only about a third of that distance to cover. The two Legion marching regiments were both involved, but Lieutenant-Colonel Girodon's 2nd Foreign with the Gouraud column had the harder fighting. Both forces set off on 9/10 May, but before marching eastwards along the Innaouen, Gouraud had to strike north to clear his left flank. On 12 May, Girodon was wounded when his troops (including Captain Rollet's mule company) met stubborn resistance around 'Tsouls Mountain' from tribesmen led by Si Mohammed el Hajjami – who was now fighting among ridges and glens that gave better cover than the plain north of Fes where Gouraud had smashed his *harka* two years previously. Once able to move eastwards, Gouraud made better progress, and his three large squares easily repulsed horsemen near the Oued Amelil. Meanwhile, Baumgarten had reached Taza on 10 May after a single night's forced march.[48]

The anonymous légionnaire of Major Met's I/1st RE at Msoun recalled that the night of 9/10 May was cold and heavy rain was falling; the column stumbled along through gluey mud, the men cursing and the pack-mules playing up. Suddenly the battalion buglers (the 'fanfare') struck up a march called *Karoline*, and

as if by a miracle, everything fell into place – the beasts behaved themselves, the mud was less sticky, and the men got their smiles back. To understand this miracle you had to understand our fanfare and our chief. 'Daddy' Met was a good légionnaire and we all adored him; an old bugler told me that he had been in the Legion for 23 years, and others told of serving under him in the Sud-Oranais, Madagascar and Tonkin ... [He was] of middle height, strong and lively; his face was lightened by a slight smile and elongated by a short, pointed black beard. He was full of solicitude and experience, kept an eye on everything, and commanded with firmness and kindness. He used to declare that with enough wine and a band he could lead his légionnaires to the ends of the earth ... He paid particular attention to the buglers, having them play popular tunes, but the one he preferred above all was *Karoline*, which he had adopted to the point that we became known as the 'Karoline Battalion'. The cannon fired, they played *Karoline*; the wounded arrived at the dressing station, they played *Karoline*; that damned *Karoline* produced a prodigious effect on the unit.

... From Msoun to Taza the terrain differed from other places in Morocco – you would think you were in the Auvergne. In some places the barley or

oats came up to your chest. It was really annnoying crossing the many fields
of wild artichokes, and we frequently had to cross streams. Little by little
the rain eased off, and marching became easier under a fine moon.

At about 4.30am on 10 May they came to the steep banks of the Oued
Aghbat, and halted for nearly an hour while improving a ford for the baggage
train. On the far side the ground was much more broken up, but by 6am,
from one of the numerous hills, the troops could see the minarets of Taza's
mosques less than 4 miles ahead. The vanguard Spahis exchanged the first
shots with Riata scouts, and at 7am Baumgarten's artillery opened fire on
groups resisting the advance:

> The 2nd Battalion of our regiment [II/1st RE] attacked the serious points of
> resistance ... thanks to accurate fire from neighbouring heights and the
> machine guns the enemy abandoned their ground. At 12.30pm we crossed
> the Oued Amelil and assaulted the hill ... At 1pm the French flag was
> floating from the kasbah, and soon our battalion was paraded before General
> Baumgarten and Colonel Boyer, our regimental commander.[49]

On 16 May 1914 the Baumgarten and Gouraud columns met at Meknassa
Tahtania about 3 miles from Taza. On the 18th, General Lyautey arrived to
review the troops, and the colours of the 1st RE, brought from Sidi bel Abbès
by Colonel Boyer, were proudly paraded in front of 6,000 men.

THE LINKING OF MOROCCO WITH ALGERIA did not end the fight-
ing in the Taza corridor, and seems in fact to have provoked fiercer resistance.
During June and July 1914 there were clashes with aggressive Ouled Bou
Rima and Metalsa tribesmen both around the Touahar pass and in the hills
to the north of Msoun. One of these actions, at a shrine called Sidi Belkassem
on 4 June, was memorable for I/1st RE. In the vanguard of General Baumgarten's column, the battalion made painful progress over ground cut up by
gulleys and hillocks, while taking heavy fire from all sides from tribesmen
who remained under cover and denied the artillery any concentrated target:

> The nearer we got to the shrine the hotter the fire got. We marched in
> skirmish lines, rifles cocked, bayonets fixed. We came under enfilade fire
> from a wild olive wood about 400 yards to our right; four légionnaires of my
> platoon fell, then the platoon commander Lieutenant Petersen, a Danish
> officer, was killed by a bullet full in the chest. The artillery raked the wood,

and enemy riders and foot fell back at a run towards the shrine ... and
seemed to form a centre of resistance on a reverse slope.

The major [Met] was riding in the midst of us; as always, the buglers were
blowing *Karoline*. We advanced by echelons; the sustained fusillade was
deafening, and the hillock on which the shrine stood disappeared in the dust
thrown up by ricocheting bullets and shell explosions. My platoon was in
the lead as we assaulted, shouting. We were greeted by intermittent and badly
aimed fire; the bounding shadows [of the enemy] disappeared into a rocky
gulley– there was nobody ahead of us. The major dismounted and came
forward to observe. Suddenly violent firing raked us from the edge of the
gulley, and we saw him fall; bullets from the rocks ahead and off to our right
tore up the ground. With a corporal and another légionnaire I ran towards
the major; the other man fell, I was pinned down, and only the corporal
reached him. He dragged him along the ground and then, with a superhuman
effort, got him up on to his shoulders and stumbled towards the rear, while
I covered them as best I could.

The rest of the platoon were up beside me now, and the 2nd Company
reached the hilltop. The firing was so intense that we could hardly raise our
heads to fire back, or use our tools to scrape up some cover. Luckily, the right
flank pushed ahead and the enemy were forced to give up the hill; when
they fell back into a valley the artillery pounded them ... The corporal
rejoined me on the hillock [and] told me that the CO was very badly
wounded; a large bullet had broken both his thighs ...

In camp that night a rumour spread through the battalion that since Major
Met would soon reach the official retirement age for his rank, only a promotion could keep him in the Army. A crowd of légionnaires gathered
outside the adjutant's tent, and after some shuffling and muttering a spokesman respectfully asked that in the name of the whole unit a request should
be sent to General Baumgarten to promote Major Met to lieutenant-colonel.
Before telling them brusquely to get back to their work, the captain promised
that the battalion officers would associate themselves with the request.
Within 48 hours confirmation was telegraphed from Paris. The narrator was
part of the escort that took the convoy of wounded and dead back to Msoun,
and he claimed that when 'Daddy' Met was lifted out of the ambulance
somebody had already given him a forage cap bearing the five braids of his
new rank. (Sadly, he does not mention the subsequent legend that the major's
amputated leg was buried by his men with full military honours.) The

battalions and mounted company of 1st Foreign remained in the Taza corridor on security duties throughout that summer.[50]

ON THE SAME DAY that Gouraud and Baumgarten began their pincer movement on Taza, down in the south-west Colonel Henrys launched a carefully planned drive to cut off a low-lying wedge of Zaian territory thrusting west from the Middle Atlas and hampering communications between Fes and Marrakesh. His objective was the riverside town of Khenifra (see Map 19).

Henrys knew that it might take Moha ou Hammou's clans two to three days to assemble and react, by which time he wanted a *fait accompli*. Three separate columns totalling some 14,000 troops struck towards Khenifra from the west, north-west and north, and by nightfall on 12 June, at a cost of only 7 dead and perhaps 25 wounded, Colonel Henrys was in possession of the blood-red town set among its orchards and willows in the curve of the Oum er Rebia.[51] Khenifra was almost deserted when the French marched in, and Moha ou Hammou showed no sign of coming in to seek the *aman* as Henrys had hoped. On the night of 14/15 June the camp was attacked in such force that Henrys was forced to use searchlights, artillery and machine guns to clear its approaches. He sent out strong columns in several directions, and on 30 June and 4 July two of these were attacked with considerable determination, suffering 94 and 43 casualties respectively in actions that came down to bayonet-fighting – a phrase that is often misunderstood.

In French histories such terms as 'taken with the bayonet' and 'body-to-body combat' are used so freely that they are in danger of being read simply as conventional tropes. Obviously, the outcome of Moroccan battles on the plains was decided by the firepower of French infantry supported by both artillery and a few machine guns. Again, most readers of military history are familiar with the fact that for two opposing Western forces to actually 'cross bayonets' has been unusual since at least 1800; faced by a determined charge with fixed bayonets the receiving side almost invariably falters and gives way before actual contact. The memoirs of twentieth-century soldiers have accustomed us to the idea that the bayonet was more useful for opening tins of condensed milk than for actual fighting. However, these accounts are all from wars where white armies fought other white armies; colonial battlefields were rather different. In the Moroccan hills, scrambling encounter-actions in overgrown and broken ground had a character quite distinct from the earlier battles against Arab horsemen on the plains. Since the highland Berbers were masters of the guerrilla ambush who deliberately chose broken ground, even battles fought by whole French brigades and battalions could easily involve a series of smaller fights at close range. In order to negate the French advantage in long-range firepower, the whole aim of the warriors' tactics was to close to hand-to-hand distance, where the odds were not just equal but often in their favour.

Although they were enthusiastic and skilled marksmen, the Berbers were products of a culture in which firearms had made face-to-face combat with bladed weapons neither obsolete nor particularly frightening, and they felt not the slightest reluctance to carve human flesh with steel. If he could get within arm's reach, the warrior with a long knife had an advantage over a white soldier trying to manage the nearly 6-foot length of a rifle and bayonet; once he had emptied his magazine the soldier was simply a rather clumsy spearman, and getting inside a spearman's reach was a game the Berbers had been playing since childhood mock-battles with sticks. The soldier, on the other hand, had been taught bayonet-fighting as a fencing exercise against another man with a fixed bayonet, which was not the same thing at all.

A heavy, sharp-pointed knife with a blade up to a foot long, in the strong hand of a man completely familiar with its use, could do immediately or imminently fatal damage in a number of ways, most of them more instantly painful and distressing than a bullet wound. A preliminary slash across the scalp could cause instant extensive bleeding, usefully blinding the soldier if a direct stab at his eyes was impractical. A stab or hard slash to the neck could lacerate the jugular vein or carotid artery and damage or even sever the spinal column. A hard stab to the chest did not have to penetrate the chambers of the heart to be effective: it could also fracture ribs and puncture lungs. A knife in the belly would usually tear into the bowel, liver, spleen, kidneys or one of several major blood vessels – piercing the aorta or inferior vena cava, for instance, would lead to immediate massive blood loss. Even a soldier who successfully protected his head and central body mass could be disabled momentarily by blows to the arms or legs to open a path to his major organs, and lacerating the femoral artery in the inner thigh was quickly fatal. And of course, if two warriors could attack a single soldier simultaneously then he was usually a dead man. The French troops soon learned these lessons, to the detriment of their morale; even in 1929 the colonial veteran Lieutenant Colonel Fabre would write:

What our troops have to fear most are these surprise attacks that can end in merciless hand-to-hand fighting, the prospect of which sometimes weighs heavily on their spirits. Such encounters are nearly always unfavourable to us, and cause four-fifths of our total casualties. They demoralize both the unit involved and neighbouring units, and increase the confidence and 'bite' of the enemy. Surprises of this sort have been numerous in Morocco, and whole battalions have been tumbled back with heavy losses by perhaps only fifty Chleuchs. It is painful to accept that it is the better led, organized and armed side that has been forced to yield ground.[52]

WHILE SOME ZAIAN CLANS did come in to talk terms with Henrys following the occupation of Khenifra in June 1914, much of the confederation was still holding together under Moha ou Hammou's surprisingly durable leadership; perched out of reach up in the hills, they continued to make swoops down on to the plain around the town. In a report to Lyautey, Paul Henrys stressed that down here the usual approach of announcing that the French came in the name of the Maghzan was counter-productive, since the Berbers had always regarded the Maghzan with loathing and contempt (a point also made by Major Ibos); they would only respond to French negotiators who dealt directly with them, not through Arab intermediaries, and who gave proper weight to their customary laws and tribal institutions.[53] Frustrated at his inability to achieve the negotiated settlement he had hoped for with the Zaians and several other tribes that followed their example, Colonel Henrys broke up his column into three brigades, one of them at Khenifra itself and the others at Sidi Lamine and at Mrirt (where the VI/2nd RE were based).

Goumiers and cavalry patrolled between them, trying without much success to seal off the hostile Berbers in the hills from the submitted clans on the plain. Moha ou Hammou continued to punish the latter with regular raids and to skirmish almost up to the walls of Khenifra throughout July 1914, which rewarded his followers with loot while weakening the fragile trust of the newly submitted in the strength of French protection. There seemed little prospect of the three mobile groups achieving more than stalemate during this campaigning season, but Henrys hoped that the next winter would weaken Moha ou Hammou's influence by forcing other clans to negotiate in order to be able to bring their beasts down to the lowland pastures. Up on the Fes-Oujda front, meanwhile, General Gouraud faced much the same situation in the hills flanking the newly opened Taza corridor, though the resistance he faced was more fragmented. He, too, could hope to consolidate when the next winter clamped down on tribal activity; but winter was still four months away when – with everything still to play for – the pieces on the board were dramatically rearranged.[54]

IN THE LAST WEEK OF JULY 1914, telegrams from Lyautey summoned his four western regional commanders to Rabat for a conference of the utmost urgency and secrecy. When they convened there on the 30th, the Commissioner Resident-General informed them that war with Germany was about to break out in Europe, and that Paris was instructing him to cut and run.[55]

15. The Lobster Shell
1914–18

During my whole period of command in the Oranais and Morocco the Legion have been my *troops – my dearest troops; and during the War of 1914–1919 they were my best resource and my final reserve.*

General Lyautey[1]

AT A MOMENT WHEN HIS TROOPS were committed to continuing operations on two fronts, Lyautey was instructed to send half of them back to France immediately. It was recommended that he give up most of the territory he had occupied, concentrating his remaining troops and European civilians in defensive enclaves around the Atlantic ports; but outside these, if feasible, he might attempt to preserve lines of communication eastwards along the Taza corridor from Fes to Oujda, and from Fes and Mèknes south-wards to Khenifra.

In practice, of course, 'lines of communication' is a phrase capable of the widest range of interpretation, and Paris was leaving the essential decisions about the future of the Protectorate in the resident-general's hands. Lyautey's response was that a general withdrawal would be disastrous both politically and militarily. In the *djebel*, Europe was a meaningless concept; every event was interpreted in purely local terms, and if the French soldiers marched away, then obviously they were admitting a defeat for which tribal leaders would successfully claim the credit. There would be massacres of Christian and Jewish civilians in the towns, and widespread uprisings in the countryside would threaten the units retreating towards the coast. Lyautey did not, of course, protest the withdrawal of his troops; this was '*la Revanche*', for which the French Army had been waiting all his adult life, and his own family home was in the Moselle border country. He sent back twenty battalions and six batteries immediately, promising more as soon as transport was available. However, his regional commanders agreed that if a thin crust of troops could be maintained around the vital centres, and if an illusion of 'business as usual' could be created, then it might be possible to hold on to what they had achieved.[2]

This would only be feasible with the continuing support of the *grands caids* of the High Atlas, to ensure that El Hiba or another like him did not seize the opportunity to come blazing back through the mountains to burn the French out of Morocco from the south upwards. At Marrakesh on 2 August, Colonels Maurice de Lamothe and Emile Mangin convened all the major southern tribal leaders to tell them of the outbreak of the European war. By far the most significant and best informed figure among them was Madani el Glaoui, and it was Madani's certainty and eloquence that convinced his fellow chiefs to reaffirm their loyalty to the Maghzan and France. His decision naturally rested on calculated self-interest; he believed that the French would ultimately be the winners, and that he could exploit profitably their now still more urgent need of his alliance.[3]

It was still only two years since General Moinier had had to use artillery on the streets of Fes, and it was vital to give the northern cities a convincing impression of undiminished French strength despite the fact that battalions were visibly marching to the harbours. To achieve this illusion Lyautey resorted to tricks that probably appealed to the theatrical side of his nature. In return for his combat veterans, he was receiving a trickle of replacement units of southern French Territorials, and these were quickly issued with sun helmets and the Legion's blue sashes to wear with their white fatigues; these men were approaching 40 years of age, but they looked convincing enough. Even European civilians were issued with rifles, boots and the red *chéchia* caps worn by Zouaves; by mixing these toy soldiers with elements of units that were about to embark Lyautey kept uniforms on the streets, and he even stage-managed a mass review of some 25,000 troops at Rabat in August. He boasted that he had 'scooped out the lobster but kept its shell'; but while he might have deceived the coffee-houses in the medinas, the frontier tribes could not see his conjuring tricks. On 4 August, the day after Germany declared war on France, two battalions marching north from Khenifra for the coast took 66 casualties in an ambush.[4]

THE LEGION WOULD PROVIDE an important part of the field forces with which Lyautey would hold (and in one respect, extend) his area of control during the next four years. Its units were not withdrawn from Morocco, although there was much shuffling of personnel to and from the Algerian depots. The Legion did not expect men to fight against the country of their birth, and most légionnaires from Germany and Austria–Hungary – about 12 per cent of the total who served during 1914–18 – were retained in North Africa while other nationalities provided the backbone for new marching regiments for the main war fronts.[5]

In a much more ambitious repetition of 1870, during September and October 1914 so-called 2nd Marching Regiments of both the 1st and 2nd Foreign, each of four battalions, were formed at the Mailly training area in France from new foreign volunteers stiffened with drafts of veterans from North Africa; three-battalion 3rd and 4th Marching Regiments/1st RE were also formed in November 1914, though these only existed for a few months. A year later the remaining légionnaires of these 14 battalions who had survived the battles in the Argonne, Artois and Champagne would be amalgamated into a single three-battalion Foreign Legion Marching Regiment (RMLE), which would serve on the Western Front with great distinction until the Armistice. The subject of this book, however, is the Legion's colonial campaigns, and the present chapter is limited to the less familiar story of the overstretched units that remained in Morocco. Like that of the British troops who spent 1914–18 on the North-West Frontier of India, their record was naturally overshadowed at the time, and has been ever since, by the infinitely more costly battles in France. Lyautey had the lowest priority for men and materiel, and experienced great difficulty in retaining regimental officers, who could only regard Morocco as a sideshow to the great national drama. It is against that background that his operations in Morocco must be considered (a brief summary of the Legion's experience on the European war fronts is given in Appendix 1 at the end of this book).

IN ALL, LYAUTEY SENT BACK to France more than he was asked for – no fewer than 37 of his 60 infantry battalions, with cavalry and artillery in proportion. His infantry in the west were reduced at a stroke from 48 to just 17 battalions, and those in the east from 12 battalions to 6. The average infantry strength available to him at any one time after autumn 1914 was about 23 battalions (with a brief peak of 30), the great majority of them in the western pillar of his now thin and shaky archway. His total strength was about 20,000 regular troops, which had to be spread along an L-shaped front totalling some 300 miles, from Khenifra up to Fes and then across to Oujda, at the same time providing a minimum garrison for the south-eastern desert. Of his battalions in the field, 5, eventually $5\frac{1}{2}$, were from the Legion, plus 3 mounted companies; légionnaires thus provided about 25 per cent of Lyautey's infantry, and at any one time probably half of his European infantry. (By November 1915 only 4 of the total of 13 Legion battalions were engaged in Europe, but those fronts were naturally the meatgrinders that consumed the great majority of wartime recruits.)[6] The only other white battalions rotated through Morocco were drawn from the 5 penal Bats d'Af, and to a lesser extent from about 15 war-raised Zouave battalions, most of them Territorials and middle-aged reservists who manned static garrisons throughout French North Africa. Lyautey's other units were 6 battalions of Algerian and Tunisian Skirmishers and 2 of Moroccans, and (the largest single contingent) a varying force of between 7 and 12 West African battalions of Senegalese Skirmishers.

This over-extended garrison would be tested by the tribes around both Taza and Khenifra as soon as the war broke out, and it would be under constant pressure for the next four years. The pattern for the Legion from spring 1915 would be a steady shift of units of the 1st Foreign from the northern front to join those of the 2nd Foreign in the west; initially this was in response to the greater and more persistent threat presented by the Zaians and their allied tribes, and later to serve Lyautey's longer term operational aim of driving a route right across the southern Middle Atlas to transform his 'archway' into a 'figure-of-eight'. The strain on their manpower due to officer transfers and unreplaced casualties would become increasingly serious by 1917–18.[7]

The French units would have help, however, and not only at a distance, from the *harkas* raised by the Atlas lords. French accounts naturally dwell upon the part played by French units, with an occasional off-hand mention of '*partisans*'; but local participation was not limited to those rag-tag gangs hired in the hope – often over-optimistic – that they would stay loyal for a single expedition in return for a rifle and a chance to loot. In all, perhaps 20 per cent of Lyautey's total forces in 1914–18 were locally raised. *Goumier* and *moghazni* auxiliaries provided a scouting screen for French columns, and to some extent replaced the nine regular cavalry squadrons that he had also sent back to France. In addition, temporary alliances were often formed with local *caids* armed by the French. The tribes never needed goading or trickery to persuade them to fight one another, and at no stage of Lyautey's operations did his aggression against one group distract others from their constant mutual warfare. The French simply channelled existing tribal hostilities to serve the Maghzan cause, and the pro- and anti-French nature of such clashes was more often a gloss than the actual *causus belli*.

ON THE OUTBREAK of war Colonel Tahon's Marching Regiment/1st RE (I/, II/ and VI/1st) was holding the eastern half of the Taza corridor. The I/1st (Major Théveney) were dispersed in companies all the way between Taza itself and Taourirt (see Map 18); II/1st (Major Duriez), VI/1st (Major Drouin), 1st (Mounted) Company (Captain Tramuset) and the sole Mounted Company/2nd RE were in various camps around Taza itself. As early as 9 August, tribesmen attacked both Msoun – to which the 1st (Mounted) were immediately sent – and a II/1st RE company camp outside Taza. Early the next day that battalion's 6th and 8th Companies went out as part of a small column under Lieutenant-Colonel de Tinan to clear a village at Ras Sirai to the north-east of the town. That afternoon they, and another company-and-a-half who had to be sent out to cut them free, returned after paying a price as high as any suffered in a single action for years: 5 Legion officers, a warrant officer and 21 NCOs and rankers killed, and 47 wounded.[8]

The months that followed introduced the northern three battalions and two mule companies to the life that the whole Legion in Morocco would lead for the next four years. The constant for all units was labour and security duties along the lines of communication – building roads and small company posts along them, holding the posts, making local patrols around them, and providing regular convoy escorts to keep the roads open along the corridors they guarded. At exhaustingly frequent intervals and in all seasons companies were also gathered to take part in Mobile Group operations – retaliatory or deterrent columns up into the hills. Their routine service along the lines of communication cost them a slow drain of casualties to ambushers and snipers, and the more aggressive thrusts into the Berber highlands were often resisted with a determined skill that exacted a higher price. The versatility of the mounted companies in particular, and the Legion's overall reputation for steadiness under fire, meant that its units almost invariably provided the vanguard for advances and the rearguard for withdrawals by mixed columns. The French term for disengagement under fire – *se decrocher*, 'to unhook oneself' – aptly conveys the difficulty of a manoeuvre that was always exploited by the Berbers. Before the first winter of the war this was demonstrated, shockingly, by Colonial troops on the Middle Atlas front.

AROUND KHENIFRA, THE KEYSTONE of the French line guarding the western edge of the Middle Atlas, the autumn was relatively quiet. By the beginning of November the regional commander, Colonel Henrys, was satisfied that during the winter the competition for the reduced area of unguarded pasturage on the left (east) bank of the Oum er Rebia would take most of the tribes' attention. Some Zaian clans, resentful of Moha ou Hammou's robust methods of encouraging loyalty, even began bringing their sick to the French infirmary, allowing contacts to be established. Moha himself was camped on the left bank at El Herri a few miles south of Khenifra, with perhaps 500 warriors and the same number of dependants. He made no provocative moves; but in the second week of November his proximity proved too great a temptation for the town commander, Lieutenant-Colonel René Laverdure.

This Colonial officer appears to have shared a fairly widespread view that Lyautey's operations were too hesitant (one must imagine the mood created by the war news from France, where General Galliéni, military governor of Paris, had saved the capital with his typically pragmatic commandeering of Parisian taxis and buses to take 4,000 reinforcements out to the front line on the Marne). Laverdure had twice been refused permission to hit villages on the left bank, and since then his garrison had been halved; nevertheless, he now took matters into his own hands. Before dawn on 13 November he marched south with the great majority of his command: 43 officers and 1,187 rankers, comprising 6 companies of Algerian and Senegalese Skirmishers, 2 French artillery batteries, a few Spahis and Moroccan auxiliary horsemen. At daybreak Laverdure surprised Moha ou Hammou's tented camp, shelled it, and sent his cavalry in to overrun it. Moha's counter-attack was driven back by infantry volleys while the camp was ransacked; success seemed so complete that some of the tribesmen even started looting their neighbours' tents alongside the *goumiers*, and two of Moha's wives were among the hundreds of captives taken. However, when the column began to withdraw at about 8.30am it came under predictable pressure from tribesmen flowing forwards again to follow it closely, and Laverdure had to use his guns to cover the retreat. At about this point it became apparent that the track back to Khenifra was no longer open; one of Moha's nephews, Moha ou Akka, had closed in behind the column with several thousand warriors of the Zaian and three other Berber tribes.

Laverdure's name was about to become indelibly associated with the worst-ever massacre of French troops in Morocco. When he ordered a company of Senegalese to force their way through to Khenifra with the wounded, many others left the ranks and followed the mules and carts in panic. The rearguard was cut off at the Oued Choubka ford, both gun batteries were overrun, the square was broken up, and individual survivors were hunted down in the scrub. The 181 wounded, their escort and a mob of stragglers, only barely reached the gates of Khenifra under cover of volleys from the two companies left there and the Berbers followed them to the very walls. Laverdure and 32 other officers were killed, along with 580 rankers; 8 cannon, at least 4 machine guns and 630 rifles were lost, with all the column's equipment and remaining ammunition.[9]

Khenifra was now defended only by Captain Pierre Croll with about three Skirmisher companies (one formed with the shaken and partly disarmed stragglers), and might even have fallen to a determined assault. As usual, however, the tribesmen concentrated on gathering up the booty from their unexpected triumph rather than exploiting it. The telegraph line was even left uncut, and Croll's cabled appeals to Henrys at Fes and Lyautey at Rabat – the first they knew of Laverdure's unauthorized sortie – brought relief after a couple of days. Colonel Garnier-Duplessis led his mobile group east from Sidi Lamine about 30 miles away, fighting his way through ambushes to arrive on 16 November. Two days later, Colonel Henrys reached Khenifra with a second mobile group, formed at Ito by Lieutenant-Colonel Joseph Dérigoin around VI/2nd RE. Dérigoin's column had marched more than 50 miles south through completely empty country – in the aftermath of El Herri the tribes had prudently moved back up into the hills, since 7,000 troops were now concentrating at Khenifra. It was not until 19 November that the légionnaires found and buried the bodies, a task that took them two days. The corpses of Laverdure and half a dozen other officers had been taken from the field for display, but were later exchanged for the release of Moha ou Hammou's wives.[10]

Laverdure's ghost was roundly cursed by Lyautey in correspondence with the War Ministry; his impulsiveness had put the delicate shell of defence at risk by handing Moha ou Hammou enormously increased prestige and influence among the Middle Atlas tribes, only a few weeks after Muslim Turkey's entry into the war beside the Central Powers had unsettled the cities. Moha's contacts with two other powerful Middle Atlas leaders, Ali Amhaouch and Moha ou Said, would now be developed, and clans from all over the Marrakesh hinterland would send warriors to join him. Lyautey had to accept that his cherished policy of political persuasion as a preliminary to military penetration simply had not worked among the Zaians, and might take much longer than he had hoped among other highland Berbers.

During the winter of 1914/15, the newly promoted General Henrys organized the northern and western fronts in three military regions: from north to south, Fes–Taza, Meknes, and Khenifra–Kasbah Tadla. These would form simultaneous Groupes Mobiles for coordinated operations by neighbouring commands; those formed at Meknes would be a versatile link between the Taza and Middle Atlas fronts, on either side of the top left corner of the French 'archway'. In the south, Garnier-Duplessis would support a defensive garrison at Khenifra, while from Ito and Kasbah Tadla his two mobile field forces would maintain – with variable success – a blockade on the highlands.[11]

UP IN THE TAZA CORRIDOR, the three battalions of 1st RE and the two mule companies spent 1915 in a repetitive rhythm of security duties punctuated by regular sorties with the mobile groups. The légionnaires marched and countermarched almost without respite, enduring the summer heat and dust of the Moulouya plains and the rain and cold of the autumn and winter hills. When periodically reassembled to join the mobile groups, they struck out from Fes, Taza, Msoun, Safsafte or Camp Bertaux to punish raids, resupply posts, reconnoitre routes and generally show the flag among the tribes. They bivouacked on scree slopes, tormented by nagging snipers; they panted up countless weary hillsides to picket the summits and ridges, only to climb down again at the risk of a sudden fusillade into their backs from above. They seldom ran into stubborn resistance, but suffered a trickling haemorrhage from hidden marksmen and small-scale ambushes. Any movement in the hills was a game of hide-and-seek, and every encounter began with a patter of shots from concealment. Somebody had to be the unlucky one – the first man over a crest, around the side of a rock or stepping clear of the trees – and as often as not the man groaning in a *cacolet* or rolled in a tent-cloth and slung over the back of a mule was a junior officer or NCO. The entries in the war diaries tap out a dull rhythm in a minor key:

22 May: Escort from Taza: S/Lt Fouquart (II/1st RE) seriously wounded.

27 June: Battalion operation near Kelaa des Sless: WO Chauvet (II/1st RE) and 3 men wounded, 1 corporal killed.

29 June: Mobile Group near Dar Caid Medboh: Lt Peyre (VI/1st RE) and 2 men killed.

15 August: Ambush near Bou Ladjeraf post: Capt Roquefort (VI/1st RE), Sgt Coggia and Pte Fremont killed.

26 November: Rearguard Fes Mobile Group near Sidi Abd el Kahman: WO Werner (Mtd Co/2nd RE), Ptes Durand and Baumert killed, Pte Raoul wounded.

10 December: Battalion operation, Djebel Bou Mihiris: Lt Ekdal (VI/1st RE) and one man killed, sergeant and 5 men wounded ... [12]

On 10 June 1915 Major Duriez of II/1st RE handed the battalion over to Captain de Larroquette and departed for France, and in August–September the unit was transferred from the Taza front down to Kasbah Tadla and then Oued Zem, to join III/ and VI/2nd RE facing the Middle Atlas. This was the first of several such transfers that would gradually shift virtually the entire weight of the Legion's deployment from the Taza corridor to the Zaian front. [13]

IN ZAIAN TERRITORY, 1915 failed to bring any sign of the hoped-for dissolution of Moha ou Hammou's confederacy. Lyautey's long-term plan was to push roads eastwards across the southern Middle Atlas to divide the tribes and give his troops access to their home country, and Major Curie's VI/2nd RE spent that summer with crowbar, dynamite, pick and shovel. They built a new post at Timahdite in the forested hills south of Azrou, escorted its supply convoys down from Ito, and drove a 20-mile stretch of road north-eastwards up the river gorges to Almis de Guigou. On 30 September General Lyautey reviewed them at Ito and presented decorations before trying out the new road to Almis by motorcar. After autumn operations south-east of Mrirt, Major Curie hoped to rotate his companies to give the men some prospect of a winter rest from constant watchfulness on the icy, sodden frontier: at any one time, three companies would be at Ito and the fourth in barracks at Meknes. Just as in the previous year, however, they would be disappointed in their hope that the tribes would stay quiet during the winter. [14]

On 11 November 1915, a strong force from Garnier-Duplessis' command was escorting a convoy with provisions for the winter along the track westwards from Khenifra towards Sidi Lamine, and in the Sidi Ammar hills the right flank guard was provided by the légionnaires of Larroquette's II/1st RE. At the Ait Affi pass (called by the troops 'Pierced Rock') several hundred Berbers hit the advance guard in very broken, wooded terrain; they were dispersed by a few shells and machine-gun clips, and their movement took them straight across the rifle sights of II/1st Foreign. The convoy kept moving under intermittent harassment from riders, but was rushed again on two occasions during that afternoon. The second attack was by some 750 warriors on foot followed by 300 horsemen; they fought to within 50 yards of the vanguard, and were only driven back by Legion bayonet charges by Captain Coste's 6th Company. The total French loss of 3 killed and 22 wounded was hardly significant, but the fact that up to 1,200 warriors of four different tribes had taken part in the ambush was. Unprecedentedly, Moha ou Hammou's league was still holding together after more than a year of fighting.[15]

In January 1916, while marching from Khenifra to Mrirt after a major resupply operation, both southern mobile groups came under attack, and Major Curie's VI/2nd RE – in Colonel Pierre Thouvenel's Groupe Mobile d'Ito – had the briskest fight. They had been marching in the vanguard when, in the usual way, they had been peeled off to picket hills on the right flank while the column passed, and there they were attacked by growing numbers of warriors. The first began to approach, sniping as they came, at 9.20am; more and more appeared, pressing attacks to close range, and it was evening before the battalion could 'unhook itself' and resume the march to Mrirt. The war diary records 16 Legion casualties among the brigade's total of 81: Lieutenant Bruyant and 9 NCOs and légionnaires killed, Sub-lieutenant Bruyère and 3 rankers wounded, and a sergeant-major and a private listed missing in action.[16] These modest losses were a good deal more damaging than the bare figures suggest, since they typically included a disproportionate number of hard-to-replace platoon leaders – on that occasion, 3 out of the 16 casualties.

Each battalion needed about 20 officers and 40 senior NCOs; the demand for battalion and company officers to replace those lost on the Western Front was insatiable, the Legion's pre-war generation of sergeants was bleeding to death, and units in Morocco would always be the last in the queue for replacements. In France, 1915 had been terribly costly for the Legion. In May and June the marching regiment of 1st Foreign had suffered some 2,600 casualties (65 per cent) in two assaults in Artois, and in September they and their sister regiment from 2nd Foreign lost nearly 1,000 more in Champagne; as already mentioned, in November all the survivors had to be consolidated into a single three-battalion regiment. At the same time, between March and September 1915 another marching battalion had been virtually destroyed in the Dardanelles.

The memoir of an American deserter (published posthumously under the byline 'M.M.' in 1924, thanks to the charity of D. H. Lawrence) describes morale at Sidi bel Abbès in 1915 as very low. The overall picture he paints of life in the single mainly German battalion of 1st RE is plausible enough, although the judgement of this thoroughly unmilitary witness does not invite respect. (His indignant whining about every aspect of life in the ranks that he, a 'gentleman', was forced to endure during his three months at the depot is unattractive. Indeed, his book is probably unique among Legion literature in including the peevish complaint 'my moustache worried me . . .').[17]

Throughout 1916 the Zaian front continued to see repeated attacks not just on convoys but on brigade-size mobile groups, and an action that August usefully exemplifies the value of the Moroccan *goumiers* if well led. On 2 August an intelligence officer named Francois de La Rocque was commanding auxiliaries with Garnier-Duplessis' mobile group on its way westwards to Sidi Lamine when a Legion picketing company found itself surrounded on a summit above the Pierced Rock pass. By the time the convoy had passed below them the company were cut off and low on ammunition, and La Rocque was sent to unhook the légionnaires with two Goums. He led half of 1st Foot Goum to within 100 yards of the tribesmen before opening fire; this allowed the légionnaires to break out, and the two companies then covered one another as they fell back by stages for some 600 yards towards 4th Mounted Goum, whom La Rocque had placed on a hilltop as rearguard. The withdrawal was successful, but Captain de La Rocque was hit four times (he survived evacuation, and while convalescent forged a medical release in order to get to the Western Front). The need for special leadership skills in such commands is, however, underlined by the fate of La Rocque's successor in command at Sidi Lamine at the end of 1916. Captain Tailharde, apparently lacking La Rocque's touch, had his throat cut in his tent by his own men and his head removed for display around the Zaian villages.[18]

*

EVENTS IN THE SPANISH ZONE during 1915–16 naturally effected dissidence in the French territory north of Taza. The Spanish commissioner-general from August 1913 was General Marina y Vega, formerly commander in Melilla. The headstrong but well-connected Colonel Silvestre, whom Marina's predecessor General Afrau had had to send back to Spain when he proved unable to obey orders, had now been promoted brigadier-general, and returned to Ceuta in a subordinate command. In the hinterland of Ceuta the dominant figure was still Silvestre's old enemy Ahmad er Raisuli. General Marina was encouraged by Madrid to negotiate with Raisuli to buy off his active hostility, but in May 1915 an attempt to do this was foiled by a 'war faction' of Spanish officers, probably including Silvestre. That turbulent soldier was recalled to Spain yet again, and in September 1915 Marina's successor, General Francisco Gomez Jordana, agreed a subsidy and other concessions for Raisuli, in return for which the Spanish hoped that he would suppress tribal resistance to their expansion. In this they were disappointed, and the ever-treacherous Raisuli continued to play off the tribes, the Maghzan, Spain, France and Germany against one another. Since he also accepted German gold, the French and British were convinced that he was working for the Germans, but – since he never delivered his promised help against the French – Germany believed him to be a British agent. They were all mistaken: Raisuli plotted, robbed and killed in his own interests alone, and his war parties continued to ambush convoys and fight Spanish troops in the hills west and south of Ceuta. (Leading a charge at a village called Biut in 1916, an unpopular, priggish but insanely brave young Spanish captain of Regulares named Francisco Franco y Bahamonde took several bullets in the stomach. His surprising survival preserved him for a more pivotal role in his country's history twenty years later.)[19]

Since Spain remained neutral during the Great War, while belligerent France had a legal status as the protecting power throughout Morocco under the Treaty of Fes, the authorities in the Spanish presidios were in a false position. Both Spanish officials and the Rif tribes around Melilla were actively courted by German agents seeking a base for propaganda, gun-running, bribery and subversion in French territory, and by 1917 U-boats were refuelling at Tangier and landing agents, cash and rifles over the beaches of Alhucemas Bay. The pre-war commercial dominance of German firms such as Gebrüder Mannesmann made this operation relatively easy, and the Spanish responses were inconsistent; some officials were pro-German, and though others did make some effort to stop arms coming in, German gold spoke loudly. One important recipient was Abd el Malek Meheddin, a grandson of Abd el Kader (the renowned Amir of Mascara, whom the French had exiled from Algeria to Syria in the 1840s). This former officer of l'Armée d'Afrique and Maghzan police chief in the Tangier zone had become a German agent, and in August 1914 he went underground to work against the French. They demanded his extradition as a deserter, but his German funding was generous enough to protect him.[20] By the winter of 1916/17 he had crossed the border to set up rebel camps on French Moroccan territory, but his activities were knocked back in late January 1917 and again that April, when his bases were destroyed by the Fes and Taza mobile groups including the Legion mounted companies.[21]

THE TAZA CORRIDOR required repeated operations into the highlands north and south throughout 1916 by the Fes and Taza mobile groups, and a particularly intense rhythm of work was demanded of the Legion mule companies. Like modern paratroopers, they were condemned to it by their very versatility and high reputation; unlike paratroopers, however, between combat operations all légionnaires exchanged rifles for sledge-hammers and were employed simply as pioneer units.

The two foot battalions still on this front were also heavily committed, and these elite 'heavy infantry' were in effect being used like alpine troops. They climbed thousands of feet a day for weeks on end, wearing out their boots, clothing and stamina, living under canvas on rudimentary field rations, often short of water in the long hot season and at other times chilled to the bone. Given the alternation of field operations with hard labour, cumulative exhaustion was inevitable, and replacements were in short supply. By May 1916, the I/1st RE (Major Giudicelli) were reduced to three companies, operating from posts and with a mobile group in the Msoun–Guercif sector. In July 1916, Lyautey ordered that the narrow-gauge railway from Algeria to Taza be extended westwards towards Fez, and Major Desjours' VI/1st RE drew the short straw of building a roadbed through the Touahar pass. The following winter the 1st Foreign's mounted company were set to work to create an airfield at Taza, since Lyautey had finally got two *escadrilles* back from France. (In 1917 his air arm, commanded by Major Cheutin, would be expanded to six squadrons; their main value was still as eyes in the sky, to some extent making up for the shortage of regular cavalry on the ground.)[22]

On the Middle Atlas front, the drain of officers to the 'real war' continued; Major Curie of VI/2nd RE had left for Salonika in February 1916 and was replaced from April by Major Auger. In service to Lyautey's plan for trans-Middle Atlas links, the mobile groups were nibbling eastwards into the edges of those ranges, and in May, Auger led his unit south from Timahdite in a column commanded by Colonel Joseph Poeymirau. (This officer was a veteran of Lyautey's staff in the old days at Ain Sefra, who later in 1916 would replace General Henrys in overall operational command when the latter returned to France.) In June the VI/2nd Foreign built a temporary home at Ain Leuh, the new advance base for Poeymirau's Meknes Mobile Group; the battalion was under-strength, with 13 officers, 39 NCOs and 598 rankers, but it had finally acquired a second machine-gun platoon.[23]

IN THE SOUTH-EASTERN DESERT, the years 1914–15 had been quiet for Captain Sainville's 2nd (Mounted) Company/1st RE at Boudenib. Camel caravans across the eastern plains to the railhead at Colomb Béchar attracted the occasional opportunists, usually from the south rather than from the Tafilalt; every now and then Sainville took a half-company out to intercept or pursue reported raiders from the Hammada, but the more usual recon-naissance patrols and escort missions across the dreaming wilderness were exercises in numbing routine. In March 1916, Captain Sainville departed for France, but soon after Captain Coutance took over things became more active. Lyautey's intention to tie a zig-zag string of roads across his 'archway', reshaping it as a figure-of-eight to separate the northern and southern Berber redoubts in the Middle Atlas, would require approaches from both west and east. In April 1916 he decided to reinforce the weak desert 'pillar' with a European infantry unit, but its nature suggested that the Legion in North Africa was nearing the end of its resources. Major Feurtet's Boudenib Com-posite Battalion – formed at Colomb Béchar with two Legion companies from the Oranais and two of *joyeux* from the penal 4e and 5e Bataillons d'Afrique – arrived at Boudenib on 8 May.[24]

On 22 May this Bataillon Mixte marched westwards as part of an 1,800-strong mobile group with III/8th Algerian Skirmishers, 15th Battalion Sene-galese Skirmishers, some Spahis, and Captain Coutance's 2nd (Mounted) Company. The pimps and draft-dodgers hauled off the streets of French cities must have been shocked by the utter emptiness of this terrain, in which the flat horizon between white sky and brown wasteland is all that the eyes can fasten upon. Wide stretches of the dreary gravel-desert west of Boudenib will not even support the usual low tufts of leathery vegetation, and single twisted little thorn-trees or dwarf palms are distributed literally miles apart. Eventually the column got into the hills and right up to the treeless plateau around Rich at the head of the Ziz gorges, where a post was to be installed (see Map 23). Picketing the crests must have been lung-bursting work; here stony heights crowd steeply in around stretches of mangy grassland, each hill seemingly born in a different aeon from another only a couple of miles away. Some are topped with jagged rust-red crags carved with fissures and caves, with masses of huge fallen boulders around their feet; others have cut faces that show pale stacked strata tipped at diagonal angles; others still are table-tops, with fretted caps of rimrock undercut by the erosion of the clay slopes, stained with red patches bleeding through the grey. At Rich, the mobile group was divided; half of the Composite Battalion began to build the post, while the other half reconnoitred downriver with the 2nd (Mounted).

As they came down into the Ziz gorges the geology changed again; the track now zigzagged in and out between interlocking curtains of red rock, each superimposed horizontal stack with its own pattern of vertical fissures, for all the world like crowded giant bookshelves, with here and there a single dramatic needle standing close but alone. Below the track on their right the putty-coloured Oued Ziz, fast but shallow, swung back and forth between pebble beaches edged with a narrow green sleeve of rushes, scrub and trees. On their way back up the gorge on 31 May the légionnaires came under fire from warriors on the tormented orange-grey cliffs that cramp the Ziz into the narrow pass of Foum Zabel; here the track on the east bank crept along a ledge around a great rock buttress thrusting out into a foaming, confined bend of the river, and the mule company lost two men. On 2 June they destroyed a riverside village at Amzoug before the column reassembled and returned to Boudenib.[25]

On 5 July 1916 the mobile group marched out again, this time heading for the plain south of the mountains through which the liberated Oued Ziz flows towards the Tafilalt. This country was roamed by the Ait Khabbash and Ait Umnasf tribes of the stubbornly hostile Ait Atta people, who had neither been tamed by the Atlas lords nor tempted to talk peace by the French. On 9 July, the column fought a significant Berber force at the oasis of Meski; the 2nd (Mounted) held hillocks north of the village in close fighting, and took seven casualties while discovering that the tribesmen were using German Mauser bayonets as daggers. The next day Coutance's mounted company made a forced march back to Boudenib in crushing heat, carrying the gravely wounded Captain Bertin of the 15th Senegalese about 51 miles in 26 hours. The rest of the column then marched north-west over the empty desert to Ksar es Souk (modern Er Rachidia), where it began to build another post, thus tying a knot to secure the bottom of the southern loop of Lyautey's planned figure-of-eight.

Inevitably, these and subsequent clashes would lead French troops towards the oases of the Tafilalt itself, where on 16 November 1916 the 2nd (Mounted) and the Composite Battalion would clash with Arabs at El Bourouj in the Tizimi *palmerie* just north of Erfoud, subsequently planting an observation post at the village of El Maadid.[26] The wealthy communities and religious brotherhoods scattered throughout the Tafilalt had for so long been a focus for resistance that they exerted a dangerous fascination over some French officers, but Lyautey was adamant that his weak force in the south-east should provoke no direct confrontation. While the sultan had preached that the Muslim Turks were heretics, the French were always haunted by the nightmare of a pan-Arabic *jihad* right across the Maghreb, and French resources in their eastern Sahara were already stretched to the limit by a serious uprising. At a time of famine, Turkish agents had stirred up the followers of the Islamic reformist Senussi movement in what is now Libya; rebellion had spread to some drum-groups of the southern Tuareg, and in the deep desert the overstretched Saharan Companies would fight at least twenty serious actions during the First World War.[27]

GENERAL LYAUTEY had returned to France periodically to confer with the government, and even he could not help but wonder about a command on the Western Front. The battlefront had rolled over his own home in Lorraine, and he had told President Poincaré that he must have a free hand to give promotions and decorations in Morocco because both officers and French NCOs felt dishonoured by their absence from the defence of the homeland.[28] In December 1916, the weak Briand administration offered Lyautey not a field command but the War Ministry, probably in the hope of borrowing a little of his lustre; untouched by responsibility for the carnage of the past thirty months, he was still a respected figure. With some misgivings he accepted, on condition that the Moroccan residency-general be kept warm for him by his old deputy General Henri Gouraud (who now had an empty right sleeve, thanks to a Turkish shell during his command of French forces in the Dardanelles).

The dominant figure in Paris was now the new Chief of the General Staff, Robert Nivelle, and Lyautey's suspicion that he himself was intended to be a figurehead with symbolic responsibility but no real power was soon confirmed. He was uncomfortable at having to answer directly to a parliamentary Chamber rich in hostile anti-colonialists, and he signally failed to apply his 'oil-stain' approach to the task of attracting allies among a class whom he instinctively despised.[29] Various generals took the opportunity to share with Lyautey their doubts about Nivelle's planned spring 1917 offensive between Soissons and Rheims. He was officially briefed on this by an old protégé, Colonel Georges Renouard (the officer who at Ain Sefra in 1904 had taken down his dictated telegram of defiance after his seizure of Ras el Ain – see Chapter 11). It was an embarrassing meeting, since Renouard had to defend to a man he respected a plan in which he clearly had no faith himself. Subsequently Lyautey tried to argue against Nivelle's breezy confidence, but was dismissed impatiently as 'a Napoleon returned from Egypt'. In the Chamber on 14 March 1917 he was shocked to be simply shouted down when he had hardly begun to speak; he resigned his portfolio, and two days later the Briand government fell. The Nivelle Offensive on the Chemin des Dames went ahead on 16 April; on 20 May, after its catastrophic failure, Lyautey left Paris to return to his old command in Morocco.[30]

ONCE HE WAS BACK IN THE SADDLE, Lyautey gave priority to preparing for his planned cut across the lower Middle Atlas, but no operation in Morocco could ever be mounted in isolation. The northern cap of his 'archway' had been under some pressure during his absence in the winter of 1916/17; I/1st RE (Major Giudicelli) had been transferred down to Kasbah Tadla in January, leaving only VI/1st (Major Desjours) and the two mounted companies to represent the Legion on the Taza front. On 13 June 1917, both VI/1st RE and 1st (Mounted) Company suffered casualties near Souk el Had south of Kifane, in an action that is worth brief description simply for its typical character.[31]

Like so many of the Legion's most punishing fights, this one saw the Berbers clinging to the rearguard of a withdrawal through wooded hills. Major Desjours' battalion got through the narrow pass of Ain el Haout only with difficulty, covered by Lieutenant Chanraud's machine-gun platoon and Captain Thiébault's 23rd Company picketing the heights on their left. When that rearguard itself began to fall back it found its flank uncovered thanks to a premature movement by a Spahi troop, and Lieutenant Veseron had to lead his platoon in a bayonet charge to recover his casualties. The Berbers continued to hang on the flanks and rear of the battalion as they withdrew, carrying their dead and wounded. From a summit to the right, Lieutenant Fetaz's machine guns covered the retreat of Captain Deckmyn's 22nd Company, but the highlanders bounded forward with extraordinary speed to surround Fetaz; some soldiers only escaped by rolling bodily down the rocky slope, and Sub-lieutenant Perret's two guns were cut off. He and nearly all his légionnaires were shot down, and in the end the survivors only got clear when 22nd Company, some Senegalese and a mountain artillery section closed up on an opposite slope and created a corridor of fire for them.[32] Meanwhile, the 1st (Mounted) were rushed as they withdrew from two jutting crags nearby; together the two Legion units suffered 3 killed and 17 wounded, with another 5 missing in action. Among the dead and lost were an officer, a sergeant, and Warrant Officer Panther of 1st (Mounted), who had saved his lieutenant under fire at Nekhila in April 1913.[33] The kind of tribesmen who killed them would be the Legion's preoccupation for twenty years.

THE BERBERS OF THE ATLAS were the products of a warrior culture not unlike that of the Pashtun (Pathans) of the Indian North-West Frontier. A mountain Berber's life depended on wresting a crop from his jealously guarded patch of land, but his honour resided in fathering sons and in fighting – to defend what the clan held, or to take what was another's. There were differences of dialect and of physical build; the northern Rifians tended to be stockier than the sometimes longer-limbed, longer-faced clans of the Atlas proper, but they were recognizably members of the same people. All had pale olive complexions and usually dark brown hair and eyes, though a minority showed the fairer colouring and pale gaze that so puzzled European academics. Mature men wore beards, sometimes a 'full set' but often only a fringe around the jawline (which some French officers copied, up to the 1950s); under a loose turban their heads were shaved except for a scalp-lock. Those who spent time among them spoke of a characteristic facial expression of reserved, watchful but lively intelligence. [34]

Like all highlanders born and bred, they had remarkably powerful legs and lungs; they could move up and down steep slopes in their woven sandals far more quickly and for far longer than most booted Europeans, and the race to or from a crest was often a matter of life and death. Since they were also completely familiar with their own wooded glens, ravines and bare ridges, they could thus exploit a cross-country mobility far superior to the mainly track-bound white soldiers with their pack-animals and artillery. Each man carried what little he needed – cartridges, *kesrah* unleavened bread or a few handfuls of parched grain, some dried fruit – in a leather satchel slung at the hip, so their 'logistics' were almost non-existent, and when needed they could seek provisions in the remote upland villages. Over a long shirt and calf-length trousers above woollen stockings or puttees they wore a loose, hooded *djellabah* robe of tightly woven mixed wool and goat-hair, in browns, greys or unbleached off-whites; this served as both a greatcoat by day and a blanket by night. Every warrior carried a rifle and a long, straight knife.

The Berbers' guerrilla tactics were classically simple, suited to the terrain and to the stubbornly individualist culture that some Europeans found so attractive. Their fieldcraft – the use of ground, light, cover and stealth to conceal movement – was superb, as demonstrated time and again by their extraordinary success in stealing rifles, even horses, from within night camps without raising the alarm. They were deadly hunters of isolated sentries and small detachments; any outpost of a few soldiers, any firewood or water party, any lagging squad delayed by crossing an obstacle had good reason to fear that lethal Berber eagerness to get within hand-to-hand range that has already been explained. In the face of a European advance they always occupied dominating heights, firing and manoeuvring individually or in small groups, falling back before superior strength only to seek the next ambush position (for this reason they could sometimes be dislodged by an apparent threat to outflank and cut them off). They were accustomed to husbanding their ammunition, and since – unlike the Arab riders of the plains – they usually took steady aim from behind a rock or tree trunk, they made every shot count.

Their war-chiefs emerged from among the most respected members of the clan councils, and their authority had to be earned by personal qualities of courage, guile and luck. Once the clan was committed, the chosen war-chief might exercise absolute authority, but his practical powers of 'command and control' were limited. The Berbers had no notion of attack or defence 'in depth' – in successive waves or lines, with reserves held back; every man was committed to the same thin battle-line. Neither did they have any concept of large-scale coordinated movements on the battlefield, nor – since each clan was fiercely independent and egalitarian – the social mechanism to organize them. However, relative lack of numbers at any particular point never deterred them from surprise attacks when the soldiers' mutually supporting formations became dislocated in the broken ground where the tribesmen chose to fight.

The Berbers had an uncanny ability to spot and exploit any mistake, and their individual tactical skills seemed to be as innate as their physical hardihood. They flowed through their hills like mercury, dispersing into individual beads in the face of strength, but coalescing instantly to overwhelm any vulnerable group. They were never more dangerous than when soldiers had to fall back in alternate platoons, opening up exploitable gaps and flanks. Captain Guennoun:

> Berber tactics rest upon two preoccupations: to use mobility to give the illusion of numbers, and to flank and surround their enemy in order to sow confusion. We have seen 25 or 30 Zaians harassing the flank of a convoy between Khenifra and Sidi Ammar on a front of [5 or 6 miles], and creating the impression that they were several hundred strong. Equally, we have seen 100 or 200 warriors oblige a whole mobile group to halt and form fronts to resist simultaneous attacks from four directions.[35]

As late as 1929, Lieutenant-Colonel Fabre would write that the French Army had not paid sufficient attention to developing a tactical doctrine for close combat that would protect the troops from such surprises. He argued for the junior officers, NCOs and men to be thoroughly instructed in a strictly limited number of straightforward 'battle drills' – *procédés* – worked out to counter the typical range of Berber tactics, which the troops could adopt at a moment's notice at the shout of a sergeant: 'Such techniques exist, but they are too little known.'[36]

THE LINK ACROSS THE MIDDLE ATLAS would be attempted by two columns: the stronger Meknes Mobile Group under Colonel Poeymirau would push south-east to meet in the hills; another, led by Lieutenant-Colonel Doury, would march north-westwards from Boudenib. Meanwhile, the Fes Mobile Group would march through the tribal territory of the Northern Ait Segrushin and Marmoucha south-east of Sefrou, to cover Poeymirau from the north; and a column from Debdou would sweep up the middle Moulouya to clear Doury's northern flank. Poeymirau began his operation in mid-May 1917 by ensuring that his southern flank would also be secure, establishing a post on the north-eastern edge of the Zaian country at Bekrite in the hills south-east of Mrirt as an obstacle between neighbouring hostile tribes (see Map 19).[37] That spring, I/ and II/1st RE were tied down in the relentless convoy warfare around Kasbah Tadla, Khenifra and Sidi Lamine, but VI/2nd RE (Major Auger) were assigned to the Bekrite force. They saw a little skirmishing and much hard labour, and in June they marched south-east to build yet another post at Itzer. By the end of June a new track along a hairpin route from Timahdite via Itzer to Bekrite was practical for motor vehicles, though only over several difficult days.

The drive across the Middle Atlas was successful, and earned Poeymirau his general's stars; on 6 June 1917 his and Doury's columns – the latter including the 2nd (Mounted) Company/1st RE from Boudenib – linked up at a spot recorded as Assaka Nidji. On the 10th the mobile group from Debdou (Colonel Maurial) also arrived nearby at Missour, where an import-ant post was established. A week later the Boudenib Composite Battalion (Major Weynaud) arrived at Ksabi about 28 miles further upriver. The next few months would be spent in improving tracks into roads, plaiting the string hung between Lyautey's 'pillars' into a rope; by late 1917 motor lorries could travel from Meknes all the way to Bekrite, and in the east from Missour and Ksabi down to Rich, although the convoys' passage naturally needed protection by pickets on summits to form a moving security corridor. Roads were no barrier to the tribes, but they allowed faster troop movements to areas of dissidence; in time they would also reverse the current of the lines of supply, so that provisions for units in the eastern ranges could come down from Meknes rather than across from far-off Algerian depots via Colomb Béchar – a long-standing drag on operations.[38] From the motorable road across the Atlas, another would be dropped southwards down the Oued Ziz, and by the end of 1917 Doury's troops would have established a new post at Midelt. However, the new access routes into the Middle Atlas were still vulnerable.

IN THE SPRING OF 1917, THE WESTERN PILLAR of Lyautey's opera-tions was being thickened at its mid-point, but not without resistance in the hills east and south-east of Sefrou – the tribal range of the Marmoucha, Northern Ait Segrushin and 'Ait Atta in the Shadows' (a far-flung tentacle of that land-hungry people). In late May and June 1917, Captain Cattin's Mounted Company/2nd RE worked on tracks between Annoceur – the gateway into the hills from the main road south of Sefrou – and a new post at Tazouta (see Map 19). This is still bleak country today, with very rough stony trails along valley bottoms between hulking naked hills, and when ordered back to Annoceur on 18 June the mounted company saw Berber signal fires on the hilltops. The troops found that drystone walls had been built across the track, and had a brisk fight before reaching Annoceur, where they stayed until 3 July. The Groupe Mobile de Fes then concentrated at Tazouta, where the footsore VI/2nd RE also arrived that day from their labours at Itzer.

On 4 July, the mobile group marched south for Skoura, at first around sandy slopes thickly spotted with scrub and small trees, and then down on to a cream-coloured plain. The change of scenery is immediate, from terrain reminiscent of dry Californian hills into something that is definitely African, with low, thorny trees and patches of wiry scrub widely scattered across a gently rolling clay plain, bright in the sun. The vanguard of the column was Major Auger's VI/2nd RE, with a Spahi squadron and a 65mm mountain battery.[39] At first the villagers that they passed seemed unconcerned, but before long the column came under fire from brush-speckled ridges a few hundred yards to the right of their track; shells and machine-gun fire silenced this, the crests were picketed and the mobile group pushed ahead, with villagers and flocks now fleeing south ahead of them. After a few miles the Oued Sebou curved in closer from the east, and the track turned eastwards up wooded slopes; when it reached a plateau at about 3,500 feet, thick trees and cultivated patches marked the village of Skoura, at the foot of a pass leading further up into steep, scrub-covered hills. There the column bivouacked for a few days, and was joined by General Poeymirau with units from his Meknes Mobile Group.[40]

The purpose of the march was a reconnaissance in force and a demonstration, not yet an occupation, and Skoura was at the end of the practical track southwards. To the east the Tizi Adni pass, rising steeply 500 feet from Skoura up the northern shoulder of the hills, was the path into the true mountains beyond – the chaotic 6,500-foot Tichoukt massif – and Poeymirau did not have the logistic resources to thrust any further. At 4am on the morning of 8 July his force began to break camp in the darkness for the return march to Tazouta.

THE REARGUARD, UNDER MAJOR AUGER of the Legion, initially consisted of his VI/2nd RE with a squadron and a battery. The combined mobile group's large baggage train delayed their departure, and it was 5am before the rearguard set off. First light had revealed tribesmen filtering down from the hills to the west and north, but the main column had withdrawn its pickets from the flanking high ground before the rearguard could catch up – always a danger when a long column 'concertina'd'. Auger sent word up the line that he needed more men to replace them, and he was sent a company each of Senegalese and Moroccan Skirmishers. These secured his flanks during his withdrawal down the wooded slopes immediately west of Skoura, and the rearguard reached the open plain and turned north without interference.

On a contour map (if such a thing existed) this stretch of plateau might seem to offer no danger of surprise; but the morning of 8 July 1917 was foggy, and thick dust kicked up from the dirt track by the convoy ahead also hung in the still air. The clay plain on either side of the track is deeply fissured here and there with natural drainage gulleys whose depth varies from knee- to head-height and more, resembling dug trenches. On the left (west) the ground is more or less bare for a margin of a few hundred yards, running back to a dark, broken line of low thorny trees and scrub along the foot of speckled ridges; as always, distance and height are difficult to judge. On the right, the eastern hills are miles off beside the Oued Sebou, but the plain rolls up to the track in low hummocks and dips, thickly scattered with stunted thuya trees, holly-oaks and patches of dry bushes to within 100 yards. When cloaked in mist, such terrain offered superb cover for the Berber riflemen who were converging on the rearguard.

The Skirmishers picketing the high ground were surrounded and attacked first, and needed artillery and machine-gun fire to help them disengage. The only way to make progress was by leapfrogging bounds, and by about 7.30– 8am the rearguard was separated into three parties each of two infantry companies. The furthest ahead were the Moroccan and Senegalese companies, which had reached a low hillock with two machine-gun platoons and a section of mountain guns. Some way behind, but making good progress towards this fire position, were two companies of VI/2nd RE; but 300 yards behind them the last two companies of légionnaires were surrounded and under heavy pressure. They were taking close-range fire from all sides, and had to resort to the bayonet to stop rushes that loomed up out of the mist. The artillery some 600 yards ahead had no clear target and dared not fire blind, and the machine guns kept jamming in the dust.

The rearguard had been fighting for hours before they finally received some support; infantry were sent back from the main column miles ahead, and off to one side Captain Cattin's Mounted Company/2nd RE, who were withdrawing across country on a parallel route, managed to fight free of their own attackers. Hearing the gunfire off to his flank, Cattin sent most of his company on in a further northwards bound while he himself led his machine-gun section across country to the aid of the VI/2nd Foreign. He managed to set up his two guns at very close range and swept the Berbers away from one flank of the embattled battalion, and at last the rearguard broke free from its tormentors; they eventually reached Tazouta after ten hours of fighting and marching. The five Legion companies had suffered 77 casualties: 43 killed, 33 wounded and one missing. As always, the higher figure for dead than for wounded speaks of fallen men being cut up by the tribesmen before their comrades could reach them.[41]

Seven days later Major Auger's mauled VI/2nd RE were 70 miles away back at Ain Leuh camp, and they remained in that sector for the rest of 1917. They were joined on 26 September by Major Desjours' VI/1st RE transferred down from the Taza front, where only 1st (Mounted) Company/1st RE now kept the Legion's red-and-green *fanion* flying.[42]

IN AUGUST 1917, UP IN MELILLA, a functionary and journalist named Mohammed bin Abd el Krim el Khattabi, the eldest son of a respected Ait Waryaghar *faqih* or teacher of the same name, was arrested by the Spanish authorities.

Abd el Krim the elder had been dealing with the Germans, and when his house was burned down during a Spanish raid he had taken to the hills with a few followers. However, these did not yet include his two unusually promising sons. The younger (whose name is usually given as Mhamed) was studying in Madrid to become a mining engineer, while the elder, Mohammed – then about 36 years old – straddled both the Spanish and the Rifian worlds in Melilla. Educated in a Spanish school there before attending the Karaouine *medersa* in Fes, in 1914 he had been appointed the senior *cadi* or Islamic judge of the Melilla region. Simultaneously, he worked both as a secretary in the Spanish native affairs bureau under Colonel Gabriel Morales, and also as editor of the Arabic supplement of the newspaper *El Telegrama del Rif*. His office duties gave him an inside view of the corruption surrounding Spanish exploitation of the Rif's mineral resources, and he became an outspoken critic both of Spanish expansion around Melilla and of the French Protectorate. In August 1917 his protests apparently became unacceptable, and he served about 18 months in Restrogordo prison. A rope was smuggled in, and the broken left leg he suffered during a failed escape attempt would leave him with a limp for the rest of his life.[43]

BETWEEN THE SUMMER OF 1917 AND THE SUMMER OF 1918, patient pressure on the Zaians brought unspectacular but useful results. While the chiefs Moha ou Said and old Moha ou Hammou would remain defiant, one by one the latter's sons and nephews opened tentative contacts with the Native Affairs post at Khenifra, and the third important leader, Sidi Ali Amhaouch, died of natural causes. Attrition worked both ways, however: no major engagements took place, but the constant round of escorts, columns, and the occasional establishment of new posts in the hills led to frequent clashes in Colonel Théveney's Tadla-Zaian Territory.

By June 1918, casualties, accidents and malaria had reduced Iler RE to just 377 all ranks, who spent the rest of the war on the Oued Zem–Kasbah Tadla–Khenifra axis. Major Desjours' VI/1st RE established a new post at El Hammam between Mrirt and Bekrite; like the other battalions it increasingly saw its companies dispersed as parts of *ad hoc* task groups as the strain on manpower became extreme. In January 1918, Major Auger led a composite battalion assembled from two companies and a machine-gun platoon each from his VI/2nd RE and Desjours' VI/1st, padded out with a Moroccan Skirmisher company, for General Poeymirau's operations around Khenifra. In deep snow that lasted until April 1918 the VI/2nd were then spread between Azrou and Timahdite to guard that northern stretch of the trans-Atlas route, before marching with spring and summer columns around Ain Leugh and El Hammam.[44] Incited by rumours of the Allied defeats in France at the time of Ludendorff's spring 1918 *Kaiserschlacht* offensive, the Northern Ait Segrushin, Marmoucha, Ait Youssi and Beni Alaham tribes were all restless, threatening the forts at El Hammam, Itzer, Midelt and Ksabi and the routes between them. In mid-June it took Poeymirau's whole mobile group three days to re-open the Tarzeft pass south of Timahdite after an ambush.[45]

Up in the Taza Corridor, on 16 August 1918 the 1st (Mounted) Company/1st RE received urgent new marching orders for the south, where a week beforehand Lieutenant-Colonel Doury's Boudenib Mobile Group had effectively been destroyed as a functioning command.[46]

WHILE LAUTEY'S ATTENTION remained fixed on his relatively fragile new link across the Middle Atlas, Doury had irritated the resident-general by showing too much interest in the Tafilalt. In December 1917, he planted a Native Affairs officer at Tighmart, south-west of the major oasis of Rissani (see Map 23). Taken together with an aggressive expansion into the Dades valley by Tahami el Glaoui's war parties, even this minimal presence provoked the Ait Khabbash who ranged the desert west, north and south of the Tafilalt.[47] When Lyautey had to send Doury reinforcements as insurance, his letter of 18 February 1918 was caustic: 'It is we who have deliberately provoked this difficulty, whereas it would have been so simple to maintain the status quo.' He warned Doury against the 'seduction of these southern mirages', which might seem to promise much but delivered nothing.[48]

On 30 July 1918, while fighting with a force led into the Dades valley by Tahami el Glaoui to chastise the Ait Atta, the elder brother Madani's favourite son and chosen heir was killed while leading a horseback charge. Whether or not it is actually possible to die of grief, it is certain that when the news was brought to him, the 60-year-old Madani el Glaoui took to his bed in his palace at Marrakesh, and died on 14 August. With Lyautey's ratification, he was succeeded in all his possessions and powers by his brother Tahami, who ruthlessly replaced many nephews with his own sons, thus reducing some 300 close relatives to dependent poverty. (Madani had said of Tahami that he was 'a dagger that one might use, but which one must afterwards discard', so the question of which brother ruined the other's line had been simply a matter of timing.)[49]

The Ait Atta unrest also led to the killing of the Tighmart post's interpreter, and Lieutenant-Colonel Doury, who was circling the Tafilalt hungrily, seems to have been happy to overreact. A *harka* was reported in the oasis of Gaouz at the southern tip of the Tafilalt, and on 8 August 1918 Doury led two battalions, a mounted company, a battery and additional auxiliaries east across the desert from Tighmart to Tinrheras. There he camped overnight in preparation for an aggressive thrust eastwards across the *palmerie* of Gaouz to the banks of the Ziz.

DOURY MARCHED at 5.15am on 9 August, and at 6.30am his scouts came under fire from a low rocky crest; a Legion platoon cleared it, and machine-gun fire into the tamarisks fringing the southern edge of the palm groves put the tribesmen to flight. At 10.30am the column halted to cook *la soupe* before pursuing.

The enemy they faced were of unknown strength; Doury's report would later number them at 1,500, but under the circumstances he cannot be considered reliable. It is known that there were at least 400 Ait Atta at Gaouz, led by a preacher who called himself Sidi Mhand n'Ifrutant. Another *marabout* named El Haouari is also mentioned, so the total number of tribesmen present may have been at least in the high hundreds (Captain Guennoun's comments on Berber tactics, quoted above pp.441, are relevant here). Whatever the number, Doury decided to divide his column into two forces; he would lead the southern, pushing straight ahead eastwards towards the *ksar* of Gaouz and the river, with Major Weynaud's Boudenib Composite Battalion (by now even more *mixte* than before, and with only one Legion company) and two mountain guns.[50] Meanwhile, Major Pochelu would cross the plantations in parallel but further north, with his composite battalion formed from two companies of the Tunisian 8th 'Algerian' Skirmishers and two from the 15th Senegalese, plus Captain Timm's 2nd (Mounted) Company/1st RE and the other two guns.

Doury and Weynaud moved off at about noon and entered the palm plantations, and by about 2pm they were heavily engaged from their left, where the Berbers were infiltrating. They had to close the baggage train and Lieutenant Montrucoli's Legion rearguard right up behind the firing line, and the 65mm guns were in action at close range. Doury sent couriers north to tell Pochelu to leave this encumbered terrain as soon as possible and to camp when he reached the Ziz. At about 2.30pm Doury ordered his force to close to their right (south) in order to start moving again; after an hour they reached the riverbank, took a Berber camp, crossed the Ziz and cleared the far side of the *palmerie*. Montrucoli's Legion company had been held as the rear reserve for most of the day and suffered only four casualties. The column camped at about 5pm; there was no sign of Major Pochelu's camp upriver, and no couriers had returned from him. Any distant sounds of combat would have been hard to distinguish from those of Doury's own action, and by the time that ended, all was quiet to the north.

MAJOR POCHELU HAD ENTERED the *palmerie* of Gaouz from the west, with Captain Timm's mule company in reserve behind the composite Skirmisher battalion. Pochelu had sent his two guns back to rejoin Doury's column, since he judged them useless in this kind of terrain. The ground between the trees of date-palm plantations is thickly cultivated with knee-deep crops and tall shrubs packed into every possible square yard. The plots are continuous in all directions, divided only by meandering irrigation ditches invisible until you stumble into them, and occasionally by mud-brick walls half hidden in the overshadowing greenery. The closely set trunks of date palms do not rise naked to a high, feathery cap like coconut palms, but throw out dense diagonal fronds and orange fruiting-branches from ground level upwards; except where old branches are pruned to allow rudimentary access tracks, they mesh together into dense barriers, confused and thickened by the bushes between. Occasionally a lane of visibility across a miniature field of lucerne opens up for a few yards, but the extent of the oasis ahead is unguessable unless it is packed against the foot of a cliff that shows above the treetops, and at Gaouz there is no such feature.

Soon after Pochelu's soldiers began to force their way into this stiflingly hot tangle-foot maze they came under fire from close range, and men began to fall without ever seeing their killers. The overlapping screens of vegetation were confusing, and the Mounted Company's report stated that significant casualties were suffered from riflemen concealed in ditches and behind walls before the Skirmisher battalion 'took up combat formation', which suggests that they were still pushing their way through the undergrowth in parallel platoon columns. Sergeant Picard was left with the Legion mule-holders under cover of a ditch, and Timm led the rest of his company forward on foot into a gap that had opened up between the two halves of the Skirmisher battalion, which was now deployed with its Senegalese companies on the right and the Tunisians on the left. In such obstructed ground they could not shake out into a single firing line, but had to advance in squad files side by side. At about 2pm the enemy ceased fire and broke contact, and Pochelu let his panting men have a few moments' rest. They were in considerable danger; this had nothing to do with individual courage, and perhaps needs a brief explanation.

From the moment when Major Pochelu's companies left the open sands and passed under the eaves of the *palmerie* they had lost mutual visibility, and thus much of the advantage conferred by their superior training, organization and equipment. The native soldiers of the composite battalion were a collective of two separate teams, each drilled and rehearsed in coordinated actions at given words of command; they were also illiterate conscripts, from whom nothing was expected but blind obedience. This human machine, with a number of 'moving parts', relied for its effectiveness on the moment-by-moment direction of officers and NCOs to make those parts function in exact sequences. The palm plantation had no real overhead canopy, but in every other respect it presented the same difficulties as true jungle fighting. The terrain and thick vegetation broke the human machine's cohesion and interrupted its internal connections (and its cohesion was in any case imperfect, since the Arab and African halves of the unit were divided by the age-old prejudices and resentments of the slave trade). If this cobbled-together machine came under real pressure and began to lose its junior leaders while its different parts could not see or hear one another clearly, then the sequence of its movements would quickly break down. The tribesmen had been at a real disadvantage out on the open sands; here in the tangled labyrinth between the trees, with visibility reduced to a few yards, their individual motivation – their very lack of reliance on any collective rehearsal for combat – gave them the tactical edge.

POCHELU RESUMED HIS ADVANCE, with the Legion company once more behind the centre in reserve. At perhaps 2.30pm the column came under very heavy attack, there was 'violent fighting before the units could deploy', and the machine began to malfunction. On the right, the Senegalese fell back; the Legion company moved forward again and charged to fill the gap in the fighting front, but tribesmen infiltrated between the platoons of Senegalese. A second Legion charge had to be made to try to clear the Senegalese left flank and restore some order; 'unfortunately, other units, nailed to the ground by heavy fire, could not follow the Legion's example', and the Senegalese began to break up in disorder.

In such a crisis the troops should have been able to rely upon their superior firepower, but to a great extent the close-set palm trunks already negated any advantage, and anyway the Mounted Company was soon reduced to carbines and bayonets only. It had lost one of its two machine guns that morning, jammed solid during the fight for the ridge outside the oasis; now Lieutenant Jorel took the other Hotchkiss forward between the légionnaires' right flank and the dissolving Senegalese companies, but soon after he took over from his wounded gunner that gun jammed too, and he carried it to the rear to try to clear it. The Legion in Morocco had by now received some issue of two new weapons: the M1915 Vivien-Bessière rifle-grenade, fired from a cup attached to the muzzle of the Lebel, and the M1915 CSRG light machine gun (the 'Chauchat'). But Captain Timm's men were already down to their last ten VBs, and with an 8-second delay fuze and 180-yard range these were difficult to drop on close targets in thick cover – they were designed for firing between shellholes and trenches in the open moonscape of the Western Front. The company's two Chauchats also jammed, perhaps predictably – this ugly and awkward weapon, assembled by the Gladiator bicycle company, was notoriously unreliable.[51]

By now the tribesmen were also getting in close among the Tunisian Skirmishers on the left, who recoiled backwards. In the centre, the Legion company charged a third time, and at that moment the Senegalese 'were led towards the rear' (the official wording). The légionnaires of 2nd (Mounted) were exposed on both flanks, and the Ait Atta pushed forward to try to hook around them in the thick cover. At about 3pm a bullet broke Captain Timm's left arm high at the shoulder. Lieutenant Jorel took command, but he too fell wounded, and the Berbers swarmed over him with knives. Sub-lieutenant Freycon had an easier death: surrounded by enemies, he held them back by windmilling his empty carbine until one of them shot him full in the forehead. Sergeant Leins and Pte Forseter tried to bring his body in, but then Leins himself was killed. Warrant Officer Regnier, Sergeant-Major Kabe, Sergeants Picard, Pommeroulie and Landers and QM-Corporal Eckhard were already down, as were five of the corporals. It fell to Warrant Officer Roque-plan, with the one remaining sergeant and three corporals, to command the company as they fought their way backwards towards the edge of the oasis. The report describes the légionnaires holding together in the middle of a nightmare confusion of Tunisians, Senegalese and tribesmen locked in hand-to-hand combat in thick cover. Lashed into the seat of a *cacolet*, Captain Timm continued to try to direct the retreat even after a second bullet smashed his face. Major Pochelu, the force commander, died after being shot through the wrist (this sounds rather puzzling, but again, it is the official wording).

At last the légionnaires saw the sun through the trees behind them. The pursuit slackened and finally ceased, as the tribesmen stopped to finish off the abandoned wounded and gather up the rich harvest of rifles and ammunition. The 2nd (Mounted) Company had lost 47 men killed, and just 7 wounded were recovered; another 2 unwounded men would soon die 'of exhaustion'. Roqueplan led them back out to the slight ridge where they had fought early that morning and organized them to defend it, but at about 5pm a sandstorm blew up. For once the légionnaires did not curse it; it provided the cover they needed to stumble away over the open desert. The sand around the southern Tafilalt is orange under a strange skin of dead black grit; normally hooves and boots would leave clear tracks, but we may presume that the wind wiped them clear that evening, and the légionnaires were not pursued. At about 9pm the exhausted survivors staggered into the Native Affairs post at Tighmart.

Lieutenant-Colonel Doury would report the total French loss that day as 238 killed and just 68 recovered wounded – the worst casualties since El Herri in November 1914 – at the hands of an enemy which he claimed to have 'almost annihilated'. How he reached the latter conclusion is unclear, and Lyautey was unimpressed; his response to Doury's report lashed the colonel for grave mistakes before, during and after his impulsive action in 'this most peripheral of zones'. The disaster at Gaouz encouraged tribesmen to rise right across the south-east; it took six months to quell the unrest, which embarrassingly obliged the resident-general to request reinforcements from Algeria.[52] Tahami el Glaoui also had to lead the greatest *harka* ever mounted – some 10,000 men – against the Ait Atta in the Dades valley, inflicting defeats in January and February 1919.

The shattered 2nd (Mounted) Company/1st RE swapped places with the 1st (Mounted) from the Taza corridor, which saw combat alongside the Boudenib Composite Battalion at Dar el Beida and other villages in the Tafilalt in autumn 1918. The posts at El Maadid and Tighmart were given up in favour of a more defensible one at Erfoud, built and occupied by the Composite Battalion, but this, too, was abandoned after a few months; the definitive occupation of the Tafilalt would have to wait many years. After Gaouz, Lyautey added this front to the already considerable responsibilities of General Poeymirau; at Meski on 15 January 1919, in the course of defeating the victor of Gaouz (Sidi Mhand n'Ifrutant), the general was seriously wounded in the chest by the accidental explosion of an artillery shell, but his task was completed by Colonel Antoine Huré.[53]

THE ARMISTICE OF NOVEMBER 1918 found Lyautey with a great deal of unfinished business in the Middle Atlas and with irritations in the south-eastern desert, but still able to boast a large measure of success over the four years of his wartime stewardship. He had held on to all the territory he had captured in 1914, and had established an important new line of communication across the Middle Atlas. Moreover, behind the thin 'lobster shell' of his Groupes Mobiles, the civil development of his Protectorate had advanced remarkably during the war years.[54]

During the First World War, the Legion lost 348 officers and men killed in Morocco – not even half of the 721 who died with the single Legion battalion in the Dardanelles and the Balkans, and a single-figure percentage of those killed or listed missing on the Western Front.[55] Disregarded at the time and now almost entirely forgotten, Lyautey's investment of these lives on France's behalf was undeniably cost-effective. It is hard to imagine how he could have preserved French Morocco without his 'dearest troops', whose relative importance there was demonstrably greater during these years than at any other period.

16. Flawed Blades
1919–22

This system of splitting up into spheres of influence a country which, while nominally one, forms as a matter of fact different political and administrative entities, is not one that can be recommended. More especially is this the case where [it] introduces frontiers that only to a very small extent are based upon natural or physical features – frontiers that pass through unexplored and unknown districts.
Walter Harris, 1927[1]

AMID THE WRECKAGE AND EXHAUSTION of 1919, the Foreign Legion needed rebuilding for an uncertain new world in which the task of identifying and balancing French military needs and resources would take some years. While Europe was awash with potential recruits, few of them were the sort of men who had typically been the source of pre-war légionnaires. The solid world of accepted identities and hierarchies that had bred the 'old moustaches' had died in No Man's Land; post-war Europe was a vast psychiatric out-patient ward, and the recruits of 1919–22 were far more heterogeneous and uncertain material than pre-war intakes. Their average age dropped markedly, to 64 per cent under the age of 25; the wider social base lifted the educational level, but with it expectations and political awareness – the newspaper-devouring légionnaire was a new phenomenon. It was hardly surprising that very few Frenchmen now enlisted, and the high proportion of Germans reversed the pre-war position with equally unbalanced results. In 1912, the Legion enlisted 23 per cent Frenchmen and 16 per cent Germans; in 1920, the figures were 3 per cent and 55 per cent.[2]

Given the recent hatreds of the World War this naturally led to mutual suspicions and, at the highest level, to anxiety over the Legion's reliability, and a consequent decision to place an artificial limit on the proportion of German NCOs aggravated resentments. Morale and efficiency were low, and the desertion rate in 1919–22 – usually to Spanish Morocco – was shockingly high. This sometimes involved whole squads, who made carefully planned escapes taking their weapons with them, and at least one group, led by a former German Army NCO, used them against fellow légionnaires.[3] Since the Legion was unique in being spared the annual convulsion of inducting new conscripts en masse, it had the potential to regain its reputation as a crack corps, but rebuilding a reliable collective morale would take several years; after all, even the immediate outward symbol – the képi – had been a casualty of the trenches.[4]

Most of the experienced sergeants who had been the guardians of continuity had gone, and out of sheer necessity too many men were given a gold stripe too quickly and indiscriminately. In 1920, it was possible to get one within a year of enlistment, but in 1921 the 1st Foreign alone still recorded a shortfall of 130 sergeants – more than 30 per cent. From that year, French Line NCOs could transfer into the Legion for twelve-month tours, but handling légionnaires required skills that Metropolitan units had not taught. Hastily promoted men lacked the natural authority that only experience brings; they compensated for their want of confidence either by becoming inflexible martinets or by seeking popularity through laxity. The new type of recruit was also less likely to give automatic respect to the small minority of old soldiers as mentors. An enlistment bounty was now offered, pay rates had improved, and with coin in their pockets (and permission to visit approved civilian brothels) the new légionnaires spent less time in the canteens listening to the old soaks' war stories – which they could often top, anyway.[5]

The officer corps responsible for reshaping the post-war Legion was equally unlike the generation that had gone into the trenches. Some pre-war veterans did return from the Western Front or prison camps, alongside commissioned rankers and a very few retained foreign volunteers, but they found the home they remembered sadly changed, and some of these survivors now regarded their German rankers as little better than prisoners-of-war.[6] The majority of the many subalterns required came either straight from St Cyr or from the Line as birds of passage, since – in order to break down the traditional walls between the home and colonial armies – after 1918 the Army introduced a system of rotating two-year postings to *théâtres d'opérations extérieur* (TOE) to give young officers experience of foreign service.

Accustomed only to French conscripts, they found their new soldiers impenetrable, and a three-month induction course at Sidi bel Abbès gave little useful guidance.[7]

Lieutenant Colonel Paul Rollet, returning to Morocco garlanded with the glory he had earned in the trenches, noted in his diary: 'Conclusions not optimistic ... post-war crisis in value of things, in value of men, above all in the moral sense – the tool is not sharp – needs recutting and retempering – the Africa Army in general and the Legion specifically.'[8] He drew up a detailed memorandum, calling for stricter selection of NCOs based on fitness for combat leadership, improvements in administration to restore a decent consistency to the treatment of enlistees, and a searching reform of the ponderous machinery of the Sidi bel Abbès depot, which in time should be moved to Morocco to tighten its relationship with the combat battalions. This memorandum was passed up the chain of command to the War Ministry, where – although approved by Lyautey, who in 1921 attained the ultimate dignity of a Marshal of France – it died of neglect in a filing cabinet. The Rue Dominique accepted the defensive objections of the depot, then commanded by one Major Riet, an officer of whom it would be noted that 'he left neither a trace nor a memory of himself' at the 1st Foreign before he was posted to the backwater of Tonkin.[9]

THE POST-WAR REORGANIZATION removed the distinction between permanent administrative *régiments organiques* and task-organized expeditionary *régiments/bataillons de marche*, so the old two-regiment structure was now inadequate. The Legion would consist of four numbered *régiments étrangers d'infanterie* (REIs) of three battalions each, though extra battalions of the 1st and 2nd Foreign would be formed to serve in the more far-flung garrisons.[10]

The 1st REI would remain at Sidi bel Abbès providing central reception, training and administrative services for the whole corps, though it would also put battalions into the field. Apart from its physical distance from the active front in Morocco, this centralization would have other malign consequences: some more or less idle and nest-feathering officers and senior NCOs would tend to accrete around these comfortable billets, where they settled into the life of the town, married too young, ticked the boxes for their pensions and future civilian employment, and skimmed off the human and material cream before it reached the front-line units.

The headquarters of 2nd REI moved from Saida in Algeria to Meknes in

42 ABOVE French hilltop post in the Rif, 1925–26.
(Fuller captions, and picture credits, will be found on pages xxxvi–xliii.)

43 BELOW Outlying blockhouse, seen from trench connecting it to
the post.

44 ABOVE The summit of Astar, looking east to west, with traces of 1925 post, photographed in 2007

45 BELOW Looking north-west from the post ruins on Astar

46 ABOVE Legion squad in a post in the Rif, 1925–26

47, 48 BELOW Légionnaire Adolphe Cooper in 1914; and Major Marcel Deslandes, killed leading II/1st RE on 18 July 1925

49a & 49b New tools
colonial warfare,
1925–26: a Breguet 1
at Taza, and Renault
FT17 tanks crossing
Ouergha river

50 LEFT Terrain in t
eastern Rif: aerial ph
of Oued Nekor valley

51 ABOVE The brothers Abd el Krim – the younger, Mhamed (left), and Mohammed

52 BELOW General Hubert Lyautey, c.1916

53 BELOW RIGHT Marshal Lyautey, 1921–25

54 & 55 ABOVE Légionnaire Albert Neal with comrades; 3rd REI, early 1930s

56 Légionnaires road-building in Morocco, 1920s–30s

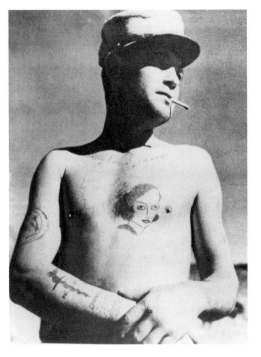

57, 58 ABOVE Légionnaire with typical tattoos; and Légionnaire Bobby Lincoln, 2nd REI, early 1930s

59 Senior NCOs' canteen at a regimental depot, 1930s

60 ABOVE & 61 OPPOSITE, ABOVE Légionnaires in action in the High Atlas, c.1932

62 & 63 BELOW Lieutenant Djindjeradze, and Trumpeter Slavko; IV/1st REC, 1932

64 BELOW LEFT Légionnaire of 1st Foreign Cavalry, early 1930s

65 BELOW RIGHT Major Prince Aage, 3rd REI, 1936

66 ABOVE Terrain in the Djebel Sahro, photographed in 1997

67 BELOW Legion camp in the mountains, early 1930s

68 TOP   Monument to the dead of 1933, at foot of Bu Gafer

69 BELOW RIGHT   View from the summit of Bu Gafer

70 BELOW   u-Skunti, the rebel leader at Mt Baddou in 1933

71 & 72 ABOVE Mt Baddou, August 1933: Berber *partisans;*
and Légionnaire Ronald House, II/2nd REI

73 & 74 BELOW Légionnaire Hunter; and General Huré reviewing Legion unit

75 ABOVE Berliet VUDB armoured carriers of VI/1st REC, early 1930s

76 BELOW Panhard 165/175 armoured car of CMA/4th REI, February–March 1934

77 ABOVE Motorized Company/4th Foreign Infantry; Foum el Hassane, 1937

78 BELOW Company jazzband at Foum el Hassane, Christmas 1936

79 ABOVE Panhard 179 armoured troop carrier of CMA/4th REI

80, 81 BELOW Sergeant Charles Milassin, Tindouf, 1939; and a légionnaire in Paris, 14 July 1939

82 The abandoned fort at Ain ben Tili, photographed in 1993

83 'À nos amis sous les sables'

Morocco. In October 1919, Lieutenant-Colonel Rollet brought his wartime RMLE back from occupation duty in the Rhineland to new headquarters at Fes, where from January 1921 it became the new 3rd REI. In November 1920, the 4th REI was created from the battalions already in western Morocco, with headquarters at Marrakesh. By 1923 the Legion's strength would be just under 13,500 men, and the establishment of the 2nd, 3rd and 4th Foreign Infantry in Morocco would be three battalions plus one mounted company each.[11]

The new designation 'Foreign Infantry Regiment' was made necessary by the long-resisted decision to form a Legion cavalry unit. In 1921, the potential recruiting pool offered by thousands of former White Russian cavalrymen – evacuated from the Crimea following their defeat in the civil war against the Bolsheviks – proved irresistible, and in March that year the 1er Régiment Étranger de Cavalerie (1st REC) was created at Sousse in Tunisia with a cadre of officers and NCOs transferred from Metropolitan and Africa Army cavalry regiments. The squadrons were formed progressively, and their lack of an armature of veteran légionnaires increased the delay in bringing them up to operational readinesss. Russians, always a small minority pre-1914, represented about 12 per cent of the Legion in 1921, and by 1925 they would provide the remarkable proportion of 82 per cent of 1st Foreign Cavalry – a striking violation of the Legion's long established melting-pot policy.[12]

IN SPRING 1920, LYAUTEY paid Tahami el Glaoui to mount *harkas*, at his own discretion, into the valleys of the Oued Dades and Todra. Some tribes of the Ait Atta people allied themselves with the Glaoua in order to retain their local dominance, while others remained implacable. Among the leaders of the latter was a *caid* of dynamic personality named Assu u-Ba Slam, of the Ilimshan clan. Another name that the French would come to know well was Belkassem Ngadi, a resourceful Ait Hammou chief who fought the Glaoua in 1920 before dropping out of sight for several years.[13]

Freed of concern for the Far South, Lyautey was reinforced to nearly 92,000 men in 1920, and his command 'surged' to almost 95,000 the following year (though Paris would reduce it again to 86,000 in 1922, and had almost halved that figure by 1925).[14] When Lyautey was interviewed for *L'Illustration* in 1921 he said that he had 82,000 field troops in 63 battalions, 29 squadrons, 24 batteries and 10 air squadrons. But of the infantry, only 57 battalions were in forward areas, and since about 20 of these were tied down in static garrisons he had only 37 units free for operations. With his usual eye to the public narrative, he claimed that 'since 1914 the whole Moroccan plain has been occupied ... All the tribes have submitted, except the three most important: the Djibala of Ouezzane, the Beni Ouarain, and the Zaians ...'.[15]

The Africa Army and Colonial regiments underwent complex reorganizations from 1919, as wartime personnel were demobilized and wartime-raised units were disbanded. The largest single contingent in Morocco was still provided by the West Africans, with up to 20 battalions; there were up to 15 of Algerian Skirmishers, and originally 6, rising to 15 battalions of Moroccan Skirmishers – originally Arab, these now began to enlist more Berbers from submitted tribes. Lyautey's only European infantry comprised between 2 and 4 of the Bats d'Af, and the Legion, which gradually increased its contribution from 4 to 12 battalions and 3 mounted companies, or about one-third of his manoeuvre units.[16]

The demands of the unrest in the south-east sparked off by Gaouz, and the general disruption following the Armistice, had reduced activity in 1919 to a more or less maintenance level, but from the spring of 1920 Lyautey could focus once more on the stubborn 'Zaian bloc' east of Khenifra. Although his Native Affairs officers had established useful contacts with Moha ou Hammou's sons and nephews, no lasting progress could be made until new posts could completely deny unsubmitted highland clans access to grazing on the right bank of the Oum er Rebia river. General Poeymirau had now returned to duty, and from April to June 1920 his mobile groups pushed the chain of posts forward; this was so effective that leaders representing perhaps half of the confederacy made terms. In the spring of 1921, old Moha ou Hammou himself, defiant to his last breath, was killed while resisting Zaian *partisans* now fighting for the French. Late that summer, after negotiations set up by Moha's sons, the last major pocket of resistance around Bekrite was eliminated by the mobile groups of General Jean Théveney and Colonel Henri Freydenberg, and the seven-year 'Zaian war' was finally over.[17]

Simultaneously, in northern Morocco the Spanish had been penetrating new Berber territory from both their western and eastern presidios. A sequence of events now unfolded that would shock Europe, and would eventually have profound consequences for both Lyautey and the Foreign Legion.

*

THE NAME RIF (in Arabic, literally 'edge' or 'border') is today applied to the whole mountain chain running behind Morocco's Mediterranean coast. More properly, it should be used only of the drier highlands in the eastern half of this strip, roughly between Targuist and Melilla, inhabited by peoples called *irifyen* – 'borderers' – in their own Berber dialect (see Map 18). The whole northern region was divided between four major groups of tribes: from west to east, the Djibala, the Ghomara, the Senadja Srir and the Rifians proper, the last being the most numerous and grouped in fewer, larger tribes. All relied upon subsistence farming; the staples were barley and wheat, and farmers kept some livestock – a household might own a cow, a mule and a small herd of goats.

To the west of Targuist the much better watered and wooded country was known as the Ghomara and the Djibala. In contrast to the parched eastern hills of the Rif proper, the fertile terrain of the Djibala has been compared to the Bernese Oberland; its population was more ethnically mixed than that of the eastern Rif and was mainly Arabic-speaking. While just as quarrelsome, these tribes were described as less austere than the Rifians, with a more cheerful outlook on life and a taste for smoking *kif*, and other Moroccans told jokes about their gullibility and impulsiveness. In the dry east, arable land was poorer and scarcer than in the west; coaxing a crop out of it required more labour and irrigation, and the Rifians of these harsher hills were famous for their dour pugnacity. In the early sixteenth century, the Arab traveller published as Leo Africanus had noted that 'All the inhabitants of [the Rif] have the balls of their throat-pipes [Adam's apples] very great, and are an uncivil and rude people'. Rifian families lived in time-washed single-storey stone and mud-brick houses, typically spaced about 350 yards apart, with their fields and orchards on the slopes nearby. Each homestead was surrounded by a hedge of prickly-pear cactus and guarded by savage dogs, and each had a loopholed pillbox sited to give the best fields of fire.[18]

Historically, the Maghzan had enjoyed a wary arm's-length relationship with the Rifians; men were periodically enlisted as soldiers, taxes were occasionally extracted, but (with some notable exceptions) the sultans were generally content to recognize local leaders and to leave these surly highlanders well alone. Some of the coastal tribes occasionally attracted European wrath by their ferocious piracy, and when the regent Ba Ahmad sent an army from Fes to punish the Ibuqquyen in 1898, their neighbours, the Ait Waryaghar, were happy to share in the killing and looting alongside the

Maghazan horde. Their victory over Bou Himara (El Rogi) on the Oued Nekor in 1908 had later cemented the Ait Waryaghar's local ascendancy and confidence. This tribe inhabited a large region west of the Nekor river, running southwards on both banks of the Rhis river from Alhucemas Bay on the Mediterranean coast, roughly as far inland as the southern limit of the Djebel Hammam massif around Targuist. They were divided into nine named segments, which were traditionally separated between five alliances, and one estimate numbers the tribe at about 40,000 people.[19]

All Rifians shared a strong regional personality, characterized by a belligerently egalitarian attitude and the pursuit of bloody vendettas, so the acquisition of a gun was every boy's overriding priority. All Berbers feuded constantly, and a great part of their complex customary law was devoted to codes of compensation for thefts and killings; however, it was noted that in the Rif really serious sanctions for murder only seem to have applied if the killing disturbed the weekly markets on which everyday life depended – the crime lay not in the killing, but in 'breaking the peace of the market'. Rifians also differed from Berbers elsewhere in pursuing deadly enmities even within the immediate blood family. A major feature of Berber society was the range of *liff* or factional pacts between individuals and groups. Any Rifian considered himself the equal of any other and resented life's inevitable inequalities; competition for relative status was constant and was pursued by means of faction. These factional divisions routinely cut across other group identities at every level; so, given the innately quarrelsome relationships between individuals, families, blood lineages and tribal segments, there were very few times when a Rifian of proper manliness was not pursuing some kind of sworn enmity, with a gun. It has been estimated that in 1900–1920 there were no fewer than 193 identifiable feuds raging within the Ait Waryaghar tribe alone.[20]

The American ethnographer David M. Hart patiently traced the successive stages of one typical Ait Waryaghar feud. In baldest summary, it began some time before 1884, and involved the family of an aged man (a fugitive since his youth following a killing in his original home region). He and his sons simply attracted the jealousy of another family, and shots were exchanged when these neighbours came to burn his house down. Other enmities – over inheritance, marriage, factional obligation and simple personal dislike – spread over time and place from this first spark. Both the original antagonists died peacefully in their beds, but by the time the rise of Abd el Krim brought the vendetta to an enforced end some forty years later at least fifteen people had died by the bullet, the knife or poison (unusually, one of the victims and one of the killers were women.)[21]

FOLLOWING THE END OF THE FIRST WORLD WAR the Spanish high commissioner, General Damaso Berenguer, became determined to punish the insolent treachery of Ahmad er Raisuli in the Djibala. Although some 32,000 Spanish troops and 8,000 Spanish-led Moroccan Regulares were based in the western Comandancia, the new Ceuta–Tetuan railway was still being cut repeatedly, and troops venturing far outside those towns risked battalion-size engagements.[22] Berenguer stripped Raisuli of his Maghzan governor's title and declared him outlaw, and in October 1920 he thrust south to capture the town of Chefchaouen, thus cutting off Raisuli's base in the Beni Aros hills from eastward access to the Ghomara country (see Map 18).

(One of the assets that Berenguer deployed in the Djibala and Ghomara soon afterwards was a newly formed volunteer regiment. The *Tercio de Extranjeros*, authorized in September 1920, was the creation of Lieutenant Colonel José Millán Astray y Terreros of the Regulares. Millán Astray had argued successfully that in Morocco the conscript army needed a spearhead unit of professionals like the French Foreign Legion, which he studied during a visit to Sidi bel Abbès in October 1919. In fact the Tercio differed in several fundamental respects, most obviously in that foreigners never actually made up more than about 10 per cent of its manpower. Pay was three times higher than that of Spanish conscripts, but discipline was even harsher. Millán Astray chose as his second-in-command the 27-year-old Major Francisco Franco, as fearless as himself but a great deal luckier. The Tercio's first three battalions went into the front line on 20 November 1920.)[23]

While Berenguer was an admirer of Lyautey's political methods, his deputy in the Melilla Comandancia was now Raisulis old enemy the impatient General Silvestre, with some 20,600 Spanish and 5,100 native troops under his command. Silvestre chose to ignore the cautionary advice of both Berenguer and Colonel Gabriel Morales, his experienced native affairs chief, and during 1920 he pushed his lines of blockhouses south and west across the plain and into the edges of various highland tribal territories, with the intention of extending Spanish control as far as Alhucemas Bay in Ait Waryaghar country during the 1921 season.

During the immediate post-war period, the Spanish authorities had given way to French pressure to extradite some Berbers who had used Spanish territory as a base for wartime attacks into the French zone. This precedent caused considerable alarm, and in January 1919 the Ait Waryaghar activist Mohammed bin Abd el Krim – now released from prison – left Melilla and followed his father into the hills. That spring, his younger brother was summoned back from Madrid, and together they began to recruit followers among their own and neighbouring tribes. In September 1920 their father died, allegedly poisoned on Spanish instructions. His former leadership in raising the tribes against El Rogi had already lent his sons prestige, and now they were by far the most informed and far-sighted personalities in the Rif. The autumn of 1920 saw the fourth bad harvest in succession and the winter of 1920/21 was unusually cold; the tribesmen were in a mood to listen.[24]

IN THE SPRING OF 1921, THE WESTERN LIMIT of General Silvestre's advance ran roughly from Sidi Driss on the coast, north of Anual, to Souk el Tleta on the upper Oued Kert, south-west of Azib de Midar (modern Midar – see Map 18). There were four main camps including Dar Drius (modern Driouch) and Anual, but many of the Spanish troops were dispersed in about 144 tiny blockhouses, each imprisoning a dozen or two soldiers.

It was later judged that some 130 of these served no sensible military purpose whatever. Lines of communication were long and poorly guarded; the light railway only reached Midar, the roads beyond there were bad (government funds for improvements disappeared into many pockets), and few posts had any intercommunication. The typical blockhouse was a one-room timber cabin with a corrugated iron roof and loopholed walls reinforced on the outside with chest-high sandbags, containing little but an oildrum for water and another for use as a latrine. Most blockhouses were sited with neither easy access to water, nor safe tracks for the convoys on which they relied for their endless diet of rice and beans (the arrival of even these was unpredictable, since much of their rations and most of the commissariat's supply trucks being quietly diverted to private rackets). The hungry soldiers sweltered or shivered in these boxes for months at a time; their clothing was inadequate and lice-ridden, their medical care derisory, their weapons old and neglected, and any kind of tactical training or even target practice was virtually unknown – some men had never even fired a rifle. Discipline in the ranks was harsh, but among the officers slackness, absenteeism and corruption were endemic. Subalterns were so ill-paid that many had to take second jobs in order to live; their wives bartered cartridges for vegetables in the Moroccan marketplaces, and captains were notorious for embezzling their companies' ration allowances. Sergeant Arturo Barea described a few officers as kindly, brave and energetic, but far too many as lazy and brutal; so ignorant of their profession that they could not even read a map, they spent their time in the bars and brothels of Melilla rather than training or caring for their men.[25]

General Silvestre had brought the local Beni Ulichek and Beni Said tribes to sullen submission by burning their crops and running off their cattle, but he had not disarmed them. During the hard, hungry winter of 1920/21 the tribes heard rumours from the west (as did Silvestre, who responded with contempt) that the brothers Abd el Krim were gathering Ait Waryghar, Ibbuquyen, Ait Ammarth, Gzinnaya, Ait Tuzin and Timsaman tribesmen in the hills. Mohammed Abd el Krim was not a physically impressive figure, but he was a charismatic speaker able to project his vision with intelligence and conviction, and his younger brother Mhamed provided him with shrewd counsel and real military talents. By the summer of 1921 they had assembled between 3,000 and 6,000 warriors, though only a small minority with black-market modern rifles. More significantly, however, Abd el Krim was not merely assembling a *harka*; he was preaching a political programme, and increasingly exercising political muscle by intimidating other Rifian chiefs who negotiated with the Spanish.[26]

Consequently, in late May 1921 one segment of the Timsaman asked the Spanish for the protection of a post planted at Abarran in their territory. A feeble sandbag enclosure, with walls just 3 feet high, was constructed for 250 soldiers and some native police. On 1 June, the native auxiliaries mutinied, killed the officers, and aided Timsaman and Ait Tuzin tribesmen in attacking the garrison, from which only about 70 managed to escape. On the same day the coastal post of Sidi Driss was also attacked, but despite 100 casualties this held out. General Berenguer arrived by ship to confer with General Silvestre on 5 June, but the high commissioner later wired Madrid that there was no cause for alarm. The next day Silvestre ordered the establishment of a new battalion camp at Igueriben, in the hills about 3 miles south of Anual, nearest source of water.[27]

ON 17 JULY 1921, ABOUT 3,000 WARRIORS from seven Rifian tribes struck all along the Spanish line. Igueriben was cut off, and after four days – and finally reduced to drinking their own urine – Major Benitez's garrison were overrun and massacred. Anual itself came under heavy fire on 21 July, the day that General Silvestre arrived there in person. Early the following morning he signalled his intention to break out. The subsequent enquiry by the Picasso Commission would report that the garrison was 5,000 strong but with only 40 cartridges per man, and that Anual was so badly sited that the Berbers could almost reach the barbed wire unseen. The withdrawal on 22 June soon degenerated into a rout, and many men were ambushed and cut down. Silvestre and his staff all died; the body of the native affairs officer Colonel Morales was handed back later as a mark of respect, but no part of General Silvestre's corpse was ever recovered. It should be noted that at Anual the Spanish troops outnumbered the Berbers.

As the survivors staggered into posts and small settlements further to the east, the plague of panic spread, provoking a wholesale stampede towards Melilla. Many posts were abandoned, with much equipment and even the helpless sick. Some blockhouse garrisons did resist heroically until they were wiped out; it was hardly surprising that others, left in ignorance by their absent officers, surrendered without a fight when offered safe conduct. (These almost invariably had their throats cut on the spot; the few captives who were spared were usually survivors of garrisons that had fought with stubborn bravery.) The news of victory spread within hours, and tribesmen poured down from the hills in their thousands to join in the killing and looting. At Dar Drius, Silvestre's deputy General Navarro was ordered to hold a line anchored on that camp, to which other garrisons were fleeing, but on 23 July (just as General Berenguer arrived at Melilla with the first few reinforcements) Navarro retreated towards Monte Aruit with between 2,000 and 3,000 men. A refugee train arriving to find Dar Drius abandoned was derailed by tribesmen and its passengers butchered.

As fugitives straggled across the waterless plain, airmen reported corpses scattered for miles along the tracks in their wake, and some of the bodies later recovered showed signs of atrocious deaths.[28] Up on the coast at Sidi Driss, just 5 out of 500 men managed to reach the ship that arrived to rescue them on 26 July. Officers at Souk el Tleta chose to lead some 1,200 men south-west towards a French border post, but only about 400 survived repeated ambushes. On 29 July, General Navarro reached Monte Aruit, a rambling adobe village 1,000 yards from the nearest water source. To his credit, he refused to abandon the sick and wounded without whom he might have been able to reach Melilla some 20 miles north. Instead he dug in, waiting for relief that never came; he had hardly any food and no anaesthetics or other drugs, and 167 of his wounded died of gangrene over the following eleven days. After agonies of endurance, the garrison of Monte Aruit surrendered to the Berbers on 9 August; General Navarro and some others were taken alive, but most were massacred at once – when Spanish troops returned there they found 2,600 unburied corpses.

Some 40,000 refugees crammed into Melilla town, and since General Berenguer discovered that the stores and magazines there were empty, it is hard to imagine what their fate might have been had the Berbers not chosen to withdraw by mid–August with their almost unimaginable loot. This included at least 20,000 Mauser rifles, 400 machine guns, 130 artillery pieces and enormous quantities of ammunition. Although it would be years before the true casualties were admitted (in so far as inadequate record-keeping allowed), in three weeks the Spanish Army – attacked at first by only about 3,000 tribesmen largely armed with obsolete weapons – had lost some 13,200 men killed, or about half the entire Melilla command. To put that figure in context: in June 1876, Custer died with just over 200 of his men at the Little Bighorn; in January 1879, Chelmsford lost about 1,360 men, of whom perhaps 700 were British regulars, at Isandlwana; and in March 1896, General Baratieri lost about 5,000 Italian troops killed by the Ethiopians at Adua. This Spanish disaster was by far the greatest defeat of a white colonial army ever yet inflicted by non-European enemies, and Abd el Krim's name went around the world.[29]

On 8 August the Spanish government fell (just one of thirty-nine administrations within twenty years). In the Djibala, troops had to be withdrawn from operations against Raisuli to be shipped to Melilla, and although others pulled back to defend only their largest posts, even some of these were overrun. Two of the most significant consequences of Anual were that captured Spanish guns began shelling surviving coastal garrisons, and that by October the younger of the Abd el Krim brothers – profiting from the 'internal lines of communication' that the Spanish lacked – was leading a Rifian force west into the Ghomara country on the Oued Lau to seek alliances.

IN FRENCH MOROCCO, this catastrophe was attributed simply to Spanish incompetence. It naturally increased unrest along the zonal frontier and attracted the interest of Moroccan urban intellectuals, but in general the population of the submitted regions remained quiet. France had no intention of becoming directly involved in Spain's problems, and while Lyautey naturally set his intelligence networks to gathering information about Abd el Krim, his focus was still on the Middle Atlas.[30]

In the spring of 1922, General Poeymirau and Colonel Freydenberg gathered mobile groups once again to tighten up both loops of the 'figure-of-eight'. They made progress at some points along the western edge of the mountains and around the headwaters of the Moulouya, and Moha ou Said – the last of the old trio of pre-war resistance leaders – was forced to flee into the highest valleys. However, although clans were brought to terms, lines of posts were inched forwards, roads were improved, and the cordons protecting submitted lowland tribes from the highlanders' raids were strengthened, the results certainly could not be claimed to vindicate Lyautey's traditional 'oil-stain' analysis. The system in which he had placed his confidence ever since Galliéni's first lessons on the Tonkin frontier in the 1890s may be said to have reached its limits in the foothills of the Middle Atlas. Here, the edges of dissidence retreated before the mobile groups, but – unlike the old days on the Zousfana and Guir – they certainly did not dissolve. Rather, each French advance compressed the irreconcilables into a denser core, not fragmenting but encouraging tribal cooperation, and under leaders such as Sidi Raho of the Beni Ouarain they struck back at any opportunity. Chipping away at its outworks was one thing, but actually breaching and capturing the Middle Atlas redoubts would demand a series of sustained operations employing every weapon in the French armoury.

Since Marshal Lyautey's comforting narrative of inexorable pacification by largely political means was now out of date, he had to reassure the politicians that there was a visible end to his current levels of expenditure. He now drew a distinction between 'useful Morocco', whose pacification would be profitable, and bleak tribal refuges that could safely be left alone once surrounded by networks of access roads and regional bases. In 1922, he predicted that in 1923 his troop numbers could be reduced from 86,000 to 78,000, and in 1924 to as few as 50,000, as he moved from a 'pacification' to a 'pacified' budget, with native auxiliaries steadily taking over more of the burden. The War Ministry was happy to cut his troop levels, but despite the real progress made in 1922, some episodes during that year's campaign hardly supported his apparent confidence.[31]

THE SPRING 1922 MOBILE GROUPS had seen eight Legion battalions committed, including II/ and III/3rd REI with General Decherf's group in the western edge of the Middle Atlas. This formation of five battalions, with cavalry, mountain guns and plentiful *goumiers*, operated between Tazouta and Skoura on the northern edge of the Massif de Tichoukt – exactly where VI/2nd RE had been ambushed five years previously (see Map 19). Although columns had planted some precarious new posts east of Tazouta, the tribes were still vigorously hostile, and the tortured terrain further south had not been penetrated. An advanced camp had been placed at Skoura in January, and at the beginning of May the mobile group from Tazouta used this as a jumping-off point for another push. Several of the officers of the Decherf Group would leave their modest marks on the history of the French empire.

The 24-year-old Lieutenant Henry Marie Just de Lespinasse de Bournazel of the 22nd (Moroccan) Spahis was the image of the aristocratic cavalryman. Tall, blond, immaculate in his scarlet regimental tunic and favouring a cigarette-holder, he in fact had rather more to offer than his appearance suggested. He had volunteered at the age of 17 and had spent eighteen months in the ranks on the Western Front before being commissioned, returning in the autumn of 1918 in time for the last battles. He had been in Morocco since January 1921, learning his new trade in an outpost on the Taza front.[32] At Tazouta he struck up a friendship with the utterly dissimilar Captain Laffite of the *goumiers*, a squat, coarse-mannered 42-year-old Breton adventurer. A mysterious pre-war past as a mercenary in the Balkans and elsewhere had led him, like Bournazel, to the trenches in the ranks of a dismounted hussar regiment; also commissioned from the battlefield, he had ended the war as a captain, with the ribbons of the Légion d'Honneur and the Croix de Guerre, and with no fewer than twelve citations. Independent command of a gang of half-tamed Berber bandits in legalized tribal warfare suited Laffite perfectly, and his audacity and cunning had already made him a legend in these hills.[33]

Major Nicolas of III/3rd REI, then 43 years old, had spent most of his pre-war career with the 1st Foreign before transferring to the Line in 1914. Wounded three times, he had returned to the Legion as Lieutenant-Colonel Rollet's second-in-command in the RMLE in September 1918; he was thus deeply – perhaps exhaustingly – experienced in both colonial and European warfare. His most senior company commander was in fact three years older than him; Captain Maire, another Breton, had languished for years as a Line subaltern before transferring to the 2nd Foreign in June 1914. After sticking it out in Morocco for the first half of the war, he had distinguished himself with III/RMLE at Auberive in 1917 and in the Hindenburg Line the following year. Tall and burly with a big black moustache, Fernand Maire was loud, fearless, ruthless, and (to judge from his memoir) a man of unreflective outlook, but he seemed to suit légionnaires.[34]

*

THE THOUSAND-MAN BATTALION of 1914, in four big companies of riflemen moving en masse (and supported by just two machine guns that nobody really knew how to employ) was long forgotten. The cruel lessons of the Western Front had created a leaner, more supple model; companies and platoons were trained to operate individually – though in close articulation – by alternate fire and movement, and junior leaders down to squad sergeant had to be able to think for themselves. In Morocco, the battalion of the early 1920s had a theoretical establishment of 700 men in three rifle companies and a separate machine-gun company.[35]

Each rifle company was supposed to have 170 men, divided into a command group and four platoons each of 35 men led by a subaltern or warrant officer, and each platoon was made up of three squads of about 11 men led by a sergeant. Two of the squads in each platoon were riflemen (grenadiers-voltigeurs), and one was based on a light machine gun (fusil-mitrailleur – hereafter, LMG); in Morocco, unlike France, this LMG squad had just one instead of three of the infamous Chauchats. Each of the platoon's three squads included a man equipped with a VB rifle-grenade discharger, and hand grenades were available to all.[36] While this increased firepower gave the battalion and company greater tactical flexibility than in 1914, it also added considerably to the physical burdens. Apart from the obviously ponderous machine-gun company, LMGs and VB-dischargers were voracious devourers of ammunition; it all had to be carried in the front line, and soldiers were loaded down with immediate-use supplies.

The bataillon d'infanterie type marocain was essentially an alpine unit, and each rifle company incorporated its own 'combat train' of eleven mules carrying ammunition, water, tools, concertina-coils of barbed wire (reseaux Brun), stretchers and cacolets. Nine more company mules carried the rations and baggage; these stayed with the assembled battalion train, along with the company's quartermaster and cooks. The point of these perhaps wearying details is that each company commander had to allocate a sergeant with at least 16 mule-drivers to the train – more, in really mountainous country – thus reducing the number of rifles in the company's firing line, which theoretically had 145 plus the 4 LMGs. Given that few battalions in the 1920s actually achieved a strength of more than 600 men and many only 500, the company in battle might have only 100–120 men instead of 170, and in broken terrain this was too few for safety. On the morning of 6 May 1922, when Major Nicolas led III/3rd Foreign out of the camp at Skoura, he had three rifle companies totalling only 253 men.[37]

*

NICOLAS WAS LEADING THE VANGUARD for a push towards the Taddoute plateau several miles east of Skoura, preceded by Laffite's 20th Goum scouting ahead on ponies. It took the battalion 45 minutes to climb the steep 500-foot Tizi Adni pass, and once they reached its head they relied entirely on the guidance of Laffite's *goumiers;* the iron-filled rocks confuse any compass, and even today there are no reliable maps of the Tichoukt massif. A couple of miles immediately east of the head of the Tizi Adni the terrain becomes chaotic, and it would have been extraordinarily difficult for III/3rd REI to reach the Taddoute plateau against any kind of opposition. However, although Captain Maire's memoir describes this vertiginous landscape, in fact the timing suggests that the battalion were stopped dead before even reaching it.

Adopting a fighting formation was extremely difficult on such ground. The manuals called for the marching column to deploy when about 800 yards from the enemy; the files were to wheel out sideways into a firing line across the route of advance, with trailing wings to watch the flanks and a reserve following behind. This was just about possible if a unit was advancing at right-angles to the gulleys and crests, stumbling down one slope and panting up the next, but that was both exhausting and dreadfully slow. In Morocco the priority was to close with the enemy quickly rather than to get the maximum firepower into the line; although a file of men made a more vulnerable target than a line, the tribesmen had no heavy weapons, so bunching was usually less of a danger than deploying too widely and becoming separated by terrain features.

The standard formation for advancing along the length of a feature was for each company to form a 'lozenge'. The lead platoon spread its LMG squad across the track in line, with the other two squads trailing back from its ends in files to form a three-sided box or blunt arrowhead, followed by the company commander's group. Two more platoons followed in parallel files on the flanks, guarding the mule train between them, and the fourth platoon brought up the rear in a reversed arrowhead of three parallel squad files. In theory the battalion's second company could do the same on a neighbouring height to one or other flank, with the third following in reserve. In practice, the terrain governed everything, and the single company was the 'unit of manoeuvre'; it had to be prepared to advance alone, defending its own flanks.[38]

At about 7am on 6 May 1922, Major Nicolas' cramped little battalion were warned by the sound of shots and the retreating *goumiers* of an apparently strong tribal force ahead, occupying a tongue of wooded ground climbing a fairly modest slope. He deployed two companies forward, the 10th on the left and the 9th on its right, with the 12th held back in reserve.[39] As his légionnaires advanced they came under immediate heavy fire, from a determined enemy who used the cover and the ground with their usual skill.

In simple language, this means that the soldiers hardly ever saw who was firing at them; now often armed with smokeless-powder rifles that left no tell-tale white puff to locate them, groups of Berbers among the rocks and holly-oaks showed themselves very briefly before disappearing, only to reappear in unexpected places, usually much closer than expected. Once combat was joined in lumpy, wooded country like this, the formal dance-diagrams of the manual could offer only vague guidelines. Company and platoon commanders, who controlled by voice and whistle from close behind the centre of their firing lines, needed constant vigilance above all else, married to a tactical instinct for ground and instant decisive reactions. Although battalion commanders usually controlled their units in person from close behind the leading companies, those companies still relied upon quick-thinking officers and sergeants; as already mentioned, the French Army of the 1920s did not practise 'battle drills' to trigger all ranks into instinctive responses at first contact. The Berbers did not give junior leaders the luxury of much time to think, and the man with the coloured képi and Sam Browne belt was a priority target.[40]

The fact that many tribesmen now had modern rifles naturally had an impact on French tactics: their greater accuracy forced wider dispersal of the troops, but dispersal had its limits if ground was to be held effectively. A company could cover no more than 300 yards of front with three of its platoons in line, so that each man was only about two paces from his mates on either side. Each platoon formed with its LMG squad in the centre, and to retain the initiative platoons had to keep moving ahead, constantly alternating between bounds forward and pauses to cover each other by shooting. Any halt other than to deliver a rapid fusillade encouraged the Berbers to concentrate their own fire, pinning the platoon down and creating a static target towards which the tribesmen were instinctively drawn. Any isolation, perceived weakness or hesitant 'floating' invited that rush from cover at close quarters that veterans described as being 'of unimaginable violence'. On 6 May the half-strength III/3rd REI lost the initiative, were brought to a halt and pinned down, and paid a price for it.[41]

Captain Duchier's 9th Company came under the heaviest pressure, from the front and right flank, and were forced to fall back; Duchier took them forward again with the bayonet and recaptured the lost ground, but at some cost. (Despite the earlier remarks about bayonet-versus-knife fighting, it was whichever side showed the most aggression that had the essential advantage. On the receiving end of a determined bayonet-charge the Berbers, like any other fighting men, would themselves 'float', and this tactic – if exactly timed, and carried out with real resolve – was successfully employed often enough for veteran officers to regard it as a panacea against any threat within 100 yards.) Following this episode, half of 12th Company were sent forward to support the weakened 9th; the Moroccans eased their direct pressure, but kept up extremely heavy fire all along the line. Laffite's mounted Goum pulled back down the pass to Skoura to try to find a way around a flank and up into the hills behind the tribesmen, but they themselves ran into another strong force and were halted with losses.[42] At about 9am, orders came up for Nicolas to simply hold his position until other units could climb the pass behind him with artillery and machine guns. The tired major's heart may have sunk on receiving an order that seemed to betray a carelessness of how this sort of encounter could develop.

Although mules with more water, ammunition and *cacolets* were sent up to them, the actual relief took what seems to have been an inexplicably long time. Whatever the reason, the fighting continued all through the morning and afternoon, with Nicolas' small companies being whittled away by casualties, and the tribesmen exploiting forwards under cover to try to pick their perimeters apart wherever opportunity offered. At last, at about 5pm, orders arrived to prepare for retreat when the guns that were now reaching the head of the pass began to deliver covering fire. The Moroccans spotted and correctly interpreted these preparations, and minimized their danger by pressing forward to 'hang on the Frenchman's belt', infiltrating between Legion platoons on both flanks. The order to begin disengaging was given, and Major Nicolas took the wounded and the rest of the mule train back about 600 yards, leaving Captain Maire in command of the three companies.

When the first couple of shells burst among the rocks above, Maire ordered the firing line to fall back, but the moment that 9th Company began to 'unhook itself' a crowd of Berbers swarmed over them in a headlong rush. Captain Duchier was shot dead; his whole company gave way, and 10th Company, finding their right flank open, were infected by this disorder.

Maire and his rearguard half-company were uncovered and virtually surrounded, and only broke out with great difficulty through a narrowing gap by halting every 50 yards to face about and deliver rapid fire (Maire claimed that at one point he had to defend himself with his walking-stick). This was the scenario that all Berber warriors longed for, and the retreat of III/3rd Foreign involved hand-to-hand fighting on both flanks. The three mauled companies seem to have had to rely almost entirely upon their own firepower to hold back the pursuit; they had been fighting for more than ten hours, they were burdened with their most recent wounded, and each time a platoon paused to fire they fell further behind, increasing the flanking tribesmens' chances of cutting the last avenue of escape.

Eventually they reached the cover provided by Skirmisher battalions advancing on each side of them, and at about 9pm the battalion got down the pass to the camps around Skoura. The day had cost them 99 casualties – 40 per cent of their strength: 17 known killed, 64 wounded and 18 missing (their bones would be discovered the following year). In his report of 10 June, Major Nicolas paid generous tribute to Captain Maire's effective command of the battalion; he himself suffered a mental collapse soon afterwards, and was evacuated to Fes on 1 August.[43]

On 12 May, when the Decherf Group took another 150 casualties less than 3 miles from Skoura, the attempted eastward advance to Taddoute was abandoned. On the 28th, Sidi Raho led some 1,500 mixed tribesmen in attacks on troops working on the road from Tazouta to Skoura, and on the latter camp. In the first week of July he attacked a convoy to Skoura; it only fought its way through after taking 70 killed and 80 wounded in a seven-hour action. The French decided that Skoura was, for the time being, untenable, and withdrew. The remnants of III/3rd REI did well in one of the convoy-escort actions of mid-May, but the battalion would be left in static post garrisons for nearly two years thereafter.[44]

IN MOST ARMIES, the battalion is the level in the chain of command at which a unit acquires a distinct individual personality. With about 600 officers and men, it is large enough to have an independent existence, yet small enough for all its members to identify with it personally. While the whole Legion was now relearning its collective sense of superiority over other corps, the dispersal of its units contributed to a special self-consciousness, and since some battalion commanders had strong personalities their units were popularly known by their names – for instance,

'Bataillon de Tscharner' as often as 'II/3rd REI'.[45] Officers who had survived the trenches, or the thankless wartime years in Morocco, kept alive the old exclusive spirit of l'Armée d'Afrique; they were not careerist box-tickers, and their unconcealed disdain for rear-echelon bureaucrats might extend to certain generals. Such officers understood and responded to the special character of the Legion; they demanded a lot of their men, but on campaign they were seen to share most of their hardships and all their dangers, so they attracted loyalty. They were strict but not petty disciplinarians; while merciless to the defiant or the dangerously negligent they could be indulgent of trivial misdemeanours, and what these '*grands caids*' regarded as trivial might scandalize officers of other corps.

There was a culture of hard drinking among all ranks, and officers tended to make the most of their quite frequent and generous leaves in Morocco's great cities. Their men appreciated colourful characters and boasted of their own commanders' real or apocryphal exploits, which all added to the Legion's swashbuckling reputation among corps with a more orthodox ethos. As long as both parties to the relationship instinctively respected the boundaries, off-duty officers might treat their men with a comradely paternalism quite foreign to most European armies (indeed, some anecdotes would remind film fans of James Warner Bellah's scripts for John Ford's US Cavalry Westerns of the late 1940s). When the veteran English légionnaire Adolphe Cooper was serving with III/4th REI – 'Bataillon de Corta' – in 1929, he was tricked into going up to Major de Corta in the bar of the Hôtel du Pasha in Marrakesh and asking him for a loan to buy a bottle. De Corta smiled, and paid for two bottles, to match Cooper's two newly regained corporal's stripes; the next day Cooper was summoned and, with equal goodwill, awarded eight days' cells, but his green stripes were spared (this was apparently a routine initiation).[46]

This is not to imply that regimental colonels were mere administrators; they often visited their dispersed units in the field, giving them a direct contact with the regimental depots on which they relied for logistic and personnel support. Lieutenant-Colonel Rollet, in particular, was tireless in his command of 3rd REI, constantly visiting his battalions, companies and posts to inspect, reward or reprimand. He fought a ceaseless war with the commissariat over his men's provisions and equipment, and during a long leave in France in early 1923 he did not scruple to exploit his wartime fame to further the welfare of the Legion old comrades' associations that he encouraged and sponsored. His high visibility did not make him universally popular, but on 9 September 1925 Colonel Rollet would be appointed to the command of the 1st Foreign Infantry and the Legion central depot at Sidi bel Abbès – an appointment with significant consequences.[47]

AS THE WINTER OF 1922/23 gave way to spring, battalion commanders began assembling their dispersed companies from the dreary posts and work-camps where they had spent the past five months, and preparing them for service in the coming season's mobile groups. The légionnaires were more combat-ready than they had been for years past, and it was time for Marshal Lyautey's big push into the Middle Atlas.

17. 'The Most Indomitable Race in the World' 1923–24

The Middle Atlas ... is a rich, populous country, and its
wooded mountains and fertile valleys provide an
admirable redoubt where the most indomitable race in
the world shut themselves off in fierce isolation.
   Marquis de Segonzac, 1903[1]

THE STORMING OF THE MIDDLE ATLAS in the spring–summer of 1923 would not, in fact, be undertaken under Hubert Lyautey's direct supervision. In March, when Captain Prince Aage of Denmark arrived with his new Legion commission and reported to Rabat for orders, he was told that the marshal was seriously ill in Fes. Laid low by recurring liver trouble while driving to a conference in Algeria, Lyautey had been rushed to his old Palais Menebhi in Fes, where doctors declared him too sick to be taken to Paris for the surgery he needed. Now 68 years old, he was a slightly heavier but still striking figure in his beautifully cut uniforms, his pale blue eyes mesmerizing under a squared cap of snow-white hair. But his relentless pace of work during nearly twenty-five years in Asia and Africa had not been without cost. For some weeks his life hung in the balance; eventually he was judged strong enough to travel to Paris for an operation, and in the meantime General Joseph Poeymirau directed the advance into the Middle Atlas.[2]

The 36-year-old Prince Aage (pronounced 'Oo-weh') was posted to I/2nd REI at Meknes, and since he was the senior captain he was appointed adjutant-major by the battalion commander Major Buschenschutz.[3] As troops gathered for the campaign the battalion marched down to Timahdite, and Aage, riding at the tail of the column with Buschenchutz, had his first experience of the traditional chore of sweating the booze out of légionnaires who had spent their last centime on wine before hitting the road:

Accustomed to commanding the comparatively docile [Danish] guardsmen, I was amazed at the sight ... later I learned that this was a practice almost customary in the Legion ... What a march that was! The sun beat down mercilessly on the alcohol-soaked légionnaires, and before we had travelled a half-dozen kilometres men began to drop out ... The major and I urged the stragglers on, dismounting after a while to throw a couple of almost insensible soldiers across our saddles like so many sacks of meal ... The day's march sobered the troops. There was no more wine to be had, and the next morning we pushed towards the hills ... The country through which we marched was exceedingly beautiful. The fields were a riot of multi-coloured wild flowers ... ahead towered the mountains, their slopes grown thick with cedars, the heights crag-crowned, with occasional patches of snow reflecting the sun's rays in patterns of deep blue and white ... [4]

On several stages of the march via Azrou and Timahdite to Arhbalou Larbi, where supplies were being stockpiled for the campaign, Aage also had his first experiences of Morocco's instantly changeable highland weather; south of Timahdite, on 2 April:

During the preceding night it had begun to snow. Morning saw a blizzard in progress ... We had advanced scarcely a kilometre when each step forward became an acute torture. In the passes, the snow had drifted to a depth of 18 inches or more. A cold wind howled down the narrow gorges, blinding men and horses with stinging particles of ice. The Spahis dismounted and led their horses; our transport mules, heavily laden, began to flounder and fall by the roadside; we called in our flank guards for fear of losing them entirely ...

Late in the afternoon we arrived at Selghert to find the post fallen to wrack and ruin. Except for the four stone walls, in varying states of disrepair, and a leaky shed, there was no shelter available. The storm continuing unabated, we had no choice but to remain where we were ... The major ordered a kitchen set up in the shed; we tethered the mules between the barbed wire entanglements and the walls, and the men attempted to pitch their shelter-tents in the churned-up mud and snow of the quadrangle ... almost as quickly as one tent could be raised, another blew down. Of firewood there was practically none, except for a few wet sticks [for] the makeshift kitchen, where the very floor was a series of pools. ... The shed was filled with dense blue smoke ... The men lined up and entered the shed in turn, only to rush out again, gasping for breath, to eat cold stew in the full sweep of the storm. ... That night the temperature dropped to 6 degrees below zero Centigrade.

By the following evening the snowdrifts were 6 feet deep, several mules had died, and the légionnaires were dumb and stupid with misery.[5]

IN THE FIRST WEEK OF MAY 1923 preliminary operations were under way. General Poeymirau's aim was to converge upon and defeat the tribes of the Tichoukt massif and a wide swathe of the Middle Atlas to the east of it. Subduing this slant of mountains and high valleys all the way across to the road and posts that followed the upper Moulouya would reduce the northern loop of the dissident 'figure-of-eight' to the Taza Pocket proper, cut off from the southern loop in the wild country where the Middle Atlas climbs into the High Atlas. Poeymirau brought to his task 20 infantry battalions (including 6 from the Legion), 12 squadrons, 15 batteries and 6 air squadrons – some 20,000 regulars, supported by numerous *goumiers*.

As part of General Théveny's Meknes Mobile Group, Colonel Callais of 6th Moroccan Skirmishers led his own regiment with I/2nd REI and a Bat d'Af from Arhbalou Larbi eastwards through the Tizi Tarzeft pass, towards a tribal stronghold among the cliffs of Bou Arfa north of Enjil (see Map 19).[6] On 12 May, however, Captain Prince Aage was recalled from I/2nd REI to join General Poeymirau's staff. Aage described 'Poey' as short, square, extraordinarily elegant, friendly, twinkling and altogether an ornament of café society, but as a workaholic when he was in the field. Irrepressibly cheerful, he put a strain on his staff by his insistence on going forward under fire to see for himself, and on sitting down for a proper lunch well within range of stray bullets. (There is something distinctly Napoleonic about all this, and one cannot but wonder whether Aage's summons to Poeymirau's staff had anything to do with his royal blood.)[7] A few days later Aage took up his new duties at Enjil, very conscious that his colleagues had years of Moroccan experience (one of them was Captain Jean de Lattre, Poeymirau's operations officer).[8] Over the following three months Aage would see combat from close range on a number of occasions, since battlefield communication between a general and his units when on campaign was still maintained by mounted staff officers.

In this 'admirable redoubt of the most indomitable race in the world', the engagements through which Aage would carry Poeymirau's orders would be consistently costly. Nevertheless, it was noticed that the Legion's morale was now recovering from the slump of the immediate post-war years, and desertion rates had fallen sharply. An outward encouragement to *ésprit de corps* was the first return of the képi in place of the awkward pith helmet and squalid sidecap; those who received them were quick to make themselves *folklorique* cotton campaign covers, as pale as possible, to set themselves apart from other troops. Such apparently trivial details can be surprisingly important to unit morale; since the men now felt that they 'looked like real légionnaires', they tried to live up to the image.[9]

ON 20 MAY 1923, the Meknes Group advanced before sunrise towards tribesmen who were holding the head and flanks of the valley of Bou Arfa. The right-hand of two columns, under Colonel du Guiny, was checked soon after 5am by heavy fire from the wooded heights on its right. His troops tried to dig themselves scrapes under constant nagging fire; in the afternoon torrential rain fell, the heat of the ground turned this to thick mist, and the Ait Segrushin warriors infiltrated forwards while the French brought up reinforcements. Prince Aage watched a horse-drawn battery of 75mm guns galloping past 'at a dead run, gun carriages swinging perilously round sharp curves, gunners clinging to their perches for dear life, while the drivers, swearing cheerfully, urged their teams to a still madder pace'. The crashing, jingling battery disappeared into the mist, and after a few moments he heard the guns begin to cough, at first slowly, then faster as they established the range and began to fire for effect.

As firing became general again on all sides, Aage was sent forward to find out why a Skirmisher battalion's frontal attack had stalled. Reporting to Poeymirau that most of its officers were down, he was sent to find and take forward on its right the first reserve battalion he met. This proved to be his own I/2nd REI; still blinded by the mist, he positioned Major Buschenschutz close to the sound of firing and then rode forward cautiously to regain contact with the Skirmishers. A breeze shifted the murk slightly, and he found himself in the middle of the hard-pressed battalion just as a group of tribesmen surged up among rocks hardly 20 yards away and shot down a subaltern and several *turcos* before his eyes. Unarmed, Aage dived from the saddle into cover, and was wondering how he could take control of the situation when Buschenschutz led the Legion battalion past him on the right with 'grim, silent purpose'. They closed with the Berbers, the Skirmishers took heart and advanced with them, and the attack rolled on. In late afternoon the tribesmen fell back, but the day had cost Colonel du Guiny 125 casualties.[10]

*

THÉVENY'S MEKNES GROUP spent the next fortnight consolidating, while 600 men blasted and dug a road through the Recifa pass so that trucks could bring supplies forward to their junction with the Fes Group at Boulemane. As always in Morocco, the camps instantly attracted a swarming retail suburb whose ramshackle streets of tents and shanties sprang up as if by magic:

> Arab merchants who sold to the troops vile cigarettes and dates of slightly superior quality; native women who were no better than they should have been; café keepers who sold native wines in the shade of skin tents; spies, whom we could not identify; mendicants who lived on our leavings; and thieves who knifed one another in squabbles over their meagre takings. It was all very colourful ... [11]

On 7 June, when temperatures reached 120°F (49°C) by 7am, the combined forces of the Southern Group (Fes and Meknes) were ordered north. Their objective was the village of El Mers, the central market and shrine for the Northern Ait Segrushin, which sat in a bowl at the southern foot of the Bou Khamouj heights. Part of Poeymirau's division would first have to take the chaotic tangle of the Tichoukt massif from the north, while the rest advanced on El Mers from the west and south across the rolling country where the tribe grew its grain. While Prince Aage was enjoying a refreshing bathe in a stream that wandered through orchards, to the north General Théveny's units struggled up steep gulches into the three-dimensional labyrinth between Skoura and El Mers, where the Berbers had successfully defied the French since 1917. The rudimentary tracks across the Tichoukt massif hairpin and switchback along ledges, and the very steep ridges, covered in holly-oak and clumps of scrub, interlock closely in sequences of folded knifeblades divided by narrow, plunging ravines.

The légionnaires had no packs, carrying all they could in two haversacks on their hips and a horseshoe bedroll; this was awkward for attaching camping tools and cooking gear, but it was more than enough of a burden for a twelve-hour day spent struggling up and down 45-degree slopes over unstable earth and scree. The columns picked their way along ledges in single file; each mule needed an extra man with a rope to prevent its 200lb load slipping on the steepest gradients, while the muleteer had to inch along the outside edge of the goat-track between his beast's head and the almost sheer drop. The opposition was stubborn, and it is hardly surprising that it took Théveny's force nearly two weeks to approach El Mers from the north;

how infantry managed to make any methodical progress through this appalling terrain almost defies the imagination.[12] For instance, on 9 June Major Barrière's I/3rd REI managed to secure a thickly wooded height on a flank, but had to hold it from 9am until nightfall against furious attacks that came to hand-to-hand range; that day's fighting alone cost Théveny's three battalions 230 casualties.

On the same day the southern force were pushing across the plain below the edge of the *djebel*. (General Poeymirau insisted that his staff sit down to take breakfast, its service slightly disrupted by a bullet that dropped the mule carrying up the mess equipment.) A Skirmisher battalion were sent to investigate a silent, wooded hill rising above the left flank, and about twenty minutes after they disappeared into the trees, firing crashed out. They had been ambushed from three sides, many officers had fallen, and shaken *turcos* were seen retreating out of the woodland; Prince Aage later heard that the unit had lost 70 killed and 228 wounded – half its strength. The I/2nd REI were sent up the hill in their turn and cleared it, though not without loss. As usual, the temperature plunged after sunset; in their freezing bivouacs the troops got little sleep, disturbed by incessant close-range sniping and by the replying machine guns until a couple of hours before dawn. After taking an intermediate ridge on 12 June, the mobile group again halted for several days to bring up supplies and prepare systematically for the next advance. Sniping was almost continual, and by night Berber women haunted the edges of the camps howling graphic threats at the Moroccan Skirmishers. Some tribesmen managed to slit sentries' throats and crept in to steal rifles, and the soldiers were ordered literally to 'sleep on their arms' in the tents – each man wrapped his rifle and buried it in a groove scraped beneath his blankets (a precaution that became habitual).[13]

EL MERS WAS TAKEN by converging attacks from north, west and south on 24 June 1923, and a battalion of the 2nd Foreign led the advance from the south towards the glowering wall of Bou Khamouj. Prince Aage was with this unit when it came under heavy fire while trying to clear Ait Segrushin warriors off high ground to the left; he describes a machine-gun crew being shot down one by one, and volunteers having to crawl out to drag the gun to a less exposed position. Artillery drove the Berbers back from their stone breastworks to a second line nearer the village, and this too was shelled before the infantry advanced again in the heat of the afternoon. About 200 yards short of El Mers village, they were held up by an outlying *kasbah* centred in an arrowhead of trenches and banks, which Aage estimated was held by as many as 1,000 Berbers (with, he claims, 'several machine guns').[14] At about 3pm all three battalions of 2nd Foreign prepared to assault this position; Aage's job was to liaise between the front line and the reserves and ammunition train, but he watched from the position of a unit delivering supporting fire. Apparently three assaults on the trenches and redoubt by the lead battalion were repulsed with significant casualties, before classic fire-and-movement by the companies and platoons of another got the légionnaires into the trenches, and the *kasbah* was finally 'bombed out' by a platoon with haversacks of grenades.[15]

SINCE BEFORE DAWN, meanwhile, other units had been picking their way down a pass from the heights of Bou Khamouj, and at about 8am were advancing on El Mers from the west. In the forefront were Captain Bastien's VII/22nd Spahis accompanied by *goumiers* led by Lieutenant Henry de Bournazel, who had been detached from the regiment to the Native Affairs service that same month. The rolling country was covered with tall barley, and as the cavalry rode through this they came under sudden heavy fire from Ait Segrushin concealed all around them. The squadron made too good a target against the sky, and were ordered to dismount and form a defensive square around their horses until infantry came up. In this perfect cover tribesmen easily drew close to the kneeling troopers, and others were attracted to join the fight, both firing down from nearby high ground and converging through the crops. Lieutenant Berger was hit three times; then Captain Bastien took a bullet full in the chest, and Henry de Bournazel took command – as so recently an officer of the 22nd he was better known and trusted by the Spahis than by his own irregulars. He too was hit almost at once, but only by a ricochet that tore his scalp, covering his face with a mask of blood more alarming than serious.

Bournazel ordered some of his *goumiers* to remount and follow him, to clear the riflemen from a low ridge that he judged the most dangerous threat. They did not, and he found himself riding up the slope alone – a single bloody-faced horseman in a bright red tunic. The Berbers concentrated their fire on him, but he got within 50 yards of the crest before his horse stumbled and went down. He stayed in the saddle and beat it to its feet again; it lurched on up the ridge, and in the face of this obvious sorcerer whom they could not seem to kill, the tribesmen fell back. By now some *goumiers* and Spahis had been shamed into following him; behind them the first double-marching infantry had at last reached the Spahis in the barley and were delivering volleys, and the first shells were bursting; nevertheless, the legend of 'the Red Man' had been born. (In the culture of the tribes, a leader's personal qualities were widely discussed, and his supposed *baraka* was a significant factor in their calculations. It was not mere bravado but shrewd psychology for Bournazel to stick to his scarlet tunic thereafter.) By noon the squadron had re-formed, and cleared several further features during the continued advance on El Mers. Prince Aage saw them coming in from his left front; he took professional pleasure in the skill with which they alternated between mounted movements and skirmishing on foot with carbines, but he noted men being shot from their saddles one after another. Altogether the El Mers campaign seems to have cost the 22nd Spahis some 200 casualties.[16]

As the sun set the tribesmen finally gave up El Mers and fell back into the hills to the east. The Legion's I/3rd REI had also been heavily engaged up on the ridges, and Major Barrière was among the casualties. That night snipers were more active than ever, and Prince Aage estimated that 40 men were hit in his camp alone. In the chill darkness he visited the casualty clearing station at the foot of the Bou Khamouj ridge:

> Huddled at the base of the escarpment was a group of hastily erected marquees, surrounded on three sides by a brown sea of stretchers, white-spotted with anxious faces. One of the tents had been utilized as an operating theatre for the more urgent cases, while others were used as dressing stations. There was as yet no means of bringing trucks up to this point, so the wounded were evacuated by mule transport.[17]

COLONEL FREYDENBERG'S TAZA GROUP was closing in from the north, and, in late June, Major Naegelin's II/3rd REI and Kratzert's VI/1st REI finally climbed on to the Taddoute plateau against stiff resistance. Meanwhile the Southern Group moved east from El Mers into Marmoucha tribal country, aiming for the plateau of Immouzer at the south-west end of the long Djebel Iblane (see Map 19). In terms of arrows on the map it looked as if the jaws of General Poeymirau's groups were closing, but in this terrain no true encirclement was possible; hills might be taken and held, but blocking all the ravines and saddles between them against night movements would have taken half the French Army.

On 17 July, Théveny's brigade occupied Ait Mahklouf south of Immouzer, and that evening the bivouac of I/2nd REI came under heavy fire from 200 yards' range while the légionnaires were still building the *murettes*. They pushed the attackers away, only for them to return in even greater strength; the Berbers were riddling the camp from all sides, and on the north-west they made dangerous progress and forced one platoon to give ground. Leading the men closest to him in a counter-charge, Major Buschenschutz took a Mauser bullet in the chest and suffered a collapsed lung – in those days always a life-threatening wound – but the counter-attack re-took the lost ground. There was no field hospital within miles; Prince Aage called for volunteers, and picked 20 men to carry and escort Buschenschutz's stretcher in relays. Despite pitch darkness and difficult terrain the légionnaires covered 12 miles in less than three hours, and the Alsatian major survived. (Aage's baggage mule was killed during the attack, and his cook served him mule steaks for days – 'not at all bad').[18]

The occupation of the Immouzer plateau in the last week of July involved three days' fighting against Marmoucha tribesmen by two columns each led by a Legion battalion – I/3rd REI (Major Susini) and II/2nd REI (Major Jenoudet). The latter unit was ordered to clear and hold a wooded hill; they had hardly reached the top when they were hit by the first of several counter-attacks, and the day cost the battalion 25 men killed and 49 wounded. The moment of first occupying a summit was among the most dangerous, since the Berbers often counter-attacked immediately before the soldiers could organize a perimeter or set up machine guns. (In such terrain one of the two-gun platoons of the battalion's MG company was often attached to each rifle company.) As the first platoons reached a crest – panting, disordered, and perhaps having lost their subaltern or NCOs during the assault – tribesmen who had dropped a little way down the reverse slope might fire into their faces and launch an uphill rush at extraordinary speed:

> It is necessary above all to nail the troops to the ground; surprised soldiers cannot manoeuvre, and may turn tail without hearing or understanding the orders they are given. The only comprehensible order [at such moments] is 'Halt!' ... This allows the men to get a grip on themselves and the officer to take them in hand and, if necessary, to force their obedience ... It is unwise to simply give the order 'Face the enemy!', which leads to confusion ... All you should ask of them is that they fight individually on the spot. Give the command 'Halt – lie down – individual fire at will – rifle-grenades, fire!'. If despite this the enemy still get within 50 yards the platoon commander should order the designated hand-grenadiers to throw two each ... We have

not given enough emphasis to hand-grenade training in Morocco, but it should play a fundamental role in close combat.[19]

The following day, as the Southern Group moved north-east along the edge of the Djebel Iblane towards a junction with the Taza Group coming south, Major Kratzert's VI/1st REI with Taza Group lost 18 killed and 36 wounded while holding off counter-attacks. On 11 August both II/ and III/2nd REI (Majors Jenoudet and Janson) had to fight their way up slopes thick with holly-oak and ilex, and Janson lost 22 men killed and 51 wounded. Jenoudet's battalion had an easier time until they reached the summit, where the exhausted légionnaires, with empty waterbottles, had to fight off several counter-attacks from heavy cover. One of these rushes got right in among them; 12 men were killed and 17 wounded, among them Jenoudet himself, shot through both thighs (he was replaced by Major Fernand Maire, the officer who had distinguished himself with Nicolas' battalion above Skoura the previous year). On 17 August the Taza and Southern groups finally linked up, before elements of the Southern moved south towards Almis des Marmoucha. On 3 September, near Souk de Ait Bazza, a series of fierce attacks on a Moroccan Skirmisher battalion *'produit un léger flottement'*; this elegantly phrased panic ('a light floating ...') was quelled by charges that cost two companies of I/2nd REI another 33 men killed.[20] These were not Western Front casualty rates, but they were significant; to put them in perspective, at the time of writing such a loss would be regarded as very serious when suffered by a British battalion not in one day but during a whole six-month tour in Afghanistan.

The year's operations wound down in early October 1923 as the autumn rains brought major movements in the highlands to an end. To 'capture' ground is an almost meaningless term in such terrain, but General Poeymirau had penetrated a great deal of new territory, brought more Berber clans at least temporarily to terms, and installed Native Affairs officers and small post garrisons in a tighter ring around the Taza Pocket. Some of these forts would be held during the winter by dispersed companies of Skirmishers and légionnaires, but the luckier units now marched back to their regular garrisons around Fes and Meknes. Three Legion battalions had earned citations in Army orders, adding the War Cross for Exterior Operations to their flags. Captain Prince Aage wrote that the 1923 Middle Atlas campaign had cost the French Army 'about 100 officers and 3,000 men killed, with wounded and other casualties proportionately numerous'; to judge by the ratios in individual actions, that means total casualties of perhaps 9,000 all ranks in six months. Marshal Lyautey could be grateful for the fact that few of these were the sons of French voters.

On 11 November General Poeymirau presided over a ceremonial Armistice Day review of the troops at Meknes. After dining his officers in great style he insisted on strolling round the noisy streets to visit the dives where his soldiers were celebrating; in the Café des Negociants he was loudly cheered and toasted by NCOs of the 2nd Foreign Infantry. Six weeks later 'Poey' was back in France, dying of septicaemia from a ruptured appendix.[21]

DURING THE 1923 CAMPAIGN, Poeymirau's operations had been supported by six of the ten air squadrons *(escadrilles)* then in Morocco, each with eight biplanes, whose major contribution had probably been short-range reconnaissance for ground columns.[22] Low flying in the thin, hot, turbulent air between the peaks was always demanding. Messages could sometimes be dropped in weighted bags, though this was highly problematic in broken country; most communication was by a simple code sequence of coloured flares fired from signal pistols, in response to coloured panels laid out on the ground pointing in a particular direction. For instance, a yellow flare meant 'Ground ahead clear', and a red one 'Danger of attack' (six-star flares, meaning simply 'Where are you?', were probably a heavy item of expenditure).[23] While some air/ground wireless communication was available to major headquarters, it was one-way: aircraft had only transmitters, not receivers, and the ground station had to signal them in the usual way with panel codes and Morse lamps. This – and the rapid movements of a dispersed enemy – limited the usefulness of aircraft for artillery-spotting.

In terms of direct support, light bombs were intimidating but aiming them was simply a matter of luck; enemy scattered in thick cover presented an almost impossible target for bombing, though strafing with machine guns could be more effective. A more generally valuable mission was aerial photography, and to make up for the lack of maps the squadrons photographed nearly 6,000 square miles of the Middle Atlas in 1923. Since the start of the 1921 campaign they had also played a supplementary part in the evacuation of the sick and wounded, flying out 1,200 casualties during those three years. The aircraft were general-purpose types, and although each squadron officially had six combat and two evacuation aircraft, additional machines could be rigged for the latter role if needed; in 1921–23 this proportion was apparently sometimes reversed.[24]

*

WHILE THE BATTALIONS of the 2nd and 3rd Foreign from Meknes and Fes had been operating with the mobile groups in the central Middle Atlas, further south, those of the 4th REI from Marrakesh had been pushing south-east from Kasbah Tadla. Resistance was not dramatic, and the knots of further posts were tied in the net that Lyautey's generals were weaving across the mountains.

The most basic function of all such posts was to lock the ratchet on the advances achieved each summer by the mobile groups; they were the visible symbol to the tribes of French determination ('if you come, you must stay'), and each spring some of them formed supply depots for that season's operations. The 'half-life' of resistance in newly penetrated country lasted several years, and the forts provided sentry-posts on the limited number of access routes between the territories of submitted and unsubmitted tribes, where reports of clan concentrations or other movements gathered by Native Affairs officers allowed the garrisons to pre-empt or interdict raids. (It was not expected that perfect peace should reign within submitted tribal areas; marauding and pillage were punished, but usually the district officers simply demanded to be kept informed of feuding, and would sometimes specifically agree to a 'fight of honour' between the warriors of mutually hostile clans in order to release tensions by giving them a chance for some limited killing. Lyautey always insisted on working with the grain of the Berber character.)[25] In times of serious trouble it was believed that an area that would otherwise tie down twelve battalions could be controlled by just four if an armature of posts was already in place.[26] Physical control obviously extended no further than machine-gun range from many of these forts, though the larger ones were soon equipped with a single gun manned by a couple of Colonial artillerymen – not for self-defence, but to extend their interdiction of nearby routes.[27]

One of the most vivid memoirists of this aspect of Legion life was a one-armed Russian, Captain Zinovi Pechkoff, who, as a 30-year-old corporal, had been gravely wounded and *medaillé* at the foot of Vimy Ridge in May 1915. Born Zinovi Sverdlov, he had been adopted at the turn of the century by the great writer and liberal activist, Maxim Gorki (A. M. Pechkoff), and had taken his name. Since his time in the trenches he had performed more confidential services for the Republic; in January 1920 he had been confirmed in the rank of captain in the Legion and posted to Morocco, where he fell in love with both the country and his enduring and ever-resourceful légionnaires.[28] On 1 April 1923, after a punishing march in heavy rain, Pechkoff's battalion of the 4th Foreign (prematurely issued cotton summer uniforms) began to build a fort for a Senegalese garrison at a spot called Koomsh:

> The crest of the mountain was thickly wooded, and in order to have a clear view of the ground around the camp we had to cut down trees that stood there like a wall ... Others with hammers and picks were to break the rocks and clear the ground so that the tents might be pitched. A road had to be made to bring up the guns, mules, horses and men ... Then the rain started to fall again; torrents of water descended on us and made the ground like jelly ... Some of the men worked through the night putting up barbed-wire defences, while others built a stone wall to protect us ... All night the rain did not stop. It grew colder and colder, and before dawn snow had whitened all the slopes of the mountains and also our tents.
>
> During the morning the snow continued to fall. Nevertheless the work had to be done. Gangs of men went to work – masons, stone-breakers, miners who drilled the rocks in order to dynamite them, men with picks and shovels who traced the outline of the post. Other men ... dug holes in the ground to make lime kilns; others cut down more trees for firewood to feed the ovens where stone was being transformed into lime ... We are the pioneers who open a new country [and] who do the hardest work. After the Legion, other men will come ... Their names will be known. But it is our men of the Legion who have paved the way with their untiring labour. Every path we make bears the pain of our men.[29]

By 15 April construction was completed, and the half-company of Africans was installed with three months' rations. There they would stay, linked to the outside world only by a mail courier twice a month, and a field telephone line that would certainly be cut by the tribesmen.

On reaching the plains again, Pechkoff was halted at El Ksiba and told that his men were to build a blockhouse on the Ifren plateau for the use of a friendly *caid* (Lyautey was still pursuing his old policy of creating armed 'home guards' among cooperative clans). This meant another three-day ordeal in execrable weather, and when the battalion hobbled back towards Kasbah Tadla on 22 April many were sick and some stumbled along behind the column, literally barefoot. Nevertheless, when the town commandant sent wagons out to meet them not one man accepted the chance to ride; this was emphatically not the Legion of 1919–20. The band and the garrison turned out to welcome them, and the légionnaires were given two days to rest, clean themselves up and draw new uniforms. When they hit town there were always old comrades and new acquaintances to drink with, and female companions happy to help them spend their pay:

> They fill up all the cafés in the small town. The main street contains almost nothing but cafés. There the légionnaire dances to the music of the mechanical pianos – his képi over one ear, his tunic unbuttoned, a cigarette in the corner of his mouth. Half-drunk, he is still filled with the vision of the desert, of the mountain, of the dust on the road, of the long marches ... He forgets himself in the rhythmic swing of an old waltz, or in the quickstep of an ancient polka. They dance their national dances, their folk dances, in a cloud of smoke and dust ...
>
> When several battalions of the Legion are in town at the same time they dominate everything ... On their two pay days [each] month ... guards on duty at the different posts in the town and camp are entirely composed of légionnaires. The patrols that are sent around the city after 'Retreat' to round up any delinquents are always composed of légionnaires. All the other troops are kept in their barracks on those days in order to avoid trouble. A drunken légionnaire ... if taken by a patrol of légionnaires, will go along with them quietly, but if taken by ... other troops, trouble will start at once. Considering himself on a higher plane ... he feels insulted if reprimanded or taken into custody by men of other units ... [30]

IN JUNE, PECHKOFF was sent with his company into the hills south of Beni Mellal to garrison a fort at Ouaouizarht (see Map 19). An independent mission in command of a company is one of the most deeply satisfying experiences in any officer's career; Pechkoff delighted in the pre-dawn departures under a black velvet sky still ablaze with stars, and in the strong, contented swing of his légionnaires towards glorious sunrises. The company marched up the western flank of the *djebel* through settled areas around Timoulilt – 'wonderful *kasbahs*, built very high of red earth, have shown us their thick walls and high towers. Superb gardens ... almond trees, figs, pomegranates and groves of olive trees' – but Pechkoff's heart sank once he had crossed the pass and saw the isolated fort in the distance below where he was to spend five months with 60 men, while the rest were dispersed.

Such posts were naturally built on high ground, to avoid being overlooked from close range and for visual signalling with those on other summits. Their sources of water were almost always lower down, so small satellite outposts often had to be maintained at some distance to guard these, or to watch some kink or saddle along the mule-tracks that were the garrisons' only link with each other and a supply base. Life in such even remoter blockhouses, held by a lieutenant with 30 men or even a sergeant with a dozen, was simultaneously tedious and nerve-racking, but even the main garrisons were so glad to see their relief arriving that the handover was accompanied by ceremonial and as good a feast as the stores afforded. After the inevitable business of resisting pressure to sign off inventories until his quartermaster- and ordnance-sergeants had applied due diligence, the new commander watched the old garrison recede into the silent distance under a thinning plume of dust, before he confronted his 'thousand duties':

> He is commandant of the post, commander of his unit, manager of the commissariat ... for the entire region. All the troops in this section of the country are supplied by me. I am a grocer, a baker (we have two ovens ...) and a butcher ... I also have to make contracts and buy the livestock. I have to deliver sugar, flour, lard, wine, and oats and hay for the animals ... Each day is full, and one does not have a moment to oneself. Everybody comes to the CO with every little thing. The nights are not very calm, either: there are brigands around the post.[31]

Nevertheless, within a few weeks Pechkoff had settled into the routine and was enjoying himself. His légionnaires had plenty to do; Ouaouizarht – little more than a rectangle of walls when they arrived – would be a supply depot for future operations, and the garrison had to build a large storehouse in addition to constructing their own barrack blocks and stores. Since it was their own temporary home that they were improving, the men turned to with a will; they suggested extra refinements, and shamelessly robbed passing convoys of useful materials. (Starved of so much by the parsimonious commissariat, all légionnaires and NCOs were inveterate thieves and scroungers on behalf of their own units. If a convoy stayed overnight at a fort it was liable to find in the morning that even its best mules and saddlery had mysteriously turned into smaller beasts and older gear – 'After all, *mon capitaine*, it is for the good of the service.')

The soldiers were confined within the fort between 'Retreat' and 'Reveille', but even in such a remote spot sutlers had built lean-to canteens outside the walls where the légionnaires instantly spent their twice-monthly pay. Pechkoff enforced proper discipline, but he learned to handle his men tactfully for 48 hours each fortnight; he got to know them as individual characters, understood what they expected of their officer, and took satisfaction in exercising man-management by intelligence rather than rigidity. By August, when a general turned up with a dozen staff officers, the captain was proud of what he had to show for his men's work: '[The VIPs] were well received on a small terrace that I had put up alongside the wall, under the branches of a giant olive tree which is one of four trees being left inside the fort. A long table was dressed by my orderly, and on it flowers had been placed in empty shell [cases] carved by the men.' Much else had changed since Major Ibos praised them in 1911, but not the 'universal handiness' of légionnaires who could make a 'rural home spring from the earth, comfortable and well run'.[32]

IN SUMMER, when the mobile groups were on the move in the hills, post garrisons often enjoyed the distraction of outside contacts, but in winter they led a much lonelier and harsher life. Throughout the year they relied on regular mule convoys and driven livestock for all supplies, but under the lashing late autumn rains the mountain tracks became virtually impassable due to wash-outs and mudslides, and when the snows fell all movement over any distance ceased. Isolated posts had to build up stores of every necessity in advance and simply shut themselves in to sit out the dreary months as best they could. This was wretched enough in a half-company fort, but in a platoon blockhouse it could threaten both discipline and mental stability; keeping his men reasonably busy, sober and even-tempered made immense demands on any young lieutenant. Telephone wires were often down, either cut deliberately or broken by natural accidents; in bad weather the signalling-lamp was only intermittently reliable, and the only method of passing very basic signals between a fort and its nearby outposts was by bugle calls.

While the tribes knew that mounting an actual assault on a post was suicidal, when the winter cut the garrisons' communications and delayed any chance of relief or pursuit, small war parties grew bold enough to close in, watchfully. At night tribesmen were often lured by the stables for mules and horses built between the outer barbed wire and the walls. After snaking in through the wire, the more ambitious lay up in the shadows at the base of the walls and threw pebbles to try to tempt a dozing sentry into sticking his head out, whereupon a swung rope would coil round his neck and drag him and his rifle over the edge. In January 1924 Captain Pechkoff lost a sentry pulled to his death in this way, and also a platoon commander shot dead as he responded to the alarm.[33]

Soldiers did not venture far from the walls without good reason, but routine sorties to bring in water and firewood were unavoidable, and these *corvées* had to be conducted as serious tactical movements. If there were any Spahis with the main garrison they rode out first and occupied high points, but in all cases the machine guns in the watchtowers were cocked, riflemen manned the walls, and look-outs scanned the surrounding terrain with binoculars while the water parties led the mules to the river or well. Such *corvées* were preceded by an advance guard which went beyond the watering point to picket any overlooking crests while the kegs were filled; the escort fell back by alternate bounds as the mule train withdrew, and when they reached the fort a rollcall was held before the gates were shut. In the afternoons another party carried out any refuse for burial and might go on to cut firewood; again, the escort advanced as if into battle, bayonets fixed and 'one up the spout', with the advance squad deployed in line and the others in files on the flanks. Wood-cutting took longer than watering and was carried out at different spots often further from the fort, so pickets in all directions had to stay alert over several hours.

The outlying blockhouse garrisons needed regular resupply and occasional relief, and were not strong enough to send more than a few men down the trail to meet the mules half way. The routes and timetables of both *corvées* and supply parties inevitably became predictable, and by the tenth time an NCO had carried out this duty without incident it was equally inevitable that he tended to relax his vigilance. Heads were hunched down into greatcoat collars out of the wind, numbed hands were thrust into pockets, and at a bend or a crest the little column began to straggle. This was the moment at which the Berbers would strike.

A few tribesmen noted for their ambush skills had been watching and remembering every detail for several days; the best shots with the best rifles occupied a height from which they could see far along the back-trail or even to the fort gates, while those with old muskets hid themselves among the rocks and trees a few yards from the track. However antique their weapons, the first blast at point-blank range could always drop one or two légionnaires in their tracks. While they were still kicking the warriors raced forward to pounce on them, thrusting their long knives into the belly and ripping upwards to gut their man and cut his belt with one upwards sweep, so that belt, shoulder braces and cartridge pouches could be wrenched free in one piece like a jacket. Snatching up the coveted Lebels, the Berbers threw themselves over the lip of a nearby gulley, leaping and sliding down the scree and out of sight in seconds, while their brothers kept the other légion-naires pinned down and those higher up covered the escape by firing on anyone emerging from the fort. The machine guns would spray the slopes and crests, blindly and with infrequent success, and by the time a strong patrol reached the survivors the Berbers were two ridges away.

The only protection against such ambushes was an Apache-like alertness and lightning reactions. At the first hint of danger the NCO shouted 'Halt! – Drop! – Fire at will!': every man had to throw himself down, whether behind cover or not, opening a rapid fire at visible enemies and into the cover around them. A few accurate snap shots might stop the immediate rush, buying precious seconds to roll behind a rock and fumble a hand grenade out of the haversack. Sometimes it worked, but seldom without the loss of the first one or two men. Lieutenant-Colonel Fabre hammered home the warning that disaster always punished the unwary sooner or later (though he was writing of the French Army as a whole, not specifically of the Legion):

> The examples are numerous. At a certain post where the water source was at some distance, three water parties belonging to different units which relieved one another there [successively] were all massacred. At another, a badly guarded work gang left 150 knife-torn corpses; at yet another, a large convoy escort was wiped out at a cost of 92 lives. None of these attacks lasted more than a few minutes.[34]

ONE EXAMPLE of a heavier than usual ambush, on 19 April 1923, is provided by the post that had now been built in the Tizi Adni pass above Skoura (as Captain Pechkoff's diary emphasized, that month saw icy rain and snow in the Middle Atlas). Captain Laixelard's small half-company of III/3rd REI had to send out half their strength that day, to resupply two outlying blockhouses and to establish a new outpost. The platoon had to start up the trail that had been followed by the same battalion under Major Nicolas for its thwarted push towards Taddoute the previous May. In the Tizi Adni the track hugs the hillside on the right (south) and the ground drops away steeply on the left, with wide views north-eastwards over the treetops to the broad Oued Sebou valley and the yellow hills beyond. On the right the stony earth slope, almost sheer at some points, is studded with rocks and thickly grown with tough little holly-oaks; after rain, deep drainage gulleys carve their way down and fallen rocks and mudslides encumber the track.

At 7.30am the 36 men were led out by Sergeant-Major Strohmayer with

Sergeants Junnot and Peronne, and they moved tactically as soon as the barbed-wire 'knife-rests' were dropped back across the gateway behind them. They advanced cautiously across open, hummocky ground, the two squads deployed side by side in line with the usual files trailing back from the outer ends; behind them the post's two machine guns were ready to cover their flanks, and QM-Corporal Thirier was manning one of the rare mortars with a crew of his company bakers. Strohmayer's platoon had only got 120 yards from the fort when, as the right-hand squad topped a small rise, the sergeant-major saw his dog freeze and growl. He shouted the order to halt, drop and fire, and immediately about 30 Berbers concealed behind clumps of scrub began an intense fusillade. The fort's machine guns and mortar opened up in support, but then a second group of tribesmen whom the patrol had already passed jumped up and charged their right flank. The trailing file of riflemen on that side and a machine gun in the post stopped this rush dead, but not before soldiers had fallen to point-blank fire.

At this point yet a third group of Moroccans were spotted further down the pass behind the post. When rifle-grenades were fired from the walls they slipped out of sight into a gulley, but then firing broke out from the high ground all along the right-hand (up-hill) edge of the upper pass. About 200 yards below the fort a group of white-clad tribesmen were seen on a summit surrounding a man in a red burnous who was watching developments intently, but the bakers' mortar bombs quickly scattered them into cover. By this time Sergeant-Major Strohmayer was down, with a bullet in his belly and a finger shot off his right hand; Sergeant Peronne took a mortal wound, and other men were falling fast. The medical orderly Private Muller, hit twice behind the right hip, kept firing until directly ordered to crawl back to the fort, where his skills would be needed. Sergeant Junnot took command and led a grenade-charge on Berbers firing from a height to cover the retreat of their main party into the gulleys, carrying their dead and wounded. The firing died away at about 10.30am; the légionnaires advanced, finding two corpses and a Lebel rifle. Strohmayer's platoon had suffered 'about half' its strength killed and wounded; but at 10.45am the new outpost was installed as ordered, and by 1.45pm the two blockhouses had been resupplied.[35]

IN 1924, DESPITE CONTINUED ILL-HEALTH that forced him to undergo another operation, Lyautey's attention was increasingly demanded by Spanish Morocco, where a surprise decision that autumn would have direct consequences for the French zone.

In the aftermath of the Anual disaster, the high commissioner General Berenguer had been reinforced to a strength of some 150,000 men and instructed to pursue outright conquest of the hostile country around both presidios. At Melilla, although Abd el Krim had generally been content to consolidate in the hills rather than trying to hold the plain, it had still taken 36,000 troops six months to re-occupy the lost territory. With new tribes joining their alliance every few weeks, the Abd el Krim brothers held the hills west of a line running roughly from Afrau on the coast down to Souk el Tleta on the Kert river south-west of Midar (see Map 20). The Spanish conscript units were employed defensively, leaving most of the aggressive fighting to the Tercio and the Regulares, who achieved results but at heavy cost. The Rifians dominated the routes up into the highlands, and they had learned to dig trenches; in the winter of 1922/23, they beat off two Spanish attempts to advance westwards around Tizi Azza, an important central pass between Anual and Dar Drius, inflicting more than 2,000 casualties.

In the Djibala, the Spanish finally captured Ahmad er Raisuli's base at Tazrut in May 1922 and compelled him to withdraw into the mountains. In the Ghomara country to the east, Abd el Krim was extending his influence; Raisuli regarded the Ait Waryaghar leader with envious hatred, but faced a choice between surrendering to the Spanish or trying to negotiate a junior partnership with the growing Rifian confederacy – an unlikely prospect. In September 1922 his dilemma was solved when Berenguer was replaced by General Ricardo Burguete, who bought off tribal leaders and reached terms that left Raisuli in his Beni Aros hills to rule the Djibala hinterland. As always, Raisuli's nominal loyalty to the Maghzan was entirely cynical, but he knew that he would not be able to gull Abd el Krim as he had the Spanish – if the Rifians reached the Djibala he was doomed.[36]

Spanish Army morale was understandably low, and soldiers and public alike were divided between those who hungered for revenge and a strong *'abandonista'* tendency. All Spain was horrified when, in January 1923, negotiations with Abd el Krim via the International Red Cross finally resulted in the ransom of Spanish prisoners taken at Anual and Monte Aruit. In return for 4 million pesetas and the release of Moroccan prisoners the Rifians handed over 326 survivors from the roughly 570 who had been taken alive. After 18 months' captivity they were in a pitiable condition, although some testified that they had been treated as well as could be expected at a time when a typhus epidemic was ravaging the Rif.[37]

*

ON 1 FEBRUARY 1923 Mohammed Abd el Krim had himself proclaimed the *amir* (prince, commander) of the Rif and demanded recognition of its independence, under a provisional government *(Jibha Rifiya)* headed by himself and a council mostly composed of his Ait Waryaghar relatives. Later French propaganda claims that he was actually seeking to usurp the sultanate were clearly false, but his ambitions, like his capabilities, far surpassed those of any previous Berber leader during colonial times. That same month the *abandonista* Moroccan affairs minister, Santiago Alba, appointed a civilian high commissioner, Don Luis Silvela, with a remit to negotiate, and in June representatives met on board ship for secret exploratory talks. It is not surprising that they failed, but it was significant that they took place at all.

Abd el Krim was now entering the period of his greatest influence in Morocco and his widest fame abroad. The *Daily Telegraph*'s man in Tangier, Colonel Repington, might refer to him as 'that interesting bandit', but commentators on the Left portrayed him as a statesman who was seeking legitimate rights of self-determination for his people. His agents maintained a network of overseas contacts among anti-colonial idealists and fringe politicians who offered encouragement, though many of these had their own agendas. Abd el Krim (the Spanish-educated journalist) was far more sophisticated than the usual tribal leader, and his communiqués – publicized as far afield as Latin America – were couched in terms designed to appeal to foreign audiences, complete with sonorous references to principles established by the Treaty of Versailles. Visiting correspondents were fed a wide range of stories about his regime's supposed capabilities and intentions; they wrote more or less gullible reports, barbed with accurate denunciations of Spanish bombing of helpless villagers, and thus created a positive image abroad.

Abd el Krim's intermediaries had long been in quiet contact with those of Lyautey, repeatedly assuring him that the Rifians had no designs on the French zone and wanted merely to free themselves from the Spanish. Nevertheless, Abd el Krim rejected the authority of the sultan for whose government Lyautey was explicitly responsible throughout Morocco, and Rifian successes were aggravating the normal hostilities among the tribes along the zonal border. Lyautey was also anxious lest international interest in Abd el Krim should encourage renewed diplomatic interference in Franco-Moroccan affairs. Despite all the foreign attention, however, apart from a few soldiers-of-fortune the only practical help on offer to the Rifians was funding from businessmen eager for mining concessions, and the *amir* was happy to exploit their greed. Besides the cheerfully venal merchants of Tangier, he was courted by representatives of German and British firms, and some of the latter encouraged him to hope for eventual British diplomatic support, despite London's absolute rebuffs to his several overtures. (His failure to recognize the vanity of this hope was a blind spot in Abd el Krim's understanding of power relationships in the outside world.)[38]

Abd el Krim's unprecedented success in keeping a pan-tribal fighting force in the field for several years, inflicting repeated tactical defeats on the Spanish Army, in fact seems to have owed very little to the sort of political vision that his foreign propagandists attributed to him, and much to the traditional attractions of such leaders: the appeal to Islam, backed by a proven ability to deliver profitable victories. In Egyptian exile in his old age he would play the tunes that the modern generation of Arab nationalists wanted to hear, denying that his war was religiously inspired, but there is no doubt that he was a devout Muslim reformer. He was deeply hostile to the manipulative religious brotherhoods such as the Derkaoua; he voraciously taxed both the tithes of their *zaouias* and the endowments of mainstream mosques to fill his war chest, and he threatened to have uncooperative preachers strangled in the marketplaces with their own rosaries. However, the reforms that Abd el Krim (the Kairaouine-trained *cadi*) imposed in the areas that he dominated were sternly orthodox, subordinating Berber customary law to *sharia* and imposing punishments for violations of Islamic codes of personal conduct that were much stricter than was usual among these tribes.

El Krim was also a tribal empire-builder rather than a constitutional nationalist, and his unification programme was equally conservative. He spread his influence as tribal leaders had always done: by diplomatic pressure backed up immediately with pillage and killing – 'if you are not with me, you are against me.' At the personal level, he forbade blood-feuds and ordered the demolition of the traditional pillboxes of Rifian houses; one innovation was the establishment of three prisons, whose inmates suffered typical Moroccan conditions. It would be quite wrong to imagine that the Rifian tribes – or even all of the Ait Waryaghar clan chiefs – flocked to Abd el Krim's banner in spontaneous enthusiasm for a 'national' cause. He built his confederacy by the usual parallel applications of persuasion, bribery and coercion, and there was a persistent story that he had two Ait Waryaghar *caids* who negotiated with the Spanish stoned to death 'to save bullets'.[39]

For obvious reasons, Abd el Krim (the centralizing ruler) distrusted the traditional system of ever-shifting *liff* alliances, but he used his power of patronage creatively to balance factional leadership within the tribes from which he drew the part-time levies who provided most of his tens of thousands of fighting men. His younger brother Mhamed also created a hard core 'regular' brigade of up to 3,000 full-time, paid fighters equipped from central arsenals. As well as Abd el Krim's green-turbaned *huffaz* bodyguard of Ait Waryaghar based at his Ajdir headquarters, these regulars were divided into five *tabors* of about 500 men, organized on the Franco-Maghzan model in companies, half-companies, platoons and squads. Officers, who owed their promotion to personal prowess, imposed severe and direct discipline, and displayed different numbers of red turban-cords as rank insignia; the 1st to 3rd Tabors were entirely Rifian, the 4th and 5th of mixed tribesmen. About 350 other regulars, distinguished by black turbans, manned some of the captured guns. (Partly prompted by the Rifians' use of artillery, the press exaggerated tales about European renegades serving as intructors and even leaders in battle. Abd el Krim would state that he never had more than a total of about 50 white men between 1921 and 1926, nearly all coerced prisoners or deserters, who were kept out of the front line and employed as technicians.)[40]

Taken all in all, it is tempting to see in Abd el Krim's Jibha Rifiya the first example of a phenomenon not unknown in our own times: a charismatic and ruthless central leadership, manipulating a diffuse pan-tribal organization that exploited modern weapons in the service of traditional guerrilla skills – a leadership articulating a simultaneous appeal to both ethnic pride and conservative Islam; understanding both the international commercial value of its local natural resources, and the narratives that appealed to parts of the international media; and with effective access to those media and the political interests that they served.

DURING THE CAMPAIGN SEASON OF 1923, while Poeymirau's columns were fighting their way up into the Middle Atlas, in Spain the machinery of the state was breaking down. There were mutinies in Barcelona and Malaga among troops mobilized for Morocco, ministers were resigning in despair, and (with King Alfonso's tacit approval) a group of generals carried out a military coup. Their choice of a leader – in the avuncular person of the Captain-General of Barcelona, Don Miguel Primo de Rivera – was interesting; although a popular and much-decorated veteran, he was known to be an *abandonista* at heart. In his manifesto of 23 October 1923, Primo promised

all things to all men, appealing for support for a carefully unspecified programme. His regime imposed strict censorship and banned demonstrations,
but also launched major public works and gave Army NCOs a generous pay
rise.[41]

The fighting on both Moroccan fronts was costly but indecisive for both
sides during the bad winter of 1923/4; more than a quarter of the available
troops were tied down in static positions, and the Army, while greatly
enlarged, had no coherent plan for regaining the intitiative. In May 1924 the
pace of Moroccan attacks picked up, particularly along the Oued Lau on the
eastern edge of the Djibala, where a series of assaults were orchestrated by
a young former soldier of the Regulares and one-time protegé of Raisuli,
Ahmed Heriro of the Beni Hozmar tribe. After shifting his loyalty to the
brothers Abd el Krim the previous year, he did not immediately try to enlist
the Ghomara and Djibala tribes explicitly in his new masters' cause, but
roused them to fight the Spanish for their own good reasons. In June, the
fighting came close to Tetuan, and by late July these warriors had isolated
the Oued Lau outpost line and were fighting off relief attempts. (Shaken by
their first encounters with armoured cars, the Berbers had quickly adapted;
they discovered that the crews' vision was very restricted, so they lay flat
until a car passed close and then leapt up to shoot through the ports and set
fire to the fuel tank. The crew of an immobilized and isolated armoured car
faced an unenviable choice.)

On 24 July 1924, Primo de Rivera arrived to visit both fronts; recognizing
the wretched state of the Army, he favoured withdrawal from the whole
hinterland and indirect rule through negotiated agreements with local
leaders, including Raisuli and Abd el Krim. This proposal to accept defeat
aroused furious resentment among the dedicated combat officers of the
Tercio and Regulares, but while Primo handled this deftly, he only modified
rather than abandoned his plans.[42] On 8 September he unveiled them: in the
western theatre all the troops would withdraw into the most northern and
western parts of the peninsula behind a new 'Primo Line' of posts (see Map
20).

The tribesmen, predictably, did not let them go easily. There were many
desperate rearguard actions, stores and arsenals were abandoned yet again,
and Sergeant Barea wrote that the Spanish ransomed some blockhouse
garrisons by paying the Berbers two rifles per soldier to allow them to escape.
With the exception of elites like Lieutenant-Colonel Franco's Tercio, Primo
de Rivera was appalled by the Army's low spirits and levels of skill, and

took personal command of operations (narrowly escaping from an ambush himself). The climax of this series of evacuations was a major operation by some 40,000 men to cut a broader corridor through from Tetuan to Chefchaouen in order to withdraw its garrison. This meant heavy fighting under torrential rains until mid-December, and the total cost of the with-drawals to the Primo Line – never admitted – was conservatively estimated at some 18,000 casualties. Worn out, but at least comforted by Primo's decisive command style, the western army settled in behind a tight line of outposts sited 500 yards apart and protected by searchlights and minefields.[43]

THE TRIBESMEN HAD CAPTURED more rich booty, the Spanish area of control had been halved, and, thanks to Ahmed Heriro, the Abd el Krim brothers had gained great prestige in the Djibala. The last obstacle there was Raisuli, and in January 1925 the younger Abd el Krim moved decisively against him. He gave Heriro 300 regulars with four machine guns and 600 Ait Waryaghar and Timsaman levies, who, on 23 January at Tazrut, captured Raisuli, his armoury and his gold. For so many years a legend of cunning and tyranny, the great brigand was now a notably diminished figure; although still only in his early fifties he had long been suffering from dropsy, and his grotesquely swollen legs would no longer support him. He was carried to the coast and then by motorboat back to the Rif, where he died (perhaps even of natural causes) at Tamasint in April 1925. Those Djibala tribes that had remained in thrall to him now came over to Heriro and Abd el Krim with some haste. Since the Spanish front west of Melilla was still stalled around Tizi Azza, by early spring of 1925 virtually the whole area bordering the French zone was unguarded and vulnerable to a triumphant and geo-graphically unified bloc of the Rifians and their allies. The still unsubmitted tribes of the zonal frontier territory were mesmerized by Abd el Krim's success, and south of them only a thin crust of the peaceful Hayana and Cherarga confederacies stood between him and the western Fez–Taza cor-ridor.

Lyautey was confronted, just 40 miles from the capital of French Morocco, by the creeping edge of what he called 'an autonomous Muslim entity, organized and modernized, supported by numerous and warlike populations exalted by their constant success against the Spanish'.[44] The marshal was exaggerating the Rifians' organization and modernity, but the immediate threat they posed was real enough. He now found himself in direct com-petition with Abd el Krim for the cooperation of the tribes who lay between them, of whom the most important were the 25,000-odd Beni Zeroual along each side of the Ouergha river valley. On the outcome of that competition depended the continuing obedience of the Tsouls and Branès further east, astride the road from Algeria; and they in turn were the gatekeepers of the defiant Taza Pocket of the northern Middle Atlas. If Abd el Krim could collapse the lintel of the French archway it might bring down much of the eastern pillar. Primo de Rivera's withdrawal from most of the zonal border had finally exposed the potentially fatal contradictions of the Franco-Spanish agreement dating from the birth of the Protectorate in 1912.

Abd el Krim's own options were far from clear-cut. Whatever his renown among Western liberals innocent of Moroccan realities, the only foreign support that could make any difference was overt recognition by a national government, and whatever their distaste for Spanish methods, no government was going to challenge France and her client sultan by endorsing Rifian independence before the fact. What Abd el Krim needed was another divided, pessimistic Spanish cabinet that could be harassed into making some hasty concession – almost anything would do, so long as it could be presented to the world as implying some measure of *de facto* recognition. Instead, he faced a dictatorship that was relatively tolerable to most middle-class Spaniards, headed by a general whose calming leadership might nurture a gradual renewal of the Army's offensive capabilities. Despite the Rifians' many tactical successes, Abd el Krim's only long-term strategic hope lay in the inherent instability of Spanish politics. In the meantime, it was clearly in his interests to avoid goading the French into active opposition.

THE FOCUS OF LYAUTEY'S and Abd el Krim's mutual sensitivity had for some time been the large and grain-rich Beni Zeroual tribe that formed the buffer between them on both banks of the Ouergha. Technically this free people lay within the Spanish zone, but since the Spanish had never come this far south they allowed the French to handle all relations with the tribe, and the influential sharifian leader of the Derkaoua religious brotherhood, whose *zaouia* was at Amjot, was in Lyautey's pocket. Domination by either their northern or southern neighbours was equally unwelcome to the Beni Zeroual, whose leaders had to make continual recalculations of the relative threats and rewards offered by each. Both the French and the Rifians would venture into their territory by the old methods of clan-by-clan persuasion, but Abd el Krim's was the rougher wooing.

In 1924, the Rifians had increased their pressure for alliances, tribute and rations, crossing into Beni Zeroual territory to take what they wanted by violence. Encouraged by Lyautey's agents, some Beni Zeroual clans took up arms to resist them during April 1924; accepting French subsidies and the insurance of a limited presence in their territory carried the risk of creeping French control, but in the face of the immediate and more violent Rifian threat it was attractive to some chiefs. In May, 12,000 French troops crossed to the north bank of the Ouergha, by agreement, to install outposts on the hills protecting the grainlands from the north. One of the units involved was the Mounted Company/2nd REI, now commanded by Captain Prince Aage, who forded the Ouergha from the assembly point at Ain Aicha and marched through a richly cultivated country between villages that were aloof but unthreatening. When the Colonial troops began building their posts, there was one Rifian attack near Bou Adel on 6/7 June, but its easy defeat increased French prestige locally. In the first week of July, the posts were finished and the covering troops marched back to Fes.[45]

The French advance had surprised Abd el Krim, and the new posts cut him off from the Oued Ouergha breadbasket in a season when the Rif was suffering yet another bad harvest. His attempt to lure Lyautey into *de facto* recognition with an offer of border demarcation talks had been rejected. Lyautey increased his political pressure on the Beni Zeroual to accept a more definitive alliance, and some leaders agreed to this divisive suggestion. In September 1924, while the Rifians' attention was held by Spanish operations around Chefchaouen, more Colonial troops were sent into Beni Zeroual country to thicken up the line of 'doorbell' outposts on the hills, and this in turn provoked those chiefs who opposed the Derkaoua Sharif to seek alliances with Abd el Krim. As winter closed down active operations, both French and Rifians stepped up their political and logistic preparations in the frontier marches separating them. While Paris was distracted by financial crises and trouble in the occupied Rhineland, Lyautey – his army throughout Morocco now reduced to about 54,500 men – continued to warn of the danger posed by the Rifian pseudo-state, and requested reinforcements to strengthen the zonal border. These were few, and long delayed; nevertheless, the marshal still had faith in his old repertoire of political manoeuvres, and was emphatically against any direct French involvement in 'Spain's war'.[46]

IT MUST HAVE BEEN during the first months of 1925, after his destruction of Raisuli consolidated his grip on the Djibala, that Abd el Krim reached the opposite conclusion. Exactly what he hoped to gain by the gamble of opening a third fighting front has been widely discussed. He and his counsellors were far too well informed to imagine that they could gain control of significant areas of French Morocco, most tribes of which would instinctively resist Rifian incursions (not on the sultan's or Lyautey's account, but on their own). His followers could raid and destroy, but could not occupy territory in any great depth or hold captured towns.

Sophisticated or not, Abd el Krim was still the son of a culture in which war between comparable rivals was the prelude to intertribal negotiations, and whatever the disparity in their resources, he saw himself as Lyautey's equal in dignity and legitimacy. He may not have grasped the fundamental differences between the Spanish and the French national moods – the one worn down by decades of failure; the other victorious, at huge sacrifice, in an infinitely greater ordeal, and motivated by an impatient sense of entitlement. He had killed many thousands of Spanish soldiers and forced their vacillating governments to treat with him; now they had fled before him again, abandoning much of what they had previously gained. Perhaps, unable fully to imagine the French psychological legacy from 1914–18, he believed that if he could shock and humiliate them by taking Fes and/or Taza he could provoke widespread rebellions and force them, too, to negotiate to his advantage. He certainly listened to those over-confident advisers – both French Communists and European mining interests – who still held out the prospect of foreign support.

Behind these calculations we may presume that he was simply carried along by the need to ensure the continued loyalty of the fickle tribes by feeding his newly enlarged domain and maintaining the momentum of his victories. Whatever the balance of reasons for his decision, its consequences would be spectacular.

18. Dropping the Baton
1925

These native chiefs . . . we know them well. They are really
simple fellows. Properly handled, they respond to
kindness. There is, of course, not the slightest chance that
this one will ever attack us.
Foreign Minister Aristide Briand, April 1925[1]

The brutal fact is that we have been suddenly attacked
by the most powerful and best-armed enemy that we have
ever had to encounter in the course of our colonial
operations.
Marshal Philippe Pétain, August 1925[2]

THE POTENTIAL VULNERABILITY of Fes to events in the Ouergha
valley is dramatized today by the shortness of the journey between them –
a morning's drive, barely 40 miles on a modern road through the arid, cream-
coloured countryside that begins immediately north of the capital. The
differences of character between the two ends of the journey are rather more
noticeable. North of the river the hills press in closely, and once you are
properly among them the dominant impression is of steepness, parching
heat, separation and privacy. Hamlets, homesteads and fields are fringed
with canebreaks, pale green cactus spotted with red flowers and the grey
blades of aloes, all standing out against slopes dark with old olive groves.
Higher up, the thin soil between the sharp brown rocks is patched with
wispy yellow grass and tough scrub, with younger olive trees – planted in
recent years, more to stabilize the hillsides than in hopes of a worthwhile
crop – somehow sucking a beggarly life out of the sun-baked earth.

These higher slopes had not yet been planted when, in May–July 1924,
Lyautey's advance initially installed 40 small posts along a shallow arc

stretching some 90 miles through the hills north of the Ouergha valley, from roughly Ouezzane in the west to Kifane in the east (see Map 20). Later that year the number was increased to 66, but apart from native auxiliaries almost the only troops defending this whole outpost line were the 2,400-strong 1st Morocco Regiment of Senegalese Skirmishers (1st RTSM). Lyautey had just 40 infantry battalions at his disposal in the whole country; of these, 19 were with General Chambrun on this northern front, and 14 of those were held back in reserve.[3]

THE POSTS were typically sited no more than 2 miles apart, each within signalling-lamp contact with its neighbours. The theoretical priorities were a high position with good intervisibility and clear fields of fire, and access to water. In practice, of course, one or more of these requirements was usually compromised, since the specific terrain features dictated everything. Very few of the posts bore any resemblance to the rectangular crenellated forts of the south, and nearly all had irregular perimeters. There are few clear photographs, and while instructional drawings give an idea of what many of them must have looked like, these, again, were naturally an ideal that could not always be achieved.

Typically a post had an outline resembling an angular 'D'-shape with circular corner bastions (see Map 21). The largest was a platform for a single field gun to cover the approaches to the neighbouring posts; since the gun needed to be revolved, this platform could not itself be surrounded by walls, but was reached through a chicane doorway in the perimeter wall. The other three bastions were slightly taller than the wall, open at the back, each with a machine gun or one of the garrison's LMGs mounted on a timber and corrugated-iron floor. The thin soil of these rocky heights seldom allowed the usual on-the-spot production of mud-and-straw bricks, and the walls and bastions were built of piled dry stones, sometimes augmented with timber and sandbags. About 7–9 feet high, these drystone walls tapered towards the top, with firing-steps, splayed loopholes and niches for ammunition spaced along the inside. A splash of cement along the top secured a jagged fringe of broken beerbottles, and on the outside a horizontal 'shelf' of pickets strung with barbed wire stuck out just below this.

Within the enclosure were a couple of small ranges of buildings – rooms for the commander, NCOs, stores and cookhouse, and a primitive barracks – built of stones bound with 'bengali' (clay mixed with a little lime) and roofed with timbers, corrugated iron and earth insulation. Spaced around these were a concrete cistern for about 5,000 litres of water, an open-air bread oven and a night-time latrine. The entrance was protected by timber and barbed-wire 'knife-rests' and a chicane wall. Outside, anything up to 40 yards from the walls to keep grenade-throwers at a distance, was a surrounding barbed-wire entanglement – one or two belts of concertina wire with sloping criss-cross 'aprons' on the outer side. On a small hilltop that distance often could not be achieved within direct sight of the walls; on a larger space the belt of wire was sometimes duplicated, with a daytime latrine, rubbish-burning pit, mule lines and sometimes even vegetable plots in the space between the two. The ideal was to keep the post as compact as possible, since the need to hold outworks simply weakened the already overstretched garrison, but sometimes an awkwardly modelled slope making a 'dead angle' forced the building of a little external MG position to cover the blind approach, linked to the perimeter by a trench.[4]

The garrisons were typically of a single platoon, sometimes of a single squad; for example, at the post of Beni Derkoul the 21-year-old Sub-lieutenant Pol Lapeyre of 8th Company, II/1st RTSM, had a French sergeant and 2 artillerymen, 2 Senegalese NCOs and 34 rankers, with a 75mm gun and two Hotchkiss machine guns. The 8th Company were responsible for no fewer than six posts spread over some $7\frac{1}{2}$ miles west to east. Less than 2 miles to the south-east of Beni Derkoul was Achirkane (Sergeant Morel), and beyond that the company commander, Captain Pietri, was headquartered down in the valley at Tafrant, with lines of sight to his posts. A couple of miles further east, another group of three posts were closely spaced on hilltops from north to south: Aoudour (Lieutenant Franchi), Dar Remich (Sergeant Peron), and, on the high and isolated summit of the dominating hill of Bibane, a post commanded by Sergeant Bernez-Cambot.[5]

On 12 April 1925, a shepherd warned Captain Pietri that a party of Rifians had come south and were pillaging the local Ouled Kassem tribe, and all that night Lieutenant Franchi at Aoudour saw flames lighting up the horizon. Pietri passed the report back, toured his posts, and was worried to note that Beni Derkoul had only about 600 litres in its cistern. He was at Aoudour on the 15th when Pol Lapeyre phoned him to report Ouled Kassem fugitives from Amjot in his wire, and by the time Pietri got back to Tafrant he could hear shooting from Beni Derkoul and the field telephone lines were dead. He was, of course, as yet unaware that a full-scale war had just broken out, which would cost the French Army more than 11,000 casualties by the end of that year.

*

NOW AT THE PEAK OF THEIR STRENGTH, the Abd el Krim brothers had more than 70,000 fighting men potentially available (though not simultaneously). The most reliable were some 7,000 Ait Waryaghar, 6,000 Timsaman, 5,000 Ait Tuzin, and 5,000 Ibuqquyen and Gzinnaya together; the remainder were a mixture of conscripted levies from tribes right across the Spanish zone, from the Anjera west of Ceuta to the Beni Bou Yahi horsemen threatening the Oujda road in the far south-east. Typically these levies, aged between their teens and fifties, were called up for about one week per month and never for more than fifteen consecutive days, so as to maintain the necessary agricultural workforce at home. Thanks to their impressive cross-country mobility they could be rotated through their nearest fighting fronts, in forces that were often stiffened with contingents from the core tribes and units from Mhamed Abd el Krim's regular brigade. The latter were the best armed, but were far from the only fighters to carry modern rifles. A claim that only about 20,000 such weapons were available has been repeated but may be considerably understated, particularly with regards to the eastern theatre.[6] In 1921–2 the Berbers had been forced to gather their own ammunition from the battlefield, with Abd el Krim's regime buying in any surplus; subsequently, gun-runners ran the Spanish naval blockade, and Rifian government arsenals were established in about eight centres. (The Taghzat tribe of the Senadja Srir people – the 'gunstock Srir', renowned weaponsmiths – had become adept at making hand grenades from unexploded Spanish ordnance, producing 450 from a single 200kg aerial bomb.)[7]

On 13 April 1925, Mhamed Abd el Krim had sent five separate *harkas* of Djibala, Senadja Srir and Beni Mestara tribesmen, each stiffened with an Ait Waryaghar contingent, south into Beni Zeroual country from three directions. These first attacking waves probably totalled about 4,000 men with the same number in follow-up forces, while Gzinnaya and Ait War-yaghar attacked further to the east around Kifane, the vital guardpost over the Branès and Beni Bou Yahi country. Showing an impressive degree of coordination, the dispersed war parties flooded through the hills inde-pendently, isolating the French outposts and bypassing them to maintain the pace of the advance. Clans that resisted were massacred and burned out, as was the Derkaoua Sharif's *zaouia* at Amjot; refugees fled south, and the tribes north of the river fell like dominoes within a matter of days. The Abd el Krims appointed their own client chiefs, took hostages, extracted taxes for their war chest, conscripted warriors to fight beside them and forced labour gangs to dig trenches. Infiltrating forces pressed on south of the river, causing destruction and alarm in a dozen places. Before the end of April they would be at Tissa, only 28 miles from the very gates of Fes, and Lyautey would be reporting that tribes that had submitted ten years previously were showing signs of shakiness.[8]

Lyautey's appeals for reinforcements that winter had brought him, early in April, Colonel Barbassat's three-battalion Morocco Colonial Infantry Regiment (RICM); fresh from the Ruhr, these were mostly young French conscripts completely untrained for colonial fighting. Acclimatized units from Algeria had also been promised, but the first did not begin to arrive even at Oujda until 21–30 April.[9] On 25 April the marshal organized his available front-line troops in three commands: from west to east, Colombat Force (Ouezzane), Freydenberg Force (Ain Aicha) and Cambay Force (Taza), all answerable to General Chambrun. The battalions, squadrons and batteries forming temporary brigade-sized mobile groups within these commands would spend the next three months frantically marching and counter-marching to and fro along the whole Rif front, reacting at short notice to every individual threat even where the situation argued for local withdrawals. Any sign of weakness provoked more tribal defections to Abd el Krim; in this deadly match any score that was conceded increased the size of the opposing team. Any ground that could possibly be held, had to be held ('if you come, you must stay'), and even when completely passive, the posts tied down Rifians who could otherwise have pushed more deeply into French territory.

Against the background of shielding the approaches to Fes and Taza, the most characteristic missions were the resupply, relief and – when it came to that – the extraction of hard-pressed Colonial garrisons. Switched from sector to sector sometimes at 24 hours' notice, the mobile groups spent almost every day of May to July either marching, fighting or digging; they often outdistanced their supplies, and in temperatures rising to 130°F (54°C) at noon and nearly freezing by night they were soon exhausted, ill-fed, filthy, and so ragged that men had to pin their torn uniforms together with thorns. They had no front line; their camps were rafts shifting around on a sea of dissidence, and while they were fighting to rescue one post to the north, others miles to the south of them would be overrun or abandoned. During these first critical months before reinforcements arrived in any numbers, the available units were mostly West African, Moroccan and Algerian, and the French conscripts of the RICM and a few Zouave companies were of limited value. Initially the hard core of the mobile groups along the Ouergha had to be provided by fewer than three Legion battalions: the II/ and VI/1st REI from Algeria, and half of the II/2nd and the Mounted Company/4th REI from the Middle Atlas. (The I/1st and the bulk of 2nd, 3rd and 4th Foreign Infantry were held back in the interior to ensure security in the Atlas during this anxious period.)[10]

Given the complexity and repetitiveness of the lunges back and forth by the ephemeral brigades, no attempt is made here to give a connected diary of their operations. What follows is a representative selection of actions fought by the two most heavily committed Legion battalions and some of the Colonial units they tried to support, set against broad phases of operations, in the hope of conveying at least something of the character of the Rif War as it was experienced by the légionnaires.[11]

THE HEADQUARTERS of the 6th Battalion, 1st Foreign Infantry was at Saida, but two companies (half of the battalion) were stationed at Kreider north of Mécheria, where they had spent a monotonous winter of drilling and route-marches punctuated by days-long sandstorms.[12] Despite the tedium of this posting, the commander of 22nd Company, Captain Zinovi Pechkoff, loved the wilderness, and often rode out alone to enjoy its silence and shifting colours. During one Sunday ride he encountered an English légionnaire from 21st Company exploring on foot, and the two struck up a conversation. Corporal Cooper was good at finding wild asparagus, which Pechkoff relished, paying for it with wine.[13]

Adolphe Cooper, no sycophant, would write that Pechkoff was the finest officer he ever met in any army; he was immediately impressed by the one-armed captain's skill in leaping up into the saddle of his grey, holding the reins in his teeth, but later the Englishman commended his brave and humane leadership in battle. Generally Cooper found French junior officers patronizing and lacking in useful experience, being schooled only in conventional European tactics. (In September 1924 this opinion was echoed by Lieutenant-Colonel Buchschenshutz of 2nd REI, who also complained that in the 1923 campaign subalterns had shown themselves deficient in practical knowledge of company weapons, being unable to fix stoppages when they should have been more expert than their men in every respect.)

During March 1925, Major Cazaban's VI/1st REI were given warning to prepare for active service; the men were not told their destination, but in a bustle of activity, weapons and equipment were checked, the men drew new uniforms, specialists were given refresher training, and medical inspections weeded out the unfit. While some of these were relieved to be staying in barracks, other older veterans were furiously ashamed to be rejected, and pulled every string they could to get back on the roster. On 19 April the final telegram arrived; it was a Sunday, and at Kreider the men were scattered around the vicinity of the camp when they heard the bugles blowing 'General Assembly' to call them in at a run from the farm and the sports fields. As they packed their knapsacks there was fevered guesswork about their destination – Tonkin? Syria? The last meal was cooked and eaten and rations were issued for the journey; the troops paraded in full marching order, the roll was called and the NCOs checked their inventories one last time. By late afternoon on 22 April the two companies were ready to march for the railway halt a few miles from the camp, led by the drums and bugles playing 'Le Boudin'. Simultaneously the HQ, 23rd and 24th Companies entrained at Saida.[14]

For Corporal Cooper the journey to Sidi bel Abbès took two days; after the overnight stop at the colon village of Perregaux many men had to be rousted out of bars, but the officers were indulgent – légionnaires did not desert when going on active service. At Sidi bel Abbès they were greeted by the central band of the Legion, and were finally told that they were on their way to Morocco. It was only when they passed through Tlemcen on the 24th and saw other troop trains heading west that they suspected that something major was going on, and when they alighted at Oujda that evening they heard for the first time of the Rifian attacks.[15] Six trains carried the battalion to Taza on 26 April, but from there they had to march the next 15 miles through the Touahar pass to Sidi Abdallah for lack of rolling stock (normally the men went by rail and their mules and horses followed by road, but in this emergency animals were also being packed onto trains). At Sidi Abdallah the companies were met by trucks that carried them to the almost empty Fes depot of the 3rd Foreign. There was no time to celebrate Camerone Day on 30 April, which was passed on the march to an outlying camp. Next morning they set off on foot for the Ouergha front along hot, dusty roads crowded with infantry battalions, Spahi squadrons, gun-teams and gaggles of native auxiliary cavalry.

On the night of 1 May the battalion bivouacked in a large camp below the rust-red hogsback hill at Tissa. There the VI/1st REI joined II/ and III/ RICM and two Skirmisher battalions to form Freydenberg Force, which marched on 3 May to Ain Aicha. The countryside was insecure, and the brigade moved in a wide, ponderous, triangular 'hedgehog' formation spread out over the dusty folds of ground and coordinated with difficulty by galloping liaison officers. It took them more than twelve hours to cover the 17 miles to the little town huddled under its jagged wall of grey crags and red fins, their arrival assuring its safety at last. From a hill above Ain Aicha the assembled officers were shown the summits to the north beyond the 5-mile wide river valley, where the chain of encircled outposts had now been awaiting support for a fortnight.[16]

THE GARRISONS ALL ALONG THE FRONT had been under pressure since 16 April; the Tafrant group of six posts held by 8th Company, II/RTSM had been under heavy harassing fire by day and night, and Beni Derkoul's platoon had been rationed to one litre of water per man per day. After a week of this, on the foggy night of 24/25 April determined assaults were made on all six posts, and the following night Lieutenant Franchi at Aoudour – encircled by Rifian trenches dug within 50 yards of his wire – lost the exterior blockhouse that guarded his water point, complete with its machine gun and 10,000 rounds. Captain Pietri managed to get aircraft to drop sacks of ice blocks into his posts to top up their cisterns – a hit-and-miss procedure, since the pilots did not dare fly too low or slowly through the Rifians' massed fire. Pietri's request for relief columns was refused by regimental HQ; on both his flanks 5th and 7th Companies were equally hard pressed – Captain Leboin's 7th Company HQ at Aoulai was under direct artillery fire, and his posts at Mghala, Ourtzagh, Bab Cheraka and Bou Hadi were holding off violent assaults.

On the night of 30 April/1 May the garrison of Bibane had to mount grenade and bayonet counter-attacks inside their own wire. The next day Colombat Force crossed the new trestle bridge that the Engineers had built from the village of Fes el Bali to the north bank of the Ouergha, but on 2 May the post at Bab Cheraka fell to Rifian shelling and assault (Lieutenant Moulin had already died of a gangrenous face wound, and it was Sergeant Boheme who signalled 'Adieu . . .').[17] That evening Captain Pietri was told that Colombat would resupply his posts and evacuate his casualties on the 3rd; under cover of this diversion Pietri himself managed to get through from Tafrant to Beni Derkoul, and found young Pol Lapeyre in determined spirits. Rifle and automatic fire had echoed around the hills all day, but when he returned to Tafrant on the evening of 3 May, Pietri learned that

General Colombat had been unable to break through the Berber trenches encircling Bibane, despite six hours' fighting.[18]

Captain Prince Aage was then serving on Marshal Lyautey's staff at Rabat. At dinner on 2 May a cable arrived from General Chambrun in Fes reporting that Cambay Force around Kifane had been beaten back and that Colombat Force was taking heavy losses, and requesting permission to withdraw all the posts north of the Ouergha at his own judgement. Lyautey refused, and ordered his staff to prepare for a move to Fes the next day. On their arrival they learned that twelve infantry battalions and artillery were promised from Algeria, but that these could not be expected for another two weeks.[19]

ON MONDAY 4 MAY the 6th Battalion, 1st Foreign formed the vanguard of Freydenberg Force as it marched north from Ain Aicha to relieve a group of posts on the 2,000-foot ridge of Taounate. This series of summits stretches for about $2\frac{1}{2}$ miles along a north-south feature above the Oued Sra, a northern tributary of the Ouergha, and from its heights some 1,500 Berbers surrounding the posts dominated the entrances to two important valleys. Screened by the usual *partisan* irregulars, the VI/1st advanced from west to east through fields of tall grain; when they were about $2\frac{1}{2}$ miles from the ridge they heard the irregulars in action, and these soon fell back. The Cazaban Battalion received their first shots as they approached the slopes of the ridge at about 8am, and after a brief artillery preparation they were ordered to attack the heights across a front of about 800 yards.

Major Jean Cazaban, who was then 43 years old, had arrived at the 1st Foreign in 1910. After four years as a lieutenant on the Moulouya front he had been among those who transferred to the Metropolitan Army on the outbreak of the Great War. He had spent four years on the Western Front with the 18th Line Infantry, during which time he collected three wounds and seven citations. He brought his accumulated experience back to the Legion in 1924 to take command of VI/1st REI; a photo of the time shows a trim, hawk-faced officer with an unsmiling expression, and Corporal Cooper wrote that he was not a commander who made any attempt to court popularity. However, he was both decisive and competent; his correspondence over the following weeks shows concern for the growing exhaustion of his 'glorious rogues, sashed with blue', while he would work himself half to death during recurring bouts of dysentery.[20]

A man of Cazaban's background could organize this kind of textbook assault in his sleep. From left to right, he deployed 23rd Company (Captain

Depesseville), 21st (Villiers Moramé) and 22nd (Pechkoff), each in line with trailing files on the flanks and each followed by its combat mule-train; behind the centre company Cazaban followed with his command group, including his bugler, runners, artillery-spotters and semaphore signallers with red-and-white flags. Captain Billaud's 24th Company was in reserve, about 300 yards behind the assault companies and ready to shore up a weakness, exploit a success or extend the line on either flank; the battalion mule-train stayed well in the rear.[21] The slopes were a mixture of rough grassland broken up by patches of trees and rocks, and terraced plots surrounding several small hamlets, all of it offering the tribesmen good cover.

As the légionnaires advanced up the slopes they could hear the whooping of the Berber women encouraging their men – 'you-you-you-you-you ...'; the intensity of the firing increased, and men began to fall. Captain Villiers Moramé took a bullet in the thigh but kept command of his central company, which became pinned down in rocks half way up the hillside; the 23rd Company on its left were a little behind, the 22nd on its right a little ahead. There is a large gulley running diagonally down the slope from top left to bottom centre; presumably Captain Pechkoff's men were climbing the uninterrupted slope to the south of this, while it presented an obstacle to the centre and left companies.[22] The battalion paused to catch its breath, and Major Cazaban called in a few more rounds of artillery on a troublesome group of buildings. Pechkoff's company took cover around a derelict walled hamlet, and as soon as their advance halted the Berbers became more aggressive, darting forwards to fire before disappearing into cover again to work around to a flank:

> With my liaison men, the stretcher-bearers and officers I installed myself in
> an abandoned *kasbah*. ... We set up our machine guns, holding under our
> fire the slope ... with its terraces of fenced gardens and houses ... soon the
> *kasbah* was full of men with shattered legs and arms or wounds in the chest,
> stomach or head. Our first-aid men and stretcher-bearers risked their lives
> many times to bring in their maimed comrades. The Legion was eager to go
> forward. We knew by experience that the longer we waited the more difficult
> it would be to attain our objective.

Eventually the battalion's eight machine guns were concentrated in a single battery and given new targets (perhaps a sign that the Western Front veteran Cazaban was among those who were uncomfortable with the new four-company structure with dispersed MG platoons). At about 2pm the bugles sounded 'Advance!', and the companies resumed their climb upwards and eastwards. Pechkoff describes them trudging

> slowly, steadily, unwaveringly, and as far as the eye could reach we saw our men going on and on, climbing the rocks, falling, climbing again, all of them in order ... We passed a [large] village on our right ... The place was searched and not a soul was found, but there were a lot of sheep and fowl wandering about the courtyards ... Before leaving [the légionnaires] stored up chickens in their haversacks ... for the evening meal.

Major Cazaban sent Baillaud's 24th Company slanting up southward behind Pechkoff's 22nd, to extend its front to the right as it reached the crest at around 2.30pm. With this support on the high ground to his right, Villiers Moramé climbed to the centre of the feature, followed by Depesseville's company on his left; by 3pm the whole ridge was in French hands, and the Moroccan Skirmishers besieged in the strongly walled post and its satellites had been relieved. The battalion's casualties were 11 killed and 53 wounded – about 10 per cent.[23] (The order and discipline with which the Legion man-oeuvred under fire is mentioned admiringly by a number of observers, but it had its drawbacks in Morocco. A multilingual force necessarily had to be trained by example and repetition, and this instilled a certain inflexibility.[24] More suppleness was needed when fighting a guerrilla enemy, and a number of units – including Cazaban's – formed *groupe francs* or 'free platoons' of picked men for patrols, counter-infiltration and night actions.)

The next morning the mobile group made a two-hour march south to establish a large defended camp on the Gara de Mezziat, a broad conical feature giving good fields of fire for defence, and views up and down the Ouergha valley.[25] At 2.30am on 6 May, the VI/1st Foreign were roused to form the vanguard for a column to withdraw the garrison from the post of Bab Ouender, marching north-east up the valley 'in the bright light of the full moon'. They remained at the foot of the hill while a Moroccan battalion climbed to the post; after hours of delay Major Cazaban was informed that the Skirmishers would spend the night there, so his unit, now providing the rearguard, could only start back for Gara de Mezziat in the late afternoon. Predictably, they were closely followed (as every retreating rearguard would be, throughout this campaign), and the difficulty of telling *partisans* from enemies in the failing light led to further delays. Immediately after the rearguard reached camp the perimeter was attacked in some strength, and during this confused firefight in the darkness Captain Pechkoff heard incoming machine-gun fire and grenades. The Cazaban Battalion lost 5 dead and 11 wounded, and the flanks of Pechkoff's pale horse were streaked with the blood of a casualty he had lifted into his saddle. Corporal Cooper believed that some Rifians actually got inside the camp, leading to 'friendly fire' casualties.[26] On that same 6 May, 18 miles to the west, the tiny garrison at Ourtzagh – little more than a hastily fortified shepherd's hut – surrendered, and when a patrol reached the site on the 13th they found the bodies of Sergeant Joandet and his 17 Senegalese grossly mutilated. That night Mghala post was abandoned, leaving Aoulai isolated.[27]

ON 9 MAY, *PARTISANS* proved their worth when Captain Mège's Beni Ouarain relieved Ain Maatouf, while VI/1st REI resupplied the airstrip camp at Mediouna. (Events contradicted intelligence predictions about the relative loyalty of some tribes; some contingents of the generally hostile Beni Ouarain and Ait Segrushin fought for the French, while some trusted clans rebelled.) That day Lyautey's headquarters issued a communiqué claiming that 'the situation is neither grave nor disquieting'. Freydenberg Force then moved westwards to the posts of Astar, Amzez and Taleghza above the Oueds Sahela and Axmer; on 15 May, Taleghza would be abandoned, Amzez came under shellfire and Taounate and other posts were assaulted. The Rifians' need to divide their modest force of serviceable artillery between the Tetuan, Ouergha, Kifane and Melilla fronts limited its use, as did the difficulty of moving guns and shells over the mountain trails by mule, but where they did get into action they were shockingly effective against the drystone defences of the posts, which the Berbers could usually hit by 'walking' shells across the ground until they got the range. A post at Bou Halima was one of several destroyed when the magazine was hit.[28]

On 12 May the first company of West African reinforcements reached Tafrant, and the next day Colombat Force mounted a resupply operation to Bibane, which had been signalling appeals for ice drops; Sergeant Bernez-Cambot had 11 wounded among his 30 surviving men. It was only 3 miles along the trail from Tafrant, but it took General Colombat six hours – and flanking operations by cavalry, aircraft and *partisans* – to fight his central column of three battalions up the steep, rocky slopes behind a rolling artillery barrage, and through two rings of Berber trenches facing outwards and inwards. Hardcore Ait Waryaghar fighters had been reported here for the past month; Rifian machine guns stopped first one, then a second unit, and Colombat had to commit his reserve battalion in order to break through –

this was emphatically nothing like any tribal campaign the French had ever fought before. When they reached the battered, roofless post the column exchanged ammunition, rations and water for Bernez-Cambot's casualties; although wounded in the neck and thigh, he himself refused to leave, so Colombat left him Lieutenant-Colonel Fèral's sappers to help restore his defences and was gone within three hours. (One of the casualties that day was a Legion officer, Captain Marc Volokhoff of 3rd REI, a Russian veteran of the Western Front who had qualified as a pilot in 1917 and was now detached to 37th Air Observation Regiment. Flying a Breguet 14 on low-level bombing missions over Bibane on 13 May, he was wounded by ground fire, and cited for his second gallantry decoration.)[29]

On 13–15 May, one of Colombat's assets was half of II/2nd REI (Major Goret), newly arrived from the Atlas, which fought in the relief of Bibane and Aoulai. Part of Colombat Force also resupplied Dar Remich, where Sergeants Peron and Fontaine and their 15 Senegalese had run out of water four days previously; the failure of a party sent out to try to reach a spring was advertised by the corpse of a Skirmisher dangling by his heels from a tree 100 yards outside the perimeter. In the Moroccan summer a man needed at least 3 litres of water daily, but in some posts this had to be reduced to half a litre, and rations of hard tack and tinned meat aggravated thirst. (In this dry heat a man hardly sweats, and when dehydrated he only urinates perhaps every second day. The saliva thickens and tastes foul, the tongue is glued to the palate, the throat feels clogged, both speech and – oddly – hearing become difficult, there are severe head and neck pains, and some men begin to hallucinate.) Again, Dar Remich was simply given water, ammunition and 20 days' rations and left to hang on as best it could.[30]

ON 21 MAY THE CAZABAN BATTALION left Gara de Mezziat as part of a Freydenberg Force mission to evacuate and destroy a group of posts about 7 miles north-east up the Ouergha valley – Srima, Bou Adel, Bab Djenane and Sidi Ahmet.[31] This country had once been thickly populated but was now abandoned; Corporal Cooper recalled passing through villages rich with olive groves, orange and fig trees and seeing 'not a soul, not a chicken, not a dog in the homesteads, where the hearths were cold but there was no debris indicating a hasty departure – it seemed to be a deliberate evacuation'. At Srima they found an Algerian sergeant and 4 survivors with the bodies of 14 dead; they came under fire from hills above, and lost 2 men killed before blowing up the post and marching on to Bou Adel to await instructions. From a hilltop Pechkoff watched Moroccan troops wrecking and evacuating the main post of Sidi Ahmet on the next height, and Cooper, being experienced with explosives, was assigned to a demolition team. Each pair of men with a short crowbar and a sledgehammer drilled a hole in hard ground at a corner of the fort to take a stick charge, detonator and 'Bickford cord' time fuse, while the other men piled up nearby all the ammunition and rations that could not be carried away.

When the charges were blown the légionnaires set off towards the Ouergha crossing in carefree spirits, and had stopped for a rest at the top of a steep wooded hill just over a mile from Bou Adel when 'one of the men from the rear came pelting up and said [the Berbers] were almost upon us'. Cooper wrote that the usual leap-frogging retreat by alternate companies broke down, and that as large numbers of tribesmen appeared on their right 'the men and even the officers lost their heads. The men and the machine guns tumbled down the steep slope in a panic. I happened to be beside Major Cazaban, so I stuck close, reckoning that I couldn't go wrong if I stayed with him'. Captain Pechkoff, whose 22nd Company had been left as rearguard with orders to hold their position until they saw the last elements crossing the river, describes a more orderly fighting retreat:

> After the smoke [of demolition] disappeared we saw groups of men clad in
> white and grey burnouses roaming around ... these groups increased in
> number as the minutes passed. I saw clearly that the retreat would be most
> difficult. Here we were, left almost alone; we had to form our own flanks
> and our own rearguard ... When the other troops were about to cross the
> river I began to send all the mules [with the wounded and the machine guns]
> back. The descent from this mountain was abrupt and precipitous ...
> I counted on the swiftness of my men, depending only on their rifles and hand
> grenades to make our way through ... When I saw that my heavy material
> and animals were reaching the river I ordered the men to retreat. But no
> sooner did we leave the strategic points that we were occupying than we
> heard the enemy yelling ... quite near. They came at us from all sides. I did
> not stop the movement. Our rearguard was formed of picked men ... who
> had proven themselves to be the most level-headed.

Pechkoff placed his rearguard concealed among the olive trees, and held their fire until the first pursuers were at close range; then he blew his whistle to unleash a volley, followed by a violent charge that won the company a little time to withdraw. However, they were still under fire all the way down to the last ridge that had to be crossed before they reached the river, and the légionnaires had to take turns carrying the wounded on their backs. On the last down-slope they were hampered by thick trees that covered attacks from behind and both flanks. Half Pechkoff's company were across the river when he and the last two platoons were cut off and surrounded; one of his runners got through to the leading *peloton*, which turned and waded back to extricate him. When the company finally began to cross together they saw that Berbers were also wading the river on either side of them, and looked certain to reach the far bank before they did:

> Nothing remained for us to do but to stop and fight, standing there [armpit-deep] in the water ... 'Fire!' was ordered. The men raised their rifles, and platoons on the left and right [opened fire] at the Rifians. They were amazed ... Some of them started to go back. Many fell. Only a few replied to our fire ... Thanks to the courage and discipline of the men we succeeded in getting across.[32]

As Freydenberg's brigade continued this operation the following day, Captain Depesseville's 23rd Company, VI/1st REI had men killed and wounded by the mistaken bombing of Amzou village by French aircraft. After a hard withdrawal, the battalion was harassed in its camp at Srima that night, and Lieutenant Fain of 21st Company took 10 men out on a grenade raid, which proved successful. (The sortie was heavily oversubscribed by eager volunteers, and may have given young Fain and his légionnaires a taste for this sort of thing that would prove fatal a couple of weeks later.) The day had cost Cazaban 5 killed, 7 missing and 29 wounded.[33]

AFTER PUNISHING AN INCAUTIOUS Rifian advance on 15 May, the Bibane garrison enjoyed a relative respite while their defences were strengthened, and a sortie on the 18th destroyed some Berber trenches. On 23 May Captain Pietri managed to reach them, and was conferring with Bernez-Cambot when Sergeant Peron at Dar Remich signalled that about 100 Berbers 'and some Europeans' were installing a cannon on a height to his north-east. That afternoon four shells fell at Bibane and two more at Dar Remich; Pietri gave permission for Peron and Fontaine to withdraw their squad inside Bibane that night. On the night of 24/25 May, Sergeant Fontaine was killed during a five-hour attack on Bibane by up to 2,000 Berbers, and about 20 shells were fired at the post.[34] Lieutenant-Colonel Feral's Engineers would soon finish their work there and had to return to Tafrant, as did two units of Skirmishers that had been left lower down the hillsides when Colombat pulled back on 15 May. The operation on 25 May to recover them and resupply the Bibane garrison once more would earn one Legion officer particular respect.

Major Marcel Deslandes had entered St Maixent as a 25-year-old Line sergeant in 1909. Commissioned into the 162nd Infantry two years later, he was wounded four times and earned five gallantry citations during the Great War. After transferring to the Legion he took command of II/1st REI based at Géryville in October 1921. Private Charles Ziegler arrived at that dreary post in February 1925, and recalled that Deslandes was a tireless conductor of tactical exercises. Slogging over the high plains with a machine gun on his shoulder, Ziegler did not realize how valuable the major's insistent lectures on 'unhooking under fire' would prove. He recalled the pipe-smoking Deslandes as a solid, reassuring presence, demanding but always just, who led by example like the sergeant he had once been.

On 6 May 1925, the 2nd Battalion of 1st Foreign departed for the Rif front; they made a four-day march over the plains in full packs 'to get them in shape' before they met their trains, and by the 19th of the month they were at Ain Defali, drawing ammunition and rations and sending their knapsacks and khaki wool winter uniforms back to stores. On 23–24 May they marched east to the flea-ridden ruins of Fes el Bali and the base camp of Colombat Force, beside the red-brown river meandering through fields of grain and poppies. Ziegler was struck by the green of the Ouergha valley after the dead ochre of the Algerian high plains.[35] The view to the north was dominated by the hulking shape of Bibane, and another man gazing thoughtfully up at it was Captain Prince Aage, now serving on the Colombat Force staff. On the evening of 24 May, a signal warned Féral that Colonel Naugés would bring 2,000 troops to break through and pull his sappers out the following morning.

CROSSING THE BRIDGE before dawn, by 6.30am Aage was at the jumping-off point for the left flank unit in a dip below the southern slope of Bibane. Morning mist hid the first Rifian trenches about 300 yards above them, but the opening of the artillery barrage was the signal for the infantry to advance and Aage followed, in a 'sort of coma' at the noise. He only realized that enemy machine guns were replying when he began to pass groups of French casualties. As the Algerian *turcos* reached the first trench, mistimed French airbursts killed friend and foe together, and Aage sent several runners back to warn the batteries, but by the time the barrage lifted Rifian machine guns were pinning down any further advance. They were sweeping the slope from a low, thick-walled stone building to the left front; the artillery seemed unable to silence it, and grenade parties had no more success. The advance was also stalled on the right; a Senegalese unit was committed in support of the Algerians, but as the morning wore on the casualties mounted with little progress made.

The Deslandes Battalion had started the day in reserve, but at around noon they were called forwards and ordered to assault straight ahead. They advanced in line to the sound of bugles, with two companies 'up' – 7th on the left, 5th on the right – followed by 6th and 8th respectively, with Major Deslandes' command group close behind the trailing inside flank files at the junction of the two lead companies. Bibane is a major feature several thousand yards wide from east to west, its broad slopes scattered with hamlets wherever anything can be coaxed to grow. The terrain on the south is steep and broken by clusters of rocks offering ideal cover, and in 1925 it was defended by piled stone 'blockhouses' and well-disguised trenches, their approaches protected by abatis of thorny Barbary figs almost as effective as barbed wire. Under a blazing sun and heavy fire from small arms and machine guns, the lead companies of II/1st Foreign fought their way upwards, but were repeatedly checked – one account speaks of seven distinct attempts.

Accounts of famous charges are always romanticized, but what seems to have happened is that at some point the battalion were pinned down by fire from a trench approximately 50 yards ahead; officer casualties had been heavy, and Deslandes had (according to one source) only seven others still on their feet. The major called them to him, told each to get himself a haversack of grenades, and explained that they were going to take the trench in Great War style. Taking his place in the centre with his own satchel of grenades, he spaced the officers along the line; at Deslandes' whistle-blast they surged forwards, hurling grenades, dropping, then springing up again to dash forward and throw another. Their men leapt up to follow them, and in perhaps half a minute they had reached the Berber trench to clear it hand-to-hand. (If they could lay hands on one, the légionnaires preferred to use a captured Mauser bayonet as a dagger rather than relying on the fragile needle-bayonet of the Lebel.)

The battalion then came under heavy enfilade fire from Rifians who were dug in on a hillock to their right flank, and Colombat's other Legion unit – Major Goret's two-company detachment from II/2nd REI – was sent against this. Perhaps inspired by Deslandes' example, Captain Demart of its 6th Company made an ill-judged attempt after only a few rounds of artillery preparation, and he and many of his men were shot down as soon as they left cover. The semaphore signallers flagged a request for more artillery before 7th Company tried a rush in their turn, but they too were pinned down (the supply of shells to the Rif front line was inadequate, and ammunition always had to be husbanded). Prince Aage reported the situation to General Colombat; after a further barrage a final effort was made at about 1.30pm, and soon afterwards uncoordinated Rifian withdrawals allowed the French to reach the post on the summit.

Typically, their own withdrawal through the grainfields to Tafrant that evening – leaving Bernez-Cambot on his hilltop with just 6 other Frenchmen and 47 Senegalese – was stubbornly contested, and had to be covered by artillery fire and four squadrons of Spahis. The operation had cost Colombat Force more than 100 killed and 300 wounded (Prince Aage actually reckoned the total at 500). From a strength of 500 committed, Major Stephani's 19th Algerian Marching Battalion had lost 132 all ranks including a company commander and 5 lieutenants; Marcel Deslandes' légionnaires had suffered 60 casualties, and the only two companies of the Goret Battalion lost 67 killed and wounded. In all, the repeated battles to sustain Bibane during May had by now cost more than 400 French killed and between two and three times that many wounded.[36]

LYAUTEY STILL HAD NOT RECEIVED any substantial reinforcements, and was wary of meeting the pressure in the north by stripping the interior garrisons any further; his great fear was that the infection might spread to the Atlas (though in the event the tribes on the Khenifra front became restless only during that autumn). The political litmus paper was Fes; there the ever-querulous business community might celebrate Abd el Krim's victories in the coffee-houses, but in fact they would far rather deal with Lyautey's regime than with a stern *cadi* from the northern mountains.[37]

Nevertheless, the cost to Chambrun's mobile groups of maintaining the posts north of the Ouergha was becoming prohibitive. On 26 May, the garrisons of five more were withdrawn and the Rifians promptly flowed forwards into the gaps, further imperilling those that remained. At Ain Maatouf, east of Ain Aicha, in the vulnerable margin where Henri Frey-denberg's and Albert Cambay's responsibilities met, Sergeant Magnien of 9th Company, 1st RTSM had already been killed, and Private 2nd Class

Berger was leading the defence of this lonely hilltop, its lifeline to the west threatened by a glowering rock cathedral overlooking the fort from about 1,000 yards away. On 30 May the platoon was withdrawn; Berger was awarded the Médaille Militaire, but he and his Senegalese were simply transferred to reinforce Warrant Officer Chrétien of 5th Company at Kouba post, where they would be wiped out a month later. With Ait Maatouf gone and the main camp of Freydenberg Force now at Gara de Mezziat, the French boys of Major Blachère's II/RICM at Ain Aicha were judged to be too isolated, and were ordered south to Tissa. During their night march on the 31st they fell into an ambush at Ouled Daoud; Lieutenants Pagnard and Bertet died with at least 30 of their men, and 37 more were wounded.[38]

WHILE THE GARRISONS of the Tafrant group of posts withstood repeated attacks in the last week of May, a new threat to Ouezzane in the north-west distracted General Colombat's attention. Close to the zonal border with the Djibala, posts north and east of this vital anchor point were coming under attack from a new 3,000-strong *harka* led by Abd el Krim's regional general, the young Ahmed Heriro.[39] The overstretched Colombat now had to deploy troops to block these approaches to the rich plains north-west of Fes, and one of the units was II/1st REI, sent west only two days after its ordeal at Bibane. The Deslandes Battalion reached Ouezzane on 31 May, and Charles Ziegler was in the ranks of 8th Company as they struggled painfully through the last baking gorge under their heavy packs:

> Worn out, shattered, with parched throats, we covered the last few kilometres; men and animals alike were at the end of their strength in the torrid heat. With feverish eyes, the officers tried to find some word, some gesture to lift the morale of their men. Mules collapsed and could not be got back on their feet. What a brilliant idea to set us on the march from Teroual at noon, loaded down like beasts in 50 degrees in the shade! [122°F] ... The last few minutes seemed like an eternity.
>
> A domed shrine appeared on the right; then, up there on the left, pinky-white amid the olive groves, Ouezzane ... What an enchantment! The white road alongside a clear, tinkling stream led us into one of the most charming little towns to be found in Morocco. Pretty red-roofed houses, in a style mixing the Arab with the Spanish taste, rose up the terraced slope ... in little gardens full of vegetables and fruit trees of all kinds. From the entrance to the town one can see the whole tableau at one glance, a masterpiece set

against the dark green of the olive groves, its inhabitants going peacefully about their business ...

On 1 June the battalion marched north to resupply the border posts on the upper Loukos river – Brikcha, Ouled Allal and Rihana. At first they saw no action, simply the usual interminable panting up and down hills to picket the convoy routes, and in his brief off-duty hours Ziegler found that a cool, shady tavern in Ouezzane had rather more to offer than the verminous villages of the Ouergha valley:

> In the square a big sign identifies the Hôtel et Café de France, a two-storey
> Spanish-style estaminet. In the corner of the room is the band – a violin,
> two *guislas* and a few tambourines – and in the middle of the floor dances
> the lovely young Ourida, dressed only in a simple veil. Repetitive, rhythmic,
> in perfect harmony – it is a delight to watch her.[40]

WHILE LÉGIONNAIRE ZIEGLER was enjoying a rare genuine taste of what the recruiting posters had cynically promised, in Paris the political classes were vociferously divided, but Prime Minister Paul Painlevé (who also held the War Ministry portfolio) had clearly understood the need to stop Abd el Krim militarily before there could be any question of diplomacy. He endorsed Lyautey's calls for significant reinforcements from the Ruhr, though not his request on 4 May for poison gas shells; he also ignored the marshal's continued reluctance to liaise with the Spanish, and sent envoys to Madrid on 14 May for extended talks. These examples seem to cast doubt on Lyautey's judgement both tactical and strategic, particularly his apparent wish to limit French operations strictly to his side of the now meaningless zonal borderline. Lyautey reported on 25 May that he had appointed General Albert Daugan from Marrakesh to command of the Northern Front; Daugan's operations chief would be General Gaston Bilotte, and General Chambrun was demoted to control of political affairs.[41]

On 4 June the prime minister reported to parliament that French casualties in the first six weeks' fighting were 1,628 men killed, missing and wounded, adding – unattractively – that 60 per cent of these were native troops.[42] He faced a restless Chamber, and some Communists were even publicly congratulating Abd el Krim for his anti-imperialist victories. Throughout the summer the government felt a need to massage the facts for French and overseas public consumption; casualty figures were understated, and there is an unmistakably Clintonesque care over the exact choice of words in Chambrun's statement at the end of May that only 'four fortifications of 40 built in 1924 were then in enemy hands'.

While Lyautey's staff were being shuffled, the movement of Colombat's battalions westwards was overstretching, in its turn, Freydenberg's defence of the central Ouergha. Mhamed Abd el Krim took advantage of this unbalancing of the French front to send strong forces across the river between Ain Aicha and Kelaa des Sless; they thrust southwards into Fichtala and Hayana tribal territory, where they would disturb the approaches to Fes for much of June. Their overture was the capture on 2 June of the post of Astar, and it was decided that with that dominating hilltop in Berber hands, the fort at Sker, a mile or so up the Oued Sra valley to the north-east, was no longer defensible.

The withdrawal of Sker's garrison would require several of Freydenberg's units, and that chosen to provide high cover by temporarily reoccupying Astar on 4 June was the VI/1st REI. Over the previous ten days Major Cazaban's battalion had been marching out daily from Gara de Mezziat to relieve and resupply posts on the Oued Sahela and Sra. The countryside was completely insecure, but although they had suffered some sniping, and Rifian guns at Taleghza had dropped shells close enough to shower Cooper's and Pechkoff's companies with dirt, they had not seen serious combat since Bou Adel – on 2 June they actually had a rest day. The following afternoon they were marched up to Taounate with two Skirmisher battalions and four artillery batteries ready for an early start the next morning. It would be an operation of no particular significance, but it stands for dozens of others fought that summer. It was hastily prepared, in unavoidable ignorance of the opposition; the resources provided were adequate on paper, but an important part of the plan failed (as plans nearly always do under the pressure of events); it was successful, if a retreat can be called a success; the terrain on which it was fought was extremely difficult; and it cost the Legion battalion dearly.[43]

THE HILL OF ASTAR is roughly teardrop-shaped, sloping up from the west towards a summit at its north-east end. It is about $1\frac{3}{4}$ miles long from west to east, and rises perhaps 1,500 feet above its surroundings. From the north and east of the summit the drops are at first almost sheer; the slope to the south is steep, but that to the west – overlooked by another, larger and slightly higher hill – is more moderate. Photographs published by Henry Clerisse in 1927 show hamlets and farmsteads on grassy lower slopes dotted with olive groves, but the upper part of the long western slope appears almost naked (as is confirmed by Pechkoff).

The abandoned post was on the north-east summit, clinging awkwardly to an east–west lip of level ground only a few yards wide between the brink of the northern ravine and the top of a stony 30-degree southern slope. The area of the post was otherwise entirely on this sharply southwards-tilted ground, as if built on the ridge and one slope of a pitched roof, and was thus very exposed to fire from the neighbouring hill a few hundred yards to the west. To the north, the outlook is a series of ridges receding towards 6,000-foot peaks about 12 miles away; to the east, the summit today overlooks the more recently built-up areas at the north of Taounate. The southern skyline is the Ouled Daoud ridge about 15 miles distant; short of that, the summit of Ait Maatouf, perhaps 9 miles south-east of Astar and easily identifiable by its accompanying rock sugarloaf, is clearly visible with binoculars (a reminder that in this terrain line-of-sight signalling with optical equipment was often practicable).[44]

The battalion marched from Taounate early on the morning of 4 June, with about 3 miles to cover to the north-western foot of Astar. Pechkoff writes that this was the first time the battalion had heavy artillery support from the start, including two 155mm howitzers. A timed barrage preceded the infantry – the Legion in the centre, flanked by two Moroccan battalions – across the intermediate ground to the foot of the hill, and then briefly hammered the slopes.[45] Pechkoff states that the Moroccan units failed to keep up; Major Cazaban writes that his own battalion reached the north-west base of Astar at 6am, and 'climbed the slopes at great speed despite brisk fire from the left flank – a big village and olive groves'.

Pechkoff's 22nd Company were half way up the western hillside before suffering any casualties, when Berbers opened fire from 'caves' dug in the slope; Pechkoff detailed most of his men to take care of these while one platoon pressed on. He writes that one of his subalterns reached the summit first as the Rifians abandoned it, and that a few prisoners were taken from the 'caves'. Cazaban times his arrival at the post at 7.20am, 'having taken only a few casualties'. However, the steepness of the final slopes defeated the mules carrying the machine guns and supplies; these had to be unloaded 400 yards below the summit for man-packing, and the mules were sent back to Taounate.[46]

No source describes the plan of the defences in any detail, and on the ground it is hard to reconcile today's vestigial remains with the theoretical layout of such posts (see Map 22). The northern edge of the summit is a level shelf perhaps 120 yards long by only 10 yards wide, with the remains of substantial drystone walls along the northern and southern lips and transverse walls at the ends and elsewhere. Centred on the steep slope south of this is the concrete water cistern, and a faint line of rubble across the slope below this suggests a second range of buildings; a formless mass of stones now lies beyond its eastern end, south of the artillery platform at the north-east corner of the summit. Southwards again, centred perhaps 120 yards below the summit, the overgrown knee-high ruin of a little building only about 5 yards long shows an internal partition and traces of rough plastering (the author's local guide, an ex-soldier, called this 'the commander's house'). There is no sign today of any perimeter walls on the east, south or west sides. In the scrub perhaps another 100 yards south of the 'commander's house' there are clear traces of an arc of trenches, backed by a couple of piled-stone *sangars* that could be MG positions, but there is no way of telling whether these date from the French or the Rifian occupations, and we know that Abd el Krim's men often dug trenches. Pechkoff writes that on 4 June 'the walls were still standing, although there were breaches here and there', and again 'we were behind thick walls and had placed machine guns on the bastions'. One striking feature is a steep staircase of little plateaux thrusting out to the north-west, well below the north-west corner of the summit, where in 2007 Graham Scott found signs of defences sited to cover both the western approach to the hilltop and its almost sheer north face.

As soon as VI/1st Foreign reached the summit they began organizing its defence, but the Rifians gave them very little time before bringing them under heavy fire and – since grenades are mentioned – pressing in closely. The fort entrance, on the west, was too exposed to use, and men had to break a new one in the southern wall. Pechkoff complains that 'we were isolated. There was no continuation of our line on the flank, because the other units did not occupy in the specified time the assigned positions' – which suggests that one of the Skirmisher battalions that had not kept up had been supposed to occupy the hill immediately to the west and south-west of Astar. The 21st Company occupied the shelves below the north-west corner, covering the access via the western slope; the 23rd held a 'hillock' to the south (conceivably the site of the still-visible trenches?), in visual contact with a Skirmisher company around a 'tower' half way down

526   OUR FRIENDS BENEATH THE SANDS

that hillside; and the 24th were apparently placed east of the 23rd 'over-looking the valley'. Major Cazaban:

> On arriving at the post we found ourselves nose-to-nose with the Moroccans,
> and had to fight with grenades. Our installation on the plateau was very
> unpleasant; the Rifs had placed snipers less than 500 yards behind [i.e. on the
> western hill], and any légionnaire who showed himself attracted a hail of
> bullets. They also had machine guns, and served them admirably. In short,
> during the day any work was almost impossible, and by nightfall the
> battalion had about 50 dead and wounded.

The légionnaires' grubby khaki drill must have blended well with the hill-side, but their off-white képi covers would make them easy to spot, and easy to count in the different positions.

The gun platform at the north-east corner of the summit was 'on the edge of a precipice'; the 75mm gun was found to have been dragged off and dumped lower down, minus its breechblock. Pechkoff's 22nd Company held the post itself, sheltering the wounded in the 'half-destroyed barracks'; the stench of decomposition led them to a shallow grave holding the corpse of a French sergeant whose charred feet and legs showed that he had been tortured, perhaps to reveal the breechblock's hiding place. (There is no further mention of the prisoners taken during the assault, and we may wonder whether this grisly discovery led to their being shot. Cooper insists that Pechkoff was a reflective and humane man, even towards the enemy; but Berbers surrendered as reluctantly as Japanese soldiers twenty years later, and given their treatment of French casualties there was no inclination to go to the trouble of guarding them.)

Pechkoff placed one of his platoons with machine guns on the artillery platform, 'formerly connected with the outpost by a trench through which one could walk to the platform unseen. Now the entrance from the post was filled up and there were 20 yards of bare ground to cover before we could enter the trench [, which we] occupied ...'. (Today the unprotected circular gun platform of beaten clay is quite evident, as is the shallow trace of an access trench with a drystone parapet.) Pechkoff's légionnaires had not been in position more than half an hour before they were

> attacked heavily from all sides. We could not believe ... that anyone could
> hide among these steep rocks. Yet on all sides we saw white and grey
> burnouses creeping cautiously from one stone to another. Our men in the

trenches and on the platform had to repel successive attacks ... Several
times the enemy reached the edge of the platform, only to be kicked off by
our men. The firing was incessant ... The Rifians came on us in a flood. We
threw hand grenades into [their] midst ... [and drove] them out of the trench
and off the platform with bayonets. It lasted for more than an hour ...

This account is extraordinary when one sees the dramatic slopes north
and east of the gun platform, but Rifians are born mountaineers with legs
like steel springs. The exposed platoon almost ran out of ammunition,
and Pechkoff describes two of his men walking insouciantly back to the
walls to collect more, with bullets kicking dust around their feet. His
company took at least 21 casualties, and a platoon from the less hard-
pressed 23rd had to come up to reinforce him. There is a suggestion that
at about 4.30pm there was an ill-informed signal requesting Cazaban to
send one or two of his companies back down to the valley – if this is
true, he certainly did not comply. Pechkoff writes that the order to spend
the night on the summit arrived in early evening; the night was very dark
and misty and the légionnaires were kept on the alert, but no attacks
were made on them despite the opportunities for infiltration offered by
the badly damaged wire.

The morning of 5 June dawned clear and sunny, but Major Cazaban was
clearly seething with impatience for orders. At 6.50am he signalled Colonel
Mativet at Mobile Group Headquarters:

1. Will Astar be re-occupied, and if so by what garrison – or will it be
abandoned?
2. Send up mules for the machine guns and battalion baggage to the base of
the slope an hour before my disengagement.
3. I have three men wounded too seriously for [carried] stretchers and will
need mule-litters for them. When I am warned of the mules' arrival I will
transfer the casualties.
4. I need two extra [carried] stretchers for casualties from 24th Company.
5. I have in all nearly 60 killed and wounded.

Mativet replied to this testy signal with assurances that the mules and
stretchers would be sent, and that there was no question of holding on to
the hill. Below it, the operation by Colonel Callais' Moroccan Skirmishers
to cover the withdrawal from Sker could be seen and heard. The dead were
buried on the hilltop and the wounded were prepared for carrying down to

the mule rendezvous. From this point the two main accounts differ in emphasis. Captain Pechkoff – writing for publication – has a signal arriving 'soon', reporting the success of the Sker operation and informing VI/1st REI that the main force would begin falling back at 7am:

'Keep strict watch to your right and left. Enemies reported in your direction. When you see the blockhouse nearest to you blown up, prepare to leave the post within half an hour ... You will become the rearguard to protect our retreat.' The nearest blockhouse was blown up. As always, the heavy material was sent on ahead. The wounded were evacuated. The men carrying the machine guns on their backs followed. Now we had to slip down the mountain as quickly as possible ... We tried to make our preparations without the enemy noticing; although we could not see them they were certainly all around us. We threw ourselves down from the summit in a cloud of dust, but we had hardly left the post when burnouses began to converge on us from all around.

In fact it was 11 am before Lieutenant Lababe arrived to announce that the mules were waiting, and the evacuation could begin. After the wounded, stores and machine guns reached the mules, the 21st Company, as the furthest from the escape route, clambered up from their outlying shelf and pulled out first, then the 22nd, followed by the 23rd; the 24th should have gone last, but apparently they were confused by flares fired by *turcos* further down the hill and left rather early, covered by a rearguard under Lieutenant Guyon. At the bottom, 21st Company took up firing positions at the hamlet of Baid. Captain Pechkoff:

The men who reached the foot of the mountain first climbed the next crest to cover by fire the retreat of those who followed; these would then stop in their turn and protect the further retreat of the first element ... Thus the enemy, hoping for a panic flight, were confronted instead by an organized withdrawal during which the steady fire of the légionnaires inflicted heavy losses.

Our pursuers lost contact, but we still had to cross some thickly wooded country. We entered the trees by platoons, separated but in contact. The woods were full of Rifians, whom the légionnaires could not spot until they were a few yards away. The men advanced without hesitation, throwing grenades. The last element, with which I was marching, was violently attacked from the right. My orderly was close beside me, carrying a grenade that he told me was 'for you and me' ... The 20 or 30 men around us were admirably calm, manoeuvring as if on an exercise, stopping now and then to take advantage of the ground and fighting the enemy one-to-one ... At last we got out of the enemy's clutches. Not far from camp we stopped to re-form our ranks; many men were wounded ...

After seeing Pechkoff in battle, Cooper wrote that the one-armed captain habitually led from the front, firing his revolver with his left hand, but would stop to check the condition of his wounded, and when one of his men was killed he would cross himself in the Orthodox fashion – Cooper once saw him kiss a dying man on the forehead.

Major Cazaban's private letter to his regimental commander is rather more thin-lipped in tone than Pechkoff's memoir, and makes clear that the brigade's staff work had left a great deal to be desired:

I assumed that we would pull out at the same time as the battalions at Sker, but for reasons which it is not my place to discuss the order to break out reached me very late, at about 11 am, long after Callais Group had retreated to Taounate. Since 6am, foreseeing the difficulty of disengaging, I had been asking for orders, and had asked for mules to be sent up to the base of the [upper] slope an hour before I was ordered to leave. They arrived only 15 minutes in advance. My orders assured me of flanking units, and battalions placed in forward reserve west of Taounate. That was not what actually happened.

After delaying my disengagement by 10 minutes to permit the removal of the machine guns and ammunition, I was already pinned down inside the post, and it took grenades [to break out – which indicates that the Rifians were within 25 yards]. The enemy who had fought at Sker had moved [south] towards Astar to encircle us and cut off our retreat. We raced down the slopes of Astar, but from the moment of leaving the post we came under machine-gun fire from the very places where our flank guards should have been, since they had long departed. We were isolated. On our leaving the summit the Rifs sent up signal flares [ordering their men] to assemble and cut off our retreat. We speeded up, but the machine-gun fire was worthy of the Great War.

We counted on the fact that once we reached the bottom we would be welcomed and supported by the reserve units from Taounate, as I had been assured. But these units had already left, and had been replaced by the Rifs. Our withdrawal to Taounate was a painful business, under fire from behind, the flanks and the front. Nevertheless, we arrived without too many [new] losses, though exhausted ...

The battalion has been worthy of its excellent reputation, and the Legion continues to have very strong ribs; unhappily, the affair has again cost us dearly – we lost 71 dead and wounded.[47]

ON THAT SAME DAY, 5 June, the darkness finally closed over the Colonial garrison on Bibane. It was their eleventh day under direct bombardment by at least two guns, which sent 20 to 30 shells a day into the post. The garrison were forced to spend most of their time on the increasingly battered perimeter, while the Rifians in the surrounding trenches were relieved every 48 hours. Even a successful air-drop of ice blocks only gave enough water for about one mug per man, and their food was semolina sopped in a mess tin of water warmed in the sun. An assault late on 1 June had been preceded by bombardment with captured VB rifle-grenades. On the 2nd, heavy fog prevented any signals contact and kept the aircraft away; down at Tafrant, where General Colombat's staff had joined Captain Pietri, Prince Aage could hear firing all that day and the next. With Rifian forces already behind him, to his left, in the direction of Fes (and others attacking his own camp every night) Colombat dared not concentrate his overstretched units to save this one position; he knew it was doomed, and so, probably, did the 23-year-old Bernez-Cambot. On 3 June the sergeant signalled that he had lost 8 more men, and asked for artillery support; he got some, but it was fired more or less blind and ammunition was too short to keep it up for long. Prince Aage wrote that at 9am on the morning of the 5th he saw Rifian shells bursting in the air above the post (if true, then a startling sign of the enemy gunners' growing sophistication). At about 4pm that afternoon he could see movement right up against the walls; soon afterwards the flashing lamp signalled 'Post done for ... Sergeant B ...' – and then the flashes stopped. Paul Colombat, with his huge white moustaches, was a sternly nineteenth-century figure; even so, Aage wrote that on this occasion the general's eyes were wet with tears.[48]

WITH BIBANE GONE, Aoudour and Achirkane were indefensible, but Colombat's request to evacuate them was again refused by Lyautey. On 7 June, Colombat had to march west for Ouezzane with part of his remaining force, leaving a Colonel Pompey in command at Tafrant; Pompey immediately signalled the two garrisons to break out the following night if they could. Lieutenant Franchi ceased signalling from Aoudour at 9pm; soon afterwards there was a loud explosion, and repeated signals asking Franchi to send up a green flare if he was receiving went unanswered. Later that night movement and grenades were heard, so the artillery fired on fixed lines and a platoon was sent out; at about 1.30am on the 8th they returned, with Franchi and almost all his 50 Senegalese. He had cut small breaches in the front walls for his two field guns, aiming them at maximum depression, and a larger gap in the side facing the escape route, where a shell crater offered cover about 60 yards outside the wall. At the last moment he pulled long lanyards to fire the two guns simultaneously, and slipped out through the darkness. After they broke through one line of enemy with grenades, Franchi ordered his men to unload their rifles, and they cut their way almost silently through a second line with bayonets and knives alone. There was still no news of Achirkane, so a 10-minute box barrage was fired around the post at 3am. Intermittent firing and grenades were heard getting closer to Tafrant, and at about 4am Sergeant Morel and some of his platoon came in, followed by others; after a first clash they had separated into their three squads, and some of each had made it.

The daylight hours of 8 June passed quietly, since there was not enough artillery ammunition to shell the Rifians swarming over the abandoned posts and recovering the serviceable guns. These were turned on Tafrant at 9.30pm that night, but although the aim was accurate the shells were duds. Post commanders had instructions to bury the fuzes separately if artillery ammunition had to be abandoned, but in this case they were apparently found within hours, because Tafrant was shelled again to some effect that evening. (That day Major Stephani of the 19th Algerian Skirmishers was killed; from a starting strength of 800 in April, his marching battalion had by now suffered about 70 per cent casualties and was disbanded.) On 9 June, Colonel Pompey was ordered to leave only six companies and a few guns in Tafrant and to march south. From Fes el Bali that night Prince Aage watched the artillery-flashes and ghostly blue-white flares as Tafrant was attacked in force. He thought the Rifians would have done better to bypass it and follow the column, which was tired and low-spirited, burdened with baggage, wounded and 1,200 mules, and protected that night only by hastily scraped trenches.[49]

TAFRANT AND TAOUNATE, isolated and under repeated attack, were now the essential remaining bastions on the north bank. They seemed capable of holding out, and so for a time did the last lonely northern outposts at Ain Bou Aissa and Beni Derkoul, but Mediouna south of the river clearly was not. The camp at this now unusable airfield east of Ain Aicha was held by about 40 French conscripts and Senegalese of the RICM, and on 10 May Lieutenant Bouscatier signalled that he was out of water and down to the cartridges in his men's pouches. The now familiar double ring of Rifian trenches surrounded the post, and the most recent attempts to resupply it had been beaten back. At Gara de Mezziat, Colonel Freydenberg ordered the mauled VI/1st REI to try to evacuate the garrison that night.

Major Cazaban decided that trying to mount a battalion attack after blundering across some 5 miles of unknown ground in the dark would be worse than pointless, and instead formed a 'free platoon' of 40 men under Lieutenants Guyon and Fain to attempt a *coup de main* to reach Bouscatier and bring his men out. Cazaban and Guyon selected them from the many volunteers who stepped forward from different companies; they wore canvas shoes or wrapped puttees round their boots, and carried only weapons and ammunition. An aircraft dropped a warning to Bouscatier to disable the guns and have his men ready for a break-out; Pechkoff writes that the white buildings at the airfield were clearly visible from the top of Gara de Mezziat that afternoon.[50] The plan was for the *groupe franc* to leave camp at 11pm, crossing the Ouergha ford to the south-east and making their way silently towards Mediouna via the abandoned post site of Oued Drader. The rest of the battalion would follow 15 minutes later to take up a reception position at the old post, where Guyon was to rendezvous if he was successful.

The plan went wrong almost from the start, partly due to the over-eagerness of men who had been rejected for the operation. The rescue party got away on time, but was accompanied by two extra subalterns who showed more courage than discipline (Lieutenants Wable and Belaygères), and was followed without orders by perhaps 15 more légionnaires. When the battalion reached the Ouergha they had difficulty finding the ford and waded the icy river at a deeper point, with the result that in the cold night air the men would thereafter be shivering and distracted. The moon was veiled by high clouds and gave a confusing light, and as the battalion made their way east in single file through tall cornfields the officers were unable to locate the Drader rendezvous (one account puzzlingly places it on a ridge, but there seems to be no such feature between the river and the airfield). The ground of these flats is cut here and there with abrupt drainage gulleys like miniature canyons, at least 6 feet deep, which must have added to the difficulty of quiet movement on a compass bearing.

Suddenly there was a shout, and a few rifle shots rang out; some troops had got disoriented in the high, swishing grain, and there is a suggestion that they ran into some of the unauthorized men without warning. Whoever was at fault, the 'friendly firing' not only compromised the operation but wounded several men, including Captain Billaud of 24th Company – which was already missing two of its officers with the rescue party. The wounded had to be carried, which added to the noise. Two hours after crossing the river, when a flurry of grenade explosions was heard perhaps a mile ahead, the battalion were still groping around in dispersed parties. It was about 2am; after waiting for a while, the furious Major Cazaban decided that the best he could do was pass the word for his companies to fall back to the ford – which was at least a fixed point for the rescue party to aim for – and set up a reception position there.

When they had recrossed the river with some difficulty, the adjutant-major Captain Chavanne went forward again on reconnaissance, but without result. Cazaban held an officers' call, and it was only then that he discovered that Lieutenants Wable and Belaygères were missing from their companies. As first light was approaching at 4am, he ordered his shame-faced battalion back to Gara de Mezziat. As they approached the camp they were met by Spahis whose commander told Cazaban that three stragglers had come in, and that he was on his way to cross the river and search for the missing Legion platoon. The mood in camp was sombre, and even more so when a full roll-call revealed that about 60 men including the 4 lieutenants were unaccounted for.

The sources are contradictory over the exact number of survivors who straggled in, but in a private letter to his colonel Cazaban wrote that it was five. They included Corporal Vietorovsky of 23rd Company; he reported that after getting lost several times the rescue party had broken through first one, then the second ring of trenches, but that only one officer and about 10 men got inside the camp. There Lieutenant Bouscatier joined them with some of his men; together they tried to break out to the south, but before they could get beyond the wire they were surrounded by hundreds of Rifians and the action broke up into a series of desperate little hand-to-hand battles in the dark. Vietorovsky had fallen into one of the gulleys and made his way back to the river alone, where he met two other survivors. One Senegalese from the Mediouna garrison also made his way to safety; the Spahis returned without having found any other légionnaires, living or dead. In seven days Major Cazaban had lost about one-quarter of his battalion, at least half of them killed.[51]

On 12 June the VI/1st Foreign paraded at Gara de Mezziat before not only Marshal Lyautey but also Marshal Philippe Pétain – the professional head of the French Army – and Prime Minister Painlevé, who had flown to Morocco on a fact-finding mission.[52] Painlevé pinned the War Cross for Exterior Operations to the battalion *fanion* and decorated 50 individual officers and men. The sonorous euphemisms of the unit citation must have caused some uneasy smiles (it called the Mediouna operation a tragically qualified 'success'), but to be decorated by the prime minister in person made the hard-used battalion feel appreciated. One of four men awarded the Médaille Militaire was a Corporal Poulet of 22nd Company, a veteran of 19 years' service in the Colonial Infantry and the Legion who had fought at Fes in 1911, with the RMLE on the Western Front, and in Morocco ever since. Pechkoff describes him as the old légionnaire of folklore: promoted and busted many times, a valuable self-taught expert in many skills, a reliable volunteer for dangerous message-running, a father to the young soldiers, but a hopeless and troublesome drunk when in barracks. Hubert Lyautey still had his matchless touch; when Painlevé had pinned the yellow-and-green ribbon to Poulet's chest the marshal saluted the veteran, took off his white glove, shook his hand, asked him about his service, and then told him to report to his tent after parade. There he sat Poulet down and poured him coffee with his own hand while they continued their reminiscences – an honour of which the légionnaire boasted far more proudly than of his medal. Sadly, it was the undoing of him; his mates got him uproariously drunk that night, he neglected his duty, and finally he had to be sent back to the depot. He was not the only admired old soldier who was straining the patience of his superiors.[53]

ON 13 JUNE, PRINCE AAGE was with General Colombat at Ouezzane, where the senior commanders were convened by Marshal Pétain and Prime Minister Painlevé.[54] The French forces were still on the defensive right along the Rif 'front', and tribal irregulars were changing sides in their thousands. Lyautey was well aware that apart from Foreign Minister Briand he had little influential support in Paris, while Philippe Pétain enjoyed huge public respect and authority. In any post-mortem on the reverses of the past two months Lyautey could point to the long delay in satisfying his request of the previous December for reinforcements; nevertheless, his confident insistence on the effectiveness of his time-honoured methods had been discredited. After so many years of unchallenged authority in his field of special expertise he was bound to feel embarrassed and resentful at close scrutiny, on his own ground, by a powerful 'new management' who pressed him, however politely, to justify his opinions. A man who habitually argues his views with passion only to then shift them loses credibility: Lyautey was now urging not only the paramount importance of military rather than political action, and full cooperation with the Spanish, but even an attempt to get the British involved.[55]

Although there were encouraging signs that the Hayana confederacy north of Fes were resisting the Rifian incursions, villages around Tissa were still being burned, and there was little good news elsewhere. While General Bilotte tried to shield the capital, and Freydenberg was barely keeping alive the remaining northern posts on his central front, Colombat Force was having increasing difficulty maintaining those north of Ouezzane. Europeans had now been evacuated from Private Ziegler's 'enchanting' town, and his unit was taking serious casualties. In the lush countryside around Zitouna, Major Deslandes' II/1st REI provided the rearguard for a convoy that was ambushed in strength on 14 June, and its 8th Company were isolated for three hours while they and the 5th manoeuvred against heavy opposition to cover one another and break free. In camp that night near Brikcha, Ziegler tried to wash away the memory of his dead comrade Kersten's bullet-smashed face with 'an excellent cold punch', mixed by the medical orderly Weisse from pilfered ampoules of chloroform, water and a little sugar.[56]

The Deslandes battalion's operations to sustain Brikcha, Ouled Allal and Rihana continued without respite, and on 17 June they made first contact with a unit of the Spanish Tercio near the Rihana border post. The Madrid talks were achieving the first steps towards coordinated if not necessarily combined operations, and both armies could now exercise rights of hot pursuit across the zonal border. During these weeks the Moroccan Skirmishers and légionnaires needed artillery support to fight their way through gorges and over ridges to reach the encircled posts, and the fighting sometimes came to hand-to-hand. The Mounted Company/4th REI, now operating with II/1st, also saw hard fighting (at Beni Rouber the doomed Private Siegel, with five tribesmen closing in on him, hurled his empty carbine over their heads to his comrades in order to save it). On 19 June, the II/1st REI were fog-bound and short of food and ammunition at Ouled Allal, waiting for a resupply convoy from Ouezzane. The first few trucks arrived with rations, but those with ammunition did not; they had been ambushed and wiped out in the pass of Brikcha, and their cargo could be heard exploding all through the night. On the 20th, the mobile group set off to march back to Ouezzane, and the Mounted Company – already badly weakened by fighting around Rihana, and now with pouches almost empty – ran into punishing fire at the pass. Private Ziegler described a disheartening scene of burned-out trucks and mutilated corpses, and the légionnaires had to tip the wreckage over the edge of the ravine before they could get through.[57] On 26 June, Major Deslandes would write to Lieutenant Colonel Rollet:

> The battalion has already been fighting for a month without interruption, and I believe that we have given satisfaction to the high command. But the young men have not stood up very well to the great fatigue that we have had to endure, which is really painful. The life that a man leads in Morocco these days is very hard and demands a strong physique to stand up to it. The battalion has lost around 100 killed and wounded since 25 May, and we have another very hard operation in prospect. We hope that we will come out of it decently.[58]

BACK ON THE CENTRAL OUERGHA, 14 June brought the extinction of Beni Derkoul post, on which the Rifians had been able to concentrate since the fall of Bibane on the 5th. On 11 June, Sub-lieutenant Pol Lapeyre had laid out a panel signal for an aircraft to pick up a message; this was hung from a cord strung between two posts, and at the seventh attempt a pilot managed to hook it with a dangling grapnel. It informed Captain Pietri at Tafrant that only 11 of the garrison of 39 were still unwounded, and that they needed water by the 14th at the latest. A night sortie to reach a spring had been partly successful, but only at the cost of three of Pol Lapeyre's Senegalese; their corpses were now dangling upside down 50 yards outside his wire, one of them with signs of a fire under his head. Stored in the post were 1,600lbs of blasting explosive for road construction work; Pol Lapeyre reported that he had piled this up with all his spare ammunition, and laid fuses to the three positions from which he fought.

His company commander had been warned that if Beni Derkoul fell, the local Beni Mesguilda tribesmen would kill their pro-French chief and rally to Abd el Krim. Captain Pietri managed to get a whole squadron to drop medical supplies, a box of medals and ice blocks, but only three blocks fell inside the perimeter. Whether or not he believed it, Pietri promised his subaltern a relief column on 16 June, and gave him the option to break out if he could, though he knew that Pol Lapeyre could not carry all his wounded and would never leave them to the Rifians. On 13 June the garrison was down to six unwounded men, and on the 14th Pietri could see tribesmen swarming all over the slopes. He had no artillery – two days previously the battery had been taken eastwards to support another sector – and the range was too long for his machine guns to make any difference. At 11am the lamp flashed 'Am under determined attack'; and at 2pm, 'Tower taken. Fire on our position. At what time should I ...'. There were no more signals; but at about 7pm an enormous fireball rose from the smoke-covered hilltop, followed by the growl of a thunderous explosion. After holding out for 61 days, young Pol Lapeyre had finally declined to let his men be taken alive. The Beni Mesguilda duly changed sides.[59]

By the end of June, 43 of the 66 French posts north of the Ouergha had been either overrun or abandoned during the ten weeks of fighting, with the loss of some 50 guns, 35 mortars, 200 machine guns, 5,000 rifles and a great deal of ammunition. The French were admitting to 1,955 troops dead or missing, plus 3,780 'natives' of imprecise definition. Rifian pressure both north and south of the Ouergha would continue throughout July. Taounate was closely surrounded and occasionally attacked; on 8 July the Rifians hit Tafrant again; on the 12th, Kelaa des Sless was encircled, and old Portuguese ruins on the heights of Djebel Amergou just south of Fes el Bali were lost. Ain Aicha was definitively relieved only on the 20th, and the last French post to fall, Ain Bou Aissa, was destroyed as late as 30 July when a shell hit the magazine.[60]

AT THE TURN OF JUNE AND JULY, while Ahmed Heriro's men were closing in on the frontier posts north of Ouezzane and refugees were pouring south to Fes, another and even more serious threat developed far to the east, where Cambay Force was shielding the northern edge of the Taza corridor.

The hills around Kifane, about 20 miles north of the Taza–Msoun stretch of the road and railway, stood between Abd el Krim's Gzinnaya allies and the vital French line of communication with Algeria through the country of the submitted Tsouls and Branès (see Map 20). Abd el Krim was competing fiercely for the obedience of these important tribes and, beyond them, for the gates to the still unpacified Taza Pocket in the northern Middle Atlas; if the clans around the corridor could be detached from the French Protectorate, then the strategic consequences might be dramatic. Since April an important part in countering Rifian pressure had naturally been played by Native Affairs officers and their local *goumiers*, and Lieutenant de Bournazel – the 'Red Man' – was leading part of Captain Schmitt's 16th Goum at the post of Souk el Djelma south of Kifane. This sector, inadequately covered by a mobile group commanded by Lieutenant-Colonel Henri Giraud of the 14th Algerian Skirmishers, was now threatened by about 4,000 Ait Waryaghar and Gzinnaya under Abd el Krim's regional general Haddu n'Muh Amyzzan, and from mid-June separate clans of the Tsouls and Branès began to waver and crumble. Although the Spahis at Kifane itself held out, smaller posts further south began to fall; some Native Affairs officers were killed by their own men, and Bournazel, isolated in hostile territory, had a narrow escape when his own Branès irregulars decided to change sides.[61]

The eastwards link between Freydenberg Force on the upper Ouergha, and Cambay Force on the northern approaches to Taza, was the upper Oued Leben, whose valley ran for some 25 miles through an almost trackless stretch of hills roughly between Ait Maatouf and Bab el Mrouj. In the fourth week of June the Rifians and their allies attacked both on the upper Leben north-west of Taza and around Sidi Belkassem on the upper Oued Msoun north-east of the town. They made considerable progress west of Taza, at one point tearing up the railway tracks, and 23–27 June was probably the most dangerous moment of the war for the French. Still with barely 60,000 troops in the whole of Morocco, General Daugan was now responsible for a discontinuous and apparently failing 'front' stretching nearly 200 miles, and in the face of Rifian successes tribes all along it were continuing to come out for Abd el Krim.

While his battalions struggled to stop the Rifians and suppress the Tsouls and Branès around Taza, Colonel Cambay actually suggested that he should abandon the town and regroup eastwards towards the Moulouya river. Lyautey refused to turn the strategic clock back ten years by sanctioning a retreat that would have left about a quarter of his troops cut off from contact with Fes, but on 5 July (by which time the immediate threat was actually diminishing) women and children were evacuated from Taza as a 'precautionary measure [that] gives the high command a greater liberty of manoeuvre'. However, by the 7th the dissidents had suffered defeats serious enough to persuade the Beni Bou Yahi on the Oued Msoun of the folly of rebellion.

That week the first of 100,000 reinforcements ordered by Marshal Pétain from the Ruhr and France finally began to arrive in Morocco.[62]

DESPITE CONTINUED SERIOUS INFILTRATION in the Ouergha sector, from late June General Bilotte was obliged to rush units south-eastwards to plug the gap on the Oued Leben, and one of these was VI/1st REI from Tissa. Such cross-country movements on foot were no less of a trial than they had been a generation before, and after a ten-hour day on the march, the exhausted and dehydrated soldiers faced hours' more labour to pitch and entrench a camp before they could eat and – unless they drew guard duty – snatch four or five hours' rest fully clothed in their bivouac tents.[63] On 26 June the Cazaban Battalion were sent against one of a pair of enemy-held hills called Bab Taza, where the Rifians had entrenched themselves and built hides with overhead cover. Under murderous fire the alternating platoons had to worm their way forwards on their bellies until they were close enough to assault each position; the 21st Company got closest, but the rest of the battalion were stalled for some time 300 yards from the hill itself.[64] Corporal Cooper, who was with the command group's escort that day, recalled that at about 4pm a gloomy-looking Major Cazaban ordered Captain Pechkoff to take his company forwards another 100 yards:

> Pechkoff, as usual, was mounted on his white horse, leading his men ... After a few minutes he rode back, very pale, and called for a drink of water. Cazaban wanted to know if there was anything the matter? 'No, I only wanted a drink', but as he wheeled his horse we all saw the white horse's side was red with blood. The bullet had gone right through the [spur-] strap on his left boot ... and out at the heel. I ran up to him and helped him from his horse [and a] *mule-cacolet* was brought ... I shook hands with him, and as he left he called out to me 'Thanks for the asparagus!'[65]

Most of the defenders later slipped off the hill under cover of darkness, and VI/1st Foreign occupied it on 28 June. Between 29 June and 17 July they were marched exhaustingly back and forth to occupy, fortify and hold various sun-parched hilltops on the upper Leben, with serious fighting on the 7th and 13th at a cumulative cost of another 35 casualties.[66]

ON 6 JULY THE WAR MINISTRY informed Lyautey of the immediate transfer of the Moroccan Division from Germany, but also of the appointment of General Stanislas Naulin, GOC 30th Corps of the Army of the Rhine at Wiesbaden, as 'commander-in-chief of troops in Morocco' with promotion to four-star rank. While Marshal Lyautey's title as

Resident-General was unchanged, he would henceforth be reduced to giving Naulin 'general instructions' while confining himself mainly to the civil government of the Protectorate. When the president's office announced Naulin's appointment the next day, it stressed Lyautey's 'entire approval' of the decision; he accepted it with outward serenity, and in fact he had asked in June for a senior general (though one to act under his orders, not to supplant him in military command).

Inevitably, however, he and the whole French politico-military hierarchy perceived the appointment as marking the government's final loss of confidence in Lyautey and in his 30-year doctrine of unified civil and military authority. General Galliéni's colonial-style improvisation might have saved Paris in 1914 and earned him a posthumous marshal's baton, but Galliéni was nine years in his honoured grave. Now the machine-generals of 1918 were going to take charge of this war, employing the massive numbers and firepower of conventional divisions and army corps with an integrated command structure, rather than *ad hoc* mobile groups cobbled together in the field by harassed colonels. On 16 July, Pétain – an embodiment of chilly pre-war Metropolitan orthodoxy who had never soldiered overseas – would return to Morocco in person for a detailed tour of inspection and to discuss with Naulin the 're-articulation of our order of battle'. By the late summer he would have no fewer than 120,000 troops on the northern front and 35,000 in the interior.[67]

FOR THE TIME BEING, however, the towns were still dependent on protection by the old scrambling methods. In the western sector, the Deslandes Battalion were operating north of Teroual as part of a temporary mobile group under Colonel Niéger, established at Zitouna on 3 July, for operations loosely coordinated with the Spanish General Riquelme. Ahmed Heriro's Djibala forces were still strangling the border posts north of Ouezzane, and on 8 July Brikcha and Ouled Allal were evacuated and blown up. All efforts to rescue the garrison at Rihana failed, and the occupants had to be left to their fate; the post fell a week later, but the surviving defenders were at least taken prisoner rather than massacred out of hand.[68] By that time II/1st REI, like all the original 'fire brigade' units, were long overdue for relief, but there always seemed to be 'one more little operation' for them. The Niéger Group's assignment on 18 July was to evacuate the posts of Ouled Hamrine and Bab Hoceine on hills above the Oued Aoudiar. Leaving their camp at Teroual guarded by the cooks and the sick, the Deslandes

Battalion marched out at dawn and climbed the south-west slopes of the Djebel Lesmed to guard the right flank of the advancing brigade. The 8th was the duty company that day, and Private Ziegler was a runner with the liaison party attached to Mobile Group HQ, so his account repeats what his friend Sergeant Maurer told him that night.

The plateau was completely flat and bare; the stones had been levelled, and the thorn bushes, aloes and dwarf palms seemed to have been cut short deliberately to deny attackers any cover. About 1,000 yards ahead Maurer could see the abrupt cliff of Hill 615; everything was quiet, but they knew the Rifians were waiting for them up there among the rocks. The companies advanced across the naked ground in the usual three-up, one-back formation; apart from the battalion's machine guns, on this occasion a support platoon also had a couple each of 37mm trench-guns and 81mm mortars.[69] When the lead companies were within 500 yards of the cliff the Rifians opened fire, looking down from their excellent concealment and cover. Men began to fall; the rest tried without success to scrape rifle-pits in the stony ground, and were reduced to crawling forwards, pushing the pathetic cover of their haversacks in front of them. The machine-gun, trench-gun and mortar crews did what they could, but without much apparent effect; the mobile group's artillery batteries were busy with other targets, and without their support the advance was agonisingly slow. It took 8th Company no less than three hours to get within 50 yards of the base of the rocks by alternate fire and rushes, but they were then pinned down, and two messengers sent back to appeal for artillery support were both shot as they ran. Meanwhile the rest of the brigade were advancing up the Aoudiar valley below them; unless Hill 615 could be cleared, their right flank would be dangerously exposed, and Major Deslandes had to get his men moving again.

A flurry of firing by the 37s and mortars did not inflict many casualties, but at least kept the Rifians' heads down behind their granite ramparts while the légionnaires made two wild bounds that got them to the base of the rocks. After Bibane, it could hardly be doubted that Deslandes would lead 8th Company up the slope in person, and just below the summit he was shot full in the chest. A hundred men saw him fall; Maurer said that they let out one terrible cry of rage and hurled themselves the last few yards, taking the crest with grenades, bayonets and butts. No prisoners were taken; and as his men heard the rumble of artillery supporting other units, and before they could even get a stretcher up to him, Marcel Deslandes died. It was three days before the mobile group managed to reach Bab Hoceine.[70]

(On that 18 July, some 2,500 miles away down at the far end of the Mediterranean, dissident tribesmen in the Djebel Druze of southern Syria opened fire on a circling French aircraft. These were the first shots in a simultaneous campaign that would convulse the French Mandate territory of Syria and Lebanon until 1927, placing a serious additional strain on French Army resources, and involving two Legion units in epic defences. For a brief summary of Legion operations in the Levant in 1925, see Appendix 2.)

WHILE THE FIGHTING RAGED in all three main sectors during July, and troop trains carried Metropolitan units towards Marseille, Franco-Spanish diplomatic feelers were nevertheless being extended to Abd el Krim. On 18 July the Madrid talks produced a joint document offering him surprisingly generous terms if he would give up his claim for an independent state and acknowledge the sultan. While Rif independence was never on the table, a considerable measure of 'such autonomy as is compatible with existing international treaties' was, together with a complete amnesty, commercial freedom to negotiate mining concessions, and (probably) a light policing presence among the still-armed tribes rather than full military occupation and disarmament. The French eventually published these terms on 14 August, and two days later the Spanish went further, stating that the sultan's authority over the Rif would be 'purely nominal'. The offer had been accompanied by a warning that if the Rifians refused, they would face joint Franco-Spanish operations to force unconditional surrender. Unable to sacrifice his prestige among the tribes by backing down from his widely published promises to lead them to independence, Abd el Krim did indeed refuse.

Marshal Pétain followed his ten-day tour by travelling to the Spanish zone for talks with Primo de Rivera to put flesh on the bones of cooperation established in Madrid. His subsequent report to the French government, released on 9 August, was the first honest analysis with which the French public had been trusted; it gave reasons for sober confidence, but did not conceal the failures. Pétain admitted that Abd el Krim was the most dangerous and well-equipped enemy the French had ever faced in their colonial wars, that his followers were brave and skilful, and that he had inflicted serious setbacks and losses during the past months. He praised the heroism and endurance of the outnumbered troops who had unavoidably been sacrificed to hold the outpost line until reinforcements could arrive. He also paid a slightly back-handed compliment to Lyautey, the 'great leader' who 'in spite of his age and the burdens of a rugged colonial career' had succeeded in defending his 'work of civilization' from this 'barbarian onslaught' (at 70, Lyautey was actually less than 18 months older than Pétain).

On 17 August, with no word of compromise from Abd el Krim, the government authorized Pétain to assume direct command and initiate his operations. He dismissed Lyautey's and Naulin's existing plan for a counter-offensive as being limited to regaining lost French-controlled territory. Assured of all the assets he needed, before winter halted active operations Pétain wanted to inflict defeats in Abd el Krim's Spanish territory, and to advance to suitable jumping-off lines for a joint spring offensive to crush the Rif utterly.[71]

ALTHOUGH THE LEGION'S NUMBERS on the Rif front would triple by the end of September, the huge multiplication of French – largely Metropolitan – strength overall would greatly reduce the corps' contribution in proportional terms.[72]

In the Taza corridor – where VI/1st REI was led by Captain Chavanne after 23 July, when Major Cazaban at last collapsed with dysentery – both the VII/1st REI (Major Merlet) and III/3rd REI (Major Boutry) had arrived during July. The bereaved II/1st Foreign, south of Ouezzane, had been led by Captain Derain, doubling up in command of the battalion and his own 5th Company due to the heavy officer casualties, but on 22 July he handed over to the more senior Captain Dolet transferred in from 3rd REI. Three further battalions from the 3rd and 4th Foreign from the Atlas would reach the front during August and September, and by late September the total Legion presence would stand at seven battalions and one mounted company.[73] But while entire divisions would be available for Pétain's counter-offensive, any hope that the burden would now pass from the units that had borne the heat of the day was to be disappointed.

General Naulin assembled three small army corps in the western, central and eastern sectors of the Fes-Taza front, each with two divisions.[74] His first initiative was to clear the Djibala attackers back from the northern approaches to Ouezzane, and from 2 August a two-week offensive by the now-General Freydenberg cleared the Djebel Azjen and Djebel Sarsar. This saw the first use of tanks in Morocco; the little two-man Renault FT-17s looked like clockwork toys as they laboured up the slopes, but although the terrain limited their areas of operation and caused many breakdowns, they did better than some had predicted. Captain Dolet's II/1st REI fought at

Djebel Sarsar on 12 August supported by fire from Spanish posts, two days after Freydenberg's French and Riquelme's Spanish troops had formally linked up for the first time in the Loukos valley. By the middle of the month tribesmen were being disarmed in thousands, and on the 18th Lyautey met General Riquelme at Arbaoua. The Legion battalion spent the rest of August in exhausting routine duties and minor clashes before marching south-east for Ain Defali, and thence to Fes to prepare for a September offensive on the Ouergha. In that sector, the Rifians had paid a heavy price on 7 August for trying to hold the captured Djebel Amergou as a base for raids in Fichtala tribal country, since their attempted defence gave the artillery and bombers an easy target.[75]

Meanwhile, north of the Taza corridor, the VI/1st Foreign established and supplied firebases and carried out exhausting picketing duties before marching from Taza on 23 July to join a concentration at Dar Caid Medbogh south of Kifane. In this eastern sector, from 17 August, General Boichut's units from the fresh 11th and Moroccan Divisions attacked to drive the Rifians out of the Tsouls country and to return that tribe to obedience. By 20 August three brigades had advanced 15 miles, and thereafter about 2,500 Tsouls tents submitted. The following week, Boichut's troops pushed into the Branès country around Smila, Bab el Mrouj and Dar Caid Medbogh. On 26 August, both VI/ and VII/1st REI were present in reserve when Colonel Corap's brigade of the Moroccan Division captured the Djebel Amseft; during this action Lieutenant de Bournazel polished the legend of 'l'Homme Rouge' by riding into battle at the head of his irregulars sporting a floating red burnous as well as his scarlet tunic, with his cigarette-holder at a jaunty angle.[76] After the Branès asked for the *aman* on 27 August, the tired VI/1st Foreign were sent west once again, being trucked to Fes on 31 August for four days of what passed for rest while they were brought up to strength for the next operation. On 4 September, Major Cazaban returned from hospital and reclaimed his battalion, and two days later he marched them up to Kelaa des Sless.

Having stabilized and advanced both his flanks, Naulin's next phase was to be a general advance in the centre to recapture all the ground lost north of the Ouergha. The troops were assembled in three 'marching divisions': the 1st and the 2nd (including II/3rd REI) would hold the line in the east and centre, while 3rd Marching Division was concentrated further west for a heavy punch northwards into the Beni Zeroual country. However, this blow would not be delivered until the progress of a simultaneous Spanish initiative, which it was hoped would transform the strategic picture, had become clear.

Marshal Pétain had met Primo de Rivera at Algeciras on 21 August for a briefing on the final plans for an amphibious operation to put a division-sized Spanish force ashore in Alhucemas Bay, threatening Abd el Krim's home base at Ajdir.[77]

THIS AUDACIOUS PROJECT had long been considered, but Primo de Rivera had now overridden those officers who drew pessimistic conclusions from a study of the Dardanelles campaign of 1915, and the success of a trial combat landing in the Straits of Gibraltar and subsequent rehearsals had persuaded the French staff that the planning was competent. Up to 18,000 troops were earmarked at Ceuta and Melilla, under the overall command of General Sanjurjo. General Saro's Ceuta force was to land first on 7 September, spearheaded by Colonel Franco with the 6th and 7th Battalions of the Tercio, followed the next day by General Fernándes Perez's Melilla force. Diversionary bombardments and smokescreens were planned, 100 aircraft were assembled in support, a floating dock had been prefabricated, and preparations had been made for landing drinking water in quantity.

Contrary currents, and last-minute diversionary attacks towards Tetuan by Mhamed Abd el Krim and Ahmed Heriro, in fact forced a 24-hour post-ponement of Saro's landings while Perez's force waited offshore, but early on 8 September 50 Spanish and French warships began a 5-hour bom-bardment. Soon after 11am the first wave of armoured barges carried the 6° *Bandera* towards La Cebadilla beach – not inside the bay, where the Rifians had long anticipated a landing, but on the outer shore of the western headland of Morro Nuevo, about 7 miles from Ajdir (see Map 20). By nightfall some 8,000 men were ashore, with 3 batteries and 10 light tanks; among the Rifians there were mutters that treachery was behind the rapid collapse of the Ibuqquyen defenders. The Melilla force was landed over the same beach on 11 September, but in all it took the Spanish 15 hard days to fight their way 2 miles south-eastwards across the horn of the western headland. On 23 September, they finally reached the bay shore at Cala Quemada; on 2 October, they looted Abd el Krim's abandoned capital at Ajdir, and the next day, with 13,000 men ashore, the fighting died away. Planning, preparation and execution had all marked a transformation in the effectiveness of the Spanish Army at every level, and the landing had inflicted a defeat from which the Abd el Krim brothers would never recover.[78]

AS SOON AS NEWS of the successful establishment of the beachhead reached Pétain, he launched Naulin's troops north of the Ouergha, into the hills for which the Colonial garrisons and Legion rescue columns had struggled so bitterly in April, May and June. With heavy artillery and air support, General Bauby's 3rd Marching Division – including both Dolet's II/ and Cazaban's VI/1st REI – pushed off from Tafrant on 10 September. The II/1st Foreign advanced via Achirkane, Amjot and Aoudour, and VI/1st joined them at Bibane on the 16th. The great hill had been surrounded and virtually cleared by Colonial and North African units during 12–15 September; the following day VI/1st Foreign were sent up to the summit, supported by Private Ziegler's 8th Company of II/1st and some Moroccan Skirmishers. On 25 May that climb had cost the Legion 127 dead and wounded, but on 16 September they took just 3 casualties from diehard snipers. On the 11th, General Pruneau's troops from 35th Division coming eastwards from Teroual had reached Ain Bou Aissa post, where they found the terrible 6-week-old corpses of Sub-lieutenant Heurzé and 22 of his 30 Senegalese. From the viewpoint of the infantryman, 1918-style firepower and methods had much to recommend them.

The Rifians withdrew northwards almost everywhere, and on 19 September the Cazaban Battalion were pulled back. They arrived at Fes on the 22nd, but the following day were sent on to Taza. As they left, the Dolet Battalion arrived in the capital, where they, too, were given four days to rest and replace their kit before they were rattling towards Taza, to arrive on 30 September. Neither battalion could be spared from the final phase of Pétain's autumn offensive.[79]

MARSHAL HUBERT LYAUTEY RESIGNED as Commissioner Resident-General of Morocco on 24 September 1925. Although his pride was certainly a factor, in effect he had been manoeuvred into this decision, and it is undeniable that he was no longer equal to a major military command. In a letter to Aristide Briand on 25 October he would express his revulsion at Pétain's insistence on applying, in Morocco, massive and ponderous Western Front-style organizations and methods, and his disbelief in their effectiveness. Although his distaste was genuine, his scepticism was misplaced, and it is certainly arguable that his own 'oil-stain' doctrine had been failing since he first confronted the Middle Atlas Berbers more than ten years earlier.

Nevertheless, it is also true that his conscientious exercise of his Protectorate had made him a popular scapegoat for both Left and Right in Paris.
The former resented his resistance to a plan to give Great War veterans
assisted status as *colons* in Morocco, and the latter his sharp eye for
attempted exploitation by bankers and industrial interests – to the end, he
had fought to save the country from Algeria's fate. In 1922 he had told Pierre
Viènot that 'My intention is to lead Morocco towards independence', and
elsewhere he had written more explicitly: 'It is predictable ... that at a more
or less distant time North Africa – evolved, civilized, living an autonomous
life – will detach itself from France ... It must be the supreme goal of our
policy that that separation is made without grief.'[80] It may seem ironic that
by 4 May 1925 he was calling for poison gas shells, but in justice this panic
reaction cannot outweigh the relative humanity of his achievements over
the previous thirteen years.

Although a government anxious to reduce military expenditure had
ignored his warnings in 1924, they still blamed him for getting them caught
up in this war, and simultaneous setbacks in suppressing the rebellion in
the Levant also played a part in Prime Minister Painlevé's decision. After a
shocking defeat there on 2 August, the Right were demanding the dismissal
of the elderly high commissioner, General Sarrail, whose military functions
were taken over by General Gamelin just as Lyautey's were handed to
General Naulin (see Appendix 2). The government's intention to replace
Sarrail with a civilian weakened their ability to protect Lyautey even had
they wished to do so. His successor, too, would be a civil administrator:
Théodore Steeg, a former governor-general of Algeria.[81]

A crowd gathered on the dockside at Casablanca when Lyautey sailed on
the liner *Anfa*. To a cacophony of sirens and ships' whistles, boats crowded
the roadstead to escort him out to sea, but his own government denied him
any naval compliments. It is pleasant to record that the British had better
manners; as the steamer passed Gibraltar, two Royal Navy destroyers came
out to provide an escort of honour, their crews lining the sides to cheer him.
On the grey quayside at Marseille on 13 October he was greeted only by a
knot of personal friends; the departmental prefect and the commanding
general of 15th Army Corps sent their regrets that they were 'extremely
busy'. Lyautey's friend Vladimir d'Ormesson would write that the only
official communication waiting for this scrupulously honest proconsul at
his Paris home was a demand for settlement of back taxes.[82]

Displays of public recognition may be fairly vain things, but a man of

Hubert Lyautey's character feels their denial cruelly, and few could deny that he had deserved better of the Republic. For some years thereafter he lived in bitter seclusion at his home at Thorey in the Meurthe-and-Moselle department; he yearned for the sunlight and beauty of Morocco, but he refused to speak of it.

THE FINAL PHASE of the 1925 operations was an attempt by General Boichut to push the French right wing northwards from around Kifane and Sidi Belkassem as far as the valley of the Oued Kert, linking up there with Spanish forces driving south-west from Midar (see Map 20).

The offensive kicked off on 27 September, and among the units committed would be Dolet's II/, Cazaban's VI/ and Merlet's VII/1st REI, Major de Corta's mobile group of I/ and II/4th REI and that regiment's mounted company, and a single squadron – Captain Bourgeois' III/1st REC – of the Foreign Cavalry. All achieved their early objectives, but atrocious weather brought the offensive to a premature halt after two weeks. French patrols actually met Spanish on 8 October at Souk el Tleta on the river Kert, but that line could not be consolidated. After General de Jonchay's cavalry brigade was repulsed at Sidi Ali bou Rekbar on 11 October, the French pulled back to Souk es Sebt d'Ain Amar (modern Es Sebt), where a series of new posts would anchor the front during the winter. The curtailed operation had still forged a solid link with the Spanish, and had put French troops on the crest of the Djebel Nador, looking north along the valley of the Oued Nekor towards the Spanish beachhead in Alhucemas Bay.[83]

THE TWO LONGEST SERVING LEGION BATTALIONS at the front, VI/1st and II/1st Foreign, had been almost continously in the field – marching, labouring, and in action – since late April and early May respectively, with only four continuous days' rest each. During those six months they had suffered significant casualties; for example, Captain Derain's 5th Company of II/1st had lost to enemy action 4 officers, 15 sergeants and 48 corporals and privates out of a maximum of 175, and sickness and drafts would actually push its total losses to about 75 per cent by mid-December. Nevertheless, neither battalion was to be withdrawn from Morocco for another month, and that month would be spent in abject misery.

After two weeks' hard labour in torrential rain, the Cazaban Battalion was moved back to Taza on 31 October, and on 2 November to Fes, where they were still under canvas. As a unit of the 1st REI, their logistic support throughout their deployment had been dependent not on Fes or Taza but on the depot at faraway Sidi bel Abbès, and – almost incredibly – it was only on 3 November that they were able to exchange their khaki cotton rags for woollen winter uniforms. They were sent to Meknes on the 5th, and at least received a warm and generous welcome at the 2nd Foreign's depot, where they were given two days' leave. On 8 November they went south by rail to El Hajeb, where they again had to bivouac in the cold and wet; on the 9th, still in pouring rain, they marched for five hours south to the post at Ito. The rain persisted; the battalion were periodically inspected by visiting doctors, and on one occasion by the local vice-president of the Red Cross, but the légionnaires still had to provide working parties. On 26 November, after more than two weeks spent rotting at Ito, the battalion were ordered to march on foot back to Meknes, and on arrival two days later they had to bivouac in the open once again.

The unit's medical officer protested about this treatment, pointing out that many of the men were exhausted, verminous and shaking with fever. Finally, on 2 December the VI/1st Foreign boarded trains for Algeria via Oujda, where they stopped over on the 4th. The following day Major Cazaban paraded his battalion, made a speech of appreciation and presented decorations; on the evening of 7 December they at last reached their depot at Saida, where they would spend the rest of the month in relative comfort. (Three NCOs and 58 men had been detached at Meknes and sent as a draft to Major Lacroix's I/1st REI down at Khenifra; they had drawn a spectacularly unlucky card – the Lacroix Battalion would be transferred up to the mountains of the eastern Rif in January, in exchange for Merlet's VII/1st Foreign at Bab Soltane, north of Tizi Ouzli.)[84]

At Saida, from Christmas Eve until 29 December, the Cazaban Battalion were able to offer a hospitable welcome in their turn to the II/1st REI passing through on their way back to Géryville; it was now the Derain Battalion, since the captain who had led 5th Company throughout the campaign had at last been confirmed in command. The légionnaires whose fatigue had worried Major Deslandes six months earlier were in dramatically worse condition by the time they were finally pulled out of Es Sebt on 10 December. Dank fog had clung to the wooded hills, every gulley was a torrent, and mudslides tore the tracks off the slopes so that mule-trains could not get through. Their sodden uniforms hung off men who were too wasted with sickness to fill them, but the medical officer's appeals for the battalion to be replaced went unanswered. Private Ziegler:

At Souk es Sebt the storms were ceaseless; worn-out tents tore like paper, and it was impossible to erect them on a ridge in the strong wind. It never seemed to stop raining . . . It rained through the tents, now as thin as cigarette-paper; it rained on our mouldy bread; it rained on our rusty rifles (which were hardly worth cleaning, because the rust would bloom again in a couple of hours) . . . Rain ran through the tents, where men sat shivering on stones with their knees against their chests. The sentries were belly-deep in mud – luckily they had nothing to fear, since the Rifs were too sensible to leave their huts. Officially the II/1st were here for road-building, but in this weather work was often impossible. The death-list grew, from fever, dysentery and exhaustion, and the battalion became skeletal. New cases of sickness were continually thinning the ranks without a shot being fired – except by the night sentries, at the jackals quarrelling over the graves of the recently buried.[85]

The number of the buried, and of those who had no known graves, was only now becoming clear. On 21 October, the prime minister had informed the Chamber that French Army casualties in northern Morocco during the six months between 15 April and 15 October 1925 had been 39 officers and 2,137 rankers killed, and 8,297 all ranks wounded – a total of 10,473 casualties (a statistic that may exclude those who, like Ziegler's comrades at Es Sebt, had died not from enemy action but from sickness and neglect). In mid-December, after two more months during which virtually no fighting had taken place, the war minister told parliament that the death toll had been revised upwards and the wounded downwards to 140 officers and 2,500 rankers killed, and 259 officers and 7,300 rankers wounded – 10,199 casualties. However, in December an additional figure was also released: 20 officers and 1,200 rankers listed missing in action, thus raising the total casualties for the year to 11,419. (Of the 1,220 men posted as missing, just 158 would later be recovered alive.)[86]

AT SAIDA, MAJOR CAZABAN was due to go on severance leave as soon as he had handed over interim command of VI/1st Foreign to Captain Villiers Moramé; the first officer to fall wounded on the slope of Taounate in the long-ago May sunshine had now taken over as second-in-command from Captain Chavanne, who was on his way to Tonkin. Of the company officers (originally 4 captains and 10 lieutenants), 4 lieutenants had been killed, 3 captains and 4 lieutenants wounded, and several others evacuated sick. Of the company commanders, only Captain Depesseville of the 23rd was still in post, and the 21st was on its third commander since May.

On Christmas Eve the major toured the barracks saying goodbye to his officers, NCOs and légionnaires. On 26 December he slipped quietly away while most of his companies were out on the exercise field; only the 21st, on barrack duty that day, saw him go, and provided the corporal's guard that presented arms as his car drove out of the gates.[87] The unit that Jean Cazaban had led for so many hard miles would soon be known as the Théraube Battalion; marshals and majors alike might come and go, but the Legion never broke its step. The holy routine of guard-mounting, inspections, maintenance, fatigues, instruction, exercises and rifle practice must not be interrupted; next spring the VI/1st Foreign, with nearly 200 new faces in the ranks, would be on their way back to the front line.

19. The Reckoning
1926–30

The Legion, by their legendary qualities of calm, bravery and devotion, remain the best troops that one could possibly have at one's disposal. Their battalions are remarkable in both attack and defence, forcing the admiration of those who see them under fire.

Captain Damidaux, 3rd Marching Division staff, 1926

They are magnificent fellows, these Berbers. They do not know the word 'surrender'; one of them will engage a whole patrol. They never run away. I admire them and I love them, but I kill them on sight.

French officer, Marrakesh, 1934[1]

THE RESTING AND REBUILDING of exhausted units during the winter of 1925/6 still left General Naulin with nearly 100,000 men in northern Morocco. One officer who considered that too many of them were being misused was Captain Jean de Lattre de Tassigny, formerly General Poey-mirau's operations officer in the Middle Atlas, who had five years' Moroccan experience.

In November 1925, when Naulin had 72 infantry battalions, Captain de Lattre wrote that it was wasteful of men and resources, and bad for health and morale, to keep 60 of them idle in wretched winter posts in the mountains or in sector reserve immediately behind them, with only 12 in general reserve. The Rifians were nursing their wounds; 30 battalions would have been ample to hold the front, where *goumiers* and local *partisans* were bearing much of the burden, and the rest should have been getting the training in anti-guerrilla fighting that they so badly needed. De Lattre put this approach down to a Great War mentality: for the men of 1918, everything had to be done on a massive scale. This gave the rank and file the impression that their leaders dared not make any move without huge numbers and overwhelming firepower, thus implying an exaggerated respect for the enemy. De Lattre argued that everything that had been achieved in Morocco had been gained by speed – by well-trained troops, lightly equipped and supple in movement.[2] It seems questionable whether Metropolitan conscripts could have been turned into anything approaching self-sufficient alpinists like the légionnaires and *turcos* in about five months. (The ideal presumably lay in some balance between the Pétain and Lyautey doctrines; but it is interesting to compare the 36-year-old de Lattre's views with his later exercise of senior command in North Vietnam in 1951.)[3] However, the French soldiers transferred from France and the Rhineland certainly needed retraining – at first, simply for movement and camping in terrain and weather that were dramatically more demanding than any they had known – and when they were sent into battle they and their officers would face some mental adjustments.

In the Moroccan hills, regular cavalry could seldom perform their European task of gathering the intelligence about enemy strengths and positions that created for a commander a picture of the early stages of the engagements to come. The *partisans* provided the most basic warning of contact but no real military information, and over wooded terrain even aircraft were largely blind. Since this weakness of reconnaissance usually made the advance to battle a game of blind-man's-buff, the infantry had to be taught the colonial doctrine of marching straight at the enemy as soon as contact was made, without waiting for any 'exaggerated' superiority of firepower to be assembled. No trainee could be given any real preparation for the shock and confusion of actual warfare, yet now they somehow had to acquire the mindset needed for fighting a fluid, 'feline' enemy with a reputation – formed by outraged reports of the 1925 fighting – that made their blood run cold.

Peacetime manoeuvres in Europe had accustomed them only to slogging across fairly level ground as obedient pawns in huge formations; even those among their senior NCOs and battalion officers who had combat experience from the Great War were accustomed to the mental comfort of close proximity to other units, under the umbrella of massive artillery support. Now, while their organization and equipment dictated that these rote-learned lessons could not simply be abandoned, there was a real need to instil initiative and confidence much further down the chain of command, so that a company of 150 men finding themselves alone did not become paralysed by a defensive neurosis.

In Morocco, the artillery were freed of their instinctive fear of counter-battery fire, and if they could get well forward they had the relatively easy task of delivering direct fire on visible targets, but in this often trackless terrain the guns (and, as importantly, sufficient ammunition) could seldom keep up with the leading infantry in any strength. The infantry company had to achieve their own superiority of firepower with their own machine guns and LMGs, and they had to achieve it anew after every movement even over relatively short distances. The flanks had to be covered with scrupulous care, though only a modest reserve was necessary to deal with strictly local surprises. The unit had to have confidence in their weapons and advance at once to feel for the enemy's flanks or gaps in his line. In defence, a single main line of resistance (with plenty of wire, if available) was normally enough; putting out little advance outposts would simply create 'honey-pots' for the Berber infiltrators of every soldier's nightmares. Rifian artillery would so seldom be encountered that there was no need for 'defence in depth', but the automatic weapons and rifle-grenadiers had to be sited for all-round defence – particularly at night.[4]

DESPITE DE LATTRE'S COMPLAINT that the number of troops holding the front line could have been halved, the hills were certainly not silent during the winter of 1925/26, and Lyautey would have been gratified by the vigorous activity of the Native Affairs officers and their *goumiers*. Gathering around them large gangs of local tribesmen whose chiefs had drawn sober conclusions from Naulin's autumn victories, these officers were preparing the way for the spring campaign by patiently chipping clans away from Abd el Krim's confederacy. For example, in December a force of 1,800 *partisans* led by just three French officers restored an expelled Marnissa *caid* to his territories north of Kifane; the core of the force was provided by Captain Schmitt with 500 'turned' Gzinnayas, and Lieutenant de Bournazel at the head of 700 Branès. Although Caid Ahmar ben Hamidou only contributed some 350 of his own warriors to the adventure, the French were quick to proclaim him as the victor in order to build up his local prestige. (Henry de Bournazel attracted attention once again, fighting with a revolver when his horse was killed under him.)[5]

In mid-January 1926, such setbacks for Abd el Krim provoked a sharp reaction to punish tribes that had sought the *aman* – not only the Marnissa, but also those on the Legion's old middle Ouergha battlefields. In the third week of the month there was renewed fighting between dissidents and

French-led irregulars around Bibane and Dar Remich, which actually led to the defeat and submission of a chief of Abd el Krim's own Ait Waryaghar. On 26 February, some 1,200 Senadja Srir began pillaging and massacring a submitted tribe in the Oued Sra valley north of Astar; fighting continued until 2 March, and although the Berbers had some machine guns it ended in useful advances by (the French claimed) *partisans* with French support only from the air. On 18 March the War Ministry claimed that the pacified zone now extended well forward of the military outpost line; the position was better than it had been before the Rifian attacks of April 1925, since for the first time most of the Marnissa and Gzinnaya were now pacified.[6]

Abd el Krim's achievement of at least a rolling or serial unity against the Spanish and French had been unique, but he had to work with the same kind of human material as any other Moroccan warlord. Even in times of success, attempting to 'govern' Berber chiefs was like herding cats, and Abd el Krim's authority had begun to fade as soon as his long run of victories ceased in autumn 1925. He had always ruled as a puritan despot, greatly respected but not loved; there had been several attempts to assassinate him, and he, too, had disposed of opponents by secret poison, open execution and selective small-scale massacres. Now he was becoming reclusive, sealed off at his new headquarters at Targuist from all but the hard core of Ait Waryaghar and a circle of trusted lieutenants. As eventual defeat became inevitable, his alliances began to crumble; he had always employed coercion, but now he had to resort increasingly to pure terror to ensure obedience. Nevertheless, in the Djibala his young general Ahmed Heriro was still loyal and – despite his defeat the previous September – still active; in February 1926, he was infuriating the Spanish by shelling Tetuan sporadically with his cleverly hidden artillery. He also raised the tribes in the Loukos valley west of Zitouna to attack French and Spanish posts, but joint operations by Generals Dosse and Riquelme soon drove them back with heavy loss.[7]

A final Franco-Spanish spring offensive was obviously coming, and in the Oranais both VI/1st REI at Saida and II/1st at Géryville were in a ferment of inspections, exercises, lectures and physical training. The company officers had been obliged to accustom themselves once more to administrative paperwork, and the légionnaires to close-order drill in spotless uniforms. Worn-out kit was replaced, and men were sent on overdue courses to qualify for NCO promotion or to familiarize themselves with new weapons, like the excellent FM24 light machine-gun that was replacing the unlamented Chauchat. During the winter, the Sidi bel Abbès depot had been shaken up by its energetic new commander Colonel Rollet, for whom the needs of the combat battalions were paramount. The training companies were now delivering droves of replacements to fill the gaps in the ranks; in January, they sent 183 to VI/1st and 205 to II/1st Foreign.[8]

EUROPEAN VICTORY may have been inevitable, but operations on such a scale would be costly, and political factions in both Spain and France were also insisting that Abd el Krim be treated justly. When his intermediaries made it known that he wished to negotiate, the offer was pursued; the spring offensive had been due to open on 15 April 1926, but on 15 March orders went out to continue preparations but to remain on the defensive. After preliminary contacts at Taourirt and Camp Bertaux, and intense man-oeuvring over the agenda, three-party talks finally began on 27 April at Oujda.[9]

The Primo de Rivera regime had been installed by a military coup, and the Army had much to avenge. (Reliable figures for total Spanish casualties in 1921–26 are unavailable, but the number of killed alone probably exceeded 50,000, perhaps by a significant margin – at least comparable to American deaths in the Vietnam War.) Nevertheless, there were those who felt satisfied by the autumn victory at Alhucemas Bay, and Primo himself had never shied from confronting the *africanistas* with Spain's need to reduce her ruinously expensive commitment. Walter Harris, whose probably unique contacts make him a convincing reporter of the intense private discussions that surrounded the Oujda talks, states that the Spanish depu-tation would have accepted the retention of their presidios and a few other strategic bases, and were willing to offer civil development as a sweetener. For the French, the deal-breaker was, as it always had been, recognition of the sultan's Maghzan and the treaties it had concluded, but both gov-ernments were prepared for lengthy negotiations over details. They were therefore frustrated to discover that Abd el Krim had apparently shackled his delegation to a rigid insistence on full Rifian independence, and the Moroccans also prevaricated over the Europeans' absolute demand for the prior release of Spanish and French prisoners before the discussion of any other terms.

The Rifian foreign minister, Mohammed Azerkan, privately told Harris that Abd el Krim was still listening to French Communist and British commercial advisors who urged intransigence on the grounds that there were still hopes of a beneficial change of government in Paris or of British intervention. Harris believed that the *amir* must also have been influenced by fear for his life if he agreed to what most Rifian tribes would see as betrayal, and by his conviction that Spain would never allow French troops to cross into her zone in any strength – he was still confident that if he faced the Spanish Army alone he could hold them off. Given their strong military position, the Europeans' stance over recognition of their protectorates, over disarmament and mineral rights was naturally fairly unyielding, but in the end the question of prisoner release pre-empted discussion of these points. On 1 May, the Europeans delivered an ultimatum that unless all the captives were handed over within a week they would withdraw from the talks. Aware of how few of those unfortunates had survived and of the condition of those who had, Abd el Krim refused, fearing that the sight of them would harden the European negotiating position to granite. The talks broke up on 6 May; in the meantime the French and Spanish had already made extensive joint political and military preparations for an immediate resumption of offensive operations, for which orders were sent out within hours.[10]

GENERAL BOICHUT had succeeded General Naulin as commander-in-chief in late January; his army was deployed in two corps, of which the eastern would play the more important role. In the west, General Dufieux's Fes Group, on the Ouergha front between Ouezzane and Ain Aicha, had 3 divisions totalling 34 infantry battalions, including 3 of the Legion. On the decisive north-east front, Taza Group was commanded by General Marty (until July 1925, the colonel of 2nd Foreign Infantry); his 3 divisions totalled 36 battalions, of which 6 were Legion units, so légionnaires provided 9 of 70 battalions, or about 13 per cent of Boichut's infantry.[11]

The Abd el Krim brothers still had a core of perhaps 12,000 fighting men of the Ait Waryaghar and their immediate neighbours in the Rif heartland. While not much more than half of the roughly 50,000 French troops committed to the key front were infantry, the imbalance must still seem gross; but 12,000 fearless and skilful guerrillas – who had been trained by shooting at an egg-sized white stone balanced on a branch – could never be negligible to the squads and platoons who had to clamber towards their hiding-places under fire. On the other hand, while defensive fighting among steep ridges and gorges would play to their natural strengths, at several points the Ait Waryaghar had unwisely prepared fixed positions that would offer targets for artillery and aircraft.[12]

The Franco-Spanish objective was the Ait Waryaghar redoubt of the Djebel Hammam, at the south of which lay Abd el Krim's new base at Targuist (see Map 20). The Spanish from Alhucemas Bay would advance to the south; those from the Melilla front would push westwards through the Timsaman and Ait Tuzin tribal country in the valleys of the Oued Kert and then the Oued Nekor. General Marty's French would push north, taking the upper Kert and the Djebel Rekbaba, to reach Souk el Tleta further down the Kert. The linked Franco-Spanish front thus achieved would then pivot on the Tizi Ouzli pass like a swinging door, advancing steadily north-westwards to the Nekor and finally the Rhis valley, Targuist and the Djebel Hammam. In the far west, an advance by Dufieux's Fes Group northwards to the zonal border would be essentially a fixing operation – it was not intended to penetrate deeply into Spanish territory to form a 'stop-line' behind Taza Group's offensive.[13]

AS SOON AS WORD ARRIVED of the breakdown of negotiations at Oujda, on the cold, wet night of 6/7 May General Dosse's 3rd Marching Division attacked on the French far right wing. Here, Major Théraube's VI/1st REI were committed to an assault on the first ridge of the Djebel Rekbaba, with Major Derain's II/1st REI among the units ready to support them at daybreak. The légionnaires assaulted up the wet black rocks of hills called 'the Stump' and 'the Dromedary', and at 3.45am on 7 May the whole crest was lit up by white flares signalling that the objectives had been taken. At dawn, tanks went clanking forwards across an ineffective ditch and into the Kert valley, where Dosse linked up successfully around Souk el Tleta with the Spanish advancing from Midar. That day on the Alhucemas front, Generals Castro Girona and Dolla advanced south-eastwards from Ajdir to the Rhis river; pushing on up it, they fought a major battle on 8–10 May at Loma de los Morabos, which cost them nearly 1,300 casualties but broke Ait Waryaghar resistance in the north.[14]

On 8 May and the following night, both battalions of 1st Foreign were heavily engaged on the Djebel Rekbaba, the II/1st standing off fierce counter-attacks in mist and rain without artillery support. Dosse's 3rd Division maintained its progress, reaching the Nekor valley on 11 May. That day the Moroccan Division commanded by General Ibos ('Pierre Khorat', the Fes diarist of 1911) was in action on Dosse's left, close to the hinge of the swinging door; the I/ and III/2nd REI, forming a marching regiment under the 2nd Foreign's Lieutenant-Colonel Gémeau, distinguished themselves by taking the Djebel Iskritten from Rifian regulars and holding the heights against counter-attacks for three days and four nights. On 14 May, the first element of the Ait Waryaghar submitted. Behind Ibos and Dosse the 1st Marching Division (General Vernois), including I/ and II/4th REI, was now coming up fast on Ibos' left as General Marty's corps front grew wider.[15]

Meanwhile, on 10–12 May, General Dufieux's Fes Group had been committed on the Ouergha front, with 128th and 4th Marching divisions (Generals Monhoven and Goubeau) – the latter including I/1st Foreign – advancing fast into Beni Mestara country east of Ouezzane. On 12 May, on Dufieux's far right wing, General Théveney's 2nd Marching Division – including I/ and III/3rd Foreign – linked up with the left wing of Vernois' 1st Marching Division from the Taza Group. In the Aoulai valley Théveney's left also linked with Goubeau's right to complete the chain; the Fes Group then pushed steadily north as tribes sought the *aman* all the way into the Spanish zone.[16]

On 19–20 May, Tercio units fighting their way southwards from Alhucemas Bay reached the Rifian base at Tamasint, and met on the upper Nekor river troops coming west from Midar; on the 21st, the Ait Tuzin and Timsaman began submitting to the Spanish in large numbers. On the same day, troops of 3rd Marching Division began climbing into the Djebel Timersgat, with the Moroccan Division well up on their left and, beyond them, Vernois' 1st Marching curling ahead to form the bottom of the bag around the Ait Waryaghar country. After little more than a fortnight of fighting, Targuist had become the visible prize in a race between the French and Spanish, and that day Colonel Corap of the Moroccan Division claimed it. In his spearhead, Lieutenant de Bournazel's 33rd Goum reached the outskirts of Abd el Krim's headquarters from the north, covered by Lieutenant-Colonel Giraud's 14th Algerian Skirmishers. Targuist was occupied on 23 May after some precautionary shellfire, and was found to be deserted. On the same day Dosse's 3rd Marching Division took the crest of the Djebel Timersgat and started down into the Rhis valley.[17]

IF THE SPANISH CAPTURED ABD EL KRIM, he was almost certain to be executed, and – for the sake of future relations throughout the Muslim Maghreb – the French government was determined to thwart their revenge. Some Ait Waryaghar were already trying to sell him; fleeing north over the Djebel Hammam to Snada guarded by his last 100-odd men, Abd el Krim sent letters to Colonel Corap asking for the *aman*. On 24 May, the senior French intelligence officer, Major de La Rocque, sent his deputy Lieutenant Montagne to Snada with a Spahi escort, while the vanguard of Corap's brigade – Bournazel's and Schmitt's 33rd and 16th Goums – camped to the south-east. On the 25th, Montagne delivered General Ibos' terms to the *amir:* immediate release of all prisoners, followed by an otherwise ostensibly unconditional surrender – although it is clear that promises were made regarding the treatment of the brothers and their families. On 26 May, the surviving 283 prisoners were finally handed over at the French camp: 25 Spanish civilians including 2 women and 4 children, 105 Spanish soldiers (but no officers), 6 French officers, 8 NCOs and 27 white rankers, and 112 Algerian and Senegalese Skirmishers. All were in wretched condition; they reported that while some captors had treated them – especially the Spanish – with deliberate cruelty, most had been merely indifferent, and that most of the deaths among them had been due to disease, famine and a lack of medical care, from all of which the Rifians had suffered equally.[18]

At 5am on 27 May 1926, the Abd el Krim brothers rode in to surrender, and were conducted to Colonel Corap and General Ibos; during the ride, Lieutenant de Bournazel and Captain Schmitt fell in behind with their *goumiers*. The brothers were allowed to bring with them 25 members of their immediate families and retinue, and 270 mule-loads of possessions and cash. Abd el Krim was calm and dignified throughout, and on 30 May at Taza he made his formal submission to General Boichut. On 14 June he was taken to Fes, and on 2 September he and his family embarked for exile on Réunion in the Indian Ocean, where he would live in retired comfort on a French government pension. The French communiqué of 27 May was clearly drafted mainly for a Spanish audience; in outlining the sequence of events it made clear that Abd el Krim and his family were in 'protective custody', having received General Ibos' assurance that they would not be handed over to any third party.[19]

The French rejected furious Spanish demands for Abd el Krim's extradition (and would retain some of the formerly Spanish territory they had occupied during the campaign). On Primo de Rivera's direct orders, the Spanish mopping-up operations that followed were reasonably restrained; most tribes submitted readily enough when it became clear that their villages would not be massacred, and some of the Krims' senior lieutenants were even taken into Spanish pay. In the Djibala, Ahmed Heriro fought on stubbornly for the rest of 1926, dying of wounds on 3 November. By that time,

55 of the 66 tribes in the whole Spanish zone had submitted wholly and another seven partially.[20]

Official French figures for their killed, missing and died of wounds during the whole Rif War from 15 April 1925 to 25 May 1926 are quoted by Henry Clerisse (1927) as being respectively 1,306, 294 and 562 – a total of 2,162 all ranks. However, since the totals for these categories already announced in the Chamber in December 1925 add up to 3,860, it seems possible to reconcile these figures only if the lower total of 2,162 refers solely to actual Frenchmen rather than to French Army losses as a whole – a distinction routinely employed by the government in order to massage the 'headline' figures downwards. Assuming that this is the explanation, then 1,167 Frenchmen alone seem to have been killed, posted missing or died of wounds during the three-week spring 1926 campaign, in comparison with 1,005 in eight months of 1925.[21] This does not seem implausible given the large late influx of Metropolitan units, but it does dispose of any idea that the final storming of the Rif was a walkover (and reminds us of Captain de Lattre's misgivings about their tactical training).

These partial figures still leave uncertain total French Army casualties for the whole war. Applying a conventional ratio of say 3:1 for surviving wounded to the claimed figures for killed and died of wounds, a guess of perhaps 16,000 French Army casualties of all categories for the whole 13-month war seems safely conservative.

HAVING DESTROYED ABD EL KRIM, the French generals could turn at once to deal with a much older frustration. Their troops had now been blooded in the Moroccan hills, and the campaigning season was far from over. Before the huge temporary reinforcement of Morocco was reversed, now was the time to crush the Tache de Taza, the last stubborn pocket of truly independent tribes in the Middle Atlas.

Poeymirau's campaign in 1923 had left the northern loop of the old Middle Atlas 'figure-of-eight' encircled by a chain of posts, and in some places chastened by the passage of a column, but it was neither pacified nor occupied. It comprised two distinct Berber territories: the smaller was that of the Northern Ait Segrushin clans in the Massif de Tichoukt north-east of Boulemane, which Poeymirau had penetrated in 1923. North-east again, this merged into the 'Grande Tache', the country of Sidi Raho's Beni Ouarain people. As physically forbidding as the Tichoukt and much larger, this was an irregularly shaped chaos of hills, ravines, soaring peaks and high cedar forest, about 40 miles deep and wide at the greatest extent of its mountainous fingers. On a modern map it lies within the area between El Menzel in the north-west, Berkine in the north-east, Ouled Ali in the south-east and Immouzer des Marmoucha in the south-west (see Map 19). The most striking feature is the Djebel Iblane range, dividing the region diagonally from south-west to north-east under various local names. At roughly its mid-point the mountains rise to the 10,500-foot peak of Tanout, and there are several other summits above 7,000 feet. The radiating ribs of the mountains divide the completely roadless Grande Tache into many secret compartments; like the Tichoukt, it was for all practical purposes closed to wheeled traffic, a heart-bursting ordeal for infantry, and in many places virtually impassable even for pack-mules.

General Boichut had begun to send troops south as soon as he could hand over his areas of operation to the Spanish, and it was in fact on 25 May, even before Abd el Krim had surrendered, that Lyautey's successor Resident-General Steeg sent an ultimatum to the mountain chiefs. If they submitted quickly the French would be generous, and there would be no reprisals for past misdeeds; if they delayed, he would deal with them as he had dealt with the Amir of the Rif. On 11 June he underlined this threat with selective air raids in the Tichoukt, and on the 23rd, two 155mm guns at Ahermoumou east of El Menzel delivered a last warning. One chief who heeded it was none other than Moha ou Said l'Irraoui of the Ait Roboas tribe, once a scourge of the Khenifra front in alliance with the Zaians, who had been forced to flee this far north by French successes in 1922. Now he rode in to Enjil to submit to General Julien Dufieux, the commander-in-chief for this operation; he promised that others would follow, but they left it too late, and on 26 June the offensive was unleashed on the Tichoukt.[22]

This preliminary bite took Vernois' 1st Marching Division only 48 hours to swallow; behind a cloud of *partisans* and under a flock of circling Breguets, three columns totalling eight battalions converged on the crests. Among them, returning to the scene of so many hard climbs and bitter fights in 1922–3, was almost the whole strength of the 3rd Foreign Infantry led by Lieutenant-Colonel Amedée Blanc.[23] Resistance was light, and the plateau was secured by the night of the 27th. Those Ait Segrushin who were determined to keep fighting melted away to the east, and met Sidi Raho at the village of Taferdoust. There the assembled chiefs agreed to resist to the end, but their resistance was to be by small groups dispersed in uncoordinated pockets all over this mountain wilderness. Sidi Raho was experienced and charismatic, but he was no Abd el Krim, and although his tribesmen do seem to have acquired grenades and a few machine guns, they did not have the booty of Anual and Chefchaouen at their disposal.[24]

FOR THE ADVANCE into the Taza Pocket, General Dufieux's forces were divided into two main formations with additional detachments; in clockface terms they were deployed around the edges of the Grande Tache as follows:

At Tamjout (12 o'clock) and Berkine (2 o'clock) were two brigades from Dosse's 3rd Marching Division, including I/ and II/4th and VI/1st REI. These brigades would move south and south-west, separated by the spine of mountains: on the west the stronger, under General de Reyniés from Tamjout, had the eventual objective of the Djebel Tizi Cherer north of the great Tafert cedar forest, while to the east, Colonel Callais from Berkine would aim for Meskedal. At Outat el Hajj down on the Moulouya river (4 o'clock), Colonel Prioux's detachment from Vernois' 1st Marching Division would stand guard to prevent any exodus of dissidents south-eastwards from the hills into the Moulouya plains. Vernois had the rest of his division around Immouzer des Marmoucha (7 o'clock), including the two-plus battalions of the 3rd Foreign. North-west of him at Tilmirate (8 o'clock) was a detachment, including the I/1st Foreign, under General Freydenberg. These two forces would move north-eastwards, also aiming respectively for Meskedal and the Tafert forest to meet the 3rd Division columns. Finally, at Ahermoumou (10 o'clock), the Mounted Company/3rd Foreign were serving with Colonel Cauvin's detachment; he was at the disposal of General Freydenberg, to help effect the link with Reyniés' 3rd Division column west of the mountains.[25]

The operation was set to start on 11 July 1926, and it was anticipated that the objectives would be achieved on the 14th. Given the extremely rugged terrain, this timetable might seem optimistic, but in the event both Dosse's and Vernois' divisions made remarkable progress from the north and south. Reyniés' Legion-heavy main force from Tamjout in fact reached the Djebel Tizi Cherer on 12 July, two days ahead of schedule, so Colonel Gendre took a column north-west to surround the Djebel Rikbat. On 13 July, the Legion mounted company from Cauvin's detachment, pushing in from the north-west towards 3rd Division's right flank, earned a citation for its conduct at the Djebel Tachkount. On the same day, east of the mountains, Colonel Callais' Skirmishers from the north met up with 1st Division troops from the south at their mutual objective of Meskedal, after the légionnaires of 3rd Foreign had taken the pass of Tizi ou Hanzi. The only element that seemed to be in trouble was Freydenberg's detachment coming up from the south-west, and the most serious fighting was to take place astride and west of the Djebel Tafert section of the central range.[26]

Freydenberg had been marching up the eastern side of the mountains, with the aim of crossing the chain north-westwards through the Tizi n'Ouidel pass to reach the Tafert forest and link up there with 3rd Division. The lead unit reached the foot of the pass on 13 July, but mistook defending Berbers for their own *partisans* and came under punishing fire. The following day I/1st Foreign took one height, but were violently counter-attacked with grenades and automatic weapons, and the dominant ground changed hands four times. On the 15th, the situation was improved by an attack near the western end of the pass by VI/1st Foreign from 3rd Division (which would bring the Théraube Battalion a second citation in army orders, and thus the right to flaunt the pale-blue-and-crimson lanyard of the Croix de Guerre TOE around the taverns of Saida). Even so, it was 16 July before the légionnaires of the I/1st managed to break through the Tizi n'Ouidel, and the tribes' resistance was still so courageous that Freydenberg's planned objectives west of the mountains had to be transferred to General Dosse.

On 18 July, Dosse received an air-dropped signal from Dufieux to the effect that since Freydenberg had made less than 2 miles progress that day due to the terrain and the resistance, and since Dosse had advanced some 12 miles beyond his own objectives, his 3rd Division must take over the clearing of the long Miat Khandak ridge. At that point Dosse's troops were spread over 25 miles and badly in need of resupply; some of them had not eaten for two days, and had been set to hunting Berber flocks in the Tafert forest. One cost of Reyniés' rapid advance along terrifying goat-tracks had been to see no fewer than 82 of his pack-mules go rolling and crashing down into the ravines below, from which their loads of food, ammunition and disassembled mountain guns could seldom be recovered. Nevertheless, he assembled two battalions and a pack-battery, and he and General Dosse in person led them north-west along the narrow crest of Miat Khandak, while Freydenberg's force slogged along the bottom of the canyons on their left, making for the Trik es Soltane path leading out of the hills towards Ahermoumou.

The high column ran into fierce resistance from Beni Zeggout tribesmen who came at them from three sides, and in the vanguard II/4th Foreign had to fight for several hours before a charge cleared the ridge; the subsequent citation mentioned that the battalion's cooks and muleteers had been sent forward to join the firing line. On 19 July the Freydenberg detachment cleared the last hill barring the Ahermoumou track, and above them Reyniés took the heights of the Djebel Sidi Ament; there he met up with Cauvin's detachment, while to their north the Gendre column finally cleared the Djebel Rikbat.[27] On 25 July, Sidi Raho made his submission to General Dufieux.

THE SUMMER OF 1926 MARKED the final elimination of the Tache de Taza as a base for raiding on any scale; it was also the last campaign season when multiple battalions of the Legion saw serious combat in Morocco. While whole brigades would be assembled as late as 1933 to form cordons for operations mounted almost entirely by native troops, and while légionnaires would see a great deal of hard marching in the process, from now on the Legion's only actual battles worthy of the name would revert to company-sized affairs reminiscent of the Sud-Oranais frontier at the turn of the century. The proportion of the Legion's total strength committed to Morocco would actually rise after the Rif War, but the nature of the remaining tasks in the still unpacified Far South (and French political expediency) would dictate a steady growth in the part played by the *partisans, goumiers* and Moroccan Skirmishers, which would steadily eclipse that of the white units.[28]

During 1926–9 the Legion would fight a number of company actions – notably, the defence of a post at El Bordj in the Djebel Ayachi south-west of Midelt, by Captain Moras' 6th Company of Major de Tscharner's II/3rd Foreign on 9–19 June 1929 – but most Legion infantry spent these years in hard labour on the road network.[29] In addition, specialist pioneer companies were formed from 1925, and these operated both individually and in concert with French Génie units.[30] Between July 1927 and March 1928 the main route across the High Atlas from Midelt down to Er Rachidia was improved by a project that became something of a monument to the Legion's skills with crowbar, hammer, pick and explosive. At the pass of Foum Zabel, Warrant Officer Michez and 40 légionnaires of the composite 31st Sapper-Pioneer Battalion drove a squared-off tunnel 90 yards long, 26 feet wide and 10 feet high through the living rock of the great buttress above a bend in the Oued Ziz gorge. They signed their work – achieved without power tools – with the seven-flamed grenade and the splendidly Roman boast that 'The mountain barred our route – the order was given to pass – the Legion executed it'. (Even on modern maps this is still identified as the 'Tunnel du Légionnaire'.)[31]

LÉGIONNAIRE COOPER OF VI/1st REI had missed the Tache de Taza campaign and the chance to swagger in the battalion's new lanyard. In May 1926 he had lost his stripes and been thrown in the cells at Sidi bel Abbès, only narrowly avoiding a general court-martial. After six months in the Disciplinary Company he was posted to III/1st REI at Ain Sefra, and in early 1929 he ended up at Marrakesh in Major de Corta's III/4th Foreign. Here he fell on his feet; he got on well with both his platoon commander, Lieutenant Vecchioni, and the interim commander of 9th Company, Lieutenant Djindjeradze. 'Djinn' was one of the Georgian noblemen who had ended up in the Legion after the Russian Civil War; he would explain that after he fled Russia the only other employment open to him was becoming a gigolo, and 'only the profession of arms seemed to me to be worthy of a gentleman'.[32] Djindjeradze, who would soon join two other Georgian princes in the 1st Foreign Cavalry, was a dandy and a womanizer who became a close friend of yet a fourth Legion prince, Aage of Denmark. However, when on duty he was a conscientious officer, and he was wounded twice. Cooper was made his orderly and spoke highly of his kindness, although the prince's late-rising habits made life awkward for his tent-striker. It was he who bent the rules to get Cooper his two green stripes back, which later enabled the Englishman to end his final year in the Legion as a sergeant.[33]

Cooper's memoir gives a useful record of a Legion infantryman's travels at the end of the 1920s; his unit was moved around a wide area of south-west Morocco, above and below the High Atlas, as a lid to clamp down on unrest that simmered but seldom came to the boil. During 1929, trouble in the Oued Sous country inland from Agadir, where alliances with client *caids* no longer seemed sufficiently effective, brought the Legion down into this far south-western region for the first time. The De Corta Battalion made an exhausting three-week foot march south across the High Atlas, climbing the green northern slopes into the woods that grew above the 6,000-foot contour. Panting in the thinner air, they eventually crossed the central watershed; here, many snowy peaks rose to between 9,000 and 12,000 feet, their misty shoulders hung with ghostly forests of centuries-old dead cedars. Wild boar and even cougars still haunted the heights, and the plentiful *mouflons* – Barbary sheep – offered tempting but agile targets to officers ambitious to improve their men's suppers of reconstituted dried vegetables and tinned meat.

Cooper writes that his officers were good to men who were on the verge of collapse, taking their packs or even putting them up in their saddles. Once they were south of the crests the slopes grew more arid and treeless; thirst became a problem, and any man who could not contribute from his waterbottle to the evening cookpot was still handed his rations raw. Such marches through almost unexplored country were planned by the Intelligence branch, who gave unit officers maps and suggested itineraries. There were no roads; the march was made by the compass, taking tactical precautions. Three sergeants or corporals took point 100 yards ahead of the leading company, spread about 30 yards apart across the route; the men followed in single file, rifle in hand, and paused at every crest or blind turn until the scouting NCOs blew a whistle.[34]

The battalion HQ was installed at Biougra, south-east of Agadir, and 9th Company were assigned to relieve a Skirmisher garrison at the post of Dar Lahoussine about 20 miles up into the foothills of the Anti-Atlas range (see Map 24). Cooper's company worked to adapt this existing *kasbah* to French standards, and garrisoned it for about six months. The local Berber tribes were certainly restless, or a Legion battalion would not have been sent this far south, but – as elsewhere in his first memoir – Cooper may overstate the amount of combat he saw. One anecdote does have the ring of truth, however, since it involves two officers whom he liked and thanked by name in print. An NCO posted to Dar Lahoussine turned out to be a notoriously cruel and devious Corsican sergeant who had made many enemies during his previous service with the 1st REI regimental police, an instruction company and the Disciplinary Company. Cooper claims that this NCO was shot in the back of the head during a patrol following a night alarm, and that all three company officers – Captain Cazeau and Lieutenants Djindjeradze and Vecchioni – quietly wrote it off simply as a death in action.

In the autumn of 1929, the whole De Corta Battalion were shipped from Agadir to Casablanca, and then rushed by rail and on foot to Oued Zem, Sidi Lamine and Khenifra in response to unrest among the Zaians. The episode seems to have been brief, but from Sidi Lamine III/4th Foreign were ordered to make a wide sweep through this edge of the Atlas – a *tour de police* – to show the flag and damp down any excitement. This was an exhausting and unwelcome mission; they marched via Kasbah Tadla to Beni Mellal, Ouaouizahrt (where Cooper was unknowingly following in the footsteps of his admired Captain Pechkoff), and finally to Azilal. There they laboured for a month to build an airfield, their sleep disturbed by Major de Corta's passion for the battalion jazz band he had formed.[35]

THE LEGION UNITS that retained their offensive role longest would be the squadrons of the Foreign Cavalry and the mounted companies of Foreign Infantry, the mobility of which allowed them to make a continuing contribution in the south, in the Legion's traditional role of providing a reliable reserve and spine for native troops and the ever skittish irregulars. The Legion cavalrymen from Tunisia were rotated through these southern postings; the 1st REC had a depot squadron at the Sousse headquarters and four sabre squadrons, and at any time at least one of these was in the Levant (see Appendix 2) and one in southern Morocco.[36]

The troopers faced the same loneliness and boredom as the infantry, but with the added difficulty of keeping horses in condition in a semi-desert environment. French horses had to be kept well away from native horses – and the waterpoints they used – if they were to avoid potentially fatal contagions. They were thirstier than mules, and more prone to a range of diseases; their digestions were also more delicate, and 'sand colic' caused by swallowing grit in dirty forage was a particular scourge. Historically (including in the First World War), French cavalry used their horses more harshly than was tolerated in the British Army. In the desert the Legion troopers had to be schooled to take the utmost care of their mounts – dismounting at every halt, inspecting their hooves regularly, keeping their manes and tails well groomed so that they could flick away the tormenting flies, and above all off-saddling whenever possible and checking for back sores. When in pursuit, their mounts could keep up a 15mph canter for a limited period, but most of the time they trotted at half that speed or walked at the same pace as a man; usually the troopers dismounted and led them for about a quarter of any march. If needed, they could keep going on one watering every 36 hours, but not on much less; they could cover up to 20 miles in a night march, but the endurance of their accompanying packhorses was a limitation over longer distances.

The rank and file were mainly Russians and Germans but most of the senior NCOs were French. The official strength of each 4-troop squadron was 4 officers and 160 rankers, but in practice this was often as low as 100 men. Even in this wilderness, REC officers (who included about 10 Russians and the three Georgian princes) maintained a traditional cavalry 'tone', and photos show that their troopers also prided themselves on a certain style – at this date a few of them, too, were still former Tsarist officers who had chosen to serve in the ranks. While issued with a bolt-action 8mm carbine the trooper still carried a sabre at his saddle, and each troop had pack-horses carrying an FM24 light machine gun and its separate 7.5mm ammunition.

IN 1927, THE SULTAN MOULAY YOUSSEF died, and the French secured the agreement of their powerful client Pasha of Marrakesh, Tahami el Glaoui, to the succession of the sultan's manipulable 16-year-old son, Mohammed ben Youssef. By 1928, El Glaoui was unchallenged in the High Atlas, but Glaoua depradations south of the mountains – particularly those of Madani el Glaoui's notoriously cruel son-in-law Hammou, who tyrannized over the family's southern fiefs from the old castle at Telouet – stirred continual unrest. The Glaoua, like the sultans of old, attempted to enforce their authority by occasional punitive expeditions rather than by the costlier and un-Moroccan method of creating a systematic network of reliable long-term garrisons. Since their methods were as violent and self-seeking as those of any other raiders, their bitterly resented interventions simply kept the cauldron seething.[37]

By now, the collective structure of the very widespread Ait Atta Berber people (never more than a sort of loose shared pride in their ancestral past, honoured in annual gatherings to elect a paramount chief of purely symbolic powers) was on the brink of dissolution. While some of their tribes had reached an accommodation with the Glaoua, others, including the irre-pressible Ait Khabbash, continued to resist violently and successfully. The Ait Khabbash were heavily involved in a tribal war that devastated the Draa valley in the south-west in 1926–7; this led to the French installing a Native Affairs post at Ouarzazate, but for years thereafter its Captain Spillmann had to proceed patiently by the old Lyautey method of clan-by-clan seduction. Further east, the richly fertile country beyond the Dades valley would be partly depopulated as a result of the age-old competition between raiding clans and rival protection-racketeers, which rumbled on into the early 1930s, right across to the still-unoccupied Tafilalt. That unlanced boil, a centre for wide-ranging activity by the Ait Khabbash among others, was also now the base of the Ait Hammou bandit chief Belkassem Ngadi. He attempted to manipulate his contacts with the Ait Khabbash – whose great numbers and black burnouses had earned them the nickname of *izan*, 'the flies' – but in practice they usually exploited him.[38]

The days of attacks on the French by whole *harkas* were long gone, and apart from occasional small raiding parties the Ait Khabbash no longer troubled the country east of the Tafilalt, where the Legion cavalry squadrons and mule-companies circulated from posts at and around Midelt, Er Rachidia, Boudenib and Colomb Béchar to maintain a general level of peace. However, this was still periodically disturbed by traditional small-scale outbreaks. One major panic right across on the Zousfana ruined tourism for several years after the GOC Ain Sefra Territory, General Clavery, was killed in an ambush on 8 December 1928. His party of a dozen men in three cars were travelling the track between Colomb Béchar and Taghit, driving at long intervals to avoid one another's dust, when they were attacked in succession. Two captains, a sergeant and two légionnaires died with Clavery; their killers were a small mixed Dawi Mani and Ait Khabbash *djich* from the Tafilalt.[39]

IN 1929, THE FIRST LEGION UNITS took an uncertain step into a future age of warfare when two new motorized cavalry squadrons were raised in the south-east; now that most convoys were motorized, the horsed escorts could no longer keep up with them. In February that year, Captain Dugas formed the VI/1st REC at Colomb Béchar; his légionnaires were drawn from the two squadrons then at the Sousse depot, and most of the junior officers and NCOs from Line light cavalry armoured car units in France. That summer, Captain Tavernot's new horsed V/1st REC were also ordered to return from Ksabi to Boudenib for motorization, but both units would be slow to receive the equipment for their new role.

In the 1920s, driving motor vehicles was far from the virtually universal skill that it was to become, and since only Tavernot's officers had any relevant experience, their men would be sent up to Meknes, one troop at a time, for a six-week basic course in driving and maintenance. When the first, under Lieutenant Lennuyeux, had finished their instruction, they were ordered to drive back to Boudenib in five big, underpowered old Berliet trucks and one White armoured car just out of the repair shop – not vehicles best suited to Moroccan dirt roads.[40] The 250-mile journey was supposed to take four days, but in the event it was eight days before a sorry procession approached Boudenib: one Berliet towing the second, the third towing the armoured car far back in the choking dust, and the fourth jerking along on three cylinders in a cloud of blue smoke. The fifth truck had been abandoned 50 miles back, stuck firmly in the broad bed of the Oued Ziz at Er Rachidia. The fledgling crews had been unable even to diagnose the causes of most of the many breakdowns, but like good légionnaires they had improvised as best they could; they used wire to replace missing bolts, soapy water for grease, and rigged a petrol-can high to persuade gravity to do the work of a broken fuel-pump.

Just ten days later this so-called 'alert platoon' and the Boudenib *goumiers* were ordered out to follow up news of a raiding party. Engine trouble delayed their departure for two hours, and when they reached the Oued Guir ford – at this season almost dry, but very treacherous going – they stuck fast, despite unloading everyone but the drivers to lighten the lorries. Even with ten soldiers pushing and digging-out each Berliet, they were still hopelessly bogged down five hours later. The amused *goumiers* had long ago left them to it, and in the middle of the night they were still sweating and cursing by the light of acetylene lamps.[41]

THE MOUNTED COMPANIES were also on notice to lose their *brêles* over the next few years, but for the time being they still operated in their traditional way, providing both cross-country patrols and labour gangs in the south-east.[42] Feeling themselves to be somewhat special, they lavished proprietorial care on their home posts, which they had either built or greatly improved with their own hands, and life between patrols followed a repetitive but fairly comfortable routine. Any feast-day that provided an excuse – Christmas, Camerone, 14 July, Armistice Day, regimental days – was celebrated enthusiastically with full-dress parades, special meals, camp shows and mule races.

Although their missions were just as punishing as they had been in the old days in the Sud-Oranais, the mule companies still attracted plenty of volunteers, from the type of men who today would apply for paratroop units and for much the same reasons. Patrols routinely involved marches of up to 40 miles in a 12-hour day, but if an aircraft found them and dropped urgent orders they might have to keep going for up to 18 hours. The usual rhythm of a patrol was three days on the march and one day's rest, and most were exercises in exhausting monotony. However, as the ambush of General Clavery's party right over on the Algerian border had proved, occasional raiding parties still ranged far from the untamed Tafilalt or ventured down from the canyons of the southern High Atlas.[43]

It may be significant that – unlike many other small fights – a defeat suffered at a spot called Djihani, north-west of Abadla, in October 1929 by half of the Mounted Company/1st REI is hard to find in the Legion's own literature, which seems to treat it with embarrassed reticence. Following the unrest in the southern Atlas in June that had seen Captain Moras' company of II/3rd REI besieged at El Bordj, the 1st Foreign's mule company had been brought across to the Oued Guir after several years of relative monotony in the Sud-Oranais. There is a suggestion that the lieutenant commanding the *peloton* at Djihani was tactically incompetent, and the word 'lassitude' is used in one of the few references. At all events, his half-company suffered 41 casualties; this was a blow to the high reputation of the mule companies and, given the tribal culture of oral exaggeration, a dangerous boost to dissident morale right across the south. One of the consequent recommendations was that machine-gun platoons should be formed within all mounted companies, which suggests that at Djihani the lieutenant must have taken on superior numbers in open terrain. By August 1930, this advice had been followed in the case of Captain Fouré's 1st (Mounted)/ 2nd REI at Er Rachidia, but it proved to be no panacea.[44]

ON THE SOUTH-EASTERN EDGE OF THE HIGH ATLAS, about half way between Er Rachidia and Tinerhir, the Oued Rheris flowing down into the desert supports a few small oases, of which one is Tadirhoust (see Map 23). There were reports of a possible Berber war party installing themselves there on a plateau near the river, and on 30 August Captain Fouré was ordered to accompany the Native Affairs officer from Tarda, Captain Gaulis, in an operation to clear them out. Fouré had about 200 légionnaires (Lieutenants Brenckle's and Garnier's half-companies, each with a two-gun MG section under Sergeants Bensel and Haefner respectively). Captain Gaulis also had at least 200 rifles under his own command: some 100 *goumiers* – half mounted and half on foot – of the 33rd Composite Goum, plus *moghaznis* from Er Rachidia and some local irregulars. Air support had also been arranged. As always, the senior Native Affairs officer would be in overall command; his *goumiers* and *partisans* would carry out the raid while the Legion company simply provided a reserve to cover their withdrawal. Captain Fouré took his company down to Tarda to join Gaulis, and the first elements of the force moved out at 8.45pm for a night march westwards, hoping to catch the Berbers at dawn on 31 August.[45]

ON THE MARRHA PLAIN the textures and colours of the ground vary widely, from a fine to a very coarse 'grind' and from black through to greys, yellows, pinks, reds and browns; even the colours of the tufts of vegetation differ noticeably over any distance. These changes sometimes occur at intervals of only a few hundred yards, and at about 4.45am on 31 August it was the white colour of the sand that led the scouts to report that they were close to the Oued Rheris and perhaps half-an-hour from Tadirhoust. Captain Gaulis halted the column and turned it back eastwards; since the ground here was absolutely flat, he wanted to get the force under cover before sunrise – first light was already dimly picking out the hills above Tadirhoust to his right. At 5.30am he stopped again south-east of the oasis, masked from it by low sand hills covered with spiny scrub. Gaulis planned to withdraw from west to east after his *goumiers* had hit the Berber camp, and he placed the Legion company accordingly. The forward half-company under Lieutenant Brenckle (1st and 2nd Platoons) took position on the edge of a rise, facing west and north-west. Captain Fouré and his command group stayed with them; he sent Lieutenant Garnier's 3rd and 4th Platoons back eastwards to a slight rise about 800 yards behind Brenckle to form a fall-back position, and they were all in place by 5.45am.

Captain Gaulis advanced westwards with his Goum; he does not seem to have had any up-to-date intelligence about the Berber camp, but he sent his *partisans* forward to feel for it. Shots were fired, but all they found was one abandoned tent, about 150 sheep and goats and three camels; the irregulars happily herded these beasts eastwards, and kept going for Tarda. Exactly what Captain Gaulis planned to do next is unclear; the shooting had revealed his presence, and the next move was up to the Berbers, wherever they were. At 6am three biplanes appeared and dropped bombs into the *palmerie* of Tadirhoust, and these were soon replaced by a reconnaissance aircraft. At 6.15am, warriors on foot approached Lieutenant Brenckle's forward half-company through the uneven ground to the north of them, but were driven off with machine-gun fire. At 6.30am, Captain Gaulis – well to the west of Brenckle – saw many riders about $2\frac{1}{2}$ miles south of him and heading eastwards fast. Ten minutes later the recce aircraft dropped a message assuring him that the enemy were in flight to the west and that he could withdraw without worries; in fact what the pilot had seen was large flocks being driven to safety, and tribesmen on foot soon emerged from Tadirhoust and started moving east along Gaulis' northern flank.

GAULIS WAS IN DANGER of being cut off from his line of retreat; a deep salient was forming, with he and his *goumiers* in the western end of a bag, and hundreds of Berbers advancing eastwards to left and right of him to form its southern and northern sides. However, Fouré's Legion company was holding the eastern neck open for him; Gaulis ordered his foot *goumiers* to fall back first, covered by his horsemen. They retreated by alternate bounds, but under increasing fire, and by 7.30am, when Gaulis reached the first rise where Fouré was waiting with Brenckle's half-company, he had himself been wounded. By this time, first Brenckle's, then Garnier's halves of the Legion company had come under attack by hundreds of Berbers advancing from the south-west, west and north, and Garnier's two Hotchkiss machine guns were giving trouble.

The foot *goumiers* reached Brenckle and thickened his firing line; their mounted brothers – several by now unhorsed – took position on his northern flank (the *partisans* had all fled by now). Captain Fouré had sent his command group back to Garnier's position; now he suggested forcefully to the wounded Gaulis that the horse *goumiers* should hold on to this forward rise while Brenckle and the infantry *goumiers* fell back on Garnier's hummock, from where they could then, in turn, cover the riders' retreat. This order 'could only be carried out in part, due to the difficulty Lieutenants Chauvin and Boulet-Desbaron experienced in controlling their riders'; this seems to mean that the mounted half of 33rd Goum took to their heels. Meanwhile, red flares from the recce aircraft warned Fouré that the Berber riders from the south-west were close to achieving an encirclement.

He had with him Brenckle's 100-odd légionnaires and perhaps 30 of Lieutenant Cède's foot *goumiers*, plus two machine guns; nearly half a mile behind him were Garnier's half-company and Warrant Officer Szencovics' command group, about 110 men, with the other two guns. Both halves of the little command were under direct attack and in danger of being surrounded. Fouré's only chance was to get them reunited on Garnier's position, and then to attempt a fighting retreat towards Tarda – about 18 miles to the east over open, rolling ground. Brenckle's mules and the heavily burdened 1st Machine Gun Section would have to lead the way back to Garnier. At 7.40am, Fouré gave the order for 1st and 2nd Platoons to 'unhook', and what would be recorded as the combat of Bou Leggou began its degeneration into a life-or-death race.

THE BERBERS RUSHED FORWARDS to occupy the rise as soon as Brenckle's men left it, and while under fire from behind the légionnaires had to use their carbines against tribesmen trying to cut them off from the flanks. As they retreated, they were at first too far from Garnier's men to be protected by any effective covering fire. The wounded Private Abandiolli was boosted up on to Private Eisenberger's back until they caught up with the mules and put him into a saddle, but he could not control the beast, and was last seen lying on the ground fixing his bayonet. Two other men were also wounded before Brenckle reached Garnier's position. Despite the fire of Garnier's 2nd Machine Gun Section and two platoon LMGs, the Berbers came within 100 yards from several directions, and Fouré had to get the company moving again almost as soon as the last men arrived. He pointed out the edge of a broad plateau about another 800 yards east as the next rallying point, and sent Garnier's 3rd and 4th Platoons back first with both the machine-gun sections.

Keeping a grip on a retreat by the fire and movement of alternating groups is more difficult than it sounds, and at the end of each bound men need a steadying pause – not only to sort out their squads and catch their breath, but to maintain their confidence that this is an orderly, controlled man-oeuvre and not a rout. Bou Leggou was always a disciplined retreat, but it seems clear that during this second bound the mutual support of the two halves of the company began to unravel under fast pursuit and relentless attack. Garnier and both machine-gun sections reached the rise and opened covering fire for Brenckle, but the latter's half-company were unable to join up cleanly. They could not simply follow in the boot-tracks of the first or they would have masked their fire, so they had to spread out to the flanks. In this terrain, occasional hummocks of sand rising a few feet above the stony surface are crowded with leggy, chest-high scrub, and it seems that the rearguard squads began to get separated among such low but distracting features. Lieutenant Cède was wounded, and his surviving handful of foot *goumiers* became mixed up with the légionnaires. Lieutenant Brenckle was hit in the shoulder, but kept going. When a bullet hit Private Eisenberger in the kidneys there was no one to carry him as he had carried Abandiolli, and he disappeared under a snarl of stabbing tribesmen.

Ahead of them, the outflanking Berbers came within almost hand-to-hand range of Garnier's men. The 3rd Platoon's three-man LMG crew were wiped out, though the gun itself was retrieved, and four other men of the platoon also fell. Sergeant Haefner of Garnier's 2nd MG Section defended himself with his revolver until he was killed, and Lieutenant Chauvin of the Goum had his brains blown out. Captain Fouré ordered 1st MG Section to rejoin Brenckle's half-company to give them some firepower, but 1st and 2nd Platoons were no longer clearly visible. During their own scrambling fight 1st Platoon's LMG crew were also wiped out; those wounded were being shoved up on to mules whenever possible, but not all could be reached in time.

By about 9.15am the situation was critical for Brenckle's rearguard half-company. We should imagine them separated into a loose skein of small groups – a dozen men here, twenty there – panting under a merciless sun across a confusing desert landscape of slight rises and dips scattered with patches of thorn-scrub and occasional rock-piles, pausing to fire back at groups of unencumbered Berber riflemen who could run faster than they could and who kept appearing and reappearing from three sides. When defeat becomes undeniable, only infantry of the highest quality can maintain their self-control while falling back under fire – especially if they have to leave their fallen to the knives of their pursuers, which naturally causes a flood of shame. Lieutenant Brenckle, weakened and in pain from his shoulder wound, was on foot with his men, trying to coordinate the fire and movement of groups that by now had become dislocated and whose NCOs lost sight of other squads for minutes at a time. Brenckle's mule-holders – about a dozen men under Corporal Bourginde, trying to lead nearly 50 animals, some with wounded men in the saddles – were getting mixed up in the fighting as they paused to pick up casualties, and mules, too, were falling under the lash of bullets. Some became uncontrollable with fear as Berbers ran among them, knifing two légionnaires and snatching the carbines that the casualties were carrying.

The commander of 1st Platoon, Sergeant Chief Cochard, was killed, and Sergeant Leu took over. Seeing that the platoon was about to be overrun, Lieutenant Brenckle ordered 1st MG Section – which had loaded up for another bound backwards – to set up their guns again to support Leu's dwindling squads. The section had already lost three men, but Privates Muller (wounded in both shoulders) and Lauber (hit in the head) managed to get their Hotchkiss on to its tripod. However, they then found themselves without ammunition – one of their pack-mules had been killed and the other now bolted – so Private Kluschka had to try to pack up the gun again to save it. Sergeant Bensel managed to get the second Hotchkiss into action, although himself under fire from only 100 yards; Privates Zimmermann and Libert fired their last eight cartridge-bands, and this was enough to buy 1st Platoon time to break free.

The 1st MG Section then had their own difficulties in withdrawing. Kluschka had his gun loaded up when the mule was hit; he had to unpack the Hotchkiss once again, and carry it on his shoulder. Helped by Private Geier, who had been hit in the throat, Kluschka tried to disable the gun as he ran (it should be remembered that the Hotchkiss weighed all of 54lbs without its tripod mount). The wounded Lieutenant Brenckle ran up to try to help them; Geier waved him on, but was then hit a second time and killed. Privates Muller and Lauber fell in their turn; carrying the second gun, Zimmermann was at the end of his strength and had tribesmen on his heels. He stopped, smashed the feed block of the Hotchkiss against a rock, and with a last effort threw the bolt assembly to Brenckle.

At that moment two aircraft swooped over at very low altitude, dropping light bombs and machine-gunning the Berbers, and the shock of this bought the légionnaires a little more time. Lieutenant Brenckle, exhausted by running and loss of blood, tried to mount his horse, but it was hit the moment his boot touched the stirrup; a few yards away his orderly, Private Fumagolli, caught a loose mule for him, but this too was shot. He finally managed to mount a mule given him by Captain Fouré's orderly, narrowly escaping tribesmen who had paused briefly to examine the wounded animals.

Meanwhile Brenckle's 2nd Platoon, on the northern flank of the rearguard, were fighting in two separated groups. Warrant Officer Schoenberger was defending himself with a carbine while carrying two haversacks of LMG magazines – a 40lb load; he and Private Sieger fell behind and both were killed. Sergeant Lay took over the platoon, which then lost two more men. The 2nd MG Section had managed to fall back with the company's rear mule party, so the four separated platoons were now fighting with carbines alone; the account states that the pressure of pursuit was so close that it would have been a suicidal sacrifice for the two remaining LMG crews to have paused to try to hold off the dispersed parties of tribesmen.

The company had covered about 5 miles when, at about 9.45am, they faced fresh enemies ahead and on their northern flank. About 20 tribesmen from a submitted clan, camped on the desert, were attracted by the firing to try to cut the retreat in the hope of winning some booty for themselves. Sergeant Lay's 2nd Platoon beat them off by a 'superhuman effort', at the cost of Privates Grabowsky and Barab caught and killed in a shallow dry watercourse.

THE BERBER FIRING began to dwindle at about 10am; they had taken many losses themselves, they too were tired, the circling aircraft were bothering them, and they wanted to gather up the weapons and ammunition of the French casualties. The last shots were fired at about 10.30am, and some 15 minutes later Captain Fouré was at last able to halt and regroup his scattered men; they had covered perhaps 9 miles since the first clashes. At about 1.15pm the 1st (Mounted)/ 2nd Foreign finally reached Tarda. Fouré's men had lost more than 30 killed and wounded, Gaulis' force as a whole about 100 légionnaires and *goumiers*, whose bodies would not be found and buried until two weeks later. Late that night, two of those posted missing, Privates Oder and Cerini, walked into the company base at Er Rachidia – a full 25 miles from the battlefield – still carrying their weapons and a pack of LMG magazines.[46]

On 30 November 1930, the company *fanion* was decorated with the War Cross for Exterior Operations. As so often, the words of the citation owed more to official 'spin' than to strict accuracy, and the actual behaviour of Captain Gaulis' men was interpreted in a liberal light. Fourés 1st Mounted Company had apparently 'succeeded in imposing itself on the enemy, stopping their movement and assuring to the end the withdrawal of the auxiliary forces which it was their mission to protect'.

Bou Leggou was not to be Lieutenant Brenckle's last fight; nor – despite the ever greater proportion of the task taken over by Maghzan units and irregulars – would it be the last action in which a Legion Mounted Company took significant casualties.

20. 'Obscure and Unknown Sacrifices' 1930–34

It is with the flesh and blood of partisans, Moroccan Skirmishers and the Foreign Legion that France is completing her conquest of Morocco. Thanks to these obscure and unknown sacrifices the work begun can be accomplished without provoking questions in the Chamber.

Pierre Scize, *Voilà*, 3 June 1933

Unstable alliance, mutual suspicion, eternal grudges and arrogant domination of their neighbours and of their clients form the leitmotiv *of the Ait Atta past, together with a sense of permanent balance through eternal violence.*

David M. Hart, *Qabila*[1]

THE TRANSFORMATION of the Legion mobile units from mounted to motorized took some time, since vehicles became available only in gradual increments, and mules would continue to be indispensable in the southern Atlas for several years. The plan in 1930, presided over by Colonel Georges Catroux (who was now commanding at Ain Sefra), was to entrust long-range desert patrolling to motorized units in collaboration with the camel-mounted Saharan Companies. The first Legion mule company to make the transition was Captain Robitaille's 2nd (Mounted)/2nd REI based at Oujda, which got its first two trucks in January 1930; but it was November before they received four Berliet VUDB armoured reconnaissance carriers, and although their official designation changed to 2nd (Motorized), the other platoons kept their mules for the time being.

The intention was to form REC cavalry squadrons each with a troop of turreted armoured cars, one or more troops of light armoured recce carriers and a troop of mechanized infantry in heavy carriers (all these vehicles being wheeled rather than tracked). The new-style Compagnies Montées of the REIs were also to have one armoured car platoon, the others being equipped with either armoured carriers or patrol trucks – 'Saharan breaks'. In the early days there was no standardization, and operating different types of vehicles simultaneously – all of them designed for European use – was a constant headache for mechanics and quartermasters. In the summer of 1931, Robitaille's company (now transferred to the Sud-Oranais and retitled Motorized Company /1st REI) had an armoured car platoon with 4 old Whites, a light platoon with 5 VUDBs and a 120-man heavy half-company with 14 Panhard 179 armoured carriers, but the workshops also had to keep a variety of support vehicles running. By 1934, the VI/1st REC had 3 Laffly 50AM armoured cars and 15 VUDBs, but also a 'softskin' inventory of no fewer than 10 different types of cars and trucks.[2]

Breakdowns were frequent, and keeping numerous spares in store in remote desert bases was a logistic nightmare – particularly as these were at the end of long supply-lines, set up to provide a limited number of items in bulk, at intervals of a month. Heavy demands were made on the légionnaire's traditional ingenuity in operating 'System D' and in knocking up improvisations in the blacksmith's shop. The Berliet VUDB armoured recce carrier ('*vehicule de prise de contact*') that equipped the light troops and platoons was a particular trial. This pig-nosed, slab-sided steel van had an advanced four-wheel-drive transmission, but since this allowed it to drive over terrain too rough for its mechanical strength the half-shafts were constantly breaking. At 4.9 tons, even before adding the necessary load of fuel, water and ammunition, it was far too heavy for its 40hp engine, and its radius of operation (of about 125 miles before refuelling) was laughable. A photograph of one lurching across a boulder-field in the full glare of the desert sun makes one wince for the crew; an inside temperature of 158°F (70°C) was once recorded.

Some of the younger soldiers were enthusiastic about this step into the future, but most veterans voiced the same grumbles that would soon be heard from cavalrymen the world over. Their mounts were alive, and had personalities; mules were willing, enduring, and could go anywhere a man could walk – and a légionnaire of '*la Montée*' could walk across anything. The new iron boxes were dead, heavy, mechanically unreliable, limited in the terrain they could cross, and so unspeakably hot that they reduced soldiers to blind, helpless suffering. Confronted with them, the légionnaire was also reduced from a proud master of his trade to a know-nothing *bleu* who had to be patiently instructed in every necessary skill by lesser breeds – which was intolerable. In March 1932, while based at Taghit with responsibility for the track down to Beni Abbès, a motorized troop of VI/1st REC completed a Saharan round trip of 1,570 miles in 55 days; no doubt the veterans, ignoring the impressive mechanical achievement, pointed out that men with mules had routinely been surpassing this average of 29 miles a day for the past 50 years. (The squadron's armoured cars had already given a hostage to military humour in May 1930, when a sniping tribesman sent a fluke bullet down the cannon-barrel of a White TBC whose breech happened to be open, and the ricochetting slug had wounded two crewmen inside.)[3]

AS THE LEGION APPROACHED its centenary in March 1931, the challenge faced by the corps went beyond updating its equipment and organization. The raising of the first integral mechanized and artillery units to join the horsed cavalry regiment fell far short of the post-1918 dream that some had nurtured of forming a complete foreign division (which had always been politically impossible anyway, due to its Praetorian undertones).[4] The Legion's *raison d'être* was fighting North African tribesmen, and it was clear that within a few years that role would disappear. It was not easy to imagine what could replace it, and the need for the Legion's continued existence was open to question by serious soldiers as well as by the political Left to whom it was a provocative anomaly. At the head of 1st Foreign Infantry and the central depot, Colonel Paul Rollet could do little to influence the ideas of the War Ministry and General Staff as to the Legion's future place in the Army. Internally, however, his powers were considerable, and he was tireless in promoting not only the well-being and morale and but also the public image of the corps to which he had dedicated his life.

Rollet's reign at Sidi bel Abbès in 1925–35 would be described as the Legion's 'century of Louis XIV, with buildings leaping out of the earth': modern canteens and shops, a sports hall and swimming pool, a theatre, and – a project close to Rollet's heart – a retirement home for old soldiers. The central band grew to 180 men, forming a 100-strong orchestra for public performances as Rollet took every opportunity to break down barriers between town and barracks. With a breastplate of medals on his old-fashioned desert tunic, he presided over regular weekly full-dress parades complete with announcements of promotions, decorations, welcomes and farewells. Round any corner officers and men might suddenly encounter 'Pil', a slight, fast-walking figure with a dog at his heels, raking everything and everyone with his electric blue eyes and demanding informed answers.

Ever since his dispiriting return from Europe in 1919, Rollet had been engaged by the need to build a spirit of continuity that would carry the Legion's special identity into the future, a matrix that could accommodate and mould whatever human material it had to work with. Compared with the British, the French Metropolitan Army has little history of regimental continuity; the fortunes of war and the serial changes of regime since 1789 have caused repeated disbandments and renumberings that have broken the genuine lineages beyond recovery, and while certain famous old names are honoured, the formal allocation of their traditions to current units has always been fairly arbritrary. The Legion had an almost unique advantage in this respect, but harnessing it would take more than simply conducting recruits reverently past the ancestral shrines in the Salle d'Honneur. Paul Rollet was a military romantic, but an intelligent one, and he understood how to nurture the legends that generate *ésprit de corps*.

It was only months before he had joined the Legion in December 1899 that the last known survivor of Camerone, Hyppolyte Kunassec, had retired after 27 years' service; Rollet's CO in the Sud-Oranais and Madagascar, Paul Brundsaux, had served with Major Marius Cecconi, another Mexico veteran; Cecconi's elder brother had been killed at Sebastopol in 1855, and their father Giuseppe had joined the Legion in 1832.[5] Yet despite such links, of which there were many, before Rollet's colonelcy the Legion had no coherent body of tradition, just a more or less vague set of ancestral memories surviving across the chasm of 1914–18 in the minds of a dwindling number of veterans. It was Rollet who decanted and clarified these memories into a rich blend of history and myth on which the Legion could feed. Remarkably for a man of his time, he instinctively understood that he had to 'take control of the narrative' if he was to protect the Legion from indifference and outright hostility.

Rollet began by perfecting the internal narrative, systematically combining the different elements – the cult of endurance and sacrifice, culminating in the annual celebration of Camerone; the guarantee of anonymity for men seeking a second chance in life; the Legion's unique uniform embellishments; the family stories and rituals – into an all-embracing sense of proudly distinct identity.[6] Rollet wanted this identity to outlast active service; the discharge certificate given in 1905 to Private Gustave Seewald looks like the sort of document you produce to allay the suspicions of a military policeman at a railway station, but that presented to Légionnaire Robert Lincoln in 1935 is the sort that a man frames and hangs on his wall.

The March 1931 centenary provided the perfect opportunity for consolidating this narrative and for broadcasting it to a wider audience, and Rollet worked towards this climax for several years. It required in particular two major programmes of fund-raising and organization. The sculptor Pourquet was commissioned to produce an imposing Monument to the Dead for the barrack square at the Quartier Viénot, to be dedicated at the climax of the celebrations; thereafter the approach to it – along which the wooden hand of Captain Danjou was paraded on Cameron Day – would be known as the Sacred Way. The monument took the form of a great bronze globe of the earth with the Legion's theatres of war gilded, supported by four larger-than-life figures in period uniforms (Rollet ensured that the monumental légionnaire wearing the pith helmet and chest pouch of the colonial campaigns had the face and forked beard of Paul Brundsaux).[7] The other visible project was the publication of a sumptuous *Golden Book of the Foreign Legion*, in collaboration with the uniform historian Jean Brunon and with colour plates by Pierre Benigni; an illustrated combination of campaign and uniform history, this would win the Prix Gobert in 1934.

The ceremonies passed off magnificently in front of an audience of thousands, not only ex-légionnaires from all over the world but also many French and foreign dignitaries and journalists, and on 30 April 1931 the precise liturgy of the Feast of Cameron was finally formalized. (It did no harm that the spring of 1931 also saw the opening of a great Exposition Coloniale in Paris, for which Marshal Lyautey finally emerged from his mourning.) Rollet's personal reward went beyond his promotion to brigadier-general and command of Tlemcen Subdivision; simultaneously the War Ministry created an Inspectorate of the Foreign Legion with Rollet as the first – and as it transpired, only – Inspector-General. His successor in command of the 1st Foreign was his old second-in-command from the trenches, Colonel Nicolas. Rollet's plan had worked; he had created a machine for attracting and integrating future recruits, and he had established a positive image of the Legion in the eyes of the French public and the wider world. (Although this would be tragically tested in the Algiers *putsch* attempt of April 1961, it survived, and Rollet surely deserves his sobriquet of 'the Father of the Legion'.)[8]

*

IT WAS ALSO in 1931 that War Minister Maginot ordered more active operations against the remaining pockets of tribal defiance in the Atlas and the South. The despotism of the Glaoua had proved unable to hold banditry in check in the southern High Atlas or to prevent outright warfare in the great west-east corridor of the Draa and Dades valleys below the mountains. Two centres of dissidence were the parallel outlying range of the Djebel Sahro, and the Ziz oases running down into the Tafilalt at the eastern end of the corridor. The recent deaths of the two secondary 'lords of the Atlas' (El Goundaffi and El Mtouggi) were drawing French troops up into the mountain passes where their levies had previously protected the new roads pushing south, and in January 1932 the French would supplant the ineffective Glaoua garrisons in the Draa valley, installing a new Native Affairs post at Zagora. Since it was intended to station an increased number of North African troops in France, there was an incentive to complete the pacification of lawless southern Morocco once and for all, but this still involved political risks. The consequences of any significant casualties among the regular troops committed – largely Moroccan Skirmishers – would be serious, and *goumiers* and irregulars were to be employed in large numbers wherever possible. Maginot would tell the commander-in-chief, General Antoine Huré:

> If you have one unfortunate engagement, I will hide your losses and I will lie
> against the evidence; but I can only do that once. If you have a second reverse
> I will be obliged to tell the truth, and then all those – like me – who wish for
> the pacification of Morocco will be swept away, like Ferry after Lang Son.[9]

General Niéger's operations in the High Atlas in July 1931 involved about 5,500 irregulars, including some 1,500 Zaians led by a son of Moha ou Hammou under the command of Colonel de Loustal. This officer was a specialist in working with 'turned' tribesmen, and his tactics would be influential throughout the remaining mountain campaigns. He would make a night march with *goumiers* and *moghaznis* screened by local scouts, halting before first light to dig in on some defensible height until regular troops and artillery could catch up with him. Mounted irregulars provided his reserve; if the dissidents attacked his new crest he would drive them back with machine guns before unleashing these *suppletifs* in pursuit, and he quite often achieved success without any casualties at all among the regulars.[10] After service in Morocco in 1930–33 the future Marshal Alphonse

Juin, who would command the French Expeditionary Corps in the Italian mountains in 1943–4, wrote of what he called Loustal's 'Tadla method':

> Imposing your will on the enemy without getting yourself killed is a matter of deception. Against an adversary armed only with rifles the way to keep casualties down is ... to meet him only when you are dug in behind wire with heavy firepower. Since you first have to go and occupy his terrain, you must employ surprise; you have time on your side, so use it to deceive him by false concentrations, diversions and misinformation. The moment will always come when – since the Berbers cannot keep a tribal force together for long – they will relax their vigilance and uncover your objective. Then choose a nice moonlit night, and jump. Send the irregulars in first to roll over the last remaining defenders of your objective, but the regulars must follow closely to occupy and organize it. At dawn the reacting enemy should find them already dug in, with wire strung and machine guns and artillery in place.
>
> To pull this off you need a perfect knowledge of the mountain terrain provided by a very sharp Intelligence service. You also need particularly well-trained troops, both irregulars and regulars, because a night advance demands a mad temerity ... It goes without saying that it is almost impossible to coordinate such an operation with neighbouring forces, [and it is certainly] for those who prefer to work alone.[11]

AT THE END of 1931 the French concentrated on the Tafilalt, from whose refuges Belkassem Ngadi's band and Ait Khabbash war parties had been intervening rapaciously in various tribal wars that were ruining the fertile valley oases between Boumalne Dades and Tinerhir. In the Draa valley the western Ait Atta tribes were being fragmented by the patient Captain Spillmann at Ouarzazate, and in November 1931 he managed to detach the once resolutely hostile Ait Istful 'fifth' from the Ait Khabbash.[12] The operation against the Ziz oases was now prepared by General Giraud's Frontier Group (Groupe des Confins Algéro-Marocains). In this terrain, Loustal's patient 'grandmother's footsteps' that worked best in the mountains had to give way to what Juin called the 'Frontier method, whose master is General Giraud'. Here speed was the key to limiting casualties: fast hooking manoeuvres by mobile units, a bold surprise attack to achieve shock, then pursuit and exploitation to the limit. Unlike Loustal's method, these tactics absolutely required tight coordination of the movement of different units drawing upon carefully pre-planned logistics.[13]

When a sandstorm stalled a preliminary night operation on 18/19

November 1931, Captain de Bournazel, with his *goumiers* and 600 irregulars, used his initiative and seized Touroug oasis on the Oued Rheris west of the Tafilalt (see Map 23); a week later 'the Red Man' was named Native Affairs chief at nearby El Glifate. On 6 December, about 150 Ait Hammou raiders from the mountains around the Todra gorge wiped out Lieutenant Chappeldaine and 30 *partisans* in the Djebel Ougnat south-east of Touroug; eight days later Bournazel caught up with them and avenged his dead. On 10 January 1932 many clans, including some of the desert Ait Atta, were reported to be submitting at the new Native Affairs post at Zagora and to the troops of the newly promoted General Catroux, now GOC Marrakesh Region.[14]

On 14 January 1932, General Giraud sent mobile columns to converge on Rissani, the southern centre of the Tafilalt complex, where Belkassem Ngadi was rumoured to be holed up. From dawn until 11am on the 15th, Giraud shelled and bombed Rissani, then sent in attacks from the north, east and south-east while the western column formed a stop-line. The village was devastated, but Belkassem Ngadi had slipped away. (He reached El Mhamid oasis on the edge of the Djebel Bani, where he joined some 500 Ait Hammou and Ait Khabbash under a warchief named Muhammad u-Bani, and continued to play cat-and-mouse with Captain Spillmann.) Henry de Bournazel's irregulars were set to guard Rissani against any return by the Ait Hammou or Ait Khabbash.[15]

The only white infantry committed were Captain Robitaille's Motorized Company/1st Foreign, who took their vehicles into combat for the first time on 18 January about 35 miles further up the Ziz, at the oasis of Meski.[16] The plan was for the mechanized infantry in their ten-man Panhard armoured carriers to advance first, with armoured cars in close support, and Berliet trucks bringing up the rear with *portée* 37mm guns to breach the walls over the heads of the légionnaires. When the first scout vehicle left the road some 1,000 yards from the objective it drew fire at once. Légionnaires disembarked to silence this, but when the company resumed the advance into the palm groves at 9.30am, the heavy Panhard 179s bogged down in deep, soft sand. After vain attempts to get them moving again it was decided that the infantry would have to put in an old-fashioned attack from about 400 yards, under what supporting fire the vehicles could deliver.

The légionnaires deployed into line, and advanced quickly across ground strewn and obstructed with fallen palm-trunks and cactus hedges, taking casualties from riflemen in the two towers of the large *kasbah*. They reached the base of the walls and jammed up against them, waiting what seemed interminable moments for gunfire support. When this arrived it was admirably accurate, blowing in the heavy timber and mud-brick gateway in billowing clouds of dust. Deafened and choking, the first squads kicked their way in through the splintered debris; more men fell to close-range fire, but the second platoon passed through them and began grenading their way through the alleyways and houses. After an hour of street-fighting, Meski was in French hands, but it cannot be said that the Motorized Company's new equipment had added much to the Legion's traditional capabilities.

That same day at Rissani, General Huré took the submission of the leaders of some 50,000 people, and this *aman* was confirmed on 26 January by Resident-General Lucien Saint in person. The great *palmeries* were now parched and yellowing from a five-year drought; the wealth of centuries was dwindling, and the submission of the Tafilalt after so many years seems to have been something of an anti-climax.[17]

THE DJEBEL SAHRO was the birthplace of the Ait Atta nation, from which their separate tribes had spread out since the seventeenth century over more than 20,000 square miles. However far they ranged they were 'tethered to the Djebel Sahro by a long rope', and their symbolic sanctuary and court of appeal was at Igharm Amazdar about 15 miles north-east of the village of Iknioun (see Map 23). In these new arm's-length operations the French regular battalions and light armour would form the cordons within which the *goumiers* and *partisans* did most of the assault work (Major Pechkoff, now leading II/4th REI, would be so frustrated by the secondary role of his battalion that he would soon request a transfer to Syria).[18] However, it seems theatrically fitting that in this final chapter of the 30-year story, the heirs to Négrier's and Lyautey's old mule companies should be the only European troops who would try to follow the Ait Atta into their last redoubt.

In November 1932, several clans, particularly in the south of the massif, had already come over to the French; others were in contact but still hedging their bets, but tribesmen who had no intention of surrendering without a fight were drifting into the Djebel Sahro from all over the south-east. The core clans were the Ilimshan and Ait Aisa u-Brahim of the Ait Atta, but these were joined by many families from a number of other tribes. Their leader was Assu u-Ba Slam, a respected warrior and chief of the Ilimshan who was a sworn enemy of El Glaoui and of those Ait Atta who had sided with him. He had a reputation as a tough but direct and truthful man, and in the winter of 1932/3 he rejected French attempts to negotiate.[19] The French reckoned his followers to be about 7,000 souls of 800 families (of which 500 were incomers), with rather fewer than 1,000 rifles, but Assu's son later claimed that he had had some 1,200 fighting men. Assu had taken some Lebels in battle with the Glaoua, and his brother Bassu was an experienced gun-runner who had smuggled rifles and ammunition from Marrakesh on mule-trains carrying sacks of henna and tea. (Only 174 of their warriors would later surrender repeaters, but that was an old trick; those who decided to surrender either hid their best rifles for recovery later, or sold them to those who were fighting on, handing in ancient single-shooters instead.)[20]

The French continued to create a ring of submitted clans around Assu's heartland, and late in January 1933 the Native Affairs chief Captain Spillmann met with u-Marir, a chief of Ait Unir rebels among Assu's following. U-Marir stressed that it was Assu's hatred of El Glaoui that was the main obstacle, and suggested that the French delay their attack in the Djebel Sahro for six months while negotiating through intermediaries. By then the French preparations had their own momentum, and Spillmann told him this was impossible; unless Assu submitted he would be attacked in twelve days by superior forces, including many of his fellow tribesmen now in French service. At this, u-Marir declared that they would fight to the death, and that the French would face three enemies: cold, rocks and copper (bullets). In this he spoke the truth; Assu had chosen to make his stand among the naked crags of Bu Gafer – the 'Wasteland', east of the snow-clad 8,900-foot peak of Amalou n'Mansour.

THE FRENCH-LED FORCES of Generals Catroux from the west and Giraud from the east closed in across the plateaux in early February 1933. Catroux's Marrakesh Group had some 4,400 Glaoua and tribal irregulars – at least 650 of them Ait Atta – and six Goums, backed by three battalions of Moroccan Skirmishers and I/ and III/4th Foreign Infantry, Captain Robitaille's Motorized Company/1st Foreign, a Spahi regiment, plentiful artillery (including a composite Legion battery from 2nd and 4th REI), and five air squadrons. The irregulars and Goums were divided between Captain Spillmann's strong *harka* advancing north-eastwards from Nekob, and Lieutenant-Colonel Chardon's force coming south-eastwards from the direction of Boumalne Dades.

Giraud's Frontier Group from the east was smaller; he had only about 1,300 *partisans*, 5 Goums (two of them led by Captain de Bournazel), 2 Spahi squadrons and a mounted Saharan Company; the Legion provided the mounted companies of 2nd and 3rd REI (Captains Fouré and Fauchaux), plus the mechanized VI/1st REC for track security. With supporting artillery and 4 air squadrons, this force was divided between Lieutenant-Colonel Tarrit's column pushing south-west via Igharm Amazdar, and Lieutenant-Colonel Despas moving due westwards. The initial plan was for Catroux's men to make the sweep while Giraud's formed a stop-line. On 13 February, both commands began moving into the central heights of the Djebel Sahro, through a cold, arid and treeless landscape of stony plateaux and dramatic outcrops.[21]

The final approaches to Bu Gafer from the north were barred by sheer cliffs, and its ultimate occupation would depend on the Spillman and Despas columns from the south-west and east respectively. Bournazel's Goums and the mounted companies of 2nd and 3rd Foreign were with Despas; these Legion companies had not yet been motorized, and were picking their way up into the heights in the old way, with riding- and pack-mules. A water column was ambushed as early as the afternoon of 13 February, and the Legion escort took casualties during a firefight across a chaotic boulder-field; that night their cheerless camp in the rocks was relentlessly sniped, sending the mules mad. On the 15th, orders came down for Giraud's units to take the initiative to try to draw off some of the defenders who were holding up Catroux's advance from the west. In cold fog the Despas column pushed on into the trackless waste of wind-swept slopes and rocky gulches, coming under frequent fire from unseen tribesmen. Progress was painfully slow, and on 16 February both eastern and western commands were more or less stalled in the clouds at altitudes of around 6,000 feet. On the 17th, General Huré arrived to take personal command, and thereafter the troops had to spend two days labouring to build tracks so that supply-mules and artillery could come up.

On 19 February, General Giraud's units – now given the assault role, despite the weaker numbers allocated for their intended mission – resumed their slow advance through a desolate landscape rich in natural defensive positions. Bournazel's Goums took a hill and cleared some defended caves; that night, high winds that cut like flint prevented the troops from raising tents or lighting anything better than the tiniest protected fires. On the 20th, icy rain added to their misery – chilling them to the bone, causing mudslides under their scrambling boots, and sending supply-mules crashing down ravines to bounce sickeningly off the sharp rocks. (Descriptions of the conditions faced by the infantry at Bu Gafer irresistibly recall accounts of the Monte Cassino battles of the winter of 1943/4.) The first gun batteries were brought forward and opened fire, but under veils of rain and mist it was impossible to locate friend from foe and the consequently tentative shelling had little effect. On 21 February, Bournazel's vanguard reached the foot of a dark granite tower nicknamed 'the Chapel'. His first attempts to make progress up it were costly, causing a distinct wavering among his *goumiers*, and before they reached the top his Lieutenant Alessandri was one of the motionless brown bundles left scattered among the rocks.

Assu u-Ba Slam's Berbers were now pulling backwards and upwards in a stubborn fighting retreat through the roots of the final heights of Bu Gafer. On 22 February, one of their rearguard parties was cut off and eventually wiped out, but the next day a counter-attack recaptured the lost ground so ferociously that the French would have retreated even further if the terrain had allowed. After stabilizing the line at some cost they were ordered to sit tight while artillery prepared the way. The Berbers, too, were suffering; they had many more mouths than rifles, and in this high desolation of stone there was hardly any grazing for about 25,000 sheep and goats that they had driven up with them. Even in the depth of winter access to water was vital, and the French advance had now driven them above nearly all the springs. Women sometimes climbed down to fetch water by night, and were killed by machine guns firing blindly into the darkness on fixed lines. (One source claims that when they were identified the Legion companies refused to fire on them.) On 25 February there was a truce while further negotiations were attempted, but firing broke out again the next day between a machine-gun platoon and Berber snipers, who shot the former's Lieutenant Bureau clean through the forehead. On the 26th and 27th the artillery pounded the heights with little apparent success; rock splinters added murderously to the steel fragments, but the boulders were so close-set that it took an almost direct hit to cause casualties.[22]

THE FIRST INFANTRY ASSAULT on Bu Gafer proper took place on 28 February, led by Captain de Bournazel's two Goums with the two Legion companies in the second wave, moving roughly north-westwards from positions on three occupied heights. Bournazel would advance from feature P2; behind him, Lieutenant Brenckle – the survivor of Bou Leggou – would follow up from P1 ('the Chapel') with his half of Fouré's Mounted Company/2nd Foreign, plus Captain Fauchaux with half of his Mounted Company/3rd Foreign. From the less exposed P3, support fire would be provided by the rest of Fauchaux's company and the machine-gun platoons of both. Only when Bournazel, Brenckle and Fauchaux had cleared three crests above them could Captain Fouré, with Lieutenant Garnier and the rest of Mounted/2nd Foreign, assault other heights on their right.

In the late winter dawn, Bournazel's 200 *goumiers* and 300 *partisans* drank mint tea and chewed a few dates, huddled in their *djellabahs* against the bitter cold and rain. Despite the low clouds and turbulent wind, a flight of Potez 25 biplanes came pitching and lurching between the peaks to drop a few bombs, with questionable accuracy. The French artillery expended a lavish allocation of shells, but the only confirmed casualties were some French supply-mules hit by accident. After an hour the shelling was lifted higher up the mountain, and at about 7am the infantry were ordered forwards.

Bournazel's first objective, P6, presented a steep tongue of rocky slope narrowing towards a defile through a cliff wall (christened 'the Mountain's Arse' by the légionnaires). This funnel would have to be climbed by a series of natural steps; about halfway up there was an outcrop on the left that might provide some cover. Above the stairway of ledges the Berbers were awaiting them on a crest. When Bournazel's two Goums had taken this, Fauchaux's two half-companies of légionnaires were supposed to pass through and assault the next balcony of the cathedral of rock brooding down at them. The *goumiers* made their painful way up the slope, but as they reached the mouth of the defile the fire from hidden defenders became heavier. They took cover behind scattered rocks, shooting back on the rare occasions when they spotted a target, and the impetus of the attack drained away. Behind them, a bullet hit the haversack of grenades carried by a légionnaire and exploded it, wounding four men badly.

Captain de Bournazel took the lead, encouraging his Branès forwards (he was not wearing his red burnous that day, just a drab smock like the rest). Amid the constant snap of near-misses and shriek of ricochets, they had almost reached the first step of the staircase of ledges when, at about 7.20am, Henry de Bournazel was hit, through the right side and stomach. He buckled, then straightened and tottered onwards; his Lieutenant Binet, Sergeant Periousse and a few *goumiers* accompanied him, but when they saw him hit a second time many others stopped or even began drifting to the rear. Two men grabbed the captain by the heels and dragged him painfully under the cover of the rocky balcony, as an excited clamour from above warned that the Berbers might try to rush down and cut up the casualties.

Behind the *goumiers* the first squads of Lieutenant Brenckle's légionnaires now clambered up into 'the Mountain's Arse'. His half of Mounted/2nd Foreign were understrength that day; he had with him only Lieutenant Jeanpierre, 10 NCOs and 70 men.[23] By about 7.40am they were so far forward that all artillery support had to cease. The Berbers were flitting among the rocks in bands of 20 or 30, firing, throwing grenades and rolling boulders down among the attackers, dropping several men each time before darting back under cover. All the rest of the *goumiers* on Brenckle's left now turned and fled, leaving Binet, Periousse and only a handful of loyal Branès with the helpless Bournazel at the high point of his advance. Then Lieutenant Brenckle himself fell, mortally wounded, and within moments Sergeant Chief Peters, Sergeant Augsten and Privates Lacoste and Schneidereit were also killed. Seeing the légionnaires of 2nd Foreign stalled, Captain Fauchaux of the 3rd strode across the slope from his place on the right to get a grip on them; halfway across he too fell, and died within minutes.

Lieutenant Jeanpierre ordered bayonets fixed and tried to get up to Binet's and Periouse's trapped handful of *goumiers*; Sergeant Jibovec and Privates Franchi, Alzua, Richard and Schmidt died in the attempt, and only the lieutenant and Privates Polak and Coghetto made it. They held out below the rim of the ledge for about 15 minutes before – since they could not advance, and were in imminent danger of being surrounded and overrun – Jeanpierre ordered them to fall back to better cover behind an outcrop about 150 yards downhill. By now the légionnaires had taken heavy casualties, and the survivors had neither the firepower nor the positions to cover the withdrawal safely and effectively. Polak was killed from behind as he slid and stumbled down the scree, and Lieutenant Binet was knocked somersaulting down the slope by the impact of three bullets, but *goumiers* dragged Bournazel part way down before abandoning him.

Private Vurusic went forward and managed to lift the captain on to his shoulders and, with the help of two other légionnaires, carried him far enough to pause under cover. They improvised a stretcher with rifles and greatcoats and forced four hesitating *moghaznis* to carry it; on their way to the rear they were joined by a shame-faced *goumier* carrying the standard of Bournazel's company, topped with the red-dyed tail of the horse that had been killed under him years before. Later that afternoon Vurusic and Private

Abassia went back up the hillside and brought in Captain Fauchaux's body. At about 4pm, Lieutenant Jeanpierre, in command of the combined légionnaires since Fauchaux's death, was ordered to fall back another 600 yards and establish a defensive night position. The four platoons from Mounted/2nd and 3rd Foreign had lost 2 officers, 5 NCOs and 15 légionnaires killed, plus 3 NCOs and 22 men wounded – roughly a quarter of the day's total French casualties of 179 all ranks.

In a freezing, flapping medical tent at the foot of Bu Gafer, Henry de Bournazel's friend Dr Jean Vial did his best for him. He piled 'the Red Man' with coats, dressed his broken right arm and injected morphine, but the belly shot had caused fatal internal damage. As pale as paper, Bournazel groaned through chattering teeth, 'Leave me alone – I'll only be here for an hour'. Later, when the morphine had taken effect, he plucked at the bloody rags of his uniform and (ever the cavalry dandy) muttered with a faint smile, 'It's disgusting to die as dirty as this, Doc.' He did not survive the night.[24]

A LAST UNSUCCESSFUL ATTEMPT to take Bu Gafer by assault was made on 1 March, with heavy artillery and air support and Moroccan Skirmisher battalions brought forward to stiffen the irregulars. Captain Spillmann was distressed by the inevitably high casualties among the Berber families and livestock, which were far more vulnerable to shellfire than the thin chains of fighting men among the rocks, but at this stage Assu u-Ba Slam's warriors shot on sight anyone attempting to parley, including a *marabout*. Thereafter the 'turned' Ait Atta advised General Huré simply to maintain a tight encirclement and wait for lack of water and ammunition to do his work for him. On 10 March the first 150 families made contact with Spillmann, who used his knowledge of particular tribal beliefs to insert a lever into this chink. On the 23rd and 24th there were further defections; and on 25 March, after 42 days of fighting, the Ilimshan led by the brothers Assu and Bassu u-Ba Slam laid down their arms in front of Generals Huré, Giraud and Catroux. These last to submit numbered 2,900 people, of whom some 500 were armed warriors. In all 4,700 people had surrendered, so up to 2,300 had died – including 500–700 fighting men – and 90 per cent of their flocks and herds had perished from thirst or bombardment. Among the dead were two of Assu u-Ba Slam's children.

It is worth considering that Assu's costly defiance – which the Native Affairs officers had appealed to him to renounce both before and during the fighting – was proud but largely pointless. The terms granted by General

Huré were hardly onerous: Assu had to submit formally to the Maghzan and in future pay the normal taxes, but his freedom from Glaoua rule was guaranteed; weapons were to be listed but could be kept; a complete amnesty was granted without the payment of fines, and Assu was confirmed as chief of the Ilimshan. The French also promised that there would be no levying of *partisans* among these hills for a year, but that summer Assu actually offered warriors to fight with the French against the very last pocket of resistance in the High Atlas. The offer was declined, but it was sincere; the last resisters included tribesmen of the Ait Atta's ancestral enemies, the Ait Murghad.[25]

THE SECOND PHASE of the 1933 offensive, the 'Mount Baddou' campaign in July–August, took place in an uncharted crumple of parched brown mountains about 80 miles across and 50 miles deep, in the eastern ranges of the High Atlas north of Tinerhir and south of Imilchil (see Map 23).

After Djebel Sahro, General Huré assembled an army of some 35,000 combat and 10,000 service troops. The usual converging movements were planned, on a grand scale: General Goudot's Meknes Group from the north with 7 battalions, including 2 of the Legion; Giraud's Frontier Group from the east with 7, plus 4 Legion mounted and motorized companies; Catroux's Marrakesh Group from the south with 6 battalions, including 3 Legion; and Colonel de Loustal's Tadla Group from the north-west with 12, including 3 Legion. Of these 32 battalions the 2nd, 3rd and 4th REIs, with a total of 8 battalions plus the motorized equivalent of a ninth, would provide the only European infantry except for a single Colonial battalion sent – with some hesitation – from France.[26]

The operations began on 7 July 1933, with simultaneous advances by the Meknes, Tadla and Frontier commands to converge on the headwaters of the Oued Dades, while the Marrakesh Group pushed north-eastwards from Boumalne Dades up the spectacular Dades gorge. For the first 20-odd miles this was broad and fertile, studded with red-brown *kasbahs* amid grainfields and orchards, but as it cut deeper into the mountains the cliffs closed in. Here it was the three Legion battalions who led the way, tasked with cutting a new motor road along the cliffs above the river. This took immense labour, choking with dust deep in claustrophobic canyons in temperatures above 110°F (43°C), and at some points men had to be lowered on ropes from the rim above to drill the first holes for charges. At least the légionnaires of 4th Foreign did not have to rely solely on explosives and hand-tools this time; General Huré, an Engineer by background, had procured dozens of 'Spiros' truck-powered pneumatic drills. As soon as a basic track had been made, these could be driven forward to improve it; Huré calculated that each did the work of 80 men, and that his légionnaires achieved a rate of 2 yards per man per day as the road crept forwards up the gorge.[27]

Their immediate goal was Msemrir, where forward supply dumps were established. Meanwhile the Meknes Group were clearing the upper Assif Melloul valley south-east of Imilchil, and the Tadla and Frontier Groups were moving south down the valley of the Oued Imdrass towards Ait Hani (in these mountains even the valley floors may be at 6,000–7,000 feet, and many of the peaks rear up to 10,000). Despite stiff resistance to the northern columns by Ait Haddidou tribesmen, the Marrakesh, Tadla and Frontier groups met on 23 July, cutting the area of operations in two. From Ait Hani the Tadla Group turned west to mop up the smaller remaining pocket in the Djebel Koucer, but the main objective lay to the east. Catroux's Marrakesh Group turned eastwards along the Tittaouine gorge (where they met their first opposition) and into the parched valley of the Assif Amtrouss, while Frontier Group pushed on further south.[28]

THE LAST BERBER REFUGE, which the French called Mount Baddou, was about 40 miles north-east of Tinerhir, somewhere in the mountain chains running north-eastwards between Tamtetoucht and Assoul. The London *Daily Mail* correspondent George Ward Price, who accompanied the operations in August, identifies the massif simply as 'the Kerdous', and implies elsewhere that it was nearly 10,000 feet high; clearly it was the highest tooth in the blade between the upper Amtrouss and Kerdouss valleys, but its exact location is obscure.[29] In the end the last tribesmen fighting for it would be the minority of warriors among some 2,000–3,000 Berbers led by an Ait Murghad chief named u-Skunti. Like the Ilimshan in February, the Ait Murghad drove their beasts up into the highest glens and fought from gulleys and caves; this was high summer, and the struggle for Baddou would be won by thirst.

There was no general engagement; a massive noose was woven with Roman patience, and was then tightened according to the 'Tadla method'. Irregulars were sent clambering up to take the first rifle-fire that would reveal the defenders' hiding-places (sometimes having to use their turbans as climbing-ropes); they were followed by *goumiers*, who held the enemy in play until they too were followed, ridge after weary ridge, by the regular infantry, who consolidated each occupied height before the next bound. This may not have exposed many légionnaires to the danger of wounds, but it was as exhausting as any operation in Legion history. Driving up the Tittaouine gorge, Ward Price noted that the vehicles made actual bow-waves in the dust as they passed the panting infantry:

> Some of the companies of the Legion that I passed on the march in the valleys of the Grand Atlas looked like processions of souls in purgatory. Under a sun that was registering 105 degrees Fahrenheit in the shade, they were ploughing along through sand six inches deep, their feet sinking into it at every step. Passing motor-lorries and mule-convoys kept them smothered in a permanent cloud of fine dust, of a kind that inflames the eyes, parches the throat, shrivels the tongue and cracks the lips. It was impossible for the men in the column to see more than two or three yards ahead. With haggard faces they plodded on, the streaming sweat clogging the dust on their cheeks into a mask of mud, an eighty-pound pack on their backs ... and sometimes a haversack full of bombs as well.[30]

After the link-up on 23 July there was a pause of about ten days to bring up supplies and position the troops for the next phase; General Huré's forward HQ came up to Ait Hani, where Ward Price arrived on 6 August after a six-hour drive from Boumalne Dades up the Legion's new road. (He found a field brothel already installed at Ait Hani, and was unimpressed by the standards of latrine discipline and water hygiene in the camp.)[31] The chain of mountains leading north-eastwards to Baddou was now being flanked on its north side by the Marrakesh and Meknes groups moving up the Amtrouss valley; meanwhile the Frontier Group had hooked left, north-eastwards up the Kerdouss valley to encircle the objective from the south.

(At this point Giraud's command also switched its line of supply: until now the Frontier Group had been provisioned from Algeria via Boudenib, but henceforward it would draw on the same rear bases as the Marrakesh force. This still meant that every bullet and biscuit had to come about 300 miles, and for the first 100 from Marrakesh to Ouarzazate the trucks had to negotiate the Tizi n'Tichka pass with its 1,800 hairpin bends, many above dizzying unfenced drops. To keep just one Mobile Group fed and supplied in the Atlas required 43 metric tons for each single day's operations, and the supply trucks groaning up the mountain roads in summer had to travel at

100-yard intervals to avoid the drivers being blinded by the dust thrown up by the vehicle ahead.)[32]

On the night of 5/6 August, half of Marrakesh Group attacked the Djebel Hamdoun, a south-west extension of the Baddou massif; the next day the Berber reaction killed 4 officers and 38 rankers and wounded another 135. On the evening of the 6th a clever ambush wiped out a convoy following the leading battalions up the Amtrouss gorge, at the cost of 100 mule-loads of ammunition; Ward Price saw with his own eyes the grossly mutilated body of a French warrant officer wounded and captured in this incident (he would later see the corpse of a Senegalese Skirmisher with the ashes of a fire in his opened belly). On the south of the mountains, the Frontier Group in the Kerdouss valley had a five-day fight from 6 to 11 August to force the Berbers back from the main water sources and up into the dry crags. The tribesmen fought hard, from caves protected by drystone walls, and it was not until guns could be brought up to deliver direct fire that the infantry made real progress in clearing them with rifle and grenade. (During the fighting in the Kerdouss the bodies of two Europeans in Berber dress were found.)[33]

Ward Price went up to the Meknes Group front in the Amtrouss valley, joining Lieutenant-Colonel Richert's 2nd Foreign Infantry at Djebel Hamdoun. He describes the stink from the corpses of unburied animals and carelessly buried men along the track, the maddening swarms of flies and the stones too hot to touch. The regiment and a section of mountain guns were camped behind wire and chest-high rock *murettes* on a stony plateau facing Baddou from the west, and after six weeks in the field the troops were dirty and ragged. Officers could at least rinse themselves – and some still sported their well-cut tunics rather than 'going native' with *gandourah* and *cheich* – but water was too short for the rankers to be able to wash or shave. (Indeed, camp-followers would sometimes crawl up to the firing-line and sell mugs of it at 5 francs, which was then two days' pay for a légionnaire with three years' service.) Ward Price interviewed – in private – two British légionnaires and one American corporal; all said they were content with Legion life, which for a man who could look out for himself was hard but just. Private Hunter, a former Royal Navy petty officer, told the journalist that he had worse memories of working as a lumberjack in Canada.[34]

In the second week of August, Ward Price witnessed a typical advance along a saddle by II/2nd REI, led – as always – by local guides, since compasses were useless among these magnetic rocks. A skirmish line of *partisans* preceded the Legion companies, which moved in file covered by others on a parallel ridge. During a pause, machine guns and Brandt mortars, mule-packed forwards, raked the next slope where movement had been seen. Between unit headquarters the communications were by wireless sets with a range of about 3 miles; closer liaison was by signal lamps powered by hand-cranked magnetos, as well as by field telephone where cable-laying was practicable, and the *partisans* were given coloured identity panels to protect them from mistaken attack by the French aircraft circling overhead.

Once the battalion had occupied a new crest, against only a little long-range sniping, they set about fortifying it with rock walls and wire. The Berbers were tireless infiltrators, and however great the imbalance in fire-power, an attack could never be discounted; shortly before Ward Price joined them, the battalion had stopped a dawn rush that came within 30 yards. The II/2nd Foreign were now facing the northern slopes of Baddou from only about 700 yards' range but across a ravine at least 1,000 feet deep. The tribesmen opposite were wary of moving around on the lower slopes, but they and their flocks wandered carelessly along the skyline; they understood that artillery from either flank could not fire freely for fear of dropping shells on the other brigade in the valley beyond.[35]

After two weeks of complete encirclement, bombardment by artillery and aircraft and growing thirst, u-Skunti was finally persuaded to surrender, largely by the example of a respected woman member of the council named Lalla Tazibout. She brought her own small group of families down under cover of night, and agreed with Native Affairs officers to go back up Baddou and try to convince u-Skunti to give up before their flocks all died of thirst. On 23 August the French sent word by *partisans* that the Berbers could come out without fear, and the next day the troops watched as their thirst-maddened flocks tumbled down the slopes towards the springs below. The families who trekked out with their laden camels, donkeys and cows were given food and water and set on the trails to rear areas, where they would be deloused, vaccinated, and given tools and seed-corn. Ward Price saw a little girl wearing a dead légionnaire's identity disc among the beads around her neck – 'Seraphin, Guilbert, 1st Foreign Infantry'; it was taken from her in exchange for a handful of coins. After a final foiled attempt to break out, u-Skunti and his last 100 or so diehards surrendered on 26 August 1933.[36]

IT ENDED, AS ALWAYS, with the *targuiba*, the formal ceremony of submission. The dirty, unshaven légionnaires brushed and polished their kit as best they could and put on their blue sashes. Detachments from all the units present paraded in a big three-sided square, with one face open towards the assembled Berbers. To the blare of trumpets General Huré rode up, followed by a glittering escort, and reviewed his troops. Then he faced the armed tribesmen of military age, who came forward between the walls of sunburned soldiers, watched by their families crouching outside. The warriors were summoned in groups to throw down their rifles in a heap: Lebels, cavalry carbines, Winchesters, old Martini-Henrys, a few flintlocks. Then the general addressed them, his words interpreted by a Kabylie officer of Algerian troops. He spoke, he said, for the Maghzan and their lord the Sultan, against whom they had rebelled. In his generosity, their sovereign pardoned them, but now they must make their submission. The tribesmen lay face down in the dust, their hands linked behind their necks, and remained lying in complete silence for one minute. At the word, they stood again. The new pact between sovereign and subjects was then sealed by the ritual sacrifice of a bullock and six sheep in the middle of the square of soldiers. Finally the tribesmen were ushered back by *moghaznis*, and the troops marched past their commander-in-chief, followed by a controlled stampede of mounted *partisans*.

Ward Price had a chance to question some of the Berbers through interpreters, and he was struck by their completely fatalistic attitude to defeat. Their rebellion had been the will of God, and so had its failure. They showed complete disregard for the sufferings of their families, for their dead, and for the seriously wounded whom they had not bothered to carry down – there had been 'quite a lot, but no doubt they were all dead by now'. Their only pressing concern was when they would get their rifles back.[37]

THIS FINAL CAMPAIGN of August 1933 was the last time that infantry battalions of the Legion in Morocco were assembled for seasonal operations, and it marked the beginning of several years of inevitable decline. For nearly 30 years – two whole generations of service – the companies and battalions had converged each spring from their scattered garrisons to join the mobile groups formed to push the frontiers of French control further into tribal territory. Now this classic cycle of military seasons had become irrelevant, and since the units remained dispersed and were used almost entirely for hard labour, they quickly lost their edge. A report of 7 March 1934 stated that their performance already left much to be desired, because when a battalion was reunited it took too long to re-accustom the companies to manoeuvring as a formed unit.[38]

However, Generals Catroux and Giraud did assemble mobile groups for one final time in the winter of 1933/4, and about a thousand légionnaires would have a voice in this last hurrah. Hardly any shots would be fired during this tidying-up exercise, and the légionnaires would undertake a great deal of backbreaking work on desert tracks and mountain ramps. Nevertheless, it was – for the last time – officially a combat operation rather than merely a 'police tour', and officers and men were happy to take what they could get.

THE LAST UNPENETRATED region of French Morocco was the Anti-Atlas range in the far south-west, between the Sous plain and the lower Oued Draa. The shallow westwards curve of that hidden watercourse marked Morocco's southern frontiers, with Algeria and then with the Spanish Sahara or Rio del Oro (see Map 24). The sparse tribes of this remote and biblically poor desert country were quite unthreatening, but a few thousand Berber incomers from far to the east had taken refuge in this last unoccupied corner. They included perhaps 350 tents of the Ait Hammou all the way from the Boudenib territory, 600 families of the stubborn Ait Khabbash from the Tafilalt, and the elusive Sheikh Belkassem Ngadi himself. In French eyes, the pacification of Morocco would not be complete until the last of these warriors had formally requested the *aman*.

General Huré's plan would be the ultimate test of the 'Frontier method' based on speed across country, and it depended upon motorized units. In the west, mounted and truck-borne troops of General Catroux's Marrakesh Group would strike south from a start-line around Tiznit and up into the Anti-Atlas, and would then turn north-east to form an encirclement. From further east, beyond a linking element commanded by Colonel Rochas, Giraud's Frontier Group would launch two columns. His right-hand force under Colonel Marratuech would peel off elements south-westwards through the mountains to link up with Rochas and with Catroux's north-eastwards hook, completing a broad 'bag' the Anti-Atlas; it would then thrust on due south towards Icht below the Djebel Bani, to meet up with the left-hand element of Giraud's command. This was Colonel Trinquet's mechanized force, which would form a mobile stop-line to cut across the southern retreat of any dissidents fleeing from the other forces and making for the Spanish Saharan border on the Oued Draa.

Starting from the oasis of Akka, Trinquet's 100 armoured vehicles and 350 supporting 'softskins' would cut south-westwards to Icht, and then divide into two prongs driving westwards to the north and south of the escarpment to meet on the lower Oued Draa, sweeping up any fugitives as they went. This force – in effect, the French Army's first trial of a light armoured brigade operating independently – consisted of three armoured car squadrons of 1st Africa Light Horse, the two mechanized squadrons of 1st Foreign Cavalry, and the two motorized companies of 1st and 4th Foreign Infantry.[39]

The operation was launched from 21 February 1934, and was a complete success. Trinquet's force reached Icht on the 25th and divided; the southern prong reached Assa on 2 March, the northern – including the Legion units – Fasq on the 5th and Goulimine on 7 March. There were minor skirmishes at Foum el Hassane, Taghjicht and Tighmert, but generally the local tribes submitted with the minimum of drama. Belkassem Ngadi and his Ait Hammou and Ait Khabbash made a last dash southwards from Goulimine for the Rio del Oro frontier, which French troops were strictly forbidden to cross. They were pursued by Trinquet's units, and the race to cut them off from the Draa officially ended in success at a spot called Mechra Chamnar on 11 March. Captain Marion's V/1st REC had in fact sent two troops some way south of the border before turning back, and it was seeing them cross that convinced the fugitives to give up, since they believed that the Spanish must be cooperating with the French to deny them refuge. In 18 days Trinquet's units had covered nearly 1,100 miles, and this first test of a wholly motorized brigade was judged a success, although their repair trucks had used up more than 7 tons of spares (25 per cent of the Laffly armoured cars had suffered breakdowns, and fully 60 per cent of the fragile VUDB carriers).[40] The formal ceremony of submission – of about 4,000 people not native to the area, with some 1,200 rifles – took place on 13 March.

The surrender of Belkassem Ngadi, and General Giraud's arrival with the Legion motorized companies at the oasis of Tindouf on 31 March 1934, closed the final chapter of the French invasion and subjection of Morocco – a story in which the Foreign Legion had been intimately involved from the first to the last page.[41]

MARSHAL HUBERT LYAUTEY DIED on 27 July 1934, at the age of 79. His wish to be buried at Rabat was honoured, despite some local objections. After Moroccan independence in 1956 the marshal's remains were exhumed and brought home, where he lies today a few steps from Napoleon's tomb in Les Invalides. In the end, he could hardly have asked for better. It could all so easily have ended in some briefly marked hole in North Vietnam – or, perhaps worse, under the gravestone of a wholly forgotten retired colonel in a village churchyard in Lorraine.

It was one minute to midnight for two kinds of North African fighting man, who had existed in a kind of symbiosis for a hundred years. The challenge of the first had called the second into being; now that the one was on the point of becoming a legend to be told around younger men's campfires, the other also faced the threat of extinction for simple lack of a useful role. However, it is logically obvious that even after the last wolf in Scotland had been killed, there must still have been a few hopeful hunters ranging the hills.

Epilogue:
The Fort at the Edge of the World

The boys who served in my time called Foum el Hassane
the arsehole of Africa.
Former Légionnaire Andreas Rosenberg, October 1985[1]

THE VERY LAST WOLVES in Morocco seem to have been about 30 Ait Khabbash Berbers who kept up intermittent banditry until July 1935; and finally one Zayd u-Mhad, whose career as a lone outlaw in the Dades valley was ended by *partisans* who tracked and killed him near Tinerhir on 5 March 1936.[2]

In the edge of the true Sahara, chiefs of the Regeibat – a numerous tribe of camel-riding raiders – surrendered to the French at Atar on 8 March 1933. Since the French-led *méharistes* of the Saharan Companies never numbered more than 800 men, the vastness of the desert would always provide refuge for small bands of incorrigible optimists, but their occasional freelance *djichs* would be no more 'political' than the activities of the last desperadoes on the American frontier. By that time the Legion's part in the watch over the northern Sahara, as heavier back-up for the *méharistes*, had been decided.

Since Algeria was the kingdom of 1st Foreign Infantry, the Algerian Sahara would be ranged by its Motorized Company. Captain Robitaille was instructed to build a post at Tabelbala, from where his company would be responsible for a huge loop of the eastern desert extending via Ouargla, Fort Flatters, Fort de Polignac and Ghat to Tamanrasset in the Ahaggar mountains. Southern Morocco continued to be garrisoned by the 4th Foreign, and the regiment's Composite Automobile Company (CMA) would remain in the Far South. After their operation with Trinquet's group in February–April 1934 they established a post at Tindouf, but on 2 May the légionnaires of CMA/4th REI were sent 90 miles north-west to the uninviting little oasis of Foum el Hassane (see Map 24).[3]

*

FOUM EL HASSANE – the 'domain of sand, horned vipers and flies' – was the point where a pass opened into the desert from the arid Djebel Bani, the southern range of the Anti-Atlas mountains. It owed its existence to a stream that emerged briefly from the rocky defile and watered a small *palmerie* before disappearing below the sands. On the southern side of the little Arab village and its palm groves, two forts would be built, one for the 300-man 19th Goum and one for the Legion motorized company. With an establishment of 284 all ranks, the CMA/4th Foreign would be the only white troops watching over more than 100,000 square miles of the Western Sahara. Their patrol circuit – south to Tindouf, south-west via Ain ben Tili and Bir Moghreim (Fort Trinquet) to Zouérat (Fort Gouraud), then north-east via Ain Abd el Malek to the cliffs of Chegga, and north-west to Tindouf and home – would be about 2,000 miles. For comparison, this is roughly the straight-line distance of a round trip from London to Naples and back, or between New York City and Pensacola, Florida.

Rivalry simmered between the 'Compagnie Montée du Maroc' and the 'Compagnie Montée d'Algérie' from the first, and on the rare occasions when soldiers from the two units encountered one another in a bar, fists would invariably start swinging. This bristling competitiveness was not eased by an apparently longstanding dislike between the company commanders. Captain Louis Gaultier of the 4th Foreign was a *pied noir* born and raised at Guelma in Algeria, and his légionnaires believed that he had wanted the Tabelbala posting for himself in order to be nearer to his family (though a glance at the map makes 'nearer' a distinctly relative term). This tension was in fact creative, since each officer pursued the rivalry by working to make his post something special. In the case of Robitaille, a former Dominican friar, this resulted in the uniquely striking design of Tabelbala, its buildings roofed with 72 shining white *kouba* domes. Foum el Hassane was more conventional; it was built like a *kasbah*, with walls and four corner towers topped with by-now purely decorative crenellations. However, Captain Gaultier and his men spared no effort – and no forgery or larceny, when requisitioning materials – to make it not only smart and soldierly, but more comfortable than anyone in this godforsaken spot had a right to expect.

The building work took many months, since in the meantime platoons periodically had to patrol in search of reported *djichs*. In early December 1934 the rhythm became more demanding and the company was divided, with an armoured and a truck platoon at Foum el Hassane and the same at Tindouf. For the rest of that month, the Tindouf half-company made wide-ranging sweeps through the desert in concert with units from right across the Western Sahara and southern Morocco; they cooperated with camel-riders of the Groupe Nomade de la Mauritanie and the Compagnie Méhariste de la Saoura, and with armoured cars of the Groupe des Confins Algéro-Marocains including the Legion troopers of V/1st REC from Boudenib. However, the men of 4th Foreign were back at Tindouf in time to celebrate Christmas 1934 in the Legion's usual expansive style.

BY 1935, THE LEGION'S STRENGTH had fallen sharply from its peak of 33,000 two years previously, to 20,445 all ranks. The seizure of emergency powers by the Nazi Party in spring 1933 had led to a rapid decline in German enlistments, from 37 per cent of all recruits in 1934 to just over 19 per cent in 1935. (It would plummet to 11 per cent by early 1937, and not only because of the harsh treatment of returning ex-légionnaires by the new regime. Many Germans of the Left would be attracted instead to the Republican cause in Spain – though some would come to the Legion, alongside many Spaniards, after its defeat in 1939.) The political turmoil in many European countries caused disquiet among the high command about the possible infiltration of the Legion by both Fascists and Communists with long-term agendas, and recruits were now scrutinized by an internal security service.[4] It became extemely difficult for a German or Austrian NCO to secure the privileged status of *sous-officier de carrière*, open to re-enlistees of other nationalities after naturalization and six years' service.

Although a posting to the better-paid and generally tranquil fleshpots of Tonkin or the Levant was still a prize for long service and good conduct, the regiments were increasingly stagnant in their long-accustomed stations. The NCO corps, while certainly the most professional in the French Army due to its high proportion of long-service soldiers, was consequently settling into a rather complacent and insular culture; a sergeant was definitely a 'Morocco NCO', a 'Syria NCO' or a 'Tonkin NCO', and there was a tendency to wriggle out of transfers. At Sidi bel Abbès – whose central services demanded large numbers of NCOs – fully half of them were married, and looking forward to the civil service careers in North Africa that usually followed retirement after 15 years in the ranks.[5] For the young and adventurous, the two desert motorized companies were virtually the only units in the Legion that still guaranteed a life reminiscent of that in 'la Légion du Papa', and in 1935 a young Hungarian political refugeee named (in French documents) Charles Milassin arrived at Foum el Hassane after his first year's training and service in the north.

MILASSIN FOUND A FORT straight out of the pages of *Beau Geste*, though with a far more humane and popular commander than Wren's 'Fort Zinderneuf'. Against the backdrop of the date-palms and the tawny bulk of the Djebel Bani, its lime-washed 15-foot walls formed a square about 150 yards on a side, surmounted by a radio aerial and a decoratively crenellated 45-foot water tower flying the tricolour. At each corner squared towers a few feet higher than the battlements protruded slightly, with slits low down in each flank from which two machine guns commanded the adjacent walls and with LMG positions on the roof-platforms. Only the towers were stone-built; otherwise the fort had been constructed in the traditional way from *pisé* (mud, chopped straw and animal dung), mixed and moulded into big sun-dried bricks by the légionnaires, with the rafters, doors and windows made from palm-tree wood. The gate in the north wall was proudly sur-mounted by the unit's title on an arched lintel, and the badge that Captain Gaultier had designed for his company in the Legion's colours: a red oval surrounded by a green cogwheel symbolizing motorized status, bearing the Legion grenade and '4' above a running ostrich, symbolizing speed in Africa, set against a horseshoe in memory of the old mule companies.

There was something unmistakably Roman about the fort's layout, with its barracks, messrooms, stores, arsenal, fuel dump, garages and workshops neatly arranged in four quarters around two large open yards, with the commander's and the lieutenants' offices in the centre. Situated about 600 track-miles from the regiment's Marrakesh depot beyond the Atlas, Foum el Hassane was necessarily self-sufficient, with its own smithy, carpentry and paint shops, fitters', mechanics', coachwork and radio workshops. The barrack blocks each accommodated 40 NCOs and privates, with their own latrine and piped-in water. Above the palm-wood ceiling a layer of rammed earth more than 4 feet deep provided insulation between the rooms and the raftered air-space under the galvanized iron roof. There was a shower-block, an infirmary, a laundry, tailor's, barber's and shoemaker's shops; there was also a small cell-block, but this seldom held anything other than a couple of rueful hangovers.

Foum el Hassane also boasted an electricity generating plant of unusual power, complete – to the légionnaires' intense satisfaction and pride – with an ice-making machine. This was a tribute to their paternal Captain

Gaultier. When word reached him that a fishing boat had run aground and been abandoned on the Atlantic coast about 100 miles to the west, that resourceful officer had sent mechanics in trucks to strip it to its ribs, and they had returned in triumph with its 250hp diesel engine. Within days the fort's workshops were being lavishly powered and the men's canteen was serving iced beer; within weeks, it had acquired a 32mm projector and was able to provide a film show every weekend. This canteen – the *foyer du légionnaire* – occupied three rooms against the south wall. At one end was a well-stocked shop selling at subsidized prices anything a soldier needed for washing, cleaning and mending, tobacco, confectionery and a wide range of other small comforts. At the other end was a library and reading room; from September 1936 the company even produced its own 12-page monthly frontier news bulletin, *'La Grenade'*. In the large central bar room and hall, accommodating about 200 men, they could drink and play billiards, dominoes or cards (but not for money).

Other than the free Sundays, the daily routine started with reveille at 5am; work began at 6.15am and lasted until 10.45am; the early lunch was followed by siesta until 2.30pm, then work resumed until evening parade at 6pm. Dinner was at 6.30pm, rollcall at 8.30pm, and lights-out at 9.30pm, or 11pm on Saturdays. After life in Depression-era Hungary, Charles Milassin remembered the food as being excellent, varied and plentiful. The basics came from the commissariat and fresh beef and mutton from Arab butchers; the fort raised its own pigs and cultivated fresh vegetables and fruit in gardens in the *palmerie*. On Sundays the cooks exerted themselves to make the food even better than usual, and the feasts for Christmas, Easter, Camerone and 14 July were 'prodigious – nobody can to eat all – 11am all big holiday, 80 per cent the people was drunk' (sic).

Apart from the daily half-litre ration of red *pinard* the men could buy beer in the canteen and, although they were never allowed more than 2 miles from the fort, in their free evening hours they could stroll out past the sand football-field to the tiny Arab bazaar. They could visit, but were not allowed beyond, a Lebanese store-cum-bar and the *souk* adjoining it; the Goum fort and the native village north of this were strictly out of bounds, and the Arabs were forbidden to come further south than the Lebanese store. The légionnaires had exclusive access to Foum el Hassane's second bar, owned by a Greek named Costas (where they could gamble their pay in strictly forbidden games of poker), and also to the establishment next door – the BMC. This was a courtyard house occupied for three or four months at a time by shifts of half-a-dozen young Moroccan girls, who were inspected by the medical officer twice a week. The brothel was open from 7pm to 9pm for the troops, then until midnight for sergeants (if any officer wished to avail himself of the facility he had to wait until after midnight). This female companionship cost a légionnaire 2 francs (about one day's pay); any who were tempted to visit a crib in the *village nègre* for 50 centimes risked the possibility of a knife in the ribs, and the certainty of disease and a spell in the cells.

MILASSIN'S MEMORIES of routine work on the fort and vehicles, punctuated by modest and monotonous off-duty pleasures, may give an unbalanced picture of life for the legionnaires. Eight-hour working days in such a climate were always tiring, hammer-and-pick work on the local tracks was utterly exhausting, and the frequent local patrols demanded much of both men and machines. A sergeant and 18 men were always on guard, and two duty platoons were always supposed to be ready to march at 10 minutes' notice.

The CMA/4th Foreign was organized in a two-squad headquarters *échelon*; a four-squad workshop platoon (in which Private Milassin served); a general purpose four-squad 'platoon employed at the disposal of the captain'; a two-squad armoured platoon, with Panhard 165/175 armoured cars and Panhard 179 armoured carriers; and four squads of motorized infantry with 2.5-ton Laffly LC2 patrol trucks. Captain Gaultier and Lieutenants de Kockborne, du Hecquet and du Part had Renault field cars with cork roofs, double radiators and extra fuel tanks; the company also had four water- and four fuel-tankers, a workshop truck and a radio car. In later years Charles Milassin could remember about 140 names, or half the company. They are the usual mix – perhaps a third French, Belgian or Swiss-French, about the same proportion Germanic, a strong minority of Russians and other Slavs, and a handful of Italians, Spanish, Dutch and Scandinavians (though also légionnaires named Grant, Doyle, Bell, and Abd el Halim). There seem to have been four other Hungarians, and Milassin remembered that one of these, Private Hegedüs, was the oldest soldier in the company, a veteran of the Great War RMLE with 23 years' service.

Twice every year, two-thirds of the company drove out of Foum el Hassane and Tindouf to make the 2,000-mile circuit around the Western Sahara as far south as Fort Gouraud in modern Mauritania. These *tournées de police* were supposed to take two months but often overran by two or three weeks. The 14hp trucks were underpowered, the going was extremely rough, and the frequent breakdowns had to be repaired on the spot. Patches of *fech-fech* – sand as fine as flour – could swallow a truck to its radiator cap, and in sandstorms all movement was impossible. Although the vehicles carried wire mesh sand-mats, the backbreaking, brain-boiling work of digging vehicles out under the Saharan sun had to be faced every few days. Inside the Laffly the NCO sat beside the driver and the eight légionnaires faced inwards along the side seats, with a 50-gallon fuel drum, an LMG, ammo boxes and tools between their feet down the middle. The trucks were also stacked and slung about like gypsy caravans with picks and shovels, the mens' carbines, personal kit and waterbottles, reserves of water, eight days' rations, firewood, and as many spare parts as the mechanics could cram aboard. The infantry's only consolation was that the ordeal of the armoured car crews enclosed in their steel ovens was even worse. It was almost unknown for shots to be fired in anger, but that did not mean that the patrols did not sometimes leave graves behind them. In the 1970s the traveller Richard Trench drove the stage between Tindouf and Chegga:

> We had left in the small hours, and by the time the pre-dawn half-light had emerged with its cold, silvery mist, Tindouf and the century that it represented had disappeared far behind us. The dawn light was easy on the eyes, and the rising red glow in the east softened the bright austerity of sand and rocks. Then the sun rose high above us, melting the colours of the desert into a single glaring tone that stayed with us all day, jarring our senses and blurring our horizons, until it slipped down in the west and the harsh light gave way to that peculiar bluish hue that always covers the desert in the early hours of the night.
>
> All along the route the landscape changed, from flat plains of gravel to neurotic outbursts of jagged rock, from slabs of jet black stone to carpets of coloured pebbles, from rounded breast-shaped dunes to skyscraping phallic buttes. The further we went into the desert, the more time seemed to slow down, until it stopped altogether and everything was as it always had been … Even the dead were clean. The first camel I saw was a pattern of shining bones picked clean by the wind, its neck twisted in a dying agony. We drove like that for three days …[6]

ON 20 DECEMBER 1935 – his sixtieth birthday, though he looked older – General Paul Rollet passed from the active list. (He would have been pleased to know how eagerly a young Hungarian recruit was responding to the culture he had done so much to create; by 1939 Charles Milassin would be a career sergeant, dedicated to a life in the Legion.) Rollet found the unstructured Paris life of a retired general intolerable, and threw himself into work for the Legion old comrades' associations with a generosity that was sometimes abused. In 1938 he also accepted the presidency of l'Association des Gueules Cassées (the 'Broken Gobs', or disfigured war veterans). He worked for this new cause with characteristic energy, and not only behind a desk; he could sometimes be seen on the boulevards of the capital in full uniform and medals, shaking a collection tin and selling lottery tickets for his two associations. When the Legion contingent arrived at the Gare de Lyon for the 14 July 1939 parade, in the snowy white-covered képis, green-and-red epaulettes and blue sashes that he had won back for them, he was there to salute them.

In May 1940, Rollet's request to return to active service was refused, and it is sad to imagine how unbearable the following months must have been for him as a helpless observer. Another 'Terrible Year' had come upon France, and a wholly new age of warfare had consigned to history the types of soldiering in which he had spent his life. He died in Paris on 16 April 1941, at the age of 65.[7]

In late 1939, the 4th Foreign, like the other three infantry regiments in North Africa, had provided drafts for new units being raised hastily in France from a mixture of serving personnel, reservists, new recruits, and Spanish internees from the grim camps in the south-west. The first 500 men went to provide a core of experience for the 11th and 12th REI (the first commanded originally by the recalled Colonel Fernand Maire), both of which would be destroyed in May–June 1940. A subsequent draft joined a rather more battle-ready unit being formed for mountain training; the 13th Foreign Legion Half-Brigade (13th DBLE) was also to see action in spring 1940, but alongside British and Polish troops at Narvik in Norway. By that time both Captain Gaultier and his rival Captain Robitaille had left the Sahara, the one for a Line command in France and the other for the 6th Foreign in the Levant. In June 1941, that regiment would face the 13th DBLE – the first infantrymen to declare for General de Gaulle – in fratricidal battle.

Although France's North African possessions survived the Franco-German armistices, the Legion's strength was greatly reduced, and the 4th Foreign Infantry Regiment was disbanded on 14 November 1940. Its remaining personnel passed into the 2nd Foreign, and its motorized company became the 8th Composite Mounted Company/2nd REI. Like the rest of the

Legion in North Africa, it would have to wait until the winter of 1942/3, in the aftermath of the Anglo-American 'Torch' landings, before it got back into the war on the right side.

After the great silence of the Sahara, Charles Milassin would hear plenty of shots fired in anger during the rest of his 25 years' service with the Legion. He would fight the Wehrmacht in Tunisia and in North-West Europe for more than two years; he would suffer several wounds, and on one occasion he would walk out of the desert to find that an unidentifiable corpse had been buried under a cross marked with his name. After fighting with the reborn RMLE in the Belfort Gap during the winter campaign of 1944/5, he would be troubled for the rest of his life by steel fragments from a 20mm cannon shell working their way out of his head and endangering his eyes. Nevertheless, he went on to serve a tour in Indochina with the 2nd Foreign, and before retiring at the beginning of the 1960s he reached the rank of chief warrant officer. Although awarded a 100 per cent disability pension, he proceeded to build with his own hands a new home in the Vosges for his wife and three children. He remained a légionnaire to his backbone until the day he died; and he always looked back with a special nostalgia to his first hitch at Foum el Hassane, where he was one of the last few hundred men ever to live the life of the Old Legion.

IN 1993, UNITED NATIONS SOLDIERS of the multinational MINURSO mission, monitoring the ceasefire in the Western Sahara between the Sharifian Kingdom of Morocco and the Polisario Front independence movement, regularly retraced part of the tracks of the old Composite Automobile Company/4th Foreign of 60 years before. Tindouf was now the centre of the main Polisario refugee camp, and one of the waypoints that the UN patrols used for overnight stops was Ain ben Tili in the tri-border region, close to where the frontiers of Morocco, Mauritania and Algeria meet. The abandoned fort was largely intact, standing silent in the middle of an utterly featureless plain.

About half a mile from the flaking walls and the sand-choked barbed wire a British officer, Captain David Craig, found a partially defaced gravestone made of coarse concrete. The name it bore began with the letters 'Tison ...'; the year of his birth was unclear, but his death-date of 12 December 1934, and his identity as a corporal in the 5th (Mechanized) Squadron of the 1st Foreign Cavalry Regiment were still legible. That corporal's resting place must be one of the loneliest on Earth, and his stone stands to remind us of a kind of soldiering that is almost entirely forgotten. The Legion had a traditional toast to their dead: '*À nos amis sous les sables*' —

'To our friends beneath the sands.'

Appendix 1

Summary of Foreign Legion operations in Europe, 1914–18

ON THE OUTBREAK OF WAR in August 1914 several thousand foreigners volunteered to fight for the Republic, and were diverted into the Foreign Legion as the only logical repository. In September 1914, the two Foreign Regiments sent the equivalent of a marching battalion each to France, commanded by Colonels Pein and Passard. In fact these were organized in four half-battalions, so that they could be completed with duration-only volunteers to form two marching regiments each of 2 battalions. During their formation at Mailly le Camp, it was decided that the flood of volunteers allowed a doubling of the original plan, and the 2nd Marching Regiments/1st and 2nd RE were each enlarged to four battalions (lettered A to D), with the armature of pre-war regulars reduced from 50 per cent to 25 per cent. Despite some unfortunate consequences, the units' performance in action in spring 1915 suggests that they had settled down well enough during a winter in the line.

At first brigaded together, by November 1914 the 2nd RM/1st RE and 2nd RM/2nd RE had been separated, the first going into the trenches near Prunay in Champagne. The second was allocated to 36th Division near Craonelle on the Aisne; now commanded by Lieutenant-Colonel Lecomte-Denis, the 2nd RM/2nd RE held its sector against German attacks in January 1915, and was relieved in May. Meanwhile, two more regiments were being raised, though their Legion identity was little more than nominal. A 3rd Marching Regiment/1st RE was formed – with very few veterans – at Reuilly barracks, Paris, in the autumn of 1914, but was finally disbanded in July 1915, the useful personnel transferring to the 2nd RM/1st RE. The entirely Italian 4th RM/1st RE, commanded by Lieutenant-Colonel 'Peppino' Garibaldi, did well in the Argonne in December 1914–January 1915, but was disbanded at the request of the (still neutral) Italian government in March 1915.

Artois and Champagne, May–September 1915

In spring 1915 the 2nd RM/1st RE, commanded by Lieutenant-Colonel Cot, were committed to the major offensive just north of Arras as part of the Moroccan Division in General Pétain's 33rd Corps. The division was in the line opposite the German-held village of Neuville St Vaast, behind which rose the wooded slopes of Vimy Ridge. The 2nd/1st's objectives were a deep German trench system called the White Works, and beyond them Hill 140, the highest point of the ridge. Zero hour was 10am on 9 May 1915; by 11.30am the regiment had advanced nearly 3 miles, taking all their objectives, and were on the summit of Hill 140. Now commanded by the sole surviving major, Collet of B Battalion, the regiment were finally relieved at 2am the next morning; from a starting strength of some 4,000 they had lost 50 officers and 1,889 enlisted ranks killed, missing or wounded. The Zouaves who relieved them were unable to hold the position against counter-attacks.[1] On 16 June the remnants of the regiment were committed to another assault from Carency en Souchez to Hill 119; again the objective was taken but could not be held, and the regiment lost another 650 casualties.

On 25 September 1915, the 2nd RM/2nd RE, now with General Marchand's 10th Colonial Division, were committed to attacks near Auberive in Champagne. Their initial objectives were trench systems around Navarin Farm on the Butte de Souain; they took several successive lines of defences and advanced about 2 miles, at a cost of 320 casualties. On 28 September the 2nd RM/1st RE were also committed to this sector, paying 627 casualties for their objectives.

The remnants of both regiments were rested behind the lines in the Vosges in October 1915, and on 11 November merged to form a single Régiment de Marche de la Légion Étrangère of three battalions, commanded by Lieutenant-Colonel Cot and retaining the decorated colours of the 2nd RM/1st RE. The RMLE went back into the second line with the Moroccan Division (General Codet) in February 1916.

The Somme, July 1916

On 4 July the RMLE, under command of 3rd Division, were committed to an assault on the ruins of Belloy en Santerre (II/RMLE were now led by Major James Waddell, a New Zealand-born veteran of Gallipoli).[2] The attack did not begin until 5pm, in heavy rain, and I/RMLE took heavy casualties from machine guns in the Chancellier trenches to their south before managing to join II/RMLE in Belloy (this was the action in which the American poet Alan Seeger was killed). The whole regiment held off counter-attacks during the night, and by the time they were relieved at first light they had lost 869 all ranks – a third of their strength. On the night of 7/8 July, I/ and II/RMLE were sent back into Belloy, and two failed attempts on the Chancellier position cost another 830 casualties; in the week since 4 July the regiment had suffered some 70 per cent killed, wounded or missing. On 15 July they were pulled out of the line, and did not return to the trenches until 5 November 1916.

Auberive, April 1917

The Moroccan Division, including the RMLE (commanded since February by Lieutenant-Colonel Duriez) was committed to the Fourth Army attacks east of Rheims on the right flank of Nivelle's Chemin des Dames offensive. The regiment would fight on virtually the same battlefield as had the old 2nd RM /2nd RE in September 1915, being assigned objectives in German trench systems on the west bank of the river Suippe opposite Auberive. The two lead battalions went over the top at 4.45am on 17 April; at about 7.30am Lieutenant-Colonel Duriez was mortally wounded by a shellburst and replaced by Major Deville. By nightfall the RMLE had made 600 yards and were embedded in the 'Gulf' trench system; there they withstood counter-attacks on the 18th, and on 19–20 April they ground their way forward into the 'Labyrinth' trenches. They were relieved on the 21st, after expending more than 50,000 hand grenades and capturing about 4 linear miles of trenches and dug-outs, at the price of around 30 per cent casualties overall (although by the night of 19 April, III/RMLE had been reduced to 275 men). One of those who particularly distinguished themselves was Warrant Officer Max Mader, who had once served with Captain Paul Rollet's mule company in Morocco.

In May 1917, command of the RMLE passed to Lieutenant-Colonel Rollet, who had been fighting with great distinction with the 31st and then as commander of 331st Line Infantry since 1914. Wounded twice early in the war, he had been recommended for promotion by General Henri Gouraud, then commanding 10th Division, who remembered him from Morocco. A reservist veteran of the 331st recalled that Rollet was loved for his unpretentious friendliness and care for his men as much as he was admired for his courage, and liked for his eccentricities (he tended to carry an umbrella in the trenches, where he was always accompanied by a dog; he clung stubbornly to his old sand-coloured Legion tunic, and it was said that the first time he was seen wearing a steel helmet was for the Paris parade of 14 July 1919). He proved to be a charismatic commander of the RMLE, inspiring a host of affectionate anecdotes.

At the time of the 1917 mutinies provoked by the carnage on the Chemin des Dames, the Legion remained rock-solid; it held a sector at Berry au Bac in June–July, and after a brief rest it paraded in Paris on 14 July, its colours decorated (for its fifth citation in army orders) with the yellow-and-green lanyard of the Military Medal. In August, the RMLE was sent to the Verdun front.

Verdun–Cumières, August–September 1917

Under Second Army, the Moroccan Division was committed to an attack on German trenches between Cumières Wood and the west bank of the river Meuse. After a six-day preparatory bombardment, the RMLE went over the top on 20 August, advancing a mile and a half to take their initial objectives in two hours rather than the four allowed. They exploited forward, and despite counter-attacks and aerial strafing took the Cote de l'Oie and Regnéville the next day. By the time the regiment were relieved on 4 September they had paid the remarkably light price of 53 killed and 271 wounded and had earned their sixth citation, at that time unique in the French Army. While the RMLE rested at Bois l'Evêque on 27 September the colours were decorated with a newly introduced lanyard in the crimson of the Legion of Honour ribbon; General Pétain told them that he was happy to keep inventing new decorations for the regiment if they continued to fight as they had done at Cumières. A photo taken of the colour party on that parade became one of the most famous of all Legion images: Lieutenant-Colonel Rollet wearing his habitual desert tunic, holding the colour with its heavy garnish of cravats, medals and lanyards, and guarded by four other individual recipients of the Knight's Cross of the Legion of Honour: Warrant Officer Max Mader and Corporals André Rocas, Jaime Dieta and Fortunato Leva.

Amiens and Soissons, April–July 1918

From October 1917 to January 1918 the RMLE held trenches in the Flirey sector, taking part in both offensive and defensive fighting. It was in a rest camp when, at the end of March, the German spring offensive burst on the Allied lines, and the regiment was rushed to the Amiens sector of the collapsing British front in Picardy. On 26 April the RMLE counter-attacked at Hangard Wood near Villers-Bretonneux, fighting alongside British infantry and tanks in chaotic terrain masked by fog; by the time they were relieved on the 28th the RMLE had lost some 850 casualties, and I/RMLE had been reduced to one officer and 187 men.

The regiment were next committed on 30 May at the Montagne de Paris just west of Soissons, holding the ridge until nightfall on the 31st against repeated attacks at a cost of about 400 casualties. Reduced to some 1,200 all ranks, on 12–13 June they held more than a mile and a half of the Saint Bardry valley sector under heavy shelling, gas and infantry attacks. On 16 June the regiment went into reserve, having lost 1,300 casualties since 26 April.

On the stormy night of 18/19 July the regiment advanced across the Dommiers plateau south of Soissons, on the left flank of the Moroccan Division and next to the US 1st Division. There was no preliminary artillery barrage to alert the enemy, and next day the Legion had both tank and air support. By the time they were relieved on the night of 20/21 July the RMLE had reached the Soissons-Château Thierry road, at a cost of 780 casualties. This success brought their eighth citation in army orders.

The Hindenburg Line, September 1918

During August the balance of General Ludendorff's 'Emperor's Battle' tipped decisively in the Allies' favour. After a month to recover, the regiment were sent into the line again on 28 August, and on 1/2 September the Moroccan Division relieved an American formation facing the Laffaux sector of the Hindenburg Line on the Mauberge-Brussels road. Rollet now had four battalions under command (the RMLE plus a Russian volunteer unit), to which a Malagasy battalion would later be attached. They advanced on 2 September, and the offensive continued without respite for 13 days and nights; on 14 September the Hindenburg Line was broken, and the regiment captured and held the village of Allemant the next day. By the time they were relieved on 15/16 September the RMLE had been reduced from a starting strength of 2,563 all ranks to 1,130 officers and men. Their conduct brought a ninth citation, and a double lanyard in the colours of the Croix de Guerre and Légion d'Honneur (an honour shared with only one other regiment in the French Army, the Morocco Colonial Infantry Regiment, RICM). At the end of October 1918 the RMLE went back into the trenches in the quiet sector of Champenoux in Lorraine, where the Armistice found them.

Legion records list 42,883 men as serving with the various units during the Great War – 6,239 Frenchmen and 36,644 foreigners of more than a hundred nationalities (including roughly 600 US citizens, heavily represented due to America's late entry into the war, and 266 British and Dominion volunteers). Of that total, 5,172 were listed as killed in action and some 25,000 as wounded or missing, the majority of the missing undoubtedly being fatalities. Total casualties were thus about 70 per cent of those who served.

The Dardanelles and Macedonia, 1915–18

In February 1915 the Régiment de Marche d'Afrique (Lieutenant-Colonel Niéger) was raised for the Dardanelles campaign, with two Zouave battalions and one from the Legion; III/RMdA (Major Geay) comprised two marching companies each from 1st and 2nd RE. The RMdA embarked at Oran on 2 March, and were landed under fire on 28 April at Sedd el Bahr, on the western flank of the Cape Helles beachhead at the tip of the Gallipoli peninsula. Penned on a very confined front under constant Turkish artillery fire, they suffered extremely heavy losses from the start. By June, fighting for the ravine of Kereves Dere had reduced the Legion battalion to about 100 men led by Warrant Officer Léon, and it had essentially ceased to exist by August. It was then rebuilt with 700 légionnaires withdrawn from Indochina, and was commanded by the New Zealander, Captain James Waddell.

The remnant of the RMdA were withdrawn in October 1915 and shipped to Salonika, as part of 156th Division in the Allied force intended to resist the Bulgarian advance through Serbia. Marched north to the Greek/Serbian border, they endured a winter retreat followed by a virtual stalemate on the Macedonian front during 1916–17. Disease caused as many deaths as enemy action, although the RMdA did see significant fighting at Monastir in September–November 1916 and at Trana Stena in spring 1917. By the time III/RMdA were disbanded on 1 October 1917 they had recorded 721 all ranks killed and probably three times that many wounded. A single company remained in Macedonia until the Armistice.

Appendix 2

Summary of Foreign Legion operations in the Levant, 1925

THE DESTRUCTION of the Ottoman Empire in 1918 had the effect of throwing an ethnic and religious jigsaw-puzzle on to the floor, and thereafter all interested parties were simultaneously trying to snatch up particular pieces and fit them into new patterns of their own devising. After 1918, Britain and France each administered some former Turkish possessions under League of Nations mandates, and the 1920 San Remo conference assigned Syria (including present-day Lebanon) to France. By the time the Mandate came into formal operation on 29 September 1923, a French army had already been operating in southern Turkey and the Levant for four years – in Syria, initially against the Amir Faisal's attempts to retain control, and later against a rash of more than 30 local uprisings and disorders between 1920 and 1925. The 4th Battalion, 4th Foreign Infantry (IV/4th REI) had landed in mid-March 1921, and was followed by V/4th Foreign early in September.[1] Locally, the French raised an only patchily reliable 6,500-man Syrian Legion from Circassians, Kurds and Armenians.

From July 1920, General Henri Gouraud, the military and political high commissioner, attempted to persuade leaders of the patchwork of different religious and ethnic communities to conclude local agreements, in order to counter any tendency towards assertive political unity among the urban elites (the nationalist People's Party did not yet represent an organized movement for an agreed model of independence). The Druzes were a population of some 50,000 inhabiting both the Djebel Druze hills about 75 miles south of Damascus and the slopes of the Mount Hermon massif south-west of the capital. A hardy people with their own secretive religion, they had a 900-year history of defending themselves among the majority Sunni Muslims. General Gouraud sent Colonel Georges Catroux to negotiate with the ruling clans, and a Franco-Druze treaty was signed in March 1921. The Druze accepted a small garrison in the regional capital, Suwayda, and the guidance of a Native Affairs officer; the French left local administration in the hands of an elected Druze governor and council.

The first governor was the paramount chief of the powerful Atrash clan, Salim al Atrash, supervised by an experienced Native Affairs officer, Major Trenga. In 1923 Salim's death led – bizarrely – to the council electing as governor not one of their own but Trenga's successor, an arrogantly impatient innovator named Captain Gabriel Carbillet, who made himself widely resented. Despite appeals to remove Carbillet and warnings of growing unrest, the current high commissioner, the 70-year-old General Sarrail, at first prevaricated and then, in mid-July 1925, treacherously arrested three Atrash chiefs.

*

AFTER PRELIMINARY INCIDENTS, on 21 July 1925, followers of the tribal leader Sultan al Atrash killed about half of Captain Normand's squadron of 12th (Tunisian) Spahis and surrounded the 200-man garrison of Suwayda. Some 8,000–10,000 rebels gathered, Maronite Christian villages were massacred, and refugees fled to Damascus. Leading a 3,000-strong relief column towards Suwayda, General Sarrail's chief-of-staff General Roger Michaud suffered a shocking defeat on 2 August at Ezra, losing about 400 casualties and another 400 local troops 'missing'. This news reached Paris just as the Painlevé government and Marshal Pétain were having to strip troops from the Ruhr to deal with the crisis of the Rif War. The two conflicts were quite unconnected, but their coincidence naturally had a powerful impact on the French public and the Muslim world.

On 19 August, a nationalist delegation agreed a pact of mutual support with Sultan al Atrash, who led thousands of Druzes and Transjordanian bedouin towards Damascus, but they were halted at Al Kiswah by French aircraft and the 21st Spahis. Nationalist Party leaders fled a French security clamp-down in Damascus, and on 9 September called for a national uprising in the name of a provisional government. Early reinforcements raised the French forces commanded by Michaud's replacement, General Gamelin, to some 20,000 men, safeguarding the cities but overstretched by widespread chaos and bloodshed in the countryside.

Al Musayfirah, September 1925

On 11 September, during preparations for the relief of Suwayda, the only available Legion units – the tired and understrength V/4th REI (Major Kratzert), and the newly landed IV/1st REC (Captain Landriau) – were posted to the village of Al Musayfirah (French, Messifré) about 15 miles south-west of that town.[2] The village had few two-storey buildings, but an old Turkish police post in the centre was overlooked by a shrine with a domed roof. Discontinous positions surrounding the police building (Post E, 'the redoubt') were held by Landriau's 178 cavalrymen, plus machine-guns and one armoured car; their horses were tethered under guard in courtyards nearby (Post F). Four sandbagged posts (Posts A–D) some 300 yards outside the village were each held by a company or a platoon of V/4th Foreign, with machine guns and two more armoured cars.

Major Kratzert was warned late on 16 September that some 3,000 Druzes were approaching from the north. Before dawn on the 17th, the northern Posts A and B were attacked, and simultaneously many infiltrators inside the village opened fire both on them and on the REC positions. About two hours of confused close-range street-fighting followed; Post F was wiped out and the squadron's horses were stampeded through the narrow streets (all were eventually killed). In the darkness repeated assaults were made on positions held by the troopers, and defenders of Posts A and B were also sending dangerous return fire into the village. A sortie had to be made from the redoubt to clear riflemen from the roof of the shrine, but daylight allowed more effective fire by the machine guns and the armoured cars' 37mm cannon, and at 6am renewed assaults on Posts A and B were driven off. (Their defence was an intimate experience: Post B was a triangle of sandbag walls only 20 yards on a side, held by perhaps 30 men, two MGs and an armoured car.)

Druzes were still both inside the village and firing on the northern posts, but an air attack early on the afternoon of 17 September was followed by a gradual disengagement, and a relief column arrived before dusk. Although wearing their traditional costume, the Druzes had been armed with Mauser rifles, and many of the 307 dead they left behind had Turkish Army belt kit, haversacks with two days' rations, and cash pay in their pockets. The V/4th Foreign lost some 30 killed and 50 wounded in the northern posts; IV/1st REC suffered nearly one-third casualties – an officer and 25 rankers killed, 2 officers and 22 men wounded. Both units were cited in army orders.[3]

Rashayya, November 1925

On 30 October General Sarrail was replaced as C-in-C by General Charles Andrea, who was faced immediately with a threat to vital French links between Damascus and the Lebanese port cities. Early in November, Sultan al Atrash's younger brother Zayd tried to extend the revolt westwards to link up with local Druze uprisings around Mount Hermon and in the mountains running north from it. The first inland range are the Lebanon Mountains, forming the western wall of the Bekaa valley; its eastern wall is the Anti-Lebanon range, with Hermon at its south-west end. In early November, rebels were in control of the eastern slopes of the Anti-Lebanon as far north as Al Nabk due east of Beirut, and were raiding into the Bekaa. To the south of that valley, on 11 November, Captain Landriau's remounted IV/1st REC – though still reduced to about 100 all ranks – joined Captain Granger's garrison at the patrol base of Rashayya, a mixed Druze/Maronite village about 6 miles north of Mount Hermon. Granger's other units were IV/12th Spahis (Captain Cros-Mayreville) and perhaps 60 remaining local gendarmes (Lieutenant Tine) – say 280 men in all.

The village was built around the remains of a thirteenth-century Crusader 'citadel' which the garrison occupied, but this was not easily defensible. Over centuries, the Norman fort had become encrusted with an organic growth of civilian buildings both inside and outside the rough 'A'-shape of the old walls. The buildings occupied as the HQ redoubt were at the north-east apex; the main gatehouse was in the west wall, close to where a vaulted tunnel also emerged inside; and the old tower in the south wall was overlooked from houses on high ground immediately outside. The crossbar of the 'A', perhaps 80 yards long, was apparently formed by water cisterns and low, discontinuous walls that separated the upper and lower courtyards used for the horse lines. The terraced interior of the complex was cluttered, and Captain Granger's garrison had to burrow new access passageways; outside, where the citadel was closely surrounded by alleys, houses and gardens, they had only been able to clear a few of the buildings abutting the outer walls and were obliged to occupy others.

At mid-afternoon on 20 November a returning watering party were fired on, and there was sporadic firing and nearby movement all night long. From dawn on the 21st, Druzes closely surrounding and overlooking the citadel opened heavy fire, and made several determined assaults until about noon. These were driven back only at the cost of some 20 casualties and heavy expenditure of ammunition, and for the rest of the day and the night of 21/22 November enemy firing continued while the attackers regrouped. From dawn on the 22nd this redoubled in intensity, with stick-grenades being thrown into the defences from houses only feet away and rushes at the barricaded entrances. At 8.20am Captain Granger was killed, and command devolved to Captain Cros-Mayreville. An air-dropped message that evening promised relief on 24 November.

The climax came from 5am onwards on 23 November; the southern tower and wall were lost to determined assaults, winning the attackers commanding positions, and a counter-attack across the lower courtyard failed. Essentially house-to-house fighting lasted all day, with rifle and machine-gun fire, grenades, and bayonet-and-sword charges being traded across an encumbered area measuring only about 100 yards by 80 yards, crowded with bucking, screaming horses (which were progressively shot down). The western gatehouse was lost but retaken, and an attack through the tunnel was driven back. Ammunition ran very short, and at nightfall Captains Cros-Mayreville and Landriau had no choice but to withdraw their troopers from the outer barricades into the northern redoubt. This was achieved only with some difficulty, and an assault across the northern courtyard had to be driven back by a bayonet-charge. By now the Spahis and légionnaires had taken about 100 casualties and were down to some 30 cartridges left in each man's pouches.

The flares of an approaching force were seen that night; a final Druze attack the next morning was half-hearted, aircraft dropped bombs on the afternoon of the 24th, and the rebels drifted away. The relief force arrived on 25 November. In their second house-to-house defence within two months Captain Landriau's 4th Squadron had lost another 15 killed and 43 wounded – half their starting strength, including a number of NCOs and men who had distinguished themselves at Al Musayfirah. The squadron was cited for the second time, bringing them the lanyard of the Croix de Guerre TOE. Rashayya was the furthest west that Zayd al Atrash's rebels ever reached.[4]

Appendix 3

P. C. Wren, 1875–1941

WREN'S *BEAU GESTE*, published in 1924, is a tale of self-sacrifice by well-born English brothers seeking the refuge of colonial soldiering in order to spare their family disgrace. It was Wren's eighth book and his first and only instant best-seller, although it was not his first exploitation of the narrative possibilities of the Legion – John Murray had published a collection of his Legion short stories as early as 1916. *Beau Geste* was the book that made Wren's name, and although a prolific writer he never again achieved comparable sales. The chronological accident of the widely reported Rif War in Morocco in 1925–6 kept the Legion in the newspapers; the novel had already been reprinted twenty-six times by 1926, when the first of several film versions was released (Herbert Brenon's, starring Ronald Coleman). The full-blooded 1939 film, directed by 'Wild Bill' Wellman and starring Gary Cooper and Ray Milland, provided a later boost to the book's popularity.

Today the novel's style and melodramatic plot seem impossibly dated, but in its own day this blood-and-sand adventure set in an exotic (if vaguely imagined) Araby appealed to a fairly undemanding readership. The 1920s were not a time for war-stories based in the real world, and such yarns as *Beau Geste* offered escapist excitements that were safely distant from the gruesome truths of the Western Front. Even so, the success of Wren's stories in fixing a formulaic image of the Legion in the popular imagination was astonishing, probably because in the English-speaking world at that time he had a fictional monopoly of the subject. Several memoirs from the ranks had been published in England before the Great War, but public knowledge of the Legion was scant. For generations after the publication of *Beau Geste*, if most people heard the words 'French Foreign Legion' their attention immediately short-circuited: even if the information that followed was factual, it was channelled through the familiar fictional matrix installed in their minds by Wren's tales.

Needless to say, *Beau Geste* is not a significant historical document, but Wren's scene-setting is clearly based on detailed knowledge of barracks life at Sidi bel Abbès in the first years of the century. His short stories are set (again, vaguely) in the context of actual campaigns, in Tonkin and Dahomey as well as the Sud-Oranais and Morocco, and many people assumed – still assume – that he had first-hand experience. Wren was a tall, strong, handsome man with a soldierly bearing; but although his Great War service with the Indian Army allowed him to inhabit the public persona of a *pukka* retired officer, he seems, in fact, to have been a second-generation product of the aspiring working class. Today that would be a matter for pride, but to the unthinking snobbery of the 1920s class background mattered a great deal, and Wren was always deliberately reticent about his early life.

In the late 1930s he declined to fill in a questionnaire circulated during the preparation of the compendium *Twentieth-Century Authors* (Kunitz & Haycraft; H. W. Wilson, New York, 1942), and the entry under his name is both vague about his life and completely inaccurate about his antecedents; like almost every other printed source, it also gives his date of birth as ten years too late. Wren allowed the assumption of previous Legion service to stand, while refusing to respond to direct enquiries and never making any direct public claim. However, he told his young stepson that he had indeed been a légionnaire, that he had been decorated, and that he had deserted after striking back at a brutal NCO.

It is certainly not impossible that Wren did enlist in the Legion and serve for a year or two before making a successful desertion, but the internal evidence of his novels and stories is not, by itself, persuasive. He could have interviewed at least one former légionnaire at length; and it should also be remembered that he lifted two anecdotes straight from the memoirs of the Legion veteran Frederic Martyn, published in 1911. One was the idea of dead soldiers being propped up around the battlements of a fort to exaggerate the remaining strength of the defenders; this story was told to Martyn during his first few days in the Legion by a veteran in a bar, and Wren in turn used it as the climax to *Beau Geste*. The other, of a French officer in West Africa finding among the enemy dead the very Chassepot rifle that he himself had carried in the Franco-Prussian War, was recycled by Wren in the short story *No.187017* in his collection *Flawed Blades* (1932). Martyn's memoir, and that of George Manington published in 1907, contain very full details of daily life in the 1er Régiment Étranger at Sidi bel Abbès in the 1890s, and accounts of service in Tonkin and Dahomey. The memoir by 'Erwin Rosen' (Erwin Carle) – *In the Foreign Legion*, first published in German by R. Lutz (Stuttgart, 1909) and in English by Duckworth in 1910 – also attracted a good deal of attention. These books alone would probably have given Wren all the basic background he needed.

For almost everything that follows I gratefully acknowledge the generosity of the writer John Ashby in sharing with me the notes of the late Brian Carter of Wigan, Lancashire (though any conclusions are my own). Carter was a tireless old-fashioned journalist who made extensive enquiries, and who corresponded with R. Alan Graham-Smith, P. C. Wren's stepson, between 1967 and 1991; Mr Graham-Smith's own more recent death in his nineties releases these memories from a promise of confidentiality. It seems important to add that he remembered his stepfather as 'a wonderful man – kind, generous and amusing, with a great sense of humour'.

WREN WAS BORN on 1 November 1875 at 37 Warwick Street, Deptford, in the East End of London. His parents were a schoolmaster named John Wilkins (Christopher?) Wren and Ellen, née Lasbury; his grandfather was Frederick Wren, a bricklayer and plasterer. The name on the birth certificate was 'Percy', and it is unclear when he adopted the style 'Percival Christopher', though this was certainly by the time of his arrival in India in 1903.

There is no firm evidence of his education, but his father was master of Duke Street School in Deptford (later Alverton Street, SE8). There is documentary confirmation that on 13 October 1894 – so at the age of 19 – Wren matriculated at Oxford with the Delegacy of Non-Collegiate Students (later St Catherine's Society, and eventually St Catherine's College); this was then a means of gaining access to an Oxford education while avoiding the full expense of membership of a college. He was apparently a keener sportsman than a student; a 3rd Class BA in history is recorded on 30 July 1898, and an automatic MA on 28 May 1901. From 29 October 1903, when India Office records (*Bombay Civil List*, 1917) confirm his arrival in Karachi to take up a teaching appointment, Wren's life is at least patchily documented. According to his stepson, by that date he was married to his first wife, whose name is unknown, and they had an infant daughter.

The gaps in his record, during which it is conceivable that he served in the Legion, are thus between his leaving school and going up to Oxford in 1894 – perhaps four years covering the ages of 16 to 19; and between August 1898 and the end of 1902 at the latest – a little more than four years, between the ages of 22 and 27. His father had apparently advised him to 'see life through as many windows as possible', and in later years he told stories of wandering around England in his teens, with a gold sovereign sewn into his clothes for emergencies. He claimed to have worked as a navvy, costermonger and deckhand; to have fought in a fairground boxing booth; and to have enlisted as a trooper in the Queen's Bays, although there are no surviving Ministry of Defence or regimental records in his name. The post-Oxford years would seem the more likely period for any putative Legion service, but medals found among his possessions (see below) would hint at the earlier period. If he actually did serve then he certainly did not fulfil a five-year enlistment, and desertion would be a plausible reason for him to remain silent – not because of any stigma, but for fear of the arrest to which he would be liable if he ventured on to French soil thereafter. In this connection one of his short stories is intriguing: *The Deserter*, in the 1917 collection *Stepsons of France*, explicitly imagines such an arrest, of an Englishman going ashore at Marseille with his new bride, from a steamer bound for India.

Between October 1903 and October 1907 Wren carried out various duties in Karachi, both as a school headmaster and simultaneously with the Educational Inspectorate for Sind. His stepson was told that during these years both his first wife and his daughter 'Boodle' died – a tragically common event – leaving him to bring up a son, probably born in 1904 or 1905 and christened Percival Rupert Christopher (nicknamed 'Fic'). In 1903, while lecturing at a teacher training college, Wren first met Isobel Mountain, a 19-year-old trainee who would later become his second wife. He was on leave from March to December 1908, and during that time Isobel married a civil engineer named Cyril Graham-Smith. In December 1908 Wren was appointed principal of a secondary school teachers' training college in Bombay, and during 1910–13 he held a post with the Educational Inspectorate at Poona. In 1910 Cyril and Isobel Graham-Smith had a son, Richard Alan (always called Alan); he was born at Behar, but the family later moved to Poona, and presumably this was when the widowed Wren renewed his acquaintance with Isobel.

Wren's first published novel, *Dew and Mildew* (1912), was followed by *Father Gregory* in 1913. Between August and October 1913 he was on special duty, preparing a manual of drill exercises and instructing a class in them, which does argue that he had previous military experience. On 16 September 1914 he was appointed principal of a Bombay high school; his third novel, *Snake and Sword*, was published that year, and *Driftwood Spars* in 1915, but none of his books had yet enjoyed any real success.

WREN'S ONLY DOCUMENTED military service began with his appointment on 1 December 1914 to the Indian Army Reserve of Officers with the rank of captain of infantry, attached to the 101st Grenadiers. (Confusingly, another Percival Wren figures in the *Indian Army List* for 1914, but this is clearly not our man. He was commissioned in 1895, served with the Poona Volunteer Rifles, and passed to the supernumary list in December 1913 in the rank of major – which may have confused Wren's obituarists.)

P. C. Wren's experience of active service would seem to have been brief and disappointing. The Indian Army provided two expeditionary forces for an attempted invasion of German East Africa (Tanganyika), and on 2 November 1914 Indian Expeditionary Force B, comprising the 27th Brigade and the Imperial Services Brigade, made a disastrous landing at the port of Tanga just south of the border with British East Africa (Kenya). Forewarned, courtesy of the Royal Navy, General von Lettow Vorbeck reinforced the garrison and had little difficulty in repulsing the attempt, and on 5 November the force re-embarked, abandoning much of its materièl. The 27th Brigade (2nd Bn Loyal North Lancashire Regiment, 63rd Palmahcotta Light Infantry, 98th Infantry and 101st Grenadiers) was withdrawn to Mombasa to join up with Indian Expeditionary Force C. The brigade was then deployed to defend the Uganda Railway between Mombasa and Nairobi against German raids from the south, strung out through unhealthy country infested with lions.

Captain Wren presumably arrived to join his regiment some time during the winter of 1914/15, but almost at once he must have joined the many who were struck down by disease, since he is listed as being on sick leave from 17 February 1915. He never served again; he left the Officers' Reserve on 31 October 1915, and is shown as being on leave from his civil employment, under various headings, until 18 October 1916. During this time his fifth book and first collection of Legion short stories was published by John Murray; *Wages of Virtue* (1916) bears the byline 'Captain Percival Christopher Wren, I(ndian) A(rmy) R(eserve)'. In later years he used the style of 'major', and a photograph that was in the possession of his stepson puzzlingly shows him in anonymous 'blues' with the insignia of that rank, but bears no date or address.

His stepson believed that Isobel Graham-Smith cared for Wren during his convalescence in Poona, where he returned to his teaching duties only between 19 October 1916 and 23 February 1917. He then took home leave; strikingly, Isobel and her son accompanied him, and they all lived with Isobel's parents in Parkstone, Dorset, during Wren's continued convalescence that year. His second Legion collection, *Stepsons of France*, and another title, *The Young Stagers*, were published in 1917, and Wren finally retired from the Indian Educational Service that November. He apparently supported himself in England by working as a tutor and schoolmaster, though details are vague; during these years Isobel made at least one trip back to India, presumably in the hope of obtaining a divorce.

The former légionnaire Adolphe Cooper told Colin Rickards, the Canadian historian of the Legion, that he had met Wren when the latter visited Sidi bel Abbès early in 1924. If he really was a deserter, then he presumably judged that after at least twenty years and the butchery of the Great War it was very unlikely that anyone who could recognize him was still serving. Cooper also claimed that Colonel Rollet instructed him to translate *Beau Geste* for him (if true, this must presumably have been in 1926, when Rollet was commanding 1st REI at the depot and Cooper was serving in the 3rd Battalion at Ain Sefra).

In 1925 or 1926, when Wren had achieved success with *Beau Geste* (in which he named the character providing the Geste brothers' love interest 'Isobel'), Alan Graham-Smith's mother finally obtained a divorce, and she and Wren were married at Bournemouth Registry Office on 3 December 1927. Wren was then 52 years of age, Isobel 44, and Wren's own son 22 or 23. Alan said that father and son had a difficult relationship; 'Fic' lost touch with his father early, and was said to have emigrated to the USA at some date before the Second World War.

Between 1924 and 1939 the Wrens lived at at least seven addresses in Dorset, Kent, Hampshire, Buckinghamshire and London. The longest period was from August 1928 to February 1934 at Westwood House, a luxurious eight-bedroom home set in two acres adjoining a golfcourse at 9 Elgin Road, Talbot Woods, Bournemouth; during work on the house Wren had a builder embellish it with a fort-like crenellated extension including a billiard room. He suffered from periodic ill-health, but by the time of his death he had published a total of 33 novels and collections of stories, the last *(Odd – But Even So)* in 1941.

P. C. Wren died of a heart attack at Moor Court private hotel near Stroud, Gloucestershire, on 22 November 1941, at the age of 66, and was buried at Holy Trinity Church, Amberley. He guarded his privacy to the last, and his obituaries are long on generalizations but short on facts and dates. (Even that in *The Times* makes him ten years too young, and gives him an inaccurate family history; attempts to link his descent to the great seventeenth-century architect's brother and to Borough Court, a country house in Devonshire, seem to be groundless, since no Wren lived there before 1890.) Isobel Wren suffered a severe stroke in 1951, and died in 1960.

AMONG WREN'S POSSESSIONS, Alan Graham-Smith inherited a full-size Médaille Militaire, and a set of three miniatures made up after the First World War – the Médaille, a Croix de Guerre avec Palme, and a Médaille Coloniale with the clasp 'Afrique Occidentale Francaise 1900'. Wren had told his stepson that he had been awarded the first two, but these decorations pose more questions than they answer. A cynic might point out that anyone can buy medals, and French decorations are not named to the recipient. The portrait photo showing Wren in major's uniform seems to show six ribbons; one might be the Médaille Coloniale, but none are easily identifiable. His Indian Army service, however brief, would still seem to have entitled him to four British decorations: the 1914–15 Star, War Medal, Victory Medal and Africa General Service Medal.

The Croix de Guerre was instituted only in April 1915, and was often awarded as a compliment to Allied personnel who served alongside French troops; however, there were no French troops in British or German East Africa in November 1914– February 1915. A retrospective wartime award to a sick British officer who had already returned to India seems odd. However unlikely, it is not wholly inconceivable in the interwar years of Wren's celebrity, when some far murkier retrospective awards of far higher French decorations caused a national scandal (in which the former intelligence officer Francois de La Rocque, mentioned in this book, played an indignant part).

The Colonial Medal clasp for campaigns in French West Africa was first awarded in 1900, with retrospective entitlement. The first Legion deployment to that theatre was of a mounted half-company formed from men of both Foreign Regiments, which embarked at Oran on 6 August 1892 and arrived at Kayes on the Senegal river (now in south-west Mali) on 2 September, with 4 officers, 120 rankers and 93 mules. They operated in Guinea and Ivory Coast with Naval Troops columns led by Colonels Archinard and Combes, and by the time of their return to Kayes in May 1893 they had taken part in 14 combats and had marched about 1,860 miles. They were then shipped back to Algeria, and were disbanded at Sidi bel Abbès on 24 June 1893. This deployment thus coincides with Wren's undocumented late teenage years. (A different medal was awarded for the 1892 Dahomey expedition.) The only other Legion elements to serve in French West Africa were the two infantry companies between February 1894 and January 1895 (see end of Chapter 5). Wren is known to have been studying at Oxford from October 1894, and a successful desertion that spring – from Segou, and many hundreds of miles down the Niger and Senegal rivers to the coast – seems highly unlikely.

The Legion Historical and Information Service does not provide records of former légionnaires to any but their proven next of kin, and without the name under which a man enlisted there is no way of even attempting such an enquiry. In 1967 they held no record of a Percy Wren, and stated their belief that he had obtained his information from a former légionnaire discharged in 1922.

In the absence of some further documentary discovery, the mystery of whether or not P. C. Wren actually served in the Foreign Legion would seem to be insoluble.

Notes and Sources

Preface

1 Charles Frazier, *Thirteen Moons* (Sceptre, 2006)

2 Quoted by Woolman, p.125, from Rosita Forbes, *The Sultan of the Mountains* (New York, 1924)

3 Dr Anderson – head of War Studies at the Royal Military Academy, Sandhurst – was attached to 1st Battalion, Royal Anglian Regiment; he is quoted by permission.

4 Dunn, *Resistance*, p.256

Prologue: 'Bloody Week'

1 *The Reality of War*, p.133

2 Michael Howard, *The Franco-Prussian War* (1961), p.57

3 Morel, p.50; Porch, *Foreign Legion*, pp.164–5; Bergot, *Foreign Legion*, pp.89–91; Geraghty, pp.82–3. The RE absorbed the 10th (Depot) Co of the 7th Line, and drafts from the 12th, 21st, 68th, 69th and 71st Line. (Michael Cox, *Orbatinfo*)

4 Porch, *Foreign Legion*, p.166; *Livre d'Or*, p.130; Garros, pp.37–8; Bergot, *Foreign Legion*, pp.94–5

5 Porch, *Foreign Legion*, p.166; Garros, p.38; Bergot, *Foreign Legion*, p.96

6 Garros, p.39; Bergot, *Foreign Legion* p.97; *Livre d'Or*, p.130

7 The eventual 'paper' strength of the National Guard of Paris was more than 340,000 men aged 20–45, of whom 104,000 formed the 'active' regiments, with 227,000 older 'sedentary' reservists. Given a total city population of some 2 million, these are extraordinary figures.

8 Tombs, pp.5, 45–7, 50–51; Horne, pp.265–75

9 Tombs, p.53

10 Bergot, *Foreign Legion*, p.98; Grisot and Colomb, pp.338–46, 358

11 In 1870 a French infantry regiment had 3 battalions, each of 8 companies; in wartime each bn normally took only 6 coys into the field, leaving the 7th and 8th to form a depot. A rgt at field strength mustered *c.*2,000 all ranks, so each bn *c.*660, and a coy *c.*110, with three officers.

12 Choisel, *RHdA*, 1981/2

13 Tombs, p.14

14 The M1866 Chassepot was a breech-loading, bolt-action rifle taking an 11mm black-powder cartridge made of paper, card, gauze and rubber. This was supposedly self-consuming – i.e. the detonation both propelled the bullet and burned the cartridge away instantaneously, so no empty case had to be extracted before the next was loaded. In fact the build-up of residue soon caused fouling, even obliging men to urinate into the hot chamber in attempts to clear it. Sighted up to 1,200m, the Chassepot had twice the range of the Prussian Dreyse; although this encouraged men to open fire too soon, the Chassepot was very effective, and its flat-nosed 25g (0.9oz) soft lead bullet made terrible, mangling wounds. In contrast to modern warfare, the majority of deaths in the Franco-Prussian War were caused by rifle fire. (Vuillemin, pp. 8–22)

15 Rank-and-file prisoners only returned in any numbers after the final Treaty of Frankfurt on 10 May. Only some 25 per cent of the Army of Versailles would be composed of ex-POWs, in *régiments provisoires* of IV and V corps (Tombs, p.99)

16 Tombs, pp.57–62, 93

17 *ibid*, pp.101–16

18 *ibid*, p.24. Throughout this text *chasseurs à pied* – 'hunters on foot' – is translated for simplicity as Light Infantry.

19 *ibid*, pp.78–9; Horne, p.308

20 Patry, p.259

21 The 'snuffbox' anyway had only half the range of the Chassepot, and misfires, fouling of the chamber and extraction problems with its brass-based cartridge case were also common. (Vuillemin, pp.23–30)

22 Tombs, pp.80–90; Horne, pp.309–11

23 Unless otherwise indicated, the account of RE operations against the Commune before 24 May is taken from Grisot and Colomb, p.354 *et seq* (Grisot was then an officer with V/RE). After that date their account is integrated principally with Gen Montaudon's memoirs, Tombs (Ch 9) and Horne (Ch 24 and 25).

24 Tombs, p.201. Until 15 Apr, Gen Montaudon's command was designated 5th Div of I Corps, and thereafter as 3rd Div. It comprised:
1st Bde (Gen Dumont) – 30e Bn Chasseurs à Pied, 39e Rgt de Marche, Rgt Étrangère
2nd Bde (Gen Lefèbvre) – 31er and 36e Rgts de Marche, 119e Rgt de Ligne
Cavalry Bde (Gen Gallifet) – 9e and 12e Chasseurs à Cheval (detached)

25 The Reffye *mitrailleuse* was one of the great French disappointments of 1870, due to a lack of trained personnel and a misunderstanding of its tactical potential; in street-fighting, however, it could be devastating. Mounted on horse-drawn artillery carriages, *mitrailleuses* were bronze jacketed 'Gatling'-type guns with 16 to 30 clustered barrels in 11mm or 13mm calibre. Cartridges were pre-loaded into a pierced metal plate that slid into grooves in the opened breechblock. Turning a left-hand crank handle closed and cocked the breech, and turning another on the right fired the barrels, at a rate depending on the speed of cranking. The practical rate of fire was about 125rpm, the practical range against area targets about 1,400–1,800 yards

26 Today, Avenue Charles de Gaulle

27 Patry, p.233

28 During the Prussian siege the National Guard had manned 9 artillery batteries. It seems unlikely that the Paris garrison had ever received stocks of the new percussion-fuzed shells, available only from Oct 1870. The Federal gunners in 1871 were probably limited to the older time-fuzed shells, which required more skill to use effectively, and had no fuze-settings for targets closer than 1,350 yds. Fuze-settings for shrapnel air-bursts were more flexible, so the Porte des Ternes battery 1,000yds from the Legion positions was also dangerous; but shrapnel was in short supply – 80 per cent of ammunition was common shell. (Stephen Shann and Louis Delperier, *French Army 1870–71 (2): Republican Troops*, Men-at-Arms 237; Oxford, Osprey, 1991)

29 Horne, pp.320–21

30 Grisot and Colomb, p.360

31 Horne, pp.325–6; Tombs, p.162

32 Horne pp.329–30, 334–9, 343–6

33 Tombs, p.129

34 *ibid*, pp.149–50

35 *ibid*, p.151

36 Montaudon, p.377–9

37 Horne pp.378–98; Montaudon, p.377; Grisot and Colomb, p.361

38 Montaudon, pp.389–90

39 Today, Place de Stalingrad

40 Montaudon, pp.397–8; Grisot and Colomb, p.362; 1871 street map, Éditions du Cadratin. The Rotunda *rond-point* (today's Place de Stalingrad) should not be confused with the more southerly *rond-point* (today's Place du Colonel Fabien, at the junction of Rue Louis Blanc and Boulevard de la Villette).

41 Porch, *Foreign Legion*, p.168

42 Montaudon, p.399; the ends of Faubourg Saint Martin, Boulevard de La Villette and Rue Puebla.

43 Tombs, p.159; Horne, pp.409–10

44 Montaudon, p.447

45 *ibid*, p.405. Today, the northern part of the old Rue de Puebla is Boulevard de La Villette, the southern part Avenue Simon Bolivar.

46 Tombs, p.165–7

47 Montaudon, p.406

48 *ibid*, p.408. Grisot (p.363) claims that his V/RE reached the summit first; and that Legion losses for the whole day were only 4 killed and 12 wounded, of whom 2 died later at the barricade in Place des Fêtes. Rumour would later claim that as many as 600–800 Federals were either killed in action or were executed on the Buttes, but such claims are beyond confirmation.

49 Montaudon, p.409; Grisot and Colomb, pp.363–4; Tombs, p.167

50 Tombs, p.161

51 Montaudon, p.411; Tombs, pp.159–61

52 Serman and Bertau, p.496. Total RE casualties for April–May are not listed by Montaudon, Grisot and Colomb, or any of the main secondary sources such as Garros; the *Livre d'Or de la Légion Étrangère* of 1931 chose to 'pass over this so-sad episode in silence' (p.130). To judge by those of other regiments, we might guess that during Bloody Week itself Legion casualties amounted to a dozen or two killed and 50 to 60 wounded, in addition to the many more suffered earlier in Neuilly.

53 Porch, *Foreign Legion*, p.168; Horne, p.418. The number killed has been hotly disputed, between unconvincing extremes, but a widely accepted estimate is around 20,000.

54 Morel, p.51; Grisot and Colomb, p.365. It

seems doubtful that all the French and Breton conscripts or the foreign duration-only volunteers were discharged before the regiment sailed; there was still a war going on in Algeria – see Ch 2. Grisot and Colomb mention Frenchmen and duration-only volunteers being discharged only in Dec 1871, when the Legion was reduced by a total of 1,200 men.

1. The Tools of Empire

1 Attributed to Gen de Négrier by the Tonkin veteran Frederic Martyn (p.286)

2 Porch, *Sahara*, pp.181–97

3 Reforms of 1889–90 gave the Inf de Marine 12 conventional 12-coy rgts; the 1st-4th in the French ports were termed 'transit rgts' or '*amphi-garnisons*', and were called upon first to provide men for temporary expeditionary forces. (Clayton, pp.312–13)

4 In 1900, provision was made for 18 white 3-bn rgts (RICs), of which 12 were to be stationed at any one time in France, and 6 plus some extras in the colonies, by rotation. At that date 26,000 of the 41,000 *marsouins* were stationed overseas. Additionally the non-European Colonial units, totalling *c*.30,000 men, were reorganized as the 1st-3rd Rgts of Senegalese, 1st-4th Tonkinese and 1st Annamese, and 1st and 2nd Malagasy Skirmishers. (Clayton, pp.313–17)

5 Clayton, pp.211–12. For the sake of brevity the Bats d'Af are usually described as penal units. In fact their purpose was not punishment, as in the Army's *compagnies disciplinaires*, but segregation; the BILAs were a '*corps d'épreuve*' – 'redemptive' combat units. Most of the rank and file were civilian petty criminals (often pimps) who had served prison sentences of not more than three months, or soldiers who had done time in military prisons and still had a period of service to fulfil. Others were new military offenders transferred from their original regiments to the BILAs – e.g. in the 1870s, men suspected of Communard sympathies, or in the early 1900s ringleaders in the several mutinies that broke out on French soil (though surprisingly, the Bats d'Af did include a few genuine volunteers). The term 'penal' does, however, correctly convey their character; a posting to these units was not the first choice of an officer, and the calibre of the NCOs selected for them may be imagined.

6 Richard Brzezinski, 'British Mercenaries in the Baltic 1560–1683', in *Military Illustrated Past & Present*, No.4, Dec 1986/Jan 1987.

7 René Chartrand, *Emigré and Foreign Troops in British Service (1) 1793–1802* and *(2) 1803–1815*;

Men-at-Arms 328 and 335 (Oxford; Osprey, 1999 and 2000)

8 Terry Hooker and Ron Poulter, *The Armies of Bolivar and San Martin*, Men-at-Arms 232 (Oxford; Osprey, 1991)

9 The most thorough English-language study of the Legion's Mexican campaign, and of the evolution of the 'Camerone legend', is that by the Canadian historian Colin Rickards – see Bibliography.

10 Rickards, *passim*; Sergent, *RHdA*, 1981/1, pp.73–89. The names of Danjou, Vilain and Maudet were only added to the rolls of honour on the walls of Les Invalides – in the Galerie de l'Orient – on 6 Aug 1949.

2. 'France Overseas'

1 Epigraphs from Ageron, p.45, and Crealock/Villot, p.1168

2 Silbermann, p.19

3 At Bône in 1834, 1,100 out of a French garrison of 1,500 died of malaria (or typhus, or cholera, or all three – misdiagnosis was commonplace). During a siege of Miliana in 1841, 676 soldiers died out of 1,200, including 542 of the 750 men of the Foreign Legion's 4th Bn. (Cohen, *JAH*, Vol 24, 1983)

4 Ageron, pp.28–9

5 *ibid*, p.35

6 *ibid*, p.45. Lucien Anatole Prévost-Paradol (1829–70), author of *La France Nouvelle* (1868) and editor of *Journal des Debats*.

7 Ageron, p.41

8 The 1845 Treaty of Lalla-Marnia with the Sultan of Morocco had dismissed the south as an uninhabitable wilderness where 'delimitation would be superfluous'. (Dunn, *Resistance*, p.139)

9 Bernard, p.145

10 Dunn, *Resistance*, p.139; Ageron, pp.36–7; Bernard, p.147–9; *Livre d'Or*, p.89

11 Grisot and Colomb, p.367. The continued willingness of Germans to enlist is a reminder of the unpopularity of Prussia in many south German states.

12 Grisot and Colomb, p.367

13 Serman and Bertaud, pp.499–500

14 Clayton, p.273

15 *Marabout* or *murabit* – an inspirational Muslim holy man, in Western terms roughly a 'living saint'.

16 Ageron, pp.50–52; the figure of 1,000 dead is from Serman and Bertaud, pp.501–2. Montagnon (*L'Age d'Or*, p.29) puts total French military and civilian dead as high as 2,700.

17 Grisot and Colomb, pp.368–70

18 The *cacolet* was an iron chair frame with uprights on one side curving up to hook over a pack-saddle. Two were slung on each mule; since the cacolet weighed 15lb and the pack-saddle 70lb, the total load with two men was close to the limit for a mule.

19 Crealock/Villot, *passim*

20 Grisot and Colomb, p.373; Crealock/Villot, *passim*

21 From the French *bouche-de-feu*, 'fire-mouth', or possibly *bouche-de-fer*, 'iron-mouth'.

22 Grisot and Colomb, pp.372–5

23 Ageron, pp.40, 56

24 Ralston, pp.67–81

25 *ibid*, pp.32–3; Serman and Bertaud pp.507, 521–2. The *Marseillaise* was restored as the national anthem only in Feb 1879, just a month after the Republic got its capital 'R' back. Bastille Day, 14 July, only became the national holiday in July 1880 – the same month that an amnesty was declared for imprisoned Communards, many of whom had been sent to the penal colony on New Caledonia in the Pacific. (Serman and Bertaud, pp.527–30)

26 Serman and Bertaud, p.506. Serving officers could sit as deputies until Nov 1875, and could stand for 30 reserved seats in the Senate until Dec 1884; thereafter only a few of the most distinguished were retained, for their valued technical advice. (Ralston, p.66)

27 Choisel, *RHdA*, 1981/2

28 A lottery still decided if men were called up immediately for five years or for only one year. The size of each annual age group was still too expensive for the Army to digest at once, and budgetary constraints would sometimes reduce the actual term of service even of the 'first portion' to less than four years, broken by long periods of leave. (Choisel, *RHdA*, 1981/2; Serman and Bertaud, p.509–10)

29 Ralston, p.81

30 *ibid*, pp.63–4; Serman and Bertaud, pp.523–4. Regimental chaplains were introduced from May 1874, but their activities would be steadily restricted after 1880.

31 Serman and Bertaud, p.512; Morel, p.52; Grisot and Colomb, p.379. Metropolitan Line coys were to have 125 men in peacetime and 250 in wartime,

giving a rgt a mobilized strength of 4,000. Importantly, however, for lack of funding it would take the Line until 1891 to actually achieve the fourth bns (Serman and Bertaud, p.563), while the Legion started from that strength. In 1875 the Legion had just over 3,000 men, giving its 4 bns around 750, so a rifle coy an average of 180 men.

32 The other categories of Africa Army troops were dispersed, one regiment of each to each of the three provinces; the other main garrisons in the Oranais were 2e Zouaves and 1er Bat d'Af (Oran), 2e Tirailleurs Algériens (Mostaganem), 2e Spahis (Sidi bel Abbès) and 2e Chasseurs d'Afrique (Tlemcen).

33 Porch, *Foreign Legion*, p.171. Young men who stayed in the occupied provinces were liable for conscription into the German Army.

34 Morel, p.52; Grisot and Colomb, p.376. By Jan 1872 the bns were stationed at Géryville, Sfissifa & Khreneg Azir (I/RE); Sidi bel Abbès, Boukhanefis and Magenta (II/RE); Mascara (III/RE and rgt HQ); and Saida and Frenda (IV/RE).

35 Grisot and Colomb, p.383

36 Charles Milassin of 4e REI recalled that even in the 1930s men who could not contribute water to the evening cook-pot were handed a raw onion with two red matches stuck in it, and invited to make their own arrangements. (Correspondence with author – see Epilogue)

37 Silbermann, pp.18, 24–5; Manington, pp.40–42; Martyn, pp.250–51

38 A penal Bat d'Af – uniformed almost identically – might replace the Legion bn; but after the mid-1870s the Zouaves, once an elite of volunteers, were seldom employed in the South. Now composed of very short-term *colon* conscripts, they were no more valuable than Metropolitan infantry. After 1875 the Chasseurs d'Afrique also ceased to be all-volunteer units recruited partly in France and partly among French *colons*, and were conscripted from settlers of all backgrounds; however, these Africa Light Horse rgts preserved both the old practice of including a minority of Arab volunteers, and something of their pre-1870 high style. (Clayton, pp.218–19)

39 To underline the importance of sticking together, the French made much of the threat of death by torture, and there are anecdotal accounts of the grim confirmation provided by charred limbs in the ashes of a fire. However, while French casualties were routinely mutilated with knives, it often took more skill than soldiers possessed to tell whether the shocking injuries to a corpse had been inflicted before or after death.

40 Crealock/Villot, *passim*

41 The withdrawal of 60 per cent of the Tunisian

expeditionary corps proved highly premature. In July–Oct 1881 successive French reinforcements had to be sent, causing the fall of the Ferry government. Although the campaign was declared over when the Convention of Marsa formalized a French protectorate in June 1883, counter-insurgency operations continued in the south until 1887. (Serman and Bertaud, pp.634–7)

42 A *zaouia* might loosely be compared to an abbey – simultaneously a centre of pilgrimage, and the college and headquarters of a *sufi* religious brotherhood.

43 Silbermann, p.19

44 A 'large guard' was a detached company, placed by day about 1,000yds out from each face of the square camp, providing four-man sentry outposts 100yds further out; at nightfall the *grands-gardes* were called in to 200yds, with their sentries 30yds beyond.

45 Dunn, *Resistance*, pp.140–43; Grisot and Colomb, pp.384–6; *Livre d'Or*, p.90; Porch, *Foreign Legion*, pp.315–16. The elusive Bou Amama would become something of a fixation for the French; although he never made another significant attack he would remain a shadowy presence on the border for 20 years, his whereabouts and intentions the subject of lively rumour.

46 Porch, *Foreign Legion*, p.316–17; Grisot and Colomb, p.392

47 *Livre d'Or*, p.315. Since the mid-1870s French infantry had been issued with the 11mm M1874 Gras, and a pair of semi-rigid 'coffin' belt pouches for its new ammunition. The Gras was a development of the Chassepot that took a brass cartridge instead of the 'self-consuming' type. (Vuillemin, pp.31–42)

48 Clayton, p.247; *Livre d'Or*, p.93; Gugliotta and Jauffret, *RHdA*, 1981/1 and /2

49 Mules are the offspring of donkey sires and horse dams. They can be of any size from a pony to a sizeable horse – 13 or 14 hands was usual for general pack-work, 14–15hh for mountain artillery pack-guns, and 15–16hh for riding and wagon-teams. Although sterile, the jacks are not impotent, and are usually gelded.

50 Gugliotta and Jauffet, *RHdA*, 1981/1

51 Porch, *Foreign Legion*, pp.312–17; Gandini, pp.25–6

52 His bride, in 1880, had been Mlle Marie-Isabelle de Juchault de la Moricière.

53 The French term *peloton* is a 'false friend' to English readers. In a cavalry context it means a troop – one-quarter of a squadron – with 30–40 men. However, in an infantry and mounted infantry context it means a half-company of *c*.100 men,

in two large platoons *(sections)* of 50, each divided into two large squads *(groupes)* of 25. These English equivalent terms are used throughout this book.

54 Bernard, p.37; *Képi Blanc*, No.83

55 The Beni Gil Arabs were a nomadic tribe of 15,000–20,000 souls living almost entirely from their sheep, which they moved over great distances on the Moroccan and Algerian high plains following the seasonal grazing. A rough proportion of one armed man for every five members of a tribe – a 'tent' – is plausible. (Dunn, *Resistance*, p.38)

56 The great Napoleonic surgeon Baron Larrey recalled of the Egyptian campaign that Arab musket balls were loaded without clipping off the casting stalk, and sometimes with two balls still linked by this into a miniature bar-shot. (Crumplin, pp.43, 52) Mr Crumplin's important study of Napoleonic military surgery also gives examples of wounds inflicted by bladed weapons.

57 *KB*, No.83; *Livre d'Or*, p.93; Turnbull, pp.72–3; Gugliotta and Jauffret, *RHdA*, 1981/1

3. *La Mission Civilisatrice* and the Straw Hat Trade

1 The first epigraph is from Prof Jacques Marseille in *L'Age d'Or*, pp.96–102. The quotation from Galliéni's letter is recorded in a number of French and English sources.

2 What follows is based partly upon an anonymous essay published as 'The Colonial Policy of France' in *The Edinburgh Review*, Apr 1893 (Pallas Armata r/p); this is a digest of various French sources, particularly Léon Deschamps, *Histoire de la Question Coloniale en France* (Paris, 1891), and Jules Ferry, *Le Tonkin et la Mère Patrie* (Paris, 1890). I also owe a debt to Robert and Isabelle Tombs, *That Sweet Enemy* (London; Heinemann, 2006), an invaluable and hugely entertaining examination of Franco-British relations over 300 years.

3 As late as 1788 France had twice Britain's gross national product, and its royal revenues were perhaps 20 per cent higher (the 80 per cent disparity being due to France's inefficient and inequitable taxation); but during the eighteenth century British governments were willing to invest a far higher proportion in wars against France – on occasion, as much as five times higher. Their ability to do so was a direct result of the constitutional settlement that had largely maintained domestic stability and commercial freedom since 1689. Britain's public finances were relatively efficient and honest, had no difficulty in raising almost limitless foreign credit; France's, conspicuously, were not. (Tombs and Tombs, Ch 3 *passim*)

4 In 1851 France retained possession of Martinique and Guadeloupe in the Caribbean; the convict settlement of Guyane on the NE coast of South America; trading posts in Senegal, W. Africa; and the islands of Réunion, Mayotte and Nossi Bé in the Indian Ocean.

5 Raoul Girardet, in *L'Age d'Or*, pp.106–34

6 Girardet, *op cit*; Ageron, p.41

7 Prof Jean Martin, in *L'Age d'Or*, pp.18–27

8 Tombs and Tombs, p.407

9 Girardet, *op cit*

10 The Colonial Ministry's remit included the 'Old Colonies' (the fragments left over from the eighteenth century), sub-Saharan Africa, Madagascar, Indochina and the Pacific islands. Algeria – 'France Overseas' – remained under the Interior Ministry and, as ostensibly sovereign states under protection, Tunisia and later Morocco came under the Foreign Ministry.

11 Eugène Étienne (1844–1921) represented the Oranais in the National Assembly from 1881 until his death. He was Under-secretary for the Colonies from 1887 to 1889, held a number of other portfolios – including the War Ministry in 1913 – in various governments, and from 1892 was the main parliamentary spokesman for the colonial group. The French Colonial Union, an association of *c*.400 firms with colonial interests, was formed in Aug 1893.

12 Martin and Girardet, *op cit*

13 Tombs and Tombs, pp.451–2

14 *JRUSI*, Vol 28, No. 77, pp. 839–40

15 Hocquard, p.243

16 Marseille, *op cit*

17 The remainder of this chapter owes most to McAleavy, *Black Flags in Vietnam*, Ch 1–3.

18 The initial cession was of Bien Hoa, Gia Dinh and My Tho provinces; the annexation, of Chau Doc, Ha Tien and Vinh Long.

19 French sources often use his Annamese name, Luu Vinh Phuoc.

20 McAleavy, pp. 99–110

21 *ibid*, pp.146, 165

22 Meyer, in *L'Age d'Or*, pp.80–91; Serman and Bertaud, p.520

23 McAleavy, pp.204–5

24 Hocquard, p.514

25 McAleavy, pp.215–22

26 The 5th Bn, divided between Mécheria and Géryville on the high plains of the Oranais, and the 6th, at Tiaret guarding the southern Tell. (Morel, p.53; *Livre d'Or*, p.94)

27 Turnbull, p.86; *Livre d'Or*, p.136; Serman and Bertaud, p.641. By Dec 1883 the Navy had in Vietnam 12 bns (four 3-bn marching rgts), and 7 btys of Naval Artillery. (Clayton, pp.212, 247, 313)

4. The Year of the Five Kings

1 *Une Campagne au Tonkin*, p.472, describing the march north to Lang Son by Gen Brière de l'Isle's column.

2 Hocquard, pp.48–50; Blond, p.115

3 Boxed petrol lamps with reflectors and lenses were used for transmitting Morse code by day and night, and were visible through the accompanying tripod telescopes for tens of miles in clear weather. A telegraph link by the British China Submarine Cable Co line to France via Singapore had been established in Saigon in July 1871, but the line from Saigon to Hanoi was not completed until 1888. (Hocquard, p.279)

4 Hocquard, pp.51–3, 104–8, 113

5 *ibid*, p.46. The first 2 bns of Tirailleurs Annamites had been raised, mainly from Christians, by an order of Dec 1879.

6 Rampart guns – Chinese-made giant shotguns, or more accurate imported rifled equivalents firing a single 2oz ball.

7 Liu's men were armed, like Chinese regulars, mainly with single-shot breech-loaders – Remingtons, Sniders and Mausers – with some American Peabodys, and even Winchester repeaters.

8 Hocquard, pp.191–201; McAleavy, pp.224–7; Turnbull, pp.86–9; Blond, pp.117–18

9 Serman and Bertaud, p.642; McAleavy, p.230; Hocquard, p.41; Morel, p.53; Turnbull, p.89

10 Charles Édouard Hocquard (1853–1911) had published papers on ophthamology, which led him to an interest in photography. In 1883 he volunteered for the Tonkin Expeditionary Corps, serving from Jan 1884 to Apr 1886. He published his account of the campaign first as articles in *Le Tour du Monde* (1889–91), and in 1892 in book form. The latter is illustrated with high-quality steel engravings of people, landscapes, urban and campaign scenes made from his own photographs; a number of these are the only known images of buildings destroyed shortly after his tour.

11 McAleavy, pp.228–30

12 As the only substantial brick buildings to be found outside the towns, pagodas were routinely used for shelter. Some of them were large complexes, but even a small village pagoda was large enough to house a platoon.

13 French companies could not compete with the initiative, energy, local contacts, language skills and self-financing conglomerates of the Chinese. (Hocquard, p.243)

14 At least two classes of coastal/river *cannonières* were employed, both with broad, shallow hulls; the earlier type drew just under 5ft and could not get into the upper rivers except in monsoon flood conditions, but a later design built by Claparède drew only 30 inches. Hocquard's images show a number of different superstructure layouts, superficially resembling houseboats, and the larger craft could transport up to 500 troops (briefly, and in great discomfort). They carried from 2 to 4 mounted weapons, either light Hotchkiss single-barrel quick-firers or Gatling-type 'revolvers', often protected by armoured shields or tubs. The larger boats had 2 tall side-by-side smokestacks and twin stern paddlewheels, and a crew of up to 5 officers and 71 ratings; the smaller single-stack, screw-driven type were an ensign's command, with a crew of 12.

15 Hocquard, p.111. Commanded by Capt Aron, the unit had arrived in Tonkin in Feb 1884 with six rather hastily and badly made balloons.

16 Hocquard, p.138; Lyautey, *Intimate Letters*, p.66

17 Serman and Bertaud, p.547

18 The traditional goals of the légionnaire (beyond, for the foreigner, French citizenship) were a sergeant's gold cuff-stripe and the Médaille Militaire. Instituted in 1852, this was the only national gallantry decoration available to French rankers before the institution of the Croix de Guerre in 1915, and it was not easily won. (The Legion of Honour was open to rankers but not as an initial award, only to long-service NCOs already wearing the Médaille.) To be *médaillé* guaranteed a légionnaire the respect of his peers and his officers, and to some extent protected him from the consequences of later misbehaviour in barracks.

19 Hocquard, pp.128–54; *Livre d'Or*, p.136; Turnbull, pp.89–91; McAleavy, pp.230–31; Blond, pp.119–20

20 Porch, *Foreign Legion*, p.209

21 Hocquard, pp.218–24

22 *ibid*, pp.541–3

23 Cohen, *JAH*, Vol 24, pp.22–36; Hocquard, pp.289, 440. The only active step to improve the chance of recovery was to evacuate the victim far from the chance of reinfection; a légionnaire who

lived long enough to be taken down to the coast had a fighting chance.

24 McAleavy, pp.231–41

25 *ibid*, p.253

26 Readers familiar with the French Indochina War of 1946–54 will recognize in this description the classic pattern of low-level Viet Minh activity in nominally French-pacified areas.

27 Hocquard, pp.185–9, 365, 511

27 Impalement involved lowering the victim vertically on to the point of a sharpened stake, so that the spike entered between the legs and – impelled by the weight of the writhing body – drove up until it forced its way out through the upper torso. If the heart was destroyed, then merciful death limited the process to a few unimaginable minutes, but that did not always happen.

28 Hocquard, pp. 329–30, 383; Charles Meyer, p.91, and Francoise Lafargue, p.133, in *L'Age d'Or*.

29 In Sept 1884, c.2,900 reinforcements and replacements were at sea en route for Indochina. The order of battle in-country was as follows (officers + rankers):

1er Bde 1er Rgt de Marche (Tirailleurs Algériens, 75 + 2,450); 2e Rgt de M (Infanterie de Marine, 36 + 2,050); 2e Rgt Tirailleurs Tonkinois (39 + 3,500)
2e Bde 3e Rgt de M (Légion and 2e Bat d'Af, 47 + 2,400); 4e Rgt de M (bns of 23e, 111e and 143e de Ligne, 46 + 2,400); 1er Rgt Tirs Tonk (41 + 3,800)
1er Chasseurs d'Afrique Half-sqn
Artillerie de terre 2 batteries 80mm
Art de Marine 4 btys '4-pdrs', 1 bty 65mm, 1 bty 95mm
4e Regt de Genie 1 coy
20e Esc du Train 1 coy
Flotte 22 river gunboats & launches (60 + 1,080)
(Source *Histoire Militaire de l'Indochine, Tome II* – hereafter referenced *HMdI*.) The first 2 rgts of Tirailleurs Tonkinois were raised in 1884.

30 The Legion coys were those of Capts Beynet, Bolgert, Bérard and Yzombart. (*HMdI*, p.97)

31 Hocquard, pp.373–81; *HMdI*, pp.98–100; McAleavy, p.260; Porch, *Foreign Legion*, p.209

32 *HMdI*, p.101; Blond, p.127

33 Sources differ over the precise number of defenders. *HMdI* gives 13 officers + 597 men = 610. Blond lists them as: CO, Maj Dominé, 2e Bat d'Af. *Légion* detachment CO, Capt Cattelin (AdjMaj I/LE); 1er and 2e Cies – Capts Moulinay and Borelli, 2 lts, 2 s/lts, 390 other ranks. *Tirs Tonk* 8e Cie/1er RTT – Capt Dia, Lt Goulet, 2 French NCOs, 160 native ORs. *Art de Marine* Lt Derappe, 2 sgts, 29 ORs. *Génie* Sgt Bobillot, Cpl Cacheux, 6 ORs. Plus Dr Vincens and 3 orderlies, a civilian commissary and 3 bakers, a Protestant pastor and an interpreter, so total 612. To these must be added Ensign Sènés and 12 ratings on the gunboat, so grand total = 625.

34 Traditional siege tactics involved the digging of a crosswise trench facing the walls at the limit of effective weapon range; from this 'parallel', saps – trenches pointing towards the walls – would zigzag forwards. Closer to the walls, another transverse parallel would then be dug to link the sap heads; the process was continued, perhaps to a third parallel, until large numbers of attacking troops could get close to the walls under cover to launch their assaults.

35 The exact weapons mounted on the *Mitrailleuse* seem to be unrecorded, but that day they were very effective against packed infantry trying to get round the east corner and down to the southeast gate on the riverbank. Two of the commonest Hotchkiss guns were a hand-cranked 37mm Gatling-style five-barrel 1-pdr firing HE shells at 50–60 rounds per minute; and a 47mm fixed-barrel 3-pdr, loaded singly by a second crewman while the gunner aimed and fired by means of a shoulder-brace and a pistol-grip trigger. (J-J. Monsuez, 'Artillerie de marine Hotchkiss' in *RHdA*, 2003/3)

36 The aim of counter-mining was to get as close as possible to the enemy tunnel – not to set off explosive charges to destroy it, but so that when the enemy charge was fired the blast would take the line of least resistance, being channelled forwards through the counter-mine rather than upwards to destroy the wall above.

37 The exact dating of particular incidents differs in the sources, usually through confusion over whether a night-time event occurred before or after midnight. It is clear that two mines were blown on consecutive nights, under the northwest wall and west corner; but it is not clear whether those nights were the 11/12 and 12/13, or the 12/13 and 13/14 Feb.

38 At this date about 45 per cent of the Legion were still Alsatians. The proportion would drop after 1889, when a law was passed allowing men from occupied Alsace–Lorraine to apply for naturalization *ab initio*, thus enabling them to enlist directly into Metropolitan regiments. (Porch, *Foreign Legion*, p.291)

39 Boisset gives 59 casualties in all; *Livre d'Or*, 14 killed and 40 wounded; *HMdI*, 16 killed and 22 wounded, including Lt Vincent. The definition of 'wounded' probably varies here; about half the higher total presumably returned to the ranks after being treated, the other half remaining unfit for duty in the hospital.

40 *HMdI*, pp.102–3; Blond, pp.125–52; *Livre d'Or*, pp.137–42; Turnbull, pp.91–7. Borelli would be inspired to write an ode in gratitude to Streibler's

sacrifice; this was more widely published than its literary merit justified.

41 L. Huguet, *En colonne: souvenirs d'extrême-Orient* (Paris; Flammarion, n.d.); Théophile Boisset, *Tuyen-Quan pendant la siège* (Paris; Fischbacher, 1885); Porch, *Foreign Legion*, p.218

42 In the Legion companies, 1 off + 31 ORs killed, 6 (i.e. all surviving) offs + 120 ORs wounded = 158 casualties, or 32 per cent of 23 Nov effectives (Bergot, in J. R. Young, p.20). For the garrison as a whole, Blond (p.152) gives 48 killed + 8 died of wounds = 56, + 208 wounded survived = total casualties 264, or 43 per cent. However, Serman and Bertaud (p.647) give as many as 297 total casualties.

43 McAleavy, p.257–8; Porch, *Foreign Legion*, pp.205–7

44 Morel, pp.53–4

45 *HMdI*, p.104; Hocquard, p.452

46 Hocquard, pp.447–51. Brière had asked for 400 mules; he got 100 (*HMdi*, p.104).

47 The order of battle of the 'teeth' arms was as follows:
GOC: Gen Brière de l'Ile; *CoS* Col Crétin, *Art Cdr* Col Borgnis-Desbordes
Ire Bde (Col Giovanninelli): Ier Rgt de Marche (Inf de Marine: LtCol Chaumont, bns Majs Mahias and Lambinet); 2e Rgt de M (Tirs Alg: LtCol Letellier, bns Majs de Mibielle and Comoy); I/2e Rgt Tirs Tonk (Maj Tonnot). *Art* (Maj Levrard: 3 btys – Capts Roperth and Pericaud, Art de Marine Capt Roussel)
2e Bde (Gen de Négrier): 3e Rgt de M (Lt-Col Herbinger, bns 23e, 111e and 143e de Ligne); 4e Rgt de M (Légion: LtCol Donnier, bns II/1er RE Maj Diguet, III/2e RE Maj Schoeffer; 2e Bat d'Af, Maj de Servières); I/1er Rgt Tirs Tonk (Maj Jorna de Lacale). *Art* (Maj de Douvres: 3 btys – Capts Jourdy and de Saxcé, Art de Marine Capt Martin)
Bn strengths were between 500 and 800; total strength of column, 7,186 combatants, c4,500 porters.

48 Hocquard, p.456

49 *HMdI*, p.105; Hocquard, pp.458–60; Morel, p.137

50 *HMdI*, p.106; Hocquard, pp.461, 469, 472, 475

51 *HMdI*, p.107; Hocquard, pp.476–8

52 In addition to 1er and 2e Rgts de Marche the relief column had 2 x 80mm mtn btys (Capts Jourdy and Pericaud), an engineer half-coy and a field ambulance; total starting strength was 86 offs + 2,348 men. (*HMdI*, p.107)

53 *ibid*

54 *HMdI*, pp.107–8; *Livre d'Or*, p.142; Blond,

pp.149–51. Both *Livre d'Or* and Serman and Bertaud (p.647) give 76 killed + 408 wounded = total casualties 484. However, *HMdI* gives 6 offs + 70 ORs killed, but 21 offs + 666 ORs wounded = total casualties 863. Again, this unexplained discrepancy may be between 'seriously' (evacuated) and 'lightly' wounded men.

55 Hocquard, pp.479–84

56 Hocquard, pp.488–90. The Chinese abandoned 3 Krupp 65mm guns + 2 Nordenfeldt MGs; French casualties were 9 killed + 45 wounded. (*HMdI*, p.109)

57 Hocquard, pp.491–6; *HMdI*, p.109

58 *HMdI*, pp.109–11. In order of march: part I/1er Rgt Tirs Tonk; 3 coys 143e de Ligne (Maj Farret); bn 111e de Ligne (Maj Faure); art bty (Capt Saxcé); and II/1er RE (Maj Diguet).

59 *HMdI*, p.111; Hocquard, pp.499–500; Porch, *Foreign Legion*, p.231

60 McAleavy, pp.271–2

61 Porch, *Foreign Legion*, p.233

62 *ibid*

63 *HMdI*, p.112

64 Porch, *Foreign Legion*, p.233

65 See *The Last Valley* (London; Weidenfeld & Nicolson, 2004) pp.109–11

66 McAleavy, p.272

67 *HMdI*, p.112

68 *ibid*, p.113

69 The court of enquiry duly found Herbinger responsible for the whole debacle, and he died in disgrace the following year.

70 Meyer, in *L'Age d'Or*, pp.80–91; McAleavy, p.275–6

71 McAleavy, p.277; *HMdI*, p.113

72 Hocquard, pp.499–502

73 *ibid*, p.500; Lyautey, *Intimate Letters*, p.84

74 Meyer, in *L'Age d'Or*, p.91; Hocquard, pp.514–23, 602; McAleavy, p.283

75 Meyer, in *L'Age d'Or*, p.85

5. General Vengeance and King Zinc-Nose

1 Martyn, p.36

2 Serman and Bertaud, p.533; Ralston, p.87

3 Ralston, p.84; Serman and Bertaud, pp.513, 561–2

4 Dutailly, *RHdA*, 1981/1. The proportion of French officers also increased as a result of casualties in Tonkin; the gaps were filled in part by giving temporary commissions for overseas service to volunteer Reserve officers, and after their tours some of these sought to extend their careers with the colours. Since the Metropolitan officer corps had only a limited number of slots for each rank, the ministry postponed the problem by channelling some of these men into the Legion under the transparent fiction of foreign status – at least for a few years, until they could apply for 'rectification' and transfer to Line units (one of these was Captain Borelli, the good soldier – but bad poet – of Tuyen Quang). Of 87 'foreign' officers admitted to the Legion between 1883 and 1895, 77 were actually Frenchmen.

5 Vuillemin, pp.59–66. On his appointment in Jan 1886, Boulanger imposed a deadline of 1 May for completion of work to marry the new nitrocellulose propellant, an 8mm bullet, and the imperfect existing Kropatschek tubular magazine system. This forced the compromise adoption of a tapered cartridge measuring fully 15mm across the base, which would cause problems for 40 years. The M1886 Lebel was issued from 1887, but required modifications in 1893.

6 Marshal de Saint-Arnaud had been both a ferocious field commander in Algeria and a leader in Napoleon III's military coup of 1851.

7 Ralston, pp.169–71; Serman and Bertaud, pp.574–80. Boulanger fled France in April 1889, and finally committed suicide in Brussels, beside the grave of his mistress, on 30 Sept 1891.

8 Ralston, pp.182–4, 188

9 Martyn's retrospective memoir, published only in 1911, was prompted by, and sharply critical of, that of the unattractively self-righteous German deserter 'Erwin Rosen', published the previous year to a scandalized reception at a time of relentless German anti-Legion propaganda. While critical of some 'barbarous' practices, Martyn pointed out that readers shocked by Rosen's book must be very innocent about life in a contemporary British barracks. He even claimed that in some ways the tougher Legion regime was superior in turning out disciplined and self-reliant soldiers to what he called the 'milk-and-water treatment' of Tommy Atkins. George Manington had no previous military experience, but (like Martyn) he already spoke good French when he enlisted in 1st RE in Feb 1890.

10 Martyn, p.39. Under a law of 29 Oct 1881 Frenchmen who had already completed their obligatory military service were permitted to enlist *à titre étranger*. This attracted men seeking the active service that the stultifying barracks life of provincial France had denied them, and par-

ticularly those who had either just failed entry to St Cyr, or who had reached NCO rank in Line units by their mid-twenties. With their superior skills such men could hope for quick promotion, 'rectification' of their national status, a commission via St Maixent, or at least the addition of their years in the Legion to those spent in the Line to count towards eventual pension rights. At that time foreigners had to serve 25 years to qualify for a pension, but Frenchmen only 15. (Carles, *RHdA*, 1981/1)

11 Martyn, pp.54, 71, 78; Manington, pp.25–6. By 1911 the planks had been replaced with iron bedsteads with allegedly flexible thin iron bands in place of springs, and the straw palliasses by hard fabric mattresses. By 1915, at least, each man was provided with a small lockable box on the shelf for personal possessions, but in the late 1880s he had to take his own precautions. ('MM', pp.202–3)

12 For those interested in such minutiae: the paybook of No.12244 *Soldat de 2e classe* Gustave Seewald (an illiterate 21-year-old shopworker from Hamm, Westphalia, who joined 2e RE in April 1903) also lists issue of a *bonnet de police* or fatigue sidecap; a flannel *calotte* or nightcap; a *couvre-nuque*, the curtained Havelock or képi-cover of folklore; trouser braces (suspenders); a pair of *souliers* (light canvas shoes?) in place of one of the pairs of hobnailed boots; two neck-stocks of bright blue calico; two handkerchiefs; a 'housewife' with sewing kit; a pair of foot-cloths; a belt, its Y-strap shoulder suspenders, three ammo pouches and bayonet frog; a haversack, mess tin, 2-litre waterbottle, knapsack, blanket, tent cloth with sectional pole, cords and pegs; and rifle No.43929 with sling.

13 Martyn, pp.106, 281; Silbermann, p.15. While a rifle company in Algeria had 250 men, there was no official limit on the size of the regimental depot companies, which could be very large. This naturally overstretched the senior NCOs, and made the three company officers almost invisible.

14 Martyn, p.61; Manington, p.20

15 Martyn, pp.101–6; Manington, pp.27–8. A high standard of smartness was demanded for the walking-out uniform, which changed according to daily orders – e.g. one evening it would be tunic and red trousers, the next it might be *veste*, white trousers and sash, and so on. With all uniforms, soldierly dignity was ensured by the belt and the long Gras bayonet, whose brass pommel and wood grips took a fine polish.

16 Martyn, pp.90–93

17 'MM', p.207

18 Rankin, p.36; Porch, *Foreign Legion*, p.222; Martyn, pp.98–100, 120

19 'MM' claimed (pp.211–12) that in 1915 the long blue waist-sash would fetch 6 or 7 francs – several weeks' basic pay for a *2e classe*, and enough to stupefy a whole barrack room.

20 Manington, pp.38, 40–42; Martyn, p.113

21 The quoted analyses are in d'Esparbes, pp.15–17; see also Porch, *Foreign Legion*, p.291; Martyn, p.112; Manington, p.36. From the sample of *c.*1,000 enlistees, the largest groups were day-labourers, farmworkers and gardeners (210) and shopworkers (103). There were also 58 cobblers and 28 tailors, 51 bakers and 25 butchers, 36 masons, 28 carpenters, 24 painters and decorators, 20 blacksmiths and – for some reason – no fewer than 70 locksmiths and clocksmiths.

22 Pfirmann, *KB* 347 and 348

23 Martyn, pp.108–10; Manington, pp.52–5 – though he gives Minnaert's name wrongly as Mertens.

24 Martyn, p.119

25 Carles, *RHdA*, 1981/1

26 Martyn, pp.32–6, 45, 77; Manington, p.29

27 Manington, p.29; Martyn, p.36

28 Martyn, pp.32–6; Silbermann, p.20

29 Silbermann, pp.31–2

30 Martyn, p.94

31 Serman and Bertaud, pp.567–8

32 Silbermann, p.25

33 This highly infectious bacterial fever is usually contracted through contamination of food or water with excrement via flies or dirty hands. During the 10- to 14-day incubation period it has no visible symptoms, and by the time headaches, exhaustion, bronchial and abdominal disorders became evident, the nineteenth-century sufferer faced about three weeks of high fever, rashes, dehydration, emaciation, delirium and a chance of fatal ulceration of the bowel. There were many ways a man could die from various complications of enteric fever, and the only treatment was nursing care.

34 Manington, pp.56–8

35 Martyn, p.183–4

36 Between 1878 and 1898 the tricolour was carried eastwards along the Senegal and Niger rivers into modern Mali and Burkina Fasso, across Niger and Chad, and finally as far as the southern Sudan. Concurrently, a thrust down the Atlantic coast added Guinea and the Ivory Coast to the western base of this band of territory, and a northwards push from the jungles of Gabon and Congo through the Central African Republic linked up with the west–east corridor in Chad. (The confusing French term 'Soudane' for the West African savannah country has been avoided here.)

37 Pierre Boilley, in *L'Age d'Or*, pp.46–55

38 For early history of Tirailleurs Sénégalais, see Clayton, pp.334–5.

39 J.D. Page, in *Journal of African History*, Vol 21 (1980) pp.289–310. Page quotes a Yoruba cleric, as late as 1880: 'Slavery is the principal source of investment and, next to polygamy, the chief thing in which wealth consists.'

40 W.A. Richards, in *JAH*, Vol 21 (1980), pp.43–59

41 Burton, *A Mission to Gelele, King of Dahomey* (London, 1864)

42 Martyn, p.242

43 Europeans reported clothing of various unit colours, and flowerpot-shaped caps of white, blue or red often decorated with appliqué emblems – crocodiles, open eyes and sharks were all noted (shark imagery was traditional to the Fon kings after they conquered the coast). See F.E. Forbes, *Dahomey and the Dahomans* (London, 1851), and J.A. Skertchly, *Dahomey As It Is* (London, 1874). For most of the quoted material on the Dahomeyan army the author is indebted to Andrew Callan and Angus McBride, '"This West African Prussia": The Dahomeyan Army 1840s–1890s' in *Military Illustrated Past & Present*, No.30, Nov 1990.

44 Serman and Bertaud, p.679

45 Behanzin's imports in 1890–92 included 400 Peabody, 250 Spencer and 230 Winchester carbines, 750 Chassepot, 250 Albini and 300 Snider rifles. (Callan, *op cit*)

46 Morel, pp.54, 60. The bns then in Algeria were III/ and IV/1st RE, I/ and II/2nd RE.

47 For note on half-coy deployed to Mali, see end of Appendix 3.

48 Porch, *Foreign Legion*, p.247. Individual officers of Metropolitan units might be posted into, or might apply for, a vacant appointment in their rank in the Africa Army. Army officers of both organizations might likewise be sent to or apply for staff posts in the Navy's colonial theatres.

49 Turnbull, pp.103–4

50 Martyn, pp.186–92

51 Silbermann, pp.55, 62

52 Martyn, p.194

53 Cohen, *JHA*, Vol 24

54 Martyn, pp.194–5; Porch, *Foreign Legion*, pp.252–6, 277

55 Martyn, pp.196–200; Silbermann, p.47; *Livre d'Or*, pp.157–8; Porch, *Foreign Legion*, p.257–9; Geraghty, pp.106–7; Bergot, *Foreign Legion*, pp.102–3; Callan, in *MI P&P* No.30; R.A. Kea, in *JAH*, Vol 12 (1971), pp.185–213

56 The rest of the campaign would be punctuated by Dahomeyan attempts to negotiate between battles, and French refusals; this reflected a fundamental difference in attitudes to warfare.

57 Martyn, pp.203–5; Porch, *Foreign Legion*, p.259

58 Or Grede, or Adegon, or Poguessa – all place-names are variously reported.

59 Callan, *op cit*; Martyn, pp.206–7

60 Martyn, pp.202, 206–9; Porch, *Foreign Legion*, pp.260–61. The incident of Battreau's rifle is only notable for the fact that P.C. Wren would later recycle it in a short story.

61 Martyn, pp.211–12; Porch, *Foreign Legion*, pp.261–2

62 Martyn, pp.226–7

63 Cohen, *JHA*, Vol 24

64 Porch, *Foreign Legion*, pp.262–5

65 Martyn, pp.217, 224

66 *ibid*, pp.32–3, 216. Martyn did point out that striking a superior in the presence of the enemy would normally have meant a firing squad; that in such circumstances the only punishments available were physical; and that while serving in the British Army he had seen men 'pegged out' as field punishment, which he reckoned was almost as bad as 'the Toad'. However, he noted approvingly that when Gen de Négrier was GOC 19th Army Corps he 'put a stop to it, and a great many other abuses'.

67 *ibid*, pp.226–9. This brought the column's strength to 69 officers and 2,000 men. (Porch, *Foreign Legion*, p.264)

68 Silbermann, p.49

69 Martyn, pp.232–4; Porch, *Foreign Legion*, p.263

70 Martyn, pp.235–41; Silbermann, p.50

71 Martyn, p.249. Porch (*Foreign Legion*, p.265) gives only 81 total French killed but 436 wounded in combat; he does not quote deaths from disease, but judges that these multiplied the combat fatalities fivefold.

72 Porch, *March to the Marne*, p.162

73 Serman and Bertaud, p.680; Silbermann, pp.55–77; Morel, p.60

74 Both coys returned to Sidi bel Abbès for disbandment on 28 Jan 1895. (Morel, p.60; *Livre d'Or*, pp.162–3)

6. Tiger Country

1 Epigraphs from 'Les Carnets du Sergent Pfirmann' in *Képi Blanc* No.350; and Lyautey, *Intimate Letters from Tonkin*, p.80

2 The passages on Lyautey's life before his posting to Tonkin are based on the Maurois biography, and Hoisington, *passim*.

3 Maurois, p.32; Porch, *March to the Marne*, p.125

4 President Sadi Carnot would be stabbed to death at Dijon in May 1894 by an Italian anarchist.

5 Maurois, p.45

6 Lyautey, *Intimate Letters*, p.46

7 *ibid*, pp.27, 44

8 *ibid*, pp.50–53. Throughout the quotations from translated sources in this text, punctuation and occasional translations of terms are slightly adjusted by the present author for the sake of clarity.

9 Lyautey, *Intimate Letters*, pp.57–9. Comparison with the contemporaneous Ferry report on the Algerian administration makes this story wholly credible. (*Edinburgh Review*, Apr 1893, pp.330–81)

10 Porch, *March to the Marne*, pp.140–44

11 Maurois, p.48; Lyautey, *Intimate Letters*, pp.68–9

12 A fifth territory, surrounding Hanoi itself, was administered directly by the civil governor-general. At the time of Lyautey's arrival 1st–4th Military Territories, from east to west, were commanded by Cols Chapelet, HQ at Mon Cai; Galliéni, at Lang Son; Thomasset, at Tuyen Quang; and Servières, at Yen Bai. (Lyautey, *Intimate Letters*, p.107)

13 Lyautey, *Intimate Letters*, p.73. See beginning of Ch 11 below, and '*l'affaire des fiches*'.

14 Lyautey, *Intimate Letters*, pp.76–8

15 McAleavy, pp.279, 283

16 Porch, *Foreign Legion*, p.239–44

17 Manington, pp.296–300

18 Serman and Bertaud, p.653; Porch, *Foreign Legion*, p.220, quoting Col Tournyol du Clos, 'La Légion Étrangère au Tonkin 1883–1932' in *La revue d'infanterie* No.525, Vol 89, May 1936, p.859; Cohen, *op cit, JAH*, Vol 24.

19 Pfirmann, *KB*, No.344; Martyn, pp.122–3; Manington, p.61

20 Martyn, p.127

21 Manington, pp.67, 86; Martyn, p.131; Hocquard, p.92

22 Pfirmann, *KB*, No.347. Many of the placenames shown on nineteenth-C French maps have changed since, e.g. on modern maps Phu Lang Thuong seems to be Bac Giang. Throughout this text and in Maps 4 and 7 the old names are generally used.

23 Pfirmann, *KB*, No.350

24 Manington, p.228

25 *ibid*, pp.121–2

26 *ibid*, p.117: Pfirmann, *KB*, No.351

27 Carpeaux, p.84; de la Poer, p.127; Sylvère, p.64; Porch, *Foreign Legion*, p.241

28 Pfirmann, *KB*, No.352

29 Martyn, pp.170–71; Manington, pp.134, 161–3, 214–18

30 Pfirmann, *KB*, Nos.353, 354; Morel (p.137) confirms the officers' deaths. Sgt Pfirmann disembarked at Algiers on 5 Dec 1889; despite treatment and two spells of convalescence at Arzew his arm was permanently withered, and he was finally invalided out of the Legion in Feb 1892. In 1936 his son Paul joined the Legion, retiring in 1961 as CO of 5e REI; his grandson Claude was also commissioned, serving as a captain in 1er and 2e REC.

31 Martyn, p.133. Normally the coys of a 2nd Bn of a regiment were numbered 5th–8th, but the Legion bns in Tonkin at that date 'formed corps', i.e. were autonomous units, so each had 1st–4th Coys.

32 Martyn, pp.140–45, 170; Manington, pp.283–5

33 Martyn, pp.176–7

34 Martyn, p.152–8; sketch and elevations Manington, between pp.100 and 105

35 Martyn, pp. 162–57, 179; Manington, pp.108–10

36 Manington, pp.125–31, 138–55

37 *ibid*, pp.34, 159, 295

38 *ibid*, pp.176–91

39 *ibid*, pp.200–203

40 *ibid*, pp.214–22

41 *ibid*, pp.229–43. Like most of his contemporaries, Manington confused malaria and blackwater fever cases.

42 *ibid*, pp.258–61

43 *ibid*, pp.264–73

44 *ibid*, pp.279–81, 296–300. Though weakened,

De Tam would remain at large in the Yen The; as late as 1909 he led another rising and he was not finally betrayed and captured until February 1913. (Serman and Bertaud, p.653)

45 Manington, pp.92–3. This re-equipment was some three years earlier than stated in standard sources, but Manington was interested in weapons and is most unlikely to be mistaken. The bolt-action 8mm Lebel M1886 had an eight-round tubular magazine under the barrel, and a practical rate of fire of up to 14 rpm if this was used – just as in the British Army, some officers preferred their men to load and fire single rounds except in emergencies, to avoid wasting ammunition. The Lebel was accurate to 1,000 yards and theoretically effective up to 3,500 yards. Its high muzzle velocity – at least 2,000fps, compared with the 1,475fps of the Gras – also gave it greater penetration; légionnaires recalled its lethal effect even against adversaries sheltering behind tree trunks. (Vuillemin, pp.59–67)

46 Manington, pp.307, 313, 329, 352. Morel (p.137) confirms Watrin's death at Ban So, 17 Aug 1892.

47 De Neuville's painting caused a sensation at the Paris Salon of 1873; see Philippe Chabert, *Alphonse de Neuville, l'épopée de la defaite* (Paris; Coppernic, 1979), Plate 7 and p.18.

48 Lyautey, *Intimate Letters*, pp.80–89

49 *ibid*, pp.87–8

50 *ibid*, pp.92–100

51 Maurois, p.52

52 Lyautey, *Intimate Letters*, pp.110, 157. The first experiment in arming tribesmen had been made on the Red and Black rivers in 3rd Territory by LtCol Théophile Pennequin. (Serman and Bertaud, p.652; Hoisington, p.12)

53 Lyautey, *Intimate Letters*, pp.108–10

54 *ibid*, pp.114–19

55 The summary that follows in this and the next chapter is based on Ralston, Ch 5, and on Douglas Johnstone, *passim*.

56 Lyautey, *Intimate Letters*, p.123

57 *ibid*, pp.133–50

58 *ibid*, pp.133–7, 286, 297, 309

59 *ibid*, pp.179–81

60 In 1947 Bac Kan was the headquarters of the Viet Minh, whose senior leadership narrowly escaped from a French parachute attack on 7 Oct at the outset of the first major French offensive.

61 Lyautey, *Intimate Letters*, pp.189–201, 225

62 *ibid*, pp.217–22, 256

63 *ibid*, pp.232–4

64 *ibid*, p.249

65 *ibid*, pp.263–8, 283; Morel, p.137

66 It is noticeable that nowhere in his letters from Tonkin does he ever mention formed Navy units, only individual naval officers leading Tonkinese Skirmishers.

67 Lyautey, *Intimate Letters*, pp.274–8. The present author has corrected some obvious errors in Mrs Le Blond's translation.

68 *ibid*, pp.289, 300, 308

69 *ibid*, pp.289–90

70 *ibid*, pp.299, 318

71 *ibid*, p.304

72 For a listing of Legion deployments in Tonkin 1897–1911, down to company level, see Morel, pp.57–60.

73 Maurois, p.63; Lyautey, *Intimate Letters*, p.319

74 Lyautey, *Intimate Letters*, p.63

7. 'A Calling Devoid of Allurement'

1 Epigraphs from *Two Campaigns: Madagascar and Ashantee* (London, T.Fisher Unwin, 1896), p.173; and Silbermann, p.115.

2 Malagasy (Fr. *malgache*) is the collective adjective for all the inhabitants, who mostly spoke recognizable dialects of the same language.

3 Jean Martin, in *L'Age d'Or*, pp.70–73

4 Queens Rasoherina (r.1863–8), Ranavalona II (r.1868–83), and Ranavalona III (r.1883–96)

5 Campbell, in *JAH*, Vol 21 (1980), pp.341–6

6 Pasfield Oliver, pp.724–5, 731 – this source draws throughout upon Gen Duchesne's report.

7 Porch, *Foreign Legion*, p.268; Gen Emile Reibell, *Le calvaire de Madagascar* (Paris, Berger-Levrault, 1935), p.50. The 200e Rgt de Ligne and 40e Bn de Chasseurs à Pied were temporary units formed by drawing lots among second- and third-year conscripts who answered a call for volunteers.

8 Porch, *Foreign Legion*, pp.269–70

9 *1er Bde (Metzinger)* – Rgt de Marche d'Algérie (Legion, I/RMdA; Tirs Alg, II/ and III/RMdA); 200e de Ligne (3 bns)
2e Bde (Voyron) – 13e RIM (men from 1er and 3e Rgts); Rgt Coloniale (bn Tirs Malgaches, mainly Sakalavas; bn Tirs Haussa; bn Vols de Réunion)
Divisional troops – escadron 1er RCA; 40e Bn de Chasseurs à Pied

38e Rgt d'Art (5 mtn and field btys) and Rgt d'Art de Marine (3 mtn btys) – 30x 80mm mtn guns, 12x 80mm field guns, 4x 120mm short howitzers 4 cies Génie; 6 cies 30e Esc de Train plus 1 cie Sénégalais (Serman and Bertaud, p.660; Pasfield Oliver, pp.724–30)

10 Porch, *Foreign Legion*, p.271; Pasfield Oliver, pp.730–31

11 The carts were supposed to move in convoys or *échelons* of 150, each of these with a total payload of 30 tons (Pasfield Oliver, p.734). Rather than sending them back to the coast empty, they were pressed into service for evacuating a couple of casualties each – a task for which these iron boxes were horribly unsuited.

12 *Livre d'Or*, p.167; Silbermann, pp.80–81

13 Pasfield Oliver, p.730

14 *ibid*, p.739

15 Porch, *Foreign Legion*, p.273; E.F. Knight, *Madagascar in Wartime* (London; Longmans Green, 1895), p.162

16 Graves, pp.476–7

17 Pasfield Oliver, p.740

18 Silbermann, pp.92–4

19 *ibid*, p.97

20 Pasfield Oliver, p.741. Melinite – so named for its honey colour – was an explosive based on picric acid, tested in shells from 1886 but not yet standard issue. The expeditionary corps had a special reserve of 500 melinite shells, in addition to 350 conventional black-powder rounds per gun. Since 1880 shells had been provided with combination time/impact fuzes.

21 Silbermann, p 99

22 Pasfield Oliver, p.742; *Livre d'Or*, p.168; Porch, *Foreign Legion*, p.274

23 Pasfield Oliver, pp.742–3; Silbermann, pp. 102–6; Porch, *Foreign Legion*, p.274

24 Shervington's letter is appended to the Pallas Armata reprint of Graves' account.

25 Graves, pp.295–6; Ellis, in *JAH*, Vol 21, No.2 (1980), pp.219–34

26 What Graves called the '12-pdr' was a 76.2mm British licence-built version of the 78mm Hotchkiss M1892; the '3-pdr' was the 47mm M1885, and the 'revolver cannon' probably a 47mm five-barrel 3-pdr piece also made by C Hotchkiss. (J-J. Monsuez, in *RHdA*, 2003/3)

27 Graves, pp.302–8

28 *ibid*, pp.354–7

29 About 1,200 were invalided out; some 1,400 Abyssinians, Somalis and Comorans had to be shipped in to replace losses, and of the combined totals around 1,100 died. (Pasfield Oliver, pp.729, 734, 767; Porch, *Foreign Legion*, p.277)

30 Porch, *Foreign Legion*, p.277. By 10 June, 130 Tirs Alg reinforcements had arrived at Majunga. On 24 Aug the *Vinh Long* (later used as an emergency hospital ship) landed 500 extra men for the 200e de Ligne, 150 for 40e Bn Chass à Pied, and 150 légionnaires. On 3 Sept, 306 men for the Inf de Marine arrived on regular mailships, plus 150 for the Vols de Réunion and 500 Tirs Haussa. In all, with specialist, service and c.240 medical personnel, reinforcements totalled 3,228 men. (Pasfield Oliver, p.725)

31 *KB*, No.374. The 'captain adjutant-major' of a French battalion was the second-in-command. Many of the more mundane tasks undertaken by a British unit's 'adjutant' were performed by a French subaltern aptly termed the 'officer of details'.

32 Porch, *Foreign Legion*, p.277; *KB*, No.282; Pasfield Oliver, p.749. The Rgt Mixte had Naval Inf, Malagasies & Hausas; Col de Lorme had 2 weak coys from 200e Ligne, 2 of Naval Inf and 2 of Hausas. The Light Column's total strength was 237 officers and 4,013 combatant troops, with 1,515 muleteers, 2,813 mules and 266 horses.

33 Pasfield Oliver, pp.751–2; Graves, p.297; Porch, *Foreign Legion*, p.278

34 Pasfield Oliver, pp.753–4; Porch, *Foreign Legion*, p.280

35 Pasfield Oliver, p.756; Serman and Bertaud, p.548; Porch, *Foreign Legion*, p.283

36 Pasfield Oliver, p.757

37 Graves, pp.298, 477

38 Pasfield Oliver, pp.757–8; Porch, *Foreign Legion*, p.284

39 Pasfield Oliver, pp.758–62; Silbermann, p.112; Porch, *Foreign Legion*, pp.285–6

40 Pasfield Oliver, pp.764–5; Silbermann, p.113

41 Pasfield Oliver, p.726–7; *KB* No.282

42 Reibell, *op cit*, p.122

43 Serman and Bertaud, p.662. The other causes were given as typhoid (12 per cent), dysentery (8 per cent), tuberculosis (4 per cent) and heatstroke (3 per cent).

44 Pasfield Oliver, pp.727, 767; Porch, *Foreign Legion*, p.286; Reibell, *op cit*, p.174; Serman and Bertaud, p.662

45 Pasfield Oliver, p.767; *KB*, No.125; Porch, *Foreign Legion*, p.286. *RMdA* – 492 died in Madagascar, 35 aboard ship, 26 after repatriation, 38 missing = 22 per cent (of original *c.*2,400 plus 280 reinforcements = 2,680). *I/RMdA* – 23 per cent (of original 818 plus 150 reinforcements = 968). *13e RIM:* 577 dead & missing = 21 per cent.

46 Silbermann, pp.115, 120–23

47 Ellis, *op cit.* This is one of those occasions when our rich English vocabulary fails us. The exact meaning is 'the last small piece of a bowel movement'; the author is informed that there is an exactly equivalent insult in Italian.

48 Pasfield Oliver, p.765; Clayton, pp.81, 335

49 The *lamba* was the garment worn by Malagasy men – a sort of hybrid of a shawl and a kilt, like the old Scottish plaid; *menalamba* meant 'red lambas'.

50 Morel, p.62; *Livre d'Or*, p.170

51 Ellis, *op cit*

52 Serman and Bertaud, p.663–4; Jean Martin, in *L'Age d'Or*, p.73; Clayton, p.82

53 In the context, 'French' must mean Naval Infantry. (LtCol Ditte's report of colonial warfare conference at École Superieure de Guerre, published Paris, 1905, by Charles-Lavauzelle; quoted Porch, *Foreign Legion*, p.285)

54 *Livre d'Or* (pp.170–72) gives some company postings.

55 Maurois, p.65

56 Serman and Bertaud, p.664; Ellis, *op cit*

57 Hoisington, p.14; Maurois, p.73

58 Again, the summary that follows is based on Ralston, Ch 5, and Douglas Johnstone, *passim.*

58 Ageron, p.63

59 In 18 months Capt Jean-Baptiste Marchand had travelled *c.*2,500 miles from Brazzaville in the French Congo. The 8 French officers included Lt Charles Mangin of the Naval Infantry; with a company of Senegalese Skirmishers and the survivors of a huge train of press-ganged porters they arrived at Fashoda on 10 July 1898. A rendezvous with a second expedition expected from Djibouti never took place, and on 18 Sept Gen Kitchener arrived, steaming upriver from Khartoum with 5 gunboats, a company of Cameron Highlanders and 2 Egyptian battalions. (Serman and Bertaud, pp.682–3; Tombs and Tombs, p.429)

60 Porch, *March to the Marne*, p.148

61 Morel, pp.55, 62. Rear echelon at Majunga; *1er Cie*, Tuléar and Ankazoabo; *2e Cie*, Tsimanandrafozana; *3e Cie*, Ambohibé; *4e Cie*, Fort Dauphin; *5e Cie*, Ilkongo; *6e Cie*, Diégo Suarez and Nossi Bé.

62 Maurois, p.73; Hoisington, pp.15–16. The article, 'The Colonial Role of the Army', was published on 15 Jan 1900.

63 Dreyfus requested and was granted another revision of his case in Mar 1904. Ministers and governments continued to rise and fall; but on 12 July 1906 the United Appeal Court decided by majority vote that the Rennes verdict was unsound, and that Alfred Dreyfus was an innocent man. He was restored to the Army, promoted, and on 22 July he was admitted to the Legion of Honour. (Johnstone, p.197)

64 Morel, pp.55, 63; *Livre d'Or*, p.172; Porch, *Foreign Legion*, p224

65 Clayton p.315; Morel, p.55. See also Ch 1.

66 Hoisington, p.17

67 Maurois, p.71. Lyautey had noted the source wrongly; the line is from Shakespeare, in *Troilus and Cressida* (Hoisington, p.13).

68 Lyautey, *Lettres du sud de Madagascar*, p.164

69 *ibid*, p.119. On 30 Aug 1897 a Naval Troops subaltern had needlessly prolonged Sakalava resistance by a gratuitous massacre at Ambiki. (Serman and Bertaud, p.664; Jean Martin, in *L'Age d'Or*, p.73)

70 Lyautey, *Lettres du sud de Madagascar*, p.302

71 Gandelin, *RHdA*, 1981/1. LtCol Brundsaux left Madagascar at the end of 1903, for 2 years with 12e de Ligne before returning to 1er RE. In Apr 1906–Mar 1908 he commanded the Rgt de Marche du 1er RE at Viet Tri in Tonkin, where he added to his reputation for imperturbability under fire. He left the Legion in Mar 1908, eventually retiring due to ill- health as a brigadier-general on the Western Front in July 1916. (*KB*, No.374)

72 Morel, p.63; *KB*, No.282

8. The Instruments of Downfall

1 Rankin, p.253. Col Rankin was at that date special war correspondent of *The Times* of London.

2 Hart, *Qabila*, pp.19–21; Harris, p.21

3 Maxwell, pp.29–32

4 Dunn, *Resistance*, p.165; Hart, *Qabila*, p.34

5 Maxwell, pp.36–44. Cresting at more than 7,000 feet, the Tizi n'Tichka climbs and descends in a continuous series of some 1,800 hairpin bends. It is the highest point of Morocco's road system, and its treacherous ledges frequently claim victims even today, especially during the winter snows.

6 In 1893, Abd el Malek el Mtouggi controlled *c.*6,000 warriors, and Tayib el Goundafi *c.*5,000; Madani el Glaoui had only 2,000–3,000 men.

(Maxwell, pp.41–2) . For the ballistically pedantic: the '77mm' Krupp gun was probably a Franco-Prussian War surplus C64 80mm breech-loading 4-pounder. In Morocco it would typically have been employed at only a few hundred yards' range, for direct fire to breach fortress walls and blow in gatehouses.

7 Maxwell, pp.40–53

8 El Rogi's true name is reported as Jilali ibn Idriss el Zarhuni; a drooping eyelid gave him a superficial resemblance to the sultan's brother Moulay Muhammad, known to be blind in that eye, who was living in secluded retirement. The career of the legendary robber baron and intriguer Ahmad er Raisuli (or el Raysuni) – brave, resourceful, cruel, and utterly unscrupulous – defies brief summary; see Harris, pp.90–98 *et passim*. It is intriguing to wonder how Raisuli would have enjoyed his portrayal by Sean Connery in the John Milius film, *The Wind and the Lion* (1975), a cheerful Hollywood fantasy inspired by one of his most insolent but less bloody exploits.

9 Tombs and Tombs, pp.436–42

10 Christopher Duggan, *The Force of Destiny* (London; Penguin/Allen Lane, 2007), pp.336–7, 345–7, 379–84. Eventually, in 1911, Italy would throw an army into the empty sands of Libya, simply because no other nation had.

11 Hart, *Qabila*, pp.13–18

12 *ibid*, pp.27–33

13 The Arabic plural of *ksar* is *ksur*, but in this text anglicized plurals – e.g. *ksars, oueds, kasbahs* – are used for simplicity.
   The journey across the mountains between the Tafilalt and Fes took about 12–15 days on horseback; caravans of 50–100 pack-animals had to pay tolls to the tribes whose lands they crossed, who provided a token escort to ensure – theoretically – their safe passage. (Dunn, *Resistance*, pp.114–16).

14 Dunn, *Resistance*, pp.31–5

15 *ibid*, pp .38–9, 59–60

16 *ibid*, pp.38–9, 52–7. The 'fifths' were the Ouled Jallul, Ouled Yusif, Idarasa, Ouled abu Anan and Ouled bil Giz. These had a loose internal clan structure, and there was no single chief of a 'fifth'. This fivefold structure – representing the five fingers of a hand, and the five elements of a traditional battle array – had ancient and prestigious roots, in Arabia even predating Islam.

17 *ibid*, pp.68–70; Hart's several studies also explain the intricacies of the Ait Atta social structure.
   For the purposes of this book, the only important point is that while there was a shared aggressive pride in Ait Atta identity, there was no effective cohesion higher than tribal *(taqbilt)* level at best, and while elected tribal chiefs had a liaison and mediation function, all segments were fiercely independent and usually mutually hostile. For the record, the basic 'wiring diagram' was as follows: the Ait Atta nation comprised the Ait Wahlim, Ait Wallal, Ait Unigbi, Ait Aisa Mzin, and Ait Isful/Ait Alwan 'fifths'. The Ait Unigbi 'fifth' *(khums)* comprised the Ait Khabbash and Ait Umnasf tribes. The Ait Khabbash tribe *(taqbilt)* comprised five clans; each clan *(ighs)* comprised between two and four lineages, each separated into sub-lineages.

18 Dunn, *Resistance*, pp.68–78

19 *ibid*, pp.31, 146–7; Hart, *Ait Atta*, pp.159–61

20 Dunn, *Resistance*, pp. 41–4

21 Purely for firearms – enthusiasts: Remington-action rifles were made in a wide range of calibres up to 12.7mm – 0.50in, the calibre of a modern heavy machine gun. After firing the Remington, you thumb back the external hammer to full-cock position by its big cocking-spur, then flip back a sturdy steel catch on the pivoting breechblock behind the chamber at the breech end of the barrel. This simultaneously revolves the block backwards to open the chamber, and brings back a small section of the chamber lip underlying the rim of the empty cartridge, acting as an extractor. Although modern drawn-brass cartridges are sturdier than the old brass foil cases with a heavier brass base, extraction must still have been simple enough unless the chamber was hot and fouled by continuous firing. You pull out the old cartridge and insert another, flip the block closed again, and you are ready to fire; 6 to 8rpm is an entirely practical rate. The rifle is comfortable to shoot; the kick with black-powder cartridges – even the 12.7mm – is hardly more noticeable than that of a 12-bore shotgun, since the parallel-sided 12.7 x 44mm holds a much smaller propellant load than, say, the longer, fatter, tapered .45in x 54mm of the savagely kicking Martini-Henry. The only obviously breakable part is the little extractor arm. The Remingtons fired by the author were a Swedish 1874 12.7mm rebarrelled in 1891 for 8mm, with nitro propellant, and an original Swedish 1876 12.7mm, with both nitro and black powder rounds. The Spanish Army's 11mm was the most common model in Morocco, although a number of others models also found their way into the country. (The Remington was also made in rim-fire, but such cartridges are impossible to reload, so only centre-fire models would have been any use to the tribes.)

22 Hart, *Qabila*, p.143, writing of the Ait Atta of the Djebel Sahro.

23 Dunn, *Resistance*, p.121–7

24 *ibid*, p.145

25 *ibid*, pp.83–101, 152–60

9. Sixty Thousand Dead Camels

1 Gandini, p.41

2 Dunn, *Resistance*, p.112

3 Porch, *Sahara*, Ch XIV. The *kasbah* of the Moroccan south fulfilled the same function as was the *ksar*, but was more deliberately designed. It essentially a walled village of tawny-red mud brick, and could be of impressive size, with crenellated walls and tall loopholed towers worthy of a Norman castle.

4 The divisional cavalry were 2e Rgt de Spahis at Sidi bel Abbès and 2e Rgt de Chass d'Af at Tlemcen, each with 4 sqns of which 3 were theoretically available for field operations.

5 Dunn, *Resistance*, pp.180–81

6 In March 1900 troops from Ain Sefra also reached Djenan ed Dar, due south of Figuig, and began to build a post there.

7 A column this size was normally allowed about 250 camels to carry its kit, baggage, tents and rations (e.g. each infantry coy had 10 camels, each officer 2), plus 750 more carrying 5 days' water. Because of the terrain, the Igli column had to carry three times that amount, or roughly 42,000 gallons. (Hale/Massoutier, *op cit*)

8 Gandini, p.46

9 *ibid*, pp.34–8

10 *ibid*, p.33; *Livre d'Or*, pp.209–10; Turnbull, pp.74–5

11 Gandini, pp.41–2.

12 *ibid*, pp.74–5; *Turnbull*, p.41

13 Tombs and Tombs, pp.432–3

14 Dunn, *Resistance*, p.177; *Livre d'Or*, p.210

15 Gandini, p.49

16 The distinction between *goumiers* and *moghaznis* in Algeria was essentially one of radius of action, although some French sources use the terms indiscriminately. Both were native irregulars; but while *goumiers* were tribesmen who enlisted for a single campaign season to accompany manoeuvre units of French troops, *moghaznis* were a longer-term localized gendarmerie. Led and armed by a Native Affairs officer, they lived with their families in tents outside his post; they drew some rations, and pay that varied according to whether they were afoot or provided their own horses (Gandini, p.15). In Morocco, from 1908, the term *Goum* would be used for a more

formally organized company of 100-plus military auxiliaries – see p.361.

17 Order by Gen Mercier, 12 July 1894. The exact administrative numbering of the *Compagnies Montées* within the two Legion regiments changed at frequent intervals, making it difficult to trace their lineage continuously, and this text does not attempt to do so. Note that in 1900, Maj Bichemin's IV/2nd RTA also had 13e and 14e Cies Montées, and Capt Droit's 14e CM marched with this July convoy from Igli to Duveyrier. (Gandini, pp.55, 89)

18 Gandini, pp.51–6. This also reproduces a photo that has been published elsewhere, mistakenly captioned as the battlefield of El Moungar, Sept 1903 (reasonably but confusingly, Zafrani has also been termed 'first El Moungar'). Guillaume's account was published in *Légion Étrangère*, Apr 1932.

19 Hart, *The Ait Atta*, p.159; Dunn, *Resistance*, pp.182, 198; Porch, *Sahara*, pp.228–32. The Ait Murghad belonged to the Ait Yafalman confederacy, enemies of the Ait Atta nation for centuries – sultans had encouraged them to block Ait Atta expansion northwards into the High Atlas.

20 Bernard, pp.155–6

21 Dunn, *Resistance*, pp.176–8

22 Gandini, p.57. Both were actually middle-aged ex-NCOs rather than the young paladins suggested by a sentimental press.

10. Blood and Sand

1 Gandini, p.62

2 *ibid*, p.13, from *Notes du Route* (Charpentier and Fasquelle, 1914). In fact Zoubia/Duveyrier was the railhead for two and a half years; south of there the tracks swung westwards to Beni Ounif, approx 5 miles south of Figuig, where a station was built in spring 1903. (Dunn, *Resistance*, p.211)

3 Dunn, *Resistance*, pp.23–5

4 *ibid*, pp.179–80, 194. The Maghzan soldiers at Figuig were Dukkalas from the Atlantic plain – see Harris's description below.

5 Dunn, *Resistance*, p.185; Maxwell, pp.73, 76, 79. Walter Burton Harris, the permanent Tangier correspondent of *The Times*, was an independently wealthy man who lived in Morocco for decades. An Arabic-speaker who could sometimes actually pass for an Arab, he enjoyed excellent contacts, and was used as a discreet conduit between many of the major players in Moroccan affairs over many years.

6 Maxwell, pp.77–8, quoting Harris, *The Morocco That Was* (London; Blackwood, 1912), no page.

7 *ibid*, p.79; Dunn, *op cit*, *JAH*, Vol 21 (1980)

8 'Flipsonn' sounds odd; could he have been British – Philipson?

10 Gandini, pp.59–62. I owe this account – like much else in this and the previous chapter – to M.Gandini's meticulous research in the Archives d'Outre-Mer at Aix-en-Provence.

11 *ibid*, p.134

12 *ibid*, p.65

13 The Legion's historical service (SIHLE) have been unable to discover any War Ministry document authorizing or regulating the grant of commissions *à titre étranger* to foreign officers. Since 1831 these had always been given or denied individually and pragmatically, depending upon vacancies, personal connections or foreign policy considerations. As noted in Ch 5 n(4), during 1871–95 the great majority of 'foreign' commissions in fact went to Frenchmen. During the 1890s, a door was opened for officers wishing to transfer from the Danish and Swiss armies, at a time when France was seeking to cement relations with those countries in competition with Germany. Selchauhansen was one of 10 Danish and 6 Swiss officers who eagerly took the opportunity of gaining active service experience; 7 of the 16 would die in French uniform during the Great War (Dutailly, *RHdA*, 1981/1). Incidentally, there seems to have been only one 'Anglo-Saxon' officer in the Legion pre-1914, the New Zealander, James Waddell (see note, Appendix 1).

14 Gandini, pp.66–70. Georges Catroux (1877–1969) graduated from St Cyr in 1896. He transferred from the Chasseurs à Pied to the Legion in 1900, serving in Indochina 1903–1906. Commanding 2e RTA, he was wounded and captured at Arras in Oct 1915. Between appointments in the Levant 1919–25 and 1926 he served on Lyautey's staff in Morocco, and was promoted brigadier-general and GOC Marrakesh Region in 1931. Governor-General of Indochina in 1939, in June–July 1940 he rejected the Armistice and a summons to return to Vichy France, and joined Gen De Gaulle in London. He commanded Free French forces in the fratricidal Allied capture of French Syria in summer 1941, and was appointed Gov-Gen of Algeria in June 1944.

15 The 75mm M1897 field gun became world famous for generations as 'the French 75'. Its revolutionary hydraulic long-recoil mechanism gave it a possible rate of fire of 20–25rpm, though 8rpm was the normal cadence in order to avoid overheating. It had been claimed that Dreyfus had passed the Germans information about its development programme.

16 Gandini, pp.65, 71–3

17 *Livre d'Or*, p.211; Gandini, pp.80–81, 131

18 Dunn, *Resistance*, pp.185–92. From Apr 1902, on the initiative of Maj Lapperine, the first *Compagnies Sahariennes* were formed to patrol the great southern voids from the Touat. Each had 200–400 locally recruited foot, horse and *méharistes* camel-riders with French cadres of Native Affairs officers, NCOs and specialist enlisted men. The first three companies were formed at In Salah, Adrar and Timimoun, mainly from Shaamba and Tuareg. Camel patrols carried food for a month and water for ten days, and marched 25–50 miles per day; this gave them an operational radius of about 600 miles. (Clayton, pp.281–5)

19 Dunn, *Resistance*, pp.196–7; Gandini, p.74. Pointurier had 30 *moghaznis*, and 1er Peloton, 22e CM/2e RE with 94 all ranks.

20 Gandini, pp.74, 128; on tribal identification, Dunn, *Resistance*, p.48

21 Gandini, p.74

22 *ibid*, pp.45–7, 79. The original chosen name was Fort Mercier, but in practice the post was simply called Taghit.

23 *ibid*, pp.75–8

24 The warriors' failure to take the 'signallers' ridge' from the west is inexplicable. Frustratingly, the current tensions on both sides of the Moroccan/Algerian frontier have prevented the author from studying the ground at any of the battle sites in the Djebel Béchar and the Zousfana valley, which lie well inside modern Algeria.

25 Dunn, *Resistance*, p.200

26 Gandini, pp.75–8

27 *ibid*, pp .89–90

28 Details from an anonymous account by a survivor, published on the 10th anniversary in *Légion Étrangère*, Sept 1913.

29 Gandini, p.111; Bergot, *La Légion*, p.111

30 Gandini, pp.121, 128–30

31 As explained above, the current security situation has prevented the author from finding El Moungar itself. However, these notes on light and ground are based on stretches of terrain south of the Oued Dadès, east of the lower Oued Ziz, and south of the Oued Guir, plus Gandini's contemporary monochrome and modern colour photos of El Moungar.
  The strength of the Shaamba is variously estimated but actually unknown; the Legion company were outnumbered by about three to one, but the ground and the warriors' fieldcraft were more decisive than the relative numbers.

32 Holtz's sketch map shows a Spahi picket ahead and right of the 22e CM, another bringing up the rear of the camel train, but none on the company's left flank. If there was one, its position during the halt is unclear.

33 See Fig 17 in this book. QM-Sgt Tisserand's sketch-map shows steep banks only at two points, on the north of the north mound and the east of the south mound. The Shaamba do not seem to have attempted to attack at either of these points.

34 The times are from Tisserand; Capt de Susbielle claimed to have arrived at 4.30pm. This description of the action is mainly from Gandini, pp.82–104, particularly the after-action report by Tisserand dated at Taghit on 6 Sept, which is the nearest to a coherent eye-witness account that exists. The anonymous veteran's account published in *Légion Étrangère* (Sept 1913) shows signs of drawing on Tisserand's; while it does not always agree, some of its additional names and details have been incorporated here. *Livre d'Or* (pp.212–13) gives only a brief summary. Any conclusions drawn are the present author's.

35 These were followed shortly afterwards by the other half of that sqn under Capt Pages, and by Lt Dubois with half of 18e CM/1er RE and some mule-litters.

36 From a morning strength of 2 offs, 7 NCOs, 7 cpls and 97 men (= 113 all ranks), Tisserand lists: *killed* 1 off, 2 NCOs, 2 cpls, 30 men (= 35, but actually Capt Vauchez then alive); *wounded* 1 off, 5 NCOs, 3 cpls, 39 men (= 48, but actually plus Capt Vauchez); *unhurt* 2 cpls, 28 men (= 30). Of the 49 wounded, 2 offs and 1 man would die later; so final casualties 37 dead and 46 wounded recovered = 83 out of 113. (Gandini, pp.98, 105)

37 Gandini, p.110

38 The second half of Capt Bonnelet's 18e CM/1er RE, and the whole of Capt Fort's 14e CM/2e RTA. (Gandini, pp.92, 105)

39 Both officers would receive posthumous citations; Sgt Charlier was also awarded the Cross, and 8 other survivors the Médaille Militaire. QM-Sgt Tisserand was naturally recommended for the Legion of Honour, but on 3 Nov the War Minister decided to give him a sub-lieutenant's commission instead (probably what he had been working towards since he joined the Legion). The *médaillés* were Sgt Perré-Dessus, QM-Cpl de Montès, Cpl Detz, and Ptes Brona, Copel, May, Ueber and Vandevalle. (Gandini, pp.107–12)

40 Charles Eugène, Vicomte de Foucauld (1858–1916); see also Fig 14, and Ch 15, n 27.

41 Gandini, pp.117–18

42 Correspondence of 30 Sept – 24 Nov 1903 (Gandini, p.122)

43 Dunn, *Resistance*, p.200; Gandini, pp.123, 125

44 Maurois, p.87

11. The Lyautey Drill

1 *Intimate Letters*, p.122. The context was the disproportionate consequences of Gen Brière de l'Ile's alarmist cable to Paris in March 1885 reporting the abandonment of Lang Son.

2 After 30 years of European peace, promotion was very slow; a logjam in 1894–1908 raised the average age for the step from captain to major to 47. At about 4,000 francs p.a., a captain's pay fell somewhere between one-third and one-half short of the income needed by even a single man for reasonable security, and the broad range of social background meant that only a minority of officers had private means. (Serman and Bertaud, pp.570–71)

3 Ralston, pp.280–83; Maurois, p.125

4 Ralston, pp.260–69

5 Serman and Bertaud, p.598

6 The involvement of the Freemasons was revealed in the Chamber on 28 Oct 1904, and André was forced to resign on 14 November. (Ralston, pp.269–70)

7 Ralston, p.278

8 Maurois, p.87. On Lyautey's religious sensibilities: in retirement he told the journalist Pierre van Paassen that if he had been Pontius Pilate, responsible for peace and order in Judea, he, too, would have delivered Christ up for crucifixion. (Van Paassen, pp.144–9)

9 Hoisington, p.21; Gandini, p.125

10 Lyautey, *Vers le Maroc*, p.144

11 Maurois, pp.104–105

12 Eberhardt stayed in the Sud-Oranais until Feb 1904, and after her return to Algiers many of her articles were published in the Arabic *El Akhbar*. This remarkable but driven young woman, then 27 years old – who travelled alone dressed as an Arab youth, and who married an Algerian Spahi – returned to Ain Sefra in May 1904, when she became friendly with Lyautey despite her more advanced opinions on Arab–French relations. She died on 21 Oct 1904 when a flash flood devastated the Muslim town at Ain Sefra. Lyautey ensured that troops clearing debris kept an eye out for her papers; many were recovered, and published posthumously. (Gandini, pp.120–21)

13 Gandini, p.127

14 Rankin, pp.34–5. For readers interested in such details: Over his greatcoat the légionnaire first wound – with the aid of a comrade – his 9ft blue woollen waist sash, to provide support for the back. He next slung on his left hip a haversack with one day's ration of bread, meat and often vegetables for the *soupe*, a plugged length of bamboo for salt and pepper, and probably his pipe, tobacco and soap. Balancing this on his right hip was his 2-litre waterbottle (not always containing water), with the handle of his '*quart*' tin mug threaded on to the sling. Over these he buckled his leather belt and Y-strap suspenders, the former with ammunition (3 packets of 8 rounds in each of his 3 pouches, so 72 rounds immediately available), and on the left hip the scabbarded needle-bayonet for his Lebel. He thus could not lift the waterbottle to his lips without disturbing the pack and belt equipment – he was not supposed to drink except at designated halts.

On his back, hooked to the suspenders, was the 'Azor' knapsack of tarred canvas over a wooden board frame. This was packed with a spare shirt, drawers and canvas camp shoes; rifle- and shoe-grease, cleaning brushes, 'housewife' sewing kit and towel; another 6 packets of cartridges (giving 120 rounds in all); a tin of concentrated soup, 24 hard-tack biscuits, an emergency ration of sweet chocolate, and two doubled bags with sugar and coffee, beans and salted rice. Rolled and strapped round the outside of the pack were a blanket and tent-cloth section with a halved tent-pole, cord and pegs, a spare blouse, stable-jacket and trousers, and a spare pair of hobnailed boots. On top of the roll, one of the stowage straps secured his *gamelle* or mess tin with cover, and a bundle of firewood was tied over all. Finally, of course, the légionnaire carried his rifle.

In addition, he also carried on the outside of his pack his share of his squad's collective camp equipment. One man in 8 carried a large flat cooking dish *(marmite)*, and one in 10 a towering 10-litre water *bidon*; one in 6 had a canvas bucket and a sack, one in 12 a hatchet, and one man in 30 a coffee-mill. In addition, each infantry company's pack-animals were supposed to carry 4 double-headed and 4 single-headed pickaxes, 8 shovels, 3 felling axes, a folding saw and a pair of wirecutters. (Rankin, pp.46–8)

15 See Ch 5, n(21) on trades in the ranks.

16 Gandini, pp.10, 17, 128, 132–3; Dunn, *Resistance*, pp.60, 214–15; *KB*, No.163

17 Dunn, *Resistance*, p.208, 214; Gugliotta and Jauffret, *RHdA*, 1981/1

18 Dunn, *Resistance*, p.207 – translation slightly adjusted.

19 Harris, pp.1–6; Woolman, pp.5–8

20 Bernard, pp.36–7, 41

21 Hoisington, p.24. In 1904 Bou Amama was indeed on the move northwards from the Tamlelt steppe, but his purpose was to explore contacts with El Rogi. By 1906, the old rebel had drifted out of history. (Dunn, *Resistance*, p.158)

22 Hoisington, p.24; Lyautey, *Vers la Maroc*, pp.76–81

23 Maurois, pp.107–15

24 Gandini, p.22

25 At this date the Cies Montées were numbered 2e and 3e/1er RE and 21e and 22e/2e RE, but, as already noted, there would be frequent administrative redesignations, depending upon which battalions where currently posted to the Sud-Oranais.

26 *Livre d'Or*, p.214; Bernard, pp.196–8; Dunn, *Resistance*, p.205–206; Gandini, pp.21–3; Clayton, p.282

27 Maurois, p.116 – author's slightly amended translation.

28 Maurois, pp.117, 130. Datelined Sept 1906 at Kenadsa; after Jaeglé's death in action the piece was posthumously published in No.8 (30 Nov 1912) of the monthly *Légion Étrangère*.

29 Bernard, p.20

30 Hoisington, p.28; Dunn, *Resistance*, pp.25, 216

31 Dunn, *Resistance*, p.208

32 Gugliotta and Jauffret, *RHdA*, 1981/1; Gandelin, *RHdA* 1981/1

33 Lyautey, *Vers le Maroc*, pp.255–6

34 Dunn, *Resistance*, pp.212, 216–18, 221–2; Hoisington, p.29

35 Gugliotta and Jauffret, *RHdA*, 1981/2

36 Porch, *Foreign Legion*, p.324

37 Gugliotta and Jauffret, *RHdA*, 1981/1, quoting Maj Poirmeur, *Notre Vieille Legion*; Bernard, p.39

38 Porch, *Foreign Legion*, pp.312–14

39 Gandini, pp.28–9

40 Gugliotta and Jauffret, *RHdA*, 1981/1

41 Gandini, p.30–31

42 *KB*, No.114

43 Gandelin, *RHdA*, 1981/1

44 In Nov 1894 the cadre of each RE was increased by 4 capts, 4 lts, 2 sgt-majs and five sgts and QM-sgts, and in 1905 by 10 more lieutenants. Such supplementary cadres were standard in the Line, to accommodate the enlargement of conscript units when raised from peacetime to wartime establishment. (Morel, p.55)

45 Porch, *Foreign Legion*, pp.289–302; Morel, pp.55–6

46 Ralston, p.300

47 *ibid*, pp.283–8; Porch, *March to Marne*, pp.110–29. The Left coalition began to break up from 1906, separating the ever more extreme Radicals from the moderate Socialists led by Jean Jaurès.

48 Woolman, p.38

49 Maurois, p.135

50 Hoisington, p.31

51 Porch, *Morocco*, pp.149–59; Serman and Bertaud, p.696. Morel (p.63) actually dates the order to VI/1er RE on 3 Aug – before the crisis – giving only about 36 hours to organize the unit before it marched out to entrain for Oran. This urgency prevented the usual selection of a picked Legion *bataillon de marche*, and VI/1st RE had its share of the poorer kind of material that was now too common – thus, no doubt, their bad behaviour in Casablanca.

52 Hoisington, p.31

53 Porch, *Morocco*, pp.166–7; Morel, p.63. Maj Provost was replaced by Maj Huguet d'Etaules (*Livre d'Or*, p.216). The reinforcements were I/2e RE (Maj Corbière) and IV/2e RE (Maj Szarvas). VI/1er RE and a bn of *turcos* from 1er RTA formed 1er Rgt de Marche de la Chaouia (LtCol Blanc, later LtCol Passard); I/ and IV/2e RE formed 3e Rgt de Marche de la Chaouia (LtCol Brulard).

54 Rankin, pp. 8, 9 and 52. The Spanish 69th Rgt (Col Bernal), which camped SW of Casablanca in a purely defensive stance, was present as a token of Spain's rights under the Oct 1904 Franco-Spanish agreements and the June 1906 Act of Algeciras.

12. Two Kinds of War

1 The first epigraph is from Rankin, *In Morocco with General D'Amade*, p.159. The second is from Moulay Ahmad Lahsin's letter of challenge to Maj Fesch at Boudenib, 29 Aug 1908; the reference in the Archives du Ministère de la Guerre is given by Dunn, *Resistance*, p.235 n(10). Since it is quoted there in an English translation, from French, from Arabic, the present author has felt free to adjust the English slightly.

2 On 15 Jan 1908 the Corps de Débarquement had:
Inf 3x Rgts de Marche de Tirs Alg (6x bns from 1er, 2e and 3e RTA); Rgt de M du 2e RE (LtCol Brulard – I/ and IV/2e RE); Rgt de M Mixte (LtCol Passard – VI/1er RE + bn from 1er RTA); Rgt de M de Zouaves (2x bns).
Cav 4x sqns Chass d'Af (from 1er, 3e and 5e RCA);

2x sqns Spahis (from 1er and 3e RS); sqn Alg irregulars.
Arty 3x field btys (each 4x 75mm); 1 mtn bty (6x 80mm, mule-pack); 2x sects Navy 37mm QF (cart-mobile, manned by sailors from *Desaix*).
Services incl Rgt de M du Génie (2x bns Senegalese).
By Apr 1908 the Corps had been reinforced to c.14,000, of which c.11,000 combat troops. (Rankin, pp.10–11)

3 *ibid*, p.17. Successful French trials of military wireless telegraphy dated from 1900. In 1908 a station on the Chaouia communicated with a ship off Casablanca, which relayed to another off Tangier, and thence to Oran, Marseille and Paris. However, the wire telegraph, the signal-lamp system and carrier pigeons also remained in use. (Serman and Bertaud, p.539)

4 Rankin, pp.54–5. On other occasions he describes columns routinely moving in two squares, one for combat and a smaller one formed by the escorted baggage, *à la Négrier*. The fighting square was actually an oblong, longer at the front and rear faces, which were formed of infantry marching in a parallel series of platoon columns 4 men wide and 10–15 deep, with intervals of about 40yds between platoons to allow them space to deploy for action – to swing outwards into a single continuous rank. The sides were formed of columns of platoons marching at intervals, or sometimes in single file. In Jan 1908 the Legion companies averaged 240 men. (Rankin, pp.25, 59–60)

5 *ibid*, p.65

6 *ibid*, p.90

7 *ibid*, p.90

8 Porch, *Morocco*, pp.170–71; Rankin, p.59

9 Rankin, pp.94, 97

10 *ibid*, pp.28–30, 112–14, 185; no correspondents accompanied this column, and his account was written up from later interviews.
    For those interested in firearms: this seems to be the earliest description of the Legion's use of machine guns. Rankin wrote that each Rgt de Marche had 'a tripod-mounted *mitrailleuse*', but that its value was dubious. It is useful to be reminded that early MGs were often distrusted rather than welcomed as battle-winning weapons, and were believed by some veterans to be a failed experiment. Several 8mm MG types were being tried out by the French Army at this period; all were air-cooled, and fed by metal strips gripping 25–30 cartridges that were passed sideways through the breech mechanism – they thus required reloading much more frequently than Maxim/Vickers-type guns fed by a continuous 250-rd canvas belt. The best of them was the

M1900 Hotchkiss (distinguishable in photos from the better-known M1914 by its T-shaped shoulder stock). A photo in Gandini's *La Légion à travers les cartes postales* (1997) shows 'a machine-gun platoon of 2nd RE at Boudenib during the Upper Guir Column', which dates it to 1908. The photo shows a sergeant, and 2 gun-corporals each with 7 men, serving a pair of M1905 Puteaux MGs, identifiable by their brass barrel-jackets with cooling fins around the whole length (a needlessly over-complex weapon, as was the more notorious M1907 St Étienne). MG crews were issued with a padded crossbelt to enable them to carry dismounted guns on the shoulder, and mittens with ringmail palms for handling the barrels, which got extremely hot in use and lacked the protective jacket of the water-cooled Maxim-type guns. (Gandini, *op cit*, p.99; Hicks and Jandot, *French Military Weapons 1717–1938*, New Milford CT; N. Flayderman, 1964, pp.121, 123)

11 Rankin, pp.164–70; Porch, *Morocco*, pp.175–76

12 Porch, *Morocco*, pp 172–4; Maurois, p.141; Rankin, pp.153–7. Gen Picquart was the officer persecuted during the Dreyfus Affair; a decent man, he had been promoted beyond his talents, probably as a deliberate provocation to Army reactionaries.

13 Rankin, p.33

14 During the parade Rankin (p.201) took the opportunity to count ranks, and noted that the average company strength was now down from 240 to about 160 men, giving a battalion *c*.650.

15 Rankin, pp.208–14

16 *ibid*, p.200

17 Fremeaux, *RHdA*, 2004/2

18 Harris, p.8; Maxwell, pp.87–8; Dunn, *Resistance*, p.231

19 *Livre d'Or*, p.221

20 The cook got 8 francs a day, though this presumably included expenses for buying food. (Rankin, pp.29, 118)

21 *ibid*, p.31

22 Hoisington, pp.32–3

23 Porch, *Morocco*, pp.189–90; Turnbull, pp.113–14

24 Garijo (p.28) mentions a major action at the summit of Ras Fourhal above Ain Sfa, where '2,000 Beni Rassen [sic] wiped out 100 légionnnaires'. No such action is reported elsewhere, and at this date 100 casualties in a single engagement would have made a sensation. This is noted simply as a reminder of the great caution advisable when consulting Garijo, which contains much good raw material but which, in the French translation from

the Spanish, has many unedited inconsistencies.

25 Bernard, p.161; Porch, *Morocco*, p.191

26 Hoisington, p.33; Maurois, pp.136–7

27 Dunn, *Resistance*, p.233

28 6e Cie, II/2e RE; 20e Cie, V/2e RE; 21e and 22e Cies, VI/2e RE; 3e and 24e CM/1er RE. (*Livre d'Or*, p.217)

29 Menabha does not appear on Bernard's 1911 map, the earliest the author has located, but is described in Gov-Gen Jonnart's report to the war minister as 10km from Talzaza and 4km W of Mougheul. (Jonnart to Picquart, 17 Apr 1908, in *Documents diplomatiques/ Affaires du Maroc, 1908/IV*, No.234)

30 *Livre d'Or*, pp.217–18; Porch, *Morocco*, pp.192–3; Lefèvre, *KB*, No.118; Jonnart to Picquart (see above). No source seems to identify the rifle coy of 2e RE from among those listed in n(28) above. Porch (*Foreign Legion*, p.321) mentions that Pierron's force also had a machine gun – which jammed.

31 Porch, *Morocco*, pp.192–3

32 Lefèvre, *KB*, No.119

33 *ibid*; Porch, *Morocco*, pp.194–5, and *Foreign Legion*, p.323; *Livre d'Or*, p.219; Gugliotta and Jauffret, *RHdA* 1981/1; prisoner reference, Dunn, *Resistance*, p.234. The fighting on 14 May cost the column only 10 dead and 22 wounded; Moroccan losses for 13 and 14 May were vaguely estimated at *c*.500.

34 Porch, *Morocco*, p.195

35 Bernard, p.163; Gugliotta and Jauffret, *RHdA*, 1981/1

36 The hesitancy of this description of the blockhouse is due to the fact that in 2007 the author's attempts to explore its remains were frustrated. From the north bank of the Oued Guir the outline of ruins is tantalizingly visible at the top of the abrupt red cliff about 1,000 yards away, but we never managed to get any closer. Maps show no vehicle-crossing for miles up or down the Oued Guir – which seems strange, but is true. While local knowledge of safe fording-places must certainly allow walkers and animals to cross, repeated efforts to drive a 4x4 to the south bank, alternating with recces on foot, all failed. The bed of the Guir is hundreds of yards wide, with a bewildering pattern of surfaces ranging from shingle-bars to mud, and we could not even reach the main water channel along the southern edge. Several slow drives through the town and along the north bank in search of a solution eventually convinced us that – as foreigners with binoculars and cameras – we had probably worn out our

welcome in this remote Moroccan Army garrison facing the hostile Algerian frontier.

The site of the main French 'redoubt' has long disappeared under the modern town, but the remains of the old *kasbah* still stand in thick vegetation near the riverbank.

37 Bernard, p.165; Turnbull, pp.81–2; Dunn, *Resistance*, p.235

38 The message transcripts do not mention specific requests for 80mm fire. The M1877 80mm *canon de montagne, système de Bange*, had a max effective range of *c*.2,700yds, about half that of the M1897 75mm *canon de campagne*, but the blockhouse at Boudenib was well within its reach from the redoubt. Perhaps it was felt to be too imprecise for night-firing so close to French troops.

39 Signals transcript from Bernard (1911), pp.378–87, quoting Lachartier, *La colonne du Haut Guir* (Paris; Chapelot, 1908) pp.40–48.

40 Bernard, p.169; Gugliotta and Jauffret, *RHdA*, 1981/1; Porch, *Morocco*, pp.198–9; Dunn, *Resistance*, p.235

13. Falling towards Fes

1 Maxwell, p.100, quoting Harris, *The Morocco that Was* (no page)

2 *ibid*, pp. 89–95

3 Woolman, pp.45–50

4 Maxwell, p.101

5 Woolman, pp40–41; Dunn, *JAH*, Vol 21 (1980); Porch, *Morocco*, pp.206–211; Maxwell, p.100

6 Harris, pp.49–57

7 Woolman, p.43; Garijo, pp.38–9

8 Woolman, pp.51–52; Harris, pp.89–91

9 Hoisington, p.36; Dunn, *Resistance*, p.237. Legion units operating on the east bank of the Moulouya in Apr–May 1910 included 11e and 12e Cies, III/1er RE; VI/1er RE; 3e CM/1er RE; 15e Cie, IV/2e RE and 3e CM/2e RE.

10 Gandelin, *RHdA*, 1981/1

11 Porch, *Foreign Legion*, p.331

12 *KB*, No.373

13 Hoisington, p.36; Maurois, p.144. Before leaving Algeria, Lyautey sprang a last surprise: at the age of 56 he married the aristocratic 38-year-old widow of a Colonel Fourtoul, thus acquiring a suitable hostess for his salon.

In 1911–12 belated reforms urged by War Minister Messimy finally lifted the status and powers of the CGS from those of a relatively junior func-tionary to those of a true commander-in-chief in time of war. Galliéni had been offered the post first, but turned it down on grounds of poor health; the difficulties facing the man who accepted it were still immense. (Ralston, pp.331–5)

14 Porch, *Morocco*, p.211

15 *ibid*, pp.213–17. Emile Mangin, nicknamed 'Projecteur' after a searchlight he had invented, should not be confused with Charles Mangin, who would serve under Lyautey in 1912–13 and rise to prominence on the Western Front during the Great War.

16 Porch, *Morocco*, pp.218–19, 228–31

17 Khorat, *En Colonne* pp.252–3.
Groupe Brulard: 1 bn Inf Coloniale, 1 bn Tirs Alg, 1 mixed bn Tirs Alg/Tirs Sénégalais, 2x ptns MGs, 1 bty 75mm, 1 bty 65mm, half-sqn Spahis, *c*.600 Goumiers Marocains.
Groupe Dalbiez: 1 bn Tirs Alg, 1 mixed bn Légion/Zouaves, 1 ptn MGs, 1 bty 75mm, 1 sqn Chass d'Af, ambulance.
Groupe Gouraud: 2x bns Inf Colo, 1 bn Tirs Alg, 3x ptns MGs, 1 bty 75mm, 1 sqn Chass d'Af, half-sqn Spahis, ambulance.
Khorat does not list 3e CM/2e RE, but Gugliotta and Jauffret (*RHdA*, 1981/1) place it with Gouraud's command.

18 Khorat, *En Colonne*, pp.246–54; Porch, *Morocco*, pp.228–31

19 The Beni Ouarain were a powerful Berber-speaking tribe, great raisers of horses and rustlers of livestock, who inhabited both banks of the Moulouya. At this date they were still expanding westwards, into the Taza corridor and towards the 'Tache de Taza' of the Middle Atlas. (Bernard, pp.25–6)

20 *ibid*, pp.19–20, 28–30

21 This account is based on the article in *Képi Blanc*, No.169, by personnel of SIHLE, the 1er RE's historical branch. Gen Toutée's divisional order of the day dated 25 May 1911 is recorded in *Livre d'Or* (p.223).

22 Khorat, *En Colonne*, pp.98–108

23 *ibid*, pp.110–16; Porch, *Morocco*, pp.222–3; Maxwell, p.103

24 Porch, *Morocco*, pp. 234–5

25 Khorat, *Scènes*, p.267; *En Colonne*, pp.180–91

26 Khorat, *En Colonne*, pp.209–11, 236

27 *Livre d'Or*, p.224

28 Khorat, *En Colonne*, pp. 212–13

29 Ralston, pp.321–2, 329

30 Khorat, *Scenes*, p.267; *Livre d'Or* (p.224) misprints '1911' for 1912.

31 Hoisington, p.39

14. The Immaculate Raiment

1 *France, Spain and the Rif*, p.55

2 Khorat, *Scènes*, pp.269–70

3 The French-built Ville Nouvelle now covers the Dar Debibagh plateau.

4 Porch (*Morocco*, p.245) gives 19 French officers and men killed on 17 Apr, 9 European civilians and 43 Jews. Khorat (*Scènes*, p.270) gives 13 officers, 40 rankers and 13 white civilians, but is unclear as to dates. The Legion bn was apparently VI/2e RE, which was camped along the Meknes–Fes road.

5 Khorat, *Scènes*, p.271; Porch, *Morocco*, pp.243–7

6 Ralston, p.324; Hoisington, p.39; Khorat, *Scènes*, p.271

7 Maurois, p.149

8 Porch, *Morocco*, p.252

9 *ibid*, p.253 ; Maurois, p.156

10 Khorat, *Scènes*, pp.272–3; Porch, *Morocco*, pp.254–6; Hoisington, p.43; Maurois, p.157. The last attacks on Fes and this sortie together cost 55 French killed and 122 wounded.

11 Hoisington, p.45

12 *KB* No.375; Garros, pp.154–5. On 3/4 June 1918, serving on the Western Front as Col Rollet's regimental sergeant-major in the RMLE, AdjChef Mader would lose an arm after leading an attack at Saint Baudry (see Appendix 1). After the war he became a well-known figure as chief custodian at the Château de Versailles.

13 Khorat, *Scènes*, pp.273–5; *Livre d'Or*, p.224–5

14 The 4e RTA were recruited in Tunisia, but such units did not change title to Tirailleurs Tunisiens until 1921.

15 *La Légion Étrangère*, No.8, 30 Nov 1912. This publication was the journal of the Federation of Societies of Former Légionnaires.

16 In Jan 1913 total Legion strength was recorded as 10,521 men, with 12x rifle bns and 4x mounted coys; so the *c*.3,500 men of 5x bns and 4x mtd coys in Morocco represented *c*.33 per cent of the corps (there were then 5x bns in Algeria and only 2x bns still in Indochina). The expanding Colonial corps of Tirailleurs Sénégalais was then three times the size of the Legion (Bergot, in Young, p.205; Garijo, p.99); and see note 21 below. 'Pierre Khorat' gives total French Army numbers in Morocco on 1 May 1913 as 54,000 – 31,000 French and 3,500 Legion, 15,000 Algerian, 8,000 Senegalese and 4,500 Tunisian – plus 12,000 Moroccans under command. (*Scènes*, p.224)

17 Hoisington, p.52. Subsequently the Rgt de Marche du 2e RE (W.Morocco) comprised I/, then III/ & VI/2e RE, and was commanded successively by LtCol Vandenberg (July 1912), Maj Denis-Laroque (Apr 1913) and LtCol Girodon (July 1913). The Rgt de M du 1er RE (E.Morocco) comprised I/, II/ and VI/1er RE, and was commanded by LtCols Tahon (1913) and Théveney (1914). (Clayton, p.231; Bergot, in Young, p.189)

18 Clayton, pp.89–90, 206, 211–12, 244–54, 262–5, 309–19. French regular military service was raised to three years in 1913; the same applied to the Tirs Alg, but Tirs Sénég had to serve for four years. New 5e–9e RTAs were raised in 1914, giving a total of 40 Algerian and Tunisian bns by that August.

19 Khorat, *Scènes*, p.274; Hoisington, pp.44–5; Maurois, p.160

20 Khorat, *Scènes*, pp.275–7; Hoisington, p.45; Porch, *Morocco*, pp.258–63; Dunn, *Resistance*, p.27. El Hiba was a son of Moulay Ma el Ainin, a great spiritual and military *sheikh* in what is now Mauritania.

21 Charles Mangin is not to be confused with Emile 'Searchlight' Mangin, former chief of the military mission to Moulay Hafid. In 1910 Charles Mangin had published a widely discussed book, *La Force Noire*, arguing for a major expansion of the Tirailleurs Sénégalais in order to offset the shortfall of Metropolitan French manpower in a coming war (the French birthrate lagged far behind that of Germany). This proposal that black troops be used not only in the colonies but in France itself was then revolutionary, but it was accepted in 1914–18; by the Armistice 45 black battalions would be serving on the Western Front, plus 26 in N.Africa and 15 in the Balkans. Mangin would be accused of using them as cannon-fodder in the failed 1917 Chemin des Dames offensive. (Clayton, pp.339–40; Fremeaux, *RHdA*, 2000/1)

22 Khorat, *Scènes*, pp.277–9; Porch, *Morocco*, pp.263–9; Maxwell, pp.110–15; Hoisington, p.48

23 Khorat, *Scènes*, pp.295–6, and *En Colonne*, p.133; Porch, *Foreign Legion*, p.324

24 *Légion Étrangère* No.8, 30 Nov 1912. In June 1913, 24e CM/1er RE at Boudenib 'formed corps' – i.e. it became an autonomous command independent of its former parent bn VI/1er RE – and was redesignated 3e CM (*Livre d'Or*, p.226).

The French Army had not yet developed a doctrine for the use of motor vehicles, but commissions had been considering the question since

1896, and in 1908 the first law was passed authorizing an inventory of French private vehicles for requisition in time of war. (Serman and Bertaud, p.545)

25 Hoisington, p.48

26 Khorat, *Scènes*, p.281. Shipped down from Casablanca, Gen Brulard relieved Massoutier on 24 December. Lt Do Huu Vi, one of several sons of a leading Saigon family, to be educated in France, gained a commission *à titre etranger* from St Cyr in 1906, and qualified as a pilot in 1911. Crash injuries on the Western Front in 1915 ended his flying career, but he returned to active duty; Capt Do Huu Vi was killed near Belloy en Santerre on 9 July 1916, leading 7th Company, II/RMLE – see Appendix 1. (Dutailly, *RHdA*, 1981/1; and see maibatrieu@hotmail.com)

27 Pernod and Villatoux, *RHdA*, 2000/1. In 1909 the War Minister, Gen Brun, had decided a turf war by ordering that both the Engineers and the Artillery should have aircraft. The first flying school and a military inspectorate were established in 1910, and the official organization of the *Aéronautique Militaire* was authorized in March 1912; this actually preceded by a year the official recognition of the Army use of motor cars. (Serman and Bertaud, p.545)

28 Hoisington pp.50–52; Porch, *Morocco*, p.298

29 Hoisington, p.47

30 Report by Col Lamothe, quoted Maxwell, p.120

31 Maxwell, p.118

32 Lyautey, *Vers la Maroc*, p.285

33 Khorat, *Scènes*, p.295; Hoisington, p.56

34 Hoisington, pp.62–3. Moha ou Hammou, Moha ou Said l'Irraoui of the Ait Roboas, and the religious leader Sidi Ali ben el Mekki Amhaouch were the most important figures in the southern Middle Atlas.

35 Hoisington, p.65; Khorat, *Scènes*, p.284; Porch, *Morocco*, p.282

36 Hoisington, p.58; Porch, *Morocco*, p.286

37 Gen Charles Mangin would command a colonial division on the Marne in 1914, an army corps at Verdun in 1916, Sixth Army on the Chemin des Dames in 1917, Tenth Army at 'Second Marne' in 1918, and French occupation troops in the Rhineland in 1919. He was nicknamed 'the Butcher'.

38 Khorat, *Scènes*, p.288; Hoisington, p.61; Porch, *Morocco*, p.284

39 Harris, p.10; Hoisington, p.37

40 Harris, p.85; Woolman, p.18

41 Hart, *Qabila*, p.36; Garijo, p.54; Harris, p.78

42 Woolman, p.53

43 Harris, p.98; Woolman, pp.55–9

44 *KB* No.473

45 *Livre d'Or*, pp.225–6; Khorat, *Scènes*, pp.297–8

46 Pernot and Villatoux, *RHdA*, 2000/1

47 Bernard, pp.20, 25–6; *KB*, No.476

48 Serman and Bertaud, p.699; *Livre d'Or*, p.226; Porch, *Morocco*, pp.284–5

49 *KB*, No.473

50 *KB*, Nos.473 and 474

51 Hoisington, pp.66–7

52 Fabre, pp.10–11. 'Chleuchs', from the name of a Middle Atlas tribal group, became the soldiers' slang for all Berbers – indeed, Morocco veterans would also use it of the Germans in the First World War. (It is sometimes mistakenly claimed to be an insult equivalent to 'nigger', but in conversation with the present author in 2007 a university-educated Middle Atlas Berber used the term with quite unselfconscious pride simply to identify his origins – like 'Jock' or 'Geordie')

53 Hoisington, p.82

54 *ibid*, pp.70–72; Khorat, *Scènes*, p.299

55 Maurois, p.183

15. The Lobster Shell

1 *Livre d'Or de la Légion Étrangère* (1931), p.227

2 Maurois, pp.184–9

3 Maxwell, pp.125–7, 134

4 Maurois, p.192; Hoisington, p.73

5 Of just under 42,900 men who served in Legion units during the Great War, about 5,140 claimed to be Germans, Austrians or Turks. Germans who had already earned French naturalization – e.g. Sgt Max Mader – did fight in France. (Bergot, quoting from *Livre d'Or de la RMLE* in Young, p.205; Carles, *RHdA*, 1981/1)

6 Hoisington, pp.73, 224 n(73); Turnbull, p.152; Carles, *RHdA*, 1981/1. In Nov 1915 the Legion had 5 bns in Morocco (I/ and VI/1er RE; II/, III/ and VI/2e RE); 3 bns in France, 1 in Salonika, 2 in Algeria and 2 in Indochina.

7 Clayton, pp.206–207, 212, 248, 263, 274–5, 340; Porch, *Morocco*, p.288; Garijo, pp.80–81

8 Heintz, pp.11, 16

9 Hoisington, pp.74–6; Garijo, pp.67–70. Apart

from Zaians the warriors were from the Mrabtin, Ait Ichkern and Ait Ischak. Details of French dead vary slightly in sources, but plausible figures are 33 French officers, c.200 French rankers, 218 Tirs Alg, 125 Tirs Sénég and 37 Moroccans. The loss was almost exactly 50 per cent in killed, and 66 per cent in total casualties.

10 Hoisington, pp.75–6; Porch, *Morocco*, p.288

11 Hoisington p.80. The GM de Ito (LtCol Dérigoin) then consisted of VI/2e RE, a bn of Tirs Alg and one of Tirs Sénég, 2x sqns of Spahis and 2x gun batteries. (Heintz, p.71)

12 Heintz, pp.5, 6, 12, 13, 17–18, 63

13 *ibid*, p.13. On the evening of 15 May 1911, Capt Duriez had tried in vain to drag the corpse of Capt Labordette up from Alouana. On 17 Apr 1917 he would be mortally wounded at the head of the RMLE on the Western Front during the Nivelle Offensive – see Appendix I.

14 Hoisington, p.81; Heintz, p.73

15 Heintz, p.13; Hoisington, p.82. The Zaian, Ait Ichkern, Ait Ischak and Ait Bou Haddou.

16 Hoisington, p.83; Heintz, pp.14, 73–4

17 'M.M.', p.220. A self-styled *littérateur* who scurried around Europe leaving a trail of unrepaid loans, M.M. organized his transfer from Algeria to Lyon after less than three months, on the pretext of his eagerness to 'fight the Boches rather than serve with them'. Once in France he promptly deserted over the Italian border. After the war he finally ran out of gullible acquaintants, and committed suicide in Malta.

18 Garijo, p.77–8. The author has been unable to identify the Legion picket; it was presumably a company from III/2e RE, whose war diary was unavailable to Heintz, the author's main source for this chapter.

19 Woolman, pp.62–3, 69; Harris, p.106

20 Harris, pp.58–61

21 27 Jan 1917, Cie Montée/2e RE; 6 Apr, 1er CM/1er RE. Abd el Malek Meheddin would quarrel with Abd el Krim in 1925 during the Rif War; he entered Spanish service, and was killed while leading auxiliary troops near Melilla before he could complete negotiations with Lyautey (via Harris) to surrender to the French and go into exile.

22 *Livre d'Or*, p.229; Heintz, p.28; Laine, *RHdA*, 1978/4

23 Heintz, pp.14, 76–7

24 *ibid*, p.43

25 *ibid*, pp.37, 43

26 *ibid*, pp.38, 44–5; Gugliotta and Jauffret, *RHdA*, 1981/1. On 5 Nov 1916 Maj Feurtet's Bn Mixte de Boudenib comprised: 2x coys Légion (Capts Blaise and Naegelin); coy 4e Bat d'Af (Lt Giacomini); coy 5e Bat d'Af (S/Lt Morel); 3x MG platoons (Lts Colin, Falcon and Grandjean – the latter killed at El Bourouj on 16 Nov).

27 The Senussi lodges had long been centres of resistance to Italian expansion in the Libyan Sahara, and in Aug 1914 the Bedouin inflicted a series of important defeats on Italian units, capturing many weapons and subverting Italian native auxiliary troops. Encouraged by Turkish officers, in 1915 the Senussi attacked British Egypt, but were decisively defeated in Feb 1916. Contact with the Senussi, easy supplies of Italian arms, and Turkish agents all spread the unrest westwards among some Touareg of the French Sahara. In Mar 1916 the fall of the besieged fort at Djanet opened a year-long series of French setbacks, including the siege of Agadês in modern Niger, the loss of other posts and the capture of French prisoners including a general (few of whom survived captivity). The missionary Père de Foucauld, long a calming influence and a useful source of information on tribal affairs, was murdered on 1 Dec 1916 at his second hermitage near Tamanrasset in the Ahaggar, by a group of incoming Ajjer Touareg. Gen Laperrine was recalled from the Western Front and given command of the whole Saharan territory, restoring the situation from about Apr 1917; although small-scale raiding continued until well after the Armistice, there were no major incidents after Jan 1918. (David Nicolle, *Lawrence and the Arab Revolts*, Men-at-Arms 208; London, Osprey, 1989)

28 Maurois, p.207

29 *ibid*, pp.213, 221, 224

30 *ibid*, pp.231–46. Henri Gouraud (1867–1946) returned to France, and commanded Fourth Army from July 1917 until the Armistice; he distinguished himself during Ludendorff's *Kaiserschlacht* offensive in spring 1918. (For his tenure of the Morocco command, see Hoisington, pp.104–108.)

31 Heintz, pp.19–20, 29–30

32 If MGs unavoidably had to be abandoned, removing the complex feed block from the receiver of the Hotchkiss disabled it efficiently.

33 Heintz, pp.20–21, 31–2

34 Vanègue, p.7

35 Fabre, pp.9–10. This tends to support the suspicion that French officers often overstated in their after-action reports the numbers they had encountered.

36 *ibid*, p.11

37 Hoisington, p.84

38 Heintz, p.38; Hoisington, p.84

39 Skoura should not confused with the large oasis on the N10 east of Ouarzazate.
The 65mm M1906 mountain gun had a hydraulic long-recoil mechanism that allowed a rate of up to 15 rpm, and broke down into four mule-loads for transport.

40 Heintz, p.80

41 *ibid*, pp.65–6, 80–82; *Livre d' Or* pp.233–4

42 Heintz, pp.21, 82

43 Woolman, pp.74–7; Porch, *Foreign Legion*, p.397

44 Heintz, pp.7–10, 21–3, 83–5. II/1er RE had been transferred south to Marrakesh in July 1917, spending the rest of the war dispersed between Azilal and other posts. (Heintz, p.15)

45 Hoisington, p.85

46 Heintz, pp.32–3, 67

47 Dunn, *Resistance*, p.243; Hart, *Ait Atta*, p.165. 'Tighmart' seems to be Taguerroumt on modern maps, on the N12 road west from Rissani.

48 Hoisington, p.86

49 Maxwell, pp.130–31, 134, 138

50 The Bn Mixte now consisted of 1 coy Légion (Lt Montrucoli, *vice* Capt Deschard sick), 1 coy 4e Bat d'Af (Capt Guerel), 1 Cie de Marche Metropolitaine (Capt Samoride) and 1 coy 8e RTA (Capt Doucet).

51 The shape of the CSRG's big crescent magazine was dictated by the sharply tapered 8mm cartridge – a legacy of Gen Boulanger's impatience to get the Lebel rifle into service back in the 1880s – and the feed mechanism often jammed. The bolt or extractor also failed frequently due to careless manufacture, and overheating routinely caused the action to seize up for several minutes after little more than 300 rounds of fully automatic fire. Even when it functioned perfectly, the widely hated Chauchat was inaccurate above 200 yards.

52 Heintz, pp.39–41, 46–7; *Livre d'Or*, pp.235–6; Hoisington, p.86

53 *Livre d'Or*, p.236; Heintz, pp.34, 48–9; Hart, *Ait Atta*, p.165–6

54 Moroccan commerce increased overall from 177 million francs to 707 million in 1912–19, and goods passing through Casablanca port from 130,000 tons to 800,000 tons in 1911–19.

55 Bergot, in Young, p.201

16. Flawed Blades

1 *France, Spain and the Rif*, p.12

2 Carles, *RHdA*, 1981/1

3 Garijo (p.111) puts Legion desertions in Jan–Feb 1921 alone at 385. At that date Maj de Corta (4e REI) reported that warnings of a mutiny and desertion plot led to two whole companies being recalled to Boudenib from Aoufous on the Oued Ziz, and that ten ringleaders were shot while trying to escape. (Porch, *Foreign Legion*, pp.392–3)

4 Jean Brunon, 'Essaie sur la folklore de la Légion Étrangère' in *Vert et Rouge*, No.19, 1948)

5 Porch, *Foreign Legion*, pp.383–8; Carles, *RHdA*, 1981/1. The enclosed world of the Africa Army shielded soldiers to some extent from the massive inflation of the post-war years; between Nov 1918 and Aug 1919 the franc dropped from 26fr to 51fr to the pound sterling, and by mid 1926 to 220 francs (Horne, *Friend or Foe*; London, Weidenfeld & Nicolson, 2004, p.362). Cooper (*12 Ans*, p.67), who re-enlisted in 1919, puts the bounty at 500fr, paid half on enlistment, half after 3 months on completing basic training. Daily pay thereafter increased after 3 years' service.

6 At the Armistice just 13 surviving foreign officers were serving with the Legion. (Dutailly, *RHdA*, 1981/1)

7 Porch, *Foreign Legion*, pp.389–90, quoting LtCol Rollet and Maj De Corta.

8 See Appendix 1 for note on Rollet's wartime service.

9 Gandelin, *RHdA*, 1981/1; Garijo, p.125

10 IV/1er and IV/2e REI were formed for Tonkin in 1920 and 1921 (the latter redesignated IX/1er in 1926), IV/ and V/4e REI for the Levant in 1921. Other bns posted to Tonkin – not as rotations, but cumulatively – were VII/1er REI (1927) and I/1er REI (1930). From 1 Sept 1930 the in-country bns formed the new 3-bn 5e REI. (*Livre d'Or*, p.147; Garros, pp.83, 124)

11 Porch, *Foreign Legion*, Ch 19 n(5); *KB*, No.394; *Livre d'Or*, p.147; Carles, *RHdA*, 1981/1. 4e REI was formed from I/, II/ and VI/1st RE and VI/2nd RE. A decree of 31 Mar 1928 would fix Legion strength at 5 inf rgts (including the *de facto* rgt in Tonkin) totalling 17 bns, 1 cav regt of 5 sqns, 4 mounted coys and 4 pioneer coys.

12 *Livre d'Or*, p.281; Porch, *Foreign Legion*, p.385; Robinson, pp.38–41

13 Hart, *Ait Atta*, pp.166–7; Dunn, *Resistance*, p.243. The Ait Hammou were a tribe of the Southern Ait Segrushin Berbers.

14 Hoisington, p.90 n(138)

NOTES AND SOURCES 655

15 Garijo, p.119. However, Turnbull (pp.152–4) gives Lyautey only 53 bns in 1921, of which only 32 were combat-ready.

16 Clayton, pp.106–107, 211–12, 252, 263, 318–19; Garijo, p.99. In 1922 there were just over 10,500 W. African troops in Morocco, with 358 white Colonial officers and 2,408 white NCOs and cadre rankers. Legion strength in Morocco was then c.5,500.

17 Hoisington, pp.88–9; *Livre d'Or*, pp.237–8

18 Hart, *Qabila*, pp.45, 55; Harris, p.86; Woolman, pp.29–31

19 Harris, pp.22, 40; Hart, *Qabila*, p.51–2. Their immediate neighbours, clockwise from the coast, were the Timsaman (NE), Ait Tuzin (E), Gzinnaya (E and S), Ait Ammarth (S and W), and Ibuqquyen (NW).

20 Hart, *Qabila*, pp.60, 66, 69, 140; Woolman, pp.23, 29

21 Hart, *Qabila*, pp.72–85

22 Harris, pp.68–9, 108–109

23 Woolman, pp.67, 144; John Scurr, *The Spanish Foreign Legion*, Men-at-Arms 161 (London; Osprey, 1985). While Franco was wounded only once, Millán Astray would lose his left arm and right eye, and was eventually awarded a special diamond-studded version of the Medal of Suffering for the Fatherland with four clasps. The difference in tone between the Spanish and French Foreign Legions is perhaps indicated by the fact that the devout and puritanical Millán Astray gave his unit a hymn called 'The Betrothed of Death', while the Legion's march '*Le Boudin*' is about Belgians not deserving any sausage. The present author has always felt that it must be significant that while the holiest relic of the French Foreign Legion is Capt Danjou's wooden hand, that of the *Tercio* is Millàn Astray's bottled eyeball, but he still cannot quite identify precisely the essential cultural difference.

24 Woolman, pp.64–6, 72, 78–9; Harris, pp.68–9

25 Woolman, pp.71, 85, 98–101; Harris, pp.69, 76–7

26 Woolman, pp.81–2, 88, 98

27 *ibid*, p.88; Harris, pp.70, 79–80

28 Woolman, p.103

29 *ibid*, pp. 89–102; Harris, pp.70–73, 80–3

30 Hoisington, p.187

31 *ibid*, p.90

32 Garijo, pp.111–12

33 'El Affrit's' luck would finally run out on 12 June 1924, when he commanded the Native Affairs post established at Skoura. Badly wounded in the thigh during an ambush while pursuing an Ait Segrushin raiding party, he bled to death. The Ait Segrushin boasted that they would dig up his body and skin it, so his *goumiers* poured cement around his coffin and booby-trapped the grave with grenades and a 75mm shell – exactly the sort of trick in which Laffite had delighted. (Garijo, p.151)

34 Garros, pp.152–3; Geraghty, pp.155–6; Bergot, *Foreign Legion*, pp.136–7; Dorian/Maire, *passim*

35 In addition to its 8 Hotchkiss guns, the MG Coy occasionally had a couple of 81mm Stokes-type mortars – 'JDs' – but ammunition was in short supply, and they are almost ignored in the tactical literature. In 1923 France had 3,000 tubes, but only the ridiculously small number of 100,000 mortar bombs in store (Stéphane Ferrard *et al*, *L'Armement de l'Infanterie Française 1918–1940*; Paris, Gazette des Armes Hors Série No.8, 1979). Perhaps surprisingly, the useful little 37mm man-portable trench gun, also issued to the infantry battalion in 1917–18, is rarely mentioned in Morocco.

36 French hand grenades were issued in separate 'offensive' OF and 'defensive' Fl models, the former designed for maximum blast and the latter for maximum fragmentation. As well as 100x VB rifle-grenades, the company mules carried 100x OF and 50x F1 (Vanègue, p.61). In practice, this over-complicated the munitions supply unnecessarily.

37 Fabre, pp.11–13; Vanègue, pp.57—63; Dorian/Maire, p.307

38 Fabre, p. 51; Vanègue, p.94

39 The account times the first clash at 15 mins after III/3e REI left the head of the pass, which in this terrain would place the action certainly no more than a mile into the hills. The author was unable to identify any particularly plausible feature among the others in this landscape. Puzzlingly, neither the *Livre d'Or* nor the rodomontade in Maire's memoir mentions the MG Coy, although 12th would be its logical number. Maire is careless over details, but both sources are clear that 11th Coy was absent, and strongly imply that all three present were rifle companies.

40 Officers occasionally wore khaki covers over their black-and-red caps, but most felt that they needed to be instantly identifiable to their men (who in 1922 wore sidecaps or sun helmets). Even those who covered their képis were recognizable; they carried no rifle – sometimes, only a cane rather than a revolver – and usually wore a pale, loose *gandourah* smock to protect their uniforms.

41 Fabre, pp.14–19; Vanègue, p.25–6

42 *Livre d'Or*, p.239

43 *ibid*, p.240; Dorian/Maire, pp.308–10

44 Garijo, pp.126–9; *Livre d'Or*, p.238

45 Albrecht de Tscharner (1875–1948) came from an aristocratic family in Berne, Switzerland, with a long tradition of French military service. In Apr 1916 he transferred from the Swiss cavalry to the RMLE on the Western Front as a captain, commanding 9e Cie, III/RMLE. He was first wounded on 4 July at Belloy en Santerre, secondly on 18 Apr 1917 at Auberive, and thirdly on 26 Apr 1918 at Hangard Wood (see Appendix 1). Retained in the Legion in 1919 and promoted major in June 1925, he then commanded II/3e REI for no less than seven years. LtCol de Tscharner retired in May 1933, after 16 campaigns and 7 wounds. (Garros, p.152; *KB*, No.343)

46 Cooper, *March*, p.135

47 Gandelin, *RHdA*, 1981/1

17. 'The Most Indomitable Race in the World'

1 *Voyages au Maroc* (1903), p.234

2 Maurois, pp.250–51

3 See Ch 7 n(31)

4 Aage, pp.33–4 (punctuation slightly adjusted throughout these quoted passages).

5 *ibid*, pp.43–8

6 *Livre d'Or*, pp.241–2; Clayton, p.107. Meanwhile (see Map 19), Col Freydenberg's Taza Group – incl II/3rd REI and VI/1st REI – would march east along the Taza corridor and then hook southwestwards. Fes Group – incl I/3rd REI – moved south to Boulemane; in early June it would be joined by Poeymirau with the whole Meknes Group, incl all 3 bns of 2nd REI and its CM. In June–Aug this combined Southern Group (Fes and Meknes) would form a pincer from west and south, while Taza Group closed in from east and north.

7 Aage, pp.59–61, 98–9. Christian Alexander Robert Aage (1887–1940), Count of Rosenborg, son of Prince Waldemar of Denmark and Princess Marie d'Orleans, was a direct descendant of King Louis Philippe, creator of the Legion. Aage was commissioned in the Danish Royal Life Guards in 1913. Like many officers in an army that would see no active service, he applied for foreign attachments, with Greek forces in 1913 and Italian during the Great War. After a year with 16e Chasseurs à Pied at Metz he joined the Legion with the rank of captain *à titre etranger* in Dec 1922. He saw active service with I/2e REI and GM de Meknes in the Middle Atlas (1923), with CM/2e REI on the Ouergha (1924), with GM Colombat in the Rif (1925), and thereafter alternated regimental

service in Morocco with staff college and staff postings in France, taking command of II/3e REI in April 1935. Prince Aage died of pleurisy at Taza in Feb 1940. (Aage, p.11; Garros, p.151)

8 Jean de Lattre de Tassigny (1889–1952) would be France's youngest divisional commander in 1940 (14e Div), GOC French First Army in NW Europe in 1944–5, C-in-C Indochina 1950–51, and posthumously a Marshal of France.

9 Garijo (p.142) quotes only 150 deserters from all Legion units in Morocco in the two years 1923–5. All French Army rankers had lost their coloured képis by 1916; a rediscovered stock of plain khaki M1915 képis began to be issued exclusively to Legion units in Morocco from 1923. (Jean Brunon, *Vert et Rouge*, No.19, 1948)

10 Aage, pp.63–7; Garijo, p.135. On the point of Aage's failure to carry a weapon, he had been advised that a revolver dragging at the hip spoiled the hang of an officer's tunic. It was long believed in many armies that an officer had no business carrying a weapon, which might distract him from his proper job: to get his men into position to fight, and then direct their fire.

11 Aage, p.71

12 From the head of the Tizi Adni pass above the present-day village of Skoura, a marginal and very narrow mountain track continues for some 16 miles of continuous hairpin bends over the successive ridges and ravines of the Massif de Tichoukt. A mere ledge, it climbs generally eastwards to about 6,500 feet before eventually turning south and dropping to El Mers at about 5,000 feet; in dry weather it is negotiable in a serious 4x4 vehicle with a transfer box, and it affords some striking views, many of them straight downwards. It is hard to imagine what would happen if another vehicle were encountered crawling in the opposite direction; despite the dramatic scenery and historical interest, it is not a detour that the author can recommend.

13 Aage, pp.73–9, 80–8; *Livre d'Or*, p.242; Garijo, p.136.

14 Aage's description (p.89) of El Mers as situated 'at the north end of a narrow valley surrounded on three sides by steep slopes' is puzzling; the terrain between the GM's overnight stop at Athia and El Mers is rolling, and the boxed-in effect he implies is certainly not evident.

15 Aage, pp.99–104

16 Garijo, pp.136–9; Aage, pp.74, 91. Garijo's apparent claim that VII/22e RS alone lost 200 dead (probably twice the squadron's strength) on that single day is one of the instances of mistranslation or careless editing that invite caution when using this source.

17 *Livre d'Or*, p.242; Aage, pp.105–106

18 *Livre d'Or*, p.242; Gugliotta and Jauffret, *RHdA* 1981/1; Aage, p.113

19 Fabre, pp.45–8. LtCol Fabre recommended that before action 2 men in each squad should be designated as grenadiers and given a haversack with 6 grenades, and that the platoon's 3 rifle-grenadiers should each carry 8 VBs, thus giving the platoon 36 hand- and 24 rifle-grenades for immediate use.

20 *Livre d'Or*, pp.243–4; Turnbull, p.159

21 *Livre d'Or*, p.244; Aage, pp.114, 117–20; Clayton, p.108

22 All air assets came under LtCol Cheutin's 37th Air Observation Rgt, HQ Rabat; 2 sqns each were based at Fes, Meknes and Marrakesh, 1 at Taza, with the other 3 in strategic reserve at Meknes. The 6 sqns committed in 1923 recorded a total of 16,500 flying hours and dropped 345 tons of bombs. (Laine, *RHdA*, 1978/4)

23 Fabre, p.31

24 Laine, *RHdA*, 1978/4

25 Pechkoff, p.20

26 Fabre, p.86

27 The military Regions were subdivided into Territories. Each Territory comprised a number of Circles, which were battalion commands; it was at this level that a major maintained close liaison with a Native Affairs officer, who controlled up to four dispersed *bureaux indigènes*. Through these he gathered information from village and clan chiefs and local agents, and formulated the advice that governed all military initiatives. These listening-posts existed in parallel with the military posts dependent on the Circle, which was the only level where political and military chains of command intersected and where action was decided – Lyautey was determined to control ignorantly impulsive junior officers. Typically, a few adjacent military posts formed a *groupe d'ouvrages* (GO) commanded by a captain stationed at the largest, usually with half his company, and responsible for a couple of satellite posts held by single platoons. (Vanègue, pp.40–41)

28 Zinovi Pechkoff (1884–1966) was born to a worker's family in Nijni–Novgorod and orphaned young, living by his wits until taken up by Gorki during the latter's internal exile in that city. As Gorki's adoptive son he travelled widely with him during his years of external exile before 1914; Gorki then returned to Russia, breaking all contact when Pechkoff chose to remain in France and enlist in the Legion. After recovering from the amputation of his right arm, mangled during the assault on the Ouvrages Blanches near Arras, Pechkoff was diverted into confidential duties as

an officer interpreter. In 1917 he accompanied French missions to Adm Kolchak in Siberia and Gen Denikin in the Crimea; meanwhile his birth-brother, Jakov Sverdlov, was one of Lenin's closest associates on the Bolshevik Central Committee and, before his death in 1919, the first President of Soviet Russia. Pechkoff would alternate between military and diplomatic duties thereafter; he was wounded again as a company commander with VI/1er REI in the Rif War (see Ch 18), commanded II/4e REI in 1933 and III/2e REI in 1937. In Aug 1940 he travelled via the USA to join Gen De Gaulle in London and served thereafter as his roving ambassador to several Allied governments, including Nationalist China, reaching the rank of four-star general in 1945. Finally retiring in 1950, he still performed occasional missions for French presidents. At his death at the age of 82 he was buried in the Russian cemetery at Ste Geneviève des Bois under the inscription he himself had chosen: '*Le Légionnaire Zinovi Pechkoff*'. (KB, No.380; Garros, p.152, also central figure in photo p.82)

29 Pechkoff, pp.26–31

30 *ibid*, pp.48–50

31 *ibid*, pp.71–2

32 *ibid*, pp.73–81, 98, 117–18

33 *ibid*, pp.108–110

34 Aage, p.138; *Livre d'Or*, pp.245–6; Fabre, pp.91–4

35 *Livre d'Or*, p.246, quoting report of Capt Laixelard; Turnbull, pp.161–2. Exact casualties not given, but presumably about 18 of the 36. There is today no obvious sign of a fort near the head of the Tizi Adni, but there is a large levelled area with some nondescript modern buildings on the northern shoulder, with good visibility down the pass and out over the Oued Sebou valley. It is overlooked from the high hillside above the south side of the pass.

36 Woolman, pp.103–106; Harris, p.126; Hoisington, p.187

37 Woolman, p.111

38 *ibid*, pp.142, 157; Harris, pp.290–9l; Hoisington, p.187

39 Woolman, p.149

40 Porch, *Foreign Legion*, p.396. The number of captured MGs that the Rifians were able to put into the field was limited by lack of skilled hands capable of maintaining them. The same limitation applied doubly to the artillery; although they had captured about 130 guns the Krims' few ex-Maghzan and white instructors struggled to form capable crews. There were very few occasions when more than 2 or 3 guns were used together, and they were often employed singly, since moving them and their ammunition over mountain tracks was difficult. (However, Mhamed Abd el Krim gathered 9 guns in cave emplacements near Tetuan in 1925.) Tactics were often limited to direct fire from close range, but occasional impressive successes included hits on Spanish warships off the coast.

41 Woolman, pp.121–6

42 *ibid*, pp.128–32; Harris, pp.129–31

43 Woolman, pp.136–45, 161; Harris, pp.138–48

44 Hoisington, p.190

45 *ibid*, p.191; Aage, pp.124, 128–36

46 Woolman, pp.170–73; Hoisington, p.196 n(49)

18. Dropping the Baton

1 Interview by US correspondent Paul Scott Mowrer, quoted Rupert Furneaux, *Abdel Krim* (London 1967), p.162. Aristide Briand (1877–1932), also a serial prime minister, occupied the Quai d'Orsay under successive administrations from Apr 1925 until his death.

2 Woolman, p.194

3 Bergot, *La Coloniale*, p.15; Hoisington, p.196; De Lattre, p.40

4 Vanègue, pp.27–38

5 Bergot, *La Coloniale*, pp.13–18; *L'Illustration* sketch-map, reproduced Clerisse. Exact 1925 positions are difficult to locate today; they are only named on copies of approximate sketch-maps, and the valleys have since been flooded by the Barrage Mjara dam and reservoir system, whose water depth – and therefore outline – varies widely with the seasons. In 2007 the author found it impossible to reconcile the course of some roads shown on quite recent maps with those that exist today, and – to his great regret – he was unable to find a track giving access to Bibane. (From a few miles north of Taounate, the Rif still has a reputation as 'Injun country' by virtue of its active drugs trade, and insistent questions from strangers are unwelcome.)

6 About that number had been captured in spring 1921 and others during the Spanish withdrawal to the Primo Line, but in June 1924 the intelligence officer Maj de La Rocque reported that up to 16,000 German Mausers had by then arrived in the Rif on ships from Hamburg. (Garijo, p.261)

7 Woolman, pp.151–3; Hart, *Qabila*, pp.198–203

8 Woolman, p.174; Hoisington, pp.193–4. However, the claim that Abd el Krim had sworn to be in Fes for the festival of Eid – on 2 July that year – was almost certainly French propaganda, to stiffen local resistance by suggesting that he impiously aspired to usurp the sultanate; he always denied it, and worded his public prayers accordingly.

9 Clerisse, v; *KB*, No.397; Bergot, *La Coloniale*, p.20. These were VI/1er REI, and 2 bns of W.African Tirailleurs Coloniaux – II/15e RTC from Algeria and I/10e RTC from Tunisia – which would reinforce 1er RTSM in the outpost line. (Clayton, p.108)

10 *Livre d'Or*, p.249; Gugliotta and Jauffret, *RHdA*, 1981/1

11 A summarized version of the French official account of operations can be found in Clerisse; Woolman gives a précis, but the great value of his book lies in the more extensive Spanish material.

12 Since 1924 a *bataillon de type marocain* had been organized in four numbered rifle companies, with the former MG coy dispersed in four 2-gun platoons between them – e.g. I/1er REI, reorganized thus on arrival at Missour, 21 Mar 1924 (Garijo, p.147). This gave greater tactical self-sufficiency to each company, but increased its mule train; bns reverted to the Line model of three rifle coys plus one MG coy after the Rif War (Fabre, pp.12–13).

13 Adolphe Richard Cooper was born in Baghdad in Feb 1899, the son of an English engineer; he died in Maidstone, Kent, in Apr 1988. After running away to sea, he joined the Legion in Oct 1914 at the age of 15, enlisting for the duration of the First World War. On 28 Apr 1915 he landed at Sedd el Bahr in the Dardanelles with III/RMdA (see Appendix 1). When wounded by a shellburst on 21 June, he was one of the very last of the original men to remain with WO Léon and the skeletal remains of the Legion battalion, and was decorated with the Croix de Guerre. While convalescing in Tunisia he was discharged on grounds of age, at the insistence of his father and British consular officials, in Jan 1916. After service with the British Army he rejoined the Legion for five years in 1919, and re-enlisted in 1924, taking his honourable discharge in Jan 1930.

In 1933 the first edition of his memoir, *The Man Who Liked Hell*, was published in England by Jarrolds; it was translated into several languages, and the French edition by Payot appeared in 1934 as *Douze Ans à la Légion Étrangère*. Cooper later told the Canadian historian Colin Rickards that it was ghost-written from his notes by a Ms Sydney Tremayne – a 'lady poet' – and that after receiving a flat fee he had no more control over it or profit from it. The book includes many colourful yarns calculated to appeal to a 1930s public, and also some outright lies about real events. Many years later he clearly regretted this first effort, and his 1972 revision, *March or*

Bust, is more honest and valuable; while some anecdotes still stretch credibility, he is specific about dates, places and units and includes other useful detail. There is no doubt that Cooper was an intelligent and courageous man who led an extraordinary life. During the Second World War, he was given a British Army general services commission and worked undercover – he claimed, for the SOE in Vichy-ruled North Africa.

14 Cooper, *March,* pp.111–14; Porch, *Foreign Legion,* p.402; Pechkoff, pp.143–9. The company officers of VI/1er REI in Apr 1925 were: *21e Cie* Capt Villiers Moramé, Lts Fain and Douplitsky; *22e* Capt Pechkoff, Lts Mauras, Blausener and Fortris; *23e* Capt Depesseville, Lts Belaygères, Royer and Lacaisse; and *24e* Capt Billaud, Lts Lique, Guyon and Wable. (Garijo, p.177)

15 Garijo, pp.176–8; Pechkoff, pp 162–70, 190; Cooper, *12 Ans,* p.132 and *March,* p.116

16 Pechkoff, pp.178–89; Cooper, *12 Ans,* p.143; Garijo, p.183

17 Fes el Bali village – now drowned by the reservoir – is not to be confused with the Fes city medina of the same name.

18 Bergot, *La Coloniale,* pp.20–22; Garijo, p.196

19 Aage, pp.161–3

20 *KB, No.397; Garijo,* p.234

21 Fabre, pp.24, 39

22 The modern town has grown considerably; however, looking at the ridge from the west one can still see a marked fault, dark with trees, running at a slant down across the hillside from the northern summit

23 *KB,* No.397; Pechkoff, pp.195–200; Garijo, p.183

24 Porch, *Foreign Legion,* pp.404–5

25 Approx 3 miles north of Ain Aicha a steep *mamelon* crowns bare slopes about 1,000 yds east of the present road from Ain Aicha to Taounate; it no longer bears the name used in 1925.

26 Cooper, *12 Ans,* pp.151–2; Pechkoff, pp.202–6; Garijo, p.184

27 Woolman, p.185, quoting Gen Pierre Voinot, 1939; Bergot, *La Coloniale,* p.10. Apart from the usual castration, eye-gouging and cutting off of ears, noses and lips, the opened stomach was usually filled with stones, grass and trash. It is difficult to verify claims that living captives were tortured; this was not generally a Rifian tradition, but there is anecdotal evidence that some black African prisoners were treated with particular cruelty.

28 *KB,* No.397; Clerisse, vi; Harris, p.216; Garijo,

p.178. Accounts of the fighting are confused by the fact that a number of small posts changed hands more than once; after initial killing and pillaging the Rifians seldom stayed on such positions to offer a target for shelling and bombing, so the French might temporarily reoccupy these hilltops.

29 During May alone the Breguets flew 1,685 sorties; 13 May was the busiest day, when 7 sqns totalled 135 bombing sorties – allowing for unserviceable machines, many crews must have flown three missions that day. The Aviation Militaire's umbrella command in Morocco was still Col Armengaud's 37e RAO, HQ Rabat, initially with 10 *escadrilles* (sqns). In spring 1925 these were dispersed in 5x two-sqn *groupes* – 6 sqns in the north and 4 in the south, with 8x Breguet 14 combat aircraft each plus 2x medevac. Between 30 Apr and mid-June 1925, the 6 sqns in the north were reinforced to 15 sqns: 6 came from 36e RAO in Algeria and Tunisia, 2 from 11e RAO in France, and one – formed May 1925 at Ouezzane by the American Col Charles Sweeny – was the '2nd Lafayette Escadrille', later Escadrille de la Garde Chérifienne, with 17 volunteer US aircrew, 4 or 5 French and all-French groundcrew. (The '2nd Lafayette' flew 470 missions over both French and Spanish zones; its participation was controversial abroad, especially after a raid on undefended Chefchaouen, and it was disbanded in Nov 1925.) In early summer 2 more sqns, at Kasbah Tadla and Marrakesh, were temporarily put at the disposal of Northern Front, raising its air assets to 17 escadrilles. (Danel and Cuny, pp.45–7; Woolman, pp.202–3; Harris, p.300; Laine, *RHdA,* 1978/4)

30 Clerisse, vi; Bergot, *La Coloniale,* p.22–3; Aage, p.166; Garijo, pp.167, 193; *Livre d'Or,* p.251

31 At this date Col Freydenberg had 6x bns – VI/1er RE, II/RICM, 2x bns of Tirs Alg, 1 bn of Tirs Maroc, and a mixed bn of Zouaves and Tirs Sénég.

32 Pechkoff, pp.217–33; Cooper, *12 Ans,* pp 155–9. Pechkoff wrote that an attempted pursuit was held off by the MGs on the south bank. Cooper claimed that the rear company were 'massacred' and that he himself was among 100 wounded, but this seems to be one of the tall tales typical of his first memoir.

33 Garijo, p.188

34 Bergot, *La Coloniale,* p.25. The bodies of one or two Europeans in Berber clothing were very occasionally recovered from battlefields, but both the Spanish and the French were over-sensitive about the part played by renegades, whom the Rifians never fully trusted or gave leadership roles. One German, Otto Noja, helped a Spanish prisoner install telephone links, including one that gave Abd el Krim at Ajdir contact with the Djibala front where his younger brother was operating, and a Serbian ex-captain of the Austro-Hungarian Army trained Rifian artillerymen.

The notorious Josef Klems, a Dusseldorf embezzler with an unsavoury record, was a self-publicist who put his name to German-language leaflets urging légionnaires to desert to the Rifians; he inspired many exaggerated tales (and P. C. Wren's short stories about 'Odo Klemens'), but he seems to have been a habitual liar. He apparently deserted from the Legion in Aug 1922 after being demoted from sergeant for falsifying accounts, and somehow talked his way into the confidence of the Beni Ouarain south of Taza, taking wives and converting to Islam (though his claim to have made the *hajj* was bogus). After offering his services to Abd el Krim in 1924 he was employed in the Djibala, where his mapping and telegraphy skills were useful, but his claim to have been an artillery instructor cannot be verified. Betrayed to the French by one of his women, he was condemned to death by court-martial in 1927, but his sentence was commuted to hard labour for life in French Guiana. He survived seven years in the *bagne* before being released, supposedly as a result of German pressure, in 1934, only to commit suicide in a Berlin prison in 1939. (Woolman, p.152; Geraghty, pp.161 and 165; Garijo, p.118)

35 *KB*, Nos.232, 337; Garijo, p.185

36 Aage, pp.169–79; *Livre d'Or*, p.252; Garijo, pp.188–90; *KB* No.232; Bergot, *La Coloniale*, p.26; Woolman, p.177

37 Garijo, p.191; Harris, p.229; Woolman, p.176

38 Clerisse, vi; Bergot, *La Coloniale*, pp.33, 36; Garijo, pp.190, 224. Ruins can still be seen on the summit of Ait Maatouf.

39 Harris, pp.220–21; Garijo, pp.190–91

40 *KB*, No.232

41 Hoisington, pp.195–8. Daugan had commanded the wartime Moroccan Division on the Western Front.

42 Hoisington, p.196

43 The sources are contradictory over how long before 4 June Astar had fallen; various details suggest that it had been lost and reoccupied more than once before that date.

44 Today the upper shoulders of Astar are almost entirely covered with olive trees and scrub, and this makes access and orientation difficult. The valleys to the north-west and north are flooded by the man-made lakes of the Barrage and Petit Barrage de Mjara; the northwards creep of the town of Taounate, and modern plantations, make it impossible to identify Sker from the top of Astar, but in 1925 it was clearly visible below. The names then used by the French for these features do not seem to be known among local people today. When trying to find a way up to the summit the author had reached a dead end on an eastern shoulder of Astar when a chance encounter with an impressive hill-farmer (a combat veteran of Moroccan Army paratroopers) led to another attempt from the west, which eventually reached 'the place where the old *mujahideen* fought'.

45 Clerisse's photos show large scrub fires started by shelling; these, and fragments of shells and aerial bombs found on the post site itself, both probably date from a bombardment in September, since the intention on 4 June was to put the post back in a state of defence.

46 *KB*, No.397, quoting a letter written by Maj Cazaban to Col Boulet-Desbarreau, CO 1er REI.

47 Pechkoff, pp.245–57; *KB*, No.397; Garijo, pp.194–6; Cooper, *March*, pp.119–20 and *12 Ans*, p.165

48 Aage, pp.179–82

49 *ibid*, pp.183–201; Garijo, p.206

50 Ain Mediouna is the name of a village cradled between high wooded hills more than 8 miles east of Gara de Mezziat, but the post at the airstrip was on a broad tongue of flat ground only about 3 miles east of the Ouergha bend, where disused single-storey concrete buildings can be seen today north of the road from Ain Aicha.

51 Bergot, *La Coloniale*, p.34; *KB*, No.397; Garijo, pp.198–9; Pechkoff, pp.259–71; *Livre d'Or*,p.251. Cooper's account in *12 Ans* (pp.169–73) is worthless.

52 Pétain, the victor of Verdun and healer of the 1917 mutinies, was Commander-in-Chief and Inspector-General of the French Army and Vice-President of the Supreme War Council.

53 Pechkoff, pp.271–5. Garijo (p.200) lists the names of all four Médaille recipients including Poulet, but Pechkoff gives it as 'Goulet', perhaps to deny readers a cheap smirk – *poulet* means 'chicken'.

54 Aage, pp.202–3. He would soon leave the Rif front, and was on sick leave for many months.

55 Maurois, p.270; Hoisington, p.199

56 *KB*, No.232

57 Woolman, pp.179–80; *Livre d'Or*, p.253; *KB*, No.232

58 *KB*, No.337. This suggests that since arriving at the front four weeks previously II/1er REI had already lost 160 men, i.e. about 25 per cent casualties.

59 Bergot, *La Coloniale*, pp.28–32

60 Woolman, p.186; Clerisse, vii and xii; Harris, p.243; Garijo, p.220

61 Garijo, pp.155, 202–3

62 Woolman, pp.199–200; Harris, pp.225–35; Maurois, p.271

63 Garijo, p.208

64 ibid, p.211

65 Cooper, March, pp.121–2. This crippling and extremely painful wound ended Zinovi Pechkoff's part in the Rif War.

66 Garijo, p.211

67 Hoisington, p.200; Clerisse, ix-x; Garijo, p.215

68 Clerisse, vii; Woolman, p.186

69 The canon de 37mm tir rapide Mle 16 had been issued to infantry battalions since 1917 to give them a weapon against protected German MG nests; it fired HE shells to a maximum range of 2,000 yds, at about 12rpm with a practised crew. It weighed 238lb, though its gunshield and wheels were often removed to lighten it, and it could be carried over rough ground by three men.

70 KB, Nos.233 and 337; Garijo, pp.213–16

71 Woolman, p.181; Hoisington, pp.201–2; Harris, pp. 240–41

72 During late summer and autumn 1925 Morocco would receive an additional 36 bns, doubling infantry strength. The first 14 of these bns arrived in Aug, with 2 MG bns, 2 tank bns, 2 cav bdes and 30 batteries.
In early Sept, 2 more air sqns arrived from 32e RAO in France. At the beginning of winter 37e RAO had 9 'sector' sqns spread along the Northern Front between Ouezzane and Guercif, controlled by local Army commands, and 9 'reserve' sqns further back, at the disposal of the C-in-C. Between July 1925 and the end of Jan 1926 5,500 sorties were flown, of which 3,000 were bombing missions, dropping 375 tons. They also took 14,000 aerial photos covering 5,792 sq miles; and in 1925 the total of air medevacs to Fes, Meknes and Taza was 987. The 37e RAO reached, at its peak, 22 sqns; to man these units many Reserve officers were given short-service commissions to fly on active service. (Danel and Cuny, pp.45–7; Laine, RHdA, 1978/4)

73 Clerisse, x; Livre d'Or, p.252. The last 3 bns to arrive were II/3e (Maj de Tscharner) and I/ & II/4e REI (forming a rgt de marche under Maj de Corta). On 24 July half of 6e Cie, II/2e REI – already badly mauled at Bibane in May – were wiped out during a convoy ambush; Maj Goret's remnant were then pulled back for security duties around Sefrou. (Garijo, p.217; Livre d'Or, p.255)

74 Initially: (west) Gen Pruneau, 128e and 35e Divs; (centre) Gen Marty, 2e and 3e Divs de Marche; (east) Gen Boichut, 11e Div and Div Marocaine. Divisions de marche mixed Metropolitan, Colonial and Africa Army units. (Clerisse, x; Clayton, p.110)

75 Clerisse, x; Garijo, p.234; KB, No.233; Harris, pp.242, 244; Woolman, p. 186; Livre d'Or, p.255. On tanks, Loustaunau-Lacau and Montjean, Revue Militaire Francaise, Apr–June 1928. At Ain Defali on 1 Sept, II/1er REI were issued some Danish Madsen LMGs, which suggests that supplies of the new French FM24 were not yet sufficient to replace the Chauchats. (Garijo, p.244)

76 Clerisse, x; Livre d'Or, p.255; Garijo, pp.222–30

77 Garijo, p.235; Clerisse, xi

78 Woolman, pp.187–93; Harris, pp.156, 162, 165, 167; Scurr, op cit, pp.16–17

79 Clerisse, xi; Garijo, pp. 227, 238–9, 244; Bergot, La Coloniale, p.36; Harris, p.246

80 Ageron, in L'Age d'Or, pp.134–9

81 Hoisington, p.204; Woolman, p.195; Harris, p.245; Khoury, p.182

82 Maurois, pp.275–7. D'Ormesson quote from Revue de Paris, 15 Apr 1931.

83 Clerisse, xii; Woolman, pp.192–5; Livre d'Or, pp.255–6; Garijo, pp.245, 248; Gandy, p.68

84 Garijo, pp.248–58

85 KB, No.233

86 Harris, pp.246–7; Woolman, p.206. Of the killed, wounded and missing totals, 780, 1,800 and 225 respectively were Frenchmen – a total of 2,805, or roughly 25 per cent of total casualties.

87 Garijo, p.255. In 1939 BrigGen Cazaban was GOC Tlemcen Subdivision, Algeria, which included 1st REI. He retired in Aug 1940, dying at the age of 98 in his native Pau in Oct 1980. (KB, No.397)

19. The Reckoning

1 First epigraph from Livre d'Or de la Légion Étrangère (1931), p.260; second from Pierre van Paassen, Days of Our Years (1939), p.271

2 De Lattre, pp.39–41

3 See the present author's The Last Valley (Weidenfeld & Nicolson, 2004), pp.112–19

4 Loustaunau-Lacau and Montjean, Revue Militaire Francaise, Apr–June 1928

5 Garijo, pp.248–9

6 Clerisse, xii – xiv

7 Woolman, pp.148–9, 198

8 Garijo, p.259

9 *ibid*, p. 261

10 Harris, pp.283–303, 310–14; Woolman, pp.199–200, 203–4; Clerisse, xvi

11 Order of battle from west to east:
Groupement de Fez 128e Div (Gen Monhoven), 9 bns; 4e Div de Marche (Gen Goubeau), 13 bns incl I/1er REI; 2e Div de M (Gen Théveney), 12 bns incl I/ and III/3e REI.
Groupement de Taza 1re Div de M (Gen Vernois), 12 bns incl I/ and II/4e REI; Div Maroc (Gen Ibos), 12 bns incl I/ and III/2e REI; 3e Div de M (Gen Dosse), 12 bns incl II/ and VI/1er REI. (Clerisse, xiii; *Livre d'Or*, p.248; Garros, p.81)

12 Woolman, pp.154, 204; Garijo, pp.261–2

13 Clerisse, xiv

14 *ibid*, xviii; Woolman, p.205

15 Garijo, p.264; Clerisse, xviii; *Livre d'Or*, pp.257–8

16 Clerisse, xx

17 *ibid*, xviii; Woolman, p.205; Harris, p.308; Garijo, p.265

18 Garijo, pp.266–9; Woolman, pp.200–201, 206

19 Clerisse, xix; Woolman, pp.207–8

20 Woolman, pp.209–13; Harris, pp.321, 329

21 Clerisse, xx; Harris, pp.246–7; and see Ch 18, n(86)

22 Clerisse, xxii; *Livre d'Or*, p.259

23 Garros, p.82. Rgt HQ, I/ and III/3e REI, Cie de Marche II/3e, and Compagnie Montée. (*Livre d'Or*, p.259)

24 Clerisse, xxiii

25 *ibid*, xxiii; *Livre d'Or*, p.259 – which mistakenly tranposes 1re for 3e Div.

26 Clerisse, xxiii; *Livre d'Or*, p.259; Garijo, p.271

27 *Livre d'Or*, p.260; Clerisse, xxiii–xxiv; Turnbull, p.170

28 In 1927 the Legion had 3 bns in Indochina, 3 in Algeria, 1 (later 2) cav sqns in the Levant; and in Morocco 12 bns, 2 sqns, 4 mounted coys and 4 pioneer coys. (Carles, *RHdA*, 1981/1)

29 After a war party wiped out Lt Lemarchand's platoon, sent out to investigate an ambush on telegraph linesmen, El Bordj was surrounded by *c.*2,000 Ait Yahia and Ait Haddidou tribesmen. Losses were 36 killed and wounded. (Garijo, pp.279–80; Clayton, pp.115, 403 n(67); *Livre d'Or*, p.264)

30 1re Cie des Sapeurs-Pionniers/1er REI had been based at Ouled Daoud during the summer 1925 fighting. (*Livre d'Or*, p.252)

31 Garijo, p.273; *Livre d'Or*, p.264. The plaques erected by the légionnaires and the Génie were removed after Moroccan independence, and on the ground it is today signposted simply as the Zabel Tunnel.

32 Gandy, p.69

33 Cooper, *12 Ans*, pp.232–4, 264

34 *ibid*, pp. 236–8; Hart, *Ait Atta*, p.3

35 Cooper, *March*, pp.142, 172; *12 Ans*, pp.241, 258–61

36 1926, III/1st REC (Capt Schmeltz) provided security Talsint-Colomb Béchar; replaced from Apr 1927 by II/1st REC (Capt Thomas – killed 25 May on recce near Bou Anane). 1928 and 1929, I/ and III/1st REC alternated in SE Morocco. 1931, III/, IV/ and V (Mot)/1st REC in region Rich-Gourrama-Ksabi. (*Livre d'Or*, pp.281–2)

37 Maxwell, pp.141, 147, 158. After Moroccan independence, Mohammed ben Youssef would reign from 1957 as King Mohammed V.

38 Hart, *Qabila*, p.91; *Ait Atta*, pp.2, 169–70

39 Gandini, pp.140–41

40 The Berliets were probably the chain-driven CBA, which had only a 22hp engine but weighed more than 3 tons empty. The M1918 armoured car had a French armoured body mounted on the chassis of an American White $2\frac{1}{2}$-ton truck.

41 Gandy, pp.72–5. See also Ch 12, n (36) for description of the ford.

42 The author does not pretend to have tracked down the full sequence, but during the 1920s there appear to have been 5 Cies Montées, either autonomous or affiliated to the four REIs. In Jan 1922 the former autonomous CM d'Algérie was redesignated CM/1er REI, based at Colomb-Béchar. In Oct 1923 the CM du Maroc became 1re CM/2e REI, based at Er Rachidia; a new 2e CM/2e REI was raised, apparently at Oujda. In Jan 1922, 2e CM/3e REI became the single CM/3e REI, based at Gourrama. In Sept 1920 the 1re CM/1er REI had been redesignated CM/4e REI, based at Boudenib, later Kerranda. (*KB, passim*)

43 Gugliotta and Jauffret, *RHdA*, 1981/2

44 Gugliotta and Jauffret, *RHdA*, 1981/1 & /2; Geraghty, p.158. The officer at Djihani (see Map 23) was a Lt Fioré, who should not be confused with the Capt Fouré whose action in Aug 1930 is described next. Since 1916 the CMs had exchanged the long Lebel rifle for the handier carbine, and by 1929 each platoon had one LMG team with 5 mules and 8 men for the FM24 and 1,350 rounds

(1 cpl, 2-man gun team, 3 ammo-carriers, 2 muleteers).

45 *Livre d'Or* (p.264), and *KB*, No.393 – from which this account is mostly taken – identify the dissidents as Ait Hammou, but Garijo (p.281) as Ait Murghad; this action took place close to the mountain home of the latter, but men of both tribes may well have been present.

46 *KB*, No.393 names 18 killed and 13 of the wounded from 1re CM/2e REI.

47 Garijo, p.281

20. 'Obscure and Unknown Sacrifices'

1 First epigraph quoted by Ward Price, p.154; second, *op cit*, p.145

2 13x 2-ton 15hp Laffly LC2 patrol trucks, 2x Laffly radio trucks, 7x field cars of three different Renault and Citroen models, a Fiat light truck, a Berliet workshop truck and 2x Chenard tanker trucks.

3 Gugliotta and Jauffret, *RHdA*, 1981/1; *KB*, Nos.376–8; Vauvillier/Clerisse *passim*; Gandy, p.77

4 Artillery: in May 1925, 1er REI had formed a Section de 80mm de Montagne de la Légion. In May 1932 cadres from 64e RACM would help form a Batterie de Marche d'Artillerie du 2e REI at El Hajeb with 4x 75mm, and an essentially identical Batterie d'Artillerie du 4e REI at Oua-zazarte.

5 Carles, *RHdA*, 1981/1

6 Details of the development of Legion uniform features may be found in Guyader (see Biblio); see also caption to Fig 81 in this book.

7 *KB*, No.374

8 Gandelin, *RHdA*, 1981/1. Rollet's promotion dated from 23 Mar 1931; in 1933 the Ministry announced that no successor would be appointed after he retired. In 1972 a roughly analogous Groupement de la Légion Étrangère was revived, with a commandant-general heading the central services of 1er RE.

9 Huré, *La Pacification*, quoted Clayton p. 403, n(71)

10 Fremeaux, *RHdA*, 2004/2

11 Juin, pp.76–9

12 Hart, *Ait Atta*, pp.172–3

13 Juin, pp.79–81. Henri Giraud (1879–1949) served with 4e RZ in N.Africa before 1914, and after 1922 he commanded 14e RTA in Morocco, where he was present at the surrender of Abd el Krim. He was captured in May 1940 as GOC Seventh Army in France; after his escape from Germany was organized in Apr 1942 he returned to Algeria. At a meeting with Gen Eisenhower in Gibraltar on 7 Nov, just prior to the Allied 'Torch' landings, he accepted French military and civil command in N.Africa, but few French troops recognized this before the assassination of Adm Darlan on 24 Dec 1942. In summer 1943 Giraud was manoeuvred by Gen De Gaulle into resigning his joint presidency of the Committee for National Liberation, and he retired from the Army in Apr 1944. Intellectually he was no match for De Gaulle; one commentator described him as having 'the incurious blue gaze of a china cat'.

14 Garijo, pp.282–3; Hart, *Ait Atta*, p.174

15 Garijo, pp.284–5; Hart, *Ait Atta*, p.174

16 Confusion arises from some sources still using the unit's former designation CMot/2e REI.

17 Garijo, pp.285–6; Clayton, p.116.
This Tafilalt occupation was followed in May 1932 by ops against Ait Haddidou and Ait Aysha Berbers around the Assif Melloul valley, south of the Plateau des Lacs in the High Atlas, by c.30 bns from Meknes, Kasbah Tadla and Marrakesh, with some Legion involvement including CM/2e REI.

18 Porch, *Foreign Legion*, p.408

19 Hart, *Qabila*, pp.91, 111. The Ilimshan were a clan of the Ait Zimru tribe of the Ait Wahlim 'fifth' of the Ait Atta people. Assu u-Ba Slam was the hereditary chief of the clan's Ait Bu Tghuratin segment, which historically had provided the bearers of an Ait Atta holy battle flag.

20 Hart, *Ait Atta*, pp.177, 180–82

21 *ibid*, pp.179–80; *KB*, No.394; Garijo, pp.289–91

22 Garijo, p.288–91

23 Not to be confused with the LtCol Jeanpierre who became renowned with 1er BEP and 1er REP in Indochina and Algeria in the 1950s – the latter did not graduate until 1936.

24 Garijo, pp.291–4; Turnbull, p.172; Vial, p.268

25 Hart, *Ait Atta*, p.182. The Ait Murghad or Morrhad were a tribe of the Ait Yafalman confederacy which had blocked Ait Atta expansion to the north-east for more than 200 years.

26 *GM de Meknès* 2x bns Legion, 4x bns Tirs Maroc, 1 bn Tirs Sénég; 2x sqns Spahis, 3x btys; 4x Goums, 1,500 irregulars.
GM des Confins 4x bns Tirs Alg, 3x bns Tirs Maroc; 3x CMs & 1 CMot Légion; 4x sqns Spahis, 1 sqn (Esc Mot) Légion; 5x btys, 1 Légion ½-bty; 2x Goums, 800 irregs.
GM de Marrakesh 3x bns Legion, 1 bn RIC, 2 bns

Tirs Maroc; 2x sqns Spahis; 3x btys, 3x ½-btys Maroc; 4x Goums, 2,000 irregs.
GM de Tadla 3x bns Légion, 4x bns Tirs Alg, 5x bns Tirs Maroc; 2x sqns Spahis, 1 sqn Chass d'Af; 6x btys; 6x Goums, 1,500 irregulars. (Clayton, pp.116–17)

27 Ward Price, p. 101

28 Clayton, pp.116–17; Ward Price, p.74

29 Air navigation chart TPC-H2A shows a peak of 10,105ft due N of Ait Daoud ou Azzi, but this seems too far W; another of 9,570ft about 13 miles ENE of Ait Daoud seems more plausible.

30 Ward Price, p.274

31 *ibid*, pp.102–3

32 *ibid*, pp.74, 98–9. The 43 daily tons for each GM comprised 17 tons of munitions, 10.5 tons of rations for the regular troops and 1.25 tons for the auxiliaries, 10.25 tons of forage for the animals – which still died at a shocking rate – plus 4 tons of miscellaneous loads such as tools and barbed wire.
Trucks and drivers were provided by the civilian firm Compagnie des Transports Marocains, which contracted to supply whatever was needed at short notice for a flat ton-per-km price scale. Most trucks were 28hp Sauer 6-ton or 32hp Panhard 5-ton with double wide-track rear wheels. All used 'unpuncturable' Viel-Picard tyres filled with a honeycomb of 900 soft rubber cells.

33 Ward Price, pp.75, 108, 138, 173, 210

34 *ibid*, pp.127–30, 151

35 *ibid*, pp.131, 133, 153

36 *ibid*, pp. 114–15, 158; Blond, p.256

37 Ward Price, pp.167–75; Blond, p.258

38 Porch, *Foreign Legion*, p.408

39 Cie Montée/4e REI was motorized on 15 Apr 1933, as Cie Mixte Automobile/4e REI (*KB* No.394). Combat vehicles Feb–Mar 1934: *V/1er REC* 3x Laffly 50 AM armd cars, 15x Berliet VUDB light armd carriers, 5x Panhard 179 heavy armd carriers. *VI/1er REC* same, minus Panhard troop. *Cie Auto/1er REI* 8x Panhard 165/175 TOE armd cars, 14x Panhard 179 carriers. *Cie Mixte Auto/4e REI* 8x Panhard 165/175, 12x Laffly LC2 trucks. (Vauvillier/Clerisse)

40 Gandy, pp.79–80; Vauvillier/Clerisse

41 Clayton, p.117; Hart, *Qabila*, p.39

42 Hoisington, p.205

Epilogue: The Fort at the Edge of the World

1 Correspondence with author. The late Andreas

Rosenberg served in the Legion in the 1940s, and was subsequently recognized as a Peintre de l'Armée.

2 Hart, *Ait Atta*, p.184. Zayd u-Mhad was an Ait Murghad, and a fellow-clansman of u-Skunti, the leader at Mt Baddou.

3 Most of what follows is from the author's correspondence with the late AdjChef Charles Milassin in 1977–9.

4 Porch, *Foreign Legion*, pp.435, 443, 448

5 Caries, *RHdA*, 1981/1

6 Richard Trench, *Forbidden Sands* (London; John Murray, 1978), pp.2–3

7 Gandelin, *RHdA*, 1981/1. In 1945 Gen Rollet was reburied at Sidi bel Abbès. In Sept 1962, on the eve of Algerian independence, his bones were exhumed once again – along with those of Prince Aage, and the body of Pte Zimmermann, the last légionnaire to be killed in Algeria – and reburied in the cemetery at the Legion retirement home at Puyloubier in Provence, near the new depot at Aubagne.

Appendix 1

Sources: Garros; *Livre d'Or*; Bergot, *Foreign Legion* and in Young; Turnbull, and Geraghty, *passim*.

1 At the time of the successful assault by 4th Canadian Div on 9 Apr 1917, 'Hill 140' was identified as Hill 145. If visitors standing on top of Vimy Ridge facing eastwards at the Canadian War Memorial turn and look over their left shoulder, they will see a more modest tribute to Cot's légionnaires and the other dead of the Moroccan Division in May 1915.

2 The life of James Waddell (1872–1954) was researched by the NZ historian Christopher Pugsley. Born in Dunedin, Waddell was commissioned into 2nd Bn, The Duke of Wellington's Regt in S.Africa in 1896. After marrying a French wife he left the British Army and, on 25 Apr 1900, obtained a commission as *sous-lieutenant* in 1er RE, serving thereafter in N.Africa and Indochina. By 1915 a captain with French citizenship, he won the first of his eventual eight Croix de Guerre avec Palme, and the Knight's Cross of the Légion d'Honneur, at Gallipoli on 4 July, and his second on 27 August. He won three of his subsequent citations in army orders within three months as commander of II/RMLE on the Western Front, and was made Commander in the Legion of Honour in 1920. LtCol Waddell retired from the Legion in 1926, and returned to New Zealand in 1950 after the death of his wife; his funeral at Levin Cemetery on 20 Feb 1954 was attended by the French ambassador.

Appendix 2

Sources: *KB*, Nos.376 and 407; *Livre d'Or*, pp.269–73, 283–6; Gandy pp.15–31, 36–49; Khoury, pp.151–9.

1 Other French troops included a 2-bn Colonial Inf Rgt of the Levant (RICL), and 5 rgts of Algerian, Tunisian and Moroccan Spahis. (Clayton, pp.275, 318)

2 17e Cie Montée, IV/4e REI had also remained in-country when that bn returned to Algeria in Nov 1924, but was stationed at Deir ez Zor on the Euphrates.

3 REC casualty figures from Gandy; *KB*, No. 376 gives 1 off and 20 men killed, 3 offs and 19 wounded. An eyewitness account of the fighting in Post A will be found in Bennett Doty, *Legion of the Damned* (Garden City Pub Co, 1928), pp.97 *et seq.*

The V/4e REI were prominent in the relief of Suwayda on 23–24 Sept, and late in Oct they operated around Damascus. In Dec 1925 they were in the Lebanon Mts; throughout 1926, in the Djebel Druze (being redesignated VIII/1er REI on 1 July); and in 1927, on the volcanic Laja plateau near the Transjordan border. The bn remained in the Levant as part of the permanent garrison, based at Horns in 1931. (*Livre d'Or*, pp.275–9; Garros, p.128)

4 IV/1er REC continued on active service in Syria until replaced by 1 er Esc in Nov 1926.

Operations by the 50,000-strong Army of the Levant continued until July 1927, by which time Sultan al Atrash had been forced over the Trans-jordan border; he finally fled to Arabia. Syria became a peaceful and, by the 1930s, a coveted posting for the three Legion units forming the core of its permanent garrison. In Oct 1939 the bns then in-country – IV/, I/ and VI/1er REI – became respectively I, II and III bns of the new 6e REI, with an attached Legion artillery battalion.

Select Bibliography

BOOKS

Aage of Denmark, Prince, *My Life in the Foreign Legion* (London; Eveleigh Nash & Grayson, 1928)

Ageron, Charles Robert, trans Michael Brett, *Modern Algeria – A History from 1830 to the Present* (London; Hurst & Company, 1991)

anon, *Histoire militaire de l'Indochine francaise, des débuts à nos jours (juillet 1930)*, Tome II (Hanoi-Haiphong; Imprimerie d'Extrême-Orient, 1930)

Bergot, Erwan, trans Richard Barry, *The French Foreign Legion* (London; Wyndham Publications/ Tattoo, 1976)

Bergot, Erwan, *La Coloniale – du Rif au Tchad, 1925–1980* (Paris; Presses de la Cité, 1987)

Bernard, Professor Augustin, *Les confins Algéro-Marocains* (Paris; Émile Larose, 1911)

Blond, Georges, *La Légion Étrangère* (Paris; Stock, 1964)

Brunon, Jean, et al, *Livre d'Or de la Légion Étrangère* (Paris; Légion Étrangère, 1931)

Carpeaux, Louis, *La chasse aux pirates* (Paris; Grasset, 1913)

Clayton, Anthony, *France, Soldiers and Africa* (London; Brassey's, 1988)

Clerisse, Henry, *La guerre du Rif et la Tache de Taza* (Paris; G. Desgrandchamps, 1927)

Cooper, A. R., *Douze ans à la Légion Étrangère* (Paris; Payot, 1934)

Cooper, A. R., *March or Bust* (London; Robert Hale, 1972)

Crumplin, Michael, *Men of Steel – Surgery in the Napoleonic Wars* (Shrewsbury; Quiller Press, 2007)

Danel, Raymond and Jean Cuny, *L'Aviation francaise de bombardement et de renseignement 1918–1940* (Paris; Docavia/Editions Larivière, 1978)

de Lattre de Tassigny, Maréchal Jean (posthumous collected writings), *Ne Pas Subir* (Paris; Plon, 1984)

d'Esparbes, Georges, *Les Mystères de la Légion Étrangère* (Paris: Ernest Flammarion, n.d., c.1912)

Dorian, Jean-Pierre, *Souvenirs du Colonel Maire de la Légion Étrangère* (Paris; Albin Michel, n.d., c.1939)

Dunn, Ross E., *Resistance in the Desert – Moroccan Responses to French Imperialism 1881–1912* (London; Croom Helm, 1977)

Fabre, Lieutenant-Colonel, *Au Maroc – Le Bataillon au Combat* (Paris; Charles-Lavauzelle, 1929)

Gandini, Jacques, *El Moungar – Les combats de la Légion Étrangère dans le Sud-Oranais 1900–1903* (Éditions Extrêm Sud, 1999)

Gandy, Alain, *Légion Étrangère Cavalerie – Royal Étranger* (Paris; Presse de Cité, 1985)

Garijo, Francois, trans from Spanish by Jean-Marc Truchet, *La Légion et les Spahis dans la conquete du Maroc 1880–1934 – La guerre du Rif 1921–26* (Guilherand Granges; Éditions La Plume du Temps, 2003)

Geraghty, Tony, *March or Die* (London; Grafton Books, 1986)

Grisot, Général P. A. and Ernest Colombon, *La Légion Étrangère de 1831 à 1887* (Paris; Berger-Lerault, 1888)

Guyader, Raymond et al, *La Légion Étrangère 1831/1945* (Musée de l'Uniforme de la Légion Étrangère; *Gazette des Uniformes Hors Serie No.6*; Paris, 1997)

Harris, Walter B., *France, Spain and the Rif* (London; Edward Arnold, 1927)

Hart, David M., *Dadda Atta and his Forty Grandsons – the Socio-Political Organisation of the Ait Atta of Southern Morocco* (Wisbech, Cambs; Middle East and North African Studies/ MENAS Press Ltd, 1981)

Hart, David M., *The Ait Atta of Southern Morocco – Daily Life & Recent History* (Wisbech, Cambs; Middle East and North African Studies/ MENAS Press Ltd, 1984)

Hart, David M., *Qabila – Tribal Profiles and Tribe-State Relations in Morocco and on the Afghanistan–Pakistan Frontier* (Amsterdam; Het Spinhuis, 2001)

'Heintz' – anon, *Historique des unités de la Legion Étrangère pendant la guerre de 1914 – Maroc et Orient* (Oran; Imprimerie D. Heintz & Fils, 1922)

Hocquard, Dr C. E., ed. Philippe Papin, *Une Campagne au Tonkin* (Paris; Hachette, 1892; edited r/p Arléa, 1999)

Hoisington, William A., Jr, *Lyautey and the French Conquest of Morocco* (London; Macmillan, 1995)

Horne, Alistair, *The Fall of Paris* (London; Reprint Society, 1967)

Huré, Général R., *La Pacification du Maroc* (Paris; Berger-Levrault, 1952)

Huré, Gén R. et al, *L'Armée d'Afrique 1830–1962* (Paris; Charles-Lavauzelle, 1977)

Johnstone, Douglas, *France and the Dreyfus Affair* (Poole; Blandford, 1966)

Juin, Maréchal Alphonse, *Je Suis Soldat* (Paris; Conquistador, 1960)

'Khorat, Pierre' (Major Ibos), *En Colonne au Maroc – Rabat, Fez, Méquinez – Impressions d'un Témoin* (Paris; Perrin, 1913)

'Khorat, Pierre', *Scènes de la Pacification Marocaine* (Paris; Perrin, 1914)

Khoury, Philip S., *Syria and the French Mandate – The Politics of Arab Nationalism 1920–45* (Princeton: Princeton University Press, 1987)

Le Poer, John Patrick, *A Modern Legionary* (New York; Dutton, 1905)

Lyautey, Maréchal Hubert, trans. Mrs Aubrey Le Blond, *Intimate Letters from Tonquin* (London; John Lane The Bodley Head, 1932)

Lyautey, Maréchal H., *Lettres du sud de Madagascar 1900–02* (Paris; Armand Colin, 1935)

'M.M.', *Memoirs of the Foreign Legion* (London; Martin Secker, 1924)

Manington, George, *A Soldier of the Legion* (London; John Murray, 1907)

Martyn, Frederic, *Life in the Legion* (London; Everett & Co, 1911)

Maurois, André, trans. Hamish Miles, *Marshal Lyautey* (London; John Lane, 1931)

Maxwell, Gavin, *Lords of the Atlas* (London; Cassell, 2000)

McAleavy, Henry, *Black Flags in Vietnam* (London; George Allen & Unwin, 1968)

Montaudon, Général, *Souvenirs Militaires* (Paris; Charles Delagrave, 1900)

Morel, Lieutenant-Colonel, *La Légion Étrangère – Recueil des documents* ... (Paris; Chapelot, 1912)

Ollier, Edmund (ed), *History of the War between France and Germany 1870–71* (London; Cassell, 1890)

van Paassen, Pierre, *Days of Our Years* (New York; Hillman-Curl, 1939)

Patry, Léonce, trans and ed. Douglas Fermer, *The Reality of War* (London; Cassell, 2001)

Pechkoff, Zinovi, *La Légion Étrangère en Maroc* (Paris; Marcelle Lesage, 1926; trans. as *The Bugle Sounds: Life in the Foreign Legion*, New York, D. Appleton, 1926)

Porch, Douglas, *The March to the Marne* (London; Cambridge University Press, 1981)

Porch, Douglas, *The Conquest of Morocco* (New York; Alfred A. Knopf, 1983)

Porch, Douglas, *The Conquest of the Sahara* (London; Jonathan Cape, 1985)

Porch, Douglas, *The French Foreign Legion – A Complete History* (London; Macmillan, 1991)

Price, G. Ward, *In Morocco with the Legion* (London; Jarrolds, 1934)

Ralston, David B., *The Army of the Republic* (Cambridge, MA; Massachusetts Institute of Technology Press, 1967)

Rankin, Reginald, *In Morocco with General d'Amade* (London; Longmans, Green & Co, 1908)

Rickards, Colin, *The Hand of Captain Danjou* (Ramsbury, UK; Crowood Press, 2005)

Robinson, Paul, *The White Russian Army in Exile 1920–41* (Oxford; Clarendon Press, 2002)

Rosen, Erwin, *In the Foreign Legion* (London; Duckworth & Co, 1910)

Serman, William and Jean-Paul Bertaud, *Nouvelle Histoire Militaire de la France 1789–1919* (Paris; Fayard, 1998)

Silbermann, 'Le Soldat' (Léon), *Souvenirs de Campagne* (Paris; Plon-Nourrit, 1910)

Sylvère, Antoine, *Le légionnaire Flutsch* (Paris; Plon, 1982)

Tombs, Robert, *The War Against Paris 1871* (London; Cambridge University Press, 1981) – in notes, 'Tombs'

Tombs, Robert & Isabelle, *That Sweet Enemy* (London; Heinemann, 2006) – in notes, 'Tombs & Tombs'

Turnbull, Patrick, *The Foreign Legion* (London; Heinemann, 1964)

Vanègue, Chef de Bataillon, *Les petites unités d'infanterie au Maroc* (Paris; Charles-Lavauzelle, 1932)

Vial, Médecin Capitaine Jean, *Le Maroc Héroique* (Paris; Hachette, 1938)

Vuillemin, Henri, *La grand aventure des fusils réglementaires francais 1866–1936;Gazette des Armes, Hors Série No.2* (Paris; LCV Services, 1996)

Weygand, Jacques, trans Raymond Jones, *Légionnaire* (London; Harrap, 1952)

Windrow, Martin, *Uniforms of the French Foreign Legion 1831–1981* (Poole, UK; Blandford, 1981)

Woolman, David S., *Rebels in the Rif* (London; Oxford University Press, 1969)

Young, John Robert, with Erwan Begot, *The French Foreign Legion* (London; Thames & Hudson, 1984)

JOURNAL ARTICLES

anon, 'Alouana ... Combat sans espoir' in Képi Blanc (hereafter *KB*), No.169, May 1961

anon, 'Il y a 50 ans au Maroc' (death of Ch de Bn Deslandes) in *KB*, No.337, July 1975

anon, 'Une figure legendaire – le Légionnaire Haberthur' in *KB*, No.373, November 1978

anon, 'Une figure legendaire – l'Adjudant-Chef Mader' in *KB*, No.375, January 1979

anon, 'Le Général Zinovi Pechkoff' in *KB*, No.380, June 1979

anon, 'L'affaire de Bou Leggou' in *KB*, No.393, August 1980

anon, 'Historique du 4e REI' in *KB*, No.394, September 1980

anon, 'Le Bataillon Cazaban' in *KB*, No.397, December 1980

anon, 'Une faite d'armes en Syrie – Messifré, 17 Septembre 1925' in *KB*, No.405, September 1981

anon, 'La defense de Rachaya, Syrie, 20–25 Novembre 1925' in *KB*, No.407, November 1981

anon, 'Images de la Légion Étrangère' in *KB*, Nos.473 and 474, Octobers and November 1987

Barreau, Jean, 'Évolution des Troupes de Marine de 1871 à 1950' in *Revue Historique des Armées* (hereafter *RHdA*), 1983/2

Callan, Andrew, '"This West African Prussia": The Dahomean Army, 1840s–90s' in *Military Illustrated Past & Present* No.30, November 1990

Campbell, Gwyn, 'Labour and the Transport Problem in Imperial Madagascar 1810–1895' in *Journal of African History* (hereafter *JAH*), Vol 21 (1980) pp.341–6

'Capitaine X', 'Admirable conduite d'un Sous-Officier du 1er Bataillon du 2e Étranger' in *La Légion Étrangère*, No.8, 30 November 1912

Carles, Lieutenant-Colonel Pierre, 'Survol de l'histoire du sous-officier de la Légion Étrangère' in *RHdA*, 1981/1, *Spécial Légion Étrangère*

Choisel, Francois, 'Du tirage au sort au service universel' in *RHdA*, 1981/2

Cohen, William B., 'Malaria and French Imperialism' in *JAH*, Vol 24 (1983), pp.22–36

Compton, Major T. E., 'The Pacification of Morocco' and 'The Downfall of Abd el Krim' in *Journal of the Royal United Services Institution* (hereafter *JRUSI*) 1923, and *Army Quarterly*, 1925 (r/p Pallas Armata, 1997)

Crealock, Major J. North, 'Algerian Warfare' in *JRUSI*, 1876: translated summary of articles by M.Villot in *Journal des Sciences Militaires*, May–July 1876 (r/p Pallas Armata, 1995)

Dunn, Ross E., 'Bu Hamara's European Connexion [sic] – The Commercial Relations of a Moroccan Warlord' in *JAH*, Vol 21, (1980), pp.235–52

Dutailly, Lieutenant-Colonel Henry, 'Les officiers à titre étanger 1831–1939', in *RHdA*, 1981/1

Ellis, Stephen, 'The Political Elite of Imerina and the Revolt of the Menalamba ... Madagascar, 1895–98' in *JAH*, Vol 21 (1980) pp.219–34

Fremeaux, Professor Jacques, 'Troupes blanches et troupes de couleur' in *RHdA*, 2000/1

Fremeaux, Professor Jacques, 'Les forces supplétives de l'armée francaise au Maroc 1912–1934' in *RHdA*, 2004/2

Gandelin, Adjudant Chef André, 'Le général Rollet ...' in *RHdA*, 1981/1

Garros, Lieutenant-Colonel Louis (ed), *La Légion, Grandeur et Servitude – Historama Spécial Hors Série No.3* (Saint-Ouen; November 1967)

Girardet, Professor Raoul, 'La France à l'heure des débats' in *L'Age d'Or de la France Coloniale, 1871–1914 – Historia Spécial* (hereafter *L'Age d'Or*), (Paris; Éditions Tallandier, Sept–Oct 1993)

Graves, Colonel Galbraith G. E., 'The Madagascar War' in *The United Service Magazine*, 1896 (r/p Pallas Armata, 1997)

Gugliotta, Georges, and Jean-Charles Jauffret, 'Des unités de légende – Les compagnies montées 1881–1950', Part 1 in *RHdA*, 1981/1; Part 2 in *RHdA*, 1981/2

Hale, L.A., 'Convoys in Southern Algeria', translated summary in *JRUSI* 1884, of pamphlet by Lt C. Massoutier, Chef de Bureau Arabe de Djelfa, originally pub by Jourdan of Algiers, 1882 (r/p Pallas Armata, 1998)

Johnson, Marion, 'Polanyi, Peukert and the Political Economy of Dahomey' in *JAH*, Vol 21 (1980) pp.395–8

Kea, R.A., 'Firearms and Warfare in the Gold Coasts from the 16th to the 19th Centuries' in *JAH*, Vol 12 (1971) pp.185–213

Laine, Serge, 'L'Aviation francaise au Maroc 1911–1939' in *RHdA*, 1978/4

Lefèvre, Sergeant, 'Les carnets du Sergent Lefèvre', in *KB* Nos.109–22 (May 1956–Aug 1957)

Loustaunau-Lacau and Montjean, Capts, 'Au Maroc francaise en 1925 – Le rétablissement de la situation militaire' in *Revue Militaire Francaise* (April–June 1928)

Marseille, Professor Jacques, 'Commerce franco-colonial – Une bonne ou une mauvaise affaire?' in *L'Age d'Or* (Sept–Oct 1993) pp.96–101

Martin, Professor Jean, 'Une spectaculaire expansion coloniale' (pp.18–27); and 'Madagascar – la conquête de l'Ile Rouge' (pp.70–73), in *L'Age d'Or* (Sept–Oct 1993)

Meyer, Charles, 'Pour que l'Indochine soit francaise' (pp.80–91); and 'Colons et planteurs au Tonkin' (pp.92–4), in *L'Age d'Or* (Sept–Oct 1993)

Montagnon, Pierre, 'La France et le Maghreb – une histoire commune de plus de 150 ans' in *L'Age d'Or* (Sept–Oct 1993), pp.28–36

Page, J. D., 'Slaves and Society in Western Africa c1445–1700' in *JAH*, Vol 21 (1980) pp.289–310

Pasfield Oliver, Captain S., 'The Madagascar Expedition of 1895–96', in *JRUSI*, 1896; translated summary from report of Gen Duchesne, *Journal Officiel*, 12–14 September 1896 (r/p Pallas Armata, 1995)

Pasfield Oliver, Captain S., 'Le Soudan Francais and recent French operations on the Upper Niger' in *JRUSI*, 1894 (r/p Pallas Armata, 1995)

Pernot, Francois, and Marie-Catherine Villatoux, 'L'Aéronautique militaire au Maroc avant 1914', in *RHdA*, 2000/1

Pfirmann, Jean, 'Les carnets du Sergent Pfirmann' in *KB*, Nos.341–54, Dec 1975–Feb 1977

Richards, W. A., 'The Import of Firearms into West Africa in the 18th century' in *JAH*, Vol 21 (1980) pp.43–59

Sergent, Pierre, 'Du nouveau sur le combat de Camerone' in *RHdA*, 1981/1

Vauvillier, Francois, 'Coup de faux dans l'Anti-Atlas ...' in *Histoire de Guerre Blindés & Matériel* No.78 (Aug–Sept 2007). After Henry Clerisse, *Le Sous mystérieux – la dernière étape de la pacification du Maroc* (Paris; Édition Mage, 1935)

Ziegler, Charles, 'Souvenirs du Rif' in *KB*, Nos.232 and 233, Aug–Sept 1966

Index

Author's note: The text, relevant end-notes and photograph captions are fully indexed, but the Appendices only for main subjects such as units and commanding officers.

Entries prefixed 'Ait', and 'Beni' or 'Ouled', refer to Berber and Arab tribes/clans respectively, unless otherwise identified as placenames. Entries prefixed 'Bou', 'Bu' and 'El' are placenames unless identified as personal titles. North African river courses are indexed under 'Oued', or 'Assif' in the Berber High Atlas, and ranges of hills and mountains under 'Djebel'.

Services, ministries and the National Assembly are prefixed 'French'. Most general categories of troops (e.g. Algerian Skirmishers, etc.) are indexed only to their first and/or few most descriptive references, under 'French Army', 'French Africa Army', and 'French Naval and Colonial Troops'; otherwise only specific units are indexed, in numerical order. See under 'French Foreign Legion' for general topics; followed by a listing of individual units, divided between pre-1919 and post-1919 organization, and between permanent 'organic' units and temporary 'marching' units.

Military ranks given for individuals are the highest mentioned in the text or notes. All grades of general officers are given simply as 'Gen', and marshals of France as 'Mshl'; the rank of major ('Maj') is used for *chefs de bataillon, chefs d'escadrons* and *commandants*, and warrant officer ('WO') for *adjudants*.

Specific types of equipment are indexed together under 'aircraft', 'weapons' and 'vehicles'.

A

Aage, Maj Prince xl, 475, 476, 477, 478,479, 480, 482, 483, 484, 501, 511, 518, 520, 530, 531, 534, 566; biog note Ch 17 n(7); Fig 65
Abadla plain 261, 263, 264, 299, 330, 571
Abandiolli, Pte 575
Abarran 463
Abassia, Pte 593
Abatucci, Gen 27
Abda tribe 289–290
Abd el Aziz, Sultan 249, 255, 273, 285, 288, 289, 290, 321, 325, 331, 337, 338, 347, 348, 349, 357, 361, 362, 365, 377
Abd el Kader 48
Abd el Krim el Khattabi, Mohammed xxxvii, 445–446, 462, 463, 465, 494, 498, 500, 501–502, Fig 51. Character of regime, 495, 496; disintegration of confederacy, 554–555; European contacts, 495, 496, 502, 556; Franco–Spanish negotiations, 542, 556–557; surrender, 559–560
Abd el Krim el Khattabi, Mhamed xxxvii, 445,